THE QUEST OF AN
UNLIKELY FIXER

Introducing Moral Selfishness, the Only Way to Heal Our Sick Planet

STEPHEN Y. CHEUNG, PH.D.

Order this book online at www.trafford.com
or email orders@trafford.com

Most Trafford titles are also available at major online book retailers.

Print information available on the last page.

ISBN: 978-1-4907-8526-4 (sc)
ISBN: 978-1-4907-8525-7 (hc)
ISBN: 978-1-4907-8527-1 (e)

Library of Congress Control Number: 2017916242

Trafford rev. 12/22/2017

 www.trafford.com

North America & international
toll-free: 1 888 232 4444 (USA & Canada)
fax: 812 355 4082

INTRODUCTION

The Fixer

I am a fixer;

I love to fix things—

A broken wheelbarrow, a neglected house, or a hurt friend.

It gives me satisfaction to make things work again.

I'll also try to fix what has been broken in me—

Hurts from a life that has seen many rejections.

Fixing things helps me to heal and grow.

God willing, I shall be the tool to fix our troubled planet,

to make it beautiful again.

A thought that appeared while taking a walk
in the evening on June 29, 2009.

I shall be the fixer. I firmly believe this book is the tool to fix our troubled planet. It shall be my quest.

Naturally, one would ask: what are the troubles with our planet? Wars, environmental deterioration, and poverty are the three majors that have caused untold amounts of global suffering, for us and other species. Unless stopped, the big three will kill most of us, together with many,

many beautiful organisms. All this suffering is mostly caused by us, a species called *Homo sapiens*, which means wise man. It is a misnomer and easily is the most flagrant type. Yes, beyond doubt, intelligent we are. Wise? Cannot be more remote from it.

The next question will be: how would one tackle these gargantuan global problems? One would credibly doubt: are these problems fixable? Would there be solutions at all? There has been no lack of proposals from great philosophers, learned scholars, and religious leaders—both present and past—who all have the wisdom and power to make changes. So far, none has shown any promise. What makes this book so special?

To have hope of fixing any problem, one must first understand the cause of the problem. Without nailing this very important step one, any attempt will be futile. Sensible? I am a biologist, more precisely, a biophysicist. From this perspective, I can see the problems of our planet have all come from one single source. It is the very nature that makes life possible—not only on our planet, but most likely in wherever life exists in our cosmos. It is the singular factor that defines life: the need to self-preserve, therefore to self-serve, or to be selfish in order to survive. To survive is a universal as well as the only goal for every living creature. To survive, one must be selfish and is naturally hurtful. There is no exception, nor there is choice. Life is selfish, and living organisms are naturally hurtful. And this fact alone is the source of all our problems.

Life being selfish is a new finding of this book. If all lives are selfish, then the next question will be: what makes our species so outstandingly bad and so tremendously hurtful? Our species is literally the cancer of the planet: growing out of control and ravaging wherever we go with very few exceptions. Why are we the most dreaded organisms by other living things? We are public enemy number one for lions, tigers, elephants, birds, reptiles, fish, plants, and trees. To them, we are gods, but very evil and cruel gods. How did we become so powerful?

What makes us so powerful? In this book, I have provided another original idea, a new theory, and a new insight. Our power has come from the unique way our species evolved—from the time our first ancestor, a common chimp, began to walk on two feet, through several stages, and eventually to us, the modern human. Our species has competed drastically different from other animals. My story does not dwell on morphological or anatomical changes—they serve as important references—rather, the focus is on something invisible and nonmaterial, something that can never be found in fossils.

Our species has abandoned the old and faithful muscle. Instead, we have relied on intelligence and cooperation to guide us, which was, and still is, a never-before-seen way. This combination was unproven and therefore highly risky, but we have overcome the impossible odds to eventually become gods to other creatures. Intelligence and cooperation have enabled our species to keep inventing simple but effective tools; it has been through the tools that we have gained godlike power.

Quite a few animals—chimps, sea otters, and some birds—use tools, but none is so desperately dependent on tools as us. Without tools, we will be pitifully unfit at any stage and for sure be eliminated in several sunrises and sunsets. With tools, we have not only handily defeated the mightiest enemies, we are also the only species that have increasingly disobeyed and ignored Mother Nature and eventually have made our own rules. We become gods. Alas! We don't have the right morality to exercise this awesome power. Like a tyrant, we use it mostly to self-serve and to indulge in short-term pleasure and convenience. This, fueled by selfishness, is the other source of the problems.

The question, then, will be: How to solve this selfish-human-god problem? The answer is definitely with the right morality, something the world still does not have. Though there are a number of existing moralities from Christianity, Islam, Judaism, Hinduism, Buddhism, and Confucianism, etc., they are all painfully outdated. None understand today's real issues. Some of the views in their teachings are also wrong. In this book, I have constructed a simple new morality that is based on the Golden Rule to solve the world's problems. The new morality is another original idea and breakthrough.

On the foundation of the Golden Rule alone, I have derived two principles that enable every person, by using common sense, to come up with his own unambiguous conclusion of moral right and wrong of a behavior or an issue. Same-sex marriage, abortion, euthanasia, or to have children freely, what has created so much debate in many of today's societies, including those most advanced countries, becomes quite easy to solve.

One of the goals of the book is to give the world a universal morality. When everyone can independently decide moral right and wrong and see an issue the same way; it will be like a universal moral traffic light. Then, we won't need authorities—who often have private agendas—to make the decisions for us and confuse us. None of the existing moral views can solve our problems; instead, they are the reasons of the problems.

When everybody knows and agrees on what is moral and is bounded by it like we obey the traffic lights, solving the global problems will be quite easy. The most effective way is for everyone to embrace moral selfishness, which is another brand-new concept. Moral selfishness has two components: (1) to be moral, and (2) to be selfish. It is opposite to the traditional moralities, which encourage selflessness and sacrifice; they are neither sustainable nor effective because they are against our nature. Moral selfishness is easy because it flows with human nature. It will be a power far greater than any form of energy we have learned to control.

And like those energies, selfishness, when under full moral control, will bring us nothing but lots of good. It will allow us to gradually transform the planet from a hellish trap to a paradise, for our benefit and for that of countless other organisms. In moral selfishness, you can be as selfish as you want provided you stay moral because morality will be the screen that separates beneficial (moral) behaviors from the hurtful (immoral) ones, and only allows the moral ones to go through. The two proposed moral principles will guide us through. With moral selfishness, the world's problems will all be solved.

This book is written following a science tradition because I am a scientist. I have defined every important concept in the book in simple terms—self, selfishness, and survival; intelligence, love, freedom, or evil. In this aspect, the book is different from traditional philosophies or even psychology, which often conveniently leaves many concepts such as a self, ego, superego, or id without definitions, and thus, is vague. In developing a theme or argument, I have gone through the trouble of clearly stating my assumptions and logic. I want a reader to fully understand what I am talking about, to criticize my ideas and logic, and to decide whether to support or to reject it.

I hope the book, because of its clarity in ideas and logic, will allow people to better understand the real issues and thus the solutions. An idea, a philosophy, or a teaching does not need to be ambiguous. Substance built upon science and reason rather than the doctrines and dogmas from authorities like Jesus, Muhammad, Confucius, and Buddha will be a better choice to tackle the planet's problems. We have been led by the authorities to dead ends for too long.

Hopefully, the new morality will unite the people of the world, who have been divided into pieces by borders, racism, and particularly religions. Then, we shall have a borderless world. Instead of wars, the globe will have lasting peace. Instead of continuously destroying our environment, we shall have clean air and water. Instead of poverty, every child that is born will be planned for and taken care of, and will have a chance to a happy life. This will be a new era. And this is the dream of the book. Again, morality will be our tool. This has been the dream of countless of people in the modern era. Unlike the other dreamers, I am very sure that this dream is doable.

Without being shy or vague, my intention of this book is to save the world, literally. It is very doable; doable because my belief is grounded on science and reason. Let me give you an analogy: If Jesus said he was going to take you to the moon, you would have every reason to doubt him. But when Kennedy declared that he would send Americans to land on the moon, no one was laughing.

The dream is doable because we now, for the first time, have discovered the source of the problems; it is a universal selfish nature of living organisms. And human selfishness, because of the power we possess, is the cause. The solution is morality—more precisely, moral selfishness. Like Kennedy's declaration to send people to the moon, our dream is based on science and reason.

The process to realize the dream will not be smooth sailing. There will be many obstacles to overcome. The religions will put up the strongest resistance because they will lose the most. There are fundamental changes in our present democratic political system, especially the way every country picks its politicians, that need to be made. Again, many politicians based on selfish reasons will fight it. I am still hopeful that the dream will one day be realized; reason and science have never failed.

TABLE OF CONTENTS

PART II

THE RISE OF THE CRUEL GODS, THE UNLIKELY ROUTE OF EVOLUTION OF THE MODERN HUMAN

PART III

THE CURE, INTRODUCING THE NEW MORALITY BASED ON THE GOLDEN RULE, THE TOOL TO FIX THE PROBLEMS

PART IV

IMPLEMENTING THE CHANGE, THE ROLE OF A GOVERNMENT AND BUILDING A HAPPY PLANET

PART I

DEFINING THE SOURCE OF THE PROBLEMS:
RAVAGING HUMAN,
THE CANCER OF THE PLANET

CHAPTER 1

A Planet Inflicted by Cancer

Some people treat our planet as a living organism—the Greeks named her Gaia, and many of us fondly call her Mother Nature. Then, the Mother is suffering from a grave and painful disease. The disease is a cancer. The cancer agent is none other than one of her children among the countless species she has nurtured and sustained. The species is *Homo sapiens,* us, the wise man and the human race, one of her latest children and the most intelligent of all living organisms. There have been many far more powerful species and organisms during the planet's three-billion-year-plus history, none—not even among the most powerful or the mightiest, including the dinosaurs and the African elephants—have caused so much hurt and damage to her. It makes us wonder what kind of animal humans are to be able to do what the powerful and the mighty can't do.

Our species began about seven to eight million years ago from a greatly disadvantaged position, from a common chimp that somehow was forced to walk on two feet. It was certainly one of nature's weirdest creations. The creature was so ill-fitted to survive that it should be destined to join many weaker species that has ended up in nature's recycle bin. Our ancestor was supposed to die within several sunrises and sunsets, or several seasons at the very most. But he did not; he miraculously managed to survive and gave rise to a number of children. They also survived, continued to evolve, made it through several transitional species, and eventually gave rise to us, the modern human.

For the most parts of our lineage's relatively short existence, our species did not show any sign of malignance. Like all Mother Nature's children, our species has lived in compliance to her rules and has

3

been obedient still. Then, things began to change. The cancer began to develop. There are three distinct stages, starting from a seemingly harmless period, to increasingly alarming, and then extremely dangerous.

Stage I: After the Discovery of Farming

If Mother Nature had been more observant, she could have noticed that our species, from the very beginning, the first chimp that began— or more correctly was forced—to walk on two feet, was bound to be a troublemaker. But she was too busy, and she had seen stranger things among the creatures she looked after. It took almost the entire 8 million years of our species' evolution to develop any symptoms. The event that has started it all was the discovery of farming by us. After farming had been fully established, our species began to grow in greater numbers. As our population grew, we needed more lands to grow food and to build houses. We began to take more and more acreage of land from indigenous species, either chasing them away or eliminating them altogether.

The lives of humans also became more complex; not everyone needed to be directly involved in producing food. Many people began to make their living by trading items. As a result, many more items besides food and shelter became necessary and were created accordingly. Farming could support far more people than hunting/gathering, a lifestyle that was gradually replaced. As always, more humans create more waste and garbage. The landscape began to deteriorate and symptoms surfaced, though hardly noticeable or any cause for concern.

Stage II: After the Industrial Revolution

The Industrial Revolution began in the eighteenth century. Like the discovery of farming, it has forever changed the way our species conducts business and lives our daily lives. We have since increasingly employed machines to do our work. With machines, we can produce much more food, clothing, and everything that we need for daily life, and in much shorter time and with much less cost and human labor. Like the discovery of farming, it appeared to be a blessing and had no ill side effects. As a result, the planet could support many more millions of people. And as a result, we needed more land to build houses, schools, factories, recreational facilities, networks of roads, and many, many more items. At this stage, our species has, without the slightest shred of doubt, become, pound for pound, the most polluting, as well as the most destructive, species that has ever lived.

Exponential number of acreages was appropriated from more and more indigenous species that were unfortunate enough to share the planet with us or lived too close. Environmental deterioration and pollution became increasingly worrisome among the highly industrialized countries. Global mass extinctions became a constant scene as we grew and expanded. If that was not bad enough, war in higher frequency and bigger scales became the norm. War not only kills us, both soldiers and innocent people, it destroys habitats and the lives that dwell in them. Within several decades after the beginning of the twentieth century, Mother Nature has seen two world wars. The symptoms of the cancer have then become full blown. Many caring people feel we need to do something to stop the cancer, yet nothing has been done or can be done because we did not know the root of the problem. And the cancer continued to develop unchecked.

Stage III: The Information Age (also known as the Computer Age, Digital Age, or New Media Age)

Even after the invention of cars and airplanes, thereby making traveling much faster for us, the planet has remained a vast place. It usually took days or weeks to get from the shore of one continent to the other. It led us to happily believe that the planet had an infinite capacity to absorb our garbage and to fully regenerate itself despite the abuses. Any biologist would tell you that our planet has an enviable system to self-cleanse, in which the wastes and pollutants from one group of organisms are happily recycled by another. So we continue to happily consume and create tons and tons of every kind of garbage in the process.

Then, the computer made its appearance. Human ingenuity allows computer technology to pick up speed in development exponentially, making the price of information dirt cheap. Computers and the Internet combined have greatly shrunk our planet. Though it still takes many hours to fly to the other side of the globe, it takes virtually no time for information to cover even the farthest apart places. The planet is still divided by borders. However, leaders in the business or political world seldom think in scope of country anymore; they now consider matters in a global context, a single entity.

Politics is also evolving quickly and is becoming far more complex. The line between an enemy and a friend has increasingly been blurred by other considerations. Business takes priority to politics, and profit routinely trumps idealism. The United States has become the biggest trading partner of Communist China. Globalization has thus hugely impacted business and trade.

One of the important consequences is it allows both goods and people to move around the planet more freely. As a result, more goods are available for consumption by people separated by a vast distance. Japanese melons, for example, can readily be shipped, still very fresh, to Hong Kong the next day after having been harvested. California produce can be flown to any corner of the globe for consumption, provided the price is right.

To accommodate the huge tonnage of goods, you need longer and bigger trucks and railroad cars. To hold more and more containers, the ships are built bigger and bigger. So are the planes for delivering the astronomical number of packages, parcels, and goods. All the transport vehicles require energy, mostly power by fossil fuel. Which, in turn, produce tons and tons of carbon dioxide, which end up in air, seas, or oceans.

People also become much, much more mobile. For families in many countries, owning vehicles powered by gas becomes indispensable. Air travel becomes more affordable, fashionable, and highly desirable. Large number of managers and executives also need to regularly fly to distant destinations for meetings. Traffic, whether on land, by sea, or in air, has quickly multiplied. And we have not taken into account the energy required and the waste created in producing all the goods and merchandize to satisfy our insatiable appetites.

Cheap information and making of ever bigger vessels and vehicles have made distributing goods much easier, and have thus greatly increased the amount of food available to people who either don't or cannot grow food in places around the world. The populations in those places grow as a result. Many of the food items shipped can hardly be categorized as necessity. Lobsters caught in Canada's east coast can quickly be delivered live to Europe or rich cities in Asia for picky diners.

To support such luxury requires burning an astronomical number of fossil fuel, which leads to further taxing of the planet.

Symptoms of a Planet Ravaged by Cancer

Suddenly, the planet no longer appears to be vast or inexhaustible; Mother Nature has finally been stretched to her limits. The ravage on her body is visible almost everywhere if one cares to look. There is hardly a cubic meter of air, a drop of water, or a square centimeter of land in her that is free from pollutants. Her wounds are everywhere and ubiquitous. She has been very sick. Her body temperature has risen noticeably; we can no longer, with good conscience, deny the serious hurt we have inflicted upon her.

There is no question that the planet is very sick. Like a sick person often does, the temperature of Mother Earth is rising. The rising temperature, global warming, is caused by the raised level of carbon dioxide we have produced, which has far exceeded Mother Nature's capacity to recycle it. As a result, it stays in the air and helps to retain heat in the atmosphere and thus raising its temperature. As a result, the weather is getting more extreme because the molecules in our atmosphere, on the average, have more energy in them. Long drawn-out droughts become more frequent—in places where it normally rarely happens. It spawns forest or bush fires besides making the land sterile. Rainfall is getting more extreme, often creating deadly floods. Tornados and hurricanes not only are more common, they are also more powerful and thus destructive.

But the extreme weather is just the tip of the iceberg. What we cannot see but is far more damaging and sinister comes from the carbon dioxide, which dissolves in water—the seas and oceans, especially. According to one estimate, we have "disposed of" 530 billion tons of carbon dioxide in the world's waters so far and we are adding one million tons of the molecules to our waters every hour. The dissolved gas raises the acidity of the water, which in turn increases the solubility of calcium carbonate, thus making it hard to form protective shells for many marine lives. There has been massive bleaching in the Great Barrier Reef from the death of many of its coral species. The once abundantly rich environment has become barren. Life must be increasingly difficult for aquatic animals, if not impossible.

Shell-forming animals and plants form the foundation of our food chain. We have yet to know the impact and consequences of this impediment. If it causes mass extinction—it is almost a certainty, just a matter of which species first, when and where—it will unquestionably wipe out the many fish species that we depend on for food. And there are over three billion people, rich and poor, who eat fish to supply 20 percent of their protein intakes in 2013. The collapse of fish species will spell famine for many and will be a calamity beyond calculating.

There is no question that Mother Nature is very sick this day. In fact, she is dying. Many mammals are disappearing; birds are vanishing in great numbers. Many reptiles, frogs, fish, and beneficial insects that were once so abundant not so long ago are difficult to find. When I lived in my native village in the southern part of China, the streams and rivers teemed with many aquatic lives, not just fish. I used to catch little frogs just for fun. Butterflies were abundant. And one could hear birds singing all year long.

I made the mistake of returning to the village sixty years after I left, hoping to relive my childhood once more. My heart was shattered when I saw my dream had become a nightmare; I almost cried. The little river in which I had spent so many hours playing, catching shrimps and fish had dried up. The bed was littered with plastic bags of all colors and sizes. Streams had become open sewage—black in color and bubbling foul gas.

But that is only one of the many parts of China that suffered this unfortunate fate. There are many places in many more countries where people live that are like that. Mother Nature is slowly dying, choking to death by the pollutants we humans have produced. We must change and we must stop this mindless crime against her. Can we stop polluting? And from killing our planet? We must change, not just for Mother Nature's sake. For ourselves, for our children and their children, and for our species' survival and for selfish reasons, we need to change.

It is not just pollution that has made lives miserable. Our love affair with war must also be stopped. War always kills lots of people; they are the lucky ones for they are spared from the many sufferings of those who continue living after. War destroys properties, land for growing food, and the people we love. To survive a war often means having to live with less food and thus constant hunger, besides the sorrow and sadness of living with families broken.

War used to be between two countries. Now, we have a government turning against its own people, killing many by chemicals. On top of that, there are groups within the country fighting and killing each other trying to gain power. The ongoing Syrian civil war has killed or wounded about half a million of its citizens, which is more than one-tenth of the country's population. It has also turned many millions into refugees, many of whom are women and children. Besides wrecking the country, the Syrian civil war, by creating millions of refugees, also spills its problems over to European countries, creating giant headaches for their politicians. Even faraway countries like Australia, United States, and Canada are not immune. We truly are living in a globalized world. How do we put an end to war in our world?

And there is widespread poverty—not just in the third-world countries like Haiti, African countries, and nations in Asia, but in very affluent countries like the United States, Canada, Australia, Germany, etc. as well. Unlike war, which usually kills a great number of people quickly, poverty kills slowly. People continue to live in drawn-out suffering, often until every drop of life has been sneezed out of them. And it will not be the end either. Children of the poor are often born into the same vicious cycle that few can escape from.

Poverty is a form of cruelty very different from war. Very few can see its true ugliness. So it is allowed to perpetuate. Though it seems to only affect some less unfortunate, it is false; in the end, everyone is hurt by it—the rich and the poor. It is the main source of social unrest and many crimes. The polarization of rich and poor often spawns riots, unrest, and crimes. That is why so many rich Africans seek to immigrate to Canada, Australia, or New Zealand. How do we end this ugliness? Is there a way to end this ugliness?

We shall continue to explore in the coming chapters. The whole book is aimed at solving the three big problems: war, pollution, and poverty.

CHAPTER 2

Life, a Very Troublesome Thing

It is debatable that love is a many-splendored thing, though there is no lack of singers singing songs praising it. The love that many sing about is, in biology, no more than an addition to sex, far from pure and noble. If there is a splendored thing in our world, it is certainly life. Life, not love, should be the many-splendored thing because the more you know about it, the more you will be amazed by it. It is so intricate, so improbable, and so mysterious.

Its origin, for example, still eludes the hardest working, the most learned, and the sharpest of minds in the scientific world. A person specializing in artificial intelligence, for example, would never fully understand how intelligence in the living kingdom is made possible, let alone be able to duplicate anything remotely resembling it. Yet, intelligence is so ubiquitous, from creatures most advanced to the most primitive, from human to bacteria. If you work in robotics, you would be so intimidated by the degree of intricacy of any insignificant animal, by its structure, function, and agility—from the very tiny to the very gigantic, from a fruit fly to a whale—that you cannot help but to feel impotent. The list goes on and on. Life, therefore, is perhaps the most splendored thing, not only on earth but throughout the cosmos.

Our search for the solution to make our planet better—to stop war, to cut down on pollution, and to eliminate poverty—has inevitably led us to question the nature of life itself. It also led us to the subsequent discovery of its nature. Despite its many splendors, life has a disturbing and sinister thing hidden at its core, making it rather ugly. A rather shocking statement, isn't it? This less than flattering fact about life has been carefully shielded by nature from us since our race began to seek understanding about things around us. It is not until now that it has been uncovered. Mother Nature has a passion to guard her many secrets; she would only grudgingly divulge them, often no more than one at a time, to those who know where and sometimes when to look, like those smart British astronomers who took advantage of a full solar eclipse to prove Einstein's notion that a massive body bends light.

Now the secret is out: all lives and living organisms have a natural tendency and need to hurt others in order to survive. They do that to self-serve, to self-preserve, and in order to survive. To live, an organism has no choice but to hurt others, often including its own kind; it is a necessity. Therefore, life is selfish, was selfish from the very beginning, has been selfish, and forever will be selfish. Life, therefore, has a dark side. To thoroughly understand this secret is crucial because it also holds the key to solving our problems.

The reason why it is so difficult to see this dark secret is: there is only one way or a particular angle to clearly see it. You need to see or define life or a living organism in an exact way to lead you there. Let me give you a couple of examples that will not lead you to the door.

Examples:

According to the definition provided by *The Free Dictionary* by Farlex, an organism is defined as:

1. *An individual form of life, such as a bacterium, protist, fungus, plant, or animal, composed of a single cell or a complex of cells in which organelles or organs work together to carry out the various processes of life*
2. *A system regarded as analogous in its structure or functions to a living body: the socialorganism.*

Or according to *Wikipedia, the Free Encyclopedia:*

In biology, an organism *is any contiguous* living *system, such as an animal, plant, fungus, archaeon, or bacterium. All known types of* organisms *are capable of some degree of response to stimuli, reproduction, growth and development and homeostasis.*

Or according to a life science textbook:

1. *They are made from structures called "cells."*
2. *They reproduce by genetic material called "DNA."*
3. *They respond to stimuli from the environment.*
4. *They synthesize an energy substance called "adenosine triphosphate (ATP)" from the environment, and they live and grow using that energy.*

You can go on and on to find as many definitions of a living organism as you please, but most of them will never lead you there and uncover this little dirty secret of Mother Nature.

Defining What Is Life

Let me give you a new definition that will do the trick. Let us define "life" as:

> *Life is a highly organized physical object, which by itself, is capable of 1) maintaining its (internal) structure for a period of time; and 2) Producing more copies of itself before the object ceases to function.*

A Physical Object Capable of Self-Maintenance

In its very essence, this is what life is, without exception. Let me explain. In our discussion, "life" and "a living organism" have the same meaning. First, it is a highly organized physical object; in particular, it has a highly organized interior. Having a highly organized interior is a prerequisite for a machine, not just an organism, to do its job. A car, for example, has a highly organized interior. From this part of the definition alone, a sharp-minded reader would immediately know that the object will breakdown naturally sooner or later. That is why any object with any degree of structure or organization will breakdown. This is why your car will breakdown, a bridge will collapse, a building will fall, and a living organism will die given time.

The spontaneous breakdown of a structured thing is a fact of life dictated by physics, by a law called the Second Law of Thermodynamics. One of the ways to understand this law is in terms of entropy, which can be explained and measured by the degree of disorder or randomness of a system. The entropy in a system tends to increase, or the things in a system tend to become disorganized. This should be a common sense, shouldn't it? This law is the reason why we have to tidy our house or apartment from time to time. When it becomes disordered to a certain point, it will eventually stop functioning. Similarly, when the interior of a living organism gets disorganized to a certain degree, it will suddenly stop functioning, a phenomenon called death.

The Second Law of Thermodynamics is also the reason every car owner needs to pay the mechanics from time to time, the City of Toronto needs to spend millions of dollars patching up the Gardiner Expressway, and a country needs a huge budget to repair infrastructure. On a grander scale, this law is also the reason our universe will die. It is the law of death; it kills everything that has any degree of structure.

To keep a structured object from becoming disorganized or breaking, work must be done to the object to repair and maintain it. It means one thing: it needs an energy supply. Now, perhaps you'll know why I have gone through the trouble of defining "life" this way. I want to lead to the fact that life, being a structured object, constantly needs energy for its maintenance. That life can self-maintain is one of the two most important concepts; it is also the one thing to look for when you suspect whether an object is living or dead.

Besides the ability to self-maintain, there is another important difference between a living and a dead object such as a bridge, a building, or a highway. Dead objects require only periodic work and maintenance: no maintenance work, no energy is required. The maintenance for a living organism, on the other hand, can never be interrupted. It needs energy 24/7 and every second. If the energy supply is interrupted for a certain period of time, death will follow shortly. How long a living organism can survive with it energy source cut off varies. For a person, cutting off his oxygen for several minutes will usually do the trick. The reason, again, is because our body is highly organized and tends to break down naturally.

The energy consumed by an organism, in effect, is to keep the entropy of that organism down to a minimum, to a level it can continue to function. Another way to view a living organism is as an object which needs and has the ability to continuously reduce its interior entropy by doing work on it. If you find such an object in nature, you are very likely to be dealing with a living organism. Interesting, isn't it?

Other than living organisms, there is no known object that is capable of self-maintenance or keeping its interior entropy down. Maybe a black hole is an exception. By sucking up the matter and energy in its vicinity, is the black hole not using them to reduce its entropy? Could a black hole be a living system? If it is, it could answer many questions, such as how life began or . . . I should stop. It is a very far-fetched thought and something far, far beyond my level! No, I am definitely not under the influence of any substance. The thought just popped up and it seems to make sense. I could not resist sharing it.

A Physical Object Capable of Reproduction

The ability to reproduce, to make more copies of the same structure, is the other feature as important as self-maintenance mentioned earlier. Like self-maintenance, reproduction also requires energy—in fact, lots and lots more energy. It is an energy-intensive process because an astronomical number of new molecules—proteins, DNAs, fatty acids, etc.—needs to be synthesized. These are all energy-rich molecules; each of them naturally costs a lot of energy to make. So this is another very important entry in the energy budget of an organism. After making the molecules, you also need to put them together to make a new individual, yet another important entry in the energy expenditure column.

To sum up, life has two distinct characteristics: (1) to maintain its interior so that it can keep functioning and (2) to reproduce itself. Both of these processes are funded by energy. The two features together are enough to separate every living organism from every machine on our planet. If you find any physical object that is capable of fulfilling these two functions, you have discovered a living organism, even if the object is not made of organic molecules like us. I am thinking about a robot that can do those two things.

Life Is Always Selfish and Must Be Selfish

Our definition of life has led us right to the doorstep of the place where Mother Nature keeps her secret. But we are not quite there yet. If it were so easy, the secret would have been out a long time ago. The next step is to ask the question: why do all living organisms do those two things? First, to maintain the interior is to prevent the Second Law of Thermodynamics from destroying its structure; to keep its structure is to allow it to continue to function.

There is a distinct purpose in the behavior of this physical object we call a living organism: it wants to continue to function. Therefore, it cannot allow the breakdown, and needs to preserve the structural integrity of its interior. To self-preserve is the only way to allow it to keep going indefinitely. To self-preserve, a living organism has to do everything exclusively to serve itself and itself only. Therefore, self-maintenance is a selfish act. Important as it is, self-maintenance is only one part of the survival story.

Reproduction is the second part, an even more important part. Why does an organism need to reproduce? The reason is simple because every living creature can maintain its interior intact for only a limited period of time; every living organism has a definite lifespan. For a bacterium, it is usually hours. Some organisms can do it for months or years; some even longer, much longer. The redwood trees, for example, can keep on going for thousands of years. Some living redwoods were born before Christ, Confucius, or Buddha, and they are still going strong. (Come to think of it, it should be a criminal offense to kill such exotic organisms for furniture, wood chips, or firewood, don't you agree?)

In the animal kingdom, some deep-sea shellfish are the champs of longevity, living more than 500 years or longer. Among mammals, the arctic whales seem to be the titleholder; some can live for more than 211 years, according to reliable information. We are not as good but still are impressive; an average Canadian male has an average life expectancy of approximately eighty years. There seems to be room for improvement.

Regardless, all organisms—you and me, a shellfish, or a tree—will fail to continue to maintain their interior after a certain period of time. In bigger organisms, the interiors do not fall apart all at once; they crumble bit by bit and one by one. I am in my mid-seventies. I don't look the same as I used to. My hair has mostly disappeared; I have a very shiny head now. More than ten years ago, I had also lost the hearing in my left ear.

I have difficulty remembering the names of friends, and finding the keys before leaving my apartment has been increasingly frustrating. I suspect that I have forgotten at least 30 percent of my Chinese vocabulary. All these symptoms are pointing to the fact that the entropy in me has been increasing steadily. When the summation of the increases reaches a certain point, one of my vital systems will suddenly fail to function and death will fall upon me. Like they say: that is it, folks!

Because a living organism has a definite lifespan, what will happen to its kind/species when an organism dies? What happens to *Homo sapiens* after I die and there will be one less organism of that particular kind in the world? So we can see that self-maintenance alone is not enough to keep the species going. And that is why every living creature must also reproduce a sufficient number of offspring before it dies. For me, I have two daughters; me and my first wife have reproduced enough children to break even.

Both self-maintenance and reproduction are selfish acts. But the two selfish behaviors serve different masters. Self-maintenance primarily serves the interest of an individual organism; to reproduce, on the other hand, serves the interest of a species, with the individuals involved often having little to gain from it and everything to lose. For a species to survive, all its members must do their best to reproduce enough copies of themselves before they die. Thus, to reproduce is the duty of an individual organism to its species. The make or break of a species therefore depends heavily on how well its members are reproducing.

The degree of success in reproduction is measured by the number of viable new copies—sons and daughters, seeds, cysts, or spores—left behind when an organism's time on the planet has expired. Biologically speaking, Bill Gates, one of the world's most successful men as measured by wealth, is not the most successful human; he does not even make it to the top billionth list of the *Who's Who of Fecundity* of our species. And for the same reason, Einstein, one of the greatest minds, was quite average compared to his contemporaries. George W. Bush, the man who turned the lives of millions of Iraqis upside down based on faulty intelligence, does not fare much better on the list either.

In view of the unequaled importance of reproduction, promiscuity of a woman is far from despicable as a priest, minister, imam, or Confucian would have her loudly condemned. Quite the contrary; it is a highly desirable biological quality. If there is one thing Mother Nature wants her children to do as frequently as they can afford to, it is to reproduce, which often involves sex. *"Make love, not war."* The message from Mother Nature is loud and clear. Surprisingly, it was John Lennon, a rock star—not a biologist and definitely not a Catholic priest—who first clearly understood Mother Nature's call.

For those that fail to pay enough attention, the penalty will be very stiff indeed: it will be the removal of the entire species from the surface of the planet, meaning game over forever for those creatures that have fallen short! The Mother has never, ever shown any mercy in punishing those who have not done enough. There will be no second chance either. Bye-bye, T. *rex.* Bye-bye, dodo birds, woolly mammoths, and millions and millions of other losers. The graveyard of extinction is full of the fossils of such doomed players—plants and animals, big and small, microscopic to humongous, aquatic and terrestrial. Goodness knows how many have vanished at some point in time without even leaving a trace.

The many species that we see today are survivors. Though luck has something to do with it—the jinxed monster lizards were case in point—none of the survivors are here by pure fluke. They all have one thing in common: they all tell successful reproduction stories that allow them to leave sufficient new copies of themselves, progeny created through DNA in their own images, generation after generation, rain or shine, in time of abundance or period of scarcity. The big white and crocs are good examples. To remain in the game, one has to be both good and be lucky—and getting lucky often certainly helps. Interest in sex often trumps other interests during mating times.

Having made it for tens or even hundreds of millions of years like the crocs and sharks does not guarantee that the species will be given a spot in the survival arena for the next round. The rules of the survival game keep changing. The weather changes, the environment will not be the same, and the players will be different. During the last few millennia, a group of new players named *Homo sapiens* has unilaterally rewritten the rules. In the blink of an eye in evolutionary time, many species—amphibians, reptiles, birds, and mammals—have been eliminated from earth by these new players.

The newcomers have barely warmed up. Mankind, through messing up the habitats of many species or by meaningless slaughter, continues to put varieties of species daily onto the train called extinction. Pandas, crocs, whales, and even some timeless sharks are onboard awaiting their departure. Despite the bleak outlook for many species, their members must continue to play the reproduction game before they die—day after day, year after year, for eons and eons . . .

There are two strategies employed in reproduction. Primitive and lower life-forms rely on producing a huge number of offspring—easily in the millions, thousands, or at least hundreds—only to leave them to fend for themselves, hoping probability will allow enough of them to make it to the next round. On the other side, higher forms of organisms, from birds to mammals, produce a much smaller number, usually in single digits, and invest a lot of time looking after the young to ensure each of them a better chance to survive. No matter what strategy a species uses, ensuring success in the reproduction game is everything.

Everywhere we look, we will find organisms, from the lowest of the low to the very top, busy accumulating whatever resources they can and channeling the excess to reproduction. In nature's survival game, there are no winners, there are only survivors. All survivors have one thing in common: they all play the reproduction game well. Give thanks if your species is allowed to play another round.

In fact, we can say that to reproduce sufficient number of offspring is the most important thing for an organism because the fate of the species depends on it. If we look at the life cycle of an organism—a fish, for example—we can usually divide it into two parts: part 1 is to get ready for reproduction, and part 2 is the actual reproduction. Before a salmon can take part in spawning, it has to grow to a certain size. It takes years of treacherous living before it finally matures and spawns. Shortly after a salmon spawns it dies. It is as if life has no more meaning after achieving the one most important goal: to reproduce. If a salmon is caught and killed before spawning, its life has absolutely no value to its species.

Another example to show the unmatched importance of reproduction is the life cycle of a virus. Among viruses, the growth phase has been deleted without endangering their survival. And self-maintenance, if any, has been kept to a minimum. All a virus does is invade a host then produce. From this strategy, we can clearly see the significance of reproduction. Again, what really counts in the survival game is whether an individual is successful in reproduction; its success as a living creature is measured only by how many "sons" and "daughters" it leaves behind. Because an individual organism can only live for a short period of time while its species can live indefinitely. A species can afford to lose its organisms; an organism can never afford to lose its species.

The Meaning of Life

"What is the meaning of life?" Or, "what is the purpose of life?" This question used to puzzle me from time to time, especially when there was nothing to watch on TV. But if we look at the question from a biological context, there is only one answer. If there is a meaning or purpose of "Life," it is to self-preserve, to self-perpetuate, to reproduce and hopefully to keep one's species around. Whether you know it or not, the meaning and purpose of life is to grow up and have children before you die—nothing more. Not difficult to understand, is it? And it also greatly simplifies the meaning of life, doesn't it?

The Interest of a Species Trumps the Interest of Its Individuals

The writing and rewriting of this book has been a continuous journey of discovery. I have my moments of eureka. Discovering that the interest of a species trumps that of its individual's was certainly one of the moments. It was almost as good as sex—or even better (I must be getting too old)—but lasts longer, to quote Stephen Hawking.

As mentioned in the previous paragraph, selfishness, as shown in self-maintenance and reproduction, serves two different masters: the individual organisms vs. its species. Though the goals of both are the same—to self-preserve and to survive. The interests of the two parties are not always in perfect alignment. Funny, isn't it? Reproduction is the part where we often see the two at odds. Strange, isn't it?

Let me explain: it is always the primary interest of an organism to self-preserve and to live as long as it can manage. However, this objective may not serve the interest of its species. For a species to successfully survive, it requires its individual organisms to give their best effort and to collectively reproduce as many offspring as possible so that there will always be a sufficient number of them to carry on the genetic relays.

As noted, reproduction is a very taxing, treacherous, and often life-ending process. If it is up to an individual, it will certainly be wise to avoid it. If that were allowed, the population of the species would certainly begin to drop. Below a certain level, the species will be endangered and therefore the avoidance must not be allowed to happen if the species is to survive. The species that failed to prevent it would have gone extinct. So when the two interests are in conflict, which party has the power to decide?

The decision always belongs to the species; an individual is powerless. And in making the decision, the species will never hesitate to hurt its individual organisms. Selfishness, no matter at what level, always spells HURT. With this rule in place, let us take a closer look at some situations.

As far as the interest of a species is concerned, an organism is no more than a gene carrier of the species where its usefulness depends on only one thing: can it reproduce? If it can, it will be most valuable to the species and should be preserved. If not, it will be useless and not worth keeping. The reproduction value of an organism therefore determines its worth within the species.

That is why in nature female organisms are far more valuable than her counterparts, the males. That is why most species will not hesitate to sacrifice the males to safeguard the females. That is why in some insects such as black widow spiders or praying mantes, the females often eat their mates during their courtships to give them some easy proteins. If it works for the species, it will be allowed and often carried out. That is also why many organisms, especially those at the lower rungs of the evolution ladder, die immediately or soon after mating. Mother Nature has never hesitated to quickly eliminate those organisms which can no longer reproduce.

How does Mother Nature do it? Mother Nature does not always resort to cannibalism where a female eats her male. Why go to such trouble if it can be done more neatly? She therefore prefers a better way to ensure that is done; she has favored using gene selection to end the lives of organisms after their reproduction. She seldom allows organisms that have passed their prime to mate either; sex in the golden age does not generally exist in the kingdom that she rules. Mother Nature is not known to be nice or considerate; she is often known as ruthlessly effective. That is the reason why many plant species are biannual or annual, and they are among the most successful. They are also the most advanced. It has taken Mother Nature a while to figure it out. Gene selection in nature often revolves around reproduction. To maximize the number of reproduction cycles, the lifespans of their individuals often are shortened to as brief as possible.

One would think only lower life forms and plants are under this cruel rule. If that is how you think, let me give you a story, a story I witnessed not long ago while traveling. It is the story of a Panamanian bitch.

The Story of the Panamanian Bitch:

A couple of years ago, I was traveling by minibus in Panama. The minibus had a number of vacant seats; it was customary for drivers to stop and wait along the way to pick up more passengers. So I was briefly stranded at a stop in a small town.

Like most towns and cities in Panama and Central America, there are often stray dogs. At the time, there were a number of them hanging around at the street corner. You could easily tell they were unwanted from their appearance. They were skinny as a rule, and their skins and bodies infected by all sorts of diseases. They were miserable and quite ugly, even for dog lovers.

Among them was a bitch that happened to be in heat. Before our bus departed, a male had noticed that. After a brief courtship, the male began to mount her. The ensuing sex scene did not bother me at all; I am a biologist. What really disturbed me and still has haunted me was the thought of what would follow several months later. The bitch would be certain to get pregnant; several puppies would be born. What kind of existence would they live?

I also immediately thought about us, the humans. One would think we would do better. Think again. What happened to the sick Panamanian bitch had happened, continues to happen, and will certainly happen to our men and women, the most intelligent animals. Unlike the bitch, we are quite aware of the hazards of having children we cannot afford, but nonetheless are too weak against the powerful sex urge, just like the bitch. The sex urge is the most important power that drives the survival of a species. It is so strong that very few people, if any, can resist it continuously. It will serve a reader well to always remember this important point—as a responsible parent or as a lawmaker.

Imagine this scenario of parents who already have several children: the family is poor, struggling only to survive another day. They both know that they cannot, under any circumstances, have another child.

And during one of the nights, they have the need and surrender to the sex drive. It only takes one single incident to get pregnant. What will happen to them and the children? Let me quote a famous line from *the Great Gatsby* by F. Scott Fitzgerald:

"One thing's sure and nothing's surer. The rich get richer and the poor get - children." It is so true, and it is also so cruel.

Mother Nature's mindless drive to force organisms, including us, the most intelligent, to reproduce despite the hazardous conditions for the participants is yet another example of the interest of a species trumping its individuals. She really does not care how many of the puppies or children will be sure to die, or what kind of existence they will live. She only cares about one thing: at the end of the day, even if one survives it is all that matters.

This rule has served her very well. As a result, many species keep on surviving and the planet achieves its balance in every habitat with every organism living in harmony. But now, humans have changed everything. This rule is the reason that the human race becomes her cancer, threatening to kill her; the chickens are coming home to roost. We must find a solution to this irony.

Before we proceed further, it will be helpful to summarize what we have discussed so far. We have defined a living organism with having two characteristics: the ability to self-maintain and to reproduce. To self-maintain is to serve an individual; to reproduce is to serve the species. The two behaviors are linked to achieve one goal: they serve to allow a species to survive. Or we can define a living organism as a physical object that always has a goal to self-preserve and to survive.

Now, we are ready to push the door open and get inside Mother Nature's living world and see games of survival at their most raw. It is not a beautiful world, especially for those of you who believe in the Disney version. So be warned! What you are going to see may shatter your ideal world and innocence.

CHAPTER 3

The Cruel Game of Survival

Let us put the special glasses on so that you can see every organism—regardless of its size, type, or in what type of habitat—in the midst of its survival. Every single one of them is doing one of the same three things: defending itself, obtaining energy mostly through food, or reproducing. Nothing more. Simple and easy to remember, isn't it? It is rather easy for us to see that they will be busy obtaining energy and engaging in reproduction sooner or later; the self-defense part is not that obvious from what we have discussed. We shall spend some time dwelling on that. But first, let us see how the various organisms get their energy.

The Three Things We All Do to Survive

1. Getting Energy

Though there is plenty of energy around us—solar, wind, wave, lightning, or from water flow, etc.—only a very limited few types of energy can be used by organisms to carry out the various metabolic activities. Contrary to fairy tales, monsters cannot eat rocks or swallow sand, for example, to get energy. The materials around us, the inorganic world, has little energy left for use by any type of organisms. Then, the question becomes: how do living organisms get their energy?

To answer this question, we can divide the living organisms on our planet into two groups from the ways they obtain energy. The first group is called autotrophs, meaning self-feeding or self-nourishing organisms. The second group is called the heterotrophs that can't feed themselves.

Autotrophs and heterotrophs are not taxonomical names; they are terms for describing how an organism feeds and gets its energy, nothing more.

There are two types of autotrophs depending on how they self-feed. The first are the chemoautotrophs, organisms that exploit the energy released/available to them during some oxidizing chemical reactions. The oxidation of hydrogen sulfide to sulfite and further to sulfate, or ammonia to nitrite and then nitrate, for example, yields free energy available to the organisms that have the enzymes to direct and control such chemical reactions. The chemoautotrophs then use the energy to synthesize more complex organic molecules. The molecules thus made have more energy stored in them; they can then be used either as energy source or for body building. That was how most of the complex organic molecules on our planet first came to exist; they were to be found only in the body of chemoautotrophs. Chemoautotrophs are widely believed by scientists to be the earliest kinds of living organisms on our planet. Many of them are also specialists, capable of making a living in the harshest environment, like near thermal vents or very acidic sulfur pools around geysers.

The second type is the photoautotrophs. This type of organism uses the energy of sunlight instead of oxidizing chemical reactions to convert carbon dioxide and water—compounds with no usable energy—into carbohydrates, energy-rich organic compounds. The carbohydrates thus obtained are then used by the photoautotrophs for energy source or materials to make other body molecules. The process in which light energy is trapped and stored in carbohydrates is called photosynthesis, when the energy in some photons of sunlight is captured by a special pigment in the photoautotrophs. The most common type of photoautotrophs are green plants—algae, *Spirogyra*, mosses, trees, bushes, and grasses. Green plants have a pigment called chlorophyll mostly located in their leaves; it is chlorophyll that traps the photons in certain parts of the sunlight's spectrum. Wherever—not just leaves—there is chlorophyll, the part can carry out photosynthesis to produce food. However, chlorophyll cannot use the "green" photons in the spectrum and reflects them, thus giving leaves of most plants their color.

At this point, a reader may doubt or even object our contention that to be selfish always means a need to hurt. Since an autotroph obtains its energy and materials to build its body by self-making them, there seems to be no reason for it to harm other organisms, correct? But that is only partly true. Let us use a maple tree as example. For it to be able to carry out photosynthesis to self-feed, it needs carbon dioxide and water. Carbon dioxide is readily available in the air; it seldom posts a shortage and therefore will not be a problem for any tree, or for that matter, any plant. Water, the other raw material for photosynthesis, will not be so freely available. In fact, getting enough water will be one of the most pressing problems for a land plant. Our maple tree will certainly be among the plants needing it.

For most plants, water comes from the earth they grow on and it usually is in short supply. To get water, the plants in the same area always need to compete. The way to compete is by sending many roots around the soil, as many as it can afford to. To grow new roots requires a supply of lots of new complex organic molecules; in short, it needs lots of energy making them. Where does the energy come from? From its leaves, of course.

So a plant that can synthesize more food will be able to afford more root growth, which in turn will allow the plant to absorb more water, together with the dissolved mineral nutrients, from the soil. Getting more water enables its leaves to make more food that can be used to grow more new everything. It is the rich get richer scenario. Competition is always like that.

Now, imagine you are a new plant, be it a maple from the same plant or another type, freshly out of a seed and trying to get established. What kind of chance would you have? From the first day of your existence, you will find yourself "squeezed" both from above and below ground. You will die of thirst and hunger pretty soon from the inability to absorb enough water and to carry out photosynthesis. You just got "muscled" out by the established trees around you, and the one that kills you may be none other than your own parent. That is survival!

If that is not bad enough, quite a few plants also secrete poisons into their environment to prevent the growth of other plants and possibly intruding into their territories. It is like a kind of homemade herbicide. So don't ever get the idea that plants are friendly and harmless. If you were the new plant trying to grow next to the established ones, you will immediately "feel" the rejection and assaults all around you. Until you die.

Competition always exists among plants; it, ironically, is always at its fiercest when growing conditions are most favorable, such as in tropical rain forests. Despite plentiful rain and sunlight, the resources will soon be exhausted because of the profuse growth of plants in the area. Plants all need the same two things, water and sunlight, which always seem to be in short supply. This is also true for lives in general, not just for plants: an environment fit for life always attracts lots of every kind of organism, all wanting to make their living there, after the same kind of resource, and thus creating the most relentless competition and causing the widest scope of hurts. Similarly, competition for resources and the hurts that come with it—the two appear to be married—also apply to chemoautotrophs. Life always involves competition, and competition always hurts.

Now, it is time to look at the hurts from self-preservation among the heterotrophs, organisms that cannot feed themselves. You know they will need energy, and you also know by definition that they cannot get it themselves. So how do they get their energy and the complex molecules to build their bodies? The answer is simple: they need to get them from somewhere; they need to ingest ready-made complex organic compounds from outside sources. And since those complex compounds exist only in the bodies of other organisms, live or dead, the answer will be obvious, isn't it?

Let us discuss the types of heterotrophs according to the types of food they consume. They can either get it from the bodies of dead organisms or from the live ones. Heterotrophs that "eat" dead organisms can either be decomposers or scavengers. Heterotrophs that consume living materials are more diverse: case 1, parasites. They get food from the bodies of living organisms much bigger than themselves. Case 2, herbivores: animals that eat exclusively plants. Case 3, carnivores: animals that eat only meat. Or lastly, case 4, omnivores: animals that eat both plants and meat.

Decomposers were most likely the first type of heterotrophs that evolved from autotrophs. Having lost the ability to self-feed, they did not have any choice but to consume the autotrophs they could find. They were the first type of organism to evolve from autotrophs and are in general much smaller organisms. They are mostly bacteria and fungi. Let us use a fungus called *Penicillium* mold as our example for discussion. A *Penicillium* mold commonly grows on a piece of bread left in the open; it also loves to grow on oranges, peaches, and many other fruits. It is also the organism that gives blue cheese—my favorite—its bluish spots. As a *Penicillium* mold grows, it secretes digestive enzymes to break down the complex organic molecules in the substrate—bread, cheese, or fruit—and then absorbs them for its own use.

At this point, a reader may ask, justifiably: "What is the hurt in the *Penicillium* mold feeding on a piece of bread, growing in a cheese, or rotting a fruit?" No, there is no hurt to the things it feeds on. Quite the contrary, by feeding on those things, a *Penicillium* mold helps to quicken the recycling of the carbon atoms tied up in those complex organic molecules. Without its help, it may take forever to free those atoms again. Having lots of carbon atoms tied up will lessen the amount of carbon dioxide available and the organic compounds to be made from them, and thus slows down the growth of every kind of living organism.

As always in nature, when there is food, there will always be many "hungry" organisms fighting for it. That means only one thing: competition. When there is competition, one competitor always tries to hurt or kill the other competitors. The competition for the same food source was what led to the discovery of penicillin by Alexander Fleming in 1928 and later saved hundreds of thousands of soldiers' lives. Penicillin is a very powerful antibiotic secreted by *Penicillium* mold capable of killing many varieties of disease-causing bacteria. It contaminated many of Dr. Fleming's cultures by killing the bacteria there. The rest is history.

Penicillium mold is one of the countless types of fungi, organisms that specialize in breaking down complex organic compounds into smaller ones and absorbing them to make their living. Fungi are decomposers; they are nature's important recyclers. Besides fungi, there are other decomposers such as bacteria, earthworms, insects such as dunk beetles and house flies, etc. As a general rule, the hurts and cruelty from competing for the same food source by decomposers are much less obvious to the unaided human eyes. Whether you see it or not, you can be damn sure that the hurt will always be there. Selfishness always hurts.

Some books put decomposers under scavengers. To be less confusing, let us treat the two separately and reserve the term *scavengers* for animals that feed on carrion. If an animal can put up with the foul smell emitted by the decomposing bacteria making their living in it, carrion or a decaying animal's body contains serious amounts of very useful organic molecules which they can use as energy source and bodybuilding blocks. There are many animals that not only can put up with it but really, really love it. The foul smell was often used by the scavengers as guide to get to the rotten food, which, literally, is rotting. Taste is often a very personal thing to animals.

Scavengers are much bigger than the decomposers. Crocs and Komodo dragons are reptiles that often make their living by scavenging. Birds like vultures, hawks, and eagles are other examples. Among mammals, coyotes, hyenas, Tasmanian devils, and raccoons are scavengers. In nature, food is always scarce and the dead body of an animal always attracts many diners, all trying to get their unfair share. Who will get more eventually depends on only one thing: who is stronger; i.e., who has bulkier muscles to operate deadly beaks and talons, or jaws and claws? As a general rule, scavengers are often predators, or vice versa. Hungry animals are not picky.

Finally, it is time to look at the ugliest selfish organisms among Mother Nature's creatures, the kinds that really, really hurt: the lives of heterotrophs that dine on living materials. We shall start with case 1, parasites. There are two types of parasites: (1) endoparasites and (2) ectoparasites. Endoparasites live inside the bodies of their hosts, whereas ectoparasites live outside. Regardless, both types weaken and harm their hosts; in more serious cases, they also end up killing them. Without exception, they cause diseases.

Many endoparasites are microscopic in size, like viruses, bacteria, protozoans, and fungi. Though they are all disease-causing agents; some are worse than others. Malaria is one of the worst; the disease is caused by a genus of protozoan called *Plasmodium,* which is transmitted by a feeding mosquito into a person's body. Malaria is quite common in tropical and subtropical regions. In 2015, more than 200 million people were infected and about half a million died. The protozoans that cause malaria live in the red blood cells of a person and eventually destroy them; the disease hugely weakens the bearer. It is one of the very common diseases when I was living in my native country. Malaria is but one kind of disease caused by parasites; there are many equally harmful and deadly ones. Again, selfishness hurts.

Endoparasites can be big and are clearly visible. Some can often exceed 10 cm or more. Most of them are worms that live inside the organs of a diverse group of animals ranging from fish, amphibians, reptiles, birds, and mammals. Endoparasitic worms affect more than a billion people on the planet every year and cause lots of human misery and suffering.

Not every parasite lives inside its host; some live outside. They are ectoparasites. They also cause diseases on top of stealing precious body materials such as blood and nutrients from their hosts. Self-preservation hurts; you can find examples from the life cycles of these organisms, most of which are animals. Most troublesome and thus well-known examples are lice, mites, ticks, and mosquitoes. Each of them is a little vampire. Besides sucking up your blood, they also leave some disease-causing endoparasites. *Plasmodium*, the agent causing malaria as discussed, is carried by mosquitoes. I was infected by lice when I was living in Hong Kong while playing with the kids from a fisherman's family. There are two ways to get rid of them: by chemical treatment or by shaving the hair. I chose the latter. It got rid of the cursed insects before I lost too many nights of sleep. I was very happy when Mother chose to dispose of my hair, together with the insects and their eggs, by burning it.

We have come to case 2, herbivores. They eat plants exclusively. I guess very few of us, even the most kindhearted, would consider eating plants hurtful. Because 1, herbivores have no choice, and 2, plants do not have feelings. An herbivore hurts and often kill the plants it eats for sure, but is it cruel? It certainly seems a bit crazy posting the question. Does it?

Case 3, predators. Here is what some will call *nature, red in tooth and claw*. The scene of a predator hunting down and eating a prey is always graphic and gruesome. Some overly sensitive and kindhearted could lose nights of sleep after watching. Invariably, flesh is torn apart and blood by the gallons is spilled, with the prey shaking and trembling before its end comes. It is hurting and cruelty at the highest level, visually at least. You get the picture and the message; let us stop.

Case 4, omnivores. They are organisms that eat both plants and meat. They are not picky and seem to get the best the world has to offer in filling their needs for energy and materials to build. Omnivores are found almost in every group of organisms, invertebrates, fish, amphibians, reptiles, birds, and mammals. Among the apes, in the degree of increasing omnivorousness, are orangutans, gorillas, gibbons, chimps, and humans.

Orangutans are almost strictly vegetarians. However, when very hungry, they may catch and eat a slow-moving loris that may happen to be around. Gorillas often supplement their diet with a small percentage of insects. Gibbons are known to eat birds. And chimps are famous for fishing for termites and making occasional hunting trip to catch monkeys. Given the choice, chimps seem to prefer meat. We humans are the most versatile; we eat vegetables and meat. And among humans, the Chinese are the kings of the omnivores. I know because I am Chinese. Hungry or not, our diet includes lots of fungi, plants, and animals, which range from insects, fish, frogs, snakes and turtles, birds, and many mammals, including dogs and monkeys for some. Chinese are almost single-stomachedly responsible for endangering many species of sharks from their love affair with shark-fin soup.

Being omnivorous means not picky in food and having a wide appetite for every kind of organisms. It certainly makes finding food easier and thus hugely increases humans' chances of survival, possibly from the very beginning. That also has made humans so destructive in ravaging the planet. We shall get back to this point in the part dealing with the origin and evolution of our species.

Before we leave this part, I need to correct myself. Not all feeding activities are hurtful and need to cause harm to other organisms. The noted exceptions are organisms that are in symbiotic relationship where two often different species of organisms live together to benefit each other without causing any harm to the other party. There are many examples in nature. To get a better understanding, I would urge a reader to google the topic. Though symbiosis is comparatively rare in nature, it is worth bringing up the topic here for one reason: selfishness doesn't always need to hurt. It can be beneficial, as indicated among the symbiotic participants, the symbionts. Nature's symbionts give us a way to exercise our selfish nature and make a living; it is to do win/win, the most beautiful behavior in a selfish world. Symbiosis is like a bright star in a dark night; it gives us a direction to live harmoniously with other organisms. We shall get back to the way to do win/win in the morality part of this book.

2.   Self-defense—In Animals and in Plants

To survive, every organism, regardless of its kind, size, and where it lives, needs to defend itself. The reason is obvious: when your body happens to have everything that other organisms need to survive, it will make you a target for their attack, will it not? Let me quote *Avatar*: "*When people are sittin' on* shit *that* you want, you make *'em your* enemy." It is not Shakespeare, but it most accurately describes nature. That is why a mosquito will like nothing more than sucking your blood, a hookworm taking nutrients from your intestine, or a tiger wanting to eat you alive.

Nothing personal! It is survival. There is one big difference though. A mosquito or tiger does not see you as its enemy. You are no more than food that happens to be conveniently around and it will be its right to take it from you. To survive another day, every creature must constantly defend itself, 365 and 24/7.

Defense among Animals

First, let us look at the strategies among animals. There are many different strategies of self-defense among them.

Bulging muscles equipped with sharp claws and teeth

The best way could be by bulging muscles. If you happen to be the top predator in the circle you live, it will be the best guarantee that no one would dare to attack you. Or you are the Goliath, like an African bull elephant, it will also assure your safety. In self-defense, size matters. That is why lions, tigers, or killer whales fear no other animals. The Americans are firm believers of *the best defense is offense* principle; that is why the country always has the biggest defense budget among the countries on the globe.

Our world is not perfect. Even the biggest and the mightiest have their nemesis. They are not always capable of defending themselves against every kind of enemy. Lions, tigers, and bull elephants do get sick; their sickness is caused by viruses, bacteria, and fungi, all of which are very small and invisible. Many parasitic insects also feed on these rulers.

Run, run, and run

We can call it the Forrest Gump strategy. If you don't have the biggest muscle, sharp claws, and teeth for defense, this strategy may suit you; it is by outrunning an attacker, by escaping. To be able to escape, an animal needs to be nimble and possess superior speed compared to its predators. That is the way a wildebeest, zebra, gazelle, or giraffe survives attacks from lions, cheetahs, or hyenas.

Not only the adults of these animals can run faster than their predators, their babies are also able to do so soon after they are born. Within hours and after a number of trials, most baby herbivores can manage to run fast enough to escape an enemy. I still clearly remember the surprise—or more correctly, shock—of witnessing how a pony learned to run soon after its birth on a documentary video. Within maybe a couple of hours, the pony can keep pace with the mother, running happily side by side with the mare. As a general rule, most herbivores can outrun their predators very early in life. What happens if you fail? You die and your species may become extinct, depending on how widespread is the failure. Simple, isn't it?

To fly away

No doubt, this is a very good way to self-defend. Insects and birds in general can fly away from danger. Like every strategy, it is not perfect, because many predators can also fly and fly even faster. Nothing is completely foolproof.

What happens if you can neither fight nor run away? Mother Nature has provided for these poor creatures several solutions:

Protective armors

There are many animals that depend on shells, exoskeletons, bony armor to protect them. With these devices for protection, the animals have to give up speed. Even if you were Usain Bolt, you won't be able to win any race in armor. But it hardly matters because they don't need to run away. They simply withdraw into the shell or armor and wait out the dangers. Snails, turtles, and armadillos are animals that don't have to run to be safe.

Camouflage

To be able to hide in plain sight of your enemy is certainly a great way to self-defend. It could be quite risky for those that have not quite perfected the art. But for many fish, insects, birds, and mammals, they are so blended in with the backgrounds that you can be staring at them and don't notice them at all. Again, satisfy yourself by googling it.

It is not only a prey that needs to blend in; even a top predator often camouflages itself. It makes it unnoticeable to its prey and thus enables it to launch a surprise attack, thereby greatly increasing the chance of success. When a prey finds out, it is too late. That is why lions and cheetahs have coats that match the background they hunt. Or even if you are the top dog, it is always prudent not to unnecessarily expose yourself to danger or you'll be someone's dinner. For this reason, aquatic animals, especially fish, all have greyish white bellies and dark backs to make them hard to spot from below or above. In a hungry world, a little bit more caution always goes a long way.

To retreat to a nearby burrow

This is another common strategy. There are many burrow or tunnel builders; they are found in every group of animals. Among mammals, many construct underground burrows for escaping their enemies. A good example is a clan of meerkats that builds elaborate tunnels that have many entrances to allow each member to take cover in looming danger. Tunnel building is not just for the weak; the strongest and fiercest also do it. The list of tunnel builders ranges from lions, wolves, hyenas, foxes, and mice, etc. The tunnels are sometimes for their puppies; they are often also for adults to hide in.

To have poisonous organs

Many animals harbor poisons in their bodies, making them very unpalatable, at the least, or fatal for consumption. Some tropical frogs, for example, have poison glands in their skin that can kill the animal that has eaten them by mistake. On my trip to Panama, I visited Red Frog Island, which, as the name implies, is home to quite a few red frogs. I came across a few of them when hiking among the trees. They are beautiful and lovely little things about an inch in length, brightly red in color with some black dots on the body. I was quite tempted to catch and hold one of them but wisely controlled my urge.

A number of species of fish also store toxins in their liver, making it fatal if they are ingested. Pufferfish is a highly valued delicacy in Japan. Only certified chefs are allowed to prepare the fish for *sashimi*. Still, there have been occasional deaths from eating *fugu*. Stonefish is another example. In general, poisonous creatures are brightly colored to warn would-be diners not to have any funny ideas. It is a wise strategy because it won't do anyone any good if it gets eaten unwittingly.

Mimicry

They are the impersonators in nature; creatures that pretend to be someone else. For example, creatures that are not themselves poisonous resembling the poisonous ones. In this case, a harmless scarlet king snake closely resembles a deadly coral snake. It is difficult for some predators to tell them apart when both species are found in the same habitat. As a result, the impersonator often escapes danger. There is a little rhyme to tell them apart. It goes like this: "Red touches black, safe for Jack. Red touches yellow, kills a fellow." Knowing that my memory is not always dependable, I would rather stay away from such creatures than try to be smart. In human societies, there are people who impersonate Elvis and make a very good living. But that is another type of story totally.

Safety in numbers

If you are a member of a large assembly, your chance of being picked up and killed by a predator will be much lower than if you are alone. It is simply probability at work. This is how most locusts survive in a swarm, fish form schools, birds flock, and herbivores in Africa plains come together to feed and form herds.

Besides finding safety in numbers, it would make it easier for a bird to escape pursuit of a hawk in a flock than doing it solo, because when there are too many targets the hawk gets distracted. Staying in a group often increases your safety and chances to survive.

An alert and observant reader may realize: we humans have none of those defensive devices! Tarzan is a myth. Our strongest will have no chance in fighting any carnivore barehanded and have any hope to win. You can be the fastest man who ever lived, but you can pretty much forget about outrunning a tiger, lion, a relatively slow bear, or for that matter, any four-legged beast trying to make you its dinner. Not only were we not born with any protective armor, our bodies are naked and therefore we're called naked apes. We don't have protective fur coats like many animals either. Humans are quite easily spotted in the environment. Our species in general has not been tunnel builders. With no burrow to hide in and our flesh not being poisonous at all, we are carnivores' dream meals. Forget about Kobe beef; human flesh is supreme.

By every criterion we have discussed we should be easy meals. Yes, most likely, our kind has stuck together from the beginning but the number in any group was likely in the tens, not remotely what you can call swarming. How do we or have we been defending ourselves? The answer is certainly not by sharp claws or powerful jaws; nor is it with speed. The answer is: we have been unique in the way we compete; a way that has never been employed in the planet's history, and will not likely to ever be repeated again. It has made us godlike and also exceedingly destructive. We shall discuss the point in great detail in the part dealing with the evolution of our species.

Regardless of what method an animal relies on, its goal remains the same: to avoid being eaten, to live another day, to survive. To increase their chance of survival, some animals use more than one scheme. Stonefish, for example, resemble the rocks in their environment; they are also extremely poisonous. Zebras, besides being very speedy, also stay in a herd. Strong as lions are, they also learn to blend in with their settings. Animals in nature are very resourceful; they always find ways to protect themselves because none can afford to fail.

Defense among Plants

How do plants defend themselves? They are immobile as a rule, so forget about running away from an animal that wants to eat them. They don't have muscles to fend off an attacker either. Does it mean they will be sitting ducks? No, or there will not be so many plants around. So plants can definitely defend themselves. In general, there are two categories of self-defense among plants: physical and chemical.

Physical means

In this method, many plants make use of a physics principle which defines pressure; i.e., pressure equals to a force applied, divided by the area of the object through which it is applied. Let us forget about physics and use our common sense. For a knife to cut through things easily, we need to sharpen it. To sharpen it is to make the cutting edge as thin (or small) as possible. Or for a needle to pierce something effortlessly, it needs to have a pointed tip; a pointed tip is something that has a very, very small area, so small that you need a magnifying glass to just see it.

Plants don't know physics, but that is exactly the kind of device many of them use for self-defense. Most people would know about the thorns on roses (should be called *prickles*) and some have actually gotten pricked by them. It hurts. Because of the prickles, few herbivores would consider eating a rose plant no matter how hungry they are. Other than roses, many plants have their stems, branches, and even leaves covered with needlelike parts that are capable of easily piercing through the skin and causing pain to would-be diners.

The physical defense devices range from thorns, prickles, spines, and trichomes. Though all of these devices are capable of piercing through your skin and thus inflicting pain, some devices are more hurtful than the others. Some plants are so densely covered with long, brittle spines and prickle that just looking at them makes you shiver. If you have made the unfortunate mistake of finding out how much it hurts, you'll not likely to forget it, ever! Deterrence is the best defense for plants.

Chemical means

Plants also use chemistry for defense. Many plants contain toxins or nasty chemicals that make them very unpalatable even if you are very hungry. In general, these chemicals either make you hate the plants, get sick, or in the extreme, kill you. Unfortunately for most herbivores, they are not born with the knowledge to tell which plants are not to be eaten. And they usually can't communicate the knowledge like humans can. So they have to learn it the hard way, most likely by making the mistake. Not nice at all.

Among poisonous plants, some actually look very cute—to human eyes at least—making them quite attractive and wanted. However, a biologist would tell you that in nature bright colors, which we associate with beautiful things, are actually loud warnings! "I am poisonous!" Every animal seems to know this simple fact and stay away, except some humans, often causing them much sorrow.

Oleander is one of them. Because oleander is so hardy and nice looking, the plants have been grown along many highways. However, the sap of oleander is poisonous and can be used to terminate pregnancy and induce abortion—from what I heard. That is why many Chinese villages forbid planting the species. The toxicity of oleander is well-known and documented. In Sri Lanka, it is a choice suicide agent because it is easy to get.

Another poisonous plant is the castor bean plant; the toxin is a protein called ricin, which can kill if it is ingested more than a certain level and has in fact been used in the so-called Umbrella Murder. Again, I urge you, the reader, to google the topic and find more interesting readings besides learning to protect yourself. After all, we are discussing self-defense here.

Unlike animals, most of the defense mechanisms employed by plants are based on hurting would-be attackers, of which most are trying to eat them. At the least, it causes physical pain, like the prickles on a rose, thorns in a crown of thorns, or spines on a cactus. At its extreme, it can kill, like the many toxins found in beautiful-looking plants. Of course, there are some that employ benign means, such having tough and heavy skins, like the leaves and trunks of many trees.

Similar to animals, some plants double ensure their safety by employing more than one scheme, such as having their bodies covered with prickles or spines and containing toxins in addition. Some also play the numbers game by having countless of them growing at the same time and place to ensure some of them would survive after a herd of herbivores has passed through. Others, such as grass, keep some parts buried and offer the blades to a grazer; it can regenerate soon after.

3. Reproduction

Arguably, and based on the interest of a species often routinely trumps its individuals', reproduction is the most important part in the life of an organism. Provided an organism can somehow reproduce enough offspring without having to grow and mature, without means of self-defense, and can't make its own food, its species can still survive. Viruses are very close to being, if not actually are, that kind of organism. Or if you were forced to give up two of the three survival activities, which two would you give up and the species could still survive? Obviously, you would not give up reproduction, because without it there would not be any more new individuals coming and the species would become extinct for sure. Reproduction can be compared to our head; it is absolutely indispensable, and without it there will be no existence.

If we can agree on the utmost importance of reproduction, perhaps we can understand biology differently: all the activities of an organism—be it a bacterium, fungus, plant, or animal—are directed to one goal, and that is to reproduce. If the collective members of a species are doing their parts, their species will survive. So reproduction is the prime deciding factor on the survival of a species and it cannot be stressed enough.

Because of its unmatched importance, every species, through gene selection, will try its best to make reproduction a stellar success. Again, using the same analogy, if you have to be weak in certain parts of your survival game, you don't want to be weak in reproduction. Pandas are animals very weak in this department. Without human intervention, the cuter-than-teddy-bear animals will certainly join the company of many losers. All the organisms on our planet today are survivors that are at least very good, if not great, in reproduction.

To reproduce, most organisms involve sex. Contrary to what you may think, it is not for the fun of the participants, the males and females. We shall explain this point in the section dealing with the morality of sex in this book. And when it involves sex, there will always be competition for mating, usually among the males. Competing to mate is another place to look for organisms—among the more advanced animals in particular—hurting and harming each other in a world driven by selfishness. In mammals, it is a general rule that mating is reserved for the strongest and the fittest. And usually, it is the males that need to compete. There is only one way to find out who is the strongest; it is in a combat where the combatants will prove their worth to sire the next generation. The defeated, besides losing their hopes to mate, often sustain fatal wounds, weaken and die from them. Nature is cruel; the privilege to mate does not come cheap.

The reproduction part of humans is rather odd by every mammal's standard. 1) Our males don't normally need to fight for mating. Rather, possibly from very early, it has been up to the females, the women, to choose her mates. 2) Sex is not always linked to reproduction; i.e., to get pregnant. Unlike most mammals, the women in our lineage have been happily engaged in sex when there is absolutely no chance to reproduce. Other than the bonobo chimps, humans are the only animals that frequently engage in unreproductive sex. This is very odd in nature; it seems to be a waste. 3) Both parents take part in bringing up a child. This is very, very unusual among mammals. To get the "fathers" involved in child caring is quite rare among all animals except among birds. I might have overlooked some examples, but we humans are the only mammals that both parents take part in child-rearing. Neither the regular chimps nor bonobo chimps—both are our closest relatives—have the fathers involved. Why? We shall discuss this point later. It is crucial to understand all these abnormalities in playing the survival game before we will understand why our species is so powerful.

To sum up, to survive, every organism has to fulfill three duties: (1) to obtain food in order to get energy and build parts for their bodies; (2) self-defense, because most organisms, except green plants and some chemoautotrophs, are unable to self-feed, and therefore need to obtain food from the bodies of other organisms, live or dead. Therefore, a living organism is under constant threat that it may become someone's meal. (3) To reproduce a sufficient number of descendants or the species will become extinct. All three survival activities can lead to hurting others because they usually require an organism to compete. Survival is selfish because it always serves the interest of the organism that partakes. It also hurts in one way or another because it requires competition; i.e., to defeat or kill your rivals.

In the following, we shall use the life histories of three organisms to show how they compete and how they hurt in the name of survival. We shall look at the life histories of a male lion, a melon plant, and the wars in the microbe.

Examples in the Cruel Game of Survival

In every language, *selfishness* is a bad word because it always implies hurt to others. I still remember in one of the nasty fights with one of my exes she pointed her index finger at me and said: "You know? You are a very selfish man." What followed was not pretty at all. Knowing what I know now, I could have responded with a smile: "You know, love, you are damn right!"

In biology, selfishness comes from a need for self-preservation; it is a universal characteristic defining all living organisms. It will most probably be also true for organisms on other planets if they exist. If human selfishness hurts, self-preservation among animals, plants, and microorganisms often kills; it is much more hurtful than human selfishness. The game of survival is always cruel.

We shall look at the life histories of several organisms in the living kingdoms to show the point. First is the life history of a lion, the top predator in the animal kingdom.

The Life History of a Lion

At birth, a lion cub weighs about 3 pounds. It is blind, totally helpless, and depends fully on its mother for milk and protection. Helpless it is, but it does not mean that the survival game will wait. From day one, a cub must learn to stay safe from its many enemies like hyenas, leopards, and eagles, which prey on lion cubs. Though not for food, buffalos and elephants hate lions; they often seek out the den where lion cubs are hiding by their scent and trample them to death. To make matters worse, a newly born cub does not enjoy the protection of its mother's pride because a lioness usually leaves her pride behind and labors in seclusion. There are times when a mother needs to leave her cubs to go hunting. When she is away, the cubs have to look after themselves. The cubs instinctively know how to stay safe during the mother's absence. To avoid detection of her cubs by enemies, a lioness keeps moving them to new hiding places several times a month before the scent in the den becomes too strong. Competition for milk for a cub begins very early too. A lioness usually gives birth to a litter of two to four cubs. Therefore, a cub has to compete with brothers and sisters at feeding time.

If a cub survives six to eight weeks, it, together with the others, will be integrated back to its mother's pride. Then, it will be much safer. But does it mean a cub will be totally safe? It depends. The safety of a cub in a pride depends on its father, the ruling male of the pride. From time to time nomad male lions will come to challenge the ruler. A king must defend his reign on his own, with absolutely no help from his lionesses. If a ruling lion defeats the succession of challengers, it will stay in power and continue to rule. Its cubs will then be safe. If defeated, all the cubs fathered by the dethroned king will be mauled to death shortly after the new ruler takes over. A lioness may defend her cubs but she is often no match for the much stronger and bigger new ruler. So there is still danger for the cubs.

A cub will depend on milk for about six months before it is weaned. The competition for milk after joining its own pride will not get easier. A cub often has to compete with cubs from other lionesses. In a pride, milk is communal. A nursing lioness does not discriminate other cubs. It is first come, first served at feeding times. If a cub is lucky, it will find itself bigger and stronger than cubs from other lionesses because it is older. It will outcompete the weaker cubs and grow bigger and stronger, and thus stretch its advantage. On the flip side, it may have to compete with older cubs and not get enough milk, and eventually may starve to death. Life is not always about playing for lion cubs. The difference between life and death is always paper thin in the game of survival.

A cub becomes fully mature in three years. It is show time for him! Unlike his sisters, he is no longer welcome in his pride; he gets chased away by his own father. His mother also wants nothing to do with him. Quite often, a newly homeless young lion will not have a brother to hang around with; he is really on his own. The survival game is now getting serious; he has no one to depend on now. It is make or break time.

First, he will have to defend himself. He has no friends, not even other lions. A herd of buffalos is not to be messed around with. Ditto a pack of elephants. Strong as he is, he is still no match for the powerful and united foes. Even a group of hyenas will challenge and bully him. Though a top predator, he is no ruler.

Second, he needs to get food. Since leaving the pride, he has been almost in constant hunger. Getting a full stomach is a rare luxury. There will be no more free meals from then on; he has to do his own chasing and killing. Inexperienced, his targets often find ways to escape. After lots of chasing, turning, and more chasing, he often comes up empty—empty pawed and empty stomached. Eventually, he will be able to bring down a gazelle. He must eat fast and gulp down as much meat as possible before the ever-present hyenas come to harass him and rob him. Alone, young, and inexperienced, he will avoid a showdown with a pack of daring and desperate hyenas.

Third, his sexual need is getting stronger and stronger. Fully mature and strong, the urge to mate—one of nature's most powerful driving forces—has been relentless upon him. In the animal world, getting a chance to mate is always very difficult for males. Among mammals, it is an extremely competitive business, so competitive that a loser can be mortally wounded in a fight with other suitors. For our young lion to have sex means to defeat the ruling male of a pride in combat. A ruling lion is never a pushover; he is always strong and at his prime. It is extremely risky and often a matter of life and death to challenge him. Besides having an edge of free food from his wives, he is also more experienced in fighting. After all, it is what he does for a living. Odds will certainly be against our young lion.

Mating is so competitive that it is not uncommon for many male mammals, lions included, to die lonely and unfulfilled without consummating the one most pleasurable act in life. Mother Nature has always favored the strongest males, giving them top priority to mate. Mother Nature is certainly not fair; she has never been fair and never will be.

If—and it is a big if—our young lion is successful, he will get his pride. But before our victorious male can claim his rightful reward with his new harem, he has dirty jobs to do. A new king often wastes no time in seeking out the cubs from the toppled king and killing them one by one. Then, surprisingly, several days after the slaughters, the mother of the lost cubs becomes receptive, so receptive that she often actively solicits the murderer for sex. So the new king is handsomely rewarded for his cruelty. This is how the game of survival works. Love, caring, and kindness have no place in nature.

After becoming a king, the months and years that follow are truly a golden period for our lion. He is strong and fit; he is almost invincible. He no longer has to do the hard work to find food; it will be done by his gals, who are the most proficient hunting machines nature has to offer. His meals are free and will be free for as long as he is victorious; he often eats first and has the first pick of a kill by baring his teeth toward his "wives," who get the food.

"How selfish!" you say in anger and disbelief. Indeed! Does our king have a choice? No. To self-preserve, he must eat well to remain strong. He does not have the luxury to be fair. For him to be strong and invincible serves the interest of the lionesses too; they don't have to worry that their cubs will get killed by a new ruler. And last but not least, sex can be plentiful and exclusively for him to take from time to time. With several "wives," getting laid will not be his problem for a while. Who says the life of an animal sucks?

But what goes up must come down. It is physics; it is also biology. A lion king usually enjoys several years of great life and then it will all be downhill. At the time he becomes a ruler, he will be slightly older than four. By the time he is ten years old, he is quite vulnerable to the never-ending challenges from young lions that are eager to take over his reign and everything he owns. When he is at his peak, he can even handle two brothers' challenge.. But as he ages, each new challenge becomes harder and harder. And after each fight, he receives deeper cuts and more wounds. Increasingly, he feels tired. There never seems to be enough daylight time for him to nap. It will be only a matter of time before the inevitable comes and the king loses his kingdom. If he wisely flees before he is badly mauled, he may be able to prolong his miserable existence a bit longer. The fate that awaits a dethroned lion, like all dethroned kings, is a tragic one. The last yelps of his children mark the end of his good life. He was once the murderer of someone's children. By the swing of a pendulum, it is his children's turn. He understands. It is the norm in a lion's world.

He has lost his harem, and everything that comes with it. Hunting for food becomes his most pressing problem. He has never been a good hunter to begin with, and having been away from the sport for such a long time does not help. On top of all that, he is much older and wounded. Yes, there are still many gazelles around. Some even indulge in jumping and bouncing to great heights near him, as if daring him. The old ruler has to swallow his pride and take the insult. What else can he do? There are always some slower creatures around; they seem easy prey. He learns, in the most hurtful way, to stay clear of those long, slender crawly things with fork tongues. He once tried to lay his paw on one. The evil creature squirted something on his face and he quickly felt the sharp pains from his eyes. He could not see for some days while hunger kept tormenting him. After days, he becomes so weak that standing up takes a lot of effort. An unyielding hunger has defeated him; he throws away his pride and tries to catch some lizards and bugs to fill his stomach. His end is near. An old and frail lion does not have the luxury to just pass away quietly. A pack of hyenas has been checking him out for a few days. They sense it is the right time. The alpha male is the first to attack him. When the old king puts up a pitiful effort to fend off the attacker, the pack becomes more confident. How quickly things change; the killer of hyenas now becomes the victim. The other hyenas join their leader.

The lion summons a roar, perhaps to psyche himself up. It too has lost its potency. Instead of frightening his assailants, it betrays his vulnerability. The hyenas all laugh. The old king soon finds himself on the ground and pain comes immediately from all over his body. He feels his belly rip open and more intense pains follow as the hyenas mercilessly tear him apart, laughing hysterically as they do so. His body spasms and he continues to moan for what seems an eternity before he finally loses consciousness.

Tragic? Yes. But there is no reason to complain. This is how an animal always dies. This is most fitting for a predator: to kill or be killed. It is a cruel existence. To self-preserve, a predator needs energy and many kinds of complex organic molecules to build its body, all of which can only be obtained from the body of its prey. The animal kingdom is no Disney World. Kindness is forever a myth.

Our second example is a plant, a winter melon from the plant kingdom. The following is the story of an evil melon.

The Life History of an Evil Winter Melon Plant

Winter melon is a member of the genus *Cucumis*. It is a vine with broad, dark, hairy green leaves that grows only in hot and humid places; it needs a lot of water and plenty of sunlight to grow. In a growing season, it produces many melons, which southern Chinese often use for making soup with pork. Cantonese love their watermelon soups.

One summer when I still owned a bungalow, I grew a couple of rows of vegetables in my backyard on a strip of land roughly five feet by ten feet. I planted several tomato seedlings, each about three feet apart from the other. I also tossed many winter melon seeds from the melon I had in between the tomato seedlings. I then covered the seeds and gave the area a generous soaking before I left.

A reader should know that yours truly is a lazy gardener; I hate to weed. After weeding the area one afternoon and getting a major backache, I never did it again. I still kept an eye on the activities in the area from time to time. The tomato seedlings became taller and developed into quite healthy plants and began to bear a few little yellow flowers.

Because the strip received lots of sunlight and the soil was fertile and well watered, everything grew there. A variety of very healthy and even faster growing weeds soon appeared and threatened to take over the area. I was a bit concerned but chose to do nothing. I am not your average lazy gardener.

About a couple of weeks later, the watermelon finally sprouted from hiding. They appeared in several patches over the area. I was relieved though a bit worried because they were so weak and frail compared to the other plants that had enjoyed a big head start. Could the young melon plants compete? I really did not care and left the area quite satisfied.

Suddenly, after many days perhaps, I remembered the vegetable garden; it was time to check the area again. I was pleasantly surprised to see that the winter melon vines were quite healthy, each with several good-size dark green leaves. Not only were they holding their ground, they were branching out to the neighboring territories and shading other plants.

By the last part of May, as the weather became warmer, things really grew—the tomato plants, the many healthy weeds, and the winter melon vines especially. The vines easily took up more than three-quarters of the entire strip and began to invade the lawn. That was not all. The vines managed to get on top of the other plants by climbing over them with the help of their gripping tendrils. The stems of some of their victims buckled under the weight of the oppressive vines while others became pale and weak because they were completely blocked out from the sun. They were all starving. It was only a matter of days that the winter melons would finish their killings and claim complete victory.

By mid-June, there were no more weeds around the melon plants; they were starved and suffocated to death. A couple of tomato plants barely survived from my occasional interventions. You think only animals can hurt; the winter melon plants are even worse. They kill and they also do a thorough job, leaving no survivors.

(When I told the story to a group of guests in the hostel in Shanghai, a Canadian girl who was teaching in Saudi at the time shook her head at the end of the story and said, "What an evil winter melon!" She was definitely a Buddhist.)

Plants fight. They fight their own kind and other plants. The fight is most fierce in places where the conditions are great for plant growth, where there is plentiful of water and sunlight. Tropical rainforests are places where the fights are most tenacious. If a plant does not somehow reach the canopy before it uses up all its resources, it has little chance to survive. I once visited a couple of cloud forests in Monteverde, Costa Rica. The forest floor in most of the places was quite dim even during midday. The ever-present clouds did not help. Though there were lots of plants in the forest, there were very few young ones on the floors. It is still the same theme of to kill or be killed. That was why there were so few plants on the floor.

The third example is the war in the microworld.

Wars in a Microworld

A microworld contains organisms collectively called microbes that are too small for our naked eyes to see. The microworld did not exist until a Dutchman named Leeuwenhoek (1632–1723) invented the microscope, which allowed him to look at living organisms that no one had ever seen before. He is credited as the father of the microscope.

Again, *microbe* is not a taxonomic term; it is a convenient grouping for every living thing which our naked eyes can't see. Microbes include algae, fungi, bacteria, and protozoa; they make up most of the living organisms—in total mass and types—on our planet. Their number is truly astronomical even within a small space inside a human mouth. They are often the toughest organisms around, living in environments often deemed to be too hostile for life to exist, such as in near-boiling water, at ocean depths of 4 km below sea level, or in brine lakes, etc. They are the extremophiles.

Like all living organisms, microbes fight and kill each other to compete for survival. The wars between microbes, unlike those between animals and plants, cannot be seen, not even with the world's most powerful microscope, because microbes often wage chemical warfare on top of the usual where the bigger eat the smaller. The wars between microbes are deadly, often leaving no survivors for the defeated.

The most brutal chemical warfare ever waged in the living kingdom was when the photosynthetic algae first appeared. They produced oxygen as a byproduct, which was released in great quantities into the ancient surroundings as they thrived. Oxygen was highly toxic to the indigenous chemotrophic bacteria and thus caused a mass extinction of those bacteria. The ancient green algae became dominant and eventually changed our atmosphere from lacking oxygen into the present-day composition.

Chemical warfare between microbes was known to scientists as early as 1897. The warfare, though cruel to those defeated microbes, can be very beneficial to humans. The chemical agents which do the killings often can be used to kill disease-causing bacteria. A well-known example is Alexander Fleming's rediscovery of the war between *Penicillium,* a green mold, and *Staphylococcus,* a bacterium, in 1928. It eventually led to the discovery of the first antibiotic called penicillin. Penicillin kills many disease-causing bacteria; it subsequently became a wonder drug during the Second World War.

As the story goes, Fleming, back from a vacation, noticed that one of his bacteria (*Staphylococcus*) cultures was contaminated by a blue-green mold and put them aside. He observed that colonies of the bacteria adjacent to the invading mold had disappeared. The mold was later identified to be *Penicillium notatum.* Curious, Fleming grew a pure culture of the mold and discovered that it produced a substance that killed many disease-causing bacteria. He named the substance penicillin after the name of the mold that produced it. Since the discovery, many more antibiotics have been found, and quite a few of them have been from bacterial sources. Thus, we can see that chemical warfare is a common thing among microbes. Chemical warfare is extremely cruel by our human standard. It is, however, of common occurrence in our planet among living creatures, especially between microbes. In nature, there is only one way to succeed. It is to compete. To compete often involves killing. Good killers are successful creatures; Mother Nature loves them most.

Like it or not, there is only one rule governing all the organisms on our planet; the one rule is to survive or to self-preserve. To survive, an organism needs to be selfish by looking after its own interest and its interest only. When there is a conflict of interest between two organisms, fighting is the only way to settle it in nature. There are always plentiful conflicts to settle. And the conflicts, most of the time, are related to obtaining energy or food, which for plants will be to secure water and sunlight. For animals, many bacteria, fungi, and viruses, food is always the bodies of other living organisms, whether they are the bodies of plants or the bodies of other animals or organisms, live or dead.

To see all living creatures fight and kill one another is the one thing Mother Nature seems to enjoy watching. To ensure that her children won't disappoint her, she gives each of them a selfish nature and a burning desire to live. Then, she encourages them to blindly reproduce, often producing far, far more individuals than even the richest environment can support. As a result, there will always be shortages in the life-sustaining essentials, thereby threatening their existence. To survive, to continue to live, the earthly creatures have no choice but to fight and often to kill to obtain the limited resources. This is how our beautiful blue planet works. Our planet is exceedingly fertile and her bountiful fertility is why competition is so brutal. Fighting is the only way the organisms decide who will get their shares of the needed energy—to eat or to be eaten—and often, who will get to mate.

We humans, despite our unmatched intelligence and power, are not exempted from this fight. We too are involved in the fight, and many are killed from time to time by other organisms. It is true that our killers are no longer lions, tigers, sharks, or crocs; they are the organisms too small for us to see. They are bacteria, viruses, fungi, and some protozoans. For them to survive, they need to live in our bodies and use our body parts to fuel their growth and reproduction. Millions of us get killed by diseases every year. Despite the advances in medicine, it will be doubtful that we can totally avoid them. Life is never easy for any organism; it will never be. We are no exception. Besides getting killed by diseases, we, despite our great intelligence, are very good at killing our own kind with wars. Unlike our killings by some diseases, there is solution to our self-killing. We shall explore the solution in the Morality section.

CHAPTER 4

Life Is Full of Suffering and
You Have No Choice

We live in a world in which every creature we come across has a reason to hurt you. Those that hurt you are not your enemies; they are often strangers. Some are also your relatives or close friends. Getting hurt is unavoidable. It does not help that to make life possible life needs to be fragile and prone to breakdown, which is an unfortunate consequence of physics. The survival game is full of hurts no matter what organism you are, as discussed in the previous chapter.

Some are luckier than others because they don't have the faculty to feel pain; they either live or die. They don't suffer. Animals are not that lucky, especially if you happen to be the most intelligent kind and full of feelings. Hardship and suffering, therefore, are big parts of an animal's existence, us included.

One may ask: life being so difficult and often cruel, why would any organism bother to participate in playing the game? Why wouldn't an animal simply give up? It could say, "Heck with it, come and kill me. I am not playing the stupid game anymore!" Well, it would make it easier, wouldn't it? But this is not permissible by Mother Nature. Hurting or killing oneself, perhaps with the exception of some members of our species, is never an option for other organisms. They simply don't know how or have that choice. Whales may strand themselves on a beach and get killed, but we are not sure whether the act was suicide. One rule about life is: no matter how tough the going is, an organism must keep on going.

Once taking a long-distance bus in Thailand, I found several little brown ants hurrying along the wall next to me; they were busy finding food. I hate ants and I was bored. So I pressed one that was closest to me against the wall with my fingertip. So that I would not get my finger dirty, I did not really squash it. The poor creature did not die; it fell on top of the narrow metal ledge several inches below. I could see its limbs badly deformed; it repeatedly struggled and tried to stand up, only to fail each time. From the way it labored, I was sure it must have hurt like hell. I knew because I had sprained my ankle a couple of times and each time it hurt and hurt.

I was a bit uneasy about my unfounded cruelty. Then, after a few minutes, its efforts paid off; the little thing did manage to get up, and before long it walked away, limping a little at first, joined its party, and resumed working immediately. From time to time, it made contact with other fellow ants, perhaps to share the information that a nasty creature was nearby.

A stern will to live dwells not only in ants; it is in every living creature. Some live in brutally dry climate, in near-boiling water or in waters where the acidity is enough to eat away flesh. It appears that an invisible whip is driving them. Not allowed to give up, every organism will try to hold on to life until the very end. Suffering is part of living and an inseparable part of life. Trying to survive even in the worst conditions is universal in the living kingdom. Life is fragile; it is also very tough and stubborn. A paradox, isn't it? In this chapter, we shall look at how Mother Nature forces animals to survive.

"Life Is Full of Suffering" ——*Buddha*

It is not surprising that almost all religions have some teachings that help their followers to deal with life's many sufferings; it is a big part of Buddhism. The Four Noble Truths, for example, are all about suffering. Let us do Zen. Let us take a look at the Four Noble Truths according to the Buddha: (I got the source from an English version.)

1. Life as we know it ultimately is or leads to suffering/uneasiness (*dukkha*) in one way or another.
2. Suffering is caused by *craving* or attachments to worldly pleasures of all kinds. This is often expressed as a deluded clinging to a certain sense of existence, to selfhood, or to the

things or phenomena that we consider the cause of happiness or unhappiness.

3. Suffering ends when craving ends, when one is freed from *desire*. This is achieved by eliminating all delusion, thereby reaching a liberated state of enlightenment (*bodhi*);

4. Reaching this liberated state is achieved by following the *path* laid out by the Buddha. (In my opinion, Jesus plagiarized Buddha. Clearly, his claim to be the only path to God lacks originality. Is the kingdom of God a liberated state of enlightenment described in Buddhism?)

Let me try my best to understand what the Buddha is trying to tell us and make some correction according to biology if necessary. (Yes, yours truly is going to correct Buddha. I am not deluded. Rather, I think science should trump religious teachings if the two are in conflict.) The first point that life tends to lead us to suffering appears to be a fact: life is a highly unstable state and therefore prone to breakdown. It also does not help that all living organisms have a hurtful nature. To keep it going needs continuous work to get food and to protect yourself; those are the areas where the troubles and sufferings come from. On top of that, you also have to deal with your sexual need when the time is right.

The second point states that suffering is caused by craving or attachments (addictions?) to material pleasures of all kinds. This seems to be valid, especially when a person becomes obsessed with money, which we all know can buy you all kinds of pleasures. When you are that obsessed with material pleasure, you'll have very little inner peace. The Buddha's view: *a deluded clinging to a sense of existence to selfhood* is quite troublesome; it contradicts with what we understand about life. To self-preserve and to cling to its existence is what makes life possible. It is not a delusion. Rather, it is a necessity and an exceedingly clear goal for every organism on the planet. Had organisms not clung to life, life would not exist. Life is a precious and wonderful thing; you need to earn it. I have to say that the Buddha is deluded in this statement. He seems to say that life is not worth preserving. Without life and the intelligence that follows, can there be enlightenment?

Point 3 states that suffering ends when craving ends, when one is freed from desire. This point could be valid for humans if the desires and wants are out of control, but will not be true for other animals like lions, elephants, or lobsters. I am not sure whether those animals have desires.

Needs, yes, but desire from a lion? Yet, we know that lions, elephants, deer, and all animals suffer from time to time. The last point is about reaching a liberated state; it is beyond the scope of this book and shall be left alone.

Despite my high regard for Buddha, I cannot agree with most of his views on suffering. Like all religious teachings, Buddha did not define many of the key concepts or bother to explain how he arrived at such views. It is stated as a matter of fact and to be taken by faith because he is Buddha. I am a scientist; I can't accept that. Let us see whether there is a biological base to explain what suffering is; in particular, whether suffering has any survival value because it is so universal. Suffering must be serving some important role in survival. Nature can definitely be cruel, but not senseless, I firmly believe.

In the following discussion, we want to look at what is suffering biologically. What are the sources? Does it help survival? And can it be avoided?

The Pleasure Principle

I believe that there must be a connection between suffering and survival, but what is the connection? Then, I got a break. I remembered the concept of pleasure seeking, the so-called pleasure principle. The pleasure principle is a concept first coined by Freud in the 1920s. The pleasure principle states that people seek pleasure and avoid pain. Freud explained the origin of the behavior by inventing three terms: id, ego, and superego, which are the three components of the psychic apparatus proposed by Freud. Like many concepts in psychology, they are very murky ideas. That is why some prominent scientists think psychology still is a pseudoscience. I am not sure any psychologist knows what they are.

Though Freud's explanation of pleasure seeking is unbiological, that pleasure seeking exists is beyond doubt. So I asked the same question about pleasure seeking: does it have any survival value? To seek pleasure and to avoid pain are obvious things to do. Do the behaviors help an animal or a person to survive?

The Discovery of The Pleasure Center

While pleasure seeking is a fact of life, the existence of a physical structure which would control such behaviors was questionable. Freud's id, ego, and superego are not real. Well, things changed in 1953; it happened accidentally. It was discovered that rats, beyond any shred of doubt, are pleasure seekers. The discovery has become one of the all-time favorite stories that psychology professors and behavior scientists love to tell their students.

As the story goes, in 1953, Dr. James Olds and Peter Milner at McGill University were researching the role of the hypothalamus in learning. By mistake, someone implanted an electrode at the septum instead of the targeted hypothalamus in the brain of the rat. Upon closing the circuit, the rodent, instead of the expected angry behavior of snarling, spitting, and teeth chattering, had the greatest time of its up-to-then miserable existence. Imagine the researchers' shock! It was not unlike a dentist finding his patient, while having a root canal, moaning in great pleasure instead of screaming in pain. Not only did the rat not shy away from the stimulus, it went after it repeatedly given the chance, the researchers later found.

Like every good doctor would in his shoes, the researcher killed the rat and dissected it to see what the heck was going on. Sure enough, the electrode had landed at the wrong spot. The rest is history. When you and I make mistakes, we usually end up paying through the noses. These guys made a mistake and became gods. The misguided electrode, besides discovering the pleasure center, also demonstrates that, given a choice, rats will seek pleasure over any other activity. In the ensuing experiments, Olds's team implanted electrodes at the same spot in other rats. Then, the rats were placed in cages with large levers and were allowed to freely press them to stimulate the septum. The rats kept pressing the lever as fast as their rodent ability could allow them, and as many as hundred times a minute for hours—talking about indulgence! They finally stopped, but not before they had spent the last ATP. It has also been demonstrated that a tested rat will ignore other goodies in favor of the lever.

Similar results were observed in other mammals, including us. Why is pleasure seeking so common in mammals? Does it play a role in survival? To answer this question, let us recap the three things an animal has to do to survive. They are 1) self-defense, which in essence is danger avoidance; 2) to get food; and 3) to reproduce. We ask: does pleasure seeking have anything to do with these activities?

The Happiness-Seeking Principle

In the following paragraphs, I shall try to explain pleasure seeking through self-preservation, which is well defined and well understood. I replace *pleasure* with *happiness* not to satisfy my ego; rather, it is to avoid confusing my view with Freud's theory, which comes with id, ego, and superego. In our discussion, the terms *pleasure, happiness,* and *joy* will all have the same meaning and be used interchangeably. *Happiness seeking* has the same meaning as *pleasure seeking* but explained in a different way. The term is also useful in seeking and practicing *moral selfishness* near the end of the book. Moral selfishness is a foolproof way to pursue happiness, which should be the ultimate goal of all our activities.

What causes pleasure? What makes us or a lowly animal happy? What triggers the feeling? Then, it becomes clear that happiness is often the result of the removal or alleviation of a stress or pain. A happy feeling always immediately follows when a particular stress is removed. Then, we naturally ask: what is stress?

Stress is what an organism experiences or feels when it encounters something or a situation which threatens its life or existence. A threat always produces a corresponding stress. For example, having nothing to eat always threatens one's existence; it produces hunger, which is stress. Hunger is stress. Having a full bladder produces an urge to urinate. An urge to urinate is stress. And depending on how full the bladder is, it produces a corresponding level of stress. Having your body dehydrated produces a thirst. A thirst is stress. So is a bleeding wound. So is not getting laid for a long period, etc. Stress is always a danger or threat to an organism's life or a species' existence.

Therefore, we can see that pleasure or happiness comes directly from the removal of a particular stress. If Freud understood this relationship, then he would not need to create those useless and confusing terms. To survive, an animal is required to keep fulfilling the three survival needs— danger avoidance, to get food, and to reproduce. Should an organism fail to meet any of them, it becomes a threat to the organism or its species, and a matching stress is produced. Thus, when an animal sees a predator approaching, it becomes stressed. To be happy again, it needs to remove the stress; in this case, to escape. Accordingly, the three needs generate three types of stresses which are of various degrees of urgency based on the seriousness of the threat. To self-preserve, an animal needs to prioritize its response in the following order:

Setting the Priority

1. The most urgent is danger avoidance, and from it, the fight-or-flight response. Is it also happiness seeking? Here, I think, is another reason why *happiness seeking* is a better name than *pleasure seeking*, because it is very difficult to connect fight-or-flight with pleasure.

   In a classic fight-or-flight response, such as suddenly seeing a black bear or a Rottweiler charging at you (the former is a real danger in the Canadian wilderness, the latter happened to me once when I was delivering a box of flowers), your sympathetic nervous system, the hypothalamus, and the pituitary glands are immediately activated. It causes the central nervous system to release a large amount of noradrenaline. In response, your adrenal medullae also secrete adrenaline, which together with noradrenaline trigger the outpouring of a hormone called cortisol. As a result, the rate of your heartbeat, blood pressure, and level of blood glucose all shoot up. As a result, most skeletal muscles in your body are ready for whatever action you will take. Needless to say, it is as stressful as it can get.

   In a wild, wild world, the fight-or-flight response will usually be over quickly. You either make it or you don't in a matter of minutes, if not seconds. And if you are lucky, the danger will soon be over and the stress subsides. With the danger and stress gone, it is time for you to relax and feel happy again. You may even joke about the incident with someone who shares the experience.

   The experience of escaping a danger or emerging intact from a stressful situation is rewarding and pleasurable. The happiness is so intense that some people actually seek the feeling, the so-called adrenaline rush, by purposely putting themselves into stressful (but safe) situations. That is why amusement parks are building ever higher and bigger rollercoasters, and the lineups for rides which offer the greatest thrills are the longest. And why dangerous sports like scaling a cliff without a safety rope are so attractive to daredevils. Though no animal in the wild kingdom will foolishly seek danger, fight-or-flight does have its reward in pleasure in a human world.

The fight-or-flight response trumps all other activities an animal is engaged in at the time. Most advanced animals when threatened will stop eating or having sex when there is a looming danger. Some years ago, a hotel in Montreal caught fire while some wife-swapping was going on. Some guests escaped covered only with bedsheets. You don't need a lot of imagination to know what they were cut short doing. See the point? When your life is in danger, sex can wait.

2. The next in urgency are things like hunger, thirst, or lacking sleep. This type of danger won't kill you right away; you have some time and even a number of days to fix it. This type of unfixed stress always produces a lot of suffering. Hunger can be so stressful that a starving person will eat almost anything to fill up his empty stomach. That is the reason why a piece of plain white bread is so delicious when you are very hungry and gives you so much joy eating it. Same applies to thirst or sleep deprivation.

3. The third on the list is sexual stress. Sexual stress is universal among animals. Its urgency varies from animal to animal. Among animals that mate only once in a lifetime—bees, ants, mayflies, and salmon, etc.—sexual stress can be the most urgent for attention. If you were one of those animals, you'll drop everything and often ignore dangers to do sex. A mammal usually has a window of several mating seasons. It is not as urgent. To mate, a male mammal usually has to compete by fighting other suitors; it often ignores bleeding wounds or feeding in favor of sex. For mammals, sex is not as urgent as danger avoidance but is certainly the next in line, often above eating.

In humans, sexual stress can wait. It is the least urgent one. Lacking urgency, however, does not mean there is absolutely no stress. Sexual stress, unlike the others, is not loud. It can be very patient but unrelenting. It allows you to ignore it when you are busy taking care of more urgent matters, like closing a multimillion-dollar real estate deal. When you've got nothing to do and when you are most relaxed, Mother Nature will quietly remind you: "Hey! It is time to do it, the species depends on you." Ever wonder why you always think about sex sitting beside a fire after a meal? You don't? Now, don't lie.

Every Animal Is a Happiness Seeker

Happiness or pleasure seeking is quite common among higher forms of animals. Chimps and monkeys obviously are capable of happiness seeking. So are the rats, cats, and dogs. We ask: are lower forms of animals also happiness seekers? For example, are birds, snakes and crocs, frogs and toads, fish and octopus, and shrimps or worms pleasure seekers? The question appears silly, doesn't it? One may conjure up an image of a shrimp or worm going to a nightclub to have a good time. How ludicrous!

But please allow me to rephrase the same question: "Are all those animals capable of seeking relief from stress, like backing away from pain, looking for food when they are hungry, and trying to find a partner to mate when they are sexually ready? Then, all of you would answer yes, yes, and yes. Therefore, we can conclude that every animal on our planet is a happiness seeker. Do you agree?

The Beginning of Happiness Seeking

When did happiness seeking begin? Considering its role in survival, happiness seeking had to begin quite early, possibly at the same time when the first living organism appeared. The reason is quite simple: to survive, the first living organism had to constantly know whether there was any looming danger, inside especially. If there was, to fix it as quickly as possible before it would be too late. Having sense a danger—a damaged cell membrane or energy running low—should generate an appropriate stress signal and thereby draw the attention of the organism to fix it. Therefore, we can safely conclude that happiness seeking began at the same time as life.

The Biochemistry of Happiness

Knowledge is a strange guest; it sometimes comes to us when least expected. The medium through which we gain our understanding can be equally weird. While a lot of our knowledge in psychology is gained at the expense of mice, rats, and some other less fortunate lab animals, some actually comes from people. In understanding the nature of happiness or pleasure, a lot of information has come from the drug addicts of heroin, cocaine, crack, or amphetamine.

Heroin is a form of morphine, which produces a kind of quiet, content, lazy, and easygoing satisfaction; under its influence, you feel totally stress free. Cocaine and crack, on the other hand, produce a sudden rush and an explosive rapture. It causes the heart to beat faster and raise the blood pressure. (Please don't think I am a druggie; I learned it from the Internet.) Both heroin and cocaine produce their highs through neurotransmitters that regulate our many moods.

What is a neurotransmitter? *A neurotransmitter is a chemical courier or messenger which is produced in one neuron and subsequently sent to a neighboring neuron to produce a certain feeling.* There are two neurons involved in the working of a neurotransmitter. One produces the neurotransmitter, the other receives it. It is mostly through neurotransmitters that we get the full spectrum of feelings like sadness, anger, depression, and happiness. Scientists are quite sure that two neurotransmitters—namely, endorphins and dopamine/noradrenaline—are the molecules that produce the two happy feelings. Heroin works through endorphins, which is a short form for endogenous morphinelike substance but is hundreds of times more potent than morphine. Cocaine, on the other hand, works through dopamine.

We can clearly see the happiness a person gets after successfully escaping from a black bear is very similar to having crack or cocaine. The happy feeling is in fact induced by our body's noradrenaline, which, chemically, is similar to dopamine.

How about eating? To be happy, you don't always have to eat pizza. A hard-boiled egg will do because it relieves your hunger, which, depending on how long you have been without food, can be very, very stressful and very unpleasant. An animal with a full stomach is certainly content, relaxed, lazy, and easygoing. I wonder whether any scientist has checked and compared the endorphin levels, say in rats, before and after eating. The happiness we see from eating is certainly consistent with that induced by endorphins. Eating relieves the stress caused by hunger and therefore is happiness seeking. The happiness of satisfying a thirst is likely to be similar to that of hunger.

The last is mating. Is mating a happiness-seeking act? It sounds stupid even to ask the question, isn't it? Well, we are doing science here, better be sure. The best answer has come from studying people, because people can tell you more clearly about how they feel when they are in love than using rats, monkeys, or chimps. In people, there are at least three stages in the mating game. The first stage is courting, which happens after two people meet and really like each other. Soon, the pair is said to have fallen in love. A person at this stage is marked by irrational thinking, characterized by sweeping generalizations, unsubstantiated conclusions, and ill-advised expectations. He, in particular, is full of life and energy, optimistic, talkative, and very confident. These symptoms, according to medical doctors, also describe the euphoria induced by amphetamines, which act through the dopamine circuit.

The climax, of course, is consummating the sex act. There are few earthly pleasures that can match it. The excitement at this stage is likely to be the combined effects of dopamine and noradrenaline. Sexual pleasure, without question, is one of the greatest and most powerful joys humans can experience; it defies poetry.

The last stage of mating is the brief period after orgasm. It is marked by feelings of security and calm, peace of mind, and a fluffy warm cloud-nine feeling (according to the book). It is not unlike the effect of heroin, which mimics endorphins. Thus, mating gives us the most complete spectrum of pleasure, and therefore is happiness-seeking of the richest kind. That is why sex is such a strong lure.

Addicted to Life

We all know that both heroin and cocaine can provide their users with pleasure, though it is short-lived. We also know that the induced pleasure makes these drugs highly addictive and the addiction ends up causing the addicts lots of harm. So we ask two questions: (1) Is the pleasure we get from the relief of a danger—a successful fight-or-flight response—for example from eating to relieve hunger or from sex, addictive since they share similar biochemistry as the drugs? In short, is a survival-driven happiness-seeking also addictive? The answer to the question is: yes, yes, and yes, all of the above are addictive. (2) Are the addictions to these activities harmful to an organism? The answer is: no, no, and no. Not only are they not harmful, quite the contrary, an animal needs to be addicted to these pleasures to self-preserve.

To see why it is necessary to be addicted to these pleasures, let us imagine every time after an antelope had escaped from a predator it would get a splitting headache or an upset stomach instead of experiencing joy. Would it run from its predator again? I would seriously doubt it. Antelopes with such a weird response would have been wiped out quickly, wouldn't they? The same logic applies to eating and having sex. Mother Nature makes it fun for an animal to engage in activities that help its survival, so much fun that it will keep doing them or become addicted to them. Instead of causing harm, these addictions are necessary if an animal is to survive.

Now, you can see the beauty of Mother Nature's design in order to make an animal self-preserve, or survive. For things that threaten the life of an animal, she creates a corresponding stress to alert or to warn the animal and to draw its attention toward removing it. If the animal heeds the warning and does something to alleviate the stress, she rewards the animal with joy; the amount of joy is often directly proportional to the seriousness of the threat. She also makes the pleasure and joy addictive to encourage the animals to keep doing the things that allow them to survive.

If an animal fails, suffering or death follows. Mother Nature offers each and every animal this deal: when there is stress, fix it or remove it and you will be rewarded with happiness so that you will love doing it. If you fail, you will be punished. You will have endless pain; you will suffer as long as you live. It is a push-and-pull combination, a reward and punishment coupling. Nothing is more powerful in motivating an animal to self-preserve than this design. That is why every animal has absolutely no choice but to obey and will do its best to live.

Pain: Mother Nature's Cruel Punishment

From the previous sections, you may get the wrong idea that fun and reward are always Mother Nature's way to persuade, to encourage, or to force an animal to self-preserve. No, far from it, for pleasure is not the only item in her bag of tricks. There is another equally potent item for her to force an animal to live. It is pain; pain is nature's strongest warning signal to an animal. Pain comes from an injury to an animal's body. If the injury is not taken care of, the pain from it can drag on for years before it kills you. An injury, big or small, often produces an intense pain. An animal under an intense pain would do anything possible to alleviate it. Lots of suffering in the animal kingdom have come from pain.

For those of us that are in our senior years, pain usually becomes part of our existence. It is because no matter how diligently our bodies work to preserve ourselves, there will come a time when age takes control of us. We will become sick because a certain part of our body is breaking down and there is no way to fix it. Our body, sensing it, will produce stress continuously and you suffer nonstop until you die. Thus, life often ends in suffering for most of us—not a pleasant thought, but true.

One of the most painful experiences I have been through came from a gout attack at the joint of my left big toe. It was painful, so painful that a gentle brush against a light blanket would produce a sharp pain. It was my body's warning that the uric acid level in my blood was too high and caused uric acid crystals to build up at the joint, which became swollen as a result. Gout won't kill you but it surely puts you in hell. Fortunately for me, there is a cheap and simple solution: taking an Allopurinol tablet daily.

But other animals don't have the same luxury. When injured, an animal either heals itself or becomes weaker and weaker as it continues to suffer until it is killed by a predator. There are lots of ways an animal can get injured in the game of survival because it has to compete. To compete is to fight. An animal often gets hurt in fighting. How much injury you get in fighting often depends on how strong you are. For the fittest, it often gets away with some minor scratches. For the defeated, it can sustain fatal wounds.

Mother Nature has no sympathy for the losers. The weak always get eliminated quickly one way or another. Unlike the previous three survival activities, Mother Nature does not reward an animal that gets injured; there is no explosion of pleasure or high after it becomes well again from an injury. The message from Mother Nature is clear: getting injured is for the weak. If you are weak, you'll suffer and suffer, and eventually get eliminated. The arena of survival is not for you!

"How great would it be if we don't have pain?" Some would wish. Actually, there are people who are born with a very rare condition called *congenital analgesia;* they are unable to sense pain—and you don't have to envy them. Failing to sense pain means having no idea what is hurting them and therefore being unable to stop danger in time to save them from a serious injury that could have been easily avoided. These individuals are at constant risk. Children with this condition suffer repeated damage to their bodies. They rarely grow up to have children of their own. Again, Mother Nature will not tolerate the weak and defective. Despite its dark side, pain is a must-have and the price worth paying if an organism is to successfully self-preserve.

Now, I hope you understand the real reason why there is suffering and there will be suffering as long as you live. Suffering comes from stress, which is a warning signal for a danger. Sometimes it hurts like hell but is for our good; it is a necessary evil. Though suffering cannot be totally eliminated, it can be minimized. How? By avoiding getting your body under stress—by keeping safe, by eating healthy, and by practicing healthy sex, if you are an adult. Contrary to most religious teachings, sex is not bad or evil. According to science, healthy sex is a great way to relieve the everyday stress, and therefore to keep a person happy. So are you going to listen to Buddha, Jesus, Muhammad, or to science?

A healthy body means every tissue and organ is doing its job well, like a well-maintained car purring along, and therefore has no need to send out any stress signal. No stress signal means no pain and no suffering.

A lot of our suffering comes from emotional hurts. A healthy mindset is the best way to reduce emotional suffering. A healthy mindset is built by a correct moral view, I believe, which according to this book is moral selfishness. Part III will deal with morality and practicing moral selfishness in great detail. When your body and mind are healthy, you have much less suffering and happiness will come naturally to you.

To show you how to become a happy person is an important goal of this book; it is the first step toward fixing our planet. The whole is the sum of its parts; a happy person is the basic component to build a better world. To fix and to build a better world for all—you and me; black, yellow, and white; mammals and birds, sharks, crocs, and the redwood trees—is the ultimate goal of the book. So far, mankind has been the troublemaker and a cancer of our planet. It will be us, and us only, who have the power to change that. And the moral view suggested in this book is the way to do it—the only way, as I see it. There is hope because moral selfishness is quite easy. All you need is a commitment to give yourself the best and work toward it. To be morally selfish, you never do anything that will hurt you eventually.

CHAPTER 5

Self and Selfishness, the Beginning

From the previous chapter, we can clearly see, no matter what organism it is—a lion, a winter melon plant, or a *Penicillium* mold—and no matter what it does (to self-defend, obtain food, or to reproduce), we can safely conclude that it is doing something related to survival, with absolutely no exception. Simple, isn't it? It makes understanding the behavior of any living organism very easy indeed, doesn't it?

"What is the lion doing, Dad?" your three-year-old asked. "It is doing something to survive," you answered. "Why?" he asked again. "Because it wants to survive." The same answer. (I have a feeling that I was not such a good dad.) But it will apply, will it not?

This conclusion applies also to us, the sophisticated humans, though sometimes it is not that obvious. For example, lots of us spend a lot of time on our smartphones checking messages and replying to them. It seems the activities have nothing to do with our immediate survival. That is true. It is because we are not like animals or other organisms; our lives are not constantly threatened. We can afford some luxury and do something just for fun, to satisfy a human need to communicate. Pleasure seeking is a well-known human pursuit.

It should be abundantly clear that the activities of any organism are not random; they all are pointing toward a singular purpose: to survive, which necessitates them to self-preserve or to self-serve and to be selfish. It may make you query: how did organisms, all of them, without exception, acquire this purpose? When did organisms first acquire this goal to pursue existence?

The answer to the *how* is extremely difficult, if it can be done. We know that a living organism has a highly organized interior, but so do many sophisticated machines we have created and they don't have a will of their own. Having a highly organized interior does not automatically generate for the machine an idea or a goal. To be able to direct all activities for survival, a living organism, or for that matter a machine, needs to be aware of two things: (1) that it exists and(2) that it wants to preserve its existence, which as discussed, involves doing the three things. Awareness is abstract. Is it possible for the first organism to know all of that?

Eventually, the question will end up on: how on earth do the interactions of some very complex organic compounds, possibly those between proteins and DNA molecules, result in producing an idea, something that seems to be outside the scopes of chemistry and physics? Not just one idea; rather, it needs two linked thoughts to come out from whatever the interactions would be for life to work. That is why it is so, so difficult, if not impossible, to explain how the will to survive has originated.

The Beginning of Life

It turns out that the answer to the *when* question is quite obvious, though it will be impossible for anyone to prove. It is a logical conclusion; there is simply no other rational choice. The moment that marked the beginning of the very first life form must also be the exact time it acquired a purpose to survive. The two should exist at exactly the same moment and should always come as a pair or life would not be possible.

Why? Let me give you a highly speculative scenario. Provided we started with two exactly alike structures, identical in every which way with one important exception: one was equipped with a will to self-preserve, the other was not. What would happen? The answer would be: the one that came with a will would continue to survive and evolve, the other would soon perish, leaving no offspring.

Granted, the example was not likely to be near the truth, if we could somehow find out what the truth was. However, it does emphasize one thing: for life to continue to exist, it must, from the very first one, the very beginning, have come with a will to self-serve. This does clarify one thing: for life to have any chance of making a start, it needs more than the right makeup of complex molecules somehow put together in the right order. It also needs to secure the will. What is the probability of that? This may make it impossible for any of us to create a living creature from a lab even if we know its makeup exactly. How would you give it the will? By giving it a jolt of electricity?

With regard to how life began on our planet, there are two schools of thought: abiogenesis vs. divine creation. From what we have discussed, what do you, the reader, think would be more likely? I think abiogenesis is an impossibility bordering on absurdity; those abiogenists are wasting their time in pursuing this theory.

Let me explain. For the first structure to become a living creature, it needed to be able to carry out the three survival activities as discussed: (1) to self-maintain when something breaks down and needs repairing, (2) to obtain energy to carry out self-maintenance, and 3) to manufacture the various building blocks to reproduce. The new organism would be working against a very tight clock with little time; it needs to get the three components working in sync, possibly in the range of hours (?), before it breaks down or it would cease to exist.

And each component, from what we know, would require the control and direction of some agents (each an enzyme?). What would be the very minimal number and kinds of directing agents/enzymes needed to be present at the moment when life began? Please don't forget that physics would not help; the Second Law of Thermodynamics would constantly cause the assembly to break down. Even if you could somehow assemble the whole thing and keep the molecules together for a little while, there still would be no guarantee that the assembly would automatically know to work together for a common purpose.

This is simply a probability argument. I don't think any of the abiogenists has the foggiest idea of how to estimate the odds. We are still very, very far from that point. But don't trust me; listen to what Francis Crick has to say on the matter of abiogenesis. This is what Crick, the atheist, has to say:

> *What is so frustrating for our present purpose is that it seems almost impossible to give any numerical value to the probability of what seems a rather unlikely sequence of events . . . An honest man, armed with all the knowledge available to us now, could only state that in some sense, the origin of life appears at the moment to be almost a miracle.*

Crick wisely did not elaborate on what "a rather unlikely sequence of events" was. I am not sure he clearly knew either.

Despite the apparent impossibility, why do the scientists insist on abiogenesis? The only reason, though none of them have admitted it, is: they all assume that God does not exist. They have intentionally omitted this very important assumption. Under this assumption, what choice do they have? Sneaky fellows!

But what if God—he does not have to be the Christian God—indeed exists? Is it such an absurd idea? Let me further remind a reader that (1) the existence or nonexistence of God can neither be proved (scientifically) nor disproved. I don't think any scientist can or wants to argue that (2) there are more people in the world who believe in God, though he may not be the same god in different religions. They are not all illiterate. So which is more rational? God or no God? With all that said, the divine creation version appears to me to be far more reasonable and rational.

It might begin this way. Again, we won't know how God did it, though we know it was about 3 billion years ago when he did it. God has created this tidy lipid sac containing some polypeptide chains, some nucleic acid segments, and some useful molecules. He then placed it in a pool somewhere in the primordial sea. He blessed it and said to the new assembly: "Now, begin to live." *Viola!* There it was, your first life form. Tell me which theory makes more sense if there is a possibility that God exists.

The divine creation theory will be much more sensible because none of the many essential compounds—protein or polypeptide chains, segments of nucleic acids, or fatty acid molecules—which were essential for life to begin have ever been found to naturally exist on earth, not in quantities so abundant that they could, by pure chance, be assembled anyway. Even if they did, then again you need to put those molecules together and somehow perform the magic to make them start working. I am not sure those scientists see it the same way. But at least, it is better than having no idea.

For those who believe in divine creation, this could be the moment when our creator said with a smile and satisfaction to the first living entity: "There! My dear little one, take good care of yourself, and may your number be as many as the stars in the galaxies one day. Yes, my little one, may you grow in size, number, and above all, in intelligence. May your children inherit all the good I have prepared for you. Take good care, my humble one, for eons from now one of your kind will be the parents of Abraham, Buddha, Aristotle, Leonardo Da Vinci, Beethoven, Newton, Darwin, Einstein, and Zhou Enlai . . . Don't despair, my beloved one, in times of tribulation—and there will be many—for I'll always be nearby to guide and protect you. Take care, my prized creation, for you are blessed and loved, now and forever."

In a way, the birth of the first living cell was similar to the birth of a star: both events require the amassing of a critical amount of substance. Though at least as important, the birth of the first living organism was not marked by any fanfare. Being the first, no other living creature was even around to witness it. Thus, the first living cell, our dearest ancestor, the one who should be remembered with the fondest memory, had the most humble and lonely beginning.

A birth of a star is grand from the moment its nuclear furnace starts firing. But from then on, it is all downhill. The birth of life, on the contrary, was obscure and humble. Unlike a star, life, after a dim beginning, kept changing for the better and kept improving. Even more than the birth of the most massive star, the beginning of life was an extremely rare and precious event in the universe. For at that magical moment when a greasy sac acquired the potent potion of molecules and a breath of life from the creator, something exceedingly unusual happened: one by one the molecules inside seemed to have woken up—first the DNA and the polypeptides, then the amino acids, and the various ions. And they said to one another: "Hey, guys, we got something beautiful going here! Let us work together and keep it going!" Suddenly, the collection of molecules had gained a purpose; they began to form a kind of union, sharing the same interests and working toward the same goal under the leadership of DNA and protein. They wanted to keep the group going and to preserve their kind as long as possible. Suddenly, there was a purpose in their existence. The purpose was to self-preserve and to survive. Strange, isn't it?

Life is also something very puzzling. How do you explain self-preservation in physics and chemistry? How would one explain the beginning of having a common purpose from a collection of zombielike molecules? From that moment on, the components which built the first living cell/organism were no longer loosely associated and yielded to the power of the Second Law of Thermodynamics by allowing diffusion to scatter them and destroy their structure. For the first time in the history of our cosmos, we had an entity which by virtue of having a membrane was able to protect itself from its surroundings. With the polypeptide chains, it was able to direct chemical reactions to maintain its form. And with the inclusion of fragments of nucleic acids, it was able, with the help of the polypeptides, to reproduce itself. We had the very first sustainable structure and thus the very first life form—a living cell! Hurrah! Hurrah! Hurrah!

This moment should have been celebrated with great joy, fanfare, and ecstasy. Until the magical molecules were assembled, the Second Law of Thermodynamics' grip on the universe was totally unchallenged—not even the most massive star would dare to disobey the law. The fire of rebellion, however small, weak, seemingly insignificant, and dim, has been lit against a tyrant whose power has no match, and is dreaded even by the most massive object in the universe, the black hole, causing it to hide. It was like a nano-David against giga-Goliath. Our universe has never run out of surprises, has it?

The Beginning of the First Self

The beginning of the first living organism also coincided with the starting point of a *self*. Then, the question becomes: what is a *self*? A reader should know that *self* is a key concept in psychology. However, like many of its important concepts, *self* has never been clearly defined. When I was writing the *Happy* book, I needed to find out what psychology has to say about the concept. I checked out a book titled *Self*, and it was a thick one with many contributing authors. I could not find a clear definition despite the theme of the book being self. Everyone had something to say, but it seemed to me that none knew what he/she was talking about precisely. Here, let me give it a definition for our discussion; it should also be useful in psychology.

Definition of a *Self*

A self always refers to a living organism or a group of organisms and yet the two are different. A living organism is a biological term which describes how a living creature is built, structurally and biochemically, and how it functions according to physics. A self, on the other hand, is a term describing the behaviors of an organism or an assembly of organisms together toward an object or objects in their surroundings, be it a living or nonliving thing. Or it describes how the organism or the group known as a self "sees" its physical world and reacts to it accordingly. Since *self* deals with the behaviors or reactions aspect, the concept is important to understand how an organism survives.

Though the concept is applicable to all living organisms—bacteria, fungi, plants, and animals—our discussion will focus on understanding how an animal self sees and behaves. An animal *self* "sees" the objects around it in two ways:

1. An object or organism that helps its survival. It generates two possible behaviors:

   A. To own the object or to fully control it for the self's exclusive use. If the organism is food, then, the self will ingest the organism, break it down, and incorporate it into its own body. Or, for useful items not to be ingested—nest-building materials, fossil fuel for us or the soil around the roots of plants—by fully controlling it and keeping it away from other organisms.

   B. If the object is another self that is not for consumption or to be controlled, then the subject self will see it as a part of its own and will cooperate with or help the organism/self. For example, in a colony of ants or bees, each individual sees the other members as parts of its self, and thus, willingly cooperates with them. Same applies to the members in a pack of wolves or lionesses during hunting. Or, organisms that are in symbiotic relationship. And it is also true among couples in love.

2. An object or organism that threatens its survival also produces two possible behaviors:

   A. If the object is inside the self—a living organism like a parasite, a toxic substance, or a rebellious member—a self will try to expel it.

B. If the organism is sharing a habitat with the self, it will be viewed as an enemy or at least a competitor and take hostile actions against it.

A *self* is different from a living organism in that it may and often consists of more than one living organism, as mentioned. A self, like a living organism, also has a boundary. While the boundary of a living organism is invariably physical—like an outer membrane or skin which separates the organism from its surroundings—the boundary of a self is often abstract. For example, a colony of termites is a single self with many individuals; the boundary that keeps them together is invisible and non-physical.

Having laid the foundation, here is our definition of a self: *a self is a living organism or a group of organisms sharing a common interest, goal, or purpose. The interest, goal, or purpose is always related to the survival of the organism or the group of organisms within that self. Therefore, we can also say that the boundary of a self is defined and drawn by the common shared interest in the group of organisms under consideration. Worth repeating is the interest is always directly or indirectly related to survival.*

The last point I want to make is: a self is a basic survival unit that is capable of fulfilling all the needs of survival. An individual living organism may not, and often *is* not. Also by this definition, a colony of ants or bees, and not an individual, is a single self, which consists of hundreds, thousands, or even millions of individual organisms. The colony is a single self because none of the ants on their own are capable of prolonging the species. Similarly, a man and his sex partner is a self, a basic unit that is capable of ensuring the survival of our species. Now, perhaps you can understand what "a missing half" really means. Romantic, isn't it?

Self is not an easy concept to grasp. From the first time I was confronted by it till now and after more than fifteen years, I still am not quite happy with the way I have defined it. Each time after writing and rewriting the definition for hours, I still think I can do better. And still it may not be crystal clear to a reader. Not to worry; there are many more examples to come to illustrate the concept as we try to explain why animals or people behave how they behave in the later chapters. The concept is crucial to understanding why a selfish animal will go against its nature to happily cooperate with instead of hurting others. It also makes it easy to understand *love,* which is directly opposite to selfishness. It is worth going through the trouble, isn't it?

The first self was also the first organism that has ever come to exist. It was likely to be some form of asexual chemoautotroph, a bacterium, which by itself could maintain the integrity of its body, harvest energy, and reproduce by fission. The self of the first living organism consisted of one lone organism; it was the bacterium. Most of today's organisms reproduce sexually—*Paramecia,* shrimps, fish, frogs, birds, and mammals, etc.—a self of these organisms consists of at least two types of individuals, i.e., a male and a female.

Regardless of whether it is a single organism or a group of organisms, the interest and goal of a self is always the same: to survive. To survive, an organism needs to do everything to serve itself; i.e., to self-serve in order to self-preserve, and therefore is selfish. From *self* thus comes selfishness naturally. The two exist in pair and at the same moment, like the two poles of a magnet.

A self is also a twosome consisting of a boundary and a goal. The goal to survive often serves to define the boundary and to separate what will help its survival from what will not. What helps its survival will be perceived as a part of the self, and therefore to be included, to work together or to give help to. An ally is thus often called an insider. Inside what? Inside the boundary of the self, the group, of course. Similarly, a competitor is someone that threatens the self's survival and thus is outside the boundary. An outsider is to be treated as a nonself, and often to be attacked. The two components—the goal and boundary—are also inseparable. If I appear redundant, it is because the concept is so important. If you understand the concept, then the behaviors of any organism, including the most cunning human, will not confuse you.

To see why the beginning of the first living organism also marked the start of the first self, let us recall how we define a living organism. It is a physical object with a highly organized interior, which, by itself, is capable of maintaining and reproducing the structure. In other words, a living organism is a physical object which by itself is capable of surviving. Therefore, a self is just another name for an organism; it focuses on the behavioral aspect of a living creature.

Now, we can understand why the first self could only be formed or born after it had acquired a membrane. The membrane was the first self's boundary; it is also physical. The acquisition of a membrane then allowed the first self to differentiate what belonged to the self and what did not and treated the two accordingly. And at the exact moment of acquiring its membrane, a self also acquired the intention to preserve its inside, the will to survive. (Connecting acquiring a membrane to procuring a selfish interest was a very special moment for me. It gave me goose bumps. I felt like the sky had opened up. And it is far, far better than sex. There is no reward better than that.)

CHAPTER 6

The Same Selfishness, Two Drastically Different Outcomes

One would expect that a world governed by selfishness where hurting others is the rule will be ugly. You know this is not true. In fact, it is just the opposite if humans are absent. Wherever you go—mountains, plain, desert, seas, lakes, and rivers—where the landscape is not spoiled by our presence, you will find beauty. Why this paradox?

How Wolves Change River

We cause great harm to our environment. Is it because we are the top predators? There are many apex predators—lions, tigers, killer whales, crocs, and the big whites—but none of them, and absolutely zero of them, is an environment wrecker like humans. Quite the contrary. They always help to build a harmonious living system where they live. Let us use wolves, an apex predator, in the place they live as our example to explain this seemingly odd outcome. The story I am going to use is called *How Wolves Change Rivers* published by Sustainable Man on YouTube, December 13, 2015. It is an interesting way to introduce an important biological concept called trophic cascade.

The title attracted my attention. Wolves are neither engineer nor they normally have anything to do with a waterbody like beavers do. How do they end up changing rivers? It is a strange story. To better understand the story, let me provide you with a brief background about the wolves that changed the river. The story began in 1900 when the US government wanted to control the predators in Yellowstone National Park. From ignorance, the government perceived wolves to be harmful and therefore to be controlled; i.e., to be eliminated from the park. As a result, the last wolves in the park disappeared in 1926.

One thing the government did not know was that the removal of the wolves, a group of apex predators, from their ecosystem would change the system drastically. Yes, wolves kill and therefore end the lives of animals such as deer; they also give lives indirectly to other organisms down the food chain, a concept central to trophic cascade. In nature, the two are intertwined; give and take, life and death often walk together.

The removal of wolves allowed the deer population in the park to thrive in number. The dramatic increase in the deer population naturally required more vegetation to feed them. But they loved the plants that grew along the riverbanks. As a result, those plants had mostly been depleted. When the plants disappeared, so did their roots. As a result, there was nothing to protect the soil along the riverbank; tons and tons of soil were washed away during heavy rains.

The plants, besides serving as food source to animals, also provided shelter for birds, insects, and countless small organisms. With the plants gone, so were the many animals that depended on them. The river was also deformed because of serious erosion, and the lands beside it became barren.

It all began with the removal of the apex predators, and the effect was passed on or cascaded down the food chain to other organisms. The tons of soil that were dumped into the river, besides changing the course of the river, also had many adverse effects on the aquatic organisms that lived there. The effect was quite widespread and the resulting landscape was ugly.

Luckily, there was a happy ending to the trophic cascade story. In 1995, the US government realized the mistake and reintroduced the wolves back to the park. The reintroduction immediately had an effect on the park's deer. They could no longer freely feed along the river. And their population was reduced. The plants along the banks were allowed to recover. Led by the renewed plant growth, the soil along the river was once again protected and the erosion stopped. Smaller animals also began to come back. Life began to thrive and things are beautiful again. The lesson learned: top predators are important to stabilize and maintain the balance of an ecosystem. Conservation of top predators allows nature to achieve harmony.

But the same cannot be said about us, the other apex predators. I have painfully witnessed what had happened to my native village, the damage caused by the villagers. Rivers and streams became filthy. Once the home of fish, shrimps, all kinds of aquatic life, they were soon occupied by and supported the growth of foul bacteria and hateful creatures, the ugliest and the most hated types.

Yes, we are apex predators, but we don't stabilize the environment we live in. Instead, we, by foolishly slaughtering and removing other organisms, are killing our planet and inevitably ourselves. We have been destroying all types of creatures that had sustained us on land and in seas. Have you ever thought about how destructive we can be or what will happen to a place or environment in our sudden absence? We now know without any doubt; we have done an experiment—not by careful design, rather by blundering into it of course—which neatly answers the two questions. To see what humans really are to our environment, let me give you another story.

Chernobyl Disaster, the Never-intended Experiment

On April 26, 1986, something went terribly wrong during a scheduled test on the emergency core cooling system of Nuclear Reactor Number 4 in the Chernobyl power plant. Some unfortunate coincidence together with a number of human errors had triggered a catastrophic disaster: the core of the reactor suffered a complete melted down. It was a level-7 event, the highest classification on the International Nuclear Event scale, and the worst of its kind ever.

An explosion took place and fire broke out, pumping lethal radioactive clouds into the atmosphere for days. The fallout from the accident created a highly radioactive area, called the exclusion zone, with a radius of 30 km. All residents in the area, including the entire city of Pripyat, had to be evacuated. The area will not be safe for human habitation for another 20,000 years, according to some report. It would likely remain a desolate area for a long, long time to come.

In an article called "Nature Thrives in Chernobyl, Scene of the World's Most Devastating Nuclear Accident" in *The Independent,* June 6, 2000, by Steve Connor, the zone has been undergoing some very astonishing changes ever since all its human residents departed. According to the article, Chernobyl, which without doubt is the site of the world's worst nuclear disaster, has proven all the experts wrong. In sharp contrast to all the gloomy predictions, it is thriving with life and has become one of Europe's richest wildlife habitats, teeming with many rare species, including some endangered ones. Many wild mammals—red deer and moose, lynx and wolves, otters and beavers, etc.—have become well established within the area. At the same time, species that do well around humans–rats and mice, pigeons and sparrows—have all suffered declines. The evacuation of thousands of residents in the area has allowed a thriving community of plants and animals in such abundance that it has shocked biologists. The area, especially the exclusion zone, despite having suffered the worst radioactive contamination in history, has proven life to be exceedingly resistant to the known damaging effects of radiation in causing mutations and birth deformities.

Amazing, isn't it? If anything precious has been gained from such a nightmarish happening, it is to show how destructive our species has been to other organisms, and nature will be a much better place in our absence. Hurting other species eventually would not serve our human interests either. If we allow our hurtful behaviors to continue, what type of planet shall we live in at the end? The difficult-to-accept truth is: in our absence, even the most hostile and barren landscape can recover; we are the enemies of other living organisms. If animals and plants could talk, they would have cursed us. Within a mere fourteen years, the exclusion zone has turned into a paradise for animals and plants.

Our Resilient Planet

The disaster, though causing a lot of hardship and pain to the local residents, has a very bright side. It is to show the resilience of our planet and its immense power to recover from serious abuse. Even in the time scale of humans, fourteen years is not a very long period and she has fully recovered. Though the ecosystem is still very toxic by our standard, the plants and animals can still live happily in our absence. If they could choose, I am sure they would happily take on the peril of radioactivity than the oppressive human.

The accident, though very bad by every measuring stick, also gives us hope. If we change our behavior and stop our abuses toward her, she will recover fully in a relatively short time. For those who don't know how lucky we are to have inherited such a forgiving planet, let me give you some examples:

According to an accepted view, our planet has gone through at least five mass extinctions, dubbed the *big five*. To qualify as a mass extinction event, it needs to be 1) widespread and 2) rapid decrease in the many types of organisms—families and genera of them—on the planet. The most well-known to us, though not the biggest, was the extinction of dinosaurs about 65 million years ago, which many believe was a result of a massive meteor that hit the earth. The impact of the collision instantly killed many organisms, but it was the ensuing freezing climate change that finished most of them. With time, our planet has recovered from events far worse than the Chernobyl disaster.

Many of those scientists also believe that the earth is on track for the sixth extinction. Unlike the previous five, this one will be caused by us, the humans, because of our love affair with fossil fuels and thus greatly increasing the level of carbon dioxide in the atmosphere to a dangerous level. We will never know how bad this one will be, but for sure we know it is coming if the current severe weather patterns are any indication. Science is still our most dependable source of information. According to science, the increased carbon dioxide will surely raise the global temperature. If allowed to continue, the big sixth will be here before we know it.

Despite the tragedy, there is a very positive fact that has come out of the Chernobyl disaster: our planet is exceedingly resilient. It gives us hope. Though we, through our selfish and insatiable pursuit of pleasure and comfort, have killed many genera and species of lovely organisms, if we stop the abuse, she will renew us with more new ones. But we must stop the abuse now.

PART II

THE RISE OF THE CRUEL GODS, THE UNLIKELY ROUTE OF EVOLUTION OF THE MODERN HUMAN

PART II.

CHAPTER 7

The Godlike Species, the Beginning

A reader at this point may question: same selfishness, also top predators, why the two drastically different impacts on the environment? The answer to this question is simple: every creature on our planet obeys the order of Mother Nature and is completely under her control, but we don't. The living organisms in every ecosystem are like the musicians in an orchestra performing a piece of symphony and Mother Nature is the conductor; the music is always beautiful and pleasing, until the modern humans joined the team. We don't and have not listened to her.

In fact, from day one, from our very first ancestor, our kind has never been obedient. The cancer seed has been sown very early. And this rebellious trait has never waned; instead, it has intensified over the millions of years as our race has evolved through several transitional stages. When it got to the modern human, *Homo sapiens*, and after we discovered farming, the cancer seed finally woke up and began to do more and more damage to the planet. Our ravaging power, like a tropical hurricane traveling over warm waters, has kept gathering power and reaching a formidable level. Unless we change our ways of treating Mother Earth, we will have her gravely harmed, killing billions of us together before the hurricane disappears and the cancer stops.

Can we change? And how do we change? The answer to the first question is yes. But to know how to change, we must first understand what the problem with our species is; we need to know how our race has evolved to become so powerful. In psychology, there is a well-established belief: if you want to understand a person, a criminal or a great teacher, you need to know the person's past, starting from his childhood.

Following this logic, let us do some detective work and trace our origins to the very first ancestor.

If the scenarios in our story are true, you'll be greatly surprised, if not shocked, that our ancestors were very marginal competitors; they were anything but dominant at the beginning and had remained weak for many millions of years since. The rise of our species has been a very interesting story, which takes about 10 million years to unfold. Like many interesting stories, sex has played a very big part at some early stages; it has helped our species to overcome a threat that would have stopped our insatiable quest for higher intelligence.

What Makes Us Human?

Before we get to the origin of humans, let us take a look at *what makes us human*. Specifically, at what stage a chimp was no longer a chimp and became a "human" instead. The first and most important criterion to qualify an ape as human is a skeleton designed for walking upright, or walking with two legs instead of four; humans are bipeds. This feature alone not only disqualifies all other apes, it also excludes all mammals—cats and dogs, lions and tigers, not to mention cattle and sheep—from the title. Birds are bipedal but they are not mammals. Immediately, a reader may sense some trouble from this definition. Why are we the only mammals, not just apes, doing it?

There are many more anatomical characteristics which are uniquely human. They include hands with opposable thumbs for multipurpose grips, loss of grasping toes, lack of large canines, and a face that sits beneath the brain case rather than protruding in front. A layman like me may ask: why use walking upright to draw the line? Why is not an opposable thumb or lack of large canines, for example, chosen to separate us from other apes? It is because those features would not have the same impact to humans as upright walking. The gradual dominance of humans over all other living creatures as we evolved has certainly been a consequence of this one singular change. The other features are probably the consequences of walking upright.

Why a Chimp? And Not a gorilla?

All biologists believe that our ancestor was a chimp. This raises the question why a chimp? Is it purely accidental? Or did it have to be a chimp? On a bigger scale, could upright walking get established among other mammals? Let us first answer the last question. Let us assume that through some wild mutations a dog, lion, cow, or an elephant was born and was forced to walk on two legs. The obvious question would be how would such a freak survive? How could it escape danger, find food, or get mature to mate?

I am not trying to be funny, but it is obvious that such a mutant would not stand a chance in a million years. The cartoonlike beast would get killed and eaten shortly after it was born for lacking mobility, which is the most important part of its survival. Therefore, a sudden loss of mobility would be the prime concern for an upright-walking mammal. Then what advantage did a chimp have over the other mammals? If a chimp was somehow forced to walk on two legs, could it survive? First, how could it escape danger? Chimps live mostly in trees and they have next to no predators in their domain. Other than leopards, they do not have any enemies to fear. They are also social animals; they cooperate to protect each other. For this reason, a leopard does not normally hunt chimps for food. Chimps are the top competitors in their domain. So if a chimp were forced to walk on two legs, it would still find refuge among trees. Together with the protection of its group, its safety would not be a big concern. Agree?

How about a monkey? Had a monkey been forced to walk on two legs, the loss of mobility would quickly spell death for the unfortunate animal. Chimps, for example, hold monkey-hunting excursions from time to time. Even perfectly healthy monkeys would fall prey to hunting chimps. A freak monkey would never be able to make it—thank goodness, or you and me would have tails! For this reason, only a chimp and not any other tree-dwelling mammal could afford a sudden loss of mobility and get away with it.

How about a gorilla? If we could choose, I think most people would pick a gorilla over a chimp. Why not? Gorillas are already ground dwelling. It would be one less adjustment to make than a crippled chimp. And if any ape is capable of defending itself from loss of mobility, it will be a gorilla. It is quite sure that prehuman gorillas had no natural predators. How about getting enough to eat? Gorillas are vegetarians;

they find food close to where they live. An upright-walking gorilla would certainly find it easier to survive than an upright-walking chimp.

Why not a gorilla then? The fact is our DNA is more similar to those of chimps than to gorillas; this alone decides we could not have come from gorillas. So the question will be is it by chance or because of some deeper reason that a chimp instead of an apparently more qualified gorilla became our ancestor? Let us assume that a gorilla had been forced to walk upright by some twist of fate. What hardships would it face? I would say very little, if any. The ape would certainly be able to hold its ground, find enough to eat, and perhaps to mate. So what is the problem with a gorilla-like ancestor? If it is a matter of look, I would certainly pick a majestic gorilla over a chimp. So why wasn't a gorilla the chosen one? The answer will likely be: since there would be no hardship, a gorilla would have no need to solve the problems associated with the sudden loss of mobility from walking upright. In nature, and among people, there are many, many of this kind of harmless trait, like the shape of the eyebrows, the color of eyes, or whether hair is straight or curly. There are few advantages and no harm; the trait is allowed to stay in the population's gene pool. The upright-walking gorilla would still lead a more or less normal life. If it had happened to a male, the guy was likely to have problems chasing or competing for gals. This disadvantage would eventually get the upright-walking gene eliminated, though it would not be immediately fatal to the gene carrier. If the gorilla were a female, she would certainly have some difficulty in mating standing upright. The disadvantage would also cause a gradual fading of the gene.

But there is another, more important reason that would have disqualified gorillas as a group to be our ancestor even if upright-walking gorillas could manage to pass that gene along. It has to do with its diet. Not only are gorillas heavily vegetarian, they are also very picky. They tend to eat juicy plant parts such as leaves, bulbs, fruits, seeds, tender plant shoots, and flowers. The fact that a gorilla has no need to drink water tells you that it gets enough water from its food.

They are not ordinary vegetarians like cows, zebras, or elephants; they are as picky as pandas.

As a result of their diet, gorillas have been limited in distribution to where the foods are. You just can't grow gorillas in the Savannah. The diet has not only limited their distribution, it also limits their population size. Diet is the reason why there are fewer gorillas than chimps or monkeys.

Why should population size matter? Because evolution is powered by mutations; it is a numbers game. A favorable mutation is rare. You need numbers to make it work. Gorillas don't have the number.

After these very crude rounds of elimination, a chimp emerged as the best candidate. It appears that it was no accident that a chimp rather than a monkey or a gorilla was our ancestor. Let us look at a chimp a bit closer to see whether it was uniquely qualified or just lucky. What advantages does a chimp have over the other apes? How did it happen? What made the chimp adopt upright walking? Was it by choice or was it forced to do so?

Let us tackle these questions one at a time. First, what made a chimp walk upright? Upright walking may not require any anatomical change, as indicated by a story titled "Back on Her Feet After a Close Call" that appears in the *Toronto Star*, July 22, 2004. Here I quote: *"Natasha, a 5-year-old black macaque at the Safari Park near Tel Aviv, began walking exclusively on her hind legs after a stomach ailment nearly killed her, zookeepers said."* The article comes with a photo which shows the weird-looking monkey walking proudly and confidently, straight and tall like you and me. The picture immediately caught my attention. But I don't think recovering from a serious sickness was the cause because the trait is acquired and an acquired trait cannot be passed to the next generation. That upright walking must be hereditary entailed that it was induced by a mutation or a number of mutations.

Was it a single mutation or more than one? A reader should know that mutation is a rare event and is usually deadly. Given the rarity of two favorable events stringing together, it was likely that upright walking was the result of a single mutation. And further, it was probably a dominant mutant gene, meaning that whoever had a single copy of the gene would be forced to walk on two feet. How could a single mutation do that? Anatomically, the mutation probably resulted in changing the shape of the pelvis, particularly the configuration of the joint between the pelvis and the upper thighbone (the femur), making it easier to walk on two legs and difficult to move on four. If a reader has any doubt, try to walk on all fours and you'll see. It is the two joints in the pelvis that make us walk upright naturally. If it was the pelvis that caused walking upright, then the pelvis should define what a human is. And that is why paleoanthropologists are so keen to find that changed pelvis.

There remains one crucial question: what advantages does a chimp have over the other apes? To begin with, a chimp is bigger than most apes; a group of chimps has no natural enemy where they live. Compared to a gorilla, a chimp is more versatile in what it eats, and therefore is able to find food in more places. But wouldn't upright walking pose a great deal of hardship for a chimp which normally spent a lot of time in trees? Wouldn't the hardship more than cancel the advantage a chimp had over a gorilla? The answer is a definite yes. Upright walking would certainly be difficult for the first chimp that started the trend. But like my favorite Chinese saying: where there is hardship, there is an opportunity. Danger and opportunity are the two sides of the same coin. Problems happen in life. You can get major setbacks, or you can come out much further ahead by solving them. Problems, by solving them, are the reasons you make discoveries, even life-changing discoveries. With this in mind, we should give thanks when encountering new problems. Upright walking would certainly pose many big problems to the first chimp.

Introducing Specific Brain Capacity

The point becomes: was the chimp capable of solving those problems? Again, we can see the advantages a chimp had. Let us take a look at the body weight vs. brain capacity/size among the apes in the table below. Chimps, as indicated by their specific brain capacity (10 ml/kg), are the smartest of all apes, and by a wide margin.

Body weight vs. brain capacity/size in apes and hominids in human evolution:

(The information was obtained from page 17 and 39, 2nd Edition of *Images of the Past,*

by T. Douglas Price and Gary M. Feinman.)

Ape	Estimated Body Weight, kg	Brain Capacity, ml	Specific Brain Capacity, ml/kg
Gibbon	20	100	5.0
Chimpanzee	40	400	10
Orangutan	73	400	5.5
Gorilla	100	600	6

Specific brain capacity has exactly the same meaning as *brain-to-body mass ratio*. When I wrote the first edition, I was not aware of the existing term—careless. After I discovered the existing nomenclature—to my great horror—I have been wrestling whether to change the term back to BTBMR. It will be an honorable thing to do. However, I have decided to keep the term for several reasons. The first, of course, is to be in line with the naming in physics. There are a number of properties that begin with the word *specific*—*specific heat, gravity,* and *volume,* etc. The name is also shorter: three words vs. five. My second reason being it will make the new concept *intelligence acceleration,* to be discussed later, easier to present and easier to grasp.

Specific brain capacity is the brain volume per unit of body weight. It is an indication of how much brain power is relied upon to help an organism to survive. A higher number means more neurons are required to operate a unit of body weight, and therefore indicates a more intense brain/neuron involvement. I shall assume that a higher *specific brain capacity* number/index will correspond to a higher level of intelligence— information collecting and processing—among different species of apes in our comparisons. We shall go back to this term and discuss it in greater detail in a later chapter.

Before humans came to exist, chimps had the highest specific brain capacity among the apes and monkeys by a big margin, making them the most resourceful creatures on the planet. If any ape could have any hope of overcoming the hazards of upright walking, it had to be a chimp and only a chimp.

Having laid the groundwork, let us explore how our species could begin from a chimp. Hopefully, we can see clearly how a chimp was uniquely suited for the role. More importantly, how a loss of mobility could be an advantage—yes, it was certainly an advantage for the long haul. It pioneered a whole new way of survival for the successive generations of handicapped chimps. It was not easy, but somehow they managed to survive, thrive, and eventually give rise to us. And even more importantly, we'll find out why and how our lineage has evolved to be gods and lead us to a cure for the planet's cancer. The following chapters are the story of our evolution; it all began when a lone chimp was forced to walk on two legs.

The Hazards of Being Bipedal

Birds are bipedal, but most birds can fly away when there is danger. For flightless birds such as ostriches, cassowary, and the emu, they have perfected bipedal locomotion for a long, long time. They have very strong leg muscles which allow them to outrun their predators. Most mammals move along with four legs. There is a very good reason for that; four legs allow the animal to move along much faster.

For an animal that normally moves on all fours to switch to two legs would spell big trouble, if not immediate death. Such an abrupt change to bipedal locomotion would invariably greatly slow down the unfortunate animal. Therefore, even many mammals are capable of moving around by two legs, but they will only do so very briefly and none will make it a habit. As discussed, speed is the way many animals rely on to escape or hunt down prey. Losing speed, especially when you are the only one that suffers such a fate, is no different from a death sentence by Mother Nature. The land is always full of speedy, powerful, hungry, and sharp-clawed and pointed teethed predators lurking day and night. Awkward-moving animals would likely be easy meals for a lucky predator who happens to come across them. Even among normal animals, a small loss of speed will soon cause them to suffer serious consequences.

There are many slow moving and flightless animals; they all have some sort of scheme, each has been proven and perfected through millions of years of evolution to be effective to protect themselves. Crocs, elephants, and hippos have size and muscle; turtles have impenetrable shells for defense. The first upright-walking chimp had none of those because it was never supposed to, and therefore had never been equipped for walking upright. As a result, it was caught totally unprepared: no hurtful claws, and its teeth were pitiful compared to those professional killers. It could pretty much forget about outrunning an enemy. So how could it defend itself, to compete with other chimps for food, and eventually mate and reproduce? There appeared to be nothing our ancestors could rely on to compete and survive.

The first upright-walking chimp must have been one of Mother Nature's cruelest jokes. But it did survive, making it one of nature's most improbable events. We know it had survived for sure because we are its heirs, an irrefutable proof of its success in doing so. With this given, our job is clear: we must come up with a solution to this big mystery.

Solving the Problem of a Changed Pelvis

We need clues, and there are quite a few of them. Let us begin to look for clues to solve this mystery. Clue #1, we know the creature belonged to a group of apes, which, as indicated by its extraordinary specific brain capacity, was certainly the most intelligent kind of animal at the time. Clue #2, the chimps are animals known to have cultures of inventing simple tools. And clue #3, the crippled chimp had something regular chimps did not have: he had gained a pair of very nimble free hands, which also happened to have a power grip.

That is it, the three clues are all we shall need to crack the mystery. With them, we should begin to see the shape, though still very out of focus, of our puzzle. Let us adjust the focus by taking a look at each clue and see what picture will emerge. Are you ready? It is so exciting!

The Clues:

Clue #1: chimps were the most intelligent apes; Definition of Intelligence

For our discussion to be meaningful, we need first to define *intelligence*. What is intelligence? According to *The New Lexicon Webster's Dictionary*, intelligence is defined as the ability to perceive logical relationships and use one's knowledge to solve problems and respond appropriately to novel situations. For our purpose, I shall simply define *intelligence* as an ability to solve problem.

Let me explain. Problem solving requires two components: (1) a database of useful facts we call knowledge or information. (2) Applying the information to come up with a solution. Both components are equally important. Problem solving is like preparing a dish: information is like the ingredients, and how you cook (applying the information), either by steaming, stir-frying, or baking, determines the type of meal you come up with. Does it make sense?

Intelligence has only one use: it is for solving problems. So this clue alone has given us some hope. When we talk about intelligence, we tend to refer to its extreme display; we are likely to associate the term with people like Einstein, Pauline, rocket scientists, and neurosurgeons. We often fail to recognize that a unicellular organism like a *Euglena* possesses a certain amount of intelligence. Even the dumbest person on earth is intelligent; i.e., capable of solving some problems. Don't ask me what information a *Euglena* would store or how it would apply the information. But I am quite certain that it would have something to do with its survival, such as staying away from a spot with an adverse pH or detecting a light source and swimming toward it. The fact that a *Euglena* can sense a number of things in its environment and makes the appropriate responses is indisputable proof of its intelligence. We shall come back to this point in a later chapter. Be prepared to discover that even a tree—yes, a tree—a bacterium, or a virus is intelligent.

Animals in general are not quite as dumb as I once thought they were. I was quite impressed to watch a program which dealt with the resourcefulness of some black birds. They can work out puzzles which are designed to prevent the birds from getting to the foods in the containers. Honestly, some of the setups would have stopped me if I were the bird. They did not stop the birds. I have since looked at birds with a renewed respect. "Birdbrain," instead of an insult, should be a compliment.

But what really, really has changed my opinion on animal intelligence was a contest in problem solving between me, yours truly, and a raccoon. I have a PhD in science from a reputable university in the States, and have prided myself for being a problem solver. I was soundly defeated by a raccoon in a game where intelligence—not brute force or use of weapons—determined the winner. Let me give you some background about the contest.

The Story of the 'Coon

Yours truly, me, lives in Toronto, which among many things is also known as the raccoon capital of the world. Years ago, I used to live in a bungalow in Scarborough. Then, in the middle of an early spring night, I was awakened by some noises from the attic. It sounded like a cat was running around up there. But I knew that the family cat Fai-Fai was not the culprit; it was too lazy and too timid to do that. Besides, it would simply be impossible for it to get into the attic. I soon went back to sleep. The problem resurfaced several nights later. And the noise was getting louder and more frequent. Some animals, I was sure, were having a party there. Being a lazy person, the problem was not pressing enough for me to take action. So I ignored it and again went back to sleep. Then, early one morning, when I was about to begin my routine walk, I passed by the side of the house and heard a noise coming from the roof. I looked up. It was a raccoon. I looked at the animal and it stared back at me, not a bit afraid. After this brief exchange, the animal disappeared in the blink of an eye. Like magic, it just vanished. Upon more careful investigation, a-ha, there was an opening at the soffit of my garage. So it was a raccoon that had been partying in my house. Mystery solved!

I also subsequently found out how it accomplished its disappearing act. A couple of the aluminum sheets covering the soffit were plied open, and the opening led to the attic. The opening was less than a foot above the sloping roof of the front section of the house. Thus, the roof provided a perfect place for the raccoon to sit down and ply open the aluminum sheets. It would take some effort, but obviously that had been accomplished.

The raccoon obviously knew something which I did not about the architecture of my house, and found a weakness in it and exploited it. If you have never had problems with raccoons, you would probably think that I had made up the story. But I was hardly alone; I later found out that many homeowners had similar problems with these resourceful animals. Obviously, every raccoon in the Greater Toronto Area knows this trick. And it was a big headache for house owners because there was an ad, *"Raccoons in Your Attic?"* if you google it. And since raccoons are not social animals, each raccoon needs to independently learn the getting-into-an-attic trick. Unbelievable, but true.

I then realized that I had a problem. I had to stop the 'coon from entering my attic again. I was going to call a trapper, but I had a better idea. Instead of doing my walk, I took a trip to a home improvement center, got myself a piece of 2 foot x 4 foot aluminum sheet with a shiny and smooth surface and a tube of heavy-duty grease. I spent the balance of the morning first to secure the metal with the shiny side up on the part of the roof leading to the 'coon's entrance. Next, I applied a generous amount of grease onto the surface of the metal. I intentionally left the soffit open; I was daring the 'coon to defeat me.

I was by nature quite mean. As I was applying the grease, I could not help giggling when I imagined how the troublemaker would try to climb up the 45-degree greasy slope. Before it could even get close to the opening, it would immediately be pulled by gravity, try desperately to hold on, lose its grip, and helplessly tumble down onto the driveway. It was simply wicked. If Einstein or Newton was right, the 'coon had a problem.

Sure enough, I did not hear any more noise in the ensuing nights. I checked the grease board on several occasions, always with a cold beer in my hand. It was so gratifying to note the many skid marks left obviously by those sliding little feet trying in vain to hold on. The skid marks began near the entrance and curved toward the edge of the roof, where they abruptly ended. And most rewardingly, there were patches of 'coon hair caught between the cracks of the eaves trough where the skid marks disappeared. Without even the slightest shred of doubt, it proved that the hapless loser did fall from there, probably not just once. Considering the height, they would have been nasty falls. I took another sip; the beer had never tasted so great.

Then, least expectedly, the noise in the attic woke me up again. I checked the clock; it was three in the morning. I knew right away there was no point trying to get back to sleep. Round 1: the coon won. I had a problem again.

There are many benefits in living in Canada's biggest city, Toronto. The home improvement center was open 24/7. While I was on my way to the center, I had come up with a couple of new ideas. I got some sturdy wire mesh and a bottle of motor oil. There were hardly any cars on the road and I was the only customer. Soon, I had everything I needed and was home in no time. I felt kind of proud about my resilience and stubbornness. There were several ways to fix the problem; I chose the way which should punish the 'coon harshly. It was getting personal.

After carefully surveying the situation, I figured out how the 'coon had defeated me. It had to get up onto the garage roof, then jump down and land on the sloping roof beyond the slippery board, and somehow enter the attic after that. It would not be easy, but obviously it could be done. My job then was to make an impassable block between the two roofs.

I cut the mesh into several suitable pieces and used them to block the 'coon's passage from the garage roof to the attic. Again, I left the opening intact. Besides being lazy, I wanted to invite the 'coon to try again. I was quite satisfied with how thorough the job was. To be sure, I applied a copious amount of motor oil on top of the grease on the once shiny board. If physics works, it would be double jeopardy for the troublemaker. After the reinforcements, the only way the 'coon could access the attic would be by flight. I knew 'coons were no birds. My spirit began to lift; I began to whistle as I applied the last part of oil. This time, the troublemaker had a bigger problem.

My solution worked. I thought I had decisively defeated the 'coon. It had been days without hearing anything. Again, least prepared, one night after watching a late basketball game on TV, when I needed to sleep most, and before I laid my head on the pillow, I heard noises from above. Being a day person, I was very tired at the time but I got back up. On such occasion, cursing and swearing definitely helped; it psyched me up. I was getting mad.

I struggled to get up, put on a heavy jacket, got myself a flashlight, and got outside to check the entrance. Sure enough, there were more patches of 'coon hair on the edge of the wire mesh and a lot more of scratch marks on the very slippery slope. But there were also some fresh "wet" footprints of the animal at the entrance. The evidence undeniably pointed to the fact that I was beaten a second time by an animal. End of round 2; again, it was my problem again!

Tired and exhausted, I was ready to give up. But defeated by a lowly 'coon? No doggone way! Tossing and turning the rest of the night, I knew one thing for sure. I could not give up! My pride would not allow me to. I spent about an hour thoroughly examining the situation the next morning. I found a tiny flaw in my previous design. Obviously, the devilishly clever 'coon was able to spot it and exploited it. What I needed to do was clear.

I immediately retrieved the leftover wire mesh on the driveway. I was so happy that I did not put the mesh away after finishing the last job. Laziness, I believed, was not always a sin, as my mother had so tirelessly drilled upon me. The repair was soon complete. I stood there to check and recheck my work. If the 'coon was to enter the attic again, it had to execute a perfect jump, make a turn in midair, and before gravity could drag it down manage to land safely on the eaves trough and then avoid the greasy board while climbing up to the entrance and somehow enter the attic. Not even an all-round Olympic gold medal gymnast would be able to complete the task. It was simply humanly or raccoonly impossible. I was 200 percent sure that the pesky fellow could not solve the problem that time.

It was one of those beautiful late afternoons in May which only came once in decades. I had completely forgotten the fight with the 'coon. I was feeling very easy and relaxed chatting with my neighbor. He asked me how I was doing in the war against the 'coon. Just as I was going to brag about my victory, the neighbor interrupted, "Look, Steve. The raccoon . . ." He pointed to the roof. I turned my head just in time to catch a glimpse of the stubborn foe completing a complex and almost impossible maneuver, overcome the first hurdle, secure its footings on the eaves, and quickly disappear behind the opening. I saw it in broad daylight but I could hardly believe my eyes. (To this day, I still refuse to believe it.) I also knew that I had been thoroughly beaten by a 'coon despite having a much bigger brain and many years of education at the highest grade. If it was any consolation, part of my downfall was underestimating the acrobatic capability of my rival. But to be fair to the raccoon, it did beat me fairly and squarely with intelligence as shown in solving the increasingly difficult problems. I was greatly humbled. I also knew that it was time for me to get some professional help.

Raccoons, from this story, are great problem solvers. Chimps are certainly much smarter than raccoons. The problems the raccoon had solved in our story were not straightforward; they required a lot of thinking from the raccoon. If a raccoon can solve rather difficult problems, now imagine what a chimp confronted with a life-and-death problem could do.

Our clue #1: chimps were the most intelligent apes before we emerged. And for that reason, they were likely also the smartest animals at the time. The question becomes was it within the crippled chimp's ability to solve the problem created by bipedalism? That is, despite the loss of speed and mobility be able to defend itself, to find food, and to compete to mate? My answer at this moment will be: I am not sure. But let us keep looking and see where the other clues will lead us.

Clue #2: chimps are animals known to have cultures of inventing simple tools.

Let us look at clue #2: chimps are animals known to have cultures of inventing simple tools. This is a very interesting and important clue because tool making has long been a human tradition, and this tradition most likely dates back to chimps, our ancestors. Using tools to get food is not unique to chimps or humans; quite a few animals, including crows, dolphins, sea otters, monkeys, orangutans, and gorillas also use tools occasionally. However, the tools these animals use are ready-made; they only need to choose and pick them up from their environment. Their tools, though very simple, are still very effective in helping them to survive. The difference between having the tool or being without it is often between being with or without food, satisfying or continuing a hunger. A sea otter with an abalone in hand will certainly testify to that.

The tools chimps and humans use often require their users to make some changes to the material, usually by removing some parts of the material, before they become suitable. Considering most apes use tools but only chimps make them, we have good reason to believe that the big jump in chimps' intelligence, as indicated by their outstanding specific brain capacity, has been substantially, if not totally, employed in tool making. We cannot overemphasize the point: having or not having tools, even the simplest kind, often spells having food or having to go hungry, or being able to defend oneself or not; at the extreme, it makes a difference between life and death.

Now, let us look at some actual findings by people who do chimp watching. In 1960, Jane Goodall first observed chimps picking leafy twigs, stripping away the leaves, and then using them to fish for termites. "The chimpanzee uses the objects of his environment as tools to a greater extent than any other living animal with the exception of man himself," Jane Goodall writes *In the Shadow of Man.*

And furthermore, let us take a look at what some chimp researchers from Ames, Iowa, USA, and the University of Cambridge in England found. They observed and filmed a group of more than thirty chimps in an area called Fongoli in Senegal, Africa. The Fongoli chimps hunt and eat squirrel-size primates called bush babies from time to time. In a span of about seventeen months, starting from March 2005, the researchers documented the chimp group using a spearlike tool to hunt bush babies on many occasions. The chimps would make fresh spearlike tools every time they hunted. How did they do it? They would first choose from nearby trees with branches of suitable length—about 18 inches long—broke the branches off, and finally shaped the twig to make it more spearlike. They peeled off the bark or shaped the twig with their teeth. The finished tool was then used to stab at holes in tree trunks where the bush babies sleep during the day. It was a trial-and-error process, but some lucky and persistent chimps would come up with some extremely precious and delicious protein. Therefore, we can safely conclude that the first chimp that got a changed pelvis had to be a tool maker.

From this clue, we can almost be certain that the first crippled chimp had made some kind of tool or tools to help him. Again, to be useful, his tool need not be elaborate, like an iPhone or car. Like the tools made by chimps, the material for making his tool should be abundantly available in his environment and easy to make. So for us to solve the crippled chimp survival secret, we need to focus on his tool or tools. Without further delay, let us get to clue #3.

Clue #3: the crippled chimp had gained a pair of very nimble free hands, which also happened to have a power grip.

Clue #3: The crippled chimp had something regular chimps did not have; he had gained a pair of very nimble free hands, which also happened to have power grip. What does this clue tell us? My answer will be he would be forced to find ways to use his hands. Regular chimps have exactly the same hands as the crippled chimp, but those hands are hardly free. Whenever a chimp moves around, the pair of hands will be busy. And chimps move around a lot.

The hands of chimps are among the nimblest hands among mammals. Those long fingers besides allowing the chimps to grasp things firmly, as in the case of holding on to branches while moving in trees. They also let chimps finely manipulate smaller objects. The fact that they can create twigs, hold on to them, and poke them into termites' nests to fish for termites are all indications of the high dexterity of their fingers. Chimp hands are very versatile; they have a lot of potential for further development in their utility. But regular chimps don't have any need to further develop them. 1) They move around a lot, whether in trees or on ground; the hands are therefore rarely idle. 2) They get more usage out of their agile hands than other apes, particularly in tool making. They are happy with what they get out of them. When you are happy with a situation, you don't want to change it.

The crippled chimp was different. 1) Because he was crippled, moving around was invariably very difficult for him. As a result, he would keep moving around to a minimum. Other than to meet his needs, he would stay at a spot a lot more than the other chimps. His hands, therefore, were often idle. 2) He was the smartest kind of animal in the world during that period. Because he sat down a lot more, he had more time to think; he had more chance to put his potent brain to use in solving whatever problems there were at the time. 3) One thing a brain does all the time is, besides thinking, demand information to be fed to it. A brain is always hungry for information. When there is no new information, the brain becomes stressed. That is why totally isolating a person from the world by locking him up in a dark room is such a torture. The crippled chimp's potent brain was sure to crave information and there was a lot of information for him in the forest. Though he sat down a lot, his mind would rarely be idle.

Now, let us look at the crippled chimp's situation. He was a very smart animal capable of solving the most difficult problem in his world. His kind had a long culture of creating simple tools. His hands were very nimble and flexible, and therefore would allow him to make tools. And his hands were mostly idle, needing some action. And lastly, he spent a lot of time thinking. We all know that to have time to think is a prerequisite for problem solving. So you can see all the ingredients for him to solve his unique problems created by bipedalism were there. And the direction for solving the problems had also been laid out for him; they all forced him toward tool making. There was no other choice. Therefore, it would be only a matter of time that he would stumble upon the solution. It was almost a certainty that he would succeed given time, because the many opportunities were waiting for him. Does it make sense to you?

Having discussed the clues, we have sketched out the shape of the solution; missing are the details. There is no way we would ever know how he had come up with the solution; all we know is he must have. That given, let me suggest a way, perhaps out of the hundreds of ways, he could have solved the problem. The following is the success story of the first crippled chimp.

The Story of the First Crippled Chimp

An unfaithful replication of DNA in the gonad of a sexually mature chimp caused something to go subsequently very wrong. As a result, a baby chimp was dealt an extremely lousy hand and was born with a disfigured pelvis. From the first step it took, it was very difficult for it to move on four limbs. Instead, it had to scramble around on two legs. Luckily, the chimp still had long arms and feet with grasping toes to allow it to climb trees, albeit in an awkward manner and at a much slower speed than other chimps. Other than the odd way it moved around, the baby looked exactly the same as the other chimps.

The life of a chimp, even normal and healthy, was not easy. The crippled chimp had three more strikes against it: (1) it had problems competing for food; (2) it was hard for it to fit in, all because it was too slow; and (3) how could it find a wife when he grew up? Imagine you were that first chimp. It would take you much longer to move up or down a tree; you might as well forget about getting to ripe fruits before the others. On land, your awkwardness would be even more obvious. Being the first ape to walk on two feet, your body was totally unequipped for it. You walked in a wobbly manner because every part of your body—the inner ears, spinal cord, torso, and even the changed pelvis, except your joints—had all been designed and perfected through millions of years to carry a four-legged animal. You would get tired easily because your legs lack thick muscles to carry your weight—a job that used to be shared by four. Avoid jumping down from any height, for you might break a bone in one of your two legs since they are not strong enough to absorb the impact at landing. Another problem, though not as pressing, was equally serious. Supposing the hapless chimp was a male, how could he ever hope to compete to mate? Among mammals, mating has always been the privilege of the strongest and the fittest. There would always be too few sexually receptive females and too many eager and horny males that were fitter and faster. How could this individual ever get the chance to spread its seed? If it had happened to a female chimp, getting lucky would probably not be a problem when she was in heat. But how could she find food for herself and her baby? Male chimps were certainly not generous or caring. Providing food and protection to a girlfriend, let alone her baby, would not be on their "to-do list." To them, sex has been a birthright. So bringing up her baby would have been double jeopardy for a female chimp with a bad pelvis.

Based on the picture above, bipedal locomotion would appear to be an insurmountable handicap which would spell "doom" for any chimp unlucky enough to have inherited it. But, was it? We know it could not have been the case or you and I would not be here today. So the picture was far from complete, something crucial was missing. Unfortunately, the clues cannot be found in the ancient bones. Just how did the clumsy apes, especially the first one, manage to survive long enough to mate?

Assuming that the road to humanity began with a bad pelvis in a chimp, what could have compensated its loss of mobility and even given it an edge? Was being forced to walk upright a curse? It was certainly not. We now know it was a blessing in disguise! How? The blessing was in the most important byproduct of the altered pelvis; i.e., a pair of free hands that inevitably came with it. Freed from locomotion, the hands became idle most of the time. If you were the first chimp confronted with a pair of unemployed hands, an important part of your body which kept drawing your attention to their idleness day in and day out, would you not want to do something about it? Remember that chimps were the most intelligent land animals during that period based on its highest specific brain capacity among the primates. Would the chimp not come up with other jobs for the laid-off appendages? Could a pair of free hands be a total waste?

Anthropologists have suggested a scenario for the first chimp to come out ahead. One of the theories proposes that the chimp was a member of a group that lived in woodland next to a body of fresh water. The water supported a luscious vegetation growth along the shoreline. There would be plenty of food for the group. In that case, the clumsy chimp would still be able to find enough food to fill its stomach, would it not?

After its stomach was filled, one can see the advantage of upright walking according to the theory. The regular chimps would go back home empty handed. Our friend with the altered pelvis could carry food back with his free hands. The food, for example, could be used to seduce an estrous female. Who do you think the female would pick? An empty-handed alpha male or the clumsy chimp with food to spare? Or the chimp could use the take-home food to make some powerful friends when sex was not an option; it might, in return, get him some high-quality protein from the friend after a successful hunting excursion. Thanks to the mutation that had led to upright walking, our clumsy chimp could become the sexiest or the most popular guy in his community.

The theory certainly makes a lot of sense. But those might not have been all the advantages. A pair of free hands could do more than carry some takeout home. We still need to answer the question: how did the chimp protect itself? Let us use the theory's settings and continue to explore with the following story.

Carried a Stick and Walked Tall

Time: Possibly as early as 8 to 7 million years ago, according to a discovery in 2002 in Chad, Africa, of a surprisingly complete skull of an individual nicknamed Toumai.

Place: An African woodland next to a body of fresh water, as suggested.

Character: Arrh, the first chimp with a bad pelvis. Arrh was a male. When our story begins, he was recently weaned.

Arrh was often alone. Because of his condition, Arrh would try to keep moving around branches or on land to a minimum. Most of the time, he stayed put at a spot that was the worst address in the whole community, a place no other chimps would want. It was where the first branch separated from the trunk of a big tree. Arrh picked the spot because it was close to the forest floor. It was a dreadful location; Arrh would be the first to get attacked by a predator such as a leopard or a big snake coming from the ground. But Arrh had little choice. Fortunately, he had the group to protect him. For safety, Arrh would instinctively try to get up to a higher branch to spend the night. Unlike other chimps, Arrh's bed was often a bare spot not covered with branches for comfort.

Arrh would get bored easily from sitting at the same spot. Like every youngster, his high metabolic rate often made him restless. A chimp of his age usually had one or two playmates. Arrh had no one; he did not like other youngsters. Not fast enough, he had become an easy target to be bullied by others at his age. His own brothers did not want to have anything to do with him either. His mother had become more and more distant. Arrh constantly missed his mother's cuddling.

To kill time, the youngster would venture down to the ground intermittently when it was safe. Occasionally, he would pick up a dead branch just to occupy his hands. Dead branches were everywhere on the forest floor. Clumsy among branches, Arrh rarely traveled among trees and thus often missed the sensation of holding on to a branch. You could say it was a chimp thing, grasping even a dead branch provided the lonesome youngster with some comfort. Playing with dead branches soon became Arrh's favorite pastime. The youngster also soon learned to stay low-key when throwing branches around; he could ill afford to enrage the alpha male while doing it. Arrh was quite smart; his bright round eyes showed that he was a quick learner.

Once in a while, Arrh would come across a branch that he liked very much. The bark was smooth and it was just the right size; it felt good in his hands. It neatly satisfied the need to keep his hands occupied. Despite the inconvenience, Arrh often chose to labor a little bit to take the feel-good branch back to his resting spot. Gradually, Arrh got into the habit of taking "home" a manageable branch after a trip to the forest floor. When Arrh got a new branch, he usually spent a lot of time examining it. He would look at it closely, feel it with his hands, and even chew on it a little. After that, the youngster would spend time playing with it, mostly by beating it against a nearby trunk. A branch freshly off the forest floor often proved not much fun to play with at his resting spot. The space was too tight. The branch would always get tangled up, making the experience quite frustrating. After a short while, Arrh would get tired and let go of the branch.

Soon, Arrh would feel a need to go down to get a branch and play with it again. However, it would not be long before the youngster would again become frustrated. The branch had a habit of getting stuck! On one occasion, he lost his temper and yanked the branch out of the jam violently. After freeing it, he proceeded to beat the branch with all his frustration against the closest object. He beat the branch so hard for so long that eventually most of the small branches broke off. By the time he was calm again, he had a much shorter and bare stick. This kind of episode was not uncommon. Arrh would get tired after the exercise, and take a nap after he had gotten rid of his frustration.

One day, and after a long rest following such a fit, Arrh found that he still had what was left of a branch in his hand. He began to examine the stick at his resting spot. It was a rare peaceful moment for the youngster.

After a while, he began to swing the stick around. Arrh liked the way his new toy felt right away; it was effortless to play with. It was a new experience. As fully expected, the stick soon hit something. But the stick did not get stuck; instead, it made a pleasing sound and bounced right off. It came as a great surprise, and it delighted Arrh immensely. Intrigued, Arrh played with his toy with a new level of enthusiasm by swinging the stick in different ways. He also paid attention to the ways the stick hit something; it produced different sounds as it hit the different parts of a tree. It was a great discovery. It pleased Arrh greatly.

At the time, the group was getting ready to head to the lakeshore for food. Slow in getting around, Arrh had learned to anticipate the activity of the group and got ready to avoid being left behind. Typically, in chimplike manner, the foraging party never hurried. Arrh could usually keep up. It was a short walk. Arrh took his stick with him. It was so much fun, he would not let go of it like the other branches. He soon found that carrying the stick was no burden; instead, the stick helped to steady his body and support his weight. Not only could he walk easier, he also walked faster. It was a new and very pleasant experience and also was an unavoidable discovery. How many ways could he carry the stick?

The shoreline supported many plants; there was a lot to eat. Arrh had learned early from his mother's examples the kind of plants to eat. Though not knowing it, Arrh was extremely lucky to grow up near a body of fresh water where food was plentiful most of the time. Otherwise, his future would have been very uncertain.

After a meal, the group usually spent some time on the forest floor. Some adults would engage in mutual grooming, and the young ones would seek ways to exert dominance. Arrh stayed at a safe corner away from the youngsters, Oow in particular. Oow was a little bit younger than Arrh. But he was the son of the matriarch, and his brothers ruled the group. Oow loved to bully Arrh because there were few chimps Oow could dominate. Though no match for Arrh in wrestling, Oow found Arrh an easy target. The trick was not to get tangled up with Arrh. Oow would usually attack Arrh when he was least prepared. He would come from behind and gave Arrh a hard push, causing him to fall face down. Arrh quickly learned to give up chasing his attacker; he accepted it. Bullying Arrh gave Oow tremendous satisfaction. Arrh, though usually not hurt, loathed Oow.

Arrh's pastime was mostly watching other members and paying attention to the whereabouts of Oow. He began playing with his new toy—the beaten stick—at his corner. Naturally, he used it to beat and hit the many objects around him; he also listened to the different sounds the objects made. There were many objects to hit—a bush, rocks of different sizes and shapes, and dead tree trunks, to name a few. And the great variety of sounds pleased Arrh greatly. It was so much fun! Arrh had never been so happy and contented.

However, his joy was suddenly interrupted. Arrh had completely forgotten about Oow. As he was moving to a new target, he felt a strong push on his back and crushed his face against a tree trunk as his body hurled forward. It hurt. Arrh got back to his feet. He gave Oow a long hard look. It appeared that Arrh had an idea.

As days went by, Arrh grew increasingly attached to the new toy. By then, the bark of the stick had completely gone from wear and tear; Arrh loved the way it felt in his hand even more. The bare stick made more pleasing sounds when it hit different items. Arrh was seldom without his stick. He once woke up without it and got very restless and anxious. Luckily, he quickly found his toy on the forest floor near the resting spot. At the time, he had developed a number of ways to hit with the stick; his favorite, however, was simply raising it and beating down on an object. It was a most natural action which required little effort but produced a very hard hit. Depending on his mood, he would apply different amounts of force with the stick. He got so mad after Oow had pushed him that he struck the stick violently and repeatedly against a bush as if it were Oow. After a while, he stopped. Half of the bush was gone. The power of the stick seemed to surprise Arrh. When Arrh was calm, he would hit targets fully under control as if to study its various outcomes.

Arrh fell in love with using the stick. Playing with the stick occupied most of his idle time; he was no longer restless or bored. He also gradually became very proficient with hitting with the stick; it almost became second nature to him. So day after day, sunrise and sunset, Arrh spent most of his waking hours playing with his toy. Sometimes, the rhythmic sounds made by the stick beating on objects were the only sounds that broke the silence of the woods. Without knowing it, Arrh had acquired the skill of using the stick effectively; he could accurately hit a target with various forces without much effort.

Then came an afternoon after a meal while every member was resting. Oow decided that it was time to have some fun with Arrh. Arrh appeared to be napping. The timing was perfect. Oow approached his target from above, moving silently between branches. At the time, a breeze stirred the trees; it rustled the leaves and covered any noise Oow made. Just as Oow laid his hand on Arrh's shoulder and before he could push Arrh off the tree, Oow saw a fast-approaching shadow and immediately felt a sharp pain across his face. Oow knew that he was smacked by something. Oow had not been careless in his approach. He was recently caught by Arrh and had paid dearly. After the incident, he always planned an attack so that he would not be caught again. He did not get caught; he got hit by something instead. Worst of all, Oow did not even know what had hit him. And it hurt a great deal. Oow gave a screeching cry and quickly retreated to a higher branch. Luckily, Arrh did not give chase. Oow sat down and felt the burning spot. He found a little bit of blood on his fingers. Since then, Oow would never try to pick on Arrh again.

Arrh knew full well what he was doing. The breeze had woken him and he smelled Oow right away. Arrh quietly got the stick ready and gave Oow a good whack as soon as he touched him. Arrh had anticipated Oow's move and responded; he was pleasantly surprised at the power of the stick. Judging from the wail, Arrh was sure that Oow was hurt quite badly. He celebrated by beating the stick forcefully against a branch; he also made some high-pitched cries as if to declare victory.

It was the first time a chimp had ever used a stick as a weapon. And it was hardly accidental. Given Arrh's circumstances, it was merely a matter of time. At a very young age, Arrh had learned firsthand the bitter taste of being hit by a flying branch. It happened shortly after he was let go by his mother. The alpha male called Gawk had a fit and began to break branches and throw them around. The other chimps quickly fled. Arrh was too frightened and too slow. He remained at the scene. Gawk began to vent his anger upon the hapless youngster by slashing at him with branches. Arrh instinctively curled up to protect himself. It appeared that sooner or later the little chimp would be badly hurt. Just when Gawk went to fetch some new branches, Arrh's mother carried Arrh to safety. It was after he was away from danger that Arrh began to appreciate the power of flying lumber.

Playing with the stick, especially at the beginning, Arrh had accidentally hit himself a few times. It caused a lot of pain. He had since learned to be more careful with his toy. As he became experienced with the stick, he also became increasingly aware of its power. Oow was the first victim of the new weapon; the victim "earned" it. Arrh hardly needed another incident to reinforce using the stick as a weapon, but it happened.

A few days after Arrh had retired his archrival with his toy, he was sitting alone on the forest floor not too far from his group. For a change, Arrh was not keen to watch the group; he preferred to play with his toy. Whacking Oow with the stick gave him a new idea. By then, hitting still objects became too easy and boring; he began to look for moving targets. There was no lack of moving targets in the woods. Arrh started by trying to hit flying things around him; it soon proved impossible. So he turned his attention to slower things, like things that crawled along nearby branches from time to time. Arrh found hitting the crawlies challenging. Normally, Arrh would stay away from them because they could sting and hurt, as he had learned. Practicing hitting crawlies was safe and also fun and began to occupy most of his idle time after beating Oow.

The exercise turned out to be rewarding in a couple of ways. After many misses, Arrh got his first hit. It was a round object with a shiny cover that could fly. Arrh hit it as soon as it landed on a nearby branch. He hit it so hard that a wet spot was all that was left. Arrh was very happy and satisfied. Instinctively, he ran a finger over the spot and sampled the fluid. It tasted like the tiny objects his mother had pulled out with a twig from a mound. It was a treat he used to enjoy when he was close to his mother. It brought back warm memories.

At the time, Arrh was very proficient with the stick. Then, a lizard slightly longer than Arrh's hand walked across the floor among the branches. At a distance deemed safe by the tiny reptile, it stopped, tilted its brownish head, and checked out Arrh with one eye. Just before it could disappear into the dry leaves, the young stick master struck with his stick. The next scene was a belly-up lizard. After a few kicks, it moved no more. Arrh instinctively claimed his prey. He had never tasted meat before; it was the most delicious thing he had ever had. Arrh was ecstatic; he celebrated by jumping up and down on the forest floor, waving his stick in the air, with the tail of the lizard sticking out from one side of his mouth and its blood dripping down the other side. It was quite a frightening scene, something that had never before happened. The young chimp looked menacing! The other youngsters stopped chimping around and began to retreat to moms. The commotion had not escaped Gawk's watch; he too chose to lay low.

Good things usually would not last, and valuable items had a way of getting lost. A chimp's world is no different; we are all governed by the same physics. One day, the stick was gone. Arrh searched nearly every corner of the woods; he could not find it. In the days that followed, Arrh was very gloomy. He stayed put most of the time at his resting place with downcast eyes. Other than joining the group in food foraging on rare occasions, he chose to be idle. Somehow, even herbaceous leaves had lost their appeal. The youngster sorely missed his toy; he had all the symptoms of an addict needing a fix.

Driven by boredom from inaction, he occasionally ventured down to the forest floor, picked up a dead branch, and swung it around. His metabolism was still high; it demanded some action. He would soon get bored and climb slowly back to his spot again. Many days went by. Arrh, though still unhappy, gradually became more active again. One day, he was on the forest floor alone, not too far from the group as usual. He picked up a branch absentmindedly. Immediately, the dead branch caught his attention; it had a smooth touch and felt like his lost toy. He looked at the branch intently and found it quite similar to his lost toy except that it was quite a bit longer. Arrh played with it for a while and took it with him when he returned to his spot.

At the resting spot, Arrh had time to look at the branch more carefully. There was something about the branch that held his attention. He began to play with it like he did with the lost toy. He tried to swing it, but the other end always got tangled up. Arrh was puzzled. The new branch was like his old stick and yet it was different. Chimps were not as smart as us; Arrh could not pinpoint the problem. Instead of tossing it away, he hung on to it. The branch gave him some comfort.

Days went by. Arrh still had his branch. He dropped the branch a few times, but always made an effort to retrieve it. Arrh often remembered the ways he used to play with his lost toy. Then it dawned upon Arrh what the problem with the new branch was. It was longer than the old stick and it got some twigs at the end, making it difficult to manage at his resting place! Once he understood what the problem was, Arrh began to remove the smaller twigs and shortened it a bit until he got more or less what he wanted—a stick that did not get stuck when he swung it.

Arrh was happy again; he began to dance by turning around and around on the forest floor, waving and swinging his new toy in different ways and uttering funny noises. If he only knew, Arrh had an even better reason to celebrate. He had learned how to make a stick from raw material. From that moment on, he would never be without a stick to play with again. Arrh began using the stick regularly to help him walk. It so happened that the new stick was perfect in aiding him to walk compared to the old one; the stick became his third leg. Being the first chimp to walk on two feet, Arrh was quite awkward in bipedal locomotion. An additional leg proved tremendously helpful. A stick had since become a part of Arrh.

As days went by, Arrh became aware of the importance of his stick. It began as a favorite toy, but it became much more than that. As Arrh matured, his need to play with the stick diminished. More and more, he used the stick to kill animals that were too quick or dangerous for other chimps to consider. A stick changed his situation. Lizards had since become Arrh's regular diet, and there were many lizards on the forest floor. As Arrh became more confident with his tool, he gradually expanded the items (some by design, some by accident) to include crawlies such as centipedes, scorpions, big spiders, and finally, snakes—creatures feared by even the lions. If there was an animal dreaded most by chimps, it will not be a lion, hyena, or leopard, it would be the snake. Snakes will not usually hunt chimps. But the mere presence of a snake, any size or shape, would instantly cause panic among the chimps. Snakes were common where the chimps lived. Worst of all, snakes invariably appeared unexpectedly; their bites inflicted great pain and were sometimes lethal. Chimps have never learned how to deal with those creatures. A chimp's fear of snakes is likely far worse than a human's fear of sharks.

At the time, Arrh was looking intently for lizards when Oow let out a loud shriek. It was a warning cry for snakes. Arrh immediately looked for a tree to climb. Before he could take a step, he saw a black, shiny, slender body gliding along very close by. Almost by reflex, Arrh struck down with his stick. It landed behind the creature's head and flattened that part of the body. Blood began to ooze from the wound while the snake continued to writhe and coil. Arrh stood there frozen. Had he known what he was doing, he would have never done it in a million years. Unlike the lizard, the fatally wounded snake did not become Arrh's meal. Even dead, the snake had power over him.

The incident, traumatic as it was, did eventually help Arrh. In the days that followed, the drama kept playing back in his mind during the daytime and often in nightmares. He finally weathered it. Seeing the incident over and over again in his mind, his fear for the snake subsided and he also began to see the power of his beloved stick. The stick had magical power; it could kill a most dreaded enemy with one blow. There were a number of subsequent encounters with the evil creatures. However, with each encounter, Arrh's fear lessened. His reactions changed from fleeing to avoidance. Eventually, he no longer chose to retreat; he beat them instead and eventually learned to eat them. It became his favorite food. His stick had transformed him from a freak with a questionable future to a member to be reckoned with.

With a stick, Arrh grew up happy and strong. It was inevitable that the confrontation between him and Gawk would take place. Competing to mate with a young estrous female called Gih triggered it. Lacking mobility, Arrh spent a lot of time sitting and watching the group. Arrh noticed that Gih's genitals got increasingly red and swollen. One afternoon, the timing was perfect; Gih was sitting on the forest floor nearby. With one hand holding his favorite stick and the other on a branch, with a swing Arrh landed in front of Gih. The gal was receptive. By that time Arrh had grown up to be a very handsome-looking fellow, strong and tall with gleaming black fur. Arrh proceeded to mount her. Gawk found out immediately. He hurried to the pair, roaring angrily.

Any other chimp in the group would quickly back off; Arrh did not. This enraged Gawk, who bared his teeth and prepared to attack. No one had dared to face Gawk in the longest time. Though obviously nervous, Arrh held his ground. Standing straight on two legs, Arrh appeared much taller and bigger than Gawk. Arrh also bared his teeth and growled; he was challenging Gawk, the fiercest and strongest male. Arrh had better be sure, for if he was defeated he would incur serious, if not immediately fatal wounds because of his inability to escape quickly. The contest, however, ended much sooner than anyone would have expected. Before Gawk could lay his hands on Arrh, a blunt object hit him on his shoulder. He felt a piercing pain and instinctively backed down. Though puzzled, Gawk was not ready to give up a chance to mate. He proceeded to circle Arrh at a distance. Soon, he was ready for a new assault at his young rival.

With cheetahlike speed, Gawk launched at his challenger; he was sure that the contender would be pinned down by him and then it would be up to him to choose what to do . . . Gawk was wrong again. He glimpsed a flying darkness from Arrh and almost at the same instant felt the heavy blow of the same blunt object. At that time, it impacted violently across his face. The blow caused Gawk to stagger a couple of steps back. He ran his fingers over his face and felt a warm fluid dripping down from the burning spot. Gawk, the once invincible chimp, knew that he was in no position to attack again. How could he win if he could not even lay hands on his opponent? Gawk quickly retreated to lick his wounds.

Arrh became the new ruler of the group. Gih gave birth to a baby months later, which, like Arrh, had to walk on two feet. Arrh lived for a long time, always had the first chance to mate with estrous females in the group, and produced many children. Some of Arrh's children inherited their king's pelvis; they also learned from the father's example to use sticks—first as toys and then as weapons. The children also became stick makers. They greatly increased the varieties of the sticks to suit their individual needs and tastes. Naturally, Arrh's children and grandchildren became rulers in the generations that followed. Arrh's descendants slowly and steadily increased in number; they became a race of stick-carrying chimps.

The end.

For sure, the story has been made up and is most likely far from the truth—if we can ever know the truth. But it hardly matters. We should be really concerned about whether the things the crippled chimp did in our story were within his ability. Given the settings, the way it happened, and to a highly intelligent being which was born to a species that was likely to have a culture of making tools, and who had gained a pair of free hands in the process, would it be probable that he would come up with a tool that would inevitably help him to successfully solve all his problems?

Let us look at the story a bit closer. In going through the story, I would like a reader to ask: would he do that naturally? Was that within his ability? Or in the real world, would that ever happen? First, let us take a look at the central character Arrh. He was very likely to be a lonely child growing up. He would be lonely because he was born defective and very different from the others. After he was weaned, he was likely to have no one to play with. The other kids would discriminate and bully him, not unlike in our human society. Even if the kids in his group did not discriminate him, there would be little fun playing with him because Arrh was quite immobile and thereby would limit the many games young chimps would love to play. Regardless, Arrh was likely to be a lonely child and also likely to have a lot of idle times.

A child, whether he is a chimp or a human, has high metabolic rate and needs to be active. Above all, he also needs to play and explore things—it is in his nature and that is the way a child learns. To keep busy, it would be natural for Arrh to come up with something to occupy himself. He would naturally look for something to play with when his survival needs were looked after. Makes sense? How many things in the forest could he find to play with? Dirt, small stones, and dead branches should be everywhere. What would you think Arrh would have more fun playing with? Then, again, it would be inevitable for him to end up using dead branches as toys because they suited a chimp's natural disposition.

If he kept playing with branches and twigs, sooner or later he would come across a stick that would make a perfect toy to play with—again, inevitably. The stick would likely be about the length of his arms, without any branch or twig, and very sturdy—not easily breakable and enough to bear his weight. How many ways could he play with a stick? I would say not more than three, and most probably one or two ways without overly taxing his young body. The most natural and preferred way would be using it to beat something nearby.

The stick would give him so much fun that once he had discovered it you would expect him to treasure it and keep it near him. You can say Arrh was addicted to playing with it. He would begin to carry it wherever he went. And how many ways could he have carried the stick? I would say not more than two, and three would be really stretching it. Again, he would inevitably and unintentionally discover that his toy was also an ideal walking aid for him, something he would exceedingly appreciate to have. Once he had discovered that—it should have been very early—he would not let go of his stick. Or, if he had lost it, he would quickly make a new one. By then, he would know exactly what kind of stick he wanted and replacing it would be easy.

Using the same stick as a weapon would very likely come last. He would first use it for self-defense. Being crippled and different, Arrh would find himself a constant target for bullying, mostly by kids of his age. One of his urgent needs, therefore, would be self-defense. And the stick would come in handy. His stick could easily be used as a beating or striking stick of remarkable power, as we shall discuss shortly. The same striking stick would also be very useful in competing for mating when he was sexually ready. Among mammals, the strongest male always enjoys the first pick, and sometimes the most picks, when competing for a female. Again, his stick would make him almost unbeatable and thus give him more chances to mate than the other males.

The last use to be discovered was likely for killing small animals for food. He then would become a complete competitor with no weakness. The simple stick was almost magical; it had fully compensated everything he was robbed of by bipedalism. And he discovered it unknowingly and unintentionally. The stick had given him power over and beyond other chimps, and had made him an awesome competitor. I hope a reader can see what a simple tool can do; it gives you much more power to do things. And modern humans have countless kinds of tools—take a look around any corner of your house and you will see. Now, you can see why we are gods to other animals. Our power has come from the tools.

In the previous discussion, I have lost count of how many times I have used "inevitably" and "unintentionally." What I want to stress is: the way the first crippled chimp had come up with the solution could not have been through reasoning and purposeful exploration; he simply did not have the required knowledge. It all happened accidentally through his daily activities. And he lived in an environment and society that would unavoidably lead him to the discovery.

This also has been the way most of our discoveries are made. First there must be a need, and second, the society has the required knowledge floating around and is ready for someone to cash it in. The discovery of penicillin was a good example. Many Chinese had found the green mold growing in their fruits and food, only Fleming, a person in the Western society, had the knowledge to know that it held the answer to curing many diseases caused by bacteria. Our central character Arrh was uniquely positioned to discover a life-changing tool.

The Power of a Striking Stick

Before we move on, we have one more issue to discuss, it is to look at the power of Arrh's stick when it was used as a weapon. Let us assume that you are the stick master and you have raised the stick to prepare for a strike. At that point, your upper arm, forearm, and the stick together should roughly form a U-shaped configuration above your shoulder, with the stick pointing back. Then, you begin to strike down. At that point, you will use the shoulder joint as a pivot to move the entire U-configuration forward. During the next stage of your striking action, your elbow will become the new pivot, which compounds with the previous movement, allowing you to further accelerate the stick as it is hurled forward. Near the end, your wrist will become the final pivot, giving the stick a last boost of speed before your arm and the stick form a straight line and impact a target. Even if you don't go all out, the action will last less than a second and the speed of the stick at the tip can easily be accelerated to over 100 miles/hour at impact. If a reader does not understand how it works, I recommend that you get a medium-length stick and carefully experiment with it. Hey, don't practice it on your Fido!

The effectiveness of a striking stick as a weapon comes from leverage. First is the speed of the attack. You don't have to be Jet Li to complete a strike in less than a second; an average person can do it with some practice. Any chimp should also be able to do it easily. How many animals can escape a speeding stick in a split second? Very few indeed, if any. Second is the force with which it hits a target. At impact, the stick hits an object with all its force concentrated in a small area of the stick, possibly less than a square inch, at the point where the speed of the stick is greatest. You don't have to be a physicist to visualize the kind of damage it can inflict.

Another beauty of a stick as a weapon is that the beating action can be repeated many times without tiring the user. If the first strike misses, you can get ready for the next strike in less than a second. So a stick is a very powerful weapon, and is easy to master. Most animals somehow learn to fear it too. Here is a story from my personal experience to illustrate the point.

More than ten years ago, my second wife and I were walking along a stretch of beach in Naxos, which is one of the many picturesque Greek islands. It was mid-October and there were few tourists. A family and their three dogs were playing at the other end of the beach. We decided to explore the beach and strolled to where the family was. As we were about 50 yards from the family, the three dogs, led by a German shepherd, began to bark and charge toward us. They were baring their teeth and were threatening to attack us. We were scared stiff. Worst of all, the family appeared to be unaware of or simply not too keen on getting their dogs under control. It was up to me to defend ourselves. Luckily, there were many egg-sized pebbles on the beach. I quickly picked up a couple, put one in my throwing hand, and raised the stone. The dogs saw it and instinctively stopped. With the breathing room, I surveyed my surroundings, and to my delight, I noticed a stick about two feet long among other debris close by. I let go of my stone and picked up the stick and immediately got into a striking position. It changed the picture. The three big dogs began to retreat to a greater distance. With a couple of stones in my left hand and holding a stick on my right, I no longer feared the animals. Then, the family came leisurely to take the dogs away. The woman assured us that her dogs would never bite a stranger. Yes, I have heard that before, most of the time from unfortunate victims. I "thanked" the woman by yelling at her for the next couple of minutes. I was so frightened and angry. I am not a gentleman by any measuring stick, but other than to my first ex I have never yelled at other women in my life. I think you probably would too if you were in my position.

CHAPTER 8

The Role of Intelligence in Survival

In the last chapter, we have speculated that our ancestor was a chimp with a changed pelvis. And we have argued that it had to be a chimp and a chimp only that would be able to survive such a huge disadvantage from a great loss in mobility arising from the tempered pelvis. One of the factors that had enabled the chimp to survive the hardship, according to our theory, was its supreme intelligence, based on its high specific brain capacity compared to the other apes and primates. I must point out that relying principally on intelligence to take a prominent role to survive instead of depending on the old faithful muscle was something very new in the survival game in the animal kingdom at the time. The regular chimps, despite all their similarities to our crippled chimp except one, have never entrusted their life-and-death matters to intelligence. They still counted on muscle to get the most important jobs done. It was muscle that gave them speed to chase down monkeys or escape danger. It was also muscle that allowed them to be kings among trees. It was also none other than muscle that allowed the males to compete to mate successfully. Like all animals, muscle makes kings.

The chimp with a changed pelvis, our ancestor, has since started a new trend. Intelligence or neurons have continued playing this leading role and have forever replaced muscle, making it play second fiddle in helping all its descendants to survive. At this stage, I think we should spend a bit of time to give intelligence a close-up.

Life Is Intelligent

We have defined *intelligence* as an ability to solve problems by a living organism. Then, the question becomes: what problems does a living organism often encounter? Well, that your body has a tendency to self-destruct is certainly problem #1. So you must constantly fight it and do self-maintenance. That takes energy. Problem #2 is you need to reproduce before you die—and all creatures die, sooner or late. That, too, requires energy besides to compete, which often is the case. Problem #3: every living creature needs energy all the time, and your body, unfortunately, also happens to be loaded with energy and every kind of vital molecules that most other creatures need. As a result, many love to eat you, dead or alive; some love to drink your blood or live inside your body. Needless to say, as long as you live, you will have problems, problems, and more pro—

Your problems always come from having to maintain yourself, to reproduce, and to self-defend. To survive, an organism must continuously and successfully solve those problems. Therefore, you can see clearly that all living organisms are intelligent—be it a green plant, bacterium, fungus, person, or a virus. Makes sense?

Let us use a poinsettia to show the point. In North America, poinsettia is one of the must-have items during Christmas. It is a December-blooming plant that originated in Central America. It has large red leaflike flowers called bracts and dark-green leaves. We all know that the leaves of plants can make carbohydrates by photosynthesis; getting energy is not a major concern for plants as long as they can get water and sunlight. Plants always make more food than they can consume; the excess carbohydrates are the source of food for most, if not all living organisms on our planet.

Every florist loves poinsettias during Christmastime; they sell like hotcakes. But the plants could be quite messy. The leaves and twigs break easily. When a leaf or branch breaks, sticky milky sap oozes out; the sap is mildly toxic. The sap is like latex; it causes an allergic reaction in some people. It can also be irritating to the skin; it can induce diarrhea and even vomiting if ingested. Most animals have learned to avoid eating the plant. The latex, which is a chemical, allows poinsettias to defend themselves. Chemical defense is quite common among plants; poison ivy, poison oak, oleander, hyacinth, and dumb canes are a few examples.

How does a poinsettia reproduce? Poinsettias are flowering plants; they reproduce by flowers, which in turn produce seeds, and seeds germinate to produce new plants. Poinsettia is a short-day plant, meaning it responds to the length of daylight less than twelve hours a day for a number of days before they produce flowers. To get the plants to bloom before Christmas, a grower needs to treat his plants with twelve hours or less of artificial light per day continuously for a period of about ten weeks. Poinsettia has evolved to use the length of daylight to time its flower production, and therefore, its reproduction cycle. Many animals, besides plants, also synchronize their reproduction cycle with a certain season.

From our example of a poinsettia, we can clearly see how the plant solves the three problems to survive. The way it solves the problems is not hit-and-miss; everything it does has a purpose directed toward the goal. It is certainly an expression of intelligence, and a poinsettia plant is without doubt intelligent. Likewise, all plants are intelligent. So are other organisms like fungi, bacteria, and viruses; they are all Mother Nature's intelligent children—they all solve survival problems. We can therefore say *life is an expression of intelligence, and is intelligent.* And most amazingly, many of them do not rely on neurons.

Animal Intelligence

Unlike plants, fungi, bacteria, or viruses, the intelligence we observe among animals all involve neurons. Why? Because animals all need speed and flexibility to react to their ever-changing surroundings. Only neurons can deliver the information an animal needs to change in speedy and flexible fashion to allow it to react quickly, either to avoid a danger, chasing down a prey, or securing a mating partner. An animal needs to know what is going on around it constantly and quickly. Where the danger, food, or a mating partner is, and then come up with an appropriate response—all within a very short span of time, often in split seconds or seconds. Too slow in any of the departments, an animal will fail the self-preservation game.

In animals, problem solving always involves neurons. Neurons do two things: (1) they collect information and build a database of useful facts, which we call knowledge or information, and (2) they apply the information to come up with a solution. Both components are equally important. In more advanced animals or animals with a more massive central nervous system, their intelligence also allows them to predict the outcome of an event long before it happens. The ability to predict an outcome often has great survival value.

Collecting Information

A useful database is not something that one is born with; it must be acquired or gathered. Information gathering is done through various sensory organs. The information is then processed and immediately applied, or stored for future applications. The brain is for central information processing and storage. Though no one can read the minds of animals, especially animals like ants, earthworms, or fish, etc., we are sure that the gathered and stored information must be survival related. Behavior biologists have demonstrated that many lower forms are capable of changing their responses to adapt after repeated exposure to the same stimulus. The capacity to learn is good proof of an ability to collect, store, and retrieve information.

I am quite sure that animals are not interested in collecting information that has no survival value. Frogs will never be fascinated by stars. Crows will not pay attention to flowers. Foxes will never be captivated by songs of birds. And wolves will not give preferential treatment to beautiful women. Humans may be the only exception. We, especially people of the developed countries, collect lots of useless information.

Let me give you an example. Many years ago, I watched an NHL playoff; the Flyers defeated the Leafs 7 to 2. If I could remember everything I saw and every little move each player made, I would have gathered tens of gigs, if not more, of information. But can I use the information to enhance my survival? Or am I getting more intelligent? Thus, watching a hockey game, tennis match, or basketball playoff does not make me any smarter. What I am trying to say is: there are different grades of information; some are simply *junk*. Collecting junk does not make a person more intelligent. (I have a hunch that watching certain kinds of TV, especially sport and soap operas, will make a person stupid. But then, I am not a behavioral biologist.)

Information, to be useful, is for problem solving to improve the chance of one's survival. For example, a hunk called David and I both want to date Judy. David does not know that Judy loves to visit botanical gardens and hates hockey, but I do. And David put a second mortgage on his home to buy a pair of tickets to see the Leafs. (If you don't know, a pair of ring-side tickets for a hot Leafs game cost $$$$.) I sold my old TV to get $$, enough for me and Judy to visit the botanical gardens in the Niagara Falls. Now, who do you think Judy will go out with?

Another example is playing the stock market. Some investors just happen to have more information than you and me, giving them an unfair advantage, making it impossible for them to lose. Those investors are not necessarily smarter; they just happen to have more valuable information. Or if you are stuck in the wilderness, then, knowing how to make a fire, what is safe to eat, and to make a temporary shelter for the night will certainly increase your chances of making it to another day, will it not? The amount of useful information contributes directly to intelligence; it makes problem solving easier. In some cases, having access to guarded information created gods. Watson and Crick were the lucky ones who happened to have access to Rosalind Franklin's findings. Once they knew DNA is a double helix, the rest is history.

Information is like food; to be useful, it must be digested and assimilated. And unlike food, there is never such a thing as too much information, provided the information has been processed. It is the undigested material that is junk; it takes up valuable storage space and confuses a mind. I know some people who love to read books. However, they don't spend time digesting the materials. They don't get any more intelligent from reading; instead, they are cluttering their minds and thus are often confused. The world has millions and millions of this kind of book gobblers. It's not how many books you read, I think; it's how much you get out of them.

Applying the Information

Provided one has the information, then the next step is to apply it to solve a problem. Quite often, it is the problem solving that separates mediocrity from genius. We all stand upon the shoulders of giants, but only a few can see further and with more clarity than others and offer solutions. Newton and Einstein had the same information available to the scientists of their times. The ways they applied the information were what made them immortal. Given the same information, the great ones can come up with a solution while most of us fail. Again, problem solving is like cooking. There are great chefs and there are lousy cooks. For an organism to survive, it hardly matters. As long as it can solve a survival related problem, it can live another day. The way it solves the problems, though, will determine its species' number.

So is there a way to grade general intelligence in a person? I believe that general intelligence has no meaning. If a person is a genius according to some IQ test and fails to better his own life or improve those of others, what good does it do? So what if you are the smartest MENSA member but have to depend on social assistance? To qualify as intelligent, a person should have a fair amount of information at his command and be able to apply the information to solve problems. The leaders and scholars of our societies are problem solvers; they solve difficult problems so that we can live better and understand more. That is why Newton, Darwin, Einstein, Watson, and Crick are such intelligent human beings. They make us smarter and enrich mankind tremendously. And so is Burt Rutan, who designed SpaceShipOne to win the Ansari X Prize. When it comes to designing planes capable of carrying people to space, very few men, if any, are more intelligent than Rutan.

General Intelligence Has No Meaning

It is meaningless to ask, "Is Einstein more intelligent than Stephen Cheung, yours truly?" I would say, "It depends. And on matters concerning women and sex, I think yours truly could beat the great Dr. Lone Stone hands down." Just kidding! But you know what I am driving at, don't you? To decide the level of intelligence, one must be specific—in what area. From the definition, intelligence is not entirely determined by birth; it can be acquired, and continuously improved upon. A person can add to his intelligence by gathering useful information and learning ways to solve problems with information. Going to school is a sure way to become more intelligent.

Predicting an Outcome

Perhaps the most valuable contribution from intelligence to survival is its ability to predict an outcome before it happens. Clouds, for example, are reliable signs of whether or not a storm is approaching. Low-hanging dark clouds always precede rain. Funnel clouds represent something nasty quickly approaching. Seeking shelter ASAP often becomes life and death. You don't actually need to be bitten by a hissing snake with an expanded hood to find out that it is dangerous. And, if you go to a certain place during a certain season you will be handsomely rewarded with lots of delicious fruits. Intelligence, through the stored information, often allows an animal to know what is going to happen and exercise the appropriate response which will enhance its survival. That is something that muscle can never deliver. That is why muscle can never be independent on its operation without the guidance of intelligence.

The Beginning of Intelligence

When did intelligence come to exist? To answer the question, I would like to go back to a section in a previous chapter which relates happiness seeking to survival. We have mentioned that happiness seeking is what helps or makes a creature to survive through relieving stresses and pains that can arise from body damage, a looming danger, hunger, or a need to reproduce. We have also mentioned that in order to relieve stress, the source of stress needed to be sensed or identified before it could be fixed. The processes of sensing stress, followed by fixing it, should date back to the very first organism or it would not be able to continue to self-preserve. Makes sense? If the first organism had no way to detect damage, how could it fix it? Not fixing the damage in time would have cost it its life, would it not? Therefore, the processes involved in happiness seeking are actually the steps in problem solving, correct? How so? Sensing or identifying the source of trouble is no different from gathering the right information, and taking care of the trouble is the same as applying the information to fix the problem—and thus relieving the stress. Therefore, happiness seeking, which is the essence of survival, and intelligence, which is solving survival-related problems, are the same things by different names, depending on how we look at it.

On our planet, intelligence began at exactly the same moment as happiness seeking, which in turn began at the same moment as life itself. The beginning of life was also the beginning of intelligence. Again, life is an expression of intelligence; life is intelligent. Intelligence is to solve the problems arising from the instability of life. By the same argument and as discussed, every living creature on the planet—an animal, a plant, or a fungus, etc.—is a happiness or pleasure seeker because each and every one will seek to relieve life-threatening stresses. Life, self, selfishness, self-preservation, happiness seeking, and intelligence all have the same beginning; they are inseparable.

The Evolutionary Trend of Intelligence

Nervous systems have evolved over time to be more complex to accommodate the ever-increasing workloads; it divides the labor into parts, each of which manages a different aspect of information: some collect it, some process it, and after processing some execute a command to solve a problem. Information-collecting devices are further categorized into departments such as sound, smell, light, electrical field, and touch, etc., and each of the information collecting is handled by highly specialized neurons. The information is then sent to a control center for processing, and after that, the decision is made whether or not to take action. In animals, an action frequently involves muscles.

A Reflex Arc

In response to certain information, the response can be very specific. For example, upon encountering a spot where the pH level is dangerously high or low, an aquatic organism's action is always to back off. It is in the organism's interest to do so ASAP. Similarly, if an animal runs into something that causes pain, it is wise for the animal to back away without the slightest delay. For a no-brainer, animals have evolved to bypass the processing center and fast-tracked problem solving by inputting a stimulus directly to the muscles to form a reflex arc. Thus, a reflex is not only a foolproof life-saving mechanism, it shortens reaction time and relieves the central nervous system from unrewarding jobs in order to allocate more resources for tasks that require serious decision making, like to buy or not to buy that new car, to call or not to call the girl, or to exercise or to watch TV, etc. Life is not simple, is it?

An Instinct

To be effective and efficient, animals have further evolved to group together several reflexes that serve the same survival purpose into a sequence of actions; the whole sequence of actions is an instinct. It is an instinct for a cardinal to sing in spring, a bull to ready its penis in the presence of a fertile cow, or a young man to automatically check out the measurements of an attractive woman. Putting an instinct into action can be quite time and energy costly and can have serious consequence if the instinct malfunctions. The animal, therefore better be sure before setting it off. Animals often pick the most reliable signal or a set of signals to start a ritual. That is why we don't hear cardinals sing in the other seasons.

Toward More Flexibility

A major trend in the evolution of intelligence in animals is toward more flexibility. That is the same as to say animals are evolving toward more massive central nervous systems, from systems built on hundreds of neurons in microscopic animals to hundreds of thousands or hundreds of millions in increasingly more advanced animals. The zenith of intelligence, a human brain, has a hundred billion neurons. With a more elaborate brain, an advanced animal can store more information, has more processing power, and comes up with more solutions and thus has more flexibility than a lower life form. A massive brain like that of humans also enables man to predict things accurately and save his life. For example, robbing a pack of wild dogs would likely be rewarding, while doing it to lions would be suicidal.

Muscle Is King in Animals

Though there has been a continuous evolution toward more elaborate brains, thus giving the animals more stored information, greater processing power, and therefore smarter animals, intelligence has not been the boss in the survival games among animals. It has always played second fiddle to muscle. Ultimately, it has been muscle that gives power to chase down a prey, make a kill, or win a mate. For this reason, the increase in neurons among animals has been kept to a minimal level, which will just be enough to serve the muscles to make them effective. Excessive investments in neurons have never brought the proportionate returns to animals. And any animal that made the wrong choice in overinvesting in neurons will soon be eliminated. This rule has been true until the emergence of the unfortunate chimp.

The Myths of Star Wars *and* Star Trek

Because of Hollywood movies like *Star Wars* and *Star Trek* for sure, most people believe that there are numerous planets in our galaxy that harbor advanced civilizations. Advanced civilizations, according to them, would be more common than McDonald's in Shanghai. We are not alone, so they believe. It is not just ordinary, scientifically unsophisticated folks who hold such a belief. Few prominent scientists, if any, astronomers and nuclear physicists, in particular, would doubt the existence of many advanced civilizations in our Milky Way. A mathematician has even manipulated numbers to prove that the probability of advanced civilizations existing outside our solar system is 1, meaning an absolute certainty. Fully convinced, they want to find and contact those civilizations. Many top-notch scientists, including the late Carl Sagan, have been diligently searching for extraterrestrial intelligence. These searchers are from Harvard, Berkeley, or the SETI Institute, just to name the big three. They use big and sophisticated telescopes to monitor certain radio frequencies for possible signals sent by outside civilizations. Besides searching for extraterrestrial signals, other astronomers are searching for planets in other solar systems. For their patience and to their credit, they have, up to April 2013, discovered 872 such planetary systems, and out of which 130 contain multiple planets. If the search for extraterrestrial intelligence is fruitful, it will give us more things to talk about other than hockey and baseball. It may also change our perspective on life. And the pope might have to send missionaries to those planets.

Existence of Extraterrestrial Advanced Civilizations Is Probably a Myth

Knowing what I know now, after having written and rewritten the possible evolution of our species, I very much doubt that extraterrestrial advanced civilizations exist outside our sun. I am not saying this because of a misguided earth-centeredness. I have good scientific reasons for my belief. 1) It is extremely improbable that life could begin by natural evolution for reasons already discussed. 2) For highly intelligent beings to evolve, it would require a number of quite, very, to exceedingly unlikely events to take place together. One of those events would require those planets to have organisms that could convert their starlight to energy. On our planet, we have green plants. Green plants had to exist before there could be animals. Green plants provided a vast biomass and energy base to support other life forms. Without green plants, our planet could still be a barren place with sparse patches of organisms. Green plants have also changed our atmosphere by creating a lot of oxygen by freeing the atoms from water during photosynthesis. The high level of oxygen allows a high metabolic rate in animals. Highly intelligent beings should have big brains, which, gram for gram, consume more calories than other tissues. Brain neurons are exceedingly energy thirsty, comparable perhaps to engines of drag-racing cars. A big brain can thus only perform at its peak in environments with a high level of oxygen to "burn" biofuels to power them. Knowing that the first green plant needed to acquire the magic chlorophyll and a resistance to nascent oxygen, one needs to ask the question: how probable was it for the first green plant (algae?) to evolve on our planet? Similarly, how likely would it be for plantlike organisms to evolve in other solar systems?

There is another reason that would make finding highly intelligent beings unlikely. We have argued that all life forms need to be selfish regardless of which planet they are found in because the physics is the same everywhere in our cosmos. To be selfish is to protect oneself, to get energy, and to reproduce. Every animal before humans came to exist has naturally favored choosing muscle for the jobs. The evolution of humans was a very lucky process predicated on several factors, one of the most important factors would be the evolution of a pair of free hands, which would become a prominent feature. A pair of free hands allows the animal to make more elaborate tools and hold on to the tools.

Some animals have hands that allow them to finely manipulate objects; raccoons, squirrels, otters, monkeys, and apes are examples. But those hands are not really free; they are important parts of their locomotion. To have a pair of really free hands is to greatly slow down the animal, making it very unfit to survive in a world ruled by muscle where speed is a prerequisite for survival. It was perhaps by many happy coincidences—already having a brain with the highest specific brain capacity was one—that the first chimp with a changed pelvis could make it. And it also happened that the chimp was a social animal and the top competitor in its environment, thus allowing it to be safe despite a great loss in mobility. It also helped that chimps lived in Africa, where lions have been kings. If the top predators were animals like tigers, which hunt alone and by stealth, then the changed chimps would not have time to get establish on land, our promised land. Those are just a few of the reasons.

Each of the above conditions necessary for an advanced civilization to evolve is in itself a very unlikely, if not impossible, event. To have so many unlikely events linked together seems extremely improbable. I would not give it a chance greater than one in a billion—that, perhaps, is still a bit optimistic.

All in all, I would not bet money from my RRSP (Registered Retirement Saving Plan) on finding extraterrestrial intelligence. If—and that will be a big *if*—there is life on other planets, the life forms will likely be microscopic organisms. It will unlikely be a rich variety of organisms similar to what's on our planet. If there are plantlike organisms that exist in the other worlds, the animals that evolve in those worlds will likely be similar to that of the early earth, nasty beasts with sharp teeth and claws crowned by muscles. Animals on the other planets, if they exist, will likely depend on simple and effective muscles than neurons. I just can't see how humanlike intelligence can exist outside our planet—unless there is God.

CHAPTER 9

The Evolution of Intelligence in Early Humans

The Misfit Chimps

It had been several million years after the first chimp with a disfigured pelvis appeared and gave birth to chimps that walked on two feet. As eons passed, the look of these creatures had changed—likely one part at a time. The changes, of course, were consequences of mutations. The way mutations produce changes is like a drunken cowboy trying to kill a wolf; he shoots in any which way and kills many cattle before getting the job done. Everything considered, it is still a bargain. Every creature needs some fundamental changes from time to time to cope. Mutation, despite its high price tag in causing far more harm than benefit, is the only game in town.

The changes, whether visible or at deeper levels, were absolutely indispensable. The reason is simple: a chimp was never designed to walk on two feet for any appreciable period of time. Bipedal locomotion meant climbing trees would be inconvenient, which meant spending more time on ground became compulsory. An upright-walking chimp often found his arms too long and his legs too short. Most of the time, the bulky arm muscles were idle; the once sure bet was a waste and the extra bulk became a burden. In fact, as those creatures began to walk more and more, covering more territories in the generations that followed, they found nothing was right—literally from his head to his toes. Walking any appreciable distance was a struggle; his body swung from side to side, and he got tired easily. Walking on two legs also raised his center of gravity, making the chimplike being less stable. Its grasping toes were simply disastrous; they were just too long, causing him to trip over every so often. His situation was not unlike playing badminton with a tennis racket or riding a 500 cc motorcycle on bicycle tires. If you were that creature, you would not laugh. Your problems, all arising from an inability to move quickly around trees, had eventually forced you to leave your home base, the trees, and venture into unfamiliar lands in search of food. It had to be an extremely desperate situation for our ancestors to make such a grim and extremely difficult choice.

Problems, Problems, and More Problems

A reader should know by now that yours truly has a habit of making statements that are aimed to shock. Having warned you, I would still say: of all the creatures that have ever been created or come to exist, none have ever faced so many problems with such frequency than the very first few generations of prehumans. Their closest relatives, the common chimps, certainly had no idea what their first cousins were going through. Living in the same woods, hunting, gathering, and eating the same kind of food in the same territory year in and year out from the time they were born until the day they died, the regular chimps were unlikely to encounter many new problems that required immediate solutions.

The trophy tools of the chimps have not gone beyond twigs for termite fishing, spearlike twigs for stabbing bush babies, or raw pebbles for nut cracking for tens of millions of years. It is not that chimps are lazier or less smart, they just did not have many problems confronting them. Obviously, the source of all the problems of the walking apes had come from the cursed pelvis. Forced to walk on two limbs, they were also forced to change their lifestyles. Before the mutation, they were living happily in woods and forests, fully comfortable in a lifestyle in trees or making occasional visits to the forest floor. The common chimps were the best of all tree specialists, with unmatched power and speed. They were kings in their domains. The changed pelvis had forever robbed the crippled chimps of their speed. Without speed, their power had no use. They quickly learned that they had to abandon trees as a source of food; they could not compete with the regular chimps. Their only hope to get food was on land, but the prospect would be equally gray. Not only were they not land specialists, the bipedal chimps had very limited knowledge, if any, about the new environment. Their ignorance had cost many lives. But they did not have any choice.

Despite the seemingly insurmountable hurdle from the loss of speed and the danger of making a living in more and more new environments and farther and farther from home, they managed to survive. In fact, they did much better than merely get by; they thrived, and their number kept increasing. If one does not want to call it a miracle, it is truly a mystery that makes quantum phenomena appear simple by comparison.

As their number increased or the climate changed, or both, they had to venture farther and farther away from their home base in search of food. Land, like any part of the planet that could sustain life, was usually fully stocked with gangs of local specialists, all of which, over millions of years, had perfected their trades. The bipedal chimps were immigrants. In a new environment, they often became food for the locals, such as wild dogs, hyenas, cheetahs, and lions. Regular chimps had no massive teeth or sharp claws; they did not need those nasty things when they were the biggest and fastest in trees. Common chimps were no gentlemen; however, they were certainly not Bruce Lees. In the new domains, our ancestors were initially outclassed even by mediocre competitors like wild dogs. Having absolutely no speed further exaggerated their weakness. It was a lose/lose combination, a fatal mix in a barbaric world. Every day of their existence was filled with problems; they had more problems than the Russian Lada, which unlike the bipedal chimps, was specifically designed to compete with other cars. Their problems were always the same: how to get enough to eat and how to avoid being eaten. In search of food, they had to cover more and more territories, exposing themselves to a greater and greater number of predators. For almost every animal on the planet, finding food means getting ready to eat. But not for the upright-walking apes; for them, it was often the first part of the problem. And there were more problems to solve before they could eat.

To eat, they often needed to use their brains. For example, they could come across a drying pool of water which contained many stranded fish. The problem would be how could they get to the fish? And catching a fish could be quite tricky; it would not be the same as catching a lizard. For those would-be diners, the muddy bank could often be a death trap. There were also crocs, hyenas, and leopards to watch out for. If they could solve every one of those problems, they would be handsomely rewarded.

Having solved the fish puzzle did not mean that they could live off their achievement for any appreciable length of time. Soon, the place would dry up with nothing left. They had to move on. Or a group might come across a turtle. They had not eaten for a while; their growling stomachs would not allow them to give it up. But how would they break an armor that had defeated tough customers like leopards, hyenas, or wild dogs, and had stood the test of time for millions of years? Or to catch a big lizard which was sheltered under a rock? Or to break the defense of a hissing snake that caused a lion to retreat? To lay his hand on a frog that always managed to jump away? Or to get fruits which were out of reach? And plant parts that were buried?

More and more, those upright-walking creatures became aware of a pattern: to eat, they had to solve some problems first, which changed from time to time and from place to place. And the solutions often did not require brute force or speed; rather, their intelligence and ingenuity would get the job done. And they knew only too well that if they succeeded, they would be immediately and plentifully rewarded. If they failed, however, they would be punished right away with disappointment and hunger. Any psychologist will tell you that there is no better way to motivate someone to learn than by a reward-punishment coupling. As a result, the awkward apes increasingly relied on their wits. Their brains, despite being the most resourceful and biggest at the time, were always taxed to the limit. Reward vs. punishment made them learn to remember more and more of the past incidents, places, seasons, times, the fauna and flora. Having information at their fingertips, they discovered, invariably made their lives much easier.

After a couple of seasons, for example, upright-walking chimps were able to figure out how to overcome the muddy bank to get to the fish faster; they could also learn how to catch them effectively. Or a turtle became an easy meal because they could crack the armor in different ways, like throwing it against a rock repeatedly or beating it with a club at a certain angle. Giving a snake a whack would take care of the nasty creature safely and quickly. And they should not eat certain things no matter how hungry they were.

Besides obtaining food, it would also greatly help them to remember certain landmarks which would lead them home or to safety. Knowing when and where certain foods could be found would also help. Knowing where predators usually hung around could save many lives. A database to predict imminent weather change and avoid being caught in a storm could be life and death. In short, the more they remembered, the easier their lives would become. Though not knowing it, the direction of their evolution had already been laid down. It was not speed and muscle they were after; they needed to upgrade their data-storage and number-crunching capacity. They were always hungry for more and more neurons, bigger and bigger brains. And millions of years before us, before we were hooked on computers with ever-increasing power, the prehumans had already developed an insatiable appetite for the same capability.

It was not only their brains, they had discovered, that would help them to survive. Their sticks and clubs were also important. It had become clear that in almost every solution to their problems they needed a club or a stick. To move along a muddy bank, for example, a stick allowed the ape to test the ground, to steady the body, and to pull away from the powerful grip of the wet clay. After getting to the fish, he could use the same stick to spear the fish and catch it one by one. Or instead of throwing the turtle around, clubbing it open proved much easier and neater. And a snake, no matter how viciously it hissed, was always an easy meal with the same old reliable tool. Buried food could be dug out; fruits that were too high were reachable by using a stick with a hook at the end . . .

It was not only for food gathering that the sticks and clubs were vital; their tools were important in protecting their lives. A club in the hand of an experienced male ape, as discussed, had bone-crushing power and a speed even faster than a leopard's paw. What they lacked in speed, raw power, sharp claws, and long, piercing teeth were handsomely compensated by the clubs and sticks. The sticks and clubs were truly magical; they transformed the apes from sure losers to powerful contenders and competitors.

The beauty of their tools was in their simplicity to use and ease to make; the material was readily available. Each individual, as he began to learn to walk, would start making a stick that suited him and carry it with him. Some individuals could carry two. A group could carry several varieties of sticks, each with a special purpose. A male, however, learned always to carry a club as the species evolved; having a club would protect him and define his manhood.

They also learned to stick together as a unit. A group often consisted of males who were either brothers or first cousins or longtime friends;

they naturally stuck together. The females, however, like those of chimps, often came from different groups. The females, especially those with children, would stay close to their group for safety. Those who failed to band together got killed quickly, with their genes that did not favor staying together eliminated.

As a group covered more land searching for food, they would come across leopards, cheetahs, a pack of wild dogs, or hyenas more often. Each of them would try to escape to nearby trees if possible. When it was too late, there would be casualties from time to time; the victims were usually the weak, like women or children. But sooner or later, as they evolved, got better at walking, more skillful with the sticks and club, made better choices of wood for their tools, and learned more about their enemies, the following scenario was bound to happen.

Introducing Cooperation, the Other Force That Powers Human Evolution

A Close Encounter of the Hyena Kind

A member of the group had made the very unsettling discovery that they were being stalked by a pack of hyenas. At the time, the group was too far from any trees, and running was certainly not an option. If they were like ordinary chimps, death was quite certain for a number of them. Luckily, every mature male had a club. The group formed a tight circle— as most social animals would do when cornered or threatened—with the males on the outer edge to face the enemies.

The alpha male of the pack was a bit confused. The pack had encountered these creatures in isolated incidents; the creatures always fled before them, clambering quickly up trees. It was a new experience for the alpha hyena that these chimps were not running away. There were few animals other than lions that dared to stand up to the pack, but these were evidently no lions.

The pack did not have enough to eat for a number of days; the rare luck of coming across these creatures seemed too good to be true. But hyenas were cautious and suspicious by nature, so the alpha hyena circled the group to check each individual out carefully, instinctively looking for ways these creatures could harm him. They did not have any horns. And the claws—if they deserved the name—were almost nonexistent. And the funniest thing of all, the creatures, in a desperate attempt to intimidate their attackers, had foolishly bared their teeth and thereby betrayed their mortal weakness: each of them had only a few pitifully small sharp teeth. Satisfied, the hyena decided it was safe to attack.

With a leap, the alpha hyena charged a "chimp." The hyena's goal was to attack the creature's throat and with its powerful jaws drag it down and go for the kill. The strategy had been perfected through millions of years of practice; it had seldom failed. But just before he could lock his jaws on his prey, the hyena felt a piercing and paralyzing pain on his back. That had never happened before. Shocked, it let out a yelp and instinctively retreated. Luckily, the "chimps" did not advance; instead, they held their ground, baring their pitifully inadequate teeth, uttering empty threats. What happened? The alpha male was more surprised and startled than really hurt. But hyenas are unparalleled in their persistence; if they were outmatched in brute by lions, they had made it up with stamina. Giving up a meal was not in their genes. The pain gradually subsided, and luckily there was no blood from the wound. So the leading hyena chose to try again. Before launching another attack, the hyena, just to be sure, wanted to check out the creatures one more time. He began to circle the group, walking calculatingly and looking for new clues. No horns, no claws, and no massive teeth. With everything meticulously checked, the picture was the same. What had hit him the first time? The hyenas had no time for an intellectual pursuit; neither could they afford to waste time chasing mystery. Driven by a growling stomach, the animal could not be distracted.

Once more, with heightened alertness, utmost vigilance, and some intricacy in disguising its real intention, the leading hyena attacked one of the prey's legs with cheetahlike quickness. The maneuver paid off. This time, the hyena hit the bullseye; it sank its massive teeth onto the flesh, and was instantly rewarded by the taste of flesh and blood. The euphoria was brief. Almost at the same instant, the hyena received a massive blow on the head. But the taste of blood made the pain bearable; it held on to the flesh and tried to take down his prey. A number of new blows landed upon his back; the hyena still held on. Success was imminent. Then, a club hit the snout of the alpha male, creating a gush of blood. The alpha male gave a high-pitched yelp, dropped the "chimp," and hurriedly retreated. Between a meal and imminent death, the alpha male had chosen life. Again, the hyena was relieved to see the group stayed at the same spot and did not go after him. Facing a group of very hostile foes and having no assurance of success, the alpha hyena decided that he had had enough and limped away. Those hyenas had since deleted the club-carrying "chimps" from their easy-prey list.

Having successfully defeated one of their most dreaded enemies, the "chimps" were overwhelmed with joy; they jumped up and down in exultation, waving their clubs and sticks in celebration. They had since become bolder in facing new attacks. They would retreat to trees if possible, but they were no longer sitting ducks. Gradually, less-powerful predators such as hyenas, dogs, and wolflike animals learned to fear the stick-carrying "chimps."

Being forced to walk on two legs was one of the greatest perils in the history of mammalian evolution. Even with what we know now, few would give them a chance to make it beyond several generations. As an informed gambler, I would certainly not bet on them making it more than a few millennia. No way, Jose! But when one is constantly face to face with death, one will be at his best. Our ancestors did just that. Instead of giving up and be killed, they dug deep and found answers with a pair of free hands and the most potent brain in the animal kingdom at the time. They turned peril into opportunity and thrived. Yin, the negative, is forever linked to yang, the positive; it all depends on the creature. Life and death, success and failure intertwine. Luck could have played a role, but it was the "chimps" that had made the best of what they got and helped to pull them through. Was it a miracle, or was it a success story of a creature against all odds?

With the above story, we shall leave behind a dark period of which no old bones have ever been dug up. Though we have no idea how the creatures looked or moved around other than they were very much chimplike, we know for sure that they had survived and overcome the lousy hand dealt to them. They even thrived after a long period of adjustments. For sure, they had made it by using their intelligence. But intelligence alone would not be able to carry them through; they were also aided by cooperation, as painted in our story, from day one, because our ancestor was a chimp, a social animal. It has been intelligence and cooperation combined and intertwined that have helped our lineage to evolve, and have carried us through the millions of years that followed.

The two forces have been with us from the very first day, have carried us, and will certainly be with us for as long as our species exists. The twosome also holds the answer of why and how our species has become godlike. The knowledge will give us a clear direction of how to fix the planet and make it a better place for us all. Tools, no doubt, have also been an integral part of our success. They, however, are products of intelligence and cooperation and do not exist alone.

In the following chapters, we shall continue to examine how intelligence and cooperation together had helped carry our ancestors through the transitional species. As shown, the twosome is intertwined; it would not be possible to discuss one without the other. For clarity, however, we can only focus on one of them at a time.

We still have many topics to discuss with intelligence; we shall continue to follow the development of intelligence as indicated by the continuous increase of brain capacity in the species to follow. The sketchy bone trail discovered by the many patient paleoanthropologists in the past decades will be the foundation of our discussion. Though many (bone) pieces are still missing, the picture that emerges is surprisingly clear for our purpose.

A Very Old Gal Called Lucy

Our knowledge of the origin of humans has, for the most part, come from paleoanthropology. Paleoanthropologists are bone diggers and collectors; they are the most careful and patient people. Like every success story, luck, in addition to knowledge, persistence, and hard work, has played an important part in their important finds. The theories on the origin of mankind have depended heavily on evidence from old bones.

From their discoveries, most paleoanthropologists believe that there were several transitional forms that link us to the first chimp. Unfortunately, our bone collections have come in bits and pieces, literally, left behind across the great span of time of many millions of years. Other than two rather complete skeletons, Lucy and the Nariokotome boy, the links that predated modern humans have been vague to totally missing. Paleoanthropologists are convinced that the very first link would certainly have retained all the chimp characteristics except, perhaps, the changed pelvis. But it was from Lucy that we began to know with some certainty what the first species that had emerged from our chimplike ancestors was like.

She may not be as famous or as sexy as Cleo. In fact, there is some doubt that she was really a woman, but few intellectuals do not know her name. Her name was Lucy, as all of us fondly call her. But it is not her name; her kind still did not have the anatomy in the throat to produce the varieties of sounds that we call a language. The gal was born about 3.2 million years ago, according to the dating method based on the ratio of radioactive potassium and argon. Her name came from a song by the Beatles called "Lucy in the Sky with Diamonds," which was played over and over again at the party celebrating her discovery. Someone in the team that made the discovery, a team led by Donald Johanson, at some point of alcohol intoxication, named the skeleton Lucy; the rest is truly history.

The team found Lucy in 1974 in Hadar, Ethiopia. Lucy was, up to then, the most complete skeleton, 40 percent, from a single hominid that was ever discovered, making it priceless. The skeleton tells us a lot about Lucy and her folks. The followings are some hard facts:

Classification: *Australopithecus afarensis*
Apelike features: Heavy protruding jaw, thick-waisted and potbellied, and a wide pelvis
Cranial capacity: 450 ml.
Height: Between 3.5 to 4 ft. tall
Weight: About 75 lbs.

What does the skeleton tell us about her kind? First, and most importantly, she walked upright. Many features—the knee joint in relation to the femur, the pelvis, the vertebral column, her ankle, etc.—clearly show that Lucy walked upright. However, some features also tell us that she was far from perfecting bipedal locomotion. She tended to swing from side to side as she walked, not unlike a model strutting down a catwalk. Secondly, no more tree climbing. Her arms had shortened substantially in relation to her legs. Though there were no bones recovered from the feet, it was quite unlikely that the feet were capable of grasping—it would unnecessarily burden the hominid to walk with long grasping big toes, would it not? Opposable thumb? It is also quite likely that Lucy's hands had opposable thumbs, allowing them more dexterity and a stronger grip on their sticks or clubs. Conclusion: From Lucy's rather (40 percent) complete skeleton—it's all relative, isn't it?—we are quite sure that she was not big; she weighed about 2/3 of a chimp. She walked in a funny way, could not run, and in fact, she was likely to have no speed. To make the situation worse, she had lost the ability to get up a tree quickly. The most puzzling fact was her brain size in comparison to chimps: it was bigger.

From the above picture, one would naturally ask: how could such a creature survive in an environment which was likely to have many predators? How did they defend themselves? From what is given, we know that they could not outrun any predators, and climbing up trees was not a regular practice or they would have kept the features that make tree climbing easier. The fact that all the features point increasingly toward more specialization in bipedal walking tells us that Lucy's type had firmly committed to living on land; they had reached a point of no return—to trees, that is.

The fact that the skeleton was preserved for such a long period of time and was discovered indicates—based on the law of probability—that their numbers were substantial; they were unlikely to be an endangered species. The most crucial piece of information is the cranial size; it is more than 10 percent bigger than that of chimps. And they achieved it with a smaller body. What does that tell us? There can be only one conclusion: Lucy represents a group of hominids that had relied heavily on their brains; they were a new breed, specialists who, instead of muscles and speed, depended on their wits and tools, naturally, to compete.

An Extremely Difficult Commitment

If I were one of the members that discovered Lucy, I would, after knowing how the hominid looked, be slightly disappointed. Is that all you have to show after such a long absence? According to most anthropologists, humans branched off from chimps about 10 million years ago. If that is the case, then after close to seven million years the hominid had not changed much from a chimp. True, a number of features show that her kind had fully committed to bipedal locomotion, and most likely had also abandoned living in trees in favor of caves. At the same time, the commitment had not brought many drastic changes; her adaptation was far from complete. She had no speed, would swing from side to side walking, and had a chimp belly. Other than a slightly bigger head and walking on two legs, their kind, I imagine, would be very much chimplike. And it had taken almost seven million years to achieve so little! Why?

I wonder whether anthropologists have ever pondered the poor showing of the new species. Was it because the commitment to bipedal locomotion was a rather recent event, say about a million years ago? If that was the case, what, then, had kept holding them back for many millions of years? For sure, the chimplike ancestors had greater difficulty in committing than me leaving my first wife. Why was it so hard for them to decide? I would think they were constantly debating over three survival issues. Number 1, of course, was their safety. If they went all out and left the woods, how could they escape to safety when predators were coming? With the sticks and clubs, they might be good enough to defeat the regular chimps; they would still be no match for even wild dogs and hyenas. Number 2, for food, they had to travel further and further from the trees they lived. Remember they were at the very beginning in learning to walk on two legs. They would get tired easily and travel quite slowly. Every step would be a bit of struggle. What distance would be within their walking capability? One kilometer and back? Two? Or three? How about the females with children? They would struggle even more, would they not? And 3, any group that had ventured away too far would find themselves more isolated. Besides the safety issue, young members would not be able to get a mate. To have any hope, they had to travel back to the trees. There, they not only could mate with their own kind, some could mate with regular chimps. Love would always be a good reason for them to go back, would it not?

So there was a constant tug of war between the three factors soon after the very beginning. Safety and reproduction needs would make them stay, and finding food would push them farther and farther away from their home base. It was a tug of war that lasted quite a few million years. It was an extremely difficult commitment to make for our ancestors. We still don't know what had eventually given them the deciding push.

Brain Over Brawn

The increase of intelligence in humans, starting from Lucy's kind, has never stopped. Before the common chimps, the role of intelligence was quite obscure in the survival game. It often involved no more than collecting information from the environment through various senses, processing the information, and, in a fraction of a second, sending an order to muscles for execution. For example, after seeing a prey, a hungry animal sends out a command to immediately go after it. Smelling something bad, it orders a retreat. Touching something that causes pain, the instruction is to back away. Though animals were many and varied in size and shape, the world remained simple, rigid, and predictable; there was no need for animals to do too much thinking.

In such a simple world, muscles were more important than the number of neurons or the size of a brain; naturally, evolution has favored brawn over brain. It was no accident that muscle, rather than neurons, had risen to prominence. Though neurons have been sending out orders, it is muscle that gives the power to get the job done. Muscle has been the real problem solver. The way muscle works is not unlike the way Shaq played basketball: there was no need for finesse or subtlety; it was all raw power. Problem solving through muscle was effective and uncomplicated; it had proven again and again to be the simplest and the most trusted way to settle conflict of interests between two animal parties. In nature, a conflict of interest between two animals was always about who would eat and who would be eaten, or who could stay to mate and who had to run away. Muscle ruled. In a world ruled by muscle, there was no right and wrong, only weak and strong. The big whites, crocs, killer whales, polar bears, lions and tigers were some of the most notable rulers of their domains, and some still are.

The picture had been the same for hundreds of millions of years. Then, the birth of a chimp with a disfigured pelvis began a new trend: intelligence began to wield its power. And rather than the mundane chores of sorting out simple messages and switching muscles on or off, the chimp was forced to work more intensively with the bits and pieces of information, to refine it, before sending out a command. In other words, the chimp needed to think often and deep to come up with a solution. The situation is not unlike countries like Germany, Switzerland, and Japan, which have little natural resources and must greatly rework and improve every piece of raw material before coming up with a product. The solutions the countries come up with require more processing and reshaping of the raw materials; they require a higher level of intelligence.

To a regular chimp, a piece of wood is nothing more than a piece of junk, which is useless in obtaining food or self-defense; old faithful, the reliable servant called muscle, can get both jobs done better and faster. To a disabled chimp, the same piece of junk could hold the answers to his most pressing problems. The answers, however, would not be straightforward; the chimp could not simply pick up any piece of wood and use it. To serve its purpose, the chimp needed first to choose the right piece, then to reshape it by shortening it into a convenient length and getting rid of the twigs which would lessen its effectiveness. Though begun as trial and error, the makers gradually learned through experience to see what the end products would be like and how to get there quickly. It took many neurons; it required a higher form of intelligence.

A bipedal chimp, in implementing the solutions to his problems, often had no need for speed or great power, of which he had neither. What was crucial, instead, was for the mind and hands to work intricately as a team. It took skill. The mind continued to provide the picture of a finished product; the hands worked step by step toward it. There was no need to rush; neither did it required bulky muscles. With the new trend, brain size had been encouraged to increase and muscle mass reduced. Given the inability to move around quickly—an inevitable consequence of bipedal walking—the new apes found it more profitable to invest in bigger brains to get greater information-cranking power and finer control of muscle movements than massive muscles. The way to do business was permanently shifted. It was a new and risky move; no animal had ever succeeded in the millions of years in dethroning muscles to crown neurons. But with every great risk often came a great payoff; it turned out to be a brilliant move.

We know nothing about how the children of the first bipedal chimp changed in the first few million years that followed. Lucy was the first hominid that emerged from that long, dark period. She was quite special; her brain capacity was amazing. To show this point, I would, again, like to use the information obtained from page 17 and 39 of the second edition of *Images of the Past* by T. Douglas Price and Gary M. Feinman. From the graph, we can extract information on body weight vs. brain size and present the numbers in the following table. The last column called *Specific Brain Capacity* has been added. We have already discussed what specific brain capacity (SBC) is in chapter 7; it indicates the intelligence level of an animal. In the case of apes, the higher the number, the smarter the animal. In the following, we shall look at the specific brain capacities of the species from chimp to modern human based on the information provided by *Images of the Past*.

Specific Brain Capacity of Chimp to Human

Primate/Species	Estimated Body Weight, kg	Brain Capacity, ml	Specific Brain Capacity, ml/kg
Gibbon	20	100	5.0
Chimpanzee	40	400	10
Orangutan	73	400	5.5
Gorilla	100	600	6
Australopithecus africanus	35	450	12.9
Homo habilis	38	680*	17.9
Homo erectus	55	1000	18.2
Homo sapiens sapiens (modern human)	60	1400	23.3
Homo sapiens neanderthalensis	65	1450	22.3

*The brain size of H. habilis has been a subject of hot debate in paleoanthropology; according to some authorities, it ranges from 600 ml to 1,600 ml.

Before we compare the specific brain capacities of the apes, let me provide you with some background rationality. The brain size of mammals, and for that matter, all animals, is always directly related to how many senses it monitors, how elaborately the information from the senses needs to be processed, and how many muscle groups it controls. For an extremely sluggish animal like a tree sloth, which has plenty of food nearby and is not required to move around much to feed, I would expect its SBC to be among the lowest of all mammals. How so? Because for a lazy animal to make ends meet, it does not need much information; neither does it need to move around much every day. Opening its eyes and stretching out a limb, it can get all the food it can consume. How much brain does it need? To stay safe, it will be well advised to cut its activities down to an absolute minimum in order not to attract too much attention from predators. So there will not be a lot of information coming in, not much to be processed, which in turn results in very few outgoing commands at any given time. The only time a sloth has to do any traveling is when a male needs to seek out a female—love always complicates things, does it not? As a result, a sloth can live happily without a lot of neurons.

A predator such as a cheetah, killer whale, an owl, or a bat represents the other extreme. Not only does it need a sophisticated tracking system of many senses and a center to continuously process the ever-changing incoming information, it also needs finely tuned muscles to give it the speed and agility in order to chase down a prey and make a kill. All in all, more neurons are required for a hunter, and therefore a high SBC index.

The SBCs of herbivores should be between that of sloths and predatory animals. And among the herbivores, a hippo, which does not need to move a lot to find food and has no natural enemy, should have a lower index than other herbivores such as an antelope. An antelope has to be vigilant all the time and be able to accelerate to top speed in seconds.

I am reasonably sure that comparing the indexes of specific brain capacity can tell us a lot about the lifestyles of an animal. A hippo should have a lower SBC index than that of an antelope. An antelope should certainly be "smarter" than a hippo, according to our speculation. But whether or not an animal is stupid or smart hardly matters; what matters is getting enough neurons for it to survive. A hippo has brawn and massive jaws; it can afford to have less neurons. In a wild, wild world, intelligence has little (survival) value. Within a species, I expect the SBCs should stay pretty close with few deviations. So will the SBCs of animals in the same genus, family, or order as long as there is no radical change of lifestyle of the animals under the classification. I don't know whether or not such a database exists. It will be an interesting research project.

With the background in place, let us look at the SBC indexes of apes and hominids in the above Table. If we look at the SBC column, the numbers are quite meaningful. For example, a gorilla, despite having a bigger body and a larger brain capacity, has more or less the same index as a gibbon or an orangutan; i.e., about 6 ml per kg. I shall interpret the similarity as equal intelligence and therefore similar lifestyles among the three. The bigger brain capacity of a gorilla of 600 ml is nothing more than to compensate for a more massive body; it still works out to be more or less the same number of neurons to control the same unit weight of bone and flesh.

The index of a chimp, which is 10 ml/kg, stands out significantly above the other three apes. What does it mean? I would say that chimps, as indicated by their higher index, are smarter than the other three. In what way? The increase in number of neurons per unit mass may mean that chimps need more neurons for sensory organs, for greater dexterity, or for information processing. Since a chimp is very similar to the other three apes in anatomy, it is unlikely that the increase is related in any significant way to monitoring the senses or controlling muscles. I suspect that chimps use the added neurons for information processing; i.e., to do more thinking. It is therefore hardly an accident that chimps are the only apes that have frequently invented and used tools.

According to the SBC and using a gorilla as a standard, Lucy, for example, needed about twice the amount of neurons, *H. erectus* required three times more, and modern humans almost four times more nerves to make a unit of body work properly. If the SBC of E.T. were available, it would be likely higher than a human's. We must catch one to find out.

Intelligence works through three components: the information-collecting part, the processing and storage part, and the application part. Obviously, the size of each of these components is related or it would be a waste. The relation holds true for most animals. In the case of the chimp, however, the information-processing part is likely exaggerated to make its SBC stand out. This new trend has continued with other humans.

Intelligence Acceleration in Hominids

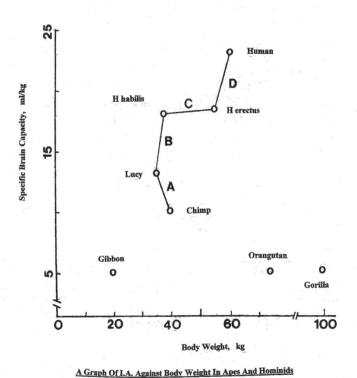

A Graph Of I.A. Against Body Weight In Apes And Hominids

A Graph of the IA between the Hominid Pairs

Intelligence Acceleration (IA)

By using specific brain capacity, we have obtained interesting information about the chimps; they have the highest index among the apes. Let us play with the information a bit differently this time. I am going to introduce yet another new concept called *intelligence acceleration*. (The term *intelligence acceleration* has been used by people selling different products; our definition is very different, rigorous, and in line with physics.) We are familiar with the meaning of *acceleration*; it is the change of speed vs. change in time. Using the same analogy, we can define

Stephen Y. Cheung, Ph.D.

intelligence acceleration (IA) as a change in specific brain capacity per unit change of body weight. To put it in a mathematical term, it will be:

Intelligence Acceleration = Change in SBC/Change in Body Weight

In acceleration, we are interested in the change of speed between two points in time; in intelligence acceleration, we are concerned with the change in SBC or intelligence level between two species of hominids while their bodies changed in weight. Acceleration is measured in meter/second/second, or comparable units. Intelligence acceleration is measured in ml/kg/kg.

To obtain an IA, we can plot the SBCs of chimps and hominids on the y-axis against their body weights on the x-axis. In doing so, we obtain a graph which is an ascending line with four segments from chimp to modern human. Very interestingly, we see as the hominids evolved their SBCs indexes, or the level of intelligence, continued to increase, starting from the chimps. To make it easier for our discussion, we shall name the segments starting from chimp to modern human A, B, C, and D, respectively. The slopes of the segments as represented by A, B, C, and D are the intelligence accelerations between the pairs of apes under consideration. An IA is a vector; it shows the direction of the acceleration as well as the magnitude. We can also calculate the value of each IA; the results are presented in the following table.

Table of Intelligence Acceleration of Different Pairs of Hominids

Direction of Connected Species	Segment	Difference in SBC, ml/kg	Difference in Body Weight, kg	IA, ml/kg/kg
From Chimp to Lucy	A	2.9	-5	-0.58
From Lucy to *H. habilis*	B	5.0	3	1.67
H. habilis to *H. erectus*	C	0.3	17	0.02
H. erectus to Modern Human	D	5.1	5	1.02

Of the four IAs, the one connecting chimps and Lucy is negative. The negative sign means part of the acceleration is achieved through a reduction of body weight; it is clearly shown in the west inclination of the vector, a point we shall come back to later. A north-pointing arrow indicates the direction of change is toward higher intelligence, with the vertical distance representing differences in SBCs. The IA between Lucy and *H. habilis*, segment B, was the greatest and most furious; it had an angle close to vertical. The next was from *H. erectus* to human, D, followed by chimp to Lucy A, and lastly C, from *H. habilis* to *H. erectus*, which was almost level, meaning the acceleration had almost taken a break. Intelligence acceleration is the rate of change in intelligence level, which should be related to the urgency for intelligence level to change to meet a hominid's needs: the higher the acceleration, the greater is the urgency.

Intelligence acceleration can either be an increase, zero, or a decrease. An increase (an upward pointing vector) means that there is a demand for more neurons per unit of body weight, which in turn means that the new animal needs more problem-solving capacity. In desperate times, an IA can sometimes be accelerated by cutting down muscle bulk, like the case of Lucy in comparison to regular chimps. If an IA is zero, it indicates that the animal pair in the consideration are quite happy with their current specific brain capacities or data-processing capabilities, therefore the values of their SBCs remain the same. If IA decreases, it means that the animal no longer needs the existing number of neurons per unit weight to survive. A decreased IA means that the animal is cutting down in activities, or the need to process information is less. Neurons are very energy hungry; keeping more neurons than needed will certainly be a waste.

The Emergence of Intelligence

We have discussed why animals in general had been avoiding investing in intelligence: Investing in intelligence means investing in neurons. Investing in neurons is like spending money in universities. It costs a lot of salaries to hire professors and research assistants. I have yet to see a university break even financially; forget about making a profit. That is why investing in universities is a luxury. Luxury does not exist in the game of survival; the game has always been tight, lean, and mean. In nature, any investment in intelligence will likely be a fatal mistake. Investment in muscles is like investing in arms and soldiers when the name of the game is to fight or kill. That is why muscles have been getting bigger and bigger among animals in evolution. Spending resources in making bigger muscles has been the safest bet. Given a choice, every animal invests in muscle.

Animals have avoided investing in intelligence until the common chimps. From its SBC, the common chimps have the highest value. And the differences between the SBC of chimps and apes are very significant—10 ml/kg vs. 5.0 ml/kg for gibbons, 5.5 ml/kg for orangutans, and 6 ml/kg gorillas. Chimps were the first apes, if not the first animal, to have invested in neurons and have proven to be very successful. The chimps did not go all out to invest in neurons; they had kept their muscles. They were, and still are, the most powerful and fastest moving apes that dwell in trees. Again, I believe that investing in extra neurons is the key that allows the chimps to invent more tools, both in frequency and types, than any other animals on the planet next to humans, their heirs. From this point of view, it seems that the highest degree of similarity between the DNAs of the two species is no accident, and it has to be that way. Only chimps could be our ancestor, and the deciding factor was its highest SBC.

It seems redundant, but I still have to emphasize the point. There are two reasons that chimps and chimps only could be our ancestors. 1) They have the highest SBC index; they have already successfully taken the most difficult step of extra-investing in neurons; the foundation had been laid down for the future species to build upon. The hominids that came after the chimps did not have to reinvent the wheel, so to speak. 2) Chimps have also got into the habit of tool making; they were the most "prolific" tool makers in the animal kingdom at the time. Tool making, which had been powered by intelligence and cooperation, was very crucial in helping the handicapped hominids to make it through. Common chimps have since stopped further investment in neurons. The intelligence-cooperation baton had been passed to the hominids. Our lineage has continued to develop and evolve along this unique and precious inheritance. The two forces have eventually made us gods to all living creatures. Evolution may and will give rise to many more new animal species, some of which will be more powerful and can move faster, but our dominance will never change.

The Toolmakers

If I were to name all the hominids, I would give them a name that reflects their most outstanding behavioral characteristic. That defining character is definitely tool making. In fact, I would go so far as naming all hominids under the genus of *toolmakers*. And according to their level of sophistication—from the most primitive to the most advanced—I would group them into different species. *Homo sapiens,* is obviously a misnomer. How wise can we be when we have turned everything we touch into ruin? The only reason why we have been great toolmakers is because humans have been born defective; our ancestors would have certainly gone extinct without tools. Tools have more than compensated for what hominids were born without, and have become an indispensable part of human existence. Though lots of animals use tools, none have depended on them as heavily and desperately as we do. Taking away the tool from any animal will only cause it some minor inconvenience—sea otters might have to use their teeth to crack abalone or switch to a fish/crustacean diet, and chimps would no longer be able to fish termites or hunt bush babies. Stripping a human of his tools would be like taking the armor away from a turtle, and you would get a pitifully unfit animal that would surely die in a few days in a wilderness setting.

How long do you think you can make it in the wilderness if you are not allowed to bring any tools with you (your clothing is a tool) and are prohibited from creating any of them? Tools have helped us to dethrone the reign of muscle. And our heavy reliance on tool making was started by a malformed pelvis; the trend is certain to continue as long as there are humans. Tool making will forever reinforce the dominance of brain over brawn. Among humans, creating new tools and intelligence are inseparable, like the two strands of DNA. The reason, again, is that we are born defective, unlike other animals.

Any anthropologist who looked at Lucy would not give her much chance to survive among the speedy and cruel land animals if she were unaided. She could not have been unaided. Therefore, she had to be aided. Then, by what? The answer becomes clear if we focus on her head or brain size. For a creature smaller than a common chimp, she had too big a head. A big head, besides unnecessarily burdening her struggle to walk upright, also required more calories to feed. Lucy's big head was more expensive to her than a fully loaded Ferrari for you and me. How could Lucy afford it? And why did Lucy's kind evolve so decidedly in that direction?

Let us first answer the "why." It was because they had absolutely no other choice; more neurons were their only hope. The scenario could be as their kind increase in number the places near the home base could no longer provide enough food for all of them. Since they could not find food in trees, they had no choice but to explore more new land territories. They had chosen hazard over starving. If we look at how she got her big head, we can clearly see that she could not quite afford it. She "bought" the extra neurons by paying for them with her flesh, muscle in particular. Her payment for more neurons was not unlike an entrepreneur mortgaging his home to buy business equipment. One could say that she was desperate, really desperate. She was more desperate for neurons than the early Chinese Communists' desire for nuclear weapons. ("We don't need pants; we need nuclear weapons!" Mao was quoted to say.) To survive, her ancestors had to make a choice between muscles and neurons; the choice was neurons. No longer nimble like a regular chimp, most of her muscles involved in locomotion had been operating at less than full capacity anyway. Her "choice" to cut muscle bulk to fuel the growth of neurons was as desperate as a poker player down to the last bit of chips going all in. The gamble turned out to be the correct path to take. It paid off. This "choice" had pulled them further and further away from the mainstream. There was no going back.

Though it had taken them several millions of years to make up their minds, they eventually committed, or more correctly, were pushed into it. From then on, it became more and more decisive, and that was when the several noted changes began to happen. And with each change to embrace bipedalism, they were pulled further and further away from the regular chimps. I am sure in bad times many of them still looked back to the good old days of tree dwelling, as you can see in the poor show of their intelligence acceleration of -0.58 ml/kg/kg. No doubt, judging from the IA, there was a lot of hesitation in the evolution of Lucy's kind.

The next stage, from Lucy (*Australopithecus africanus*) to *H. habilis*, was the most breakneck. The IA. at this stage was 1.67 ml/kg/kg, almost three times of the preceding stage. It was the greatest intelligence acceleration in the history of humans and will be unlikely to ever happen again. Why? We may never know the circumstances that drove those hominids. But one thing was certain: neurons, like real Cialis, are not cheap; hominids would not "buy" them unless they needed them really badly. One thing was sure: the hominids after Lucy's stage had the most urgent need for intelligence to get them through. The stage should represent the period of time when the lives of early humans were most difficult and exceedingly challenging; they were hungry for neurons to solve their never-ending problems—so hungry that every bit of increase was quickly consumed. That is why we don't see any relax in intelligence acceleration before the hominids got to *H. habilis*.

Some of the added neurons were no doubt spent in balancing the body to improve upright walking. Some were employed to give their hands more dexterity. But a great number would certainly be engaged in storing useful information on types of edible food, landmarks, and weather changes, etc. Data processing, thinking, and particularly tool making would have certainly taken up a lot of the newly acquired neurons. Their tools were likely quite simple, sticks of different shapes and sizes for various jobs. The unprecedented intelligence acceleration indicates one thing: these hominids were constantly confronted by new problems that often needed new solutions.

Why did they encounter so many problems? They faced so many problems because they were not supposed to live where they lived. After leaving—or more correctly, being forced to leave—the forest, they had been living lives of never-ending changes since. When you have changes, you are guaranteed to have problems. An established professional like an accountant, doctor, or lawyer will not encounter many new problems. I have been through five major career changes—high school teacher, university research associate and lecturer, florist, and real estate broker— before I became a restaurant owner and now a full-time writer. I have gone through lots of problems. As a result, I lost all my hair, one flower store, two wives, and two houses, just to name some changes. Don't want any problem? Then don't make any changes.

If changes were the reasons that created their needs for more and more neurons, then where did the changes arise from? The reason was always the same: in search of food. And to do so, those hominids needed to travel to new places frequently. The transitional hominids from Lucy to *H. habilis* were wanderers and opportunists. They followed where the food would take them. Each new place would offer different kinds of food at different times. There would be lots of things for them to remember: the geography, change of seasons, and the appearances of various plants, just to name a few. And to get to the food often required problem solving, as already discussed. Besides new food, a new place also often came with new kinds of hazards to watch out for and to remember.

The Handyman

Homo habilis, handyman, was the name given to a collection of fossils which were supposed to belong to a hominid. The collection included some fragments of hand bones, the mandible, an isolated tooth, and pieces of skull discovered by a team led by Louis Leakey in 1964. Though the authors believed that the bones belonged to one individual, it is questionable, according to some experts, that the claim had much validity.

Why the name? According to John Napier, the medical doctor who helped Leakey to analyze the bones, the hand bones are quite modern and are capable of the power and precision grips, both coined by the doctor. A power grip is the way a person holds a baseball bat, a hammer, or a tennis racket; it involves the palm, the thumb, and all the other fingers. As the name implies, a power grip allows you to exert a lot of force on the object, like hitting a tennis ball over 100 miles per hour. A precision grip involves a thumb plus one or maybe two fingers; it is the way a person holds a needle, a fork, a scalpel, or a ballpoint pen. A precision grip employs only the fingertips; it allows you to delicately control the movements of the object you are holding. A jeweler, a surgeon, or a painter uses a precision grip a lot.

While a chimp is capable of a power grip, it does not have a precision grip because it lacks an opposable thumb long and flexible enough to touch its other fingertips. Tool making often requires a maker to have both types of grips. *H. habilis,* according to Dr. Napier, had both and that was one of the reasons for the name. Another reason was the many primitive stone tools found among the remains of the hominid.

The species *H. habilis,* unlike Lucy's species before or *H. erectus,* that followed, fails the rigorous taxonomic requirements that usually define a species. The brain capacity of the species, for example, varies from 600 ml to 1,600 ml—a huge range. From the points already discussed, I would favor a cranial capacity about 600 ml for the species. In the evolution of a lineage like humans, you won't find any sudden jump or substantial deviation in any one feature, especially for a feature as important as the brain size. A brain size of 1600 ml, as compared to modern humans' 1,400 ml, just does not even make common sense. Again, be warned that yours truly is not an expert. But I hope you can see my logic. The size and shape of the bones included in the species also diverge greatly, to the degree that there has been disagreement on whether or not the species is sexually dimorphic. Despite the controversy surrounding the species, the species has been widely regarded as the missing link between Lucy and *H. erectus*. We are anxiously awaiting future finds to provide us with more information.

Having discussed the background, let us try to visualize how the hominid would look. Based on *Images of the Past,* the handyman stood less than 5 feet tall, weighed in slightly heavier than Lucy at about 40 kg—almost the same as a common chimp—with an impressive brain capacity of 680 ml. The transition from chimphood to humanhood was more than half completed from the head down. The potbelly found in Lucy's kind had disappeared a long time ago.

Based on the picture presented, I would speculate that the hominid could walk confidently with head held high; he no longer swayed from side to side as he moved along. It was likely that he could run, but don't bet on him to win any race against today's athletes. One would find *H. habilis* in groups of ten or more, with men slightly outnumbering women, and one to two children. The members, men in particular, are closely related. When traveling, one would expect to see a male carrying a couple of sticks, one for food collecting and the other mainly for combat.

There is little doubt that *H. habilis* were cave dwellers. Each day, a small group of several men would carry their sticks and clubs and set out in search of food. Unlike Lucy's species in which the two sexes often traveled together for safety, women and children were unlikely to join the men. Having lived in the same area for generations, women knew it would be safe to stay behind and look after their children. The women would sometimes venture out to nearby places as a group to gather food. To join the men, the women had discovered, would create problems for the men and put themselves and the children at risk.

The men were not hunters, neither were they strictly gatherers. It was likely that they would start the day slightly after dawn; it would be pointless to stay at the cave while the stomach kept growling. In the early morning, most of their dreaded predators were deep in sleep, and there would be all kinds of delicious little creatures to be found, like snakes, frogs, and lizards, which would come out early and disappear when the sun was high. By the time the sun reached its zenith, the men would likely get enough small animals and tender plant parts to eat. It would be a good time to take a short nap. They knew the area well. To rest, they would choose a shaded spot far away from the lions. Instinctively, they would stay close together, each with his club nearby.

By early afternoon, they would be ready for some excitement. Fully rested, refreshed, and alert, they would set out again. It would be a good time to look for the catch of the day. The group was looking for a chance to rob some canines or hyenas. Robbing wild dogs, hyenas, or even a cheetah was nothing new to the group. Nobody knew how and when the practice got started, though it was inevitable that it would happen. When it came to *H. habilis,* they had accumulated enough experience from countless encounters with small predators to learn that beating the beasts was not impossible; they had little fear of the canines or the hyenas. The practice was likely started when some very hungry male hominids came across a small pack of wild dogs feeding on their fresh kill that they finally took the plunge.

It was likely to happen this way, in a late afternoon. The group had a bad day, and most of the members were still hungry. Then, they spotted a pack of wild dogs near a big tree where they regularly rested. From the commotion, the pack was in the midst of feeding on something. So the strongest of the hominids decided to take a look; the group followed closely. The pack, the hominids found out when they got closer, was feeding on a small antelope. It was obvious that the wild dogs had made the kill quite recently for there was still a lot of the antelope left.

The members looked at each other as if to decide; then they nodded and grunted in unison. They had made up their minds. They were going to rob the pack! It would be a risky business; canines would never be happy when someone interrupted their meals. But the hominids were desperate. So the hominids stayed close and approached the feeding pack warily. To summon their courage, they began to roar and grunt louder and louder, baring their pitiful teeth and raising the clubs as they shortened the distance between the feeding pack.

The pack stopped eating. The alpha male came forward to face the slowly advancing gang. It, too, bared its teeth and growled with stifled roars which betrayed its intense rage. The pack stood behind the leader. Soon, neither the group nor the pack would take another step forward.

The hominids held their ground and readied their clubs, fully raised in striking position. The alpha male made the first move; like the wind, it launched at the leading hominids, instinctively going for the throat. But the canine was no match for the speed of the club; the attack was doomed even before it was launched. It saw the clubs coming, but there was nothing it could do to avoid them. It let out a pained yelp as it tumbled head-first to the ground. It quickly got back to its feet and began to retreat, tucking its tail tightly between its legs. Sensing victory, the group roared loudly and began to charge the pack. The other wild dogs followed their leader and fled. The hominids jumped and shouted in exultation. Then, they carried the prize home as the wild dogs watched from a safe distance.

Months, also possibly a couple of years, after successfully robbing wild dogs, hyenas became next on the list. Hyenas proved to be much tougher customers. They were stronger, more stubborn, and ferocious; they resisted fiercely and inflicted more painful and damaging bites. But the hominids were hard pressed. Driven by hunger and tempted by a handsome reward would sometimes outweigh the risk. Raiding a pack of hyenas was full of unpleasant surprises. However, with any risk, sometimes came a reward; the payoff would also be far more lucrative. In desperate times, stealing from hyenas was often a risk the hominids could not afford to pass up.

Looting a cheetah had turned out surprisingly easier than robbing a pack of hyenas. They would be dealing with a lone defender. A cheetah, other than often impossible to hit, did not offer much worse of a bite than a hyena. Lions, whether singly or in a group, were a totally different matter. Even during their most desperate times, the hominids had never considered stealing from the king of the beasts. The hominids had more than once witnessed a lion in action, from a great distance of course. The king could kill an alpha hyena in one quick blow. They knew that lions were in a much higher league.

So this was one of the many ways I imagine the hominids would make their living based on their morphology; they were opportunists and risk takers. When they got to *H. habilis* stage, the various groups had also likely settled down. They were far from strong and fit. Besides the uncertainty of their anatomies, we also know little about the flora and fauna in their environment. We may never know for certain what they ate and how they got their food. But one thing is certain, they had to rely on their brains all the time, especially during their transformation from Lucy's kind to the *H. habilis* stage. Their way of life explains why their brain capacity kept expanding, accelerating at the greatest pace.

Without doubt, they had survived with their tools. The hominids' tools had always been simple to make and easy to use; they were sticks and clubs shaped from branches of trees—fresh or dead, as the situation dictated. And because they were still not quite strong and were still learning how to walk efficiently, their tools were likely to always serve two functions. One as a walking aid, and the other as a weapon. To cut up the animals they had stolen, they also made simple cutting tools out of stones from time to time. As the hominids evolved, their dependence on the sticks as walking aids gradually waned and their love affair with the tool as a weapon steadily waxed. It was not that humans were excessively cruel in nature; it was their weakness and pitiful physique that necessitated such dark passion. The trend continued.

It should not be surprising that humans had applied their intelligence very extensively in weapon development from the very beginning. For them, intelligence, not muscles, was their special asset in survival, in self-preservation, self-serving, and selfishness. When the issue was whose meat was to serve as building block, the simplest solution was to kill. And they had relied upon their tools to do the killings. Weaponry has certainly played a central role in the survival of humans dating back from the first chimp to modern day. It always has been, and it always likely will be. If raiding wild dogs, cheetahs, or hyenas were a way of life for the early hominids, then sooner or later they learned that using clubs and sticks to fight hungry animals was a very bad way of doing business. It was always close combat with little distance separating the flesh from those sharp claws and powerful jaws. They would win most of the battles against cheetahs, leopards, wild dogs, or hyenas, but most of their victories would come with a price. To say the least, it would be a big problem living a life of a raider. The raidees always fought back, and nine out of ten times the bites from their raidees hurt like the bites of venomous snakes. And until they could solve the problem, the hurt would continue. Sooner or later, one of them would, like those of us who have to sweat for our rice and noodles, inevitably query: "There has got to be an easier way to make a living!" Once someone began to think in that direction, it would be a matter of time before someone, possibly in the late stage of *H. habilis,* discovered a new weapon, the first projectile. Again, please allow me to guess how the weapon could have been discovered.

A Story of the First Projectile

If the early humans did discover this weapon, the question will be: how did they discover this highly useful weapon? One of the hundreds of possible scenarios leading to the discovery could be as follows.

A group of *Homo habilis* had been living in a large cave for a while. Near the entrance was an area covered with pebbles. The area was a favorite place for the group to spend their leisure time because it was nearby, dry, and clean. It was close to sunset at the time when our story begins. The adults were sitting in the area and several pairs of adults were engaged in mutual grooming, which was a favorite pastime. Close by, a couple of kids were playing. Once in a while, one of them would pick up a pebble and toss it around for fun. Small stones were fun to play with; they were smooth and nice to handle, and would bounce around and make crisp sounds. Young hominids were energetic and playful; they would try more things than adults.

At the time, there were several small antelopes grazing at a short distance away. Then, one of the kids inadvertently tossed a small stone in the direction of the herd. The stone landed near the herd and frightened the animals; they took off in a hurry. The unexpected result from the errant stone made the kids very happy; they jumped up and down in joy.

A young lone male adult had been watching the kids play; he too was delighted to see how the stone had created such a commotion among the animals. It did not take long before a herd of animals came to graze in the area. At the time, the kids had returned to their mothers. Remembering what had happened not long ago, the adult picked up a pebble and tossed it deliberately at the herd. To his great surprise and delight, the pebble actually hit one of the animals. The animal gave a loud cry as if its life was going to end, causing the herd to flee in panic.

This time, all the adults saw the incident. In their small and tight circle, it would be rare that someone did something without the others knowing it. The adults celebrated with the pebble thrower, like our modern-day baseball players do after their team scores a homerun. Since then, throwing stones at grazing animals became the group's favorite pastime next to grooming.

A guy named Kack was particularly addicted to the game. Kack was in his late adolescence; he did not have a grooming partner like his older brother Ark. Kack usually had a lot of time to kill; he began to pick up pebbles and toss them around even when there were no grazing animals nearby. He had another reason to play with pebbles other than to kill time. He remembered an incident which happened shortly after he was old enough to join the adults on wild dog or hyena raiding. At the time, the group was trying to rob a pack of hyenas. Being new, he was quite timid and was at the back of the gang. Ark, like the other members, was grunting and roaring, trying to intimidate the hyenas. The empty threat had no effect; the hyenas stood their ground, growling and snarling at the hominids. Ark mindlessly picked up a pebble and tossed it at the hyenas. Ark's gesture was not unlike a chimp throwing branches at other chimps to intimidate or to relieve his stress. The pebble caused the pack to panic; the animals instinctively backed down. After seeing that nothing followed, the hyenas quickly resumed their aggression.

Ark was totally unaware of the incident after the raid. Not Kack, he remembered it clearly. The stored information would have been washed away sooner or later if Kack had not witnessed the power of a flying pebble on the grazing animals. Something about a pebble had bugged Kack for a while, but his less than 700 ml brain could not quite nail the reason. Early hominid was carefree by nature; Kack soon stopped thinking about it. Kack immediately connected the two incidents together when he saw the effect of a stone tossed toward the grazing animals. Kack was the first one to see and understand the power of a purposely tossed stone. This, perhaps, was what a bigger brain would be capable of.

After playing with an assortment of stones and pebbles, Hack came up with a preferred type: round and smooth stones that fitted comfortably between his fingers. He tossed them around in different ways; he even tried to copy the way Ark did it. After trying several different throws, he developed an action which remotely resembled the way a pitcher threw a baseball. The stance came naturally and effortlessly, allowing him to throw a pebble to a greater distance. Kack was no Cy Young, but using the technique he could throw a stone farther and with more accuracy than any other adult in his group.

Satisfied with the throwing stance and achieving a good distance, Kack began to practice on targets, which would be a natural next step.

A target could be a big rock, the trunks of trees, or small animals that caught his attention. Hitting a target gave Kack a lot of joy each time. Kack got a lot of pleasure from target practice; he became hooked on the new game.

It had been many sunrises and sunsets and from rainy season to dry times since Kack started throwing stones and pebbles around. He did it as a pastime; he was the only one still doing it. With practice, he had greatly improved both in distance and accuracy; Kack had become the undisputed champ of the stone-throwing game. However, the honor did little to improve Kack's standing in the group; he still did not have a grooming partner. Then, the unavoidable happened; it took place during a late afternoon. At the time, some of the members—the children and females in particular—were gathering around what was left of a small deer that the group had snatched from a cheetah. Kack, like the other males, had long finished eating; he was sitting at a spot on the outer skirt of the group to keep watch. Habitually, he had a pebble in his hand; he would turn it around and feel it from time to time.

Kack spotted several wild dogs pacing back and forth well within a stone's throw. Wild dogs were no threat to the group, as Kack had learned long ago, but they were nuisances and sometimes would attack an unattended child. Kack did not like wild dogs, and for that matter, any wild animals. He decided to chase them away. But before he let go of his pebble to pick up his club, which was always within reach, he got an idea. He rose unhurriedly, walked a couple of steps toward the pack. The wild dogs heightened their alert, retreated a little, but stayed. Kack then stopped, took aim at the closest animal (likely to be the alpha male), and stepped into the throwing action. The stone left Kack's hand, sped toward the alpha male much faster than a cheetah chasing a gazelle, and smacked the wild dog at the chest area. The poor animal let out a yelp and began to take flight as rapidly as its four legs could carry it, with its tail tucked tightly between the legs. The pack followed.

It was indeed a historical moment. A number of other members, males and females, witnessed the event; they jumped up and down in great joy. Unbeknownst to the other members, though, it had dawned upon Kack that he had found a more powerful weapon than his striking club! In his mind, he clearly saw the potential of the pebbles. He had just discovered the first projectile. A new drama in human history was about to take place.

Time: Some sunrises and sunsets later. The setting: A group of hyenas had killed an antelope, and an all-male group of several club-wielding hominids had been stalking the hyenas, and had just caught up with them before the hyenas could do any serious feeding. The group, of which Kack was a member, had tried to raid a pack of hyenas a while ago with a dreadful result. During the raid, Mook, the leader, had one of his legs badly mauled by a defending hyena. Luckily, Mook's brother Kar came in time to his aid and attacked the hyena. The hyena let go of Mook; Kar carried him away. The group had since become quite reluctant to raid hyenas.

The group did not have much meat for a while and their women were not too happy. For a number of reasons, they decided to try again. Mook was still limping; he remembered the last episode well and would not lead. Kar was no different; the brothers stayed close together behind their new leader. Ark became the new leader, partly because of an urge to seek recognition and mostly from stupidity, if you could read Mook's mind. Then, Kack made his move; he deliberately chose to walk in front of the new reluctant leader, his brother. Ark, though concerned, was quite happy that someone had replaced him. Kack approached the feeding pack cautiously, holding a stone in his throwing hand and carrying the club in the other. They stopped at a spot well within the distance Kack could throw a stone accurately at the pack. The hyenas were getting edgy; a couple of them stopped eating, baring their teeth and growling at the group. A showdown between two groups of hungry animals was imminent: a handful of hominids against a pack of almost twice as many hyenas. Even one on one, the odds of hominids winning by muscle was anything but certain; they were also outnumbered. But the leading hominid did not merely count on muscle to win. The place they stood had an ample supply of stones and pebbles; the coincidence was hardly an accident.

Kack initiated the attack. But unlike Mook the brute, Kack did not want to endanger his group at all; he had it planned. He signaled to the group to stay behind him with a grunt and gesture. He then assumed his throwing stance, aimed, and raised his arm. The group caught a brief glimpse of a shadow speeding toward the hyenas and almost at the same time heard a pained whine from one of the beasts, making it back quickly away from the food. Alarmed by the pained yelp, the pack stopped eating instinctively. However, they held their ground and refused to give up the hard-earned antelope. Kack bent down to pick up another stone; the others immediately understood and copied him.

With the success and the hyenas not attacking, Kack became more confident. He took aim again. The stone left his hand hissing and landed on the head of the closest hyena almost at the same time. The hunting party could see blood gushing from the stunned beast. Then, the other members began to roar as they threw stones at the pack. The pack began to withdraw. Then, stones began to rain on the hyenas; the pack had lost any will to resist. Kack let out a loud war cry and charged at the pack with his club raised; the others followed. The pack quickly retreated. The hominids claimed their prize.

It was a great victory! It was easy and simple. And best of all, none of the raiders got even a scratch. It became a new way to do business for those hominids. The group happily carried the reward home. As leader, Kack got the first pick of the freshly killed animal. Kack soon got a grooming partner, but he never stopped practicing stone throwing. Kack's children, as well as the children of other members, also acquired the skill from their fathers.

The end.

Up to the stone-throwing stage—if that ever happened—the early hominids (likely to be *Homo habilis)* were not hunters; they did not have the speed to keep up with their prey. Stone throwing, useful as it could be in raiding smaller predators such as hyenas, cheetahs, and wild dogs, was neither effective nor a dependable weapon for killing. No matter how well a hominid could master the skill, he could not kill a sizable animal with stones. Nonetheless, with the projectiles, early hominids found it much easier to loot other hunters.

From Stone Throwing to Spear

Long before they discovered throwing pebbles, hominids had already learned to use their sticks to stab and kill small animals. After they became experienced with stone throwing, then stick throwing would be a natural extension. Sooner or later, some would reason that throwing a stick instead of a pebble could be more effective in seriously wounding a targeted prey. The invention of spear throwing could happen not too long after hominids had mastered the skill of throwing stones.

Throwing a spear involved the same throwing stance; it was a simple switch from a stone to a spear. Unlike the accidental discovery of using stones as weapons, spear throwing could be invented through purposeful exploration. It was likely from trial and error before they came up with the right type of stick to throw and kill. Some might have begun throwing their clubs to attack and found it ineffective and thus had abandoned using them. There was another reason why spear throwing should follow stone throwing. Without securing another reliable weapon, it would be unsafe and downright stupid to throw away the sticks, your only weapon.

Once hominids had invented spears, they could do their own hunting instead of depending on hyenas or wild dogs to do the dirty work. Being able to hunt had made their meat supply more reliable. Their future became more secure and they could gradually even stand their ground against the mighty lions. *Homo habilis* possibly started using spears at a late stage. They would enjoy more meat, allowing them to grow even stronger and smarter . . . The journey continues.

CHAPTER 10

The Price Tag of Higher Intelligence

Brain power, as every modern human knows, is more useful for making a living than muscle unless you happen to have muscles like Arnold the ex-governor or King James. Beyond any doubt, continuous increase in brain capacity is one of the most important developments in the evolution of early humans. And as far as we can see, the increase has been all blessings; there seems to be no bad side effects from a growing brain. How could it be otherwise? Intelligence, more than anything, has allowed us to invent all kinds of weapons and tools which have helped us to be much stronger competitors. Since Lucy's type, humans could also store much more information in their brains to remember more things, to learn new tricks, to predict outcomes based on past experiences. It was like getting an extra dimension to compete. But has having a bigger and bigger head always been a blessing? The answer is no. At a certain period, it posed a serious problem for hominid moms and threatened to post an insurmountable limit to humanity's insatiable quest for higher intelligence.

Nature's Biggest Growing Pain

To see how a bigger and bigger brain became a big problem, let us take a look at the table that shows the brain size of hominids again. Let us concentrate on the early hominids compared to the chimps.

163

Primate	Estimated Body Weight, Kg	Adult Brain Capacity, ml	Head (Brain) Size Compared to Chimp
Chimpanzee	40	400	1
Australopithecus africanus	35	450	1.125
Homo habilis	38	630	1.58
Homo erectus	55	1000	2.50
Homo sapiens	60	1400	3.50

If we use a chimp's head size as a standard for comparison, we can see that the brains of *A. africanus* and *H. habilis* were 12.5 percent and 60 percent larger respectively. The two species achieved brain growths with less or little change in body weights. When it came to *Homo erectus,* brain size had grown to 1,000 ml, about 2.5 times that of chimps. So far so good, right? Well, if you are as ignorant about human child birth as I once was, it would certainly seem OK. But if you know something about female genitalia, especially the vagina, which is also the birth canal, like Uncle Yat did, you will sooner or later ask: "How do they do it?"

Uncle Yat's Not-So-Popular Query

Uncle Yat is somehow related to my father's eldest sister. He stayed with my family for two years when I was attending junior high school. Although Yat is my uncle, he was only eight years older than me. At the time, Yat was preparing for the entrance exam to the then only medical school in Hong Kong. He was, like most playboys at his age, also rather busy dating. Once in a while—often after dinner during the family time and out with a girl the previous night—he would wonder and think out loud, "How does a woman do it?" Of course, I did not have the foggiest clue of what he was talking about. And occasionally, he would add, "How can a baby pass through such a small hole?" I would still be lost. Before the playboy could go any further, Mother would bluntly put an end to the topic.

It took me a number of years to eventually understand what Uncle Yat's query was. And like Uncle Yat, I was quite baffled by the same thing. Childbirth, some would say, is one of nature's miracles, or God's cruel punishment to women, according to some Christians. My eldest daughter was born when I was in my third year of graduate study at UCLA. I would have had a chance to witness this wonder of nature, the birth of a human baby, if my friend Edwin had not caused more than headaches for those medical staff in the delivery room of the university's teaching hospital a couple of months earlier. At the time, the university implemented a new policy to encourage the husbands to take part when their wives were giving birth. The husbands were supposed to calm the wives and make the deliveries easier for every party. The policy had obviously worked well before Edwin came along.

At the time, Edwin was a first-year medical student. It would be fair to say that he knew a fair amount, on paper at least, about the birth of a baby. Based on what I had gathered from Edwin's wife, Winnie, months after their first child was born, I learned that she had gone through a difficult delivery. Edwin was an exceedingly protective and loving husband. At the beginning of the labor, Edwin was calm and cool; he tried to ease Winnie's anxiety by telling her jokes. Edwin always came up with the most hilarious jokes. The jokes worked, but not for long. Then, the woman began to moan; the moaning got louder and louder and at shorter and shorter intervals. Nothing Edwin did could help. Edwin would have gladly switched positions with Winnie if he could. Edwin became very concerned; he began ordering the staff to do this and to follow that. Edwin really lost it when his woman began to scream and writhe and the doctor and nurses appeared to be unresponsive. Edwin then yelled at the professor and nurses, ordering them to follow such and such procedure. When the nurses and doctor failed to follow his orders, he tried to take over. The professor had to call in the security guards, somehow got Edwin restrained and escorted out of the facility. No more participation of fathers-to-be for a while. I still have not seen how a baby is born. And thanks to Janet Jackson's halftime performance in the Super Bowl, I don't expect to see it on TV in the foreseeable future.

Those Troublesome Bigheaded Babies

Childbirth, besides being the most painful thing (according to what I have read), is also a dangerous business. There is a saying in Chinese: "A woman giving birth is paper-thin to King Yam-Law, the ruler of the dead." Laboring mothers in industrialized countries are luckier nowadays; they can choose, even without obvious medical reason, to deliver their babies by Cesarean section instead of by natural birth.

For those lucky men who are old enough to know, a vagina is not that roomy. In its resting state, it has a circumference of about 3 inches. I still have a problem seeing how a baby can pass through the canal. Childbirth, if it is no longer a life-threatening issue for well-off women in developed countries, is still a frequent cause of death for laboring mothers in poor nations. Now try to imagine the hardship an early laboring hominid woman had to go through.

To see what hardship those early hominid mothers had to face, let us use an average newborn human baby as a reference. At birth, the head of a human baby is about 25 percent its adult size, which will be between 350 and 400 ml, with a circumference of about one foot. To allow the head of a baby through, the vaginal wall must stretch at least four times its normal length. Since the head is the bulkiest and is the most rigid part of a baby's body, head size sets the upper limit on the size of a baby. If the head can go through, the rest will be relatively easy.

If you think stretching a piece of muscle four times its resting length is not that hard, go to your supermarket and buy a piece of flank steak or chicken breast and try to stretch it. Muscles are designed to contract, not to stretch. So it brings up a question: is a baby's head size of roughly 350 ml the maximum modern mothers can handle? Or does the head size at birth in general represent the limit birth canals can stretch?

Let us take it to a bigger scale, we ask, "Among mammals, do the sizes of the babies at birth represent the maximum their mothers can handle?" To answer this question, we need to ask another question: how does a mother decide when to give birth? I am relatively sure that nature plays with two factors. One overriding factor is the odds of survival of a newborn, which is directly related to how mature a baby is at birth. The other is the safety of the mother in carrying the fetus, and the ease of giving birth to it. It is quite certain that the degree of maturity of a baby is directly related to its size at birth: the bigger a baby, the more mature it will be. Then, the size at birth represents the maximum which the females of a species can provide their babies before they have to leave the protection of the wombs, isn't it? Then, the question will be why is it important for animals to give their babies maximum allowable maturity at birth? Because the outside world is dangerous and babies are one of the most sought-after food by predators.

A baby animal—regardless of how strong it will be later—is at the weakest and most vulnerable stage of its existence. Though mammalian mothers will always be around to look after their babies, there are limits to what they can do to protect and provide for them. If you happen to be an herbivore like a water buffalo, a zebra, or an antelope, you often have to run for your life. When a cheetah is trying to run you down and kill you, your first priority is to run and escape; you don't have the luxury of taking care of your baby. I am sure that a cheetah would love to have a baby antelope for dinner. Without the protection of the mother, how can a baby antelope survive?

In escaping predators, a baby antelope, zebra, buffalo, or horse is on its own; it has to run fast enough to escape shortly after it is born. Zebras, antelopes, and horses are among land animals with the most developed and mature babies at birth for good reasons. Babies of herbivores, as a rule, can outrun their predators because the survival of the species depends on it. And that is why it is important to give birth to as-mature-as-possible babies. For this reason, mothers of herbivores only bear a lone baby at a time.

We all know that not all mothers are as lucky as cows, zebras, and horses. If humans were like horses, then childcare would not be an election issue. Among mammals, babies are born with different degrees of maturity and are able to take care of themselves at different levels. Predators like lions and tigers have several cubs, which are less mature than a baby pony. Nonetheless, in a couple of weeks they are able to run and instinctively hide when their mothers go to work. Cubs of lions and tigers are weak, but they are not totally helpless. It does not take long before they can fend for themselves. They are born mature enough that their odds of survival are high. With the exception of the marsupials, mammals in general give birth to babies with maximum degree of maturity their mothers can afford.

If we can agree that babies are born at the maximum developed stages their mothers can afford to give them, then why are human babies so helpless at birth? Is giving birth to such ill-fitted babies the best human moms can do? Our closest surviving relatives, the chimps, have babies that can, by themselves, cling to their moms within days after birth. Why are human mothers so anxious to get their fetuses out of their wombs that they give birth to babies that are far less ready for the world? Do you know that humans are the only mammals other than marsupials that get stuck with hopelessly dependent babies for the longest time? Marsupials have pouches to carry the babies; we don't. A marsupial can abort its babies in the midst of their development and suffer relatively little loss of time or resources. A human mom, despite giving birth to a very immature baby, has invested heavily in her child. Are we, for a change, singled out by Mother Nature for unfair treatment?

What if a human mom were to give birth to babies that are as mature as baby chimps? The obvious consequence of having a more mature baby would be a newborn with a much bigger head. I have tried but failed to find statistics on the head size of newborn chimps. Let us assume that it is about 1/3 its adult size because a baby chimp is more mature than a human newborn, which has a head size of 1/4 of its adult measurement. For humans to give birth to babies as mature as baby chimps, the head of a newborn would be over 460 ml instead of 350 ml. I am not sure any superwoman could handle that.

There must be a reason for humans to give birth to babies with head size around 350 ml instead of 460 ml. The reason, from our argument, is any further increase would pose serious danger for a human baby to make it safely through the birth canal; 350 ml is therefore roughly the maximum allowable development limit. Why? If there is room to spare, would Mother Nature not allow it to make it easier for both the mothers and the babies?

To see the danger posed by brains that have kept getting bigger, let us try to see the hardship those early hominid mothers had been through during their labor. We ask, "What would be the head size of a newborn of *A. africanus, H. habilis,* and *H. erectus?* It is highly doubtful that archeologists will ever dig up the skulls of those babies, so please allow me to do some speculation.

How do we find the head sizes of babies among the hominids? Let us assume that the head size of a newborn chimp is 1/3 of its adult size, which is 400 ml, then, at birth, the head size of a chimp will be around 130 ml. This will be the starting point. The head size of a newborn human baby is 350 ml, which is ¼ of 1400 ml, the adult size; this shall be our end point. We then can construct a graph using these two points as anchors and draw a straight line through them. In so doing, we are assuming that the change of baby head sizes among the hominids follows a linear relationship as defined by the two points. Then, we can obtain the head sizes of different hominid babies if we know their adult head sizes, which are more or less known.

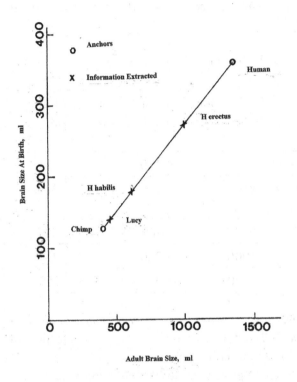

Head Sizes at Birth vs. Head Sizes of Adult Chimps, Hominids, and Humans

From the graph, we can obtain the head sizes of the three hominid infants at birth from their adult sizes; the figures are presented in the following table.

Head Sizes of Hominids: Adults vs. Babies

	Adult Brain Capacity, ml	Brain Capacity, at Birth, ml	Ratio of Baby Brain Capacity to Adult Size, %
Chimpanzee	400	130	33%
Australopithecus africanus	450	140	31%
Homo habilis	630	180	29%
Homo erectus	1000	260**	26%
Homo sapiens	1400	350	25%

** Pages 183–184 of The Wisdom of Bones, In Search Of Human Origins by Alan Walker and Pat Shipment comes up with 231ml cranial capacity for the H. erectus baby, which would grow to about 900 ml adult size. If we use 900ml, instead of 1,000ml, the graph will yield a cranial capacity for the H. erectus baby of 240 ml instead of 260. Considering the simplicity of our method, the graph does seem to have some value.

A. africanus, with an adult head size at 450ml, would have babies with head size about 140 ml, heads of babies of H. habilis about 180 ml, and H. erectus at about 260 ml, which would have doubled those of chimps. We can clearly see a trend of decreasing maturity among the newborns, as indicated by their corresponding lowering percentage in the head sizes. If this is true, it would indicate the babies of A. africanus would be like those of chimps and more mature at birth as compared to humans. The babies of H. habilis, lagging 4 percent behind those of chimps in maturity, would take some time to develop to a stage comparable to newborn chimps. And *H. erectus* moms would have to spend almost as much time as their modern human counterparts to look after their babies. Also, be reminded that those head sizes were likely to be the maximum allowable by their corresponding mothers. The question then becomes: how could a mother-child pair of *H. erectus,* if not *H. habilis,* have any chance of surviving?

The Hazards of Being a Hominid Mom

The hazards of being a hominid mom began long before she got to the *H. erectus* stage and was not limited to giving birth to babies. It started as soon as the prehumans had made the commitment to abandon the trees as their homes. If you look at the length of time it took to get to *Australopithecus afarensis,* the first species that evolved from chimp, you will be puzzled by its magnitude. This first step took close to seven million years out of the total length of 10 million years to get to us, the modern human. And *Australopithecus afarensis* had very little to show for it in terms of morphological and anatomical changes other than the fact that they had since firmly committed to bipedal locomotion. What was holding them back? It must have been an extremely hard decision to make. Can you blame them? To commit, your problem would always be your safety. When you saw a pack of hyenas or a lion come charging, how would you get to safety quickly? Committing to walking on two legs would have made it almost impossible to get up trees fast enough. You would be dead nine out of the ten times. Not to commit meant that you would have to live very close to some trees for safety. It also meant that you needed those grasping toes, which meant that you could not walk very far without tripping. A bummer, isn't it? Your other problem would be where would you get food? You could forget about getting it from trees because you were too slow to compete with monkeys, and above all, your closest relatives, the chimps. Not only they did not welcome you, they, in fact, hated you. Stronger and faster, they could easily hurt you in trees. So other than at desperate times, you would not think about getting up a tree, would you?

Most of your food had come from other places. Not picky, there were quite a few things to eat. Bugs might not fill you up, but they were loaded with proteins and would sure beat a growling stomach. Snails were plentiful in nearby shallow waters. They had lots of meat; you just needed to pick them up and break their shells with a small stone to get them. Berries were plentiful during some seasons. Monkeys and chimps would not compete with you because they were too far away from the trees they lived. You could also find many juice plants near a river. With a stick that helped you walk, you could also use it to dig up some pretty nice things. Though nervous, you began to drift farther and farther away from the trees to find food as eons passed.

Then, after many million years of hesitancy, the balance tipped to the commitment. They might not have much choice. It boiled down to competing with chimps or facing the claws and jaws. They chose the latter, to face the claws and jaws. The choice, without their knowing, would also unavoidably lead to steep and steeper price tags. And of the two sexes, unfairly the females had ended up paying most of the price.

Australopithecus afarensis would certainly be a very nervous and scared bunch of animals. I don't care if you were the fittest male in the group; you would still be no match for any of those animals that tried to eat you. Imagine you were a female like Lucy. It could not get any lousier, could it? Now, put yourself in her position with a baby in your arms and you hear some hyenas howling nearby. You did not pass out, did you? What I am trying to say to you is: in the more or less 10 million years of evolution to modern human, some of our ancestors, especially those early species like *A. afarensis,* would have lived a very hazardous existence. For the males, the level of danger would gradually decrease as each new species evolved. A male *H. habilis* had very well adapted to bipedal locomotion; he also had a much stronger power grip. With his striking club and the support of his brothers and cousins, he could self-defend very successfully. A group of males would almost be unbeatable. The situation for males got even better for *H. erectus.* If they were not kings of animals, they were pretty close. They could often defeat lions and were to be feared by most animals. These improvements in security did not apply to our female ancestors. In fact, as the situations of their male counterparts got better and better, the females' were getting worse and worse. 1) To begin with they were weaker physically than their males. 2) They had to, over their lifetimes, bear and look after a number of children. Childbearing is the biggest burden and hazard for most female mammals. This burden to our female ancestors was far heavier than to all other mothers. Let us look at each of their burdens one by one.

Childbearing has always been a very risky business for mothers. For an early female hominid, carrying a developing baby inside her body would put her at a serious disadvantage and at greater danger. To start with, she would need more food during gestation—both for herself and for her growing baby. At the same period her body would need more and more food, her mobility would gradually be less and less. Pregnant or not, speed had never been a hominid's strong suit. Carrying a baby, especially near full term, would render the mother-to-be exceedingly immobile and thus most vulnerable. So getting enough to eat and eluding predators would become a progressively more serious problem for her. When it got to *H. erectus*, the loss of mobility was quite severe and so was the resulting danger.

If you think that was tough, the period during pregnancy was only a small part of her problems. Then, it would be childbirth. At stake would be a totally helpless hominid almost paralyzed from the pain of labor. Just at a time when she is most defenseless and least mobile, the smell of blood that always comes with childbirth would broadcast to the cruel and hungry animals, advertising the weakest moment of her life, inviting attack to her and her baby. Again, the danger from childbirth would progressively be greater and became greatest among *Homo erectus* mothers.

If she was lucky enough to survive childbirth and recover from it, her real work had just begun. At birth, a baby of *Homo erectus,* as indicated by its projected head size, was quite likely to be premature like a human baby, and be totally dependent on the mother for everything for several years. Even without having to provide for her baby, an *H. erectus* mom would find it very difficult to find enough food for herself; she had to do it for both while caring for and carrying her baby around. And if that could be done, she had to escape the claws and jaws of the ever-present predators. A premature baby was certainly a consequence of a growing brain; unmatched intelligence did come with an extremely steep price after all.

Childbearing was certainly the source of a female hominid's most miseries. Unfortunately, this was an inescapable fate for her because bearing children, as many as she could, was the only reason for her existence, biologically speaking. For the survival of the species, she must bear children—as many as her body would allow her—to the day she died. To understand her fate, let us see how many years a female hominid likely would spend having children.

We know chimps reach sexual maturity at about thirteen years old, and (human) girls reach the stage at about fifteen. So we can safely assume that a female hominid would be somewhere in between; they should be ready to have children at fourteen at the latest. The gestation period for chimps is seven to eight months, whereas for humans it is about nine. From this, would it be eight months for a hominid? Then, how many more years were required to care for a newborn until he or she could more or less move around on his own before she could have another child? Chimps need about two years and humans without childcare help about five. Does three and a half sound fair?

With these numbers, we can do some simple arithmetic and speculate on how many years a female hominid would spend in childbearing. Before we do that, we need one more assumption, it is, in order to keep the species going, how many of her children had to survive to maturity to repeat the cycle? Without getting fancy, I shall assume the infant mortality rate for those prehumans to be 60 percent; i.e., four out of ten would survive. For the species to continue, we need, on the average, 2.5 individuals to have some safety margin. Then, each female needed to produce about six (2.5/0.4 = 6.25) children before she could afford to die without endangering her kind. The span of the gestation period for six children would, allowing some downtime, require at least six years having six babies. Since some of her children died before reaching maturity, and among them some died before they could walk, we assume that she needed to look after three of them for three and a half years before those children could be on their own to walk around and follow the mothers. From that, the mothers would, in average, spend about 10.5 years babysitting. In total, she would spend close to sixteen years with a child under her charge after she began to have children at fourteen. Because of this burden and some other hazards, female hominids were unlikely to live long past thirty years old, which would translate to a very nasty fact that she would live very, very nervously for more than half of her existence.

I am quite sure that this ever-present feeling of insecurity must have existed in women of our lineage; it should be also quite unique that few other mother animals share it. A female chimp with her baby has similar dangers, but they can quickly get up the trees and will be safe.

So a mother-and-child chimp pair can be as relaxed as a male. A mare and her pony can count on their speed to outrun a pack of hyenas. A mother wolf has a den to hide her cubs in while she goes hunting; she may lose a cub or two, but her life will never be overly burdened with danger. A mother kangaroo simply puts her joey in the pouch and off she hops. We can go on and on, but I'll bet you anything that you won't find any female animals dealt a lousier hand than our female ancestors. This lousy hand began shortly after we branched out. Through Lucy, we can imagine how tough life must have been for those early female hominids. Their lives hardly got better when their male counterparts had seen great improvements from the handyman on. Just the opposite. They got worse as we proceeded up the evolutionary tree. So this fear for her safety and that of her children became something she had to cope with and find solutions for.

This unrelenting fear, unpleasant as it had been, was, however, a necessary evil for her survival. Had she been fearless, she would have let her guard down, failed to seek protection, and be eliminated quickly, together with her no-fear genes. To survive, she had to be fearful all the time. And the fear became firmly ingrained in her genes. This fear became inherent and had made her constantly feel insecure and always look for protection. This insecurity should still be an integral part of the psyche of the present-day women. It has a root likely to go back to the very beginning of our lineage—a root slightly less than 10 million years old. This insecurity is unlikely to serve any survival purpose for today's girls, who, in general, live securely under the protection of law and are increasingly becoming more financially capable; it may one day disappear, but it may take a long period. Therefore, if you ask what a woman wants most? It would be security and not a 10-carat diamond.

The many, many years spent in childbearing and the hazards that accompanied it were certainly very grave problems for both sexes to solve, not just for the females, if the species was to continue. Those hominid moms needed help and they had to get them from someone somehow or our intelligence would not get too far, and likely would have stopped around Lucy's stage. But how? The obvious answer would be for a hominid mother to get someone to provide her and her baby food and protection during those long dark years. "No way!" You'll say. Human nature has always been selfish. It is so now; it would be more so then. And we are talking about barbaric times when food was very hard to come by, and one's own safety was always at risk. Who would have food to spare and a willingness to share? Who would be foolish enough to risk his life for your protection? What would the person get in return?

These are tough questions to answer because what those hominid mothers needed was some devoted and almost selfless lovers. They had to be noble characters. And given a selfish human nature, noble characters simply did not exist in primitive and barbaric times. It will be almost impossible even in today's most civilized and caring societies. But don't worry; we know they must have found the solution because we are here. We shall continue our story in the next chapter. And with this, we shall temporarily leave our discussion on intelligence in aiding our evolution, and move to the other equally important force of the twosome: cooperation.

CHAPTER 11

Self, Bond, and Cooperation

We mentioned earlier that intelligence and cooperation were the two forces that have helped our species to evolve through the many millions of years of dark times. We have already discussed the contribution from intelligence. It is time to introduce the role played by cooperation.

In the previous chapter, we have posted a very difficult question: In a selfish and barbaric world, who would provide protection and food for those hapless hominid mothers during their pregnancy, childbirth, and the several years after their children were born? Without help, it would be certain death for the infants, and most likely also for the mothers because of the many perils in their primitive world. Who were those noble characters? Before we can answer the question, we need to lay down some groundwork about cooperation.

Selfishness and cooperation are opposites. How do we get one selfish human to help another? How do we reconcile such a paradox? Let us first define what cooperation is. Cooperation, according to *The New Lexicon Webster's Dictionary of the English Language,* is *working together to a common end.* Thus, to cooperate is to share the fruit or what is obtained at the end from working together. Cooperation is a phenomenon usually observed between animals of the same species, which often belong to the same pack, group, or colony. Despite being seemingly incompatible with a selfish nature, cooperation does occur in nature, especially between members of the same species. If it happens, cooperation always greatly increases the competitive edge of the members involved. Through cooperation, an army of ants becomes one of the most formidable forces in nature, capable of overwhelming animals thousands of times more powerful than any individual ant. A pride of lionesses is the most efficient hunting machine. And before finding a mate which is also a hunting partner, a lone wolf is a lousy hunter with a very uncertain future. The list goes on.

Without exception, cooperation always empowers its participants, giving them a seemingly unfair advantage over noncooperating animals. Because of the huge advantage, one would expect to see cooperation widespread among animals. But it is not; rather, it is a rarity. Why, then, is cooperation atypical in nature? If it is indeed so great, why isn't it a rule rather than an exception? There are two reasons that cooperation is rare in the animal kingdom. The first reason is undoubtedly due to the universal selfish nature of all living organisms; it is natural for an organism to hurt another organism, even its own kind, in order to gain an advantage to self-preserve. Just open your eyes and you will see plenty of it going on around you—one animal hurting another animal, a person hurting another person, a sister hurting her brother, or a presidential candidate hurting his or her counterpart.

Another drawback of cooperation is that the reward from cooperation is not immediate. A participant often needs to give up immediate gratification before getting a benefit. It is not unlike trying to lose weight by giving up potato chips, ice cream, pizzas, or by doing hours of sweaty exercise daily. An animal requires foresight to see the benefits of cooperation to commit to it. It also requires trust, believing that the other party will look after your benefit in return at the end. In a barbaric world where food is difficult to come by and hunger is the rule, an animal that is stupid enough to trust another needy animal is likely to be game over pretty quickly. Foresight and trust make voluntary cooperation impossible among selfish and ignorant creatures. These are the reasons why cooperation has been the exception rather than the norm in the animal kingdom. To cooperate is, without question, opposite to an innate selfish nature. Then, the obvious question will be what makes a selfish organism change so drastically from hurting to cooperating with other members? The answer will be: it depends on the animal under consideration. Some have no choice, some by instinct, and yet others are by choice from learning. We shall use some examples to elaborate the different types of cooperation.

Conjugation, the Most Primitive Form of Cooperation

Our first example is *Paramecium,* a microscopic animal about 0.25 mm in length. This microbe was probably among those first observed by the Dutch biologist after his invention of the first microscope. It is a solitary organism which lives in stagnant water, hunting bacteria, yeasts, and other still smaller organisms for food. It can neither see nor hear; it can, however, sense dangerous chemicals and back away from them. This tiny animal usually has no need to cooperate with other *Paramecia* except during the time of sexual reproduction, which is often triggered by unfavorable environmental conditions. A harsh environment somehow creates an urgent need and drives the tiny organism to reproduce sexually. If a compatible partner is found, the two *Paramecia* then join together physically to form a conjugating tube and exchange gametes. After that, the two *Paramecia* separate and become rejuvenated, live happily alone, and reproduce asexually by fission many, many times after. A fairytalelike story, isn't it?

To cooperate in sexual reproduction is almost universal, and often is the only type of cooperation among most animals. To reproduce, even the most antisocial or the laziest will go against their nature to seek cooperation with their sex partners. They cooperate because sexual reproduction offers much greater advantages than asexual ways; skipping sexual reproduction will eventually make a species unfit for survival. That may be why there are not many organisms which do asexual reproduction exclusively; they were and will be, one by one, washed away by the evolution tides.

Mother Nature does not give animals the choice either. When an animal matures to a reproductive stage, the sexual urge will be irresistible. To relieve the sexual stress, the animals will comply. *Paramecia's* cooperation in sexual reproduction is likely firmly wired. Once the act is consummated and the urge subsided, the animals will resume their natural behavior.

Cooperation among Ants

Our next example is a colony of leafcutter ants. These ants are insect gardeners; the workers cut fragments from leaves, petals, or other plant parts with their mandibles and carry them back to the nest where they grow fungi with them. They harvest the mycelia of the fungi to feed the larvae. The leafcutter ants are very common in Central America. When I was in Panama, Ecuador, and Costa Rica, I saw quite a few parties of these ants on the floor of every forest I went to. With each ant carrying a fragment of leaf, a team of them formed a line, obviously hurrying back home. It was quite interesting as well as impressive to see them so occupied with what they were doing, carrying such huge loads in comparison to their tiny bodies and going at such great pace.

There are two genera of leafcutter ants, *Atta* and *Acromyrmex,* making up about forty species. A colony begins with a potential queen, which is a female reproductive ant. After a nuptial flight and having mated with one or more male ants from different colonies, her hard work begins all on her own. She gets rid of her wings shortly upon landing. Then, she has to find a suitable place to build herself a small nest, which is a small underground chamber that often requires a lot of digging and rubbish removing. When the nest is big enough, she seals off the entrance from outside for safety. She is ready to lay her first batch of a few eggs at spaced intervals. During this period, she also starts her fungus garden with material she took with her from her old colony prior to the nuptial flight—these ants also have a culture of giving dowry. If successful, the mycelia of her fungus culture will later serve as food for her first batch of larvae.

As her first batch of eggs hatches one after the other, she begins to nurture the larvae. Since she cannot go out to find food and her fungus garden has not been established, she has to obtain the nutrients from breaking down some of her nonvital body components, such as those bulky useless flight muscles. To survive, making hard choices is often part of the game, and we have seen it in Lucy's type in buying extra neurons.

On top of looking after her "babies," she also manages her fungus culture and keeps everything in her nest clean and tidy. It is one of the most taxing periods of her young royal life. A queen typically loses about 35 percent of her weight before the first batch of workers take over her daily chores of housekeeping and foraging for food. The tolls on the potential queens are high after mating; typically, about 97 percent of them will succumb to the various awaiting hazards (predators, bad weather, failing health, or failed fungus gardens) and fail to establish their colonies during some points—another snapshot of the survival game.

The 3 percent of the potential queens will be successful and live to enjoy their queenships. With the number of her daughters growing up and helping, a queen no longer needs to multitask. Her only duty then is to lay eggs and produce more and more female workers for her colony. For cultures—Chinese, Indian, and Islamic—that discriminate against girls, they have a lot to learn from biology. Females are far more valuable in nature.

There are several types of workers based on the widths of their heads; workers are all sterile females. The smallest workers are the newly hatched and have head size less than 1 mm in width; their duties include looking after the larvae and tending the fungus garden. The next type has head widths around 2 mm. They are the soldiers that patrol the ground near the colony and the foraging line of the leafcutter ants; they attack selflessly and fiercely any intruders that get too close to their territories. The third type is the actual leafcutters, which pinch out leaf fragments and bring them back to the nest of the colony to nourish the fungus culture. They make up most of the colony. The last type are the Yau Mings in the colony. They have body length of 16 mm and head width about 7 mm. They are the giants and the last defense of their colony, and are often responsible for clearing heavy debris from the foraging trails or carrying very heavy loads back to the nest and thus are the multifunctioned, heavy-duty machineries of the colony.

Besides a queen, an ant colony can have millions of workers and they have different duties. However, they have only one goal, which is shared unconditionally by all: it is the survival of the colony. Their sharing of this one interest is complete, so complete that each and every one of their individual selves is perfectly aligned toward achieving it. Everything an individual does is for the colony and the colony only; individualism does not exist in ants.

The cooperation in leafcutter ants is not by free choice; they cooperate because they are wired to do so. It is in their genes to cooperate. Somehow, through some mutation or mutations, the inborn hurtful behaviors have been changed and the changed insect begins to cooperate. If cooperation is indeed a consequence of mutation or mutations, and given the highly improbable nature of a favorable mutation, it may require at least hundreds, if not thousands or even millions of bad mutations before a good one will pop up, "forcing" a previously hurtful insect to cooperate.

With this reasoning, we can expect only animals which are present in great numbers on our planet would have a chance to beat the unlikely odds to become cooperative. Once established, the cooperative trait will be passed along by the species that evolves from it. To attain the very high level of cooperation of ants and bees, it could have required many cumulative favorable mutations, which in turn should require a population size of astronomical magnitude and a time span of over millions, tens of millions, or even hundreds of millions of years of successive favorable mutations to achieve. With this rationality, it seems hardly an accident that insects and only among insects have some ever achieved the highest degree of cooperation. Mammals will and should never be able to attain the same height of mutation-driven cooperation.

One of the reasons that makes the cooperation in an ant colony so thorough and high is the way a colony is structured. There is only one individual, the queen, that is capable of reproduction. The rest of the female members are sterile; they are not burdened by a reproductive need and therefore have no need to compete with each other for reproduction. Thus, one major source of conflict of interest among them has been eliminated. And there is no male in a colony, thus further ensuring no possible disruption. Try to imagine a human colony like that. There would never be any sex crime, will it?

Cooperation among Mammalian Hunters

Our last example is the cooperation observed among hunting mammals, such as a pride of lionesses, a pack of wolves, or a group of chimps. The reason we group these animals together to discuss their cooperation is that they share a lot of common features in their behaviors. A pride of lionesses are always sisters or genetically closely related females. A pack of wolves often consists of children—brothers and sisters—from a mating pair. And a group of chimps, unlike a pride of lionesses, are from closely related males—brothers or nephews. These animals hunt as a unit in full cooperation with one another. They are highly effective. However, as soon as the prey is brought down their cooperation ends and the members in a hunting party will compete against each other to get as much to eat as possible. Some cooperative animals will even bare their teeth and show aggression to other members during feeding.

Given that animals are all selfish, it is very doubtful that the cooperation among hunting mammals is entirely from free choice. Their inclination to stay in a group instead of being solitary is certainly wired. By staying together, the animals may have somehow learned that cooperating can give them a better chance of a successful hunt than going solo. They have to be all social animals; there is a lot of (wired) friendly feeling among them. It may just be a natural step for them to cooperate in hunting. Hunting requires a lot of flexibility and split-second decision making; the way they cooperate is highly unlikely to be an inborn behavior. Mammals are likely the most intelligent animals on the planet with the highest index of specific brain capacity. It may not be that hard for them to learn and to foresee the advantages to cooperate. The immediate breakdown of their cooperation at feeding supports this point.

Self and Cooperation

How do we reconcile the seeming contradiction of selfishness and cooperation? What happens to the selfish nature? I think we can apply the concept of *self* to resolve this apparent contradiction. Let us review the concept of the *self*. We have defined a *self* as a *living organism or a group of organisms defined by a goal, purpose, or interest.* The goal, purpose, or interest of an organism is always self-preservation or survival. For a *self* to exist, it needs a boundary to separate what is inside from what is outside, and therefore what belongs to the self from what does not. The boundary can be physical in nature or can be purely psychological. To pursue its interest, to self-preserve, will dictate how a *self* "sees" the other objects or organisms and behaves accordingly. Let us examine how a *self* "sees" the world. Though we have discussed the concept when *self* was first introduced, it does not hurt, though could be a bit redundant, to go through it again so that a reader can get a firmer grip of this difficult concept.

A *self* (of an animal) constantly screens the objects or organisms outside its boundary and "sees" them either as helpful or harmful to its survival. For an object that helps or boosts the animal's survival, the self will seek to possess it. To possess something is to include the item as part of its *self*, either inside the physical (self) boundary or the psychological one. Eating something, for example, is to include the food inside its physical boundary and integrate it into the self. Likewise, harmful molecules will be eliminated from the physical boundary by excretion.

The urge to possess something is also to exclude other parties from having it. When an animal is trying to possess something and is interfered with by another organism, whether it is of the same species or a different one, the animal will see the interference as a hostile act which threatens its survival. When the animal sees its survival endangered, it will defend it. Fighting is a universal method of self-defense in the animal world. That is why selfishness often leads to fighting.

Not everything an animal wants to include inside its *self* is to be consumed. Nest-building animals also "see" their nest-building materials as vital to their survival. Before mating, an animal will screen the environment for materials suitable for building its nest. Suitable materials will trigger the animal's urge to possess them. Though not to be included inside the animal's physical boundary, the nesting materials are to be included inside the boundary of the animal's psychological *self.*

During hunting, each lioness in the group "sees" each other as vital for a successful hunt and therefore its survival. As a result, their selves merge into one and are united by the same goal, and therefore each will happily cooperate with the other member. Each lioness is still selfish. Their cooperation with the other serves the same self, which is for the pride. Therefore, selfishness and cooperation can coexist in harmony. In English, we have the words *insiders* and *outsiders*. *Insider* is someone to be included into the group, which is a self, because he or she shares the same interest. An *Outsider* is outside the self, not to be trusted and to be excluded.

Selfishness and cooperation will be in conflict when two organisms see each other as competitors for some limited resource, and that is the most common situation in the animal world. That is why selfishness leads to hurting in most situations.

Bond and Cooperation

We have discussed, from the concept of *self,* that cooperation between organisms is actually still self-serving. Therefore, a cooperative behavior is consistent with the selfish nature of the cooperating organisms. We are going to look at how cooperation is achieved.

In order for two or more organisms to cooperate, they must share a common (nonconflicting) interest. But how do the potential cooperators know that they indeed share the interest? It will be very dangerous for an organism to proceed and to find out later that it is a trap. To ascertain the shared interest is genuine, the organisms must be brought close together and interact. This need to first interact is very important because an organism can assess whether the other party is worthy of the risk.

For two sexually ready *Paramecia*, the interaction should be quite brief and also precise. Since *Paramecia* cannot sense many things—can't see, and don't have much other senses—it is likely that each will use some chemicals, some kind of water-soluble pheromone(?) to signal the readiness. Once the signal is verified, they will happily cooperate, which is conjugating with one another. This type of merging of two selves is physical and visible. Still, each conjugating *Paramecium* retains some parts of its body that is not shared.

In an ant colony, a worker has a lot of time to interact with other members. Right after its hatching, a larva is looked after by the older ants. Then, it matures to a stage for it to begin tending the larvae. Then, gradually it is promoted through the ranks and becomes a forager. This system ensures the safety of the cooperating members and thus the colony. Having grown up in a colony, all the members will carry the scent unique to their colony, which serves as their chemical IDs. It is a foolproof system. Therefore, a worker ant can fully trust the system and freely cooperate with any ant carrying the same scent on its body.

For the hunting mammals, the need to closely associate with a potential cooperator will almost automatically disqualify all outsiders, even of the same species. Wolves, wild dogs, hyenas, lionesses, and chimps never cooperate with members from another pack or group; the interaction to outsiders is always hostile. Cooperating mammals are (wired) social animals. The puppies grow up and play together; they interact favorably with each other and stay within the same group before they become sexually mature. As a result, each has learned that it will be safe to cooperate. It is during the time when the potential cooperators interact with the others that each establishes its trust of the others. The established trust leads to the formation of a bond. The formation of a bond always precedes cooperation. Between conjugating *Paramecia*, the bond is physical, and so is the merging of the two selves, which involves the partial breakdown of their boundaries to become one. Between cooperating ants, the bonds are purely psychological, so is the merging together of their individual selves. So are the bonds and the unions of the selves between a pack of wolves, a pride of lionesses, and a group of chimps. Physical bonding and merging of selves are the most primitive forms of cooperation; they have been replaced by psychological ones among cooperating animals as they evolve.

The Strength of a Bond

A bond, whether it is material or abstract, often differs in strength. The strength of a bond is related to the survival need that creates it. The more vital a need is, the stronger will be the bond thus created. When a need disappears, so will the bond. Between the conjugating *Paramecia*, the bond is strong enough to allow the exchange of the gametes to complete. Once the exchange is complete, the need is gone and the conjugation tube disappears together with the merging of selves. Among ants in a colony, their needs to cooperate never end as long as they live. Their bonds, though abstract, are unbreakable. "Till death do us part" is a vow taken by many wedding couples. I have taken the vow twice and have broken it both times. Only ants and bees are able to honor their commitments. The bonds among a hunting pack of hyenas or wolves are intact as long as they are chasing their prey. As soon as they have achieved the goal, their bonds are greatly weakened, if not totally disappear, and their cooperation ends. Then, it will be every hyena or wolf for itself, trying to get as much to eat as possible.

We can also relate the strength of a bond to the degree of merging or union of the selves among the cooperating organisms. Between two conjugating *Paramecia,* the union is only skin deep, involving the disintegration of part of their boundaries to allow the conjugation tube to establish. There is minimal overlapping between the two selves; most of the contents of each *Paramecium* are still separate. The strength of the bond between two conjugating *Paramecia* is therefore as strong as the physical properties of the membrane of the tube, which is rather weak. The overlapping of the selves of the ants with their colony is at the opposite end; their self is completely merged with that of the colony and therefore is at the maximal level of overlapping. That is why the bonds between the ants and bees are the strongest in nature.

Among a pack of hyenas, their selves only partially overlap with the other; there is a big area of the self in each hyena that is still unshared. And the unshared area is to get as much to eat for itself as possible, often at the expense of the other partner, when an opportunity comes; this part of the unshared self is still hurtfully selfish. From hyenas and wolves, we should watch out for the partners we are cooperating with, for the parts of their unshared selves, because if you are not careful you will be hurt. That is why some sisters or brothers will not hesitate to hurt other siblings. The bonds between cooperating hunters are much weaker than those between ants of the same colony and thus will break when conflict of interest arises.

The Unlikely Bonders

We have looked at three examples in the spectrum of cooperation; they are all strategies in the survival game. In our examples, the organisms which form bonds and cooperate are from the same species, and often from the same mother, a common ant queen, or from the same parents, such as the members of a wolf pack or a pride of lionesses. Our planet has a vast number of animal species. Weird things occur from time to time. Sometimes, unlikely bonding happens, and as a result, an odd friendship develops between two most unlikely participants. The Internet and the widespread use of cameras in cell phones have recorded and made known quite a few of such strange bonders and their behaviors.

In *A Goose Is a Man's Best Friend* you will find the story of Hernandez and his goose Chacho. Or from *Man, Goose Form Odd-Couple Friendship* on YouTube you can enjoy the short video of the friendship between Dominic the person and Maria the goose. In both cases, the bonds between the men and their feathered friends are quite strong. In light of what we have discussed, it is very difficult to see what survival value this type of odd friendships offer. The two pairs of organisms involved are as different as can be; they belong to totally different classes: mammalia vs. aves. To put thing into perspective, the last thing they have in common is both are warm-blooded and classified under *Chordata*, animals with vertebral columns, which also include fish, frogs, lizards, etc. I can only say that since we live in a cosmos built upon a bizarre world of quanta, nothing should really surprise us. Or the bird that initiated the bonding was the result among some countless weird mutations which in some case did not kill the stupid bird. If the man the bird was bonding with were Chinese, the weird gene carried by the bird would soon be eliminated. "We are going to have roast duck tonight, thank you very much."

While some of the trans-class friendships don't make much sense, the trans-order bonds between us and our truly best friends, dogs, can readily be explained in terms of survival. From the point of view of a dog, an owner offers almost everything necessary for its survival— shelter, protection, and food, though sex is often eliminated from the list. Two out of three isn't bad. Therefore, there are plenty of reasons for a dog to befriend a man. Since an owner is vital for a dog's survival, there is a reason for a dog to become possessive; that is why a dog will not hesitate to defend and protect its owner when danger arises. From an owner's point of view, a dog also has plenty to offer. It provides protection and companionship plus some other services: a blind person and his guide dog, a policeman and his German shepherd, a hunter and his retriever, or a cowboy and his sheepdog are some of the examples.

In the cooperation between organisms of the same species and between members that are closely related, the overlapping or sharing of their selves is often more or less equal. Each *Paramecium*, for example, will invest the same amount of its content in conjugation. Or each pack-member hyena will share a certain portion of its self in hunting and reserve some portion for itself and itself only, whereas each and every ant will put everything it has into the colony and share it with the others. An ant does not have anything outside the colony.

So how will the sharing of selves be between a dog and its owner, two species from different orders? For sure, there will be a very big part of a person's self that he does not share with his dog because a person's interests will be many and some are far more important than the wellbeing of the dog. In a dog's case, it is very likely that there is very little, if any, part in its self that is private to the canine. Like an ant serving its colony, there is very little that a dog will not do for its owner. In a dog's mind, it and the owner are one; the dog is likely to have completely included its owner as a part of its self. That is why a dog will fearlessly attack someone who tries to harm its owner. In the dog's psyche, attacking its owner is no different to directly attacking it. You may see the dog as a noble and selfless animal; I still see a self-serving SOB. The difference in the degree of the sharing of selves in the psyches of the two will make them behave differently in life and death situations. A man is more likely to abandon his dog in danger than vice versa. It is more likely for a dog to risk its life to save the owner than vice versa. If an owner has limited resource, he will be more willing to spend money to buy medicine for his sick kid than his sick dog if both need medication. I know some people will call their dogs their children, but when the "children" are sick and become financially too draining the "children" are often put to "sleep." This should not be taken as unfair to our loyal friends; it is simply a practical matter of who needs who more. If you are really desperate for something or some person, like a dog needs its owner, then you may end up paying with your life for it.

The dog is in a very lousy position to overshare its self, leaving very little room for its own. But the dog has no choice. The degree of dependence for survival between a dog and its owner is not equal and therefore the consequence isn't either. You would think only dogs would overshare their selves; think again. Sometimes, people, in the name of "love," will foolishly do what dogs are doing. There are many love songs that have lyrics like "I'll die for you" or "I can't live without you." When you find out your honey does not share as much her *self* as you do—as evidenced in his or her "doesn't care" behaviors, your overcommitment often results in a lot of hurts. Sounds familiar? Be warned, especially if you are a romantic type! But you are hardly alone; I have done it a couple of times and I am likely to repeat it. Some people never learn.

CHAPTER 12

Noble Lovers or Sex Junkies?

The Puzzling Big Penis, Big Breasts, Naked Body, and More . . .

Anthropologists are still baffled by quite a number of sexual features and behaviors unique to us, the modern humans. First, for example, of all the primates, including the much bigger and stronger gorillas, men have the biggest penises, according to anthropologists. I first learned this fact from an article by Jared Diamond. The knowledge always puts a smirk on my face; it is very reassuring. However, I also learned later that men's testes are smaller than those of chimps, though still bigger than those of gorillas, and for that matter, the rest of the apes and monkeys. It disturbs me quite a bit. Why the incongruity? You can call me greedy or ungrateful, but shouldn't we also have the biggest set of testes? If a penis is likened to the wheels and testes to the motor, shouldn't the biggest set of wheels also be equipped with a V12?

Next is the constant sexual receptiveness of women. Other than female bonobo chimps, our women are the only exception in the animal kingdom that are always sexually receptive. Then, there is the concealed ovulation, so-called because women, unlike all other fertile females in the animal kingdom, do not want to publicize the time when they are ready to procreate; they hide their ovulation from men during the narrow window of time when they are fecund.

If these are not enough to confuse you, there are more. How about the pairs of big breasts of women? Do you know that women, on average, have the biggest breasts among apes? Forget about the skinny monkeys! And I am not only talking about divas such as Pam, Madonna, Janet, or Dolly. Women's breasts are just far too big in biological and physiological context. It sounds like I am complaining. No! I'm not. It is just so mind-boggling. Human breasts are way out of proportion in comparison to the other apes, including gorillas and those promiscuous bonobos. If nursing babies is the deal (should it be otherwise?), do women need such big breasts? Size, according to physiology, has little to do with the amount of latte produced; most of the bulk in the breasts is functionally, as far as milk production is concerned, useless fat. And if you ask any biochemist, the price tag of the astronomical number of fat molecules required to build the "mounds" is not cheap. In nature, fat is far more expensive than silicone gel. How about the period when the service is not needed? What is the point in wasting precious resources to maintain those massive and expensive dry fountains?

And there is the issue of a hairless/naked body. There should be at least half a dozen of equally plausible theories explaining such a biological oddity. If you ask any animal, it will tell you there is nothing more sick-looking, ugly, and unsightly than one that has lost its fur. There are breeds of dogs and cats with naked bodies. I won't touch any of them with a 3-meter (I favor going metric) pole. Perhaps a lion or hyena may tell you that hairlessness is great; it sure saves the diner the trouble of swallowing a fur coat when eating a human.

Last and not least is the repositioned vagina; the birth canals in women are tilted frontward. Why? Oh yes, one more: a female common chimp or bonobo is polygamous; usually, she practices first come, first serve in picking her sex partners when she is in heat. We are monogamous; most anthropologists think the trend started with *Homo erectus,* if not *Homo habilis.* How and when did the transition take place? What caused the change?

Oh, I have almost forgotten the prolonged lovemaking—I might have taken it for granted (just kidding). Male chimps or gorillas get it over with in seconds; three strikes and it will be over. A man with a bit of experience will not lose it before ten minutes. One of my friends claimed he could sustain it for hours. (Didn't he have better things to do?) I should not leave out orgasm, which is also unique to humans.

Not surprisingly, there are many theories explaining the advantages of our big penises. According to some, a big penis has little to do with enhancing reproduction, which, I think, is valid. However, it is not a total waste either. If you are not a biologist or biochemist, you may not know why having a big penis is wasteful; it takes a lot of ATPs and useful

191

molecules to build an XL penis. A big penis carries a steep biological price tag, like a woman's out-of-proportion breasts. Why not max the return by investing in muscle building? Or invest in neurons? Why the extravagance? Well, extravagance does sometimes serve a purpose: it is a true form of advertisement telling your rivals that you are exceedingly rich and strong, so much so that you can afford to be wasteful, according to some scientists. The situation can be compared to guys buying million-dollar antique cars which they only use on the odd sunny weekend or not at all. Lots of gals fall for guys like that. The seemingly useless cars serve to eliminate the pretenders and make it simpler for their owners in dating games. I guess the theory should also apply to big breasts. Do women need to go out of the way to attract males? Not from my experience. Each unique feature, like the concealed ovulation, prolonged lovemaking, or a hairless body has attracted a number of fascinations.

No disrespect to the hardworking, knowledgeable, and always inquisitive scientists and their convincing arguments, but their theories seems to me like pieces of unrelated jigsaw puzzles. Or it is like several musicians playing together—one playing Mozart, the other Beatles, and yet another singing Abba. Other than making a lot of noise, it appears senseless. What if those sexual features follow a central theme, like many of our anatomical adaptations to upright walking? And what if all the goodies—likely to have happened one at a time, through practice or lucky mutations—occurred stepwise to give the early humans more sexual pleasure? Yes, I am saying that the features are specials and extras thrown in by Mother Nature primarily for humans to enjoy sex. Each feature heightens the sexual pleasure and was designed to make humans more and more addicted to sex! You can either say they are gifts or traps. With this assumption in mind, let us again examine the features one by one and try to see whether or not they would increase our sexual pleasure. At this stage, let us not be concerned with the sequence in which the features might have evolved; we may never find out.

For Your Sexual Pleasure Only

Big Penis: Some would argue that size matters not, and I am inclined to support such contention. It certainly would not hurt to have an oversized male genital, a.k.a. OMG, would it, guys? And if I were granted three wishes, I would certainly burn one in the penis department. Though bigger is not necessarily better—according to some surveys—and a penis the size of an English cucumber may not bring more pleasure to its owner or his partner than a bananalike organ, if a man is unfortunate enough to be smacked with a chimp-size penis he may have a problem satisfying his partner. All on my side? (Honestly, I have never seen how bad a chimp's penis is, have you? The reason can either be it is too small or too short, or both. In either case, it will be nasty all the same.)

Big Breasts: Again, bigger may not be better, but if you ask guys, the majority of them would tell you that breast size is one of the very important things they look for in gals. Most guys would, and within limits, prefer gals with bigger breasts any day, provided other things are more or less equal. There is a reason why all swimsuit models have navel-orange-sized breasts, and most popular female entertainers own bosoms that quicken heartbeats. Forget about blondes have more fun. Most hedonistic men will tell you that they spend lots of time and attention on women's breasts during lovemaking. I am reasonably satisfied that big breasts do give more pleasure, though not necessarily more milk. If a guy insists that breast size has nothing to do with sexual pleasure, I respect that and would say, "I am glad you do."

Holding It Longer: From what I have heard, experienced men usually will not ejaculate sooner than ten minutes during sexual intercourses. On the other hand, the nervous chimps and the edgy gorillas will lose it within seconds after penetration; strike 1, 2, and 3, and you are out. If we can agree on sex being highly pleasurable, is it not true that a half-hour ride is far better than a few seconds? If a man always ejaculates prematurely, he has a big problem—not only for himself—because women usually don't reach orgasm before tens of minutes.

Always Receptive: Hockey fans will forever remember the 2004–2005 season with all kinds of negative emotions. Likewise, baseball fans will tell you how they suffered when the players were on strike. One thing every man should be grateful for but rarely acknowledges is the constant sexual receptiveness of his girlfriend or wife—unless, of course, he does something stupid, like not bring home enough bacon, smelling like a rat, or having bad breath. We are all guilty of taking things for granted; men often forget that we are the luckiest creatures on the planet. Our women are open to sex 24/7 and 365, like a Tim Horton's or McDonald's.

Repositioned Vagina: Mother Nature repositioned the vagina by tilting the canal toward the front, making it quite natural for face-to-face copulation. One would say why bother? Do you know that face to face is the most preferred position? I don't think the ease of doing it is the main reason for its popularity. Rather, the unmatched level of pleasure is the main reason. Other than the acrobatic bonobos, humans are the only mammals that can do it face to face, and we do it naturally. I have yet to see cats or dogs doing it—thank goodness. For a change, I am not aware of any theory on this one. Scientists are a morally very wary bunch; you don't want your name to have anything to do with such a woman's private part.

A Naked Body: Mother Nature has so drastically reduced the thickness of the fur of hominids—whether in stages or by one clean stroke of mutation—that we essentially became naked, which, objectively, makes us the ugliest mammals on the planet. What good does a naked body serve? Of course, it would reduce the drag when swimming. But neither penguins nor seals go naked! Or a naked body makes it easier to cope with the African heat in hunting. If that is the case, why are we the only medium-sized mammals that go naked? Don't the wild dogs, hyenas, cheetahs, or antelopes have the same need? Lacking the thick skin and size like an elephant, rhino, or hippo, doesn't the lack of protection from fur result in more harm than the advantage gained from thermal regulation or drag reduction?

But if you will excuse my "dirty" mind—yes, I have been called that by some friends for the pleasure-increasing theory—I think that a naked body serves one thing and one thing only: it is to increase sexual pleasure. For those who disagree, I would suggest for them to leave their clothes on the next time they make love. The excitement of two naked bodies rubbing against each other is not unlike the fireworks on July 1 for Canadians (or July 4 for the Americans), with all the sensory organs firing like crazy in the night sky.

If you don't think that is beautiful, I don't know what is. Bipedalism, besides freeing our hands for other chores, also allows humans to naturally fully embrace one another, making it possible for almost every square centimeter of the lovemaking couple's skin to be touching and rubbing against each other. No other mammals come close to that.

Female Orgasms: The phenomenon of women reaching orgasms or sexual climax is certainly quite odd in the animal kingdom. I am not saying that a woman will get an orgasm every time. But some women do experience such intense pleasure from time to time, depending on a number of factors, of course. Orgasm is certainly uniquely human. Though bonobo chimps do sex far more often than humans—before they eat, they will routinely first have a quickie or someone getting edgy will be a good time for another one—it is highly unlikely that any female will ever have an orgasm. To the bonobo, sex is a form of greeting and peacemaking. We should also note that whether a woman has an orgasm or not does not affect her chance of getting pregnant, though I have heard a theory that having it will increase her likelihood of having a daughter later. I love the guy—and I have two daughters.

Then, it begs the question what survival function does female orgasm serve? I would say it gives more pleasure to both the woman and her partner, making them love sex more. Female orgasm is an unfailing signal that the girl is enjoying the sex as much as her man. Without reaching orgasm, sex will just be some tiring and invariably frustrating work for a woman, and sooner or later she will not welcome it. Her orgasm will also heighten the sexual pleasure of her man. There are few things in life as satisfying to a man as giving his woman the ecstasy of an orgasm. It makes you feel like Caesar the Conqueror.

If we look at each individual feature alone, it does seem to serve a different need or function. Sure, a big penis can be a great advertisement for its owner. So are the bouncy breasts. Longer copulation before ejaculation, however, does seem a total waste of time if reproduction is the only goal. Constant receptiveness, which can be closely linked to concealed ovulation, may be for other survival-related activities. A repositioned vagina may make it less messy for a woman to pee. And a naked body may serve other more urgent purposes. But what if those features do serve a central purpose? Then, one can arrive at no other conclusion than they have been installed for our sexual pleasure; it is a dream sex package! Any scientists who deny it would risk being ungrateful. If I had Gandalf's power, I would return a chimp-sized penis to guys like Diamond naturally, because he has been the most vocal. If they are still unrepentant, then shorten their good time before ejaculation, and reinstall the fur coat . . . Just kidding! Sorry. So can I get you to temporarily agree that it is a dream sex package?

Then, the obvious question will be why would Mother Nature want to make sex more fun for humans? A fatal flaw in the Dream Sex Package hypothesis is that as far as an incentive for having sex is concerned, there is no animal on the planet that needs further motivation. In plain and simple English, no female animal on the planet in heat ever has a problem getting laid. To have sex is hard-wired among animals; there is no need to make it fun. Animals have absolutely no choice but to comply when they are sexually mature. In fact, sex for animals in general is a big drag. Not only is sex no fun, it often costs the lives of its participants—most die shortly after it, like mayflies and salmon. Some die doing it, like certain male spiders and praying mantes. For clumsy creatures like sloths, armadillos, crested porcupines, or turtles, sex, besides being no fun, is likely to be all hard work. Can you imagine how much easier and simpler would life be for the animals without getting bugged by sex?

The reason that sex does not have to be fun for all the animals except for people and bonobo chimps is that it only serves one purpose and one purpose only, and that is to reproduce. When the time is right, animals have no choice but to comply; Mother Nature does not need to make it fun for animals. We know that sex in bonobos is not always for reproduction. It is a form of socializing, like a hug between friends in some parts of Europe, or handshaking, with a message: I don't mean you harm. Sex, whether it is hetero- or homosexual, creates peace in a group of bonobos.

If sex also serves other functions in humans, then what is it to justify the many extras? The package is certainly not cheap. Big penises and big breasts are extremely pricey. Longer copulation not only endangers the mating couples, it is likely to be a waste of time, as far as reproduction is concerned. How about the constant receptiveness of women? How do we explain such sexual oddities in humans?

There is another very odd thing among the features, so odd that it does not seem to make any sense at all. It is almost like a plot or conspiracy. If you look at those oddities again one by one, you will see that women have contributed more of those odd features to make sex fun for men than men's contribution for women. Again, if I can get you to temporarily agree that the features are for enhancing our sexual pleasure, then there is only one male contribution: it is a big penis. Holding it longer is at best questionable. I think it serves men's interest more than that of women's, if you ask me. The majority of the goodies have come from women!

Few will disagree that female bodies are more naked than those of men. They are smoother by a wide margin, and feel much better to touch by an even wider margin. On top are those big enticing breasts, the 24/7 receptiveness—rain or shine, especially when it rains—and the conveniently forward-tilted vagina to make it possible to wrap your arms around her, to kiss her lips, or suckle her nipples while having sex. Why have women so disproportionately done more during evolution to make sex more fun?

We men are very lucky. No other animals, including the chimps, our closest relatives, have come close to having so many features. Since most of these goodies—big penis, big breasts, and repositioned vagina, etc.—required changes at the gene level, the changes could only happen through lucky mutations. Because these "goodies" could not be preserved, it is almost certain that we will never know at which stage of the evolution a certain trait made its appearance. One by one, it might have taken Mother Nature many millions of years to complete the delivery. However, we are 100 percent sure that when it came to modern human, we have received the full installment of the dream package. And if our sexual-pleasure theory is right, there will be no more goodies to come because there will be no more need or advantage in having them.

The lopsided female contributions to sexual pleasure might mislead you to think that women have, since great antiquity, been more interested in sex or they were promiscuous. That is why they have offered so many; they want to make men want it. How could it be otherwise? If that is your conclusion, you cannot be more mistaken. Any man will tell you that women being promiscuous is a myth; at best, it is a rarity. You may say I am ignorant (or very unappetizing), but I have yet to meet promiscuous women. (Brad Pitt might want to dispute the point.) You should also know that compared to men, women in general are not that interested in sex. To say that women are not that interested in sex may be an understatement. There is a big gap in the sexual appetite between the two sexes. The gap has likely existed throughout the long evolutionary road. Not just today. How big is the gap? Sexual urge of men should be about ten times stronger. It is so because sexual need is driven primarily by the level of testosterone. Men have far more of the stuff in their blood than women, roughly a 10 to 1 ratio. It may not translate directly to the actual numbers of ten men vs. one woman. That the huge sexual appetite gap exists is a fact any man active in dating will testify. (The huge gap in sexual appetite not only exists in humans, it is a fact among apes and monkeys, lions and seals, etc.) As a result, men, in general, find it much more difficult to get laid than women. Men, in general, are always hungry for sex. It is true now. It was true since ancient times.

Let me tell you a real story to show the point. I visited Thailand a couple of times. Wherever I used the toilets—Bangkok, Chiang Mai, or Krabi, etc.—I would, often when I was urinating, sometimes in the middle of it, find a woman cleaning the washroom. Quite often, she would be only a couple of feet away from me. Understandably, I was quite uneasy and felt naked when I first encountered the situation. More and more, I realized that this is a common practice in Thailand. And it has never caused any concern. Can you imagine the other way around? Other than Thailand, there are other countries like Japan, China, and countries in Central America that also have the same practice.

So it is puzzling, isn't it? For many million years, the women, through mutations, have been finetuning their bodies to make them much more fun for men to have sex with. At the same time, they have been playing a hard-to-get game. They really have little interest to engage. Why have they been playing this game? Why? Well, be patient, my dear reader; it is a long story.

The First Quantum Leap—Down from Trees to Caves

At the time our story began, eons had passed and the early hominids had abandoned tree dwelling for many, many generations. They had, instead, made their homes in caves. It is quite likely that the move had been made somewhere between the walking chimps and Lucy's type. The change in a place to sleep was likely sudden and is not unexpected. Without grasping feet, an upright-walking ape would have to labor to climb up a tree to sleep at night; he could lose balance and fall to the ground during sleep. There was no pressing reason for them to continue living in trees, especially when they had to travel farther and farther away from the forest to obtain food. As they could better defend themselves with their sticks, they also feared fewer animals. The first group probably discovered cave dwelling during one of their food-gathering excursions.

During a season when food was scarce near their home base, they might need to go farther and farther to get enough to eat. It was quite conceivable that eventually, during one of the food-gathering outings, they had traveled too far to get back home; they had to look for a place to spend the night.

Not nocturnal nor a top predator, it would be against their survival instinct to sleep in the open, rendering themselves vulnerable to attack from all directions. It would, therefore, be natural for the group to look for a shelter. The primary targets would be some tall trees. If trees were not an option, they had to look for an alternative as night began to fall. A cave, then, especially a large one if it happened to be around, would be a natural choice. If the cave was occupied, the early hominids could evict the occupants with their weapons. Top predators, in general, were not cave dwellers. We know that few animals could defeat or harm the stick-using apes. And once they had tried sleeping in a cave, they would not want to go back to sleeping in trees. A cave offered better protection from the elements, was easier to get to, more comfortable, and there was no danger of falling to the ground during sleep. With number and weapons in their favor, not many animals would dare to attack the group. Cave dwelling gradually became a new way of life for the early hominids, our ancestors.

Switching to cave dwelling might not appear to be a big deal for a group of early hominids other than changing a place to sleep, but the consequence was far reaching. It gradually changed the way members interacted with each other and eventually would lead to the formation of family units (millions of years down the road). Let us explore how living in a cave could have affected the behaviors of a group of early hominids.

Let us assume that the group had been living in a cave for a while and had settled down. There might be days, especially during seasons when food was plentiful, that the group got enough food early. Instead of staying out and unnecessarily exposing themselves to dangers, they would likely return home sooner. Or they had successfully stolen some meat from wild dogs, so the group headed home. After the group had eaten and rested, the sun was still quite high on the horizon. There was still a long period before it was time to sleep. What would the members do? The early hominids were highly intelligent animals; it would be unlikely for them to just sit around and do nothing, like lions. Being social animals, they would have the need to interact with one another. Living in a cave and on the ground, it would be much easier for the members to get to one another and stay together comfortably. So they would interact even more than chimps when they had nothing to do. What type of interaction? Each and every member had a full stomach—some probably had too much to eat because of the abundance of food—it would be unlikely that any individual would be in an aggressive mood for several reasons. To begin with, they were closely related individuals, brothers, cousins, and nephews like in a group of chimps. And after generations using sticks as tools and weapons, I would assume that fighting between members for dominance would be reduced to a minimum because a fight with weapons would cause serious injuries to both parties and therefore to be avoided. And most importantly, early hominids needed to stick together more tightly than chimps; their survival had demanded greater unity from each and every member to face the many and ever-changing adversaries. Anything that weakened their cooperation would spell doom to the group. A group of early hominids would likely have a leader, but its dominance over the other members would be less overwhelming than a leader chimp. In such a setting the interactions between the members would likely be peaceful in nature. Younger members would play with one another to kill time. Pairs of more mature hominids would take up mutual grooming. I am no chimp; but I believe that grooming would be quite pleasurable for the chimps. Mutual grooming is a very popular pastime for monkeys and chimps. We all enjoy being groomed. We shall therefore assume that mutual grooming between pairs of hominids was the most common pastime and focus on the consequence of this pastime among cave-dwelling hominids.

Mutual grooming could take place between two hominids of the same sex; the pleasure produced from grooming would likely strengthen their friendship. Or it could be between a pair of the opposite sexes. In that case, it could lead to a sexual preference in favor of a grooming partner when the female in a pair was in heat. The reason was simple: mutual grooming would be pleasurable for both parties; it would make a female hominid like her partner more than other males. A male partner would have an unfair advantage in picking up the first sign that she was receptive. A male hominid, like a chimp or a man, would always look for sex. Sex, in comparison to grooming—and for that matter all other survival activities—produces much more intense pleasure and thus would be far more addictive, as we have mentioned in a previous chapter. Unlike the pleasure produced by thirst, hunger, or escaping enemies, a young male's appetite for sex is seldom fully satisfied. In the case of a male grooming hominid, he would always look for and try to get sex from his partner.

Because grooming is in itself pleasurable, it will help to create a bond between grooming partners. Sex is the most important part of survival; it is no accident that sex also generates lots of pleasure. Whereas grooming is not that important to survival and we can expect the bond created by grooming alone will be weaker. It would be also natural that among hetero pairs, the males particularly, would become very possessive of their partners. A possessive feeling, as discussed in the concept of self, would cause the male to protect his partner. Without knowing it, the selves of the pair would merge gradually. The self-boundary of the male, in particular, would include more and more his female partner. He begins to see his partner as a part of him. When that happened, he would be increasingly willing to share things valuable to survival, food in particular, with his female partner.

What we want to establish here is: grooming is a pleasurable activity; it will help to create a bond between the grooming partners regardless whether a pair is homosexual or heterosexual. Grooming between heterosexual partners would give the males in grooming pairs an advantage to have sex with their partners when the females were sexually receptive. As a result, the bonds between heterosexual pairs would grow stronger over time depending on the frequency the pairs having sex; the more frequent, the stronger the bonds. The bonds would cause the selves of the pair to merge. The selves of the males in the heterosexual pairs, in particular, would include more and more of their partners', again depending on the level of sex they had. When a male's self includes his partner, it would make him more willing to protect and share food with the female. How much a male is willing to protect and share with his partner would depend on how much sex they had.

The last point worth reiterating will be: cave dwelling would favor mutual grooming to develop naturally more than tree dwelling. I hope this relation between grooming and sexual activities, and the natural merging of selves that would happen, makes sense to you because we shall continue to develop along this theme.

Without the hominids knowing it, sex had gradually become an important force that shaped both the behaviors between the two sexes and evolution of our species. Our theory will also help to explain the many human anomalous sexual features. Now, let us see whether it will lead us to solving the puzzle of the "concealed" ovulation.

The Puzzle of the "Concealed" Ovulation

Among animals, it is common for fertile females to advertise the time when they are sexually receptive. The ads may be chemicals, sounds, or visual signs, which can readily be picked up by the males of the same species. Since the windows of receptiveness are usually narrow, failing to advertise her fertility is sure to doom the species. Modern women, however, are marked exceptions to the rule. Other than certain subtle mannerisms that can be easily picked up if you are experts—so they claim—women give no signal that they are fertile. And, more often than not, a woman herself has no clue when one of her ovaries has laid an egg.

Naturally, one would ask a number of questions. How do women get away with concealed ovulation? Why do women conceal it? And when did the practice begin? The first question is easy to answer. Women can do without advertisement because they have a hot item that every man wants. Any marketing expert will tell you that if you have an extremely hot product, like the Maple Leaf playoff tickets, you don't need King James to promote it for you. Men are constantly horny, being endlessly whipped by their male hormone produced by a pair of potent testes, which are second only to chimps' in size. A woman does not need to give a signal; she gets more begging for sex than she can handle. Hot girls get more guys knocking at their door for sex than they want.

The question becomes why do women conceal it? And when did the practice begin? There are many persuasive theories about the concealment. I think it will not hurt to add one more. I don't think women have chosen to conceal their ovulations; rather, they find the signal useless and often irritating, like candidates' signs after an election, and therefore got rid of it. When did the practice begin? For sure, modern women did not start the trend to be fashionable. And I seriously doubt that we can ever hope to pinpoint the hominids that began the practice because the signals, the flashing red genitalia inherited from chimps, would only be skin deep and would not allow the signals to be preserved. To take a not-so-educated guess—I am no bone digger—I would pick a very early time in human evolution, mostly likely prior to Lucy. Please allow me to explain.

Several factors could have led to junking the signal. The first one I can think of would be upright walking. In upright walking, the position of the genitalia would be pointing downward instead of horizontal like in chimps or monkeys, thereby making the signal less visible, and as a result, weakening its effectiveness. This alone would make dumping the signal a matter of time.

The other factor could be the decreasing need to advertise. Concealed ovulation was likely to happen long after mutual grooming had been established in hominid groups. A fertile female would naturally pick her grooming mate over the other males because she would like him more for the reasons given. There already was a strong bond between her and her male. When you have an acceptable taker lined up for a limited item, you don't waste time in advertising it either.

The last one I can think of is that the signal would cause some unnecessary complications to an otherwise satisfactory arrangement. The signal would undoubtedly create some commotion in a group, and caused squabbling, if not fighting among males for the female who would rather mate with her partner. If males in a group continued to fight over females, some males would incur injuries from the competitions. The fighting over females would also make them less cooperative with each other in facing danger. Both situations would lead to weakening the competitive edge of the group.

All in all, it would neither be in the interests of the individuals, nor that of the group to have gals flashing red asses around from time to time. Flashing red genitalia became bad news. As a result, there was an evolutionary pressure to get rid of the signal, the faster the better. Any group of hominids that had females concealing their ovulation would be stronger because it reduced internal struggles. Concealed ovulation would also allow the males to downsize their testes. In the chimps' world, for a male to have any chance to mate, he has to be ever ready and he also needs to be fast, super-fast like a Ferrari, to get its penis in gear. Mating is more competitive than racing for the males. It would be more than embarrassing for a male to be stuck at neutral when the signal was flashing. So every male chimp needs serious horsepower and therefore a pair of super-sized testes. Not those lucky males who had their gals lined up; they could take their time. So gone were the good old days when a female would suddenly pop up a red signal and every male would be ready to do business. When hunting season is over, it will be a waste to keep a loaded gun. It would certainly be expensive to maintain a pair of chimp-size testes when a hominid did not have to compete like a chimp. With only one client to serve, a pair of slightly above-average testes would do mighty well for the males. Survival, again, has always been lean and mean. When energy was difficult to come by, waste has no place in a lean world.

Once ovulation had been concealed, the many benefits of grooming became more obvious. At the very least, it would promote friendship. And friendship, as discussed, would promote cooperation between grooming partners. If sex was an added bonus of grooming, it would further strengthen the bond between the pair, making them stick together more closely than a pair that only groomed. In their daily activities, like food gathering, defending against predators, and dealing with other members, the pair would look after each other's interest. For a female hominid, she would naturally get more goodies from her willing male partner. A stronger bond was likely to translate into a competitive edge within a group. In food gathering, a pair of strongly bonded hominids could easily bully a lone member to get a better choice and bigger share of food. The pair could also outcompete a pair of no-sex groomers because the bond between the latter would be weaker, making them less willing to work for each other. The bond and the cooperation created between groom-only pairs would break up much sooner than sex-and-groom pairs when there was danger. The same would apply when it came to facing predators. A male of a groom-only pair would leave a partner when death was imminent. The male in a pair of groom-and-sex hominids might not abandon his partner so readily despite great danger. When it came to bedtime, a groom-and-sex pair would have first pick of a safer and more comfortable spot to sleep because they were more united. I am not sure whether a groom-only pair would have a strong preference to sleep together. As a result of a weaker preference, they might not put up a struggle to get a better spot.

Besides the edge from heightened cooperation, the psychological benefits to a groom-and-sex pair would be significant. Because of more sex, I would rate the level of overall happiness of a groom-and-sex pair highest. Next would be groom-only, with a no-groom-and-no-sex loner dead last. We all know, from medical research, that happiness boosts a person's immune system. It would follow that a groom-and-sex pair would be more resistant to sickness because they were happier. If our speculations are valid, then we can expect groom-and-sex pairs to be the strongest and fittest in a group because the pairs would get better and more food, sleep in a more comfortable spot, and feel satisfied, which is the same as happy, more often. And since survival favors the strongest and fittest, there would be pressure to increase the level of sex in a group besides grooming, would it not? Then, there would be a constant pressure in the course of human evolution to promote more sex between members because of the many benefits sex provided; i.e., higher cooperation between the partners and better health of the partners. Does it make sense? Then, the big penis, enlarged breasts, constant sexual receptiveness, long copulation before ejaculation, naked body, and repositioned vagina suddenly begin to make sense! They all increase the sexual pleasure between men and women and would be favorably selected upon when any one of the traits appeared through some lucky mutations.

Each feature in the package would enhance the pleasure of sex in a stepwise fashion. With the realization of each feature, the joy of sex would be heightened, thereby creating an even stronger bond. A stronger bond, in turn, would increase the willingness to cooperate between the pair. A hominid who first received an XL penis would likely be able to satisfy his partner more, bringing her greater joy, causing them to be more attached to each other, and making them even more willing to cooperate. The same applies to a pair of breasts with more fat, naked body, or repositioned vagina. More and more, there would be a higher percentage of hominids with bigger penises, females with bigger breasts, and males who could copulate longer. Any deficient hominids would have difficulties competing and be eliminated in the eons that followed. That is the reason we men have bigger penises than chimps or gorillas; we have gone through many rounds of elimination and survived.

From the above, I would strongly argue that all those odd human sexual features—at least seven of them—are for one purpose and one purpose only, and they were to give greater and greater sexual pleasure to the successions of human species that had inherited more and more of the features in the package. The heightened sexual pleasure was to bind the partners together stronger and stronger, making them both more and more willing to help each other and eventually merge their selves into one.

It is also an appropriate time to answer another puzzling question. We have identified that at least five of those odd sexual features—a pair of bigger breasts, a forward-tilted vagina, a naked and smooth body, constant receptiveness to sex, and female orgasm—are from the females. It is also a scientific fact that women are, in general, not as hot on sex. So why were our women ancestors so anxious to make sex pleasurable for their men despite their relatively low appetite for it? It was like someone who was not that interested in eating kept coming up with a variety of great dishes. Why? Obviously, it is to please. To please whom? And for what?

The sex was to please their men, to get them hopelessly hooked on sex. When that was achieved, the women would get their men to provide for them and protect them when they were most vulnerable. Do you still remember the hazards of being a hominid mom? Who would be the noble character that would selflessly provide her food and protection when she got pregnant, during childbirth, and the years following the birth of a child? The provider had to be her sex partner, who was likely to be hopelessly addicted to sex with her because sex was so pleasurable. And sex had become increasingly more addictive as more and more sexual features were realized through lucky mutations. As our female hominids climbed up the evolutionary ladder, they would increasingly be burdened by childbearing and childbirth, needing more and more help from the other members. The many hazards, no doubt, would constantly threaten women of Lucy's type; they could not climb up trees fast enough and the moms also needed to protect and provide for their children. They would appreciate some help from someone from time to time, wouldn't they?

Because of the continuous increase in head size of the newborns, successions of hominid moms would increasingly find it more difficult to get enough to eat and to be safe from predators during those many long years of childbearing. Not only were those needs very difficult for anyone to provide; she also would need them for several continuous years, a very long period of time in a hominid's life span. She was in an extremely tight situation—and that would be an understatement, wouldn't it? So whether she and her baby would live or die would boil down to whether or not she could find that noble character, wouldn't it?

For our ancestral females, it would be like beauty contests to win lovers. They all tried to outdo others in being sexy. But the stakes would be much, much higher; it was a matter of life and death, literally. A hominid mom and her baby would die if she could not secure a faithful lover before she got pregnant. She and her baby would also die if she thought she had a partner but who was unfaithful and left her during the time she needed help most. To take time to make sure that her man would be faithful was one of the reasons why she could not afford to be as eager to have sex as her partner; her low appetite for sex would serve her well. She could spend time to check out her lover and make sure he would be reliable before she had a baby with him. She would have time to find out from the willingness of her partner to give her food, in time of danger to protect her. Before she was sure, she would say to her partner, "Grooming, yes; sex, no, not so fast, Romeo."

In those beauty contests, it would be easy to see the advantage of gals who were sexier and offered more sexual goodies. Everything being equal, the first gal who had a naked or a far lesser hairy body would have guys fighting over her. So would a gal with the first tilted vagina, a pair of aces, who would never say no, and who would moan and gloom and yell, "Yes, yes, yes!"

It will be impossible to ascertain which feature had come first. It would not change the picture much. The important thing was each one would enter the human sexual scene eventually, over the many millions of years, and give those lucky gals who got the new features extra advantages in securing their lovers, providers, and protectors. With little doubt, the gals like Lucy's type would have less—might be one or two of the goodies. Those "Handy Gals" might have a couple more. And when it got to the females of *H. erectus*, Mother Nature might have completed her deliveries because they would need help during their childbearing years most. How many items and thus how complete the package a hominid gal got was likely to parallel how desperate her need would be. Was the parallel a coincidence? Or by design? What do you believe? Do those odd sexual features each play a different role or together serve only one purpose? What makes you think what you think? Does it make sense?

The Question of Sexual Dimorphism

Some paleoanthropologists hold that early hominids, like *H. habilis* if not Lucy's type, were sexually dimorphic. Sexual dimorphism is common in polygamous mammals where the males are significantly bigger than the females. Sea lions, elephant, lions, seals, and gorillas are good examples; the exaggerated size difference is required to keep a harem. And only a dominant male has the privilege to mate. Sexual dimorphism could never have occurred during the course of evolution of our species at any stage for several reasons. To begin with, the chimp, our undisputed forefather, was not sexually dimorphic. Second, sexual dimorphism is linked to polygamy, and a dominant hominid would not care to provide for or protect his females. One would also expect the male hominids, if they were polygamous, to fight constantly against one another in competing to mate. Please bear in mind that the early hominids were newcomers and marginal competitors on land; they were still struggling to walk on two feet. They could not run, had little muscle, and lacked powerful claws and jaws; they had nothing which could hurt other animals. I would give them next to no chance to survive if the males in a group were constantly fighting.

I would insist that besides their tools, weapons, and intelligence, another crucial part in the survival of early hominids was their unity as a group and in their willingness to look after each other. Based on this assumption, any situation that would weaken their unity would bring about their demise. Sexual dimorphism would erode the males' unity. On the opposite end, anything that would enhance cooperation between the hominids would allow them to compete more successfully against the cruel animals around them.

One more point about sexual dimorphic mammals. They are usually the top competitors in their domains. Could the same apply to the early hominids? Lions, gorillas, elephants, and sea lions are all top competitors in their territories. The males of these animals never cooperate; they don't need to. To give the most powerful male all the right to mate serves the species better.

Male hominids like Lucy's type and *H. habilis* had committed to land dwelling in a relatively short period of time; they were still very fragile and questionable in terms of long-term survival. Not only could the males of these two species not afford to engage in internal fighting, they needed to stick to each other, looking after each other much more so than the male chimps. When facing imminent danger, these males would always stand up for each other with their striking sticks ready. Cooperation, not just between a sexual pair, rather between males was likely to be one of the important keys for them to survive despite their so many weaknesses. With this rationality, I would expect the cooperation among male hominids in a group was much tighter than among chimps even at the beginning stages; it would also heighten as our lineage evolved.

Nature's Crazy Glue

There is no denying that sex is very pleasurable for humans. The fact that it is very pleasurable also makes it extremely addictive. Bonobo chimps may have sex more often, but I doubt that they ever reach cloud nine. One may ask, almost all animals have sex, why don't the others get addicted? The answer is they rarely get to do sex repeatedly. Most animals, like insects and fish, only have sex once in a lifetime. Most birds and mammals need the hormones to keep up the sex drive. When the mating season is over, none of them want sex. To get addicted, one needs to get repeated exposures and the hormones to drive it. Humans have those.

Then, the question becomes why are we lucky enough to have a constant appetite for sex? The reasons are quite simple. To begin with, male chimps are always interested in sex. It is the females that need some persuasion. A scenario that had led to more female sexual receptiveness might be like this: a pair had been grooming partners for months; she and he got along really well. He was a good partner, attentive, gentle, and his touch always made her feel good. She was very fond of him. Several days earlier, after the group had robbed a pack of wild dogs of a small antelope, he shared the meat he got with her. Male hominids always had the first picks of meat, I believe. He was by her side in every food-gathering trip and was willing to let her have her share. And when there was danger, he was always there to protect her. Everything seemed to be going her way except for one nuisance which happened from time to time. He wanted sex; she was not ready and had turned him down many times. He was persistent and becoming more annoyed at each refusal. (This could be my projection from experience.) What should she do next time? How would you coach the female hominid? I think the female hominid should give in once in a while even if she was not in the mood for sex. Am I a male chauvinist pig? I could be, or I could be talking some business sense.

Consider the following observation. I remember watching a program many decades ago in which a researcher had provided some bananas to a group of chimps. As days went by, a pattern emerged. The alpha male began to hog the bananas, grasping as many as possible, much more than his fair share, and leaving some female chimps without. Chimps, like all animals, are selfish, though I did not know it at the time; still, nothing was out of the ordinary. Then, a female chimp approached the male, who still had several bananas; she allowed him to mount her despite her not being in heat. Sex for a banana! The researcher had shockingly witnessed the first documented case of prostitution in chimps. They don't call it the oldest profession for nothing. No more bananas for the chimps since.

If the banana experiment provides any information about whether a nonestrous grooming hominid in our case would yield to the persistent sexual advances of her partner, the answer, I believe, would eventually be a "yes," albeit a reluctant one at the beginning. The nonestrous female soon found out that it was not a bad tradeoff. In essence, it was a fleeting nuisance (those ancient males were still very much chimplike when it came to sex) in order to keep the established goodwill intact and the nice things that came with it. I would call it a win/win situation; both parties got what they wanted, granted the female had to make a petty concession to put the deal together. Nothing is really free; it is true today and would be true in antiquity.

If the scenario was not too far off, then sex would gradually be added to grooming, because sex would be pleasurable for the male hominid and therefore habit forming. Provided a female would put up with it (and there was a lot at stake), the male would keep looking for sex as part of a grooming deal. Then, he would be increasingly hooked to the female, increasingly willing to provide service and goodies, hanging around her more often and willing to please her.

In the worst scenario where the female did not enjoy sex at all, the bond between the two would one-sidedly become stronger, making him care about her more, to do more for her. The situation is very common in our modern societies; lots of guys are willing to do a lot to please their gals to get sex. From my many years as a florist, I happen to know a lot of guys who won't buy flowers for their moms but would pawn their watches to buy roses on Valentine's Day. And guys usually spend more money on Valentine's Day than Mother's Day unless they are in financial troubles.

Regardless of how the females became continuously receptive, they would, once they acquired the taste, enjoy sex as much as the males. I would think that the constant sexual receptiveness of modern women has a very long root; it could date back to a very early stage in the evolution of our species. For a trait—in this case, receptiveness to sex—to be retained for millions of years, it should, at the very least, not be harmful to the species, and in most cases, be beneficial. It was sex, I firmly believe, that had been the main driving force in promoting and intensifying cooperation between men and women in human evolution.

With quantum leaps in their sexual pleasure made possible by each feature, hominids would spend more and more leisure time having sex and thereby enhancing the bonds between the mating pairs. A pair of hominids heavily bonded through sex was like modern-day lovers; each was willing to share, to care, and to give. And they would do so willingly out of free choice. The lovers became totally selfless despite their selfish nature. Why and how? Because when the two were deeply in love, their individual selves would have fused into one; every seemingly selfless thing they did to each other would still be self-serving, serving the fused self of the pair. There was absolutely no incongruity between selfishness and selflessness in their case.

Definition of Love

Here is one of the strangest things in our cosmos. Sex, which, according to all current moral views, is often viewed as bad, dirty, sinful, and to be prohibited or harshly suppressed, has given birth to love, something that is universally considered beautiful and noble. Love is like a white waterlily, pure and perfect, though it comes from dirty water and a filthy pond. According to our model, sex yields love through a dirty trick; i.e., addiction, which is another lowly creature in morality. The way love works goes against our apparent selfish nature. The beauty of love, thus, lies in its seeming incongruity and weirdness.

Before we proceed any further, it is necessary to clarify what we mean by love, which is one of the most used and also the most confusing concepts in our daily vocabulary—the other one is freedom. People who don't know what *love* means, I have discovered, are often quite well educated; they often have a bachelor's degree or higher. To show you my point, let us look at some of the most popular ways *love* is used:

"I'll kill myself if I cannot see you again; I love you more than anything."
"I love you so much; please don't leave me to join the army."
"I just love chocolate."
"I love my dog." Or,
"I love you; I'll give you one of my kidneys if you need it."

Are we all talking about (true) love?

In order to tell love from not love, let us give *love* a definition. I would like to define love as: *Love begins with a caring feeling/emotion of one individual toward another. If we put caring and love in a scale from 1 to 10, with a higher value corresponding to a more intense feeling, caring will top around 3 and love will be from 5 or higher.* (Please don't be overly concerned about why I have picked 5 instead of 4. To understand the difference is more important.) *What differentiates the two? Love is different from caring in that love can only be apparent in action, through giving, which is a conscious and unconditional act for the benefit of a willing receiver of the act.* It is a mouthful but is necessary to make it as clear as possible.

Let us study the definition carefully. First, love starts with a caring feeling or emotion; a loving person cares. A person who does not care has no love to give. A caring feeling alone does not constitute love; love needs action. We all know that talk is cheap. If someone says he or she loves you but would not do anything for you, the person is just bullshitting you. (It is quite surprising that many people willingly fall for that—again, I am talking from experience.) To qualify as love, it must be shown in action, which is by giving something of (survival) value or performing a beneficial act.

A conscious act is an act by choice, an act which is planned or fully intended. There is no accident in the act. If someone intends to hurt you but ends up helping you, it is not an act of love. You should thank your lucky stars and not the SOB. To qualify as love, an act must be free from any attachment or condition, or it becomes a deal or business transaction. The last point of having a willing receiver is crucial; without a willing receiver, an act, no matter how great it could be, becomes a nuisance. If someone does not need my attention or care, then no matter how beneficial my intended act will be, it will still be irritating or annoying to my intended target. I think good-looking people, especially the beautiful and the famous like pop singers and movie stars, would agree most with this part of the definition.

Having defined what love is, let us examine the above series of statements to see whether any of them qualifies as *love*. The first is not love. There is no gift or benefit to the receiver, who may be unwilling to stay in the relationship; it is a popular form of manipulation. The second is not love either. The person does not give anything; he/she demands the targeted person not to leave and join the army, and therefore is not love.

The third one is also not love; there is no willing receiver. Chocolate is not a living object. Most pet owners truly love their pets. They willingly and unconditionally do a lot of nice things for their pets, which certainly will be happy and willing receivers of the kind acts. It is love. The last one is also true love. It is a conscious decision from a willing giver despite the fact that the gift would cause him/her a lot of pain and endanger the giver. The act is unconditionally offered for the sole benefit of the receiver. If it is true and not just talk, it will be a high-grade love. By the same token, organ donors and people who donate their blood regularly are loving folks. The act benefits other people who should be more than willing to receive their gifts. I salute you folks.

Let us also use this definition to see whether certain phenomena in nature are acts of love. I am thinking about parental care of the young. A mother croc spends quite a bit of time looking after her hatchlings. Is this an act of love? I think that if a mother croc has chosen to do it and knows full well what she is doing it is love. If she is governed by instinct, it is not. What is your vote? What about a lioness looking after her cubs? Is it by choice or instinct? Since lions are quite advanced and intelligent animals, we have reasons to suspect that it is by choice. But then, I remember seeing a documentary which showed a new ruling male lion killing the three cubs of the toppled king. I was shocked to watch the lioness, the mother of the slaughtered cubs, actively soliciting the murderer for sex in the days that followed the killings. It has changed my mind; maybe it is instinct for a lioness to care for her young. How could she forget so quickly? Human mothers would never do such a thing.

Then, how about the chimps? Does a mother chimp care for her young out of choice? Or for us, the modern human, does a mother have a choice of not loving her newborn baby, especially after she has seen and held the child? I think a great part of parental love is wired; it is too important a matter for any species to leave it to the free choice of a mother. However, I think human mothers do have some choice. Occasionally, there are mothers who would go to parties for several consecutive days and nights without checking on their children who desperately need their care. If those mothers were not bad enough, there are cases where mothers use their own babies as weapons for self-defense and offense against the babies' biological fathers. We humans, unlike most lowly animals, do have some choice of not loving our babies. But the limited free choice is not supposed to be used for partying or using their babies as weapons; it is likely a design for mothers to self-preserve when, and only when, by giving up their babies it would allow or even enhance their chance to survive, a point I shall pick up again in the morality of abortion.

So love is a very strange thing, isn't it? It makes some people—despite their selfish nature—choose to do things even for the benefit of unrelated people. How did love, such an improbable thing, begin out of selfishness? Are we, the humans, the only creatures capable of love? The answer is no. Monkeys and apes are capable of love; they show it when one monkey or ape is grooming another. Grooming another animal is an example of love in action. Why is grooming a form of love? Because it was likely to be a conscious choice of the two intelligent animals involved, and it was performed for the benefit of another monkey or ape which would be a willing receiver of the act. And by definition that was love, a weak form of love nonetheless. Please remember it was only a starting point; therefore, don't expect too much.

If we accept mutual grooming in primates was the first act of love in nature, then the question is what made two monkeys or apes engage in mutual grooming in the first place? The answer, I think, could be 1) they had nothing better to do; they were bored. Mutual grooming would relieve the boredom, which was a form of stress. Monkeys, and apes in particular, were the most intelligent animals before human; they had the biggest brain-to-body mass ratio. Intelligent beings will get bored when they are idle. And 2) grooming, in itself, is pleasurable to both a giver and the receiver. Both reasons point to happiness seeking. Other than happiness seeking, there is no reason for one monkey to sit patiently to groom the other monkey, or for one chimp to groom another chimp. We have already argued that all animals do certain things—knowingly or unknowingly—for one reason and one reason only: it is for pleasure or happiness, which leads to survival. Following this argument, then, love, from the very beginning, has to be a pleasurable act and a rewarding experience for both giver and receiver.

I am quite satisfied with the assertion. Why? Because there is nothing that forces a monkey to groom another monkey; likewise, there is nothing that obliges the receiving monkey to stay. Both monkeys have to be willing, and therefore, it has to be pleasurable for both. Agree?

Before we proceed further, we need to clarify an important point. The point is: love is a pleasurable act for a giver and the receiver, but not all pleasurable acts are acts of love. Love is just one of the parts under the "pleasure" umbrella.

Now, please sit tight, because here is the shocking consequence. We have argued that anything which generates pleasure is potentially addictive. Since love is pleasurable to both giver and the receiver, an act of love is addictive, albeit a very healthy and beneficial addiction. Love being addictive not only has very strong backing from biochemistry, as discussed, the symptoms of someone who has lost a loved one are indistinguishable from those of a junky craving a fix. Sadness, depression, and loss of interest in food and work are commonly observed signs among the brokenhearted. In more severe cases, the victims are willing to give up anything to get back a loved one. When that is impossible, the person even perishs. When a person's happiness, sense of wellbeing, and meaning for existence all come from another person, isn't that substance dependence? Instead of a chemical, the "substance" is another person. Most people would agree that love is a double-edged sword. When a person is in love, he/she feels wonderful. If cut off, it hurts like hell, often making a person nonfunctional, and at its extreme, commit suicide. If that is not an addiction, I don't know what is.

Obviously, chimps are quite capable of love and attachment to a degree similar to that of humans. I once watched a documentary called *People of the Forest*.

The Love Story of a Young Chimp

People of the Forest: The Chimps of Gombe (1988) is the title of a wonderful TV documentary sponsored by the National Geographic Society. It is about a group of chimps in Gombe National Park, Tanzania, Africa. Directed by Hugo Van Lawick and written by Jane Goodall and Hugo Van Lawick. The story was filmed in the park where a group of approximately twelve chimps lived.

There was an alpha male, the head of the group, and an alpha female or matriarch. The story revolves around the matriarch and her several children, the second to the last child especially. To make a long story short—the documentary spans twenty years of nonintrusive observation by Goodall—the matriarch, after giving birth to two elder sons and a daughter, produced this very cute young chimp named Charlie. After this little guy was born, the matriarch, probably because of her age, did not have any more children for a number of years. The situation allowed Charlie to hang around his mom much longer than normal and had enjoyed the mom's undivided TLC. What a lucky little fella! Then, the matriarch gave birth again to another child, her last son. As a result, Charlie became a distant second for the matriarch's attention. Charlie was very unhappy; he often tried to force himself back to the mom, competing with his much younger brother for the matriarch's affection. Invariably he was turned away, though gently, by the matriarch. I used to think chimps were wild and rough animals; my opinion on them have made a 180-degree change after seeing how gently and caringly the matriarch turned away her overly attached son. The matriarch would shame a lot of human mothers by comparison.

Then, Charlie got a break. His younger brother died. With the youngest chimp gone, our little fellow once again became the center of the matriarch's attention; he was on cloud nine again. Without warning, the next scene shows the matriarch's dead body lying face down in a small creek that runs through the forest. The little guy tried and tried to get a response from his mom; he failed of course, and eventually accepted the fact. We may never know whether or not chimps can comprehend the meaning of death. Regardless, the little guy had since lost interest in everything. He did not want to join the group in any of their activities; neither did he eat again. He resigned to a tree next to where his mother's dead body laid, built a nest at the treetop, and never left even when his group went away to a new forest. He died many days later, of hunger maybe, but surely from heartbreak. The little chimp was definitely a strong testimony to love; he was also undoubtedly a victim of a fatal addiction.

The moral of the story could be love is a dangerous affair. Of course, it can make you most happy when it works. But if it does not, the double-edged sword can cut you very deep. We have discussed how all survival activities (like danger avoidance, eating, and reproduction) are basically driven by happiness seeking. Happiness/pleasure creates addiction, and addiction forces an animal to seek ways to repeat these activities. Not only are these addictions totally harmless, they are absolutely vital. One might wonder why has evolution created love, something that can be very sinister, which not only causes great pain but also kills when it goes wrong? If survival is the goal, is love overkill?

To answer this question, we need first to understand how love works. The ultimate purpose of love is to bind two people tightly together. Much more than the other addictions, love operates in an exaggerated reward vs. punishment system. If the bond is kept intact, the participants will be handsomely rewarded with a happiness and joy that defies poetry. On the other hand, if the bond is broken, then the victim suffers very severely, so severely that he or she may lose the interest to live. Unlike hunger or danger avoidance, love does not inflict much physical pain. The pain goes much deeper and often causes irreparable damage to the survival instinct of a victim. This might be the reason why Buddha teaches common people to stay away from love if you can.

Then the question will be why did nature evolve a way to bind two people so tightly together? The answer, I think, was to give hominid moms a hand, without which a growing brain could not be sustained. It has been a long detour. In chapter 10 we have discussed the hazards of being a mom in the early days of human evolution. With the head size of their babies getting bigger and bigger, and without a change in their anatomies to keep pace, the moms were forced to give birth to increasingly immature babies to avoid killing both the baby and the mom in labor. This option created a helpless infant, and thereby endangered the mother-and-child pair for months and years after. The only way for the pair to survive was by having someone willing to look after them, a selfless lover. A selfless lover was a male hominid hopelessly addicted to sex with the mother of his child. His addiction or love made him willing to take care of the mother-and-child pair even at great cost. When the continuous growth of intelligence of our species was threatened, Mother Nature had to use the strongest medicine called "love," passionate love that can be overdosed and kills. This, my romantic friends, concludes the very long story of the greatest love!

Forming Families

If you were another animal, even if you were a chimp, our closest relative, and look at us, the humans, you would find that any which way you look at us we are a very, very weird type. Unlike any mammal, we walk on two feet. And ever since then, things about humans have become weirder and weirder, so weird that other than some basic characteristics

Stephen Y. Cheung, Ph.D.

we share with mammals there is very little in common in the ways we do things, even with the chimps.

Other than the many puzzling sexual features, we have one more very odd behavior; it is human males take part in bringing up the children. Most of us grow up with both parents taking care of us; we take having two parents for granted. We therefore think that it is a norm for mammals to do that. NO, NO, NO! It took me quite a while to realize that humans are the only mammals that involve two parents in bringing up their children. Male chimps don't; male monkeys don't. Male gorillas don't and male lions, male horses, pigs, male . . . None of them do. Interesting, isn't it? Naturally, I wanted to know why. So I googled *Paternal Care*. According to *Wikipedia*, only two groups of mammals, us and some rodents, have the "fathers" involved. But none, absolutely *nada*, provides a satisfactory reason based on biology to explain the odd involvements of the males. The reason could be 1) that is not important, or 2) they simply don't know. It is almost like *love* and *freedom*; few people actually know what it is.

But that is hardly a trivial matter in the animal kingdom. If you look at all the animals, birds—and not every bird—are the only advanced animals that involve both mating partners to bring up their chicks. Sparrows, eagles, penguins, and puffins—just to name some more familiar names—are birds that involve both parents. Why? Before we answer the question, we need one more piece of information. They are, as far as I know, all animal-eating birds; they are birds of prey. They feed on animals that move very fast and are thus difficult to catch. It will be impossible for a single mother to get enough food for her growing chicks. In nature, there is an unspoken rule, the rule is to keep it simple. When one parent can do the job, don't involve two. And the reason that most mothers go solo is males are very selfish and unreliable; they are only interested in sex. Once that need is satisfied, most of them will depart without saying goodbye. The rule of thumb that every mother knows is if you can do it solo, never involve your "husband" or you will fail. Makes sense?

The nature of every living creature is selfish, then why will some males stay? It could be either they don't have any choice; it is a wired behavior. Or if they don't, the species cannot exist. Choose the one that makes you happy. If this argument is valid, then obviously the human

218

females have no choice but to rely on the help—both in protection and food—from the males.

In the previous chapters we have dissected how the mothers of our species have been put into the many insurmountable hardships, and sex as a lure has, until recently, been their only salvation provided by Mother Nature. Now, having a broader view, I hope you can appreciate the difficulties of our species more. The females, in particular, have borne an extra heavy load. And understand what has made us so very odd among mammals. We are truly unique.

Knowing that it is rare among male mammals to get involved in bringing up the family, our next question will be when did humans begin to form families? The puzzle of 1808 provides the clue.

The Puzzle of 1808 (*Source: The Wisdom of Bones*, chapter 8*)*

KNM-ER 1808 is the ID of a hominid specimen where KNM-ER stands for Kenya National Museum-East Rudolf. The specimen has posed an interesting puzzle and serious intellectual challenge to its discoverers, a team led by Richard Leakey and Alan Walker, the same people who many years later also found the Nariokotome boy. Please allow me to explain the puzzle of 1808 (pronounced as "eighteen oh eight," as its finders fondly call the specimen).

The discovery: The specimen was discovered in 1973 in Kenya. More than any other fossil specimen, the bones came in thousands of small fragments scattered over an area about the size of a football field. To make identifying it more challenging, the fragments of the specimen mixed together with skeletons of many animals such as crocs, turtles, hippos, antelopes, and giant baboons, each numbering in the hundreds. Needless to say, it would take many, many hours to sort out the forty-some-thousand pieces of bone mixture and put those that belonged to the hominid back together. Paleoanthropologists are a rare breed with the greatest patience.

The identification: The specimen, though very fragmented, is rather complete; it belonged to a mature female *H. erectus* who lived about 1.7 million years ago.

The background: The individual, from the condition of her bones, had suffered from a bone disease which obscured the shape of almost every piece except the skull and teeth. The followings are some pertinent facts.

The symptoms: The bone disease had been both widespread and severe. The bones of the arms and legs of 1808, in particular, were coated with about half an inch of "woven bones." Woven bone is a pathological bone growth which is rapidly deposited. The growth occurs under one of the three conditions: (1) when an animal has to grow very fast, (2) when broken bones heal and rejoin, and (3) disease. The extensive nature of the growth in 1808 points to a disease.

The diagnosis: It took a whole team of top-notch doctors at Johns Hopkins Medical School to work out an opinion. (For those who are medically inclined, the evidence presented before the conclusion was reached was both engaging and illuminating.) The 1.7-million-year-old patient had probably died from hypervitaminosis A, i.e., ingesting too much vitamin A.

Some relevant facts on vitamin A: Regardless of diet, an animal takes in vitamin A throughout its lifetime. The excess vitamin is stored in the liver, where it never breaks down. A carnivore tends to eat the livers of its victims and thus accumulates lots of vitamin A in its liver, similar to the way a shark or a tuna fish builds up mercury levels in its body.

About hypervitaminosis A: How does one get the disease? From mega-dosing on vitamin A, of course. Vitamin A poisoning can come from taking too many vitamin A tablets, or eating the livers of predators such as polar bears, hyenas, wild dogs, lions, and leopards. Much of our knowledge of the disease has come from some unfortunate polar explorers, like the Australian Sir Douglas Mawson, who seemed to have a nasty habit of getting stranded in desolate frozen places with nothing to eat other than their sled dogs, their livers in particular.

The disease is brutal. Besides being extremely painful, it immobilizes its victim. (For an in-depth description of the disease, please read *The Wisdom of Bones*. Be warned that you may end up reading the whole book and lose precious bedtime.)

The puzzle: In order to preserve the original buildup, I would like to quote a paragraph on page 134 of the book:

> *"To have such extensive blood clots, she must have been completely immobilized with pain. Yet, despite her agony, she must have survived her poisoning for weeks or maybe months while those clots ossified. How else could her blood clots have been so ubiquitous; how else could they have*

turned to the thick coating of pathological bone that started
us on this quest?"

The author's interpretation of the puzzle: Again, I quote
from the same page:

"The implication stared me in the face: someone else took
care of her. *Alone, unable to move, delirious, in pain,*
1808 wouldn't have lasted two days in the African bush,
much less the length of time her skeleton told us she had
lived. Someone else brought her water and probably food;
unless 1808 lay terribly close to a water source, that meant
her helper had some kind of a receptacle to carry water in.
And someone else protected her from hyenas, lions, and
jackals on the prowl for a tasty morsel that could not run
away. Someone else, I couldn't help thinking, sat with her
through the long, dark African nights for no good reason
except human concern. So useless as 1808 was for telling us
much about normal Homo erectus *morphology, she told*
us something quite unexpected. Her bones are poignant
testimony to the beginnings of sociality, of strong ties among
individuals that came to exceed the bonding and friendship
we see among baboons or chimps or other nonhuman
primates."

And more from page 135:

"Lacking all evidence, I don't know who cared for 1808 or
if it was one or several individuals. Probably, the protector
was a relative of some kind, *because social groups among*
early hominids were likely to have been largely coincident
with kinship groups. Whoever stayed in the area until 1808
died undertook a serious commitment. The thickness of
ossified blood clot coating on her bones tells us that 1808
survived this excruciating and debilitating disease not for
a few days but for weeks or even months. The costs and
risk of caring for her went well beyond those routinely faced
by nonhuman primates or elephants. The bones of 1808

221

> *thus speak of the appearance of a truly extraordinary social bond."*

Needless to say, Walker is exceedingly thorough in his analysis. I don't know much about pathology, but it is very unlikely that the diagnosis of the Johns Hopkins team is wrong. And from the condition of her bones, it is certain that 1808 would have been sick for quite a long time before her death. Given the time and place she lived, it is very clear that there was someone there to selflessly look after her before she passed away.

As a person who likes to argue—a fact both of my exes would wholeheartedly agree to—I would like to say something about the caretaker of 1808. It was very unlikely that the protector and provider would be anyone except her lover. Why? The author has convincingly pointed out that the protector *undertook a serious commitment,* so serious that he/she had thought very little about his/her own safety. Such commitment requires the strongest bond. In nature, only two types of bonds will be strong enough to qualify. One is that between a mother and her infant. In this case, 1808 was certainly not a child. The other is that between lovers. The protector had to be the lover of 1808. Not just any lover either, he was a lover of the most devoted type, one who was hopelessly attached to 1808, and one who was likely to be passionately involved with the dying woman. In the concept of *self,* the protector had completely included 1808 inside his self-boundary and treated her as his very own. Why? The clue comes from her disease; it was likely that she needed to eat more than one carnivore liver to contract it. The author, for some reason, did not speculate on how 1808 got overdosed on liver, which should yield some precious additional information to the case. Any liver at the time of *H. erectus* was likely to be ounce for ounce more precious than fresh Alaskan king crab legs. Such a delicacy would be a treat that belonged exclusively to the top hunter who made the kill. And since hunters would not normally kill carnivores for food, the rarity of their livers, then, should more than double its value. If you were that top hunter, would you save the liver, take it home, and give it to a friend, a brother, or sister? I don't remember the last time my mom saved her most favorite snack for me, forget about my old man, who was usually too keen to self-preserve.

It seems like I am complaining; I am not. I just want to bring out a point. The point is it would take a tremendous amount of tender love to make someone give up a most prized treat to another person. The fact that 1808 got the disease tells us that she would have eaten more than one carnivore liver. It was hardly a one-shot deal, thus making it very unlikely that 1808 had inadvertently or somehow consumed the toxic treat. The carnivore livers were gifts. They were gifts of understanding and love. They were as valuable as diamonds. Walker and his team have yet to understand the role sex plays in evolution; it is something new in our book. Their inability to see the protector and provider as the lover is understandable. I don't think a special social bond was strong enough to make the person commit, not then or even today.

Alas! The young (hominid) lover did not know it was poison he was giving her. After more than 1.7 million years, we can still see the sorrow that must have consumed the young man, watching helplessly as his most loved companion suffered. Other than bringing her water once in a while, he would be with her most of the time. Nights and days, he stayed close to her with his spear and club nearby. In the end, she died. It was likely that she felt a warm rain pouring on her face as she took her last gasps. Beyond doubt, she had suffered lots of pain. But certainly, she had died contented, at peace, and feeling secure to have her lover, the only man she had ever known, embracing her tightly as the last shred of her awareness faded away. Even after almost two million years, her bones still bear witness to a story of the strongest love to those who can read it. And quite likely, her lover followed her shortly after.

A Classic Example to Showcase Intelligence and Cooperation

Before we proceed, I would like to use the manner in which the team has solved the puzzle posed by 1808 to showcase how intelligence and cooperation work together. The two forces that have been helping our species from the very first walking chimp to now, nonstop.

To solve the puzzle presented by 1808 requires several levels of intelligence and cooperation. Level 1 was to collect all the bits and pieces of bones, both those belonging to the various animals and to the hominid. Then, the first part of their job, I would think, was to sort out the hominid bones from the animal bones. The job requires knowledge and many experts working together. To a layperson like yours truly, I would imagine that would have been an impossible job. But the sorters have the knowledge to tell the difference. Then level 2 began. It would be grouping the small bits and pieces, likely to be thousands of them, into different parts of the hominid's skeletal system. "This goes to the skull, this piece belongs to the femur, and the next one is a tooth . . ." I cannot imagine how those experts decided which piece belonged to where. For example, how would they tell a piece belongs to the left tibia instead of the right? Can you imagine the kind of knowledge the job would demand? Again, it should have involved many people.

Level 3 would be toughest; it would require certain specialists of the team to assemble the pieces into one of the many parts of the skeletal system, such as the skull or a bone in the limbs, for example. If you have tried to complete a jigsaw puzzle, you have a rough idea of how difficult it would have been. I have never finished a more than 500-piece two-dimensional puzzle. The team had to work with three dimensions, often with pieces missing. Again, it required data or knowledge, deep knowledge, and putting the knowledge to use by a team.

Level 4 was to identify the specimen from the assembled pieces. The team would then apply what they already knew about *H. erectus* to decide that 1808 was a member of the species rather than belonging to another hominid group. Then, it would be the matter of sex. The team, again based on information provided by the specimen, applied their knowledge to determine 1808 to be a woman. Level 5 was a crucial step in cracking the puzzle. To solve the problem, they must first find out what kind of disease killed the woman. To come up with a correct diagnosis, the author sought the cooperation of the experts who were among the most knowledgeable pathologists. Level 6 was the most crucial step, without which all the efforts would have been wasted in a defective specimen. The value of the specimen was not to provide detailed structural information on *H. erectus,* as pointed out by the authors; rather, 1808 provided a rare opportunity for the anthropologists to "see" the social structure of the species. It has proven to be priceless. It was specimens like 1808 that allowed scientists to conclude that *H. erectus* had strong social bonds.

The case of KNM-ER 1808 not only is a classic example of how intelligence works, it also beautifully demonstrates the importance of cooperation. From the discovery to drawing a conclusion, it involved many people working together for a common goal, for their mutual benefit. Each level requires a different skill and different participants. In the end, a satisfactory interpretation was reached. No other animal group can use intelligence and cooperation together at such high levels.

One thing will always mark human endeavors: behind every great human success story, one will always find intelligence interlace with cooperation.

If the interpretation on the caretaker of 1808 is valid, then *H. erectus* had all that was needed to form families. Though not bound by law or contract, a couple was willing to stay together, happy to share, willing to give, and the man was committed to taking care of the mother-and-child for a long time, which would not be an easy task by any stretch of the imagination. It had been a love story that had taken 8 million years to unfold—from mutual grooming to family forming, according to our highly speculative sex-package model.

A Dance of Mind and Lust

From what we have discussed so far, a lot had happened in the early stages of human evolution. We have found a continuous increase in the intelligence level as indicated by the increases in the brain size, something exceedingly rare in the evolution of any animal. Developing concurrently was the level of cooperation among the early humans. So one naturally wonders whether or not the two processes had been related. The question becomes have intelligence and cooperation evolved together during the entire period of human evolution? One way to look at the relationship between the two is by asking the following questions. Has the evolution of human intelligence been aided by cooperation? And, has the evolution of cooperation been made possible at certain stage by intelligence?

Cooperation Has Helped the Continuous Heightening of Intelligence

Let us focus on whether or not intelligence got help from cooperation. From the previous chapter, our sex-based cooperation has played a critical role in providing faithful males to take care of *H. erectus* mother-and-child pairs, making it possible for those helpless bigheaded *H. erectus* children to survive after birth. The involvement of male hominids in caring for their pregnant companions was unlikely to have happened overnight; rather, it was likely to have evolved together with monogamy. Chimps, our ancestors, are not monogamous. When did monogamy occur? Which hominid group got the trend started? Sex was certainly the driving force for monogamy; sex was like an invisible rope tying a male to his woman. Then, the question becomes after the realization of how many sexual features was monogamy firmly established? From *H. habilis*? Or even earlier?

Though we may never know the answer for sure, I don't think there was a clear cut-off line which we can confidently say from *H. habilis* or *H. erectus* that our species has establish monogamy. If our depiction of Lucy is valid, then from the females of her kind on they would have needed some help from some males whether they were pregnant or not because they needed to spend a lot of time walking on land and they were still ill-fitted for bipedalism. When they became pregnant, their needs for help would even be more urgent. Then, the question becomes what would be the relationship between them and their helpers? With the knowledge we have, we can pretty much rule out the helpers were relatives or friends; it points to their lovers.

Besides the strong cooperation between sex pairs, the cooperation between members of a group, particularly among the males, could have helped early hominids to grow bigger brains and be smarter. How? By better defending themselves and by helping them to venture into greater territories to collect food and to steal from wild dogs and hyenas at a later period. Higher quantity and quality of food was likely to fuel the brain to grow larger and thus to get smarter. The level of cooperation between the male hominids was expected to be much higher than those among male chimps. It was unlikely that they would squabble for food after a successful hunting or food gathering. As our ancestors evolved, male members should gradually become more and more united. Their unity has likely been intensified by the increasing extent of the many dangers as they traveled to places in search of food. Because the males in our lineage need to be united to face the increasing level of danger, they can never afford to fight among the members. This factor alone should nullify any theory that claims we had ever been sexually dimorphic. Sexual dimorphism and cooperation between males can never coexist.

The last point was the sharing of information. Though the hominids could not talk to each other, according to the research of Walker, they were very tight social animals and thus had the need to communicate with each other. Their forms of communication would likely include observing how other members solved problems—making tools for example—gesturing, facial expressions, and different utterances. Through communication, each member was able to learn and share more information with others than any other social animals. More information, by definition, makes a person smarter. Cooperation certainly has helped our lineage to be more intelligent all along.

Intelligence Has Also Helped the Continuous Intensifying Cooperation

Has intelligence helped to intensify cooperation? Since all living creatures are selfish and intelligence is primarily for solving survival problems and therefore intrinsically self-serving, therefore one would expect that intelligence would be against cooperation. And that is why most animals decide not to cooperate. However, among humans the answer is surprisingly a "yes" in several ways. First, intelligence, instead of instinct, was the reason why the early humans—possibly from the time they began to venture farther and farther away from their forests in search of food—had chosen to cooperate, to become more united than ever before so that they could better defend themselves against predators. Their cooperation in self-defense was certainly a learned behavior and thus a decision based on intelligence.

Second, intelligence enabled early hominids to invent and improve their tools, which were likely to enhance their ability to find food and thus have a better chance to survive. Their tools often had multipurpose use: as weapons as well as for obtaining food in many ways and getting it in less time. As a result, they had more time for leisure, which would certainly be spent in happiness-seeking activities such as mutual grooming or sex for some. We have argued that both would heighten the cooperation between members.

Third, intelligence had also helped hominids to remember places and times to find certain food or overcome obstacles to get to it. Spending less time in getting food would always give them more leisure time and in bonding.

From the very beginning, our ancestors had been aided by intelligence and cooperation; the two forces that powered the evolution of our species have always been tightly linked. The first that came to help was intelligence; it gave the bipedal chimps their tools and weapons. Then, cooperation enhanced the group's survival by allowing them to better defend themselves, to explore more territories, and to get more and better food. Better nutrients then allowed the hominids to grow stronger bodies and bigger brains, and thereby continued to make the early hominids smarter in problem solving, such as improving their tools and weapons. Better weapons together with stronger bodies made them better food gatherers by improving their efficiency in food gathering, thus giving them more free time for pleasure, meaning more mutual grooming and more sex. The positive feedback cycle continued . . .

It has been like a dance between intelligence and cooperation through time. Intelligence first stepped up, pulling cooperation to a new height. Then, it was cooperation's turn to lift intelligence to yet a higher level. In the many millions of years that followed the appearance of the first crippled chimp, the pair has kept on dancing; each partner has taken turns to hoist the other up, making the hominids smarter and more cooperative, and so increasing their competitive edge along the way.

It is a beautiful picture, isn't it? I could almost hear *Swan Lake* as the pair waltzed along. Then I see dark clouds gathering in the horizon, with flashes of lightning. The darkness is closing in fast. There is a looming ugliness that threatens to stop the dance and destroy our planet. If one could stay sober from the intoxication of the music and not be dazzled by the dance and look at the pair closely, one could perhaps see that someone is pulling the strings. The puppeteer is none other than the grand master named survival. Alas! Both our cooperation and intelligence are powered by self-preservation. How can a dance of two selfish partners be sustained? How do we stop selfishness from halting the dance and destroying all the beautiful things? Or can we ever hope to stop selfishness, the foundation upon which life is built?

Aided by the twosome, our species has kept getting more powerful; the pace of the dance between the pair has not shown any sign of slowing down. Quite the opposite, the pace quickened after *H. sapiens* had acquired spoken language. The invention of written languages for the first time has simultaneously boosted intelligence and cooperation. If you think written language is powerful, it is no more than a horse pulling the pair uphill. The inventions of PCs and the Internet are like rockets that also carry intelligence and cooperation together, sending the twosome to the sky. With PCs and the Internet operating, there appears no limit to our power.

There has never been so much knowledge—math, physics, chemistry, biology, political science, social science, etc., etc.—readily available to everyone through the Internet. The readily available knowledge makes everyone much, much smarter than was possible. Sharing knowledge is one form of cooperation. Language, computers, and the Internet have given us more power than we can truly fathom; they make us gods. In writing and rewriting this book, I become aware of the seemingly limitless knowledge one can get if he has the tool.

With our technology, our intelligence and cooperation together, we are traveling at sonar speed, so is our power. There is a great danger in traveling too fast with godlike power; we can easily lose control and perish. And from the many ominous signs that keep popping up, we are certainly losing control of our power. Many, especially the scientists, see the danger. We are accelerating toward a cliff that has no bottom. Help! Would someone come to help?

Ali Against Tyson

Empowered by the entwined advances of intelligence and cooperation, the early hominids had success beyond the dreams of any animal group. Early hominids defeated wild dogs first; the hyenas, cheetahs, and leopards next; and eventually the lions. They were so good in fighting that they ran out of worthy opponents. It looked like Mother Nature had no more entertainment; her passion to see living organisms fight finally was spoiled. Was it?

How naive! For Mother Nature, the real show had just begun. It will then be humans against humans. It would be better than matching Ali against Tyson at their primes. It was champion against champion, a nonstop show of clashes of the titans.

The record-smashing success of early humans had allowed them to populate most of the African continent. Eventually, their numbers were so great that they kept running into each other. As conflicts kept happening, fighting between humans became more often and deadlier. Humans, despite our unmatched intelligence, were still like other animals. Intelligence had not changed their way in resolving conflicts with their own kind; it only helped them to be deadlier. Like animals, muscle was the only way to settle a conflict. Unlike animals, power was no longer decided only by muscle; instead of sharp claws and massive jaws, it was measured by the levels of their cooperation and intelligence. Thus, hominoids that only groomed but had little recreational sex were likely to be gradually eliminated in wars by those that had more sex. Hominoids that ejaculated quickly were replaced by those that could hold it longer. Soon, bigger penises became a prerequisite to win females. Then, the group again was replaced by groups that had big penises and receptive females. Later, hominid groups in which females had bigger breasts and repositioned vaginas would yield more intelligent and more cooperative fighters. Eventually, any hominid group that came with less than a complete package was soon disqualified. Without exception, the losers were those that were less addicted to sex. Let there be no misunderstanding. Sex has been one of the crucial forces that has carried us here. And many of the "wise" that came eons later thought sex is sinful, dirty, and bad! Talking about ignorant and ungrateful!

The Demise of Lions and Tigers

From what we know, it is likely that humans evolved around 10 million years ago from a crippled chimp. If you like to bet on sports such as horse racing, NBA, or hockey, and if you were around to see the appearance of the handicapped chimp and bet on its future, I don't think you would give it any chance to survive more than a month, forget about making it to adulthood and having children. The fact is after 10 million years (which is not that significant on an evolution scale) the chimp with a malformed pelvis had not only survived, its descendants became the undisputed ruler of the globe and are capable of wiping out any species. Can anyone ever hope to estimate the odds of such success? It would not surprise me (if it could be done) that it would be one of the most improbable events in the cosmos.

How did our ancestors achieve such a phenomenal level of success? A right combination of very lucky mutations at the right times and at the right places would not hurt. But we know mutation occurs in all creatures. What makes humans so special to be able to take advantage of the lucky mutations? Did we get help from an unknown source?

Being blessed with either a rising intelligence or an increasing cooperation would have made a species dominant in the animal kingdom. The ants and bees have cooperation, look at their success. Humans have both from the very beginning. Our intelligence and cooperation are not hard wired, thus allowing us to consciously improve them. It is just not fair for the lions, tigers, hyenas, and wild dogs to be condemned to live side by side with humans. Forced to compete with creatures that had pocketed growing intelligence and heightening cooperation, they were doomed given time. What would your chance be if your enemies are gods?

Fairness is a myth. There has been only one rule from day one. The rule was simple: no right and wrong, no fairness, only the weak and the strong. Weak and strong, if it should be an issue, would be decided in combat. And every kind of weapon and treachery is welcome and encouraged. Fight you will, till death if necessary. This simple rule was all that was required to settle conflicts and disputes. The rule has served Mother Nature well.

After watching the big white, crocs, dinosaurs, tigers, and killer whales, she might have gotten bored of the show where muscle always wins. She asked, "What if . . ." And soon after, a chimp with a distorted pelvis was created. It was meant to be a cruel joke. Over the eons, Mother Nature has carelessly or intentionally created many such unfortunate players to kill the intermissions; most were quickly eliminated, leaving no trace of their brief and tragic existence.

Despite being hugely handicapped, the chimp did continue. Had such a pelvis happened to any other earthly creature, it would have had absolutely no chance of making it through several sunrises and sunsets. But not that chimp; it did not get disqualified right away. This chimp had something going for him that Mother Nature did not see; it had the most resourceful brain and a pair of unemployed hands gained from the tragic event. Better than just passing the test, the chimp proved that he could compete; his kind began to increase. He had also begun to rebel against Mother Nature. He showed Mother Nature that he would not accept what was given to him; he could make up for what he was born missing with his brain and his nimble hands.

Like their cousins, nephews, and nieces, the disadvantaged chimps stuck together and even more. Unlike the common chimps, they increasingly traveled outside the forest to find food. It was a very risky move. As a result, some of them were taken down by lions, cheetahs, hyenas, or wild dogs. To better defend themselves, they learned to stay even closer together than the tree chimps. After many, many generations of using sticks as weapons, the handicapped chimps began to master the tool. Hyenas and wild dogs were first to feel the bite of striking sticks and quickly learned to fear them.

Risk taking had its reward for those smart and cooperating chimps. They not only surprised Mother Nature and survived, they thrived. The stick-carrying chimps unilaterally redefined strength, which had lasted for more than hundreds of million years. Instead of muscle power, pointed teeth, and sharp claws, it became brainpower, cooperation, and tools. The balance began to tip in favor of the bipedal chimps.

Despite their physical weaknesses, humans eventually outcompeted their opponents, which were among the fittest from tens of millions of years of in-combat training. How was that possible? It would have been impossible if the newcomers had played by the old rules, counting on muscle to win. But they did not fight barehanded, they had tools. They did not confront their opponents alone, they ganged up. And most importantly, hominids did not rely on instinct, they exercised intelligence, which gave them flexibility in their actions. Hominids would avoid their enemies if the odds of winning did not favor them, and return to attack when their chances improved. They were as good as Mao Zedong in guerilla warfare against bigger, stronger, and faster enemies.

As if the hominids needed more help in making the already lopsided fights in their favor, they kept getting better. They got smarter with every increase in their brain size. They became more powerful through the amplified levels of cooperation, and deadlier with their ever-improving weaponry. And above all, their knowledge or information database never stopped growing and thereby multiplied their existing advantages. The bad news for other creatures is that our unfair advantages are still compounding with each passing generation.

It had not taken a long time before the reigning kings were dethroned; even the lions learned to flee from the once lowly animals that looked like chimps but could not climb up a tree quickly. *H. erectus,* if not *H. habilis,* regularly defeated lions through cooperation, intelligence, and their spears. Today, we put the once mighty kings—lions, killer whales, tigers, elephants, and polar bears—in zoos or amusement parks for entertainment. Defeated, these pitiful kings have no choice but to accept the humiliation. But that will not be enough for us to spare them. Men, the selfish gods, have not learned how to wield the power wisely; we continue to ravage our environment everywhere we go. Like cancers, we have been ending countless beneficial species, wantonly killing our living planet.

Archeological records indicate that early humans began to migrate out of Africa around 2 million years ago. They were *Homo erectus*. *Homo erectus*, as indicated by fossil records, was quite modern with the exception of perhaps more body hair and a smaller cranial capacity. The tools of these early humans were more elaborate; they had cutting stones, tools made of bones, and above all, wooden spears. *Homo erectus* had also discovered the use of fire and perhaps was able to make a fire whenever they needed it.

If I were to pick a time to be human other than the current period, to be a spear-throwing and fire-using *Homo erectus* would certainly be cool. Why not? There were lots of wild animals for the taking and few competitors. For a change, they could enjoy meat regularly instead of having to depend on other animals to do the killing. And best of all, they could barbecue as much as they wanted. The less fortunate groups of hominids (*Homo habilis?*) that happened to share territories with them were quickly wiped out or assimilated; there was only one species of hominids left—the spear-throwing and barbecuing hominids that uttered fragmented language and loved sex. *Homo erectus* had brought human success to a new height. How successful? So successful that they were forced to migrate out of Africa. The big continent, after only several million years, was getting too crowded. After killing and replacing all their ancestors, they would keep running into one another. No doubt they were, up to then, the most successful and deadliest humans, but that did not mean that they could live happily and peacefully from lacking other enemies. Instead, they faced never-before-seen levels of hazards. To show how difficult and challenging their lives must have been, let me take you back to the intelligence acceleration between *H. erectus*, the modern human (chapter 9). It is 1.02 ml/kg/kg, the second highest in magnitude as compared to the jump between Lucy and *H. habilis*.

Why were their lives so difficult? Because their enemies were often their own kind, the greatest competitors on the then planet. When one group of *H. erectus* bumped into another group, they would not shake hands; they often began to kill the others. This is exactly what a selfish creature would do. To avoid confrontation with their own kind, some groups of *H. erectus* had chosen to get out of the continent altogether. The timing of the great exodus from Africa closely coincided with the appearance of the species. With their superior wits, tight cooperation, and deadly weapons, they conquered wherever they went. Within a very short period, they had spread to almost every part of the Eurasian continent. Some even went as far as Java.

Today, all of our ancestors except the chimps are gone. The common chimps have survived because they lived in trees. With no conflict of interest with hominids, they have been spared. One thing is glaringly clear. As our kind evolved and our power grew, we had always killed our own kind and had left no survivors. Is today any different? What if Hitler and the Japanese had won WWII?

Was *H. erectus* the first group that started emigrating? After watching a program on the Discovery Channel which staged a hypothetical showdown between a lion and a tiger, it occurred to me that our ancestors would have had no chance to evolve in territories ruled by tigers. And tigers have ruled pretty much everywhere in Europe and Asia. Why? Tigers hunt differently than lions. Lions live in groups in grassland; it would be relatively easy to spot a group of lions and avoid them. Tigers are solitary and often hunt among trees by stealth. If a tiger decides to hunt you down, it will patiently stalk you and eventually attack you when you are least prepared. It is no secret that humans are part of a tiger's diet.

I lived in a village in southern China when I was a child. From time to time, I heard stories about tigers taking people away. Our stick-wielding chimps would not have had a chance to evolve in lands patrolled by tigers. Does it make sense? Then, it dawned on me that *H. erectus* might not have been the first group of humans that began the journey out of Africa. The journey could have begun with *H. habilis*. If that was the case, one naturally asks where were those hominids? Why have they left no record outside Africa? I think those stone-throwing and stick-wielding *H. habilis* had become tiger food, likely one at a time until the whole party was consumed.

There could be a number of reasons why *H. erectus* was the first kind of human to successfully settle down in new lands. The invention of spears was one of the most important reasons. Imagine the first encounter between human and tiger. If the humans were *H. habilis,* how could they defend themselves? By using their striking sticks or by throwing stones at the beasts? I don't think they would have had any chance.

Now, what if those humans were *H. erectus?* They had spears, which would allow them to put some needed distance between themselves and an animal that was in every way as strong and powerful as a lion. A spear is a more effective weapon. It can, in experienced hands, fatally wound a tiger. Having a primitive language would likely help them to warn other members, to coordinate an attack or a retreat. And the strong bonds between members of a family would make them defend their loved ones more fiercely. Furthermore, they could make a fire when they needed one, and we know that all animals instinctively fear fire. And what if one of the members had fought a lion before? He would certainly share his experience with the others, would he not?

One more reason. *H. erectus* might have domesticated some canines when they emigrated. They could surely use the service of their four-legged friends. Their dogs would give them warning and therefore gain them some precious time to prepare before a tiger could launch a surprise attack. Some other hominid groups could have ventured out of Africa before *H. erectus,* but they did not stand a chance to survive with tigers around.

CHAPTER 13

The Modern Humans, Masters of Reshaping Nature

Homo erectus, with their wooden spears, broken languages, and the taming of fire, had become the new rulers of the planet, bullying all animals big or small. Successful they surely had been; the heirs of the planet they were not. Like all the other hominids before them, they disappeared from the planet. Bones of *H. erectus* have not been found again since about 130,000 years ago. Perhaps they too, like the other hominids they had replaced, were hunted down, slaughtered, and eventually driven into extinction by groups of smarter and more cooperative modern humans that had evolved from them. We may never know what caused their demise; our bits and pieces of knowledge in archeology have been gained, besides through countless hours of backbreaking and snail-paced digging and cleaning, from gifts granted by Lady Luck.

Where did the modern human come from? Of course we have come from *Homo erectus.* There are two notable views on the rise of modern human from *Homo erectus.* 1) The *African Eve Hypothesis* favors a single common origin in Africa. And 2) The *In-Situ hypothesis* or *multiregionalism* holds that modern humans originated in multiple sites at different times from groups of *Homo erectus* that lived in the various sites. Both the archeological finds and DNA/amino acid sequences between humans from different continents favor the *African Eve Hypothesis,* an origin of modern humans from a group of *Homo erectus* about 200,000 years ago in Africa.

The Nariokotome Boy—Almost Perfect

One would wonder what type of change or changes would be required to make the jump from *H. erectus* to *H. sapiens*. The answer turns out to be not that much, not in terms of the skeletal system anyway. One of the most amazing fossil finds made by a team led by Richard Leakey and Alan Walker in 1985 provided the answer:

> Site: The slopes of Nariokotome sand river, Kenya
> Period of the specimen: About 1.8 million years old
> The specimen: The most complete fossil of *Homo erectus*, which provides the following information:
>> Sex: Male
>> Age: About ten, possibly under thirteen, as indicated by the incomplete emergence of his molar teeth (the find is thus nicknamed the Nariokotome Boy)

What do the bones tell us?

1. A hominid with features very similar to modern human: a tall and slender build, over 5 feet and likely to be more than 6 feet at maturity
2. Long legs compared to early hominids like Lucy, would likely walk and run like modern humans
3. Brain capacity close to 1,000 ml, much smaller than that of modern humans
4. Facial features and smaller molar teeth suggest a softer, high-quality diet that could include substantial amounts of meat
5. From his proportions of skull to pelvis, it would be likely that females of such hominids would give birth to immature infants to allow the baby's head to pass through the pelvic opening (we have discussed that, haven't we?)

For more detailed information about the discovery and the various studies on the specimen, please read *The Wisdom of Bones* by Alan Walker & Pat Shipman.

So the Nariokotome Boy obviously had all the looks of a modern human except a smaller head. Then, the required jump from *H. erectus* to modern human, according to Leakey and Walker's Nariokotome Boy, appears to be just that of the head size. The question will be what had caused the brain size to increase? For the brain to increase about 400 cc, I would think you need at least three factors working together: (1) there was a demand, (2) the hominids could afford it, and (3) some favorable mutations needed to take place.

Was there a demand for the brains of *H. erectus* to increase? Increase in brain size means raised intelligence. A demand in higher level of intelligence can always be equated to the level of difficulty faced by the species and thereby requiring more data-crunching power. The more problems an animal needs to solve, the more its intelligence will accelerate. The greatest intelligence acceleration observed on the road to *H. sapiens* was between Lucy's type and *H. habilis*. The jump between *H. erectus* to *H. sapiens* was second.

In the last chapter, we have speculated that *H. erectus* would likely become the rulers of all animals, the mighty lions included. Having few animals to fear, what then would their problems be? I think the problems of the hominids would simply be from having too many of them. Even the big continent was getting crowded. Their unmatched success also had created overpopulation. How would you compete with a rival who was in every which way as good, as fit, and as competent as you were? You would have a big problem, would you not? It was likely to be the heat of competition and overcrowding which had driven some of them to emigrate. And as long as bipedalism was concerned, the physique of *H. erectus* was as fit as it could get. Then, the only advantage could be gained would have to come from intelligence, wasn't it? So a demand for a bigger brain was certainly there.

(If we can assume that the fierceness of competition would create an urgent demand for higher intelligence attained only by brain growth, then the African Eve Hypothesis will be more attractive. Why? *H. erectus* which lived outside Africa were unlikely to face so much competition from their own kind. They would likely have enjoyed relatively easier lives. Thus, there would be little demand for higher intelligence and a larger brain.)

Could they fuel the brain growth? It is highly likely that *Homo erectus* were successful hunters and would have been eating meat rather regularly, so they could afford the price tag of a bigger brain. An increase in brain size was more likely to happen among those hominids who were already more successful. It would be like the rich getting richer. The demand would certainly be there, and they could afford the price. It then became a matter of waiting for the right mutations to happen. And because mutation happens randomly, it would take many hurtful mutations before the right one appeared. The mutation(s) required to happen would also favor the African Eve Hypothesis. It would be very unlikely that the other regions would have a population size big enough to drive the mutation factor.

Regardless of how modern humans have evolved, Mother Nature had finally given birth to a group of creatures that began to openly disobey, challenge her, and take away her control. The chickens are coming home to roost. By their unmatched brain size, their ever-increasing level of cooperation, and aided by their evermore complex tools and inventions, humans have been more and more successful at reworking the rules of the survival game in their favor. Over the past billions of years of natural history on the planet, never has there been any organism which out of its free will tells Mother Nature straight in her face: "I don't like what you have given me, and I am going to change it." Humans, with their supreme intelligence, was the first group of animals to understand that they didn't always have to accept what Mother Nature had given them.

The very first handicapped chimp had started a trend to mess around with Mother Nature's plan. The luckless chimp, according to our story, was supposed to die because it would not be able to compete for food and gals; it invented a tool—a striking stick—and had outcompeted its contemporaries. Though many animals—even some of the supposedly stupid birds—use tools occasionally, none have ever so willfully tried and so extensively reshaped the materials to suit their needs as humans have. The branches did not always come in convenient size, shape, or length. The handicapped chimp reshaped them by eliminating the unwanted branches, and often shortening them to get a stick that pleased the maker.

When we look at human evolution, we can either look at the process as changes in body shape and size, or as a continuous exercise of reshaping nature to suit their needs. It began with the reshaping a fallen branch. Eons later, some pieces of stones were tampered with, and then different kinds of materials such as bones, branches, and stones were reworked and combined to form something desirable. Bit by bit, the scope of human meddling with Mother Nature's designs kept on growing with the passing of time, and thereby incrementally giving them more control and power over nature and other animals. By the time *H. erectus* appeared, they had replaced the lions and tigers to become the new rulers of the planet, and there was very little the Mother and those toppled rulers could do to stop them.

Reshaping things to become tools had handsomely rewarded the hominids. Hominids had become increasingly addicted to the practice. They kept expanding the variety of things they could work on. Then, modern humans began to manipulate living organisms to serve them. This was about 100,000 years ago. They first began to manipulate plants and then animals, and direct them for their service or consumption. Without doubt, the domestication of plants, which eventually has evolved into full-scale farming, has been one of the very few events that has tremendously helped to shape human evolution. Farming has completely changed the lifestyle of early humans from nomadic to sedentary, and from creatures with no more than a handful of simple possessions to people that began to own items like homes, animals of labor, pots and pans, TVs, cars, and cell phones, and rockets . . .

Global Warming—A Welcome Relief

How did farming begin? Who were the first farmers, and what did they grow first? What had motivated them to farm?

Before we try to answer the above questions, it would help to get some background information on the timing which had marked the beginning of farming. Most interestingly, farming began in very different parts of the world independently and at a relatively narrow strip of geological time. The first farming community began approximately 8500 BC in the Fertile Crescent, part of which is modern-day Iraq. In China, it began in a region of the Yellow River roughly around 7500 BC. And it was 3500 B.C. in the Americas—Mesoamerica, Andes, and Amazonia. Was it accidental that farming all began at roughly the same time? Or was there a common driving force?

It seems no accident that farming began independently in vastly different geographic areas within a relatively narrow geological period of 5000 years. And the common driving force was likely to be the latest trend of global warming. While global warming is a very frightening thing nowadays, it was a blessing once upon a time. Let me explain.

The global temperature has never been stable. It has been fluctuating as far back as we can tell, dating back to the past 70 million years, according to some pretty reliable scientific findings. The evidence has come from the varied ratios of oxygen isotopes in the carbonate of the shells of some marine animals that once lived on the ocean floor of the Caribbean. The ratio of oxygen isotopes changes with temperature of the ocean, and each ratio represents a different temperature reading.

This is how scientists found out the temperatures of the past. Scientists first drilled some parts of the ocean floor in the Caribbean to obtain samples which contained layers of sediments. Each layer was then assigned a geological time according to its position. And finally, the ratio of oxygen isotopes in each layer was determined to get a temperature it represents. From the oxygen isotopes method, it has been found that global weather has come in cycles of 100,000, 40,000, and 20,000 years, possibly coinciding with the activities of our sun. One of such cycles began approximately 195,000 years ago, which happened shortly after the emergence of *Homo sapiens*. The cycle began with the planet's temperature taking a dive and zigzagging its way down to hit the lowest point around 130,000 years ago. Life should have been very rough for our ancestors, the early modern humans. One would expect to find several fur coats in every cave.

The last Great Ice Age which happened about 20,000 years ago was the coldest time from a cooling cycle that began eighty thousand years ago. After the deep freeze, the global temperature began to climb sharply. We are, if the past records are any indication, likely to be amid a warming trend which may last for tens of thousands of years. Just this alone will raise the global temperature. Anyone who bets on the current global warming to continue will be like putting his money on Nadal winning on a clay court.

Warmer weather had resulted in more rainfall, which together with the raised temperature allowed more vegetation growth, and the population of wildlife jumped accordingly. The cornucopia of food had given modern humans more leisure time and allowed them to settle down. At the time, humans had certainly reached the current level of brain capacity. It was highly likely that they had long acquired fully developed languages, making exchange of fine ideas possible, heightening their cooperation to a new height, and inevitably leading to the discovery farming. But how? There are a number of theories and hypothesis on the origin of farming. For a thorough and rigorous academic treatment of the subject, I would recommend Jared Diamond's *Guns, Germs, And*

Steel. (Diamond, if you remember, is the guy from whom I learned that humans have the biggest penis among primates. It has been one of the most illuminating, as well as feel-good learning experiences for me.)

As always, I am not fully satisfied with any of those hypothesis and theories. In the following, I shall once again draw on my imagination to provide a way in which farming could have first started in the Fertile Crescent, China, or any of the agriculture centers. Let us say it had happened in the Fertile Crescent. Again, I am not a scholar or an academic person. Treat it as a fairytale. And please be extremely careful in quoting me; it could make people laugh.

The Fertile Crescent is roughly a semicircular area of land that includes Mesopotamia to the east, which also contains Euphrates and Tigris rivers. The central part of the Crescent borders the Mediterranean Sea, with its southwestern arm formed by Upper and Lower Egypt, which contains the Nile. At the time farming began, it supported a wide variety of plant species such as wheat, barleys, peas, muskmelon, as well as wild animals like goats, sheep, cattle that were suitable for domestication. The world's first farming community began in the Fertile Crescent about 10,000 years ago.

At the time, our ancestors were hunter-gatherers. They were likely to be quite happy. They might not be Adams and Eves, but they lived literally in paradise. Why? After thousands of years of a gradual increase in temperature, the area should have one of the most luscious vegetation as well as large herds of grazing animals which took advantage of the outburst of plant growths. With their wooden spears, the abundance of wildlife around, the biggest brains ever, and a fully developed language that made communication easier, hunting and killing animals of their choice should have been uncomplicated and almost effortless. Even in a not-so-good day, the sun would still be high when a hunting party would return home with their kills. And it would be unlikely that they needed to travel far from their hunting grounds either. It would certainly be like living in paradise.

Although we call them hunter-gatherers, the modern human at the dawn of farming had almost certainly divided hunting from food gathering for a long, long time. Men, being stronger and able to run faster, would hunt exclusively. Women, being more patient and having to take care for their children, would certainly be responsible for gathering fruits and edible plant parts.

The two jobs required different physiques and temperaments. Hunting is physically demanding; a hunter must be strong, fit, able to run fast, willing to take risks and face danger. All of which suit the disposition of men. Because of the many possible dangers, taking women and children to hunt would not be wise. Food gathering, on the other hand, could be done at a much slower pace and could be interrupted from time to time, making it easier for the gatherers to look after their children while gathering. If hunting could be compared to a 100-meter sprint, then food gathering would be like a marathon. It would not be viable for the hunter-gatherers to do both jobs together as one unit. The division of labor would work very well.

It was bound to happen either when the women gatherers were able to protect themselves with their sticks, or there would not be much danger for the women to venture out together with their children. With the great number of plants to choose from and a variety of fruits available in different seasons, it would not take much time before a food-gathering party would get more than enough for the day or even the coming days. The mothers would always bring the children along, using the field trips to teach the youngsters the knowledge they had accumulated over generations. The following could be some likely scenarios.

"Yes, this is good. See the red color, love? That's the best time to pick them."
"No, this type will give you a stomachache. Stay away, sweetie."
Or, "Now, let us dig up this plant. We shall find the best tasting part at this time of the year. Remember the way the leaves look, honey?"

With such a perfect lifestyle, why would anyone bother to farm? Any farmer in a third-world country would tell you that you don't do it for fun. It would definitely be a backbreaking way to make a living for those first farmers who did not have any machinery to help them. I spent several early years with my mother in a village in Guangdong, a province in southern China. My mother did all the farming in the family; she took care of the rice field, grew sweet potatoes, fed the chickens twice a day, and looked after my sister and me. She rose at dawn, got to the field to work when the sun was hardly up, and returned home just before dusk. So why did the early modern humans give up a relatively easy and far more exciting lifestyle of hunting-gathering in favor of fun-less, backbreaking, and extremely demanding farming? I am quite sure choosing to work hard will not be a human character, certainly not mine.

Were they stupid? Well, they had attained a brain size similar to ours, they could not have been so dumb. And I believe that laziness, if it does not hurt you, is more a virtue than a vice, and a crucial attribute for survival. It helped to conserve energy as well as to limit your exposure to predators. Then, were they so smart as to see the advantage of farming at the time? I would not think so either. Given that farming had never before existed, how could our ancestors possibly dream of such a thing, let alone see its potential and want to do it? Even if they could see the future with some kind of crystal ball, could they afford to do it? Remember hunter-gatherers did not have fridges; their food reserve at best would not be for more than several days. They could not possibly afford to give up their regular jobs and suddenly take up farming. We all know that medical doctors and lawyers make shitloads of money, and assuming you can handle the academics, how many people can afford to pursue the lucrative careers if you have children to feed and a car loan and mortgage to pay? Any crazy hunter-gatherer who dared to try would soon be starved to death. So *farming cannot be a conscious, practical, or sensible choice*, according to Diamond. And I agree with him 100 percent. If farming was not by choice, then it had to have happened accidentally, or came as a byproduct of another activity, like the intensified cooperation arising from sex addiction.

How did farming get started inadvertently? In the following I would, through daydreaming again, come up with a story in the way farming could have been started. If you think the story on the invention of sticks or the evolution of intelligence is far-fetched, wait until you read the story. (No, I was not smoking pot! I just happen to have a very vivid imagination, a logical mind, plus some science knowledge.)

A Story of the First Gardener

The first farmer, or more correctly the first gardener, was likely to begin tending some plants as a rewarding hobby. We all know that people, like animals, do things for one simple reason: the activity is pleasurable, or they do it to seek happiness because the activity makes them happy. Let the story begin.

Fielda the First Gardener
Time: Once upon a time, roughly 10,000 years ago.

Location: Somewhere in the highlands along the Tigris River.

Setting: A small village consisting of some closely built round houses on a small stretch of level space along a hillside and next to a natural spring. The houses had short stonewalls and conical roofs made of small bundles of reeds and dried grass. In front of the houses was an open courtyard where adults and children socialized and played.

The courtyard was marked by a crude semicircular short stonewall of similar style to the house. Leading from the courtyard outward was a small trail created by foot traffic. The trail followed the gentle slope of the hill and led to a big freshwater lake, which was surrounded by layers and layers of hills and mountains. There were several small villages dotting the shores of the lake. The far end of the lake was a part where no villager had ever traveled. It led to a world the people there had absolutely no knowledge of.

It was midsummer and the weather was hot and dry. The landscape surrounding the village was shades of brown and yellow as the tall grass on the higher ground began to dry up from lacking moisture. Scattered along the hillside that surrounded the lake were some olive trees. There were small groups of wild goats, sheep, and gazelles busily grazing among the golden vegetation.

The sun was several olive trees high on the horizon; it was late morning. The village was quiet. It appeared that all the inhabitants had left their homes in search of food. The men had gone out in small groups quite early; some of them headed for the lake to catch fish, while some went hunting. The women also left later together with their children. Each woman carried a sack made of animal skin to keep the gathered food in. The sacks were practical and fashioned differently, reflecting the artistic tastes of their makers.

The village looked empty. Then, the laughter of a child broke the silence; the sweet, happy sound had come from the side of a house next to the village's spring, which had been losing its vigor since the dry season began. The villagers loved the spring all the same. It was a source of their happiness and many blessings. After emerging from the rocks, the spring gave birth to a tiny waterway that meandered along the slope and reached the lake. Along its journey to the lake, the "rivulet" encouraged an enthusiastic growth of vegetation, which starkly contrasted the surrounding wilting grass. But the vibrancy of the vegetation could hardly match the sprawling vine that had almost taken up all the space between the house and the spring. At the time, an elderly woman was quite busy working among the rich dark green leaves of the vine. A naked small child about a couple of years old was fully occupied chasing a small white butterfly several steps away.

"Be careful, Kida sweetie. Don't run too fast," the woman said to the boy who was trying to catch the tricky flying bug rather than watching his steps. The woman was half naked and wore a piece of worn-out skin from her waist down; the skin served more to cover her lower body than for warmth. It had been a custom of the villagers—young girls particularly—to cover that part of the body to avoid evil spirits. From the look of her limp and wilted breasts, the woman had lost her fecundity for many years; she was not the child's mother. She was crouching on the ground and attentively checking the vine. From time to time, she parted some leaves to peek at what lay beneath the dense greens; she often smiled as she was doing it. There were several melons at various stages of ripening. And from the color of a couple of the melons, they would be ready soon.

The old woman's name was Fielda. She was the oldest person in the village. She came to the village to live with her two "husbands," who were brothers, when she was very young. Over the years, she had produced more than a handful of children, and out of whom three sons and a daughter had survived. Both of her "husbands" had passed away long before the grandson was born. She had been living in the same house since she came to the village. At the time, she was living with her three sons, the sons' two "wives," and the only grandson.

Fielda had not joined the young women to gather food for a number of years. She dropped out rather abruptly and mostly against her wish. One morning, Fielda woke up with a piercing pain in one of her hip joints, which had nearly rendered her immobile; she stayed home that day. When the pain eventually went away—after many sleepless nights and days living with a throbbing pain—she could no longer walk the same way. The ailment had greatly slowed her down; she was no longer able to keep up with the other girls. Since then, the old matriarch had been staying home. Her first grandson Kida was born the next year. She naturally helped to take care of the baby; the young and inexperienced mother was more than happy to accept her help. After Kida was weaned, he stayed home with the granny when the mother went to work. It was a happy arrangement for every party—the young mom, the child, and the grandma.

Looking after Kida was an easy and rewarding job for Fielda. The child got the granny's undivided attention and love; she got a satisfying and rewarding job. Fielda loved to work; she felt useful and wanted again looking after Kida. As if she would need more reasons to be happy, she got herself another job, she became a part-time gardener tending the vine that had occupied the space next to the spring during the previous summer. Looking after the vine was far less demanding than taking care of Kida. It was almost as rewarding. How did Fielda become a gardener? Fielda had picked up the pastime rather innocently.

***

A couple of years earlier in one early afternoon of the late summer, the girls returned home from a food-gathering outing. One of Fielda's daughters-in-law, named Shemmie, had, among the many items, a round fruit which was about the size of her grandson's head. Fielda had never seen the fruit before. The fruit was yellowish, had a rough and heavily netted skin, and a musky smell. Shemmie was the one who found the fruit; she had once tasted the fruit long before she came to live with the family. Shemmie recognized the fruit by its unusual skin; she remembered how good it tasted.

A bit later, the men also returned; they brought home a turtle, some shellfish, and several palm-sized fish. The girls could not wait to show their men the fruit. Shemmie was particularly vocal, gesturing to her men with great fervor on how she found it and how good it would taste.

One of the men—a tall, dark, and muscular person in his prime—took out his "knife," which was a slender piece of bone about the length of a hand, with sharp cutting edges on both sides, and cut open the fruit. The fruit's unique fragrance exploded to fill the little room. It had a pinkish-orange flesh and countless tiny whitish inclusions. Everyone cheered. The man divided the fruit into pieces so that everyone got at least one; Fielda got the largest piece. It did not take long before the fruit was completely consumed.

The open space between the spring and Fielda's house was damp all year round. With plentiful sunlight, vegetation growth in the little area would have been fierce even without a steady deposit of fertilizers by the youngsters from using the space as a latrine. Since retiring from food gathering, Fielda had taken up the job to rid the area of the ever-encroaching weeds, some of which would somehow manage to sneak into the living space of the house.

It was late spring when Fielda decided to keep the intruding plants in check. The girls had been complaining about crawlies getting into the house because of the invading flora that occupied the area. Fielda had not been well and had not paid much attention to the spot. She could hardly recognize the space when she got there; the weeds had grown almost as tall as she was during her lengthy absence. Among the weeds, a strange new plant caught Fielda's attention almost right away. It was a vine that was not found in her neighborhood. Fielda did not even have to look closely to tell the newcomer apart from the regulars because it was so different. It had big dark-green leaves, a prostrate stem, and above all, some showy yellow flowers, which had attracted a number of bugs hovering around the area.

For a short while, Fielda could not decide whether or not to pull up the stranger plant. It would require a lot of work. She chose to first get rid of the other weeds around the house. Then, Fielda noticed a fruit about twice the size of an olive along the vine. She looked at the fruit closely. The fruit was green, indicating that it was far from ready for picking; Fielda had a lot of knowledge about plants from her many years of food gathering. The prospect of fruits had tipped the balance in favor of keeping the vine. Having decided, Fielda proceeded to clear up the area and left the vine alone.

A number of days went by before Fielda went back to the area again. By then, the vine had borne many more bright yellow flowers and had taken up all the open space; it had also begun to cover a corner of the roof of the family's house with its leaves. The vine had made her job much easier by preventing the proliferation of weeds in the area. Fielda was delighted. Then, she remembered the bigger-than-an-olive fruit and decided to look for it. Where was it? Fielda could hardly remember; she had come across the fruit most unexpectedly many days earlier. With Kida having a nap, she had a lot of time to spare. She proceeded to find it. As an experienced food gatherer, she knew it would not be hard to do.

After surveying the surface and finding nothing, Fielda began to look under the leaves. She carefully parted the dense foliage systematically and peeked through the opening, starting from the edge. "Oohvah!" Fielda exclaimed in joy. She had barely parted many leaves aside when a fruit almost the size of her fist popped up from nowhere. Fielda looked at the fruit closely. She could hardly contain her excitement because the fruit, though smaller and still green, had the markings and look of the most delicious and exotic fruit she had ever tasted the summer before. Fielda remembered the fruit well; she had even dreamed about eating it a couple of times. Again, her experience told her the fruit was not yet ready.

Thrilled with the unexpected find, Fielda became eager to spend more time with the new plant and studied the plant with a renewed interest. It was not just any other plant; it was none other than the one that would produce the tastiest fruits. To be more comfortable, she dropped her knees to the ground and began to examine the plant with undivided attention. She turned over some leaves, felt the leaf surface gently, and looked at the small threadlike things that wrapped around other plants. As she followed the vine, Fielda also did some weeding. As a mother of several children, taking care of things was her second nature. And looking after the plant which delighted her had come easily and naturally.

Having examined some leaves and the vine, Fielda then switched her attention to the many bright yellow flowers. At first, Fielda looked at the brightest and the most beautiful ones. Her interest, however, was soon captured by the wilted and wilting few. After she had examined a number of them, especially those most wilted, it had become increasingly clear to Fielda that it was the flowers that had produced the fruits. At the bottom of each wilted flower was a very tiny fruit! She did not need a biology professor to show her the point. Her broad knowledge on plants had helped her to make the connection. There were a number of fruits at various stages of formation, and most of the young fruits still had what undoubtedly were the remains of the once colorful blooms. Fielda had never been so happy and satisfied. It was a totally new kind of happiness; it lasted much longer than eating meat, holding her grandson, or seeing her sons bringing home killed animals. Fielda could not wait to share the discovery with every member of the family, Shemmie in particular.

As soon as the food gatherers returned, Fielda, instead of eagerly emptying the sacks to check what was inside, got hold of Shemmie and dragged her to the vine, which was by then also quite familiar to Shemmie. The old woman began to show Shemmie flower by flower what she had learned, highlighting the flower-and-fruit connection. Shemmie was both astounded and delighted with the knowledge. Fielda was particularly proud to find out that her smart and knowledgeable daughter-in-law had known next to nothing about fruit formation. It was one of nature's biggest secrets that Fielda had discovered. The discovery brought great joy and satisfaction to both women. From that day on, Shemmie would habitually look for fruits when she came across flowers. And the practice served her well. Shemmie, as years went by, became the most prolific gatherer in the area.

It had been many, many days since Fielda had discovered the new plant and the flower-to-fruit secret. Getting up in the morning had been much easier for her. Her eagerness to find out what had happened to the fruits during her absence had greatly eased her pain. Each morning, she would first visit the vine, check the fruits, and look at the wilting flowers. She was one happy old woman. Each and every fruit had kept growing bigger, and there would be many more coming as the vine kept producing flowers. With each passing day, a couple of the fruits began to look more like the one her daughter-in-law had brought back. Fielda had tried hard to resist the urge to pick the fruits prematurely. She also had kept Shemmie updated.

Then, the day had come. Fielda had been focusing on the first melon she first discovered for several days. She had many times resisted picking it against her urge. It was dawn when Fielda woke up; she got up right away. With the help of her walking stick, she headed immediately for the vine. She was limping and could be in some discomfort, but one would not know it from her quickened pace; her mind was totally occupied with anticipation. Fielda could smell the fruits even before she got to the vine. The air was still; the musky fragrance got stronger with each of her limping steps forward. It was surprising to see how an old woman could hobble along so fast. Once again, Fielda held the fruit in her hands. Just as she was trying to lift the fruit gently to smell it, it dropped onto her hands. Fielda yelled and shouted in great joy; she freely let the long-imprisoned emotion out. The moment marked the realization of a long buildup.

A great commotion took over the living quarters. First Kida began to cry, then Fielda's eldest son came dashing out with his spear and hurried to the matriarch. Fielda's celebration had woken everybody up. Soon, everyone gathered around the matriarch, who was holding the fragrant melon with tears of joy. She passed the melon first to Shemmie and from Shemmie to the husbands. Each member then took turns to feel and smell the fruit. Naturally, Kida had his turn. The family had the most delicious fruit for breakfast that morning. Everyone agreed that it tasted far better than the one Shemmie got. It was not to take credit away from the young woman; rather, it was something homegrown and the first in human history—though they would not have known it! The family got many more of the exotic fruits from the wonderful vine. At the peak, the vine had produced so many melons that the family could hardly keep up with the supply. After a few had gone moldy, Fielda gave some away.

***

Fielda had been waiting for the return of warmer weather since the day her favorite vine dried up last year. It broke her heart as the weather became colder and colder, and as she helplessly watched the leaves of her loved plant turn moldy, yellow, and eventually die *en masse*, leaving many of the young fruits wasted. The sun had finally begun its return journey; the days were getting longer and warmer. Then, it was spring again for sure because weeds around the house began to grow rapidly. Fielda was hoping that spring would revive her withered vine like it had given life back to so many dead vegetation. But it was not to be; instead, the vine had rotted completely.

Fielda had not lost her hope; she would visit the space once occupied by her loved vine each day. Once in a while, she would get rid of the weeds in the area just in case her plant would somehow find its way back. After taking care of the vine last season, Fielda had learned that getting rid of the weeds, besides making it easier to spot the fruits, would in some way encourage her plant to grow better. It could also be a way she expressed her feeling to the dead vine to which she had become attached. For whatever reason, she had a need to work the area; it had become a habit.

Then, it happened one morning. As Fielda was pulling up some weeds near the edge of the house, something caught her eyes. She had uncovered a patch of new plants that had been shielded from her sight. The plants were still quite short and tiny; they had emerged from the earth not long ago. What really stunned her was that the biggest plant bore two small leaves that looked amazingly like the leaves of her beloved vine. After tending the vine for more than a season last year, Fielda knew every little thing about the plant. She looked more closely and was convinced that those were the same kind of leaves. A great joy filled Fielda; the new plants had revitalized the old woman and swept away all the gloom in her heart. Her loved plant did, after all, find its way back home.

Encouraged and energized, Fielda began to study the new growth carefully; she found other clues which suggested that the new growth was certainly the same as her dead vine. Amidst the new growth, there were a number of tiny white and roundish objects with pointed ends. Fielda remembered those tiny objects very well; they looked the same as those found inside the melon. Fielda spit them out while Kida and her children swallowed them. "Yes. You must be my beloved vine. You have finally found your way home! You know how much I missed you." Fielda was talking gently to the plants, and felt the new growth with her fingers tenderly.

Everybody in the family noticed the sudden swing in the matriarch's mood. She smiled most of the time and began to hang around the space where the new growth was. Again, she found it much easier to get up in the morning, and making her way to the space was no longer a struggle. It was a new experience for her; it was as if those were her children. Sometimes, even Fielda would get confused whether she cared more about her grandson or the vine that had returned from a long absence. They were so small and fragile; watching them was like watching her children, except the children could never grow as fast as those green little things. To Fielda, looking after the young growth was as joyful as caring for her grandson and far less demanding. Fielda loved both of them as much.

The new vines never stopped surprising Fielda. And the one new thing Fielda had discovered was exceedingly interesting, heartwarming, and fulfilling. On the day Fielda discovered the new patch, she spent a lot of time examining the new plants. She picked up some of the small whitish objects to examine them. After feeling them between her fingers and then studying them up close, she found they were empty and the pointed ends were open. Fielda could not make much out of the empty shells and soon forgot about them. Then, a number of mornings after, Fielda spotted something in the area. Right away it held her attention. A few small plants had apparently just come out from the earth during the night before. What had made the plants so unusual was that a couple of them had their "heads" still partially wrapped inside the tiny whitish object. The picture right away reminded Fielda of the birth of a baby. Fielda had given birth to a number of children and had assisted in quite a few childbirths; the sight of a young plant about to come out from the ivory-colored envelope was shockingly similar to the birth of a child. She instinctively knew that she had witnessed the birth of one of her favorite plants! She suddenly connected. Fielda had learned another biggest secret of nature; she had found out that her favorite plant had come from the tiny, hard, whitish thing! *Eureka!* (Funny how people would express the same joy in the same way. Eons later, Archimedes would utter the same word after discovering buoyancy equals the weight of the water displaced.)

Like never before, Fielda was very anxious to tell the other girls about the secret she found. As soon as Fielda spotted the gatherers returning, she waved and yelled at Shemmie, prompting her to hurry up. Shemmie did not get back to the house to unload her sack; she was grabbed by the matriarch and led to the side of the house where the new patch of growing green was. Fielda was trying to explain to Shemmie what she saw, but there was no need for words, because the young woman also made the association quickly. The two looked at each other in disbelief. They hugged each other for a long, long time, again sharing the happiness and joy in the discovery and the knowledge.

***

Fielda became a gardener each year from midspring to late summer. She loved to take care of the plants that had never failed to abundantly yield the exotic melons. With each passing growing season, she had learned more about her plant. Kida had joined the other men to hunt a while ago. Fielda, besides looking after her other grandsons, continued to care for her vine. With the help of Kida and other family members, she had enlarged her garden and grew many more vines. And the vine had repaid the gardener generously. The family could no longer keep up with eating so many of the melons during the peak season. They gave away many of the exotic fruits to neighbors and relatives.

Fielda always passed her knowledge to Shemmie, who was as enthusiastic about the vine as the matriarch. After Fielda passed away—not before she had lived many, many happy growing seasons, and given away a countless number of the delicious melons—Shemmie became the gardener in Fielda's place. Shemmie also passed her knowledge to other women in the family; they too became happy and willing gardeners when they could afford the time.

Generations went by, and when it got to Kida's great-great-great-grandchildren, the number of villages in the lake area had multiplied and Fielda's village had long since been replaced by larger and better houses. The villagers not only kept up with the tradition of growing the productive vine, some had learned to grow other plants too. The new crops that they grew had gradually been expanded from the muskmelon to include peas and then wheat and barley. And like Fielda who had started the trend, it was always women that spent time looking after the crops. The men remained hunters for many, many generations after their women had begun growing. But unlike the men, the women had stopped going to the field to collect food. They did not need to, for they could grow all they needed and more at home.

The end.

How Was Farming Started?

The story is fake. However, I am absolutely sure that farming did not and could never have existed prior to many people having begun to grow plants (at a small scale) over many years. Farming requires a body of knowledge about plant growth which could only be acquired and accumulated by many people doing it for a while before it could be viable. Given that humans had never grown any plant before, the questions become how was the trend started? Why did the first grower do it? Who was the first grower? And at what stage did farming become a regular practice? Let us answer those questions in sequence.

How was the trend started? Since growing plants for any purpose had never existed, it had to be an accidental discovery instead of the result of a purposeful search. Does it make sense? There could be hundreds of ways the discovery could be stumbled upon. Our story is only one of the many possibilities. It was discovered accidentally by someone because growing the first plant was so much fun.

Why did the first grower do it? The answer is simple. Like everything a person, an animal, or an organism does, it has to be survival related, and therefore for happiness seeking. Our central character Fielda, in growing a vine, got plenty of the exotic melons. The vine, a melon plant, was very easy to look after. Once the plant got established, Fielda did not even need to clear the weeds because it was a fast grower. It would outcompete the weeds. The vine also kept on yielding its many secrets—the flower-and-fruit connection and the birth of a plant from a seed—to Fielda and thereby made her very happy. There were plenty of other rewards too—the praises and gratitude of her family and neighbors. Growing the plant let her feel great to be able to contribute again. Fielda had gradually become addicted to the new hobby. The never-ending rewards for a chore that did not require too much hard work were the reasons she kept doing it season after season.

Who was the first grower? First, let us decide the gender. Was the first grower or gardener a man or a woman? I am almost sure that the first grower had to be a woman. Several reasons point to the choice. The physique and temperament of a man would be suited to hunting. Hunting was exciting, glamorous, and prestigious. Given a choice, no capable male would spend lots of time in gardening in ancient times. Growing things did not require great physical strength. Rather, it required patience, attention to detail, and endurance, and it was not prestigious. Only the temperament of a woman could satisfy those requirements. Another important point that favored a female discoverer was, to be able to discover something, one needed a certain amount of knowledge in the thing to be discovered. It was hardly an accident that the Frenchman Jean-François Champollion was the first one to crack the secrets of hieroglyphics. Would a man or a woman know more about plants at the time? Women, because they were career gatherers of plant products for food, would naturally possess more knowledge on plants than men.

Then, the question becomes what type of woman? A busy woman that had to go out to gather food every day, or someone who was capable of gardening and had to stay home for some reason? A crippled old woman would nicely fit the job description. Despite her disability, she would have no difficulty in getting accepted by her family; she would have the needed leisure time. A disabled old man, even if he were knowledgeable in plant matters—a far-fetched assumption—would not be allowed to stay in a prehistoric family. It was true in great antiquity, it is still true in modern societies. That is why yours truly has been very conscientious to be independent.

Everything considered, farming can only be a viable practice after many years of gardening by many people. Gardening was likely an accidental discovery by a woman, and the discoverer was mostly likely to be a retired old woman who picked it up as a hobby because it made her happy and was very rewarding.

Our last question will be how did gardening evolve into farming? To see how farming could have evolved from gardening, let us get back to our fictitious story. It would be unavoidable that the switch would eventually take place. After Fielda had cultivated the muskmelon for several seasons, the villagers and the food gatherers, Shemmie in particular, would begin to see the advantage of cultivating over gathering. With a minimal initial investment in getting the plant started and some occasional tending, the plant began to yield a return. First, it produced one or two muskmelons and paused; then, it would give abundantly, often producing more muskmelons than the family could consume before they rotted. Sooner or later, someone would realize that Fielda, by staying home and looking after several vines which occupied a small amount of space and very little of her time, would bring home more food than the combined effort of all the women in the family during the peak of a growing season. They had to be complete morons not to see such a simple fact!

As a result, when the weather was suitable, more and more women, even the capable ones, would choose cultivation over gathering, which could still be dangerous during those ancient times—wild animals, treacherous terrains, and males from other tribes, etc. As more and more people picked up the practice, it would be natural for someone to start growing other varieties of crops and learn more about plants. From the first gardener, they had learned to grow a crop from seeds. When people started growing seeds, instead of fruits for food—wheat, barley, and oats were plentiful in the area—they could store the excess to last them until the next harvest. Then, for the first time in human history, our species will be forever freed from the day-to-day worry of getting enough to fill up our stomachs.

Farming, the Then Most Massive Manipulation of Nature

The *"I don't like what you have given me, and I am going to change it"* mentality of early humans was the source of discontent that had led to their interference with, and rebellion against, Mother Nature. Though the scope had been limited and small—some branches, pieces of animal parts, or stones—when it began, the interferences had brought them great results. For millions of years, their interferences had often been in creating more deadly weapons for self-defense. As a result, they eventually became king of all animals. Farming was a huge leap in human meddling with nature; it was much, much more massive. Instead of changing bits and pieces of dead materials, humans began to change the lives of many, many living organisms. Acres and acres of native vegetation, together with their animals—insects, rodents, snakes, and birds—were eliminated or evicted to allow the cultivation of a single species of plant that served the farmers' need. Instead of depending on nature to provide, the early farmers created their own food source.

From that stage on, Mother Nature was no longer the only power that dictated the life and death of living organisms; early farmers took some of that power away. If deciding life and death is the province of God, then the early farmers got the first taste of what it was like to be God. It was something which proved to be extremely addictive. Though the scope was still small and limited at the beginning from a global perspective, it was only the infancy of a long, long trend to come.

The early farmers quickly learned the benefits of farming. Farming, like the wave created at the middle of a pond, continued to spread to more communities and areas. The continuous growth of farming led to many, many changes which kept giving our species more and more power. Because of our selfish nature and lack of moral sense, our power has allowed us to be even more hurtful to other species, and often, to our own kind. Our power to ravage the planet kept growing with every new success. Farming was also a launching pad for more and more intrusions to come. In farming, we began with the domestication of plants; the next stage would be animals—naturally.

Domestication of Animals

After mankind began farming for many, many generations, there would come a time when the early farmers found that they had less and less meat on their tables. The reason was easy to see. With the ever-expanding population (a point to be discussed in greater detail later) and everybody getting meat from Mother Nature, sooner or later there would not be enough grazing animals to go around. Humans were not Mother Nature's only customers; lions, tigers, and hyenas needed meat too.

Farmers depleted their source of meat in two ways: (1) they took grazing land away from animals, and (2) they kept killing them for food or to protect their crops, both of which would cut down the wildlife population. So the early farming communities were increasingly pressed with the issue: "How can we secure enough meat to keep our families happy?" It was a problem that needed to be solved. Most people crave meat after not having it for a couple of days. I grew up in a farming village. My family—my mother, sister, and me—could not afford to have meat regularly; few farmers in our area could. Luckily, there were a number of festivals in a year. To celebrate each festival, Mother would kill a chicken or buy some pork, and we would reacquaint ourselves with the wonderful taste of meat. Above all, I loved chicken! I remember praying to a deity to bless me with the good fortune of having chicken every day when I grow up. Now, I have chicken almost every day—a classic case of be careful what you wish for.

The situation of the early farmers would be much worse than that of my family. After supper and before they went to bed, an elder would often tell stories about the good old days when they had meat more often, when there were still quite a few goats and wild boars to hunt. "How wonderfully delicious barbecued game pork had tasted." The storyteller would shake his head and sigh, dearly missing those bygone days. Sooner or later someone would begin to ask, "Is there another way of getting meat other than from the wild?" And by asking the question more often, someone would begin to look for a solution. Before they popped that very question, the early farmers would still pin their hopes on Mother Nature; they were passive. By asking the question enough times, someone would inevitably propose, "Why don't we grow the meat ourselves?"

To solve a problem, the first step is often asking the right question. *"Why don't we grow the meat ourselves?"* It would be the question to help them to focus their attention on the possibility of growing some meat instead of hunting it. It boils down to whether the early farmers had the knowledge to pose the question. The answer would be the early farmers were certainly knowledgeable enough to ask the question. After discovering farming, early farmers knew that they did not always have to depend on Mother Nature to provide; they could grow what they could not find in the wilderness. They had been growing plants for food for centuries, if not millennia. But growing plants and growing animals are totally different matters. Just because you are a good tennis player does not mean that you will automatically be good at ping pong, don't you agree? How would they know that animals could be domesticated? A valid point, isn't it? Growing plants and growing animals would require different sets of skills, setup, and knowledge. But I am also convinced that those things could be learned over time—most likely through trials and errors—once they began doing it. The crucial point will be: granted that the early farmers had the knowledge to grow plants, how could they be sure that animals could be domesticated to justify attempting it. Is that correct?

Domestication of Dogs

According to an article titled "The Origin of the Domestic Dog" by Jessie Zgurski, humans have certainly domesticated dogs for at least 14,000 years—thousands of years before farming began. According to the article, dogs have an origin from the wild wolves of Eurasia. However, by using another method called "molecular clock" which compares the number of different nucleotides in the sequences of dog DNA and wolf DNA, scientists have obtained another number in the period of time required to reach the current difference. The method has established that dogs have been domesticated even earlier, well over 100,000 years ago. It is therefore quite certain that by the time farming was established some canines had been domesticated for many thousands of years. And it was quite possible that dog meat had been part of the early farmers' diet, like in South Korea and many southern China villages. However, being always skeptical of the established beliefs, I would go as far as saying that humans could have domesticated dogs on and off at least since the later days of *H. erectus* or even earlier.

To see how this would be possible, let us first take a look at the ancestors of dogs. Dogs are members of the Canidae, which includes over thirty species of canines, such as wolves, jackals, coyote, foxes, bush dogs, and African wild dogs, etc. Though a pack of canines are capable of hunting small grazing animals and rodents, I would not be surprised that a great percentage of them have counted mainly on scavenging. Lacking the power of lions, the endurance of hyenas, the speed of cheetahs, or the stealth of leopards, they could not afford to rely solely on hunting. In Africa, the daily death toll among animals was likely high all the time. There were likely a lot of chances for those canines to come across animal carcasses of elephants, lions, zebras, and giraffes. (Well, you should get the gruesome picture.)

I think that there should be a number of behavioral differences, or body language if you wish, between top predators and scavengers. Among them, scavengers should, in general, be less aggressive and less inclined to attack humans than predators like lions and tigers. The size difference between an adult human and a typical canine certainly did not favor a canine, and humans also had clubs and spears. Canines are smart animals; it would not take them long to learn to respect humans, the *H. erectus* at the time.

For a number of reasons, we believe that *H. erectus* were true hunters. They would eat meat regularly. Partly from having a lot of meat and partly from lacking powerful teeth, *H. erectus* would consume most of the more tender meat of their kills and throw away the tough parts such as the skin or bones, often with some meat attached. In seasons of plenty, *H. erectus* might discard animals with quite a bit of meat left. Sooner or later, some canines would learn to follow humans around in anticipation of getting leftovers. Makes sense?

The dogs would likely choose to wait around humans to get their turn for food rather than attack the humans. Once they had learned that hanging around humans would equate to getting food, some would seek out humans and wait at a distance deemed to be safe. There would be a lot of chance to get leftovers from *H. erectus*. The pack of canines that followed a group of *H. erectus* should be small and likely less than four or five. Why? There would not be enough food to go around the animals, and the humans would not be comfortable with a big pack of canines constantly hanging around them. The constant association between the canines and humans could make the two become more comfortable with each other's presence as time progressed. From the humans' perspective, the canine seldom posted any threat or danger; any aggressive males would either be chased away or simply eliminated. With their skill in throwing spears, it would be unlikely that an intended target, an unwanted male canine, could consistently escape. *H. erectus* were likely to be capable of tender emotions; they were family men. I don't think they would enjoy senselessly killing any dog that had depended on them for food regularly, not unless the animal began to pose a threat to their safety. From the canine's point of view—yes, a canine should have its own point of view too—the humans were related to its survival. They could give him food or they could kill him. It would constantly monitor the signals of the humans, and from which gauge its response. A signal could be prospect of food and get into position, imminent attack and be prepared to retreat to safety quickly, unsure of an attack and be very alert, or no danger and relax. During their initial association with humans, the signals the canines received would likely often be *imminent attack and be prepared to retreat* or *be alert.* As they got used to being around humans for food, they would become more and more relaxed, and eventually would even see humans as their friends and incorporate the humans into their selves.

The outcome was certainly odd in the animal kingdom. Due to a selfish nature, a canine would normally see even its own kind as a competitor, if not an enemy. *Dog eats dog* is common. Gradually, some canines, through their learned experience with humans, had learned to see humans as their friends and their benefactors. Were the canines stupid? How did they learn to trust humans, an equally selfish animal? How did that happen? And how could or did so odd a thing happen? The answers to these questions are linked to the way a canine define its *self,* a concept we have discussed. The outcome would be inevitable, though unintentional, for both parties. Unbeknownst to both, they had built a friendship through mutual selection and screening. Among the canines, those that were not comfortable with being so close to humans would choose to leave after several unpleasant encounters; those that remained had a disposition to befriend humans. From the canines' point of view, humans not only provided them with food, they also gave them protection from fierce predators like lions and hyenas. After the invention of spears and fire, few predators would dare to venture near the humans. After hanging around humans for a while, a canine would learn that it would be safe too.

As time went by, some dogs would learn that certain gestures, such as smiling a bit when approaching a human—yes, dogs do really smile— rigorously wagging their tails, or passionately licking a human's hand could increase their chance of getting accepted, if not getting fed, and learned to keep doing it. Gradually, only those dogs that did one of those things would have an edge in their dealings with the humans; the eager-to-please dogs not only did not get their backs whacked or their behinds kicked, they could often be at the receiving end of bones with serious amounts of meat. If you were the dog, would you not perform one of those tricks conscientiously? I certainly would. I would practice those tricks whenever I had the time—and there would be a lot of spare time—like a newly hooked golfer until I had perfected each one of them. It was a competitive world. I would increase my repertoire in pleasing humans to outcompete my other relatives. Even not for food, I would want to get petted instead of getting whacked.

For those dogs that were either too proud or did not know how to please humans, they not only did not get any food, they would receive very rough treatment, and some could get themselves killed. So, gradually, the behavior of dogs toward humans would be shaped in the direction of tameness, friendliness, and an eagerness to please. The dogs were also conditioned to relate to humans as providers of food and safety. So the dogs got themselves a pretty good deal in befriending humans, did they not?

To those *H. erectus*, dogs might begin as a nuisance or could even pose a danger to their children. In response, they could systematically eliminate those dogs, the males in particular, that were either wary in the presence of humans or the aggressive type. And for safety reasons, a massive breed was unlikely to be allowed to linger around. Though it has been quite well proven that the dogs today have originated from gray wolves, the dogs *H. erectus* kept were likely to be smaller canines such as the dingo, African wild dogs, or certain types of foxes—the less threatening types. An *H. erectus* group was likely to be dealing with the same group of dogs and their descendant's generation after generation. If you were in the dogs' position, would you leave a human group that kept feeding you? Or would you allow another group of dogs to share your territory? I am no dog and I know next to nothing about how a dog reasons, but I would bet you anything that 1) the dogs would never leave on their own, and 2) they would defend their territory fiercely against any intruders. Their lives and wellbeing depended on it. The humans would likely help the dogs they knew to fight the intruders; it would be in their interest to have animals they knew well and even love to hang around.

The continuous contact between the same pack of dogs and the same group of humans had allowed the humans to select dogs with traits they wanted. "Are you sure?" you ask. We have the answer from the taming of Siberian foxes in Russia. It only took fifty years of selective breeding to tame the breed. It would not be that far-fetched that some canines had been tamed as far back as the time of *H. erectus*.

Humans had good reasons to let a few friendly dogs stay. Dogs, even during those early days, were likely to provide similar types of services to the humans, such as guarding a home/cave, helping in hunting, and playing with and protecting the children. They could be trained or selected to do those things. It was a win/win situation for both humans and their pet dogs.

If our speculation is true, it would be highly likely that some of the tribes had brought their dogs with them when migrating out of Africa and helped them to survive in lands patrolled by tigers or other deadly predators.

Which Animals to Domesticate?

The next question they would ask was likely to be: "Which animals should we try to tame?" Some morons could suggest taming lions for food and would quickly be rejected because 1) they were dangerous, and 2) it required meat to grow them, and that was exactly what they did not have. So the targeted animals should be quite harmless and manageable, and those they could afford to feed. With the shopping list, the early farmers began the quest to tame various animals. They proved to be quite successful, according to the information from *Guns, Germs, And Steel* by Jared Diamond. Sheep, goats, and pigs were among the first to be tamed around 8,000 BC. The cow was tamed later in 6,000 BC. The horse, donkey, water buffalo, and camel were the latest to join the list. Please note that the animals were tamed at different agricultural centers. Water buffalo, for example, were tamed only in the southern part of China, where yours truly come from. Believe it or not, I used to ride a water buffalo while taking it out to feed when I was around seven years old.

Not all wild animals can be domesticated, for one reason or another. Gazelles, for example, have not been tamed despite the animal being abundantly available and having undoubtedly been captured a few times by early farmers. Through trial and error, the early farmers found that some animals such as sheep, goats, and cattle could be kept alive and around indefinitely. Some of the captured animals could also produce babies in captivity.

The domestication of animals ensured the farmers a reliable source of animal protein and thus freed the early farmers from the heavy dependence on wildlife. A steady supply of high-quality proteins would certainly greatly enhance the health of its people and make them stronger. Domestication of animals was one of the most important practices powered by farming. The taming of animals empowered mankind enormously. All the essentials were there for further progress. Taming of animals was yet another step in the ever-intensifying attempts to control nature rather than accepting it. With the successes, humans had justifiably earned the title as the undisputed ruler of all creatures on the planet in every sense of the word. From Mother Nature's hand, we have seized ownership of a number of plants and animals. Humans have continued to become more and more powerful, as well as more hurtful. The sweet taste of power has only increased our thirst for it. Humans' unquenchable thirst for power without a correct moral guide can only mean trouble, trouble, and trouble, for the planet and ourselves.

The Consequences of Farming

The discovery of farming was easily up to then the most important human achievement on the long road to civilization, making the taming of fire look pale in comparison. While the use of fire had made the early humans eat better and sleep safer, it did not directly lead to other significant human inventions or discoveries, or drastically change their lifestyles. Farming had a much further-reaching effect in human histories over the millennia that followed. The following were some of the more important outcomes of farming on human societies.

Population Jump

One of the most important factors that limit the size of a population is food. Before the discovery of farming, a hunter-gatherer required many more acres of land to satisfy his food requirements. The reasons were 1) nature produces few edible plants or plant parts suitable for human consumption, and 2) hunter-gatherers had to compete with many other animals for the same categories of food. With farming, we change an ecosystem through promoting the growth of a few types of crops while eliminating all other indigenous plants and animals. Thus, farmers require far less land per capita for food production than hunter-gatherers. If ten acres of land were needed to feed one hunter-gather, then one acre or much less land would be enough to feed a farmer's family. Farming magnified the carrying capacity of the same piece of land ten times or more by eliminating all other plants except the intended crop. The exact figure may vary; the overall picture will be more or less the same.

Food supply also became more stable for the early farmers. After the farmers had successfully grown wheat and barley, which produced seeds that could safely be stored for years, they solved the problem of uncertainty of food supply that had plagued all previous humans. Mortality rate was down; the population grew faster. The lives of hunter-gatherers were much less certain; they would never know what the next day would bring. They would eat a lot when animals were plentiful, and starve during lean seasons. They often would either feast or famine, not unlike many of today's real estate agents. The drastic fluctuations in food availability were likely to take their toll on the weaker members of a family. Together with the many hazards related to hunting-gathering, mortality rate among them, infants and the elderly in particular, would likely to be a lot higher than in a farming community.

Besides having a more reliable food supply, farmers did not have to move around, thus allowing them to build better shelters and own more tools at their disposal. Every farmer's house, even at the beginning of farming, was likely to have a bed where they could sleep in greater comfort and safety. For farmers, a rainstorm, especially at night, could be something to enjoy in the safety of their homes. Hunter-gatherers, in general, needed to be more mobile to follow their prey; the lifestyle would not allow them to build permanent shelters or to have too many belongings. Besides their weapons, a group might carry some gadget to make fire and something to carry water in. A wandering lifestyle, besides being more taxing, would also be more dangerous; the mortality rate of hunter-gatherers would certainly be higher.

Claiming of Land Ownership

To hunter-gatherers, a piece of land did not have a fixed value. If there were animals to be hunted, they would stay. If not, they would leave. Hunter-gatherers had absolutely no interest in land ownership. To farmers, a piece of productive land was their livelihood. Land was where they grew their crops; they would invest a lot of time on their land—sowing, watering, fertilizing, weeding the field, chasing wild animals away. Farmers would have very strong incentive to guard that piece of land. It would literally be a matter of life and death to defend a piece of crop-producing land from intruders.

There is an unwritten universal law about land ownership in nature. If an organism occupies a spot and can defend it from intruders, the spot becomes its property. A maple tree, for example, by growing at a particular spot can successfully exclude all other organisms from occupying that space; it owns that space. Birds do the same thing during nesting season. Each pair would claim a certain territory and defend it fiercely. It would not take early farmers long to learn that their survival would be tied to a piece of productive land, and would defended it and claim it to be their own.

Emergency of Nonfood Producers

Farming, from the beginning, was much more cost effective than hunting-gathering. It did not require acres and acres of land to produce enough to feed a family either. While hunting-gathering would require every pair of capable hands (and feet) to take part in food earning, farming is not as demanding as to require everybody in a family to get involved most of the time. Even at the very early stage of farming, a farmer was often able to produce enough food to support some nonfarming members. As they knew more about promoting plant growth and incorporating more varieties of crops—after many generations, for sure—a farmer would be able to support more and more nonproducers. In North America, there are not many farmers, but each farmer can easily produce enough to feed hundreds of people. The early farmers were not nearly as good, but for each farmer to feed several nonproducers would not require superhumanly effort either. As a result, farming created a new group of people, a class of nonproducers of food.

Men's Rise to Power

Who were those early nonproducers? Some of them were the old, the disabled, and infants of course. Because of the quantities of excess food, a farming society could afford the luxury of feeding those who did not get involved in food production. Besides the disabled men and women, there

The Quest of an Unlikely Fixer

would also be many healthy and highly capable people. They were mostly young and strong men—the husbands and sons. The nonproducers were seldom women. Able or not, young or old, most of them had to farm. So the question becomes what would those highly capable males do? They were unlikely to be idle for sure. The first full-time occupation for those strong and capable males would likely be as security guards. Why? Their service would be in high demand. With the land producing food, how would the early farmers protect the fruits of their labor? Remember, there were no policemen or even governing bodies. And the role of security guards would suit the male temperament and physique perfectly. If there is one thing that men are undoubtedly better at than women, it has to be fighting or physical combat. Men, in general, love to fight. Even an otherwise peace-loving man would enjoy watching a boxing match. Men love physical games; it is in the male genes. Survival of the fittest means excelling in competing for food and in mating, both of which depend heavily on how strong physically a male is. It has been that way for hundreds of millions, if not billions of years; the strongest male in a group always gets the first crack to mate with a receptive female. Mother Nature has always handpicked strong fighter males and gives them the most chance to leave their genes. Muscle has always ruled.

After harvest, the men in my village would spend many hours each day practicing kung fu. There was a *see fu* and there were many eager students. They practiced with real weapons—long knives, swords, long sticks, and all kinds of gadgets—often yelling and shouting as they practiced. I was too young to participate, but I remember eagerly wanting to grow up so that I could be like them. The villagers did not learn kung fu to keep fit; they fully intended to use it in land disputes, which happened between neighboring villages from time to time.

The role of security guard could begin with defending a family's land. How well the males successfully carried out their duty would depend on how strong they were physically and their number. A family with three young strong males was likely to fare much better than one with an elderly male. Any martial arts teacher or military person can tell you that despite the difference in spelling and meaning there really is no difference between defense and offense. When an American president talked about a defense budget, he was aiming at making weapons that could be deployed in invasions. The role of security guard would naturally evolve into offense. Consider this scenario. Imagine the situation of a woman farmer during those early farming years. One day three young, strong musclemen show up on your field to claim all the mature muskmelons and your only protector was your aging husband. What could you do to stop them? Again, remember, there were no policemen or any kind of government; the human race was still uncivilized and was governed by law of jungle. Gradually, strong males, because of their muscles, began to impose their wills upon a community. It would not take too long for people to realize that the more males a family had, the stronger the family would be. A strong fighter represented power. A trend that strongly favored boys instead of girls thus began.

With all the benefits, it would be every boy's dream to grow up and become a security guard in early farming communities. It would not hurt if a boy had a strong elder brother as mentor. The number of security guards in a stable farming community would gradually increase; the size would depend heavily on the productivity of their lands and the number of (women) farmers supporting them. Among the security guards, leadership was likely to be decided by strength and size. The strongest boy would become the undisputed leader who would rule his community. Eventually, the security guards evolved into armies of soldiers; then the heads of the soldiers became rulers and kings. Men's rise to prominence and power was certainly a consequence of farming.

Enslaving of Women

In a hunter-gatherer community, adult males were hunters and the main providers. It would be unlikely that a hunter male would enjoy much more privilege in his family. When there was practically no accumulated wealth, there would not be much benefit to have power over others. Men and women were likely to be equal partners. Their relationship would most likely be harmonious, loving, and caring because each party needed the other to survive. Farming forever changed this harmonious relationship. Farming, even at its primitive stage, produced wealth in the form of surplus food and other household items. Though they did not get much involved in the hard labor, men learned to impose their strength and power over the weaker members, the producing women, to get a bigger share of the accumulated wealth. Some women might stand up to protect their interest or they might have tried to reason with their men, but why argue if you could simply beat up your women and get what you want? The smarter men soon learned.

Out of necessity, men might have innocently taken up the role of guarding their own fields against intruders and the occasional grazing animals. They soon learned that with brute force they could make their own rules and get what they wanted right away. It would not be hard to imagine how a part-time security guard could change into a full-time position. It would be an easier job than working in the field. It would also be much more rewarding. By simply beating your opponents, you got what you wanted—food for sure, and the choice of women too. Thus, it was likely that taming of women by men followed farming shortly. It was also so thorough that almost no woman could avoid it. Unlike the taming of plants and animals, domestication of women for men's service took neither trial and error, nor knowledge nor skill. It took only muscles. Women are still second-class citizens in many parts of the world. Men were no different from the male lions. They didn't take much part in farming but had claimed a lion's share of the returns. It seems an irony that it was likely a woman that discovered farming, and the discovery ended up turning women into men's possessions or slaves for many. After many millennia, many of them are still not free today.

The Invention of Written Languages

Written language, a writing system to convey thoughts and ideas, was certainly a human invention driven by need. It would naturally follow spoken language, which certainly existed many millennia prior. As the human population expanded—a consequence of farming— communities were formed around farming centers. The population size of these communities also gradually increased. Not every member in a community would be directly involved in farming. There were likely to be more and more nonproducers who engaged in other trades. From time to time, the nonproducers needed to offer their services in exchange for food and other items. Thus, trading between people began. To facilitate trading, some type of record keeping would be desirable. And a ruler of a big community would certainly charge his people some form of "tax"—a certain amount of wheat, barley, melons, or even animals—in exchange for his protection or land lease. It would also be necessary to have some sort of record keeping on who had paid and how much, etc. For whatever reason or reasons, the first written language was created around 3000 BC in Mesopotamia, or even a bit earlier in Egypt according to some scholars.

Of all the tools that had ever been created, or of all inventions that had come to exist up to the time, none have ever been as important as a written language. A written language has further raised the power of our species to a never-before-possible height. And it is still propelling us forward. As discussed, mankind has risen from obscurity to kingship through two intertwined forces: intelligence and cooperation. Before the invention of written language, no tool has ever aided us in both areas. A written language not only aided us in both areas, it has also done so in many immeasurable ways.

First, a written language makes us more intelligent. Intelligence, as defined, is the capability to solve problems. And to solve problems, you need useful information. The most useful information, without any doubt, is scientific facts. A written language makes mankind more intelligent by helping to spread science to every part of the globe where there is a written language in use. From science comes technology, which in turn allows us to create all kinds of gadgets to make our lives easier and less boring.

Second, written language allows mankind to cooperate beyond the confines of time and space. Thus, we still can share Confucius, Plato, or Einstein's ideas by reading their writings even though the person is long dead. With written language, time no longer impedes human cooperation. Written language allows us to communicate with friends and loved ones separated by tens of kilometers through letters, emails, or other social media. Cooperation through sharing of ideas is thus made easy and very precise with written language.

Let us see how precise and how much information can be shared in a simple equation, like $E = M \times C \times C$. (or M C square) The sharing of ideas in experience or scientific findings has no boundary. Thus, written language raised our intelligence together with our cooperation at the same time.

Written language is what makes the fast-paced scientific progress possible, the industrial revolution possible, the invention of computers and the Internet possible. The Internet in particular has further raised the cooperation and intelligence of our species to never-dreamed-of levels, making us truly godlike. There is no limit, it seems, to how powerful we can become. But, isn't there? Remember the gathering dark clouds? Remember what really powers us? With every incremental increase in power, our hurtfulness is also raised to a new level. Can we handle the ever-growing power? Would selfishness destroy us before we can get very far? Is there hope? Can our intelligence, a servant of selfishness, help to solve this puzzle masterminded by the big boss?

Having Choice

An animal has very little choice, if any. Every day in its existence, it is burdened with the problems of self-preservation or survival. For many, it will be to avoid being eaten and/or getting enough to eat. Then, it will be breeding season when every mature member is forced by Mother Nature to procreate. Having no choice means an animal is never too far away from death; there is little time to relax, and no leisure. How long can a pride of lions relax after killing a water buffalo? How long can their food last before they have to kill again?

Up until the discovery of farming, humans had little to no choice. Our species was not unlike other animals; our survival had been constantly at risk. Farming forever changed that. Many nonproducers came to exist. They did not have to worry about making a living at all; they could venture into other activities which were not directly survival related—singing, combing hair, keeping track of the coming and going of seasons, or stargazing, etc.—and still lived well. In other words, they had choice.

We can define what being human is in many, many ways. Our anatomy is certainly one way, ability to create many tools is another, or having the ability to communicate by language is yet another. I would certainly add having choice as the most relevant one.

In many parts of the world, there are still hundreds of millions, if not billions of people who regularly struggle to survive. Millions rely on scavenging to make ends meet. In Africa, India, and third-world countries, there are people who make their living among garbage dumps, sifting through garbage for something they can sell. Even in a rich country like Finland there are people in Helsinki who collect discarded beer bottles to make money. Each bottle earns them about two-thirds of a euro. These people are certainly human, anatomically fully capable of making tools, and some even speak English. Are they human in terms of having choice?

We often use the word *civilized* or *civilization*. What does it mean? How would you define *civilization?* I would define being civilized is when you have choices. A civilized country is where its people all enjoy lots of choices, have enough food, live safely and comfortably, and don't have to worry about survival most of the time. A civilized country is also where all its citizens enjoy equal rights. With this definition, Scandinavian countries, Japan, France, Germany, and Canada are certainly more civilized than Africa, Egypt, India, Iraq, or China before the current government. And among them, Egypt, India, Iraq, and China were places where the world's oldest civilizations were born. What happened to these countries except China? Why have these countries failed to keep up? There is only one answer, I think: most of the people in these countries are ignorant in science.

Is Farming a Blessing?

Is farming a blessing to mankind? Not if you happened to be a woman during the early period or even today in some parts of the Muslim world. Other than that, with so many good things farming has brought us it would be hard to argue against it. But is it really? On the surface, farming looks great with few side effects. It appears to be the best deal humans have ever had: Farming has offered mankind more stability in food supply, enabled us to stay put instead of drifting along with the animals, and to invest time to build houses so that we can sleep comfortably in safe places away from the beating of the elements and attack of man-eaters. Farming has made life much more predictable and safer. We know as long as we do our part—following the time to sow, to water, to weed, and to fertilize—we can expect to reap enough at harvest time to provide us with food year-round. With the pigs, goats, and chickens we keep, we can have high-quality proteins and meats from time to time. Mother Nature no longer holds all the cards to our survival. Gone were the days when humans would not know whether or not they would have anything to eat, where to sleep, whether they would be attacked by beasts, or survive to see the sun rising again the next day. But is farming an all-good deal? Or is there such a thing as a 100 percent good deal?

We know all too well that even modern-day good living tends to cause obesity and the health problems that come with it. Though farming, even at its infancy, must have created a few obese people—mostly men—for the very first time in the history of human race, it would hardly qualify as a problem. The predicament that came with farming was the never-before-seen rate of population growth. We all know too well that land does not grow. I would be horrified to wake up in the morning to find that my backyard had doubled in size. I would rather die than have to mow a bigger lawn. Sooner or later, a successful farming society would face a shortage of land to feed the added mouths. Driven by survival, those thriving farmers had to somehow find more land to grow crops. Humans, through their success, began to find that they were trapped by Mother Nature's most favorite trick: too many organisms and not enough resources. What will an animal do facing such a situation? They will fight and kill each other for a bigger share of the resources. Men are no exception.

So those successful farmers had no choice but to invade their neighbors. The first type of neighbors to go would be the hunter-gatherers, if any were left. And after the weaker competitors were gone, it would be war between farmers of different communities. Farming leads to overpopulation; overpopulation inevitably breeds war. In human history, the initial sweet taste of farming has always turned into a bitter aftertaste of war.

One does not have to be a history scholar to note the inseparable relationship between farming communities and war. The history of China, for example, is a history of wars of its farmers through the passing dynasties. The earliest written history of China, *Spring and Autumn,* which was written slightly before Confucius, is a story about the wars between the various tribes living along the Yellow River, a region where farming began. And the Chinese were not, are not, and will never be overly aggressive people; the high regularity of war in China has been a natural outcome of the success of its farmers. History has never been my forte, but I am quite sure that the driving force of wars in the early eons was overpopulation, an inescapable outcome of farming. So the best we can say about farming will be it is a mixed blessing because it leads to overpopulation.

Hunter-gatherers were likely to engage in wars between neighboring groups occasionally, but the scale would never be as big and would be less frequent as the wars between the early farmers. The successful hunter-gatherers, *Homo erectus,* had the luxury of expanding into other continents; the farmers had no such luck. I believe that every creature on the planet has the right to self-preserve or to live. The early farmers did not kill their neighbor so that they could create a playground for their children; they had to kill in order to live. When a person's life is threatened, he has no choice. When he has no choice, morality can no longer apply. The early farmers did not know the deal they were getting into when they began to farm. If a person did not know the consequence of his actions, how could he be liable or be condemned?

Farming has given us wealth beyond our dreams; it has also created problems that can eventually put an end to our existence. Life is full of ironies, isn't it? A curse becomes a blessing, and something that appears too good to be true is also the root of war, something extremely evil. Or, to survive we must be selfish, and for the survival of the species we have to cooperate. How do we find a way out of the paradox?

CHAPTER 14

The Domestication of Humans

To domesticate, according to *The New Lexicon Webster's Dictionary,* means to *tame* animals *and teach them to live with man and under his control.* Obviously, if we change the word *animal* to *humans* the meaning still fits. To domesticate is to rule. Humans, after taming plants and animals for our services, have become increasingly addicted to changing more living creatures around us. Some even learn to domesticate men and women to serve them. In domesticating a plant or an animal, the purpose may not always be for food. I have several indoor plants in my living area; I have absolutely no intention to use the leaves of the *Hibiscus,* African violet, or the *Coleus* for cooking or salad. The plants serve to bring some nature into my home. A dog is another example; it is often trained to serve us. In the same way, some very smart people, mostly men, learned that it would be far more profitable to domesticate, to control, and to shape other people to serve them. "But humans are highly intelligent. How would you domesticate a person?" You might object. There are two ways: by muscle or by mind control.

Domestication by Muscle

Domestication by muscle is the most primitive way to control other people. This form of domestication invariably involves violence. A domesticator does not seek consent; instead, he demands unquestioned submission from those to be domesticated. His demand is always backed up by force if needed. Any resistance to the domesticator will be met with violence—beating and torture. To get what he wants, a domesticator often will not hesitate to kill anyone who dares to oppose him.

Historically, domesticators first appeared in farming communities. They were the strongest males in their circles. In those lawless early communities, muscle ruled. A strong male, by beating up whoever dared to say no to him, got his way. From fear of physical abuse or getting killed, people quickly learned to live under his rules. As discussed, women were the first group of people domesticated by violence. Muscle men and their kind eventually became tribal heads, kings, and emperors. Even today, we still have quite a number of countries ruled by strongmen despite the wide spread of democratic belief. Invariably, strongmen rule countries where education level is low and people are mostly unskilled. Bosses of criminal organizations like drug cartels and the Mafia also rule by muscle.

There is one common underlying principle employed by muscle domestication: a domesticator always unilaterally sets the rules to be followed, he enforces the rule by muscle. Domestication by muscle is the oldest as well as the most barbaric form of controlling people. In essence, it treats other humans like animals.

Attempts to domesticate humans by muscle will, once in a while, occur on a massive scale. It happens when one country seeks to control another, like the invasion of China by Japan and Germany attacking European countries in WWII, or the US and Britain assaulting Iraq. War, because of the number of people involved and properties destroyed, is the ugliest form of domestication by muscle; it is also the most evil. Strangely, the world's moralities often do not condemn war. Just the opposite. The people of a winning country often glorify war. Wars have been where immortal soldiers and statesmen are born. Why is war exempted from existing morality? Why the inconsistency? Something could be very wrong.

Domestication through Indoctrination

It did not take some smart leaders too long to find out that beating people to submission was not the best way to govern them. To control by muscle could only be done on a small scale, to a few people, and it would last only as long as you had the muscle. People controlled by you will hate you and seek every chance to kill you. It is no different to being in a jungle. The most effective way to domesticate people is to control their minds by doctrines set by you, the controller. It can be done on a massive scale to millions, and it can last indefinitely.

How do you control the minds? The only way is by education. You need a lot of teachers working for you. For mind control to be effective, the education has to begin at a very early stage when the minds are still empty, ignorant, unspoiled, and eager for information. One of the consequences of having a big brain is that it always craves information. There is no better time to indoctrinate a person than when he is young, when he will greedily gulp down whatever information fed to him. The information-hungry character of a brain makes mind control easy; you don't have to fight resistance. And the beauty of doing it young is that the indoctrination will easily last a lifetime.

What do you teach the young minds? You always teach them what is right and what is wrong. But what is right and wrong? The young minds do not have to know; you, the controller, will dictate it to ensure that they will follow it and grow up under your control to serve you. "But how do you explain it to the young minds?" Not to worry. You set the rule that your doctrines or dogmas do not need to be explained or justified, and are never to be challenged. The way to make it work is by drilling the concept that the doctrines have come from God. You, the controller, must keep pounding this message to the young minds and continue doing so as they grow up. Most of today's doctrines were formulated thousands of years ago by priests or past teachers when mankind was still very ignorant; they then were passed from generation to generation by the enforcers of the doctrines.

But what is a doctrine? A doctrine is a simple statement of right and wrong; it is something alleged to be universally true and absolutely cannot be doubted or challenged. In the following discussion, *doctrine* will be used interchangeably with *dogma*, though the two terms have different meanings according to the Catholic Church. Let me give you some samples of doctrines or dogmas from different cultures:

An emperor is the son of heaven (God); he should be absolutely obeyed.

A woman should always obey her husband.

You shall not kill.

Stephen Y. Cheung, Ph.D.

Sex is the source of all evils.

Same-sex marriage is evil.

To live a blameless life, one must obey Jesus.

A priest or teacher never has to explain or justify a dogma or doctrine; it is stated as fact and truth. It is to be obeyed without question. From the samples, we can see that a doctrine could be sensible, like *you shall not kill, sex is the source of all evils,* or *a woman should always obey her husband.* (It made sense thousands of years ago.) Some were difficult to prove or disprove, like *to live a blameless life, one must obey Jesus,* or *an emperor is the son of heaven (God); he should be absolutely obeyed.* None was downright absurd at the time the doctrines were created.

Not every young mind would grow up to continue to accept the doctrines given to them. What happened when some begin to challenge the doctrines? So the controllers need serious muscle to back up their claims and to suppress their challengers. In every case, a challenger will end up guilty or sinful of challenging or rebelling against God. The penalty often is death. Regardless where you find the controllers, they ultimately always use the Almighty to back them up.

One of the problems with doctrines will be that there are as many gods (religions) as there are sets of doctrines. How can you tell a true god from a fake one? You cannot, because God does not have (neither does he need to) a habit of explaining himself. To make matters more confusing, the very same God Yahweh has, according to the different religions—Judaism, Christianity, and Islam—given different sets of often conflicting dogmas to their believers. So who is right and who is wrong? Who should you believe?

If one really wants to know more about God, a civilized or scientific way, I think, should be sharing the information with an open mind with full intention to learn from the other. Has that been the way so far? Nope! In fact, it never has and never will. Why not? You may wonder. Because there is too much at stake. At stake is an exclusive ownership of the Almighty, and from it comes the power to control a huge mass of humanity, a power far beyond that of kings or emperors. When the stake is so high and when the name of the game is the power to control people, there is only one way to settle it: it is by muscle, just like crocs and sharks, lions and tigers do. As a result, Jews and Muslims have been at war for centuries; same applies to the Christian and Muslims. And in some cases, even Christians against the Catholics. "But they all believe in the same God?" You are confused.

In recent years, there have been some discussions and exchange of ideas between the religions from time to time, but I seriously doubt that the participants had any intention of truly listening or fact-finding. The exchanges have been no more than PR. The Jewish consider themselves the chosen. Christians hold that Jesus is the only son of God. They and they only will go to heaven and the rest of the world, including the followers of the other two religions, will end up in you-know-where. Or Muslims claim to get the Koran directly from God's messenger vs. the other two religions, which are holding on to texts full of human errors.

A planet ruled by morality coming from doctrines and dogmas will always be full of conflicts and wars. Doctrines and dogmas serve only the selfish interest of those controlling their religions. Despite the desire for peace, we can never realize it as long as we follow doctrines. Is there any hope that our intelligence will one day untie this Gordian knot?

Indoctrination of the Chinese

For more than two thousand years, the Chinese had been, and millions still are, ruled by doctrines of Confucius (551–479 BC) or Confucianism. Despite changes of dynasties—from Han, T'ang, Sung, Yuen, Ming to Qing—the mind of practically every Chinese person, poor and rich, very learned to the illiterate, had been ruled without the briefest interruption by Confucianism. It had turned every Chinese person into the servant or slave of an emperor or ruler. Beyond any doubt, it was the ultimate form of domestication of people. Unlike the mind control of any religion, there had absolutely been no resistance to Confucianism until the recent decades, until China had been repeatedly defeated and humiliated by foreign powers, starting with losing to the Great Britain in the Opium War.

There is a Chinese fable. As the story goes, an old herdsman lost a horse. When someone tells him the fact, the old herdsman replies with a smile instead of alarm: "It can be a blessing." A gain is often hidden in a misfortune. The repeating defeats and humiliation have finally awakened some Chinese as they began to see the toxic nature of Confucianism. But the mind control of Confucianism cannot be so easily undone. A big part of it still remains in many minds, including that of the Communist leaders. Instead of totally abandoning it, people just pick and choose the parts that suit them and use it to form their moral mosaics. The Chinese are morally a very confused bunch. My parents, especially my old man, was a faithful follower of Confucianism. I did not clearly see its poison before I turned sixty.

Why is Confucianism so powerful? It is because Confucianism has been tirelessly endorsed, promoted, and fully supported by every king and emperor who ruled China. The Han emperor Wu-Di (156–87 BC) was the first to endorse and hoist Confucius to a godlike status by giving him the upmost honor of Supreme Saint. Why then were kings and emperors so anxious to kiss Confucius's ass, for the lack of better words? To sum it up, kings and emperors, according to Confucius, were literally sons of heaven (*heaven* is a Chinese version of god). As a son of god, a king or emperor was the rightful ruler of all people on earth. To quote Confucius: "If the emperor/king wants you to die, you must die without questioning." And many, including Qin-Shi-Huang's eldest son, a loyal follower of Confucianism, did commit suicide without questioning and thus forever changed Chinese history. Confucianism demands absolute obedience of the subjects to an emperor; it certainly made an emperor's job easy and his reign secure. If you were an emperor, would you not love Confucianism?

Every king and emperor had since honored the tradition and often tried to outdo the others in bestowing Confucius with never-ending praises and honor. Confucianism serves the interest of two groups of people only: parents, and ultimately, a ruler or emperor. And any person who dared to question or disobey the saint would be viewed as the worst kind of rebel and be mercilessly eliminated. Not just the involved rebels, slaughtered like cattle together were the rebels' nine social circles, which began with his immediate family members, parents, brothers and sisters, nieces and cousins, uncles and aunties, and extended to include friends and associates and teachers, etc. Quite often, hundreds to thousands of people, including many innocents—children, servants, women, and people who had absolutely no part in the rebellion—were killed during a cleansing. The so-called rebellions frequently had no basis at all. And it did not have to be a real rebellion. Sometimes it was very questionable. In the Qing Dynasty, someone—whether knowingly or coincidentally—had written: "The breeze knows not to read, how it dares turn the pages!"

Breeze can also be taken as *Qing people*. At the time, the emperor was sponsoring a number of literary projects like editing and correcting some classical Confucian/Chinese literature. Being sensitive and always suspicious, the emperor took it as an attack and arrested the writer, who was later chopped into two pieces at the waist, together with his nine circles of associates and acquaintances. It was exceedingly cruel and no solid proof was needed. That was the kind of cruelty an emperor was often capable of and the kind of power he commanded.

Confucianism is the only reason that the Chinese culture has remained intact despite the country being conquered many times by outside tribes, the Mongolians and the Qing for example. Khan had conquered China and ruled the land for a number of years. The Mongolians quickly reinstated and reinforced Confucianism to help them to rule. The Manchurians did the same thing after they became the rulers. They too quickly wholeheartedly embraced Confucianism; they thoroughly accepted the Chinese value. Within a couple of generations, most of them became Chinese. Chinese culture is the most powerful cultural melting pot, and all credits should go to Confucius.

The preservation of Chinese culture, which essentially is keeping Confucianism, has come with an extremely steep price to billions of Chinese people, because Confucianism is a very evil way of governing. According to Confucius, an idealistic world could only be achieved by two doctrines: (1) an emperor is the son of god (heaven); he therefore has absolute power over his subjects. And (2) parents, especially the father, are rulers of a family and should be obeyed by their children without question. To enforce these two doctrines, the best way is through education. Confucianism was all the teachers taught before the Qing Dynasty was gone. From the two doctrines, you can see what a mad genius Confucius was. He gave a ruler and parents so much power that none could turn down his thesis. If you were in their position, would you not? With the support of a ruler and parents, drilling the doctrines into the young minds would be very easy, would it not?

Though China has been without an emperor for decades, Confucianism is still going strong. Many Chinese parents still believe that they are always right and emphasize the high moral virtue to be filial. I was taught from an early age on that talking back to parents would be a moral sin. No wonder my parents loved Confucianism. With such godlike power, it would be very hard for any ruler not to abuse it. And because human nature is selfish, most emperors and rulers often did. Through Confucianism, they could rightfully treat their subjects like slaves and cattle to exploit and kill them. Bad rulers far outnumbered the good ones, and by a huge margin. You can count all the good emperors with the fingers of one hand; the rest were rotten. It is not surprising that the history of China has also been a history of suffering of its people. Europe had many kings and emperors; none of them had ever enjoyed nearly as much power as their Chinese counterparts.

For their selfish interest, kings and emperors loved Confucius more than their own dads. Rulers and emperors propped up the supreme authority of Confucianism with two additional methods. 1) They belittled any idea that differed from Confucianism. That is why science had no chance to develop in China for more than two thousand years. The many competing philosophies that once thrived around Confucius's time were discredited as trivial. 2) There were annual official exams to pick only Confucian scholars to fill the many lucrative as well as highly prestigious government positions. To have any chance to work for an emperor, you needed to thoroughly study *the Four Books*, which were the analects of Confucius. The practice had been maintained almost to the very last Chinese emperor. The emperors' unanimous favoritism of Confucianism had made studying it the only game in town; teachers only taught *the Four Books*. China was like a restaurant that only served ramen. People who were interested in other branches of knowledge often found themselves unemployable by the government, and also looked down upon by Confucian scholars. Law school, accounting, mathematics, physics, or any science subject did not exist in China for more than two thousand years. As a result, the intelligence and creativity of the Chinese had been stifled since Han-Wu-Ti. The Dark Age in China began about 140 BC and was never interrupted even after the many foreign invasions.

Have you ever heard about the four major Chinese inventions? They have not changed for almost a thousand years while some so-called barbarians, according to Confucian followers, have succeeded in sending spacecraft to the moon, Mars, and other solar systems. I am getting sick and tired—besides hugely embarrassed—to hear some Chinese still enumerating them with such pride.

CHAPTER 15

Putting Things into Perspective

In the Introduction of this book, I have suggested that wars, environmental deterioration, and poverty are the three major issues ravaging our planet. And we want to fix it. To have any chance of fixing a problem—in this case, our sick planet—we must first know the cause of the problem, correct? From what we have discussed in the previous chapters, the sources of our planet's problems have, other than some natural disasters, mostly come from us, the human race and the people of the world. We all contribute to them and therefore have an obligation to fix them.

We are the sources of the problems because 1) we are selfish in nature and thus are naturally hurtful, and 2) we have godlike power. Instead of being fully controlled by Mother Nature, we make our own rules, which often cause more hurt than good. Let us see how our selfishness is responsible for causing war, environmental destruction, and poverty.

Let us start with wars. In wars, the ruin to human lives and to the environment of course is through our tools, the many weapons. But the weapons are used by soldiers who are under the command of a leader, who, in a democratic society, is ultimately either a president or a prime minister. How does a president make a decision to commit his country to war? In the best scenario, it is for the benefit of the invading country. Even with this scenario, it is one country hurting another one for the benefit of the invading country. It is driven by selfishness, though it serves the whole country. More often than not, a war is driven by the interests of a few elites of the country, and in the worst possible case, by the greed and ego of its leader in pursuit of power and glory. A dictator often starts a war for personal gain, totally disregarding the wellbeing of his people. War is one country hurting the other; one collective self harming the other. The worst and the most unnecessary are wars where ruling parties try to hold on to power and turn against their own citizens. Besides hundreds of thousands of innocent people getting killed, many ecosystems are destroyed as collateral damage. Without doubt, wars are driven by human selfishness and greed, which often have no survival connection. In nature, selfishness is directly related to survival. Organisms fight each other to survive and an organism often has no choice. The wars between human societies often bear no relation to the survival of the countries initiating the attack. Again, wars often serve the interest of an elite few who are friends and allies of the leaders. The current civil war in Syria is just that. I don't think anyone would have trouble identifying whose interest the war serves. Considering the hundreds of thousands of innocent people killed and millions more displaced, the persons who decided to launch it are evil. War is the ugliest expression of human selfishness.

Next, let us consider environmental deterioration. With the increasing frequency of severe weather, we can no longer deny with what we know in science that global warming is real. And it is mostly man-made. If a reader has any doubt, I would strongly recommend him to watch *An Inconvenient Truth* by Al Gore. Carbon dioxide is the main culprit. Though every person on the planet contributes to the production of carbon dioxide to the atmosphere, only some are guilty. A person, like every living organism, always pollutes as long as he lives. Even the first living organism was a polluter. It produced metabolic wastes and dumped them into its surrounding water. Pollution is part of the living process and is unavoidable. But we need not worry about the quantity of carbon dioxide and waste produced metabolically; they can be fully recycled by plants, which in return give food and oxygen back to us. It is the carbon dioxide and the waste produced from our tools, the various machines, and vehicles that are the real culprits.

If we look at the carbon dioxide emission among countries in tonnes per capita, then most people in the industrial countries are roughly at the range of mid-teen tonnage per capita. I live in Canada, and like most Canadians, drive my car almost every day, though I would take TTC when I am not in a rush. I also travel quite a bit—I love it. I have a feeling that my carbon footprint will be way over that of an average Canadian, possibly close to 20, if not over. With this knowledge and being a person wanting to fix the problems of the planet, am I going to give up my lifestyle? My answer will be: No way, Jose. "What!" I can almost hear you scream in disbelief. So what will that make me? A selfish person, no doubt. Being a selfish person, I don't believe in sacrificing my interests even to save the world. Neither will I ask other people to sacrifice theirs. Sounds familiar, doesn't it? It is almost John Galt.

Please note that I am talking about reasonable use. I am sure people like Al Gore and David Suzuki will have very big carbon footprints because they both need to travel a lot to promote their messages. Their big carbon footprints are justifiable. Having a big carbon footprint and being green are not mutually exclusive. Neither Al Gore nor David Suzuki are hypocrites. So it brings us back to how do we solve the carbon dioxide problem? *One thing is sure, no thing is surer*: asking people to make sacrifices like giving up driving or staying home more is not going to work. For that matter, asking people to go against their selfish interest is bound to fail. To cut down carbon dioxide emission globally, we need most people in the world to agree to do it and do it wholeheartedly. For that to happen, a government needs to take a lead role and not leave it to the voluntary participation of its citizens. Again, please remember people are selfish. Therefore, the participation of governments is crucial for its success; we need laws to promote and to reinforce conservation.

And this, again, is easier said than done. Take Canada, for example, a country whose people are known to be nice and considerate. Canadians as a whole are also quite educated and are quite environmentally mindful. However, Canada is still very behind other developed countries in its efforts to cut down carbon dioxide emission. Why? Because easily over hundreds of thousands of Canadians, besides the provincial governments, depend heavily on the dirty oil sands for incomes. It is not a secret that the many processes in the production of gas from the oil sands are very polluting to the lands, rivers, and air. Even if the prime minister has the will, how can you get people whose incomes are from the oil sands to agree? Not just the CEOs of the oil companies, affected are more than one hundred thousand of directly involved workers, and we have not included the people employed by the secondary industries created from it. It is great to save the world down the road, but how can I feed my family? For any solution that has any chance to work, we must first consider how to solve this problem: how a government can take care of the needs of the people affected. To survive is every human's basic need and right; to survive, we all need incomes. I would take part to save the world, but not by asking me and my and my family to go hungry.

Not looking after the people affected will certainly create very strong and stubborn resistance; they will fight you. You don't want to fight people who are desperate. It is also a government's job to look after its citizens. The question then becomes: with the needs of people under consideration, can a government, especially of a country like Canada, still take part in saving our environment by weaning its dependence on the dirty oil? The answer will be yes, Canada can. There are lots of examples. Some countries like Sweden, Denmark, and Germany have been doing just that. They try to satisfy 100 percent of their energy needs from renewable sources. Some countries might make an excuse for not doing it by saying they don't have the knowledge and technologies, or the education level of its people are not as high. If you google "How 11 Countries Are Leading the Shift to Renewable Energy," you will find countries like Costa Rica, Nicaragua, and Uruguay are topping the list. Those people are not even close to the top in the level of education compared to Canada. So no more excuse for Canada. It takes political will of its prime minister. And more importantly, Canada needs a plan to make the switch. The Canadian government does not have a comprehensive plan. Not yet.

The hope of halting the environment's deterioration always begins with the leaders of a country. To have any hope, the leaders must first figure out a way to look after the livelihoods of the people affected by the switch. All the technologies are there waiting. All that is needed will be a workable plan of execution. Educating its people about the urgency of abandoning fossil dependence is also crucial. Without that, the prime minister is only dreaming.

Last, but not least, let us deal with poverty. How do we solve it? Unlike the damages caused by wars and to environment, poverty is not the result of greed or living in luxury. It is directly linked to survival, and therefore is driven by self-preservation, selfishness itself. Poverty is always the result of having too many people to feed and to house and lacking enough resources. It is true for a country and is true for a family. What then is the reason behind having too many people to feed and to house in the first place? The driving force of poverty is blind or unplanned reproduction; i.e., having no plan for the children. Reproduction among poor parents is often blind and unplanned. It is driven by Mother Nature, who does not give a damn whether the children will be poor or rich, happy or not. She does so against our interest. Why and how? Every person will hope for a happy life. For a person to have any hope to have a happy future, he needs to begin life with caring parents who have enough time and money to properly look after him for a number of early years. And he also needs to have a chance to receive good education so that he can acquire a skill to make a living. This wanting to have a good start in life should be everybody's interest, but you need to have caring and able parents.

Whether you will have a good life or a rotten one is the least of our species' concern. What our species wants is for it to continuously survive. For *Homo sapiens* to survive, every (sexually) mature person must try his or her very best to have children, as many as biologically possible. You say, "That is no fair! How can it be so?" Whether you like it or not, this is truth! The interest of *Homo sapiens* and yours as its member do not always agree. When your interest is in conflict with that of *Homo sapiens,* the species, guess whose interest will prevail or who will be the boss? The interest of *Homo sapiens* will always trump yours! Though this fact seems to be cruel to you, the individual, but it is mandatory or there will not be any more humans in the future.

This rule that the interest of a species trumps that of its individual applies to every living organism on our planet. That is why those Romeo praying mantises get eaten during lovemaking and the noisy cicadas die shortly after having fun. Producing the greatest number of progeny has always been priority number one for the survival of a species. Mother Nature does not leave this utmost important matter to the free choice of its organisms either. To ensure that its individuals will all do their best to reproduce, she uses tricks. Her trick is through hormones. She uses sex hormones which will control the developments of sex organs, the production of sperms or eggs, and in animals, also give them their sexual urge. In the animal kingdom, sexual urge is so powerful that almost none can resist it. When it is time to reproduce, most animals will obey their sexual urge and have sex, which leads to reproduction. Most of them will have sex in the face of great danger and disregard the dire consequence. Still remember the sad story of the Panamanian bitch? She was sick and was struggling just to survive; she was still willing to have sex and was going to have a number of puppies. The tragic fate of them all had been sealed; there was no escaping it.

You would think with our intelligence and knowledge we can do much better than the bitch, can't we? Let me give you another story. I got to the bus terminal of Sao Paulo when it was dark. Under the overpass near the bus terminal, there were close to a dozen homeless people sleeping. Among them was a young couple sleeping and embracing each other. They immediately reminded me of the bitch. Sooner or later, they were going to have a child. What chance does their child have to grow up having a good career? We are not that much different. People who absolutely should not have any more children keep having more. It only takes a moment of weakness or ignorance to procreate; people who are already poor are most vulnerable.

Poverty is not controlled by any gene and yet it is often passed from one generation to the next. Poor parents always give their poverty to their children, by ignorance or carelessness. While struggling, they still produce more poor children because of their biological needs. That is the reason why *the poor get children.* And when their children grow up, they often become poor, and they in turn produce more deprived sons and daughters. So the cycle goes on and on. When most families in a country are poor, you will always have a poor country. Poverty is also inheritable at the national level. How do we break this cycle? It will be next to impossible because Mother Nature is not the only party that is responsible in perpetuating poverty. She gets help from most of our existing moral views, the view of the Catholic and Christian Church, in particular. The erroneous belief that life is sacred and procreation should be encouraged regardless make putting an end to poverty impossible. Pure and simple: poverty is the result of ignorance on the part of the parents and those who want to end poverty but have absolutely no clue of its source and cause. Without the knowledge and armed with an erroneous moral view, those kindhearted followers passionately help to make sure that poverty will forever be in the world.

Human selfishness, like selfishness in every living creature, always ends in hurt, though it can be unintentional, like how poor parents keep having children. But this is only one part of the whole problem. Another question that needs to be addressed is that all living organisms are selfish, yet in a natural setting living organisms work together to create a very harmonious ecosystem; none of them could continuously damage the environment. Each creature occupies a niche to build a balanced habitat, in the same way a musician plays in an orchestra to make beautiful music.

Unlike any other living organism, humans destroy their environments most of the time. We ask: powered by the same selfishness to survive, why such glaringly different results?

Why do we always have to be destructive? Where does our power come from? We are so destructive because we have godlike power and don't know how to wield it to do good. How did we get to be so strong? To answer the question, we have traced the rise of our lineage from the very beginning, from the time our first ancestor emerged from the common chimp. We have theorized that our lineage, from the very beginning, had been almost fatally handicapped because what has defined humanity is an ape walking on two feet. Our species has been born defective from the start. Because of the many overwhelming hazards that came with bipedalism, the chimp had to come up with solutions or it would die without leaving any heirs.

The most pressing challenge that arose from bipedalism was a huge loss of speed to that chimp. Losing speed meant that it could no longer compete for food in trees, it would be difficult to escape danger, and eventually it had difficulty in competing for mating. Luckily, our ancestor, the first bipedal chimp, was then the most intelligent kind of animals on the planet. It did find the solution, and the solution had come from his tool, likely a multipurpose stick. With his tool, he managed to more than overcome all his problems; he had competed successfully. It survived and eventually thrived.

A simple tool was the answer to all our ancestor's problems. What is a tool? A tool is something that an animal is born without, something of great value in aiding the animal to overcome its survival problems. Many animals use tools available in their environment to aid them to obtain food occasionally, but none have ever so desperately depended on tools to make it to the next day like a human. Luckily for the first bipedal chimp, the first human, he came from a species, and likely the only species at the time, which was able to regularly create simple tools. While other chimps could still happily survive without tool, our first ancestor would not. Without it, our first ancestor would be dead in a matter of months, or at best a number of years. Thus, from the very beginning our lineage has been hopelessly reliant on tools for survival. This complete dependence on tools is the first key to understanding the secret of our power. A tool is the source of our power.

The hazards of having to walk on two feet have thus forced all humans to depend on tools. The dependence has also shaped the direction of evolution for our lineage. Having lost speed, crippled chimps could no longer count on muscles like regular chimps in competing. They were forced to use their brains. Luckily, the crippled chimp's kind had the most powerful brain on the planet then, another happy coincidence. As a result, the crippled chimps had abandoned muscle and hired neurons as boss to take control. Neurons have helped our species in several ways. First, naturally, was and has been to help us create and improve the tools. Second was to remember more and more facts, thus providing the brain with more information for problem solving. Third was to allow them to reason with increasing clarity, and to see the consequences of things to come; in other words to allow them to predict future events.

Using neurons as boss, based on what had been observed in the past hundreds of millions of years of evolution in animals, had never been successful and therefore never before existed. It was an extremely risky move, which is an understatement. But our lineage has proven history wrong. Not only have we made it, we have done it in flying colors. Using intelligence instead of muscle to be boss for survival is the second key to understanding the secret of our dominance.

It would be naive to assume that tools and intelligence are the only two things that have helped us. If our first ancestor was a loner, it would be highly questionable, even with the help of its tool under the command of the then most powerful brain, that it was able to make it through a couple of generations. Our ancestor was a social animal—another very happy coincidence. The first crippled chimp got help from the group he was living with in avoiding predators and in sharing information, especially in tool making. Our lineage has been born to cooperate, though limited in scope, from the very beginning. As we evolved, we have not only intensified the investment in neurons, we have also deepened and widened the cooperation between the members in a group at the same time. More and more, the increased cooperation is by choice. The high degree of by-choice cooperation is thus the third key to understanding where our power is from.

Though there are three things that have given us our godlike power, our power has been the results of the continuous and combined working of intelligence and cooperation. Tools are merely products of the twosome working together; they are the expressions of intelligence and cooperation. Tools are not parts of our body; they are the media through which we wield our power. Though tools are doing all the damage, it is the intelligence and cooperation driven by human selfishness that is the real culprit and master. The twosome has kept working together as we evolve. That is a very strange thing in nature. Every living creature depends on intelligence to solve the three survival problems. But very few get aid from cooperation. Though there are highly cooperative insects such as ants and bees, for example, their cooperation is not by choice. It is wired in their genes and is thus very rigid. But the high degree of cooperation in humans has been by choice. The increased cooperation between members possibly started shortly after those crippled chimps began to venture out of their forest in search of food. We have inherited a limited cooperation from the common chimps and have further intensified it by choice. Since our cooperation is by choice, it is from reason and thus is intelligent, and therefore is much more flexible and can be improved and changed, which is hugely superior to those wired to cooperate.

Choice cooperation is not supposed to happen among selfish and highly intelligent animals like chimps; selfishness is the opposite of cooperation, like water and oil. Because the two don't mix, it is doubtful that the cooperation among chimps is by choice. Either way, their degree of cooperation is quite limited. From this, we have reason to doubt whether those first-generation crippled chimps, with a chimplike specific brain capacity, were capable of seeing that they needed to heighten their cooperation to carry them through. Lucy's type, with a specific brain capacity at almost 13 ml/kg—about 3 ml/kg over that of chimps—obviously had the required additional neurons to break through the intelligent barrier to allow them to see the necessity to cooperate. A heightened cooperation was the prerequisite before they could leave the trees for good.

With the twosome working together, we have evolved to be the most powerful creatures on the planet; we have conquered and defeated even the mightiest and replaced them as the rulers of our domains. With each victory over our once worst enemies came many rewards. We became addicted to conquering and crushing things that are blocking us. We became cocky and erroneously thought that we can keep on doing it. Then, we began to fight Mother Nature and try to control her. In doing so, we often inflict lots of damages to her, to suit our needs sometimes or just for convenience. If you look at the evolution of our species, we have, since the very first ancestor, been rebellious to Mother Nature. And after discovering farming, we even began to take power away from her. With the accumulation of scientific knowledge and aided by our increasingly powerful technology, we have become bolder and more aggressive; we began to control and even try to enslave Mother Nature. With intelligence and cooperation, we have replaced Mother Nature and become gods to many living organisms.

Alas! We are short-sighted gods with no correct morality to wield the enormous power. Like a tyrant, we let our selfishness run wild. As a result, we often leave a trail of destruction wherever we go. We must stop our fight with Mother Nature. We must stop hurting her because we now know that we are a part of her. Hurting her is no different from hurting ourselves. We need to show our love to her because we are a part of her.

The Solution—Again by Intelligence, Cooperation, and Tool

I am 100 percent sure that we can solve the problems yoking our planet because now we can clearly see the reasons behind it; more than ever, we now have a clear target. The target is certainly our natural tendency to harm from human selfishness and our godlike power. The way to solve the two problems is by a new, correct morality. Then a reader may ask, don't we already have many moralities in our world? And the existing moralities have not worked, or we would not have this mess. Why is this new morality different from the others? There are a number of reasons that all existing moralities have failed. (1) None have clearly identified that selfishness is the problem and the only problem. Not knowing the source of the problems will not lead to a solution. (2) Most of the existing moral views are religion based and their most important goal is to promote the worship of their own gods. Their moralities are primarily the ways to lead their followers to eternal lives; to lessen the sufferings in this world plays a secondary role at best. (3) All the existing moralities, though, cannot clearly identify selfishness as the target; nonetheless, they all target selfishness as an undesirable quality. They try to fight it or deny it; they preach selflessness and promote sacrifice. Because both are against our nature, they are bound to fail. (4) None of the existing moral views is based on scientific facts and are often erroneous. To view sex as evil instead of a possible ally is one of the examples.

To sum up, the existing moralities lack intelligence: no understanding of the problems and the source, and therefore have failed.

Knowing why the traditional moralities have all failed, we can learn from it. Our new morality will target human selfishness. Fortunately, our existing wisdom has some teachings that specifically prohibit human selfishness, though without people actually knowing it. It is the Golden Rule. Therefore, in our new moral model the decision maker is the Golden Rule. Using the Golden Rule and the Golden Rule only keeps things simple. We use the Golden Rule only for two reasons: (1) it is universal; the essence of the Golden Rule is in the teaching of every major religion. And (2) it is tailor-made to deal with human selfishness, which is our target.

One of the reasons that traditional moralities have not worked is because they have too many rules; having too many rules often leads to confusion as to what is more important and therefore which one to follow. Some rules even contradict the other. Having one rule only has allowed us to avoid all the pitfalls of the previous moralities and makes moral decision simple. The golden rule–based morality will be the tool we shall use to solve today's many problems; the tool which targets human selfishness is the contribution of intelligence. We also need to cooperate by having everyone agree that human selfishness and our godlike power are the roots of all our problems. We also must agree to control and guide our power to beneficial use. To achieve that, we need a correct moral code that every nation and culture can accept and agree to be bound by it. Without having the people of every country accepting the proposed morality, we will still do things the old ways. Once the universal moral code is accepted, it will be our moral traffic light. Then, we can all clearly see what is morally right and what is morally wrong. With intelligence, cooperation, and the new moral tool working together, we can fix and save our planet.

There is hope. It can be done for sure, but it takes time. And more than anything, we need more people to participate. In part III, I am going to introduce the new morality to you. I would ask a reader to read it critically, because whether or not you are going to use it depends on whether it makes sense to you or not. The hope of our troubled world hinges upon your participation.

PART III

THE CURE,
INTRODUCING THE NEW MORALITY BASED ON
THE GOLDEN RULE,
THE TOOL TO FIX THE PROBLEMS

CHAPTER 16

A New Morality

In part III, we are going to discuss the tools we shall depend on to fix our sick planet. Our first tool is knowledge, particularly from science. Science gives us knowledge based on facts that have withstood many rigorous tests; trustworthy information that we can make decisions upon. Scientific information is the main source of our intelligence. Applying the information, we can solve the many environmental issues: finding renewable energies, setting the limits of our fossil fuel consumption, how to meet them, and better managing waste, etc. Science will guide us in deciding what is harmful and to be banned, or what is beneficial and to be promoted. In particular, it will help us to better understand sex, will allow us to enjoy sex to the fullest, and eventually will enable us to get rid of the most important source of poverty, which is blind procreation.

The other tool is education, which is the duty of a government to provide. Education should at least achieve two goals: (1) to teach students the knowledge to decide moral right and wrong, and (2) to give students, at the end of their education, the skills to make a decent living.

Since there are lots and lots of information on the Internet on environmental conservation and education, I shall leave them to a reader to satisfy and educate himself; I don't have much to offer on the two subjects anyway. So without further ado, let us plunge into the most important tool that we shall count on to fix and heal the world. Let us discuss the new morality.

Stephen Y. Cheung, Ph.D.

Predicting the Probability to Harm or to Attack

Case I: A Tiger Attacking

In part I, we have argued that life is selfish and selfishness always ends up hurting other organisms, including one's own kind. The motivation to hurt always comes from a need to self-preserve. To self-preserve, an organism needs to do three things: (1) to self-defend,(2) to obtain energy to do the many kinds of survival related works, and (3) to reproduce. The needs from the three areas thus allow us to predict the probability of an animal, especially those at the more advanced level of evolution such as a tiger, an elephant, or a water buffalo, to launch an attack at another animal. Let us put the prediction in the following equation:

$$P = N - F \quad (1)$$

Where P is the probability that the animal under consideration will attack a target animal. N is one of the animal's three survival needs—food, safety, or sex. F is its fear of the consequence, or the factor that will hold it back. The values of P, N, and F are all between 1 and 0. When P = 1, the animal is certain (100 percent) to launch an attack. N = 1, the particular survival need under consideration is at its maximum. If the need is for food, it means the animal is extremely hungry. F = 1 means the fear is at its maximum; so will the holding-back factor be. When P, N, or F is zero, the factor under consideration is extremely weak; i.e., the probability to attack does not exist, the animal has no need for food, no sexual need, and no need to self-defend, and fear does not exist. Easy to understand an animal, isn't it?

Let us use an example of a very hungry tiger which happens to come across a lone child. We ask, what is the probability of the tiger attacking the child? In this case, N will be 1 because it needs food most, and F is 0, meaning it will be fearless; therefore, P = N − F or P = 1 − 0 = 1. It is quite certain that the tiger will attack the child 10 out of 10 times, a certainty. Make sense? At this stage of discussion we don't have more precise figures on the values of P, N, or F other than their ranges.

What if the same tiger sees the same child, however the child is accompanied by several soldiers, will the tiger still launch an attack? I would say very unlikely. The probability will be next to zero, if not zero, because the tiger's fear of the consequence will be close to 1. Tigers are very intelligent; they are good survivors. They don't just count on muscles, they use their heads too to make good decisions. The reader may want to use a different animal with a different need to predict its probability to harm others just to get some feel of the equation.

Before we leave the probability of an animal to initiate an attack, I would like to stress the fact that an animal usually attacks in response to one of its three needs at a time. It can be for food, self-defense, or to mate. It will be rare, if it happens at all, that it will be driven by two needs at the same moment.

Case II: A Person Attacking

Case I is only for academic interest; it has little practical value. Everyone knows that a tiger is a man-eater; you don't need to find out whether it is hungry to stay away. The reason I want to bring forth the equation is to introduce the following equation, the equation for predicting the circumstance a person will harm another person or persons. For a person, let us express the probability to harm others in the following:

$$P = (N + W) - (M + F) \quad (2)$$

Where P, N, and F are still the same as equation (1). For a person, P will be decided by two more factors: W is the wants, such as power, a big house, designer shoes and clothes, expensive cars, a Rolex, or diamonds; a want can also be abstract like fame and recognition. Please note that sex is a need (N) and not a want. M is the person's moral sense, which comes from one's upbringing and education. W and M also range from 1 to 0, 1 being the strongest and 0 being nonexistence.

Now, we are ready to have some fun. Please consider the following scenarios.

A sexually needy man attacking

For a number of reasons that we shall discuss later, every society has many sexually deprived men; they need sex but have no way of realizing it. It is a hidden danger that exists in every society, particularly in a society governed by morality that sees sex as sinful, dirty, or ugly animal-like behavior.

Let us use a guy named Bruce as our example. Bruce is young and strong and is very average looking. He is a temporary employee with a moving company. Bruce lacks social skills; he does not know how to talk to gals. For a number of reasons, he does not have a girlfriend and his sexual need is always strong. Bruce comes from a poor family and has little education other than finishing primary school; Bruce's moral sense is lacking.

Let us assume that one night Bruce happens to come across a gal in his neighborhood whom he has secretly been fantasizing about. The gal was walking along in a dark alley. Under this setting, what will be the probability (P) of Bruce assaulting the girl sexually? Let us use the equation to analyze the situation.

The factor driving the attack is certainly Bruce's sexual need (N) which is very strong all the time. His N will be very close to 1. What will be holding him back? There are always two factors: a person's moral sense and his fear of punishment in a lawful society. We have assumed that Bruce has very little moral sense because of his upbringing. His M is therefore close to 0. So the only other factor that holds him back will be his fear for punishment. In this case, Bruce knows that he will not be caught because there is nobody around; his F is therefore close to 0. So the probability of Bruce attacking the girl, $P = 1 - (0+0) = 1$. It is almost a certainty. It is common knowledge that a lot of crimes happen in places where the victims are alone and no one will witness them; sexual crimes are among them.

A young man with many wants but no skill becoming a gang member

The everyday news of North America's big cities—Toronto certainly is one of them—often includes gun violence. Most of the cases involve young blacks killing other blacks; most are also gang members dealing drugs—from what I have gathered. So the questions become: why have young blacks led the gun-violence scene? What kind families do they come from? And what drives them to this kind of violent lifestyle? I am fully aware that labeling those criminals black will make many politically correct people call me a racist and attack me. But between not pointing out the problem as I know it and being politically correct and nice, I would rather take the risk. Scold me if you want to vent your anger, but please give me a reason. Is making a sensitive comment which is based on a lot of observations and what a person believes to be valid and not based on one's prejudice wrong? Or, to be "considerate" one would sacrifice the truth, and in so doing let some tragedies continue? Gun violence has happened too frequently; too many young lives have been wasted and too many mothers' hearts shattered. We need to stop it from continuing to kill our young people. Pretending it is not a black problem will not stop it. Please hear me out: together with this, my nasty labeling, I have also come with a solution.

First, let us look at the probability (P) of a young black becomes a gangster from our equation:

P = (N+W) – (M+ F).

P is driven by two factors, a survival need and wants. It is counterbalanced by two other forces: a moral sense (M) and a fear (F) of consequence. A person, like an animal, can be motivated to attack the other at any given time by only one of the three needs. That is where the similarity ends. An animal does not have wants; it will never attack others because of a want or wants, something that is not immediately related to its survival. A person, on the other hand, can launch an attack on others because of his need or his wants. This, if you think of it, makes people more unpredictable and more dangerous than tigers or lions.

Make no mistake. Those young blacks did not kill one another to satisfy a survival need—to buy food, clothes, or to get a place to live. In North America, a person's survival needs are guaranteed by the government. Often, it is the wants he is trying to satisfy. And his wants are many and usually very expensive. Take a look at what he wears and you will see they cost a lot of money. From the head down, he usually wears the attire of the sports team he supports; in Toronto, the teams will be the Blue Jays or the Raptors. A hat of the team and a jersey of a popular player will set you back about a couple of hundred dollars. Then, there will be blue jeans and shoes, all have to be name brands—another couple of hundred dollars. And you need more than one set; a minimum of two or four perhaps? He does not usually eat at home either, and not many eat at McDonald's regularly. Then, there will be his car, a car that can turn heads. In October 2016, a young black got killed while driving; the car he was driving was a luxury SUV and a rental. We can go on and on. But you get the picture, don't you? These young men need serious disposable income to support their lifestyles. How do they get the money? They are not professionals like doctors, accountants, or lawyers. No, most of them don't finish high school and lack any skill. So we have many young men in our society that have very expensive tastes and wants but don't have the ability to support them. You can see the trouble brewing, don't you? They need easy money. There is no easier money than getting it the quick way: by holding up banks, gas stations, convenient stores, or dealing drugs.

I like to get easy money too, but I won't do it because my moral sense won't allow me and I don't want to be locked up in prison either. Not for those young men with many wants. As a group, they have little moral sense and they also pride themselves on being fearless or having no fear. What can happen to them if they get caught? Jailed for a number of months or years? It will be no more than some inconvenience at the most, or as part of the costs of doing business.

Our system in dealing with criminals is a joke; imprisoning a person can hardly be called punishment. In fact, most prisoners have better lives than a lot of hardworking people. I know because I have changed careers several times and often have worked my butt off, close to twelve hours daily, 7/365, and no vacation for a number of years, just to pay my mortgage and car loan. If anything, our prisons serve to harden criminals; they are the universities or graduate schools for the-not-yet-there young offenders.

So what do we have? We have many young, capable men who have lots of expensive wants but can't satisfy them the right way. They have little moral sense and are fearless. What will be the probability of them going bad? Almost a certainty, isn't it? It is a lifestyle operating under the law of the jungle; getting killed is a matter of sooner or later. Where do those young men come from? What kind of families do they grow up in? The fact that many of them will end up criminals tells me that their families, their parents, or single mothers (it is no secret that many of them are from single-mother families) have failed them by not providing the love, care, and the environment for them to grow up successful. They are the unavoidable results of growing up with parents who have absolutely no plan for them and thus have failed them.

Here I hope a reader will not see young men becoming gangster being unique to blacks, or that it is in their genes. No! They are just a natural consequence of our selfish human nature. We all have a natural inclination to hurt. However, that hurtful tendency is often countered by a person's moral sense, which can usually be imparted by parents and education together. From our example, we can also clearly see that a person without a moral sense is more dangerous than an animal. He will have one more reason to harm others: his wants. We can also say that a person without morality is worse than an animal. If calling people "animals" is an insult, from what we have discussed it seems a compliment.

Let me reiterate. A young black becoming a gangster is NOT in his genes. Look at Obama, he can be a president. But the fact still is many of the gangsters are young blacks. Among people killed by guns, young blacks have been disproportionally higher than the size of their population. I hope lawmakers would start tracing the problem to the offenders' families because that is where those young blacks are from. Until the sources have been cut off, the killings will continue and the tragedies go on. Black lives matter. I hope it is not just a slogan. Make them matter. I shall bring up the solution to this problem in part IV, the new way to govern.

Did or didn't Donald grab women's private parts?

To me, American presidential election had been quite boring until Donald joined the race and became the undisputed but very controversial Republican candidate. Donald is very unconventional, or I should say extremely unpredictable. He has never failed to come up with new surprises and shocks. His strategy has worked much better than the others'; he has blown away the several very worthy opponents like they are no-names and claimed the candidacy by a huge margin. By talking tough and glaring political incorrectness, he has won the support of millions of Americans who are very unhappy about the government's softness in treating illegal aliens, Mexicans in particular, and letting Muslims in. Nice politicians, with their mindfulness in being politically correct, won't do any of those. That makes Donald stood out like a crane among pigeons; to those Americans, he is certainly the man to make America great again.

Then, the mother of all bombs dropped. On October 7, 2016 at 4:27 p.m., *The Washington Post* made known a 2005 tape titled: "I Grab Women by the Pussy . . ." Since Janet's unfortunate "wardrobe malfunction," the Americans have not been shocked by such tsunami of the sexual kind for years. Since the tape was made known, eleven women have, up to October 20, 2016, come forward and accused Donald of sexually attacking them. Donald, like any shrewd man, has denied, denied, and denied all of them; he knows more psychology than many professors. So our job is, based on our equation, to throw some light on the subject. Did or didn't Donald *grab women by the pussy?* Was he just bragging? Or did he actually do it?

Since we may never find out the truth and nothing but the truth, we can only do the next best thing; i.e., use a bit of what we have discussed (the probability argument) to come up with an educated (or not so educated) guess. Did or didn't he do it? Let me remind you that the prediction from probability is valid for events that happen over many, many tries, like throwing an unbiased dice over thousands of times and the results of the occurrence of each possible outcome observed. Regardless, I don't think Donald will ever be so naughty as to do it again.

Number 1 factor to consider is what drove Donald to do it, if he in fact did it. I don't think it is his unbearable sexual need. Donald is a star and is very well-known; many women would let him do it—according to Donald. Donald is married and not so young like a bull anymore. So if Donald wants anything, the last thing, perhaps next to money, will be sex. So it was likely that it was his *want,* not *need,* that had powered him; his sexual need, if it existed at the time, would be secondary at best. Donald loves power. He craves power and will do anything to satisfy this *want,* and grabbing women's private parts, breaking their last defense as he pleases, and humiliating them are surely the most gratifying ways to feed his ego. This daring behavior will certainly make him an alpha among the machos. Donald's *want* in proving his manhood and power is likely to be close to 1 all the time, which makes him very dangerous. A leader that loves power is very prone to start wars, like a man who digs muscle cars is inclined to speed. Americans will likely start wars with Donald the man as president. Watch out!

What could have held Donald back? It would either be a moral sense or fear, or both. From what I have seen so far, Donald is certainly a very shrewd businessman who is great at avoiding paying taxes, but morality does not seem to be his forte. Or how could a guy of his status talk like that in a country which prides itself in having a very high moral standard? And Donald is fearless; he knows the system too well to have any fear of something so trivial—to him. With his money, he can have the service of the sharpest legal minds money can buy. "Sue me. See if I care!" Rich people often get away with murder in America. Fear is not in Donald's dictionary.

So Donald has an ego as big as Mt. Everest to feed, he has very little moral sense, and is absolutely fearless. What is there to hold him back? And those were his own words. What more proof do we need? So what do you say? Did he or didn't he?

Before we leave this part of the discussion, I would like to stress three points again:

1. A person, like an animal, will not hurt others from fear of the consequence; this is a common factor holding a person or an animal back.
2. If a person has no moral qualms and has no fear of the laws, he is much more dangerous than a beast.
3. The best way to make a society safe is definitely by imparting on its people a strong moral sense. Though both fear and moral sense can hold a person back from hurting others, moral sense will be a much superior way of achieving it, because instead of policing each person will be his own policeman. A society with a strong moral sense is a safer society, so is a country or a planet. Therefore, morality, more than any other branch of knowledge, should be the foundation to build a society, country, or world.

We Are living in a Morally Confused Planet

In the previous section, we stressed that morality will be the best and the most effective way to prevent a person from hurting others. In this statement, I am assuming that 1) the person has the correct moral sense, and 2) he will be bound by his moral sense. The problem with our world is we don't know what a correct moral sense is. Even if he knows, his moral sense could be overridden by other issues that he thinks is more important. In a morally confused world, there are many faces of morally defective people. We shall look at some of them.

The Good

Many people, out of good intention and a genuine belief that they are doing good deeds, have done a lot of harm to the society. In some cases, what they have done borders on cruelty. I am thinking about people who are very active in preventing euthanasia; they do it because of their flawed morality.

The Pitiful and the Exploited

The end of the Iraq invasion also marked the beginning of a new wave of suicide bombers. Hurting one's enemies by suicide is the saddest form of offense, and an attacker fully knows his consequence; he expects to die and kills as many of his enemies, and innocents, together. Some do it for a very honorable cause and are heroes to their countries, but many, I believe, are misguided and used.

During a sea battle between the Chinese navy against an invading fleet of Japanese warships in WWII, the Chinese fleet was grossly outclassed by the invaders. Almost all the Chinese ships were destroyed shortly after the encounters. The outdated planes of the Chinese air force sent to counter the enemy fleet were pitiful by comparison to the Japanese steel and cannons. Confronted with certain defeat and the prospect of letting the enemies in, and thereby putting the lives of millions of loved ones at the mercy of the enemies, the pilots, one by one, dived and hit the enemy's flagship with their planes, and eventually sank the Japanese equivalent of Battleship *Bismarck*. It was both a sad and glorious story. This kind of suicide bombers are to be remembered and honored. But can we say the same of those Middle East suicide bombers? In our story, the soldiers in the Chinese air force were killing enemy soldiers. But in the Middle East, the bombers were killing more innocent people than the targeted. How do you justify that? What drove them to commit such a sad way to kill? In light of a need to survive, a common goal shared by every living organism, what kind of power can override such a deep instinct that roots at the beginning of life?

It must be hatred, an emotion quite unique to humans, that makes them do it. When you hate someone strong enough, you will seek to kill that person more than anything, including your own life. It is also likely powered by a strong moral sense, whether that moral sense is flawed or not. People who commit suicide bombing believe 1) they are morally right; they are doing it for Allah. And 2) there will be a reward after they get themselves killed. Though there could be exceptions, most of them were ignorant and easily manipulated and exploited. It is such a sad thing, not only for the used and exploited, but also for the many innocents that have lost their lives from such ignorance. What pity!

The Ugly

Yes, my choice is none other than the ex-Ontario Premier Dalton McGuinty. Surprised, aren't you? In the animal kingdom, cruel animals always have the look to go with it: the hood of a striking cobra, the angry look of an eagle, or the rage on a lion's face when it kills. Or, in fairytales, a wicked person always has a twisted look that warns you. Not McGuinty. He has the look of a movie star; he always smiles and is so charming. He knowingly screwed the taxpayers. What made McGuinty so ugly was what he did to the Ontario taxpayers and the people who voted for him. McGuinty was the premier that cancelled the contracts to build two gas-fired electricity plants in Oakville and Mississauga. Why? To save the two Liberal seats in the 2011 provincial election. The cost? More than $1 billion, a sum that puts the scandal among the costliest in the province's history.

So what was the big deal? Do you have any idea how many people would die because of the money wasted? Let me assume that each $10,000 could save the life or change the future of one person—you can pick your number—then, more than 100,000 people could have died or have their lives ruined from McGuinty's decision. He clearly chose to do it and could not be ignorant of the consequences because he cowardly resigned before the whole scandal surfaced and thus did not have to answer the voters. In light of the number of lives lost and ruined, McGuinty did not simply make a mistake; he knowingly committed a crime against the people who voted for him. He bit the hands that fed him. Nasty dog!

Why did he choose to do it? Because he had no moral sense? I don't think so. He has got lots of education and has been brought up in a respected family; he could not have been ignorant. He chose to be loyal to his party over the people who voted for him. If he had moral sense, it was a twisted one at best. In essence, he ignored his moral sense (I am assuming he had it), and did it because he knew the system too well and the people of Ontario could not do anything to him. There was absolutely no accountability in the system. Thus, he had no fear of the consequence of his action despite causing huge damages to Ontarians. If that is not ugly, what is?

The fact that we have these different faces of morality, all believing that they are righteous and doing the right thing, shows that we live in a morally very confused time. It is such an irony considering the level of knowledge we have achieved in science. In biology, we know a living organism to its very basic level—its structure, its genome, biochemical makeup, the kind of physics operating inside, and much more. In understanding our cosmos, we are quite certain about its starting point and the forces among the smallest particles involved in holding the whole thing together. And in medicine, we have wiped out many diseases that have terrorized humanity since antiquity. Despite all these achievements, we still don't have a united moral view, like a united view in science or traffic light signals, to govern our planet.

Then, one might think that a united morality is not important or more people will work toward finding it. If that is what you think, consider this. What if the world did not have unified traffic signals? Then driving in another country or even in a different city would be very dangerous, won't it? This is exactly the state morality is in. Every country has its own view. This can be dangerous too. Doing something permissible in one's culture can get you executed in another country. With the moral views so different, there will never be solution to wars, poverty, and environmental deterioration.

The confusion is caused by our world having too many moral views. As a start, every religion has its own brand of morality; there are as many moral views as there are religions. And since not everyone is religious, the atheists have created their own kind of no-god moral views. The morality presented by Immanuel Kant is among the more well-known.

By doing away with God, Kant's morality is based on reason. It was a great start and Kant was in the right direction in unifying the moral views. However, Kant's brand of morality has not advanced much since his passing. His many followers still have no answers to many of today's moral issues like war, pollution, same-sex marriage, euthanasia, prostitution, or whether a well-off country should or should not accept more refugees from Syria or Africa.

Ideally, morality is supposed to help build a happy world where people live in harmony with one another and our environment is protected. If that is the goal, then all the existing moral views have failed and failed miserably. Not only do people in the globe not live in peace, wars and miseries are everywhere you look, even in advanced countries. As long as these conditions exist, people will keep coming up with new morality and try to solve the problems. But regrettably, there are very, very few scientists, if any, participating in the search. People who do morality are still philosophers that have little science training; they don't have the right tools to solve moral problems.

Human Rights Movement—the New Moral God

There is a newcomer. It is called *human rights*. For people who are interested in this brand of morality, I would recommend an article called "Human Rights 101-AAAS" by Sam McFarland. From this article, I got a brief view of the movement. A reader needs to know that my understanding on this subject is quite limited. Please read my view on this subject with great caution.

The concept of human rights is relatively new compared to the religion-based moralities. The movement began after WWII in response to the cruelties seen in the war, particularly what Hitler did to humanity, to the millions of Jews especially. Human rights are moral ideals. The movement is full of noble ideas about what a human being should be entitled to. One thing that is always true about morality is leadership has always been competitive. To be a leader in morality, people always try to outnice the other. The field of human rights is no different. After several decades, it has evolved to become highly idealistic, with little consideration for the different political environments. According to this ideal, the rights a human being has should apply to every single person on the planet, regardless of the economic conditions of a country. These rights are dreams, and the dreamers have no idea of how to realize them. The dreamers are quite enthusiastic in imposing their dreams to the world with no authority to do so either. As a result, many of the rights are not enforceable.

Nations that reject some of the rights are quite advanced, not just the third-world countries. For example, how would a country look at the problem of using torture to get information from a most hated enemy? Without question, torturing someone is exceedingly cruel. But can it be ever justified? Based on the high ideal of human rights, it is never justifiable. In the 2016 American presidential election, Donald Trump makes it an election issue by proposing the use of torture on some of America's worst enemies. He won the election.

Human rights also prohibit death penalty and restriction of religion freedom. China is a country that has been repeatedly accused of a long list of human rights violations, such as lacking religious freedom or too frequent use of death penalty. It is quite fashionable for western leaders (the ex-Canadian Prime Minister Stephen Harper, for example) to insult China with human rights violations on many occasions while Canada's own human rights records under Harper's watch were less than shiny. Other than the inability to solving the many pressing problems, human rights have added to the already confusing moral situation, adding not-needed fuel to international conflicts.

The morality based on human rights is very problematic because the concepts of human rights, their very foundations, have been messy from day one. *"The concept of human rights implies that basic rights belong to every member of the human race,"* a quote from McFarland's article. From this simple statement, it is quite obvious that the universality of human rights is an assumption and an unprovable thesis, and nothing more than an unsubstantiated claim.

Please let me explain. For a person to have any rights, the rights need to come from a certain governing authority that has the power to grant the rights. A Canadian, for example, has many rights; his rights come from the Canadian government. Or a child's rights often come from his parents. What is the authority that gives these basic rights to every member of the human race? For atheists, they are certain to reject the notion that it is God that gives people such rights. Other than God, who would have this power? Without the proper authorities to give such rights, will the rights be enforceable? And who should have the power to enforce the many rights? Quite often, every one of the human rights is debatable for countries that object to it. The organization that promotes human rights has no answer for any of those objections.

The second fatal flaw of the concepts is it lacks moral foundation for those universal rights. Again, let me quote a sentence from the article: *When they have finished (drafting the Universal Declaration), philosopher Jacques Maritain summarized, "We agree about the rights, but on condition that no one asks us why."* Again, this should be obvious. The many rights are nothing more than claims; no reason on the claims has ever been provided. If human rights are good for anything; they sure have created tens of thousands of jobs and thus help to reduce unemployment worldwide. There must be more than thousands of Canadians making very good incomes from this piece of moral junk.

Despite its uselessness in solving any real issue, human rights, benefited by their amorphousness, have kept on growing like weeds after a summer rain. Human rights have replaced God or been placed above God by their believers. In Muslim countries, the death penalty not only is justified, it is condoned by their God. I urge you to spend a bit of time studying the Sharia Law to satisfy yourself if you doubt this statement. Many politicians find human rights useful to score political points; they are phonies. While criticizing a country for violations, the politicians also eagerly court the noncompliant country for business. Saudi is one of the worst countries for its lousy human rights records. Canada, despite its self-appointed role as a human rights defender, also eagerly sells billions worth of armored vehicles to the country. Human rights are garbage.

If you can't help being confused, moral view will be the last thing you want to be confused about, because it is so, so important. For an ordinary person, his moral view is his road map for his everyday activities, especially in dealing with others. For lawmakers, their moral views will be the basis for making a country's laws. A moral view is the foundation of a country's laws; a moral view decides a country's values and helps to create laws to uphold those values and rid the country of the unwanted ones. Examples are many. If we consider stealing undesirable, then it will be immoral and the person caught stealing is breaking the law and will be punished accordingly. Same applies to telling lies, driving drunk or at unsafe speed, etc.

Different cultures have different values set by their religions; therefore, their laws also reflect such variations. In countries that still hold extramarital sex as sinful and a very serious immoral act, the punishment for breaking such a law can be death. In most western countries, adultery is not such a big deal, and there is little consequence for the adulterers. Or, in Muslim countries, citizens do not have religious freedom; only Islam is legal. Infidels are punishable by death. In most western countries, religious freedom is guaranteed.

Ideally, a good or practical moral view should be the instrument to serve its people and is the foundation for creating laws which build a happy society. And a happy society or country is where the people enjoy the maximum degree of freedom and have comfortable lives. If we can agree on the two goals as the measuring sticks, then countries in our world have different degrees of happiness. The most successful countries are those that provide their people with safety and rich material lives, while those failing countries are where people suffer the miseries of wars, unhealthy environment, and poverty. The marked differences are the reflections of the different levels of the people's moralities. Our moral view should be the foundation to build happiness. Yet, even among the best countries—Japan and Scandinavian countries—there are still issues that don't have clear answers. As a result, people still suffer unnecessarily. My favorite examples are same-sex marriage, abortion, euthanasia, prostitution, or going to war.

The latest (2016) issue that has been troubling many leaders of advanced European countries, the United States, and Canada, etc. is the question of accepting refugees from Syria and many poor countries in Africa. How do you decide one way or other? Accepting too many will cause lots of problems—financial, how to assimilate these groups with different religions and drastically different values into the society, and security. Not accepting them will give the countries a guilty conscience from their high moral expectation created by the unreal moral view. Unable to resolve the morality, the issue creates a rift among the countrymen. So how do you, the lawmaker of a country, deal with these huge moral headaches? Should we continue the old course just to be nice, without knowing the hidden dangers, or find a new morality to solve them?

I believe it is time for many of the more advanced countries to consider junking the old moral system and look for a new solution. I also believe that a person who recommends or champions breaking something should morally be responsible for fixing it. The latest Brexit is a very valuable lesson. The leaders championing Brexit quit after they succeeded in breaking the country's relationship with the other European countries. They have no solution to the big mess they have created. The Brits, to their horror, found out after following their leaders that the emperor is naked! How morally irresponsible is that? You just don't wreck something and say, "I have done my job," self-congratulate, and walk away, thereby leaving people who have counted on you to continue leading them lost in confusion. What a bloody shame and pity!

I won't break something without offering a solution. I am quite confident the new morality will do the job. It is based on a new knowledge that human nature is selfish and how to work with it, not against it. We also have a clear direction of how to fix the problems of our planet and build a better one. For the first time in human history, we have all the tools we need.

Introducing Our Objectives of the New Moral Model

Without any doubt in my mind, the way to fix our planet and then build a better one should begin with a correct moral view. Therefore, let us first define what our new moral view should achieve. It should be the foundation to make laws that give people the maximum degree of freedom without harmful effects; it should also lay the foundation to give people stable, safe, and comfortable material lives. The moral view also should give a person a road map to happiness and a successful life; it should be the source to supply a country with valuable building blocks, the people.

From what we have discussed following the evolution of our species, the morality should lead to enhancing the cooperation and intelligence of the people. A highly cooperative society will be a happy country; a highly intelligent country will give people the best material comforts. If you can agree on these goals, the new morality will be the tool.

Besides the principles from the new morality, we shall rely on science to provide us the information to solve problems. Science will be the main source of our intelligence. And since the one thing that will destroy cooperation among people is selfishness, therefore the main target of the proposed moral view is to deal with this selfishness. Should we mercilessly suppress it or work with it?

Any proposed morality will be a failure if it cannot solve the biggest three problems plaguing our planet: wars, poverty, and the hurt and harm we have inflicted on our environment. Let us never lose sight of these objectives by keeping asking this question: Will the new morality achieve the three ultimate goals? Can it work?

Building the Model from the Golden Rule

Building the new moral model involves two steps. Step 1: Choosing the right criteria to decide what should moral right and wrong be; the criteria are the components or ingredients. Step 2: Assembling the components to create a tool or machine for moral judgments. I am using the word *machine* because it will be the way it works: very rigid and precise, and will produce the same conclusion no matter who uses it—like a machine; some common sense required, of course.

Since we want our moral code to help us build a rich world with plenty of other species, then our moral code should be extended to include protecting some species that are beneficial, if not all. While I have no moral qualm in wiping out some blood-sucking mosquito or pesky fly species, mindlessly slaughtering sharks, snakes, whales, tigers, leopards will certainly be no-nos. It is time to extend our moral obligation to include other species and environment; it also serves our own interests.

The Golden Rule

What criteria should we choose to decide moral right and wrong and how many? Since the goal of the new code is to stop people from hurting others—a natural tendency from having a selfish nature—our focus will be specifically on whether harm has been caused or not. If an act causes no hurt to anyone, it should not be a moral concern. In other words, harmfulness is what determines the morality of a behavior; i.e., no harm done, then it is not immoral. How do we decide whether or not harm has been done? Then we need science. Scientific knowledge will have the final say on whether or not a behavior is harmful if in doubt. Our existing moral views are old. Many of the allegedly bad or harmful behaviors have no support from science at all. Our attitudes toward sex, for example. To view sex as evil, dirty, and something to be avoided is a wrong label according to science. Our misunderstanding of sex has been the reason for lots of human suffering. It is time to retire the old myths and let science take charge in judging real harmfulness, and from it the moral right and wrong. Let the facts speak for the issues.

Using harmfulness as the only deciding principle appears to be a solid choice for what we want to achieve. But there is an important consideration. Since our model is to be used to solve global problems, will everyone accept harmfulness and that harmfulness only is what should determine the morality of a behavior? Will every country, religion, or culture support it? Let us do some research among different religions and cultures and see whether we can find the needed common ground.

It was a daunting task for me. I was a biologist. I did not know much about the moral field. Just when I began to lose hope, my luck changed. *The Toronto Star* on September 29, 2001, had an article by Ron Csilag titled "The Reciprocity Entreaty." It was exactly tailor-made for what I wanted. The article was about the Golden Rule. To avoid infringing on the copyright, I shall not quote the article. A reader is encouraged to google *versions of the Golden Rule* to satisfy himself.

The Golden Rule is based on the principle of reciprocity. It teaches us to be considerate by always asking ourselves the question in dealing with others: *If I were at the receiving end of what I am going to do, how would I feel?* And it is so simple and makes so much common sense that even a dummy or idiot can understand it. Best of all, the rule has come from the leaders or teachers of the world's most popular religions, those who had in the past given us the present-day moralities. So the Golden Rule fits the universality requirement beautifully; the concept is one of the very few widely accepted beliefs before science.

Interestingly, all the great religions and teachers have been saying the same thing and mostly have taken a prohibitive tone. They seemed to know our natural tendency to hurt. And curbing our hurtful tendency is exactly what our model is aiming at. The Golden Rule is like the laws of our societies: *Do not speed. Do not drink and drive. Or do not text while driving.* The "*don't*" in the Golden Rule is not specific; it covers everything and anything that is hurtful to others, and we all understand what that is. While many behaviors covered by the *don'ts* are unquestionably bad, there is one common behavior which causes a lot of harm and is very widespread. Many even endorse it as morally OK or desirable. And that is forcing one's beliefs or values upon others. We ask:

according to the Golden Rule, is it moral to force one's beliefs or values upon others? A belief can be religious, philosophical, or based on science. A receiving party can be a total stranger, a student, or even one's own child. To put it in the Golden Rule's format, it will be: *If you do not want others to force their beliefs on you, should you force your beliefs upon others?*

There are many ways to force one's beliefs upon others. It could be by violence, intimidation, brainwashing, or propaganda through newspapers or TV channels. Parents forcing their beliefs upon their children is quite common, and they do it with the best of intention—love. Granted, does it make it right to force a belief upon someone under your care? I once asked my younger daughter when she was five, "Quan, what would you like to be when you grow up?" She replied with a smile and conviction, "I want to be a garbage collector." OMG! It took me a long while to figure out the possible reasons why she would choose such a lousy job. It was our different perspectives. To me, a good job is something prestigious, something I love doing, and also makes good money. But to a five-year-old, a good job is something fun. Riding outside a garbage truck on a sunny, breezy afternoon and get paid for tossing bags into the truck certainly looks fun to her. Luckily, she soon changed her mind. She wanted to be a nun instead! Oh Lord, why me?

If my daughter were twenty-one at the time and still wanted to be a garbage collector, should I respect her decision? (I apologize for my prejudice against garbage collectors. From where I came, collecting garbage is a shitty job and makes shitty money. Above all, no decent girl would want to marry such a loser.) I always remember how "uncle" Lai had spoiled my fun in a chess game. At the time, I was living in a new subdivision close to the high school I was teaching in. I liked playing chess. However, like the way I have been conducting my life, I have never planned more than two steps ahead before making a move. I ended up losing most of the time. It was difficult for me to find an equally lousy player to make the game interesting. Lucky for me, I found Yeung, a neighbor; he was that player. Yeung and I were in the middle of a chess game when "uncle" Lai came along and stood behind me. Lai was in his seventies; he was a loner. Just after I had finished a "brilliant" move, I heard "uncle" Lai say, "No, no, no!" And before I could do anything, he had retrieved my move and changed it. One move led to another, and pretty soon the old man was making all the moves for me. I "won" the match, but I felt absolutely no joy. If it were up to me, I would certainly have preferred to do it my way. Even losing—and that happened all the time—I would have more fun.

While forcing one's beliefs upon others could be motivated by love, attacking others because they hold a different belief is certainly self-serving. I used to do it a lot, especially arguing with one of my exes. Soccer fans are notorious for their intolerance of their rivals. Brawls frequently break out after a match, if not during a match. One would think only soccer hooligans would attack others. Hardly! In Mexico and some Asian countries, it is not uncommon to see politicians involved in fistfights for having different ideas in running a city or country. I have seen some of those videos; it beats *The Three Stooges*. How about science professors? You would think with their education and their beliefs in academic freedom and pursuit of truth they would be more civilized. In writing a chapter of the *Happy* book, I was surfing the Internet for information on the possible causes leading to the extinction of the monster lizards. I was shocked to read and sense the ferocity with which one party of an alternative theory was attacked. The "criticisms" did not have to do with hard scientific facts; some of the things were very personal, not unlike the verbal fights between hawkers in the poor Hong Kong neighborhoods. Scientists are supposed to be an intellectual bunch that take pride in advancing the truth based on hard data; they are expected to be objective and courteous. It is quite inexcusable to see an authority in a certain field who for personal gains tries to push his pet theory by heat rather than by light—an expression borrowed from Edward O. Wilson.

The attacks in academia would be like child's play compared to the cruelty with which the Catholic Church attacked and prosecuted the scientists in the past centuries. As a result, many scientists still bear the grudge of the bygone eras; many top-notch scientists often deny God. And there are the centuries-old fights between Muslims and Christians, Jews and Palestinians, or Shiite and Sunnites. Some of the cruelest killings on our planet have been done between groups worshipping the same God. Does it make sense? Should we kill someone just because they do not believe in the same thing as we do or have a different set of values? Should one be attacked because he believes that the universe was created in a Big Bang, apples are more delicious than oranges, or brunettes have more fun than blondes? Is attacking another party based on a difference in belief an exception to the Golden Rule? Or is forcing one's beliefs upon others in compliance with the Rule?

Lay not on any soul a load that you would not wish to be laid upon you, *unless their beliefs are different from yours.*

Treat not others in ways that you yourself would find hurtful, *unless their beliefs are different from yours.*

So always treat others as you would like them to treat you, *unless their beliefs are different from yours.*

And so on, and so forth.

But nowhere in the Golden Rule has the exception been made. So what do you think? Should we attack others because they have different beliefs? Should we force our beliefs upon others? I am in favor of making *forcing one's beliefs upon others* something prohibited by the Golden Rule. What do you think? Are we all on the same side?

It then brings up a very interesting point. Is it OK for me to force my beliefs in the Golden Rule upon you, the reader, as a principle to build the moral model upon? I strongly believe in the Golden Rule. But the Golden Rule also says that I should not force it upon anyone. A belief is a belief regardless. What should we do? With such an understanding, and in full compliance with the Golden Rule, our subsequent discussion on morality is therefore only a proposal or a suggestion. I really want to sell it, but it will be up to you to decide whether to buy or not to buy it. So please keep in mind that the model is only a suggestion, and feel free to toss it into the recycle bin if you are not comfortable with the Golden Rule as a deciding principle.

Some of you may be skeptical about the usefulness of the Golden Rule for our model building. The concern will be that the Golden Rule has been around since antiquity and been a component of all moral models. It has also been proven ineffective, if not useless. The irony about the Golden Rule is everybody knows it but hardly anyone takes it seriously as a moral guideline. Using the Golden Rule in our model would be like a coach using a fifty-some-year-old long retired quarterback in the Super Bowl. Why do you think it will be different this time? This concern has been raised, in fact, several times in the past years after I have first published the model in the *Happy To Be Morally Selfish* book. It is a valid concern, if not an objection.

There are several reasons contributing to the ineffectiveness of the Rule. 1) In every morality there are many competing values like integrity, honesty, trustworthy, and loyalty. The Golden Rule was just one of them; it can easily be lost among those seemingly more important virtues. 2) The Golden Rule, when compared to the dogmas of a religion or a teaching, is often far less important. There are many dogmas that trump the rule if in conflict. And religions have little interest in crowning the rule; it does not bring them much benefit. There are more important messages to spread, like Jesus is the only son of God, or Muhammad is the only true prophet, etc. 3) For the Golden Rule to be effective and useful, it is assumed that people are all equal. This belief was never honored until modern democratic societies came into existence. When some people were at a higher class than others, the Golden Rule had no teeth. For example, an emperor in China would never give a damn about the Rule, let alone be bound by the Rule. If an emperor decided that you should be killed for whatever reason, you would be dead. Not vice versa. Following an emperor, the many government officials were higher in social status than ordinary citizens. They had absolutely no interest in following it when dealing with ordinary people other than to talk about it. 4) There seems to be no consequence for violating the Rule. And lastly, 5) to make the rule effective in moral decisions, you need to allow people a freedom of choice, which did not exist before true democracy had been established. We shall discuss *freedom of choice* shortly.

From the above, the Golden Rule has been so routinely trumped by other "virtues" or people for convenience that it has been weakened to the point of being a piece of useless furnishing in a moral house, like a fireplace in a Chinese-Canadian home. Everyone wants it in his morality, but no one pays much attention to it. Confucius, for example, was one of the people who taught the Golden Rule. But I don't think he believed in it personally, or he would not have proposed giving an emperor unlimited power, allowing him to break the Rule at will.

For us, the Golden Rule is a godsend. It is tailor-made for building our model because the target of our morality is selfishness and the Golden Rule is tailored exactly for that, though people who proposed it might not have known it. To make our moral model effective, the Golden Rule, and it only, will decide morality. Its decision will be supreme in every moral consideration. There is absolutely no exception to the ruling from it, regardless of who the person is. Nobody is above the Golden Rule in moral considerations. Simple, isn't it?

Reshaping the Golden Rule to Get the Two Criteria for Moral Decision

The Golden Rule is definitely the principle we have been looking for to decide morality. To be useful, however, we have to reshape it without changing its essence a bit. The Golden Rule just tells us *do not* but fails to mention what consequence will follow if we *do*. It is like you teaching your three-year-old son, "Don't touch the hot plate!" and not telling him what will happen if he does.

Our job becomes obvious. To make the Golden Rule useful, we need to ask two questions: (1) What if someone violates the Golden Rule, i.e., he does something he would find hurtful when it happens to him, yet still intentionally does it to another person? Then, we can pass a judgment. Such an act will be immoral and the person has committed a moral wrongdoing. Makes sense? The second question will be why would someone do such a thing anyway? From the knowledge that human nature is selfish, we know there can be only one motive; i.e., to gain something of value to his survival from his victim. In most societies, that something of value to survival will be money. For men, there is another reason; it will be for sexual gratification. The answers to the two questions allow us to come up with the first moral principle:

1. To Intentionally Hurt Others for One's Own Gain is Immoral

For something to be classified as immoral, it must be (i) intentional and (ii) for the self-gain of the person who initiates the behavior. Now, the Golden Rule is almost ready to be deployed.

2. Not Allowing a Receiving Party the Free Choice is Immoral; Defining Freedom

While hurting others for self-gain is immoral according to the Golden Rule, there are many cases where the "victims" are happy and willing to be harmed. How do we decide the morality where a "victim" does it out of his free choice? Therefore, before we can come up with a moral judgment, we should also consider whether the party being hurt has the choice to partake. The freedom to choose is highly valued in all democratic societies. It will thus be our second criterion for moral consideration.

Let us elaborate on the meaning of free choice to oust some of the common misunderstandings before we proceed. Free choice, of course, is having a freedom to choose. Then, the question becomes: What is *freedom*? If you check a dictionary, it often has the meanings of *without* or *exempted from* restriction, restraint, confinement, or being forced to . . . While the description is not wrong, it can be misleading. It is often taken as you can freely do what you want. And that is the reason why so many people don't actually know its meaning.

Freedom is an oxymoron or a paradox because freedom is always defined by boundaries. To be free, you need to do things within a number of boundaries. To be continuously free is first to know your boundaries or you will lose freedom in no time. Our freedom is limited by three boundaries. 1) Physical boundary: We all have to obey the laws of physics and you can only jump so high, run so far and fast, and can only live in environment with oxygen, etc. 2) Financial boundary: Money often decides how free a person can be. In winter, we all love to vacation in the Caribbean, we can't. We have to work to make money to pay mortgage, car loan, and grocery, *and tax*. Before the tax-freedom day, all you make goes to the government. And 3) moral boundary. Moral boundary is the most difficult one. If you don't know what is moral and what isn't, then you have no choice but to be told by some authorities—your clergy, rabbi, imam, or politicians, for example. It is not an enviable position. You are not unlike a little kid who often has to ask for approvals and permissions from your dad and mom. You will be bounded by many rules and views given to you that often don't make sense; you can also be exploited.

I feel much freer ever since I have established my new moral principles in this book about ten years ago. I don't need other people to tell me right from wrong. I form my own judgment in moral matters. It gives me lots more freedom than people going to the church, following the Koran, Buddhism, or Confucianism. If you want to be truly free in the moral department, know your moral boundary. Moral boundary includes the laws of the land, our moral duties and obligations—to our family members, friends, employers, and others. In our new morality, our obligation also includes to other species and the environment.

Only within the constraints of the three boundaries then can a person be free. The three boundaries are comparable to the three dimensions of space; they define the space you can truly be free in. It is like a rectangular aquarium containing water set by your physical, financial, and moral boundaries. Within the defined space, you are like a gold fish and can freely swim within the confines of the boundaries. So there is no such thing as absolute freedom. Once you cross the boundaries, your freedom will soon end. If you want to be free and want to fly like a bird, you can get yourself killed in no time. If you spend more than you earn, your freedom will soon be taken away. Or if you cross a moral boundary, you will likely be in trouble with the law. For an animal, the moral boundary and financial boundary do not exist. It has only the physical boundary; physics only dictates its daily survival activities. But it is a brutal existence. I would rather have three boundaries than one.

People in highly civilized countries such as the US, UK, Canada, etc., often misunderstand individual freedom as something without obligation or boundary. I am talking about the right to bear children without restrains. Often, poor single mothers or couples on welfare are allowed to freely have children without the capability of providing for them. It is their rights, according to the laws of the land. What do you think? I think having children is a right which should also come with some obligations, like owning a house, or a car. A person must pay for it. Failing that, it will be immoral, according to our new moral model. Why? We shall explain the issue later.

Even more ridiculous—and this one is homegrown in Canada—is the so-called freeman on the land movement. With a misguided (or intentionally distorted) view of freedom, these people—believed to number around 30,000 in Canada—are nothing but trouble for those who are unfortunate to deal with them. A senior Calgary woman rented a unit of her duplex to a freeman. The freeman declared his rental unit as "embassy." He almost completely wrecked the unit and refused to pay the agreed rent. It made my blood boil reading the story. Make no mistake, these are immorally selfish guys who specialize in hurting people for their own gain. They are criminals. I would send them one way to the great Canadian wilderness. Isn't freedom what they want?

Having explained what true freedom is, let us explore what *freedom to choose* or *freedom of choice* means. Let us define it as: *every clear-headed, well-informed, and mature person, when not under undue pressure, has the right to freely (within the three confines) choose and decide a course of action that best serves his individual interest.* I think we all understand what clear-headed, well-informed, and mature mean. I want to draw your attention to *best serve his individual interest.* In our new moral model, freedom of choice usually means whether or not the person is forced into the situation or by choice. We ask: is it the person's choice?

After including freedom to choose as another component, we have all we need to build our moral "machine." To recap, our moral model has only two principles: (1) to hurt another person intentionally for one's own gain is immoral; and (2) to force another person to partake is also immoral. Though there are two principles, both are from the Golden Rule. The Golden Rule is truly golden; it is the only foundation upon which we shall build our morality. Therefore, our model shall be very simple, coherent, and will never ever contradict itself.

Putting the Two Criteria Together to Build the "Moral" Machine

Asking the Questions

We have two principles to decide morality. If you intentionally hurt another person for your own gain, it is Immoral. There are hundreds of ways—stealing, attacking, sexually assaulting, cheating, drinking and driving, etc.—one person can hurt another. Before we can judge a behavior, we need first to find out who is hurting who, correct? How? By asking questions. Isn't that simple? What questions and how many? We only need to ask two very simple questions. No trick, promise!

1. *Whose interest does it (an act or a behavior) serve?*

    We are exceedingly intelligent creatures; we won't do things without a reason. What is the reason behind our dealings with others? To show the point, let me tell you a story.

    Years ago, I was doing some research in the Badlands, Alberta. I was with a group from the Botany Department of U of Toronto.

During one of the weekends, the group visited a small town call Red Deer. I was strolling along Main Street trying to kill some time. Then, I heard a girl say a sweet hello to someone. I turned my head to the direction where the hello was from, and saw a rather pretty blonde young girl across the street. As soon as we established eye contact, she said another sweeter and louder hello to me, and signed for me to walk across to meet her. At the time, I had not shaved for more than a week. There are men who would look macho and irresistibly sexy by not shaving. Yours truly was definite not one of them. Five foot five and Chinese in a small Albertan town, I knew it was not sex that the girl was interested in. (I am one of those animals that always first think of sex when a pretty woman talks to me.) I instinctively obliged to her bidding. "Would you like to make a small donation . . . ?" She popped the question with a most charming smile as soon as I was at a distance of several arms' length away. I quickly made a U-turn. I also cursed myself for being so heartless to a possibly worthy course. The moral of the story: there is always a reason for someone to do something.

2. *Who is getting hurt, or at whose expense?*

You can choose either version. It serves to ID the victim.

We are almost ready. Simple, isn't it? I don't think any reader should have any problem understanding the questions, and later on, in applying them.

The next and final step is to find out whether the initiator and the receiver of the act both have the freedom to choose, or if anyone is forced into the situation. How? By asking the third and final question, of course!

3. *Do both/all parties involved have the freedom to choose?*

Under many circumstances, question 1 and 2 together are enough to lead you to a right moral conclusion. But in some weird circumstances, we need Question 3. It will allow us to decide with great certainty. The third question is the key question that empowers our moral model, making it so effective. Our planet never lacks strange animals or weird behaviors. In some situations, the "victim" is a willing participant who is not intoxicated and knows exactly what he is getting into. In other words, the "victim," out of his free will and to serve his individual interest, has chosen to be hurt.

Example: A German computer expert named Armin Melwes confessed on December 3, 2003, that he had killed and eaten an allegedly willing victim named Berliner Bernd Juergen Brandes. Melves got his victim through advertising in the Internet: *"Come to me. I'll eat your delicious flesh."* Brandes, forty-three, was among the more than 400 that answered the ad and the only one picked. According to Melwes, the victim had the desire to be killed and eaten and did not appear to be disturbed when he decided to volunteer. Brandes knew exactly what he was getting into and was willing—according to the cannibal. How would you judge the incident morally? When a victim is a willing participant, we can call it a *Commander Zhou Beating General Huang Scenario*. It is a classic case in which one party is happy to inflict the pain—beating in this case—while the receiving party is willing to take it. The story took place near the end of the Han Dynasty during the prelude of a deciding battle between the two kingdoms at war. Commander Zhou and General Huang, the soldiers of the invaded country, put on a show in which Commander Zhou, on top of mercilessly beating General Huang, also humiliated him in the presence of the other generals for Huang's alleged insubordination. General. Huang then used the beating and humiliation to sell it to the commander of the invading army. The commander bought the show, to his total demise at the battle of Russet Cliff on the Yangtze River.

The third question is quite crucial to determining moral right and wrong. If you don't believe that a mature, well-informed, and clear-headed person can freely choose a course of action for himself, you will have difficulty with the moral decision based on the third question. We shall look at the moral issue of the man-eater's case in a later chapter. Used together, the three questions allow us to come up with a clear moral conclusion all the time.

That is it, folks. Now we have a brand-new, complete, and fully working machine to tell moral right and wrong. How do we know? Why don't we find out? Why don't we take it for a test drive? Hold it! Before we do our test drive, maybe we should be a bit more critical and let us look at the components of this new machine again to see any of the components is faulty. The model is based on one fact: human nature is (hurtfully) selfish. To control and guide this selfish nature, we employ the Golden Rule, which, in essence, is stating that (i) hurting others for self-gain is immoral, and (ii) not allowing the receiving party a freedom of choice will also be immoral. Are you comfortable with the fact and the rule? Are we on solid ground or on shaky foundation? Our model is built upon them. If any one of the two above is wobbly—i.e., that human nature is noble and naturally giving, or the Golden Rule is defective—then our conclusions will be wrong. I urge you to spend a bit of time to critically think about them before proceeding. If you have objections, put them down for later reference.

For those who prefer to adhere to the teachings of the church or the moral guidelines from your mother-in-law, the following discussion may offend you. Please be warned.

Testing the Model

Let us first test our brand-new moral model with some pretty easy stuff such as lying and stealing, to which we already know the answers. The tests will allow us to see whether the model really works, and if it does, get some feel to using it—just like test-driving a car. Let us do it.

The Morality of Stealing

Scenario 1:

Person A unwittingly left his wallet which showed a bunch of $20 bills on his desk. Person B happened to pass by and took the wallet, not knowing person C was watching. Let us first decide the morality of stealing in this case. B stole the wallet of A. To see the morality of the incident, let us ask the three questions.

1. In taking the wallet, whose interest did it serve?

Ans. B's interest.

2. At whose expense?

Ans. At A's; he suffered the loss.

3. Did both parties in the event have the freedom to choose?

Ans. B had the choice, A did not.

Conclusion: From the Golden Rule, *it is not morally acceptable to hurt another person for one's own gain and it is wrong to promote one's interest at the expense of another person.* B stole the wallet from A, who suffered some financial loss. B had the choice, not A. In essence, B chose to do something to promote his own interest at A's expense, while A had no choice in the matter. So B was immoral. And stealing in this case was immoral. Our model is working!

Scenario 2:

In 2003 in Toronto, we had a rather high-profile politician suspected of using taxpayers' money to pay for part of his and his family's trip to Europe. If proven true, the thief might as well say goodbye to his political future. Let us again use the three questions to decide the morality of the politician's action:

1. Whose interest did it serve?

Ans. The politician's personal interest, which was not entitled.

2. At whose expense?

Ans. The taxpayers', mine included.

3. Did both parties in the event have the freedom to choose?

Ans. The politician had the choice; the taxpayers did not.

Conclusion: The politician is definitely immoral. Clear and simple, isn't it?

Scenario 3: *"Heinz dilemma"*

Let us look at another example on the morality of stealing. Will there be any circumstances that justify stealing? The following example is taken from the second edition of *Psychology* by Bernstein, Roy, Srull, and

Wickens. The example is called *Heinz dilemma*, which is on page 67 of the textbook. And here I quote:

> *In Europe, a woman was near death from a special kind of cancer. There was one drug that the doctors thought might save her. It was a form of radium that a druggist in the same town had recently discovered. The drug was expensive to make, but the druggist was charging ten times what the drug cost him to make. He paid $200 for the radium and charged $2000 for a small dose of the drug. The sick woman's husband, Heinz, went to everyone he knew to borrow the money, but could only get together about $1000, which was half of what it cost. He told the druggist that his wife was dying and asked him to sell it cheaper or let him pay later. But the druggist said, "No, I discovered the drug and I'm going to make money from it." So Heinz got desperate and considered breaking into the man's store to steal the drug for his wife. Should Heinz steal the radium?*

So what do you think? Should Heinz do it or not? Before we try to answer the question, let us see what the textbook has to say. The story is used in the book to show how people judge morally as they get older and learn more. According to L. Kohlberg as quoted by the text book, there are six stages in the development of moral judgment, with stages 5 and 6 topping the moral judging scale. For example, stage 5, according to Kohlberg, is characterized by respecting rules and laws but knowing their limitation. Stage 6, the highest level of moral reasoning, is typified by following universal ethical principles such as justice, reciprocity, equality, and respect for human life and rights. Both stages 5 and 6 of moral reasoning conclude that Heinz should steal the drug because saving a life is more important than respecting laws and property.

With the background, what do you think? Should we apply the three questions to find out?

1. In stealing the drug, whose interest does it serve?

Ans. Heinz's and his wife's, who together could be viewed as the same *self* because the couple shares a lot of common interests and therefore should be considered as one party.

2.   At whose expense?

Ans. The druggist.

3.   Do both parties in the event have the freedom to choose?

Ans. Heinz has the choice; the victim, the druggist, does not.

Conclusion: Heinz is immorally selfish. Heinz is clearly hurting the druggist for his own benefit and therefore has committed a moral no-no according to the Golden Rule and our model! So what happens? Why the opposite conclusion? Let me remind you that Kohlberg, according to the book, says stealing the drug is *a conclusion from the highest levels of moral reasoning*. And yours truly, according to the model, has concluded that stealing the drug would be selfish and immoral. And let me further remind you that Lawrence Kohlberg is a prominent scholar specializing in human moral reasoning development—search the name and you will see. I, yours truly, have, up to the time of writing this part, done nothing that qualifies me to speak on the subject. I am not an academic person. I was still a real estate broker when I was writing this part of the book. Having said that, I guess the contradiction arises from the different criteria used for moral judgment. If the sick party had been Heinz instead of his wife, I wonder what the verdict from the book would be. And if there is a moral in the story, it will be that morality has been a murky issue because of the lack of a common standard. I have not read any of Kohlberg's publications. It would be interesting to see what are the assumptions and grounds upon which he builds his moral reasoning.

Kohlberg cites *justice, reciprocity, equality, and respect for human life and rights* as the ground. Great! But how and under what circumstances should those noble universal moral ethical principles be applied? Isn't it the *respect for human life and rights* the exact reason why we have poor parents freely procreating? So the current confusing moral views of the world are not only created by religions, we also have scholars like Kohlberg, who obviously is a follower of Kant's moral reasoning, helping to add to the great moral confusion. With confusing moral views come laws that do not make sense. And there will be more confusing issues to come from the existing views.

If it were up to me, I would change the central character from Heinz to Ullrich, who is a neighbor of the sick woman, and would add some spice to the story by mentioning that the woman is a widow with two very young children to look after. With the changes, let us look at the morality of the stealing again:

1. Whose interest does it serve?

   Ans. That of a sick widow who also has two very young children to look after.

2. At whose expense?

   Ans. Primarily at the druggist's expense, but also at Ullrich's because he is likely to be caught and prosecuted.

3. Do both parties in the event have the freedom to choose?

Ans. Ullrich has the freedom; the druggist does not.

Conclusion: Ullrich steals the drug for the benefit of a person who is likely to be a willing recipient of the gift. Ullrich does not expect anything in return from the beneficiary of his act; there is nothing attached to the gift. It is a classic example of love by our definition. Above all, Ullrich puts himself in serious jeopardy in benefitting an unrelated person. Out of love, he willingly sacrifices himself for something he believes in. We have the highest form of morality; we have a most noble character. Sacrificing for a belief or course—in this case to benefit an unrelated person in need—is the noblest act. The stories of such acts warm your heart, make you feel secure, and regain hope in humanity. They are people like blood donors, firemen who are willing to risk their lives to save the trapped persons, mothers who give their lives to save their children, and doctors who willingly and intentionally infect themselves with diseases to find the cures. They are selfless people; they are true heroes and saints. Do you agree?

One may be concerned about the druggist, who is certainly a victim of Ullrich's selfless act. What about him? It is tough being a moral judge, isn't it? My feeling is it is not a perfect world. We often have to pick the lesser of two evils. Ullrich has made a choice to hurt a party whose loss will be much less in comparison to the good the action brings to a sick widow and her children. And he has absolutely no other choice than to steal the drug. To relieve your conscience, the druggist should have bought insurance, shouldn't he? What if he doesn't? Not my fault, is it?

The Morality of Lying

Scenario 1:

Let us continue the scenario in case 1. Someone called the police. C came forward and told the police officer that B took the wallet. B denied it. He was lying. What is the morality of B's lie? Let us ask the three questions:

1. Whose interest did it (the lie) serve?

    Ans. That of B. He knew he stole the wallet; he lied to try to get away.

2. At whose expense?

    Ans. At A's.

3. Did all parties in the event have the freedom to choose? Or was the victim a willing participant?

    Ans. B had chosen to do what he did; A had no choice.

Conclusion: In denying his stealing, B tried to protect his own interest, which was to keep the money and avoid legal consequence. His financial gain was at the expense of A. The whole thing was B's choice. A was an unwilling victim.

So what do you think? Does the model work? Now, let us move on to a more sophisticated case of lying.

Scenario 2: Bertrand Russell's Dilemma

Lying should be immoral, regardless. However, in his book, *The Conquest of Happiness,* Bertrand Russell, one of the sharpest logical minds of the twentieth century, has the following to say about lying:

> *Take again the question of lying. I do not deny that there is a great deal too much lying in the world and that we should all be the better for an increase of truthfulness; but I do deny, as I think every rational person must, that lying is in no circumstances justified.*

I envy the guy. Not only does he think with great clarity, he also writes beautifully and forcefully. *Russell denies that lying is in no circumstances justified,* which is more or less the same as saying that lying is justified in some circumstances. (I hope I am getting the double negatives right.) He, however, does not specify the circumstances. Instead, he gives a personal story in which he has chosen to lie. Let me dramatize the incident from the accounts of his book:

Time: Probably a weekend afternoon
Place: An English countryside
The Beginning Scene: The professor was strolling along on the countryside, possibly with a pipe in his hand (Did he smoke?), enjoying the scenery
The event begins to unfold: A very tired fox was laboring along and entered the scene. It was panting heavily as it pushed on. It then disappeared behind some bushes. A short while later, a pack of noisy hunting dogs entered. They were followed closely by a group of riders, all impeccably dressed in the traditional hunting outfits. The leader, a manly fellow with neatly trimmed mustache, asked the professor, with a typical English gentleman's accent, "Pardon me, sir. Did you happen to see a fox passing by?" "Yes, of course. As a matter of fact, the little fellow just went that way a couple of minutes ago," the professor replied cheerfully, deliberately sending the party to the wrong direction. The chase resumed.

Here is the professor's moral conclusion about his deliberate lie: *"I do not think I should have been a better man if I had told the truth."* What do you think? Do you agree with the professor, or would you condemn him for lying? Let us ask the questions:

1. Whose interest did the lie of the professor serve?

   Ans. The fox's.

2. At whose expense?

   Ans. The hunters' and also at the professor's.

Should we ask the third question?

On the other hand, let us pretend that the professor had not lied. Would he be more moral? Let us ask the three questions again:

1. Whose interest would the professor have served?

   Ans. Those of the professor and hunters who hunt the fox for fun.

2. At whose expense?

   Ans. The poor animal, an innocent party which was literally trying to save its skin, and which was unlucky enough to cross paths with a bunch of humans who would take pleasure in killing fox.

3. Do all parties in the event have the freedom to choose?

   Ans. What do you think the fox would say?

Conclusion: This brings up an interesting case in which two parties are partaking to hurt an innocent third party who has no choice but to suffer the consequence. The colluding parties can be viewed as one self that shares a common moral view: It is OK to kill fox for fun. In essence, one party—the hunter and the professor—is hurting another party, which is the innocent fox. If the goal of our new moral model is to build a happy planet, then we owe other animals a moral obligation to protect them. If the professor had not lied (or if he had told the truth), he would be immoral. What do you think?

The professor lied. In doing so, he had absolutely nothing to gain in terms of money or material. He did it to protect an innocent party, a fox.

He was likely an animal-rights person. If you were the professor, would you lie?

Scenario 3: *Mayhem in Congo*

The professor's story, though interesting, might be a bit trivial in the bigger scheme of things. I would like to cite another story that I have read from *Time,* June 16, 2003, titled "Mayhem in Congo." The following is the story according to *Time:*

> *Albertine is a hero in Bunia. When militias from the rival Hema and Lendu tribes started hacking and shooting their way through this hillside town in northeastern Democratic Republic of the Congo last month, the 46-year-old herbalist used her modest stone house and compound to shelter more than 150 people from both ethnic groups. "When Hema militiamen knocked on the door to find Lendu, the Hema would deny there were any Lendu," says Albertine, who won't give her real name for fear of reprisals. "When Lendu militiamen came looking for Hema, the Lendu would say, 'You think we would stay in the same compound as Hema?' We all save one another."*

When an act is not self-serving and instead is motivated by protecting the innocent from cruelty, especially when the liar has nothing to gain and everything to lose, do you think it will be immoral to lie? Do you agree with the professor that lying is, under some circumstances, justified? If your answer is "yes," what will be the circumstances for you?

The Morality of Not Apologizing

Scenario: *"Love means never having to say you're sorry,"* or *"I have done my best."*

"Love means never having to say you're sorry" is a line made famous from *Love Story,* a 1970 film with Ryan O'Neal and Ali MacGraw as the leading stars. The phrase is almost as catchy and popular as *"Frankly, my dear, I don't give a damn."* I have to admit that I did not at the

time understand what the phrase meant, and I still cannot understand what it means today. If I were to write the line, I would put it as *Love means wanting to say I am sorry as often as the situation calls for it.* This should explain why I am not a screenplay writer. It sucks, doesn't it? But seriously, I am not trying to be cute or clever by saying the opposite. Let me give you a story to show the point.

Once upon a beautiful Saturday morning in a park, there were many people taking advantage of the lovely weather. Some were jogging, some in-line skating, some power walking, and most of them just strolling along the path, stopping occasionally to listen to the birds sing or to smell the flowers. Among the joggers was a very fit young man. From his outfit, the guy was likely a professional. And among the slowly walking people was a young family. At the time, the father was carrying his son on his arm and walking besides his wife. The other two-foot-something son was next to the mother. Then, just as the jogger was passing the family, the little boy ran sideways and placed himself in front of the jogger. The jogger tried his best to avoid the boy but failed. As a result, the little boy got knocked down and suffered a small scratch on one of his knees—nothing life threatening. The little boy began to cry, and the parents tried to comfort him. Now, let us play the moral judging game again. If you were the jogger and were allowed to say one of the following two things—i.e. "I am very sorry; are you OK?" or, *"I tried my best to avoid the boy; it is not my fault"*—Which one would you choose? Again, let us apply the three questions to the hypothetical situation, one at a time.

Case 1: Suppose you choose *"I am very sorry; are you OK?"*

1. Whose interest would the apology serve?

   Ans. The boy's parents.

2. At whose expense?

   Ans. The jogger who did try to avoid the accident.

3. Did both parties in the event have the freedom to choose?

   Ans. The jogger had the choice to say what he did; the boy and his family did not.

Conclusion: The jogger was not self-serving. Because he cared about other people, he apologized and put himself in a no-win situation. Selflessness and caring are noble Godlike qualities similar to love; the jogger was a moral person.

Case 2: Suppose your answer is *"I tried my best to avoid the boy; it is not my fault."* And further go on to lecture the couple that they should know better than to let the boy run around in a park, blah, blah, blah . . .

1. Whose interest would it serve?

    Ans. The jogger's.

2. At whose expense?

    Ans. The boy's parents, who would certainly be very unhappy that their son got knock down.

3. Did both parties in the event have the freedom to choose?

    Ans. The jogger had the choice to say what he said; the family did not.

Conclusion: The jogger certainly cared more about himself being right than those he had hurt, albeit unintentionally. In so doing, he also hurt the parents' feeling. The jogger was selfish and uncaring—the traits of a bad person and a person to be avoided. Had the jogger lectured the parents, a fight would likely be started—I would punch the SOB. On second thought, I should check out his size first.

"Love means never having to say you're sorry" is like Zen, few people really understand it. Elton John comes up with an explanation: *sorry seems to be the hardest word.* Indeed! It is so easy and simple a thing to say *I am sorry.* And yet, it takes superhuman effort to utter the words sincerely. Perhaps next to climbing Mt. Everest, it is the hardest thing for men—and some women. I cannot agree more with Sir Elton John.

Then, the simple phrase evolves into *self-love means never having to say you're sorry.* And eventually, it becomes *self-serving means it will be extremely stupid to say you're sorry.* People who hold the view of the last version are not dummies or idiots. Quite the opposite. They are smart, sharp, and exceedingly successful people. They are the CEOs, presidents, prime ministers, and the pope. Take the invasion of Iraq for example. It is pretty clear that it was based on faulty intelligence. So instead of saying, "Sorry, America, I have erred and please forgive me." Or more appropriately, "Sorry, Iraqi people, I have made a very stupid mistake." What did the president say? I am sure you know what Mr. Bush has said so convincingly for so many times. How moral was Bush doing that? We shall discuss the morality of the Iraqi war in a later section.

From my personal experience, there are very few words that have more magical healing power than a sincere *"I am sorry."* It allows the victims to begin healing. It is such a simple and important thing, and yet very few people will do it. If anything, our culture appears to be heading to *"Never say I am sorry."* Doing that is extremely stupid. Any legal counsel will tell you it implies admitting guilt, and makes you liable. Whose interest does it serve? In sexually abusing many children under their care, the Catholic Church has reluctantly agreed to pay the victims. But there has been one thing the church refused to do for a long time: sincerely apologize to the abused. Withholding the apology makes it next to impossible for the victims to close an ugly chapter in their lives and begin the healing processes. I believe the Church did it for self-serving reasons. It was certainly not an act of love or care, as they so often preach. Above all, it is immoral according to the Golden Rule. To save face, the Church chose to keep hurting the many innocent followers instead of apologizing. Make no mistake, the church was not serving God by withholding the apology. Whose interest did it serve? And at whose expense? To me, it is beyond immoral; it is an evil act beyond any doubt. Why? Because it was so unnecessary. To save face, the Church has chosen to continue to inflict the hurt to their innocent followers. What do you think?

The Morality of Smoking

The following information has been obtained from *www.stop-smoking-center.net*.

Fact: Cigarette smoking has been identified as the most important source of preventable morbidity and premature mortality worldwide. Smoking is responsible for approximately one in five deaths in the United States.

From 1995 to 1999, smoking killed over 440,000 people in the United States each year. This includes an estimated 264,087 male and 178,311 female deaths annually.

Fact: Excluding adult deaths from exposure to secondhand smoke, adult males and females lost an average of 13.2 and 14.5 years of life respectively because they smoked.

Fact: Smoking cost the economy over $150 billion in annual healthcare costs and lost productivity between 1995 to 1999, including $81.9 billion in mortality-related productivity losses and $75.5 billion in excess medical expenditures.

Fact: Over 85 percent of smokers say that cigarettes are addictive. Sixty percent of light smokers (one to fifteen cigarettes per day) have at least one indicator of addiction. The high rate of relapse is a consequence of the effect of nicotine dependence.

Fact: Ten years after smoking cessation, lung cancer risks are the same as in nonsmokers, and fifteen years after smoking cessation heart-disease risks resemble those of nonsmokers.

Some adverse health effects of smoking:

- Cigarettes contain at least forty-three individual cancer-causing chemicals, and smoking is directly responsible for almost 90 percent of all lung cancers.
- Smoking causes most of the cases of emphysema and chronic bronchitis.
- Smoking during pregnancy accounts for 20–30 percent of low birthweight infants and up to 14 percent of preterm births. Approximately 10 percent of all infant deaths are attributable to smoking.
- Apparently healthy full-term infants of smokers have been found to be born with narrowed airways and impaired lung function.
- Smoking by parents (secondhand smoke) is associated with adverse effects in their children such as exacerbations of asthma, increased upper respiratory infections (colds, ear infections, etc.), and SIDS (sudden infant death syndrome). Children under eighteen months of age are very susceptible to secondhand smoke causing lower respiratory tract infections.
- Secondhand smoke is responsible for 3,000 lung cancer deaths annually in US nonsmokers.

From the above information, it is very, very certain that smoking is hazardous to health, and it kills. With the given, let us look at the morality of smoking.

Scenario 1: Smoking alone in a private property

1. Whose interest does it serve?

   Ans. That of the smoker.

2. At whose expense?

   Ans. At the smoker's and no one else.

3. Do both parties in the event have the freedom to choose?

   Ans. The question is not applicable to situations when there is no other person involved.

Conclusion: The smoker does it at his only risk. A person has a freedom to choose his action, which includes doing something that harms himself. Other than putting a burden on the public health system, smoking in private is a morally neutral issue. Like smoking alone in a private property, masturbation is morally neutral. Unlike the former, it is very healthy.

Scenario 2: Smoking with a nonsmoker present

1. Whose interest does it serve?

   Ans. The smoker.

2. At whose expense?

   Ans. The smoker and those who have to inhale the secondhand smoke.

3. Do both parties in the event have the freedom to choose?

   Ans. The smoker has the choice, but not those who are forced to inhale the secondhand smoke.

Conclusion: The smoker pursues a self-serving interest and knowingly chooses to harm other people around him. It is a selfish act, and therefore is immoral. This is the reason why smoking is banned in most public area in North America. It is a decision based on science. Bravo!

Scenario 3: Smoking during pregnancy

1. Whose interest does it serve?

   Ans. The pregnant female smoker.

2. At whose expense?

   Ans. Both the mother and her fetus.

3. Do both parties in the event have the freedom to choose?

Ans. The mother has the choice, not her fetus.

Conclusion: In developed countries, most smokers know the hazard of smoking, to themselves and to the fetus. A pregnant smoker knowingly and gravely harms her child. It is inexcusable, and it should be a crime. I therefore think that smoker females should be banned from bearing babies before they kick the habit.

The morality of (heavy) drinking

Excessive alcohol use is bad for the health. Drunk drivers cause accidents and kill innocent people. Like smoking cigarettes, drinking also harms the people who are closely related to the drinker, though in a different way. Heavy-drinking parents often lack the ability to take care of their children, and are often abusive. From what I have read and heard, in almost every case where there is a problem child there is usually at least one alcoholic parent in the family. And for the longest time, I used to look down on people who panhandle. An article titled "Fetal Alcohol Disorders (FAD)" from *Toronto Star* has changed my point of view. Please allow me to quote parts of the article:

> . . . *People whose brains have been irreparably damaged by alcohol flowing through the umbilical cord long before they were born are estimated to make up at least half of Canada's homeless population.*

> . . . *After years of study, specialists now know that alcohol dehydrates the brains of babies born to mothers who drink. The gray matter shrinks. The surface, which should be wrinkled, is interrupted by smooth patches. The damage is irreversible. Children affected have low IQs, trouble learning and poor judgment. They can't make the connection between cause and effect or right and wrong. Frustrated by their inabilities, they often become violent. Many end up living on the street, themselves addicted to alcohol or drugs. Many also end up in prison.*

. . . One man diagnosed at age 46 broke down and cried. All his life he'd been told he was bad, that he just wasn't trying hard enough.

How sad and unfair. He got a major rotten deal, did he not? The paper also includes some statistics. What happens to children suffering from the effects of alcohol abuse in the womb? Studies show:

95 percent will have mental health problems
68 percent will have "disruptive school experience"
More than 50 percent of males and 70 percent of females will have alcohol and drug problems
55 percent will be confined in prison, drug or alcohol treatment centers, or mental institutions
82 percent will not be able to live independently

Talk about having the odds stacked against you! Children from alcoholic mothers have next to no chance of living a normal life. If driving impaired is criminal, what kind of offense should it be for carrying a baby impaired? Sadly, FAD has been plaguing the people of the First Nations for many centuries. From time to time, there are depressing stories of teenagers committing suicide, babies being neglected, abandoned, or even killed in Canada. With a total population of approximately 700,000, such sad incidents are out-of-proportionally high. And that is not all. The First Nations also have an out-of-proportionally high number of beggars and drug users in the big cities of Canada.

One wonders what reason is behind such sadness. The answers can be 1) they are, as a group of people, stupid and inferior, or 2) they are equally intelligent but have no chance of developing to their full potentials. Let us consider the first possibility. We know that the aboriginal people in the American continent came from Asia. Saying that they are inferior is like saying the Chinese, Koreans, or Japanese are stupid. Yours truly, me, I am Chinese. I believe the people of every race on our planet are the ultimate survivors after hundreds of thousands of years of natural selection from their environment. That there is an inferior race is a myth. Instead of inferior, the people of the First Nations, genetic wise, should be far better than average "white" or "yellow" people. All the First Nations people are of mixed blood from Asian and European races. Hybrid vigor being superior is a biological fact. So they can't be inferior.

What causes their misery? The answer has to be alcohol and heavy drinking of their mothers, as indicated by many such studies. The heavy drinking of pregnant women is the reason that most of their children suffer some degree of brain damage long before they are born. That is the source of their collective misery. With this knowledge, how to fix the problem will be up to the Canadian government, and more importantly, up to each of the chiefs. Looking at the mothers when they are pregnant will be a good starting point.

The Holocaust was cruel and tragic, and the human toll was in the millions. But the tragedy is unlikely to ever happen again. Today, alcohol is doing much greater harm to the people of the First Nations by damaging the brains of their defenseless fetuses. Once that happens, their lives are ruined and there is no remedy. Even more tragic is the fact that those babies were harmed by none other than their own mothers, those who were supposed to love and nurture them. But can you blame the mothers? What if you know they too have been damaged? Are we going to allow the cycle to continue until the last of the once brave and proud people is gone?

Heavy drinking hurts. It hurts the drinkers and those who are close to them. It is the primary cause of many family problems. Heavy drinking also damages some vital organs like the liver, heart, and some other parts of the body. It kills.

So what is the morality of heavy drinking? Why don't we ask the three questions?

1. Whose interest does it serve?

   Ans. That of the drinker.

2. At whose expense?

   Ans. Obviously, the drinker will suffer a lot of harm from his drinking; also those who are close to him/her. In the case of pregnant women, their drinking gravely harms their babies, who have no chance for happy lives and are doomed to a miserable existence. Their drinking should be more than simply immoral; it should be a very serious crime next to homicide. To stop this crime, I think a governing body should enact a law which bans heavy-drinking women from having children. There should be severe penalty for breaking the law.

3. Do the parties involved all have choice?

Ans. The drinkers have the choice, not their victims.

Conclusion: Heavy drinking should be a crime. There are many victims afflicted by a heavy drinker. It is a worldwide problem. However, all the governments in the world have not treated it as a serious problem. Alcohol continues to wreck the lives of millions of people every year. In our discussion we have been limited to heavy drinking. How about moderate drinking? According to the most updated knowledge, drinking in moderation is beneficial. Alcohol has been deeply rooted in every culture and is associated with happy occasions. Despite much harm heavy drinking has caused, there appears to be no moral ground to ban alcohol for everyone. Whether it is harmful or beneficial varies from drinker to drinker. Education and good parental guidance should be the way to handle alcohol drinking. What do you think?

Smoking Marijuana

On August 22, 2013, Justin Trudeau, the young leader of the Canadian Liberal Party, disclosed to *Huffington Post Canada* that he had smoked pot since he became a member of parliament. The volunteered information caused quite a stir in the political circle in a country where moral right and wrong is often murky. Since then, most of the politicians in the country, when asked whether they have ever smoked pot or not, mostly admitted that they had tried the weed in their distant past. Whether or not to legalize some marijuana use has from time to time surfaced and been hotly debated.

Before we discuss the morality of smoking pot, let us first look at what some studies on the use of the weed tell us. If you google the pros and cons of smoking marijuana and choose *ProCon.org*, you will find an article under *Medical Marijuana, Top 10 Pros and Cons*, on "Should Marijuana Be a Medical Option? In the article, ten pros and cons are presented, starting from (1) physicians' perspectives on marijuana's medical use, (2) medical organizations' opinions, (3) US government officials' Views, (4) health risks of smoked marijuana, (5) treating AIDS with marijuana, (6) marijuana for the terminally ill, (7) marijuana vs. Marinol, (8) addictiveness of marijuana, (9) "gateway" effect, and (10) medical marijuana debate and its effect on youth drug users. A reader is encouraged to review the article and reach his conclusion.

From what I read, the pros side seems to have a stronger case. Based on facts, smoking cigarettes, beyond doubt, is hazardous, whereas the harm caused by smoking pot is at best questionable. And it is far less addictive. The puzzling fact is no one has said anything about banning cigarettes while smoking marijuana is still criminal and immoral in many parts of the world. Personally, I had come across a number of priests and pastors who smoked cigarettes when there were people around. No one makes an issue of it. I am confused by how people draw their moral views. Shouldn't the degree of harmfulness be the only criterion? Again, let us be clear about one point: yours truly has absolutely no intention of promoting pot smoking. I am not a dealer. During a trip to Germany, I smoked weed in several occasions. It did not do anything for me—no hallucination or crazy behavior. I have since no more desire to do it again. It is not addictive based on my experience.

What I am trying to say is morality should be based on harmfulness as indicated by facts from research, and not based on perception. If smoking pot is proven harmful, we should certainly ban it. But so far, the data is mixed. Many doctors even claim that pot has medical value. The harmfulness of pot is far from conclusive as in the case of smoking cigarettes or excessive alcohol consumption. If you ask me, the banning of marijuana is all political, with no real benefit to the public. To help generate some badly needed revenue, it should be legalized so that the profit from the drug goes to the growers and government instead of some criminals.

The Morality of Same-Sex Marriage

Of all the moral issues we are discussing or going to discuss, I just love this one because it has helped me to successfully defend the model for the first time after the book was published. The successful defense has also given me a much-needed boost on my confidence in the value of this moral model. I was totally new in the field at the time.

Here is what happened. It was the first time I went to a book show called "The Word on the Street" in Toronto. With no experience at all, and selling a book on how to judge morality—a sensitive and potentially explosive subject—I was very nervous. The book show was on Queen's Park, a space in front of the Legislative Assembly of Ontario Government. It is a couple of minutes' walk from the University of Toronto downtown campus. About noon and shortly after people began to come in, a man who had all the look of an academic type approached my booth. He carefully read my sign, which introduced the moral model and its usefulness. Above all, it promised to solve all moral dilemmas. He then walked toward me and remarked: "You have some guts to make this kind of claim. What makes you think you can do that?" The guy was asking me a question to which he had no interest in the answer. He was obviously offended and just wanted to air his feelings. Not knowing how to answer, I asked him a question: "How would you decide moral right and wrong?" "I would use loyalty, justice, reciprocity, equality, and respect for human life, compassion and . . ." He gave me a list of things almost like a reflex. (It happened when I was least prepared. I might not have gotten the list 100 percent right. But the essence is there.) I was quite sure that morality and ethics were his specialty. After he finished, I said to him, "Very well then, how would you use those criteria to decide the morality of same-sex marriage?" I then stared at him, waiting for his answer. The guy just stood there and stood there, apparently putting every one of his neurons to work. After what must have felt like eternity, he kind of muttered, "I am in a bit of hurry, but I'll be back before you close." With that he quickly disappeared. I never saw him again for the rest of the book show.

Like the issue of marijuana, same-sex marriage has been on and off the Canadian political scene for as long as I can remember. Both should have been no-brainers according to our model. However, the lack of a clear-cut way to tell moral right and wrong has unnecessarily complicated the issues. On June 10, 2003, Ontario's highest court rewrote the definition of marriage to include same-sex couples on the grounds that denying gays and lesbians the right to marry *offends their dignity, discriminates on the basis of sexual preference, and violates same-sex couples' equality rights under the Charter of Rights and Freedoms.* The decision legalizes same-sex marriage.

The court gives the following reasons for the decision:

"A person's sense of dignity and self-worth can only be enhanced by the recognition that society gives to marriage, and denying people in same-sex relationships access to that most basic of institutions violates the dignity." And further: *"Preventing same-sex couples from marrying perpetuates the view that they are not capable of forming loving and lasting relationships and not worthy of the same respect and recognition as heterosexual couples."*

The reason I want to use same-sex marriage as an example for moral decisions, other than out of convenience as the news happened to appear on the day I was desperately looking for something interesting, is to show how moral decisions are often made in our society. I have read the wordings that have led to the court's decision several times, but I still don't quite understand what the words mean. *To enjoy the same sense of dignity, self-worth, and respect.* What do those grand words really mean? Are they not the exact words that the Catholic Church has often used in opposing same-sex marriage? I am confused. How does our society decide what is moral and what is not? For some reason, the scientists who would usually have a black-and-white view on many issues are surprisingly quiet on same-sex marriage. Most of them wisely stay away from moral issues lest their applications for funding be jeopardized. Or they are as confused as others—a very strange thing indeed.

To show the murky nature of moral decisions, I would like to quote a sentence from a *Time* article I have read a long time ago (I have no idea on which issue), and I quote: *"Lacking harmfulness does not imply lack of wrongfulness."* Unfortunately, the writer, after making the statement, has not given any example or elaborated on what connection was between harmfulness and (moral) wrongfulness; it beats Zen. Would it not be rational to decide morality on the ground of harmfulness? If something is harmless, how can it be morally wrong? How would one define right and wrong? Shouldn't we all have a part in its decision, like picking a president or prime minister?

Now, let us see whether the three questions would offer any help in seeing the morality of same-sex marriage?

1.   Whose interest does same-sex marriage serve?

347

Ans. Some same-sex couples.

2. At whose expense?

    Ans. Nobody; there is no victim. Or you may argue that it puts *H. sapiens* at risk. But are we an endangered species?

3. Do both parties in the event have the freedom to choose?

    Ans. Yes and yes.

Conclusion: Same-sex marriage should be moral according to our model. It is something two mature people have chosen to do out of their free will. The union serves the interest of the couple and does not harm anyone or a society. It should be viewed the same as a heterosexual marriage.

Next, let us look at the morality of those who go out of their way to ban same-sex marriage.

1. Whose interest does the objection serve?

    Ans. That of the groups that object; namely, those Christians whose voices are loudest, some conservative Chinese, and the Muslims. We should also include Putin and the president of Uganda perhaps.

2. At whose expense?

    Ans. The same-sex couple; they cannot legally live together and can do without the harassment.

3. Do both parties in the event have the freedom to choose?

    Ans. Those who oppose have the choice, not the gay couples.

Conclusion: Objecting to same-sex marriage violates the Golden Rule in two ways: (1) the objectors force their beliefs upon other individuals that only heterosexual unions are holy, and (2) they hurt other people for their own gain, which is to promote their beliefs. And there is no research that shows same-sex marriage harms our society in any way. If there were any harm from same-sex marriage, it is that the union produces no children. But do we need more people on our overpopulated planet? How about heterosexual couples that don't want any children? I would interfere if pandas, the snow leopards, or the humpbacks—definitely not the gay penguins (story to immediately follow)—were to engage in homosexual activities.

The lack of a makes-sense morality not only causes lots of heartaches among humans, the birds could also suffer from our decision. I would like to quote you a story about same-sex penguins in the Toronto Zoo. (Source: CBC News Toronto, November 10, 2011.) It is a "sad" love story between two African male penguins named Pedro and Buddy, which, I think, will brighten your day. According to CBC, the two birds came to the Toronto Zoo about a year ago. The two have eyes only for each other and have been spotted swimming and sleeping together by sharing the same nest. Their behavior has caused a lot of concern and unease for the zookeepers. They were soon separated because "the penguins are an endangered species," so the zoo officials claimed. The separation is to redirect the pair's interest to the other females. But the zoo officials did not fool everyone. It was really about same-sex union, and in this case, that of two birds. Even the often sexually confused Americans are having a great time with the interference.

> "Tough love: Toronto Zoo to separate 'gay' penguin couple"
> ——TIME's website.
> "Birds of a feather? Zoo to split up same-sex penguin pair"—— msnbc.com.

Jimmy Kimmel called it Brokeback Iceberg. The zoo has been overwhelmed with calls from concerned citizens about the breaking up of the unfortunate pair; one of the callers was allegedly from a group called the *Canadian Society for Gay Animals*. Ha, ha, ha.

The Morality of Littering

From El Coca to Nuevo Rocafuerte, Ecuador, is a very interesting trip. There is only one way to travel, and that is by boat down Rio Napo, which is the biggest river that feeds the Amazon. The boat trip lasts fourteen hours or more for a cargo boat, and slightly more than seven hours, even upstream, for a fast passenger ship. It cost me US $12 for each way, and I would highly recommend it. It lets you experience Amazon traveling and see a lot of the river scenes without costing an arm and a leg.

Midway up or down the river, the boat makes a scheduled stop for passengers to buy lunch and use the "bathrooms," which were whatever private corners one could find nearby—for both sexes. The break lasted only about thirty minutes. Because of the long lines, some passengers bought the takeouts and took them back to the boat. Then, I saw something really disturbing: the locals all happily and conveniently threw their plastic containers into the river after they finished eating. Not all Ecuadorians litter. People in Cuenca, for example, are quite aware of protecting the environment. There are a number of rivers passing through the city, none of them have litter problem. Why the difference between the people of the two locations within the same country? I am sure it is education. Most passengers were from people living along the river; they may not be able to get as much education as those in Cuenca. They don't know trashing the river will come back to hurt them and their country eventually; it also hurts others. They may not know the Golden Rule.

Plastic containers have the following impact: (1) they will become eye-sores for everyone, (2) they pollute, (3) they may be swallowed by some fish and harm them, and 4) they will end up in the Atlantic, and unless removed, will stay in our oceans for many thousands of years. It takes a long, long time for plastic to break down naturally.

Littering is an immoral act, you only need to ask the three questions. People litter for convenience. They not only hurt others, they also hurt themselves because making their own environment ugly will discourage tourists from visiting their country. They also hurt the environment by creating eye-sores and harming the species that inhabit it. Big fish, sharks for example, often mistakenly ingest plastics, and since they are indigestible, the plastics give them serious indigestion, weaken them, and kill them. If building a beautiful planet is our goal, littering must be stopped. Littering hurts.

Not only in Ecuador, litterbugs are common in many tropical countries that depend on tourism. Unfortunately, we are sharing the same oceans and seas with them. There should be some international campaign to educate these people before our blue planet becomes a big garbage dump.

With that, I would like to conclude the test drive on the new model. So how is the handling? Do you like it? Is it user friendly? If you like it, why don't you take it home and test the model on the many moral issues that have bugged you and your girlfriend, wife, or whatever. Issues like whether or not you should go to Bangkok without your wife, use the mortgage money to buy a set of fancy golf clubs, or the morality of squeezing the toothpaste at the middle rather than at the end, as you have been repeatedly told. I hope a reader finds it easy to use. And for those who still don't, do not despair. There are more examples to come. Perhaps I should mention that the model is not for dummies or idiots. (Sorry, just kidding.)

The model could also be used as personal guidelines when you are not sure what action you should take. Our moral model is based on two guidelines: (1) *Whenever you deal with another person, never hurt him/her for your one-sided gain.* (2) *Even if you are doing something with an intention to benefit another person, girlfriend, spouse, or friend, etc., allow him/her the freedom to choose.* You will never go wrong with these two guidelines. It will make you morally impeccable, very popular, very successful, and above all, a very happy person. These two guidelines are very simple and easy to understand. You don't need an IQ of a rocket scientist or neurosurgeon to fully appreciate them. The three questions make deciding morality simple and foolproof for everyone. I hope it will eventually take away the monopoly from the priests and authorities, who often have hidden agendas and who don't always serve our interest. Who says moral decision making needs to be complicated?

CHAPTER 17

The Morality of Sex

We have established a simple way to tell moral right and wrong by using the two principles we have derived from the Golden rule: (1) it is immoral to intentionally hurt others for one's personal gain, and (2) whatever you do, even to benefit the receiving party, you still should allow the party the freedom to choose. Therefore, it is immoral to force others into accepting something. The way to know who is hurting who and whether freedom of choice is given is by asking the three simple questions. We have tested our new model with several common issues where we already agree on the moral verdicts in most cases. We have found the model performing very well, provided clear answers to some previously difficult issues such as lying and stealing can be moral under some circumstances. It is very user friendly. It is simple to apply and it always produces a definite answer. By it, we have greatly simplified moral decision making. With the new model, I hope everyone will be able to take part in morality discussion. The future of our planet depends on everyone taking part.

In this chapter, we shall use the model to explore and discuss the morality of sex, which is the most difficult and most confusing issue, as well as an issue that has caused so much human misery. The morality of sex is difficult and confusing because (1) we have been using the wrong criteria to tell right and wrong, and (2) the priests and the wise who gave us their moral views knew practically nothing about the two roles sex fulfills in humans: the biology aspect and the bonding role it has taken up in the evolution of our species. If you don't understand the problem, you can't solve it. It is that simple.

The priests and the wise are not the only people that are ignorant about sex. The ignorant include today's many top-notch biologists. Other than the biological aspect of sex, its role in reproduction, most biologists still are unaware of its role as a bonding agent. Not knowing this important part, sex and the morality of it will remain messy and fussy and unsolvable. The goal of this chapter is to give the readers a more complete view of sex. Hopefully, the readers will participate actively in solving the sex problem that has been plaguing our species shortly after the discovery of farming.

Make no mistake, sex can be beautiful and healthy, or it can be very ugly and harmful. The side that shows up depends on the person's understanding of it. If you know how to handle sex, it will serve you well and bring you happiness and promote your health. Or if you are ignorant, it will become a shapeless malice that keeps haunting you and even destroy you. That is why most people in the world, including the highly educated and otherwise most intelligent people, fear it or are ashamed of it. In either case, people try to avoid it. The phobia of sex or its shameful view, like the Golden Rule, is universal but in a very negative way. It is time for us to rectify it. Not fully understanding sex always brings harms. There are often two harmed parties: the person himself and the many innocent victims hurt by him, sometimes through good intention. The harm does not end there, because people will pass their wrongful views to their children. The children will in turn perpetuate the erroneous views. Because of the widespread of hurt from ignorance, we don't have the option not to understand sex fully.

Sex is a difficult problem because of the general ignorance. Many developed countries include sex in their high school curricula, but that does not mean that students will understand the subject better. The biology aspect—the genitals of male and female, how we can get pregnant, or how sexual diseases are transmitted—does not tell you the whole story. As important is the knowledge of the awesome lure of sex because it is one of the three forces that power survival. Its power is so great that it is simply humanly impossible to resist in a sustainable way. Preaching moral restraint to young people, who are both curious and full of libido, as the way to fight sex is bound to fail at some point. Statistics will show you that it is not working. We also have failed to warn the kids about its dangers. It could ruin your life, and you only need to do it wrong once. Sex is both very pleasurable and healthy, but it is also very dangerous. Any sex education that fails to properly warn our kids is a failure. Education should be teaching our kids how to make the right choice in sex.

There is a good reason for the biologists' collective ignorance of sex, because traditionally sex has been viewed as dirty, filthy, shameful, and even sinful. It is a behavior likened to that of animals. This concept is so prevailing and pervasive that very few people, particularly the highly educated, biologists or not, in a society can be immune from it. Because of this shameful view, virtuous people, including reputable scientists, will consciously stay away from this topic—not to talk, not to see, and not to think about sex. To many biologists, sex is still taboo. That is why biologists like J. Diamond have still missed the point, they are puzzled by the many unusual human sexual features. It is so obvious that they are collectively to enhance our sexual pleasure, but they can't see it. They have failed because sex is a dark and scary alley to them.

Besides not daring to venture into the sex world, scientists, biologists in particular, are also very afraid of getting involved in any moral conversation. Prominent biologists like Dawkins and Wilson know lots about sex, and they have powerful logical minds. Yet they have carefully chosen to avoid using their knowledge and wisdom to make any moral implications. In *The Selfish Gene*, Richard Dawkins, a professor at Oxford University writes:

> *This brings me to the first point I want to make about what this book is not. I am not advocating a morality based on evolution. I am saying how things have evolved. I am not saying how we humans morally ought to behave. I stress this, because I know I am in danger of being misunderstood by those people, all too numerous, who cannot distinguish between a statement of belief in what is the case from an advocacy based simply on the gene's law of universal ruthless selfishness would be a very nasty society in which to live . . .*

And

> *This book is mainly intended to be interesting, but if you would extract a moral from it, read it as a warning . . .*

You cannot be more thorough than that in distancing yourself from any association with morality. Dawkins is hardly an oddity in the scientific circle in detaching himself from moral issues. Edward O. Wilson of Harvard University has the same concern:

> *The moment has arrived to stress that there is a dangerous trap in sociobiology . . . The trap is the "naturalistic fallacy" of ethics, which uncritically concludes that what is, should be.*

The two top scientists' fear of getting involved in moral issues is likely the tip of the moral-phobic iceberg among biologists and scientists in general. When the sharpest minds refuse to take part, morality will forever be left to religions and philosophers with little scientific training to decide. And their decisions often have little logic or facts to back them up; they are based on declarations and claims. Unless we start a change, our morality on sex will remain confused for a long, long time to come. People will continue to suffer endlessly as a result . . .

The Big Sex Phobia

Sex is so closely linked to our survival that problems from it will continue to surface in almost every aspect of our daily lives, confronting us, demanding us to come up with a solution. There will be no hiatus before we solve it. Lacking understanding, sex is still like a mighty evil spirit which seeks every chance to destroy us. Our fear of sex is quite real and there is no escaping it. You can become a monk or a nun, but it does not mean that you will be immune from its disturbance. Our fear makes us lose our ability to reason. The ways our societies deal with any perceivable sexual infraction is often quite out-of-proportionally harsh. There is a big sexual phobia pervading North America. In rare occasions, the phobia could also unintentionally produce some lighthearted and hilarious moments too, like pixilating the images of mating cicadas by CBC.

Stephen Y. Cheung, Ph.D.

The Pixilation of the Mating Cicadas by CBC

On June 5, 2013, the Canadian Broadcasting Corporation (CBC) broadcast the emergence of cicadas in some city during its evening news. The insects emerged to do one thing and one thing only: have sex. And it takes seventeen years for every one of the Romeos and Juliets to get ready. It is a matter of survival to the species and very elementary biology. Then, the TV screen showed two mating cicadas with their united tails pixilated! It was so hilarious! It was certainly the best joke I have come across for the longest time. But to joke was certainly not the intention of the brains behind it. As usual, the Internet and comedy shows were having a lot of fun at the expense of CBC. The following is the title of an Internet article:

> *O Canada! CBC pixilates video of mating cicadas. When the video shows them mating, the reporter says, "You really don't want to watch—it's kind of yucky."*

"It is kind of yucky." It could as well be shameful and gross too. This was perhaps the best snapshot of how Canadians view sex. As you know, CBC is a Canadian crown corporation. It is Canada's public broadcaster; its opinions and stands often reflect Canada's position in lots of issues. And Canada is one of the most civilized, scientifically and technologically advanced countries. It is not Haiti or the Dominican Republic. To qualify as a reporter in CBC, you need serious intelligence and knowledge in lots of areas. If a person of such caliber can have this kind of view, imagine what the ordinary guys and gals think about sex. Ignorantly scary, isn't it? With this background knowledge, the separation of the gay penguins by the Toronto zookeepers no longer appears to be for conservation, does it?

The "No Consent" Chanting

The confusion and phobia could fuel a lot of public outrage, like the 2013 frosh week chanting by some cheerleaders in St. Mary University. A fifteen-second video shows some orientation-week leaders—both men and women—chanting the following again and again, spelling out the word *young* by shouting: *"Y is for your sister, O is for oh so tight, U is for underage, N is for no consent, G is for grab that ass, SMU boys we like them young.*" Students said the chant has been used at frosh week for years. What is wrong? Here is a relevant feedback. *"It's derogatory, really. Underage. No consent. It's saying that's OK. It's definitely not. It's a bad message. It's saying we like the frosh girls, we like them young. It's not good, it's not cool," said Shannon Neville.*

There are several key words in the comment: *underage, no consent,* and *we like the frosh girls, we like them young.* First, *underage.* I would think a first-year university student should be about eighteen. Is eighteen underage? Would an eighteen-year-old understand what she is doing or is she too young for sex? Given the common participation of teenagers in sex these days, I don't think they are underage, not the freshmen anyway. I don't think we should overreact to this one; it is certainly acceptable. The *no consent* is the most disturbing one. It boils down to rape. Rape only serves the interest of the rapist, mostly that of the man, at the expense of a woman, the victim. *No consent,* meaning giving the woman no choice. It is not OK regardless how old the woman is. It is therefore immoral and a serious crime. This is what we should focus our censorship on.

I don't think there is anything wrong about declaring how they like the frosh girls; *i.e., they like them young.* It is a matter of taste. Who wouldn't like them young? Again, the no consent is the most troubling and the only issue that we should deal with. The comment also shows that the commentator, Shannon Neville, does not quite understand the issue, which should only be the *no consent.* For university students to glorify the *no consent* is inexcusable. They should have enough moral sense to know rape is never OK. How can you explain such major screwup? But can you blame them? When it comes to moral issues, we don't have clear guidelines. And when it comes to sex, authorities are totally confused. Students in UBC were chanting exactly the same lines a bit later, and UBC is one of the very top universities in Canada. No matter where you look in Canada, it is confusion, confusion, and confusion.

The Suspension of Harvard Men Soccer Team over Sexist Emails

No doubt, Canadians are very confused when it comes to the morality of sexual issues. But please don't forget we Canadians are the little brothers of the Americans; we copy them. So when it comes to sexual issues, one would wonder whether the Americans are doing better. On November 4, 2016, the Harvard University president okayed suspending the men's soccer team for the remainder of the season. The reason? The university discovered the team members had several years' history, at least, of writing and circulating (among the men's team only?) sexually very explicit "scouting reports" on the women's soccer team's new recruits. On top of the many "disgusting, degrading, graphic, and insulting" terms used, the report, in particular, ranked the girls' attractiveness on numerical values based on the fantasized sexual positions of the women and their theorized sexual inclinations, etc., according to one source. The "scouting report" is considered very degrading to women, and the university feels it is necessary to take very serious action to reflect its "zero tolerance" for such behavior.

I have tried but failed to find the actual wordings in the original emails. And I am not sure whether the "report" has been made public, or circulated among the team members exclusively. From the various reports on this incident, I got the feeling that the boys of the soccer team had not actually committed any sexual assaults on the women. I doubt whether any rape has been committed by any of the team's member. Let us put things into perspective. Those are young bulls at their primes and full of testosterone in their blood. Having strong sexual desires and fantasies is certainly normal for them, and for that matter, any healthy man. I am certainly one of them. I think about sex all the time when I see a beautiful woman. But there is something called self-restraint. The boys have not actually crossed the line. If the "report" was only for the team members only, then there is absolutely no reason to suspend the team. It is quite healthy and natural for boys to fantasize about sex. To punish them will be serious spying and violation of their freedom, the freedom to sexually fantasize without crossing the moral line. It is a clear case of overreacting due to sex phobia. If a society starts censoring people's thoughts and fantasies, where would it stop? It should have been a nonissue. The incident, more than anything, shows sex and moral ignorance at its highest level. If Harvard, the very top learning institute on the globe and the zenith of human intelligence, can screw up on sex, it is quite worrisome.

The Nipple Tsunami

If the suspension of Harvard's men's soccer team sounds harsh, the reprimand and punishment that Janet Jackson received from her *wardrobe malfunction* during the halftime show in the 2004 Super Bowl was certainly way excessive and unjust considering American culture. I was watching the Super Bowl with a friend. Being a day person, I was dozing off long before the halftime. Just when I was quietly snoozing away, I heard my friend exclaim, "Waah!" I instinctively knew that I had missed something big and became fully awake. I got right up, hoping to catch an instant replay, but there was none. So I asked my friend what had happened. And here was what he said, "Can you believe that? Janet Jackson bared her breast!" By the excitement, thrill, and animation on my friend's face, I was sure that I had just missed something more spectacular than an impossible catch leading to a touchdown. Damn! Such has been my luck that I always miss the highlights of a game or show. The most spectacular scene in a movie always comes up when I go to the washroom. I would not be surprised if Big Foot had walked by, waved to me, and I would not see it. I ended up brooding over it the rest of the evening.

It turns out that my misery was unwarranted. I did get many second chances to see the incident over and over again in the news the day after. After all, life is fair. However, the replays were not aired in the sports channels, they were on international news instead. The bared nipples, despite its much-too-brief duration, had generated, through some force more mysterious than dark energy, a ripple effect of celestial proportions. In a matter of several hours after the exposure, it hit the American public like a tsunami. The diva's exposed bosom had drawn a greater single-day hit on the Internet than the 9/11 terrorists attacks. Wow!

There was heavy "carnage" on the days that followed. First, the apologies:

- MTV (and CBS?), which produced the show, apologized to every possible offended party;

Timberlake (the guy who pulled it off, just in case you didn't know) apologized: "I am sorry that anyone was offended by the wardrobe malfunction (which has since become an instant classic)."

- Jackson apologized by saying that the incident, being a last-minute stunt, went awry.

- Last and not the least, Labatt's, a Canadian brewer, apologized for its Super Bowl ad featuring a long, deep kiss between two women.

Second, the casualties:

- Jackson, Timberlake, and a former bandmate of Timberlake all got canned from hosting future shows, awards, and big games.

- Countless viewers, men and women, were seriously offended; some even suffered deep emotional scars.

Third, the fallouts: Fear and phobia shrouded the whole North America continent.

- Tape delay has been installed and will be a way to do business in the foreseeable future for all networks to prevent similar incidents from happening.

- NBC forces *ER*, a popular hospital drama, to edit a brief footage showing a senior woman's breast (on the operating table?).

- Powell, the FCC chief of the US, issued a very strong statement on the incident: "Like millions of Americans, my family and I gathered around the television for a celebration. Instead, that celebration was tainted by a classless, crass and deplorable stunt." (What a righteous man. America will be proud of you.)

- And most seriously: A Tennessee woman named Carlin filed a suit seeking billions of dollars in damages against every party that had anything to do with the incident on the following grounds: *The acts caused viewers to suffer outrage, anger, embarrassment, and serious injury.* I do hope the Tennessee woman could get something out of the very terrible mishap so that she may use some of the nipple money to seek top-notch psychiatric treatment; she certainly would need it.

The dust has finally settled. One wonders what the fuss was about. Why? As a person hooked on sex, I have regularly seen naked breasts on TV fashion shows during family hours, and nobody has cried foul. If sex is the issue, then Miley, Madonna, Jennifer, Britney, Christina, Janet for sure, and many, many others have been much more explicit and provocative in simulating sexual intercourse in their performances with full intention to stiffen the viewers' flabby organs than the half-time show. Has anyone complained? No, sir.

After the incident, even the possible glimpse of a senior woman's breast in *ER* has become taboo. I think our American friends have a major phobia of bared breasts. Obviously, the fear has nothing to do with how they look. If you ask me, they are something absolutely beautiful. I will pick naked breasts over Picasso or Van Gogh on any given day. Obviously, it is causing moral corruption that makes the bared bosom so, so daunting. Sex is shameful, dirty, and evil, according to the wise of old. Thou shalt fear it and hide it.

If sex is really the issue, should we not be concerned about the vivid sex faking by both male and female singers and performers? It has been so widespread that there is a new term coined for it: *twerk*. The most passionate twerkers are Timberlake, Bieber, Lady Gaga, and Cyrus, etc. If you don't think that should be a concern, just watch how some children perform it, if you have a chance. Many of them too are twerking like their idols! Have the parents said anything? Why the incoherent? What is the moral guideline? If the American public can embrace Elvis the King's hip thrusting many decades earlier, why not a pair of harmless, ordinary, naked nipples, albeit belonging to a diva who has a slightly above-average bust? I don't know about the American children. I am hopelessly confused.

Shall we use our three questions to test the morality of the nipple-baring episode from an unfortunate malfunction? (I am already addicted to the newly minted phrase.) Whose interest does it serve? Ans. The performer's? Or being too eager to please, she might have wanted to give her male audience more than their money's worth? The fact is we don't know. Should we give her the benefit of doubt? At whose expense? Ans. I doubt many people who were in the stadium would be able to see it. Most people who had witnessed the incident were likely watching it on TV. And the duration of the exposure was so short—possibly in the range of nanoseconds, like the length of time you would have to glimpse the tennis ball from John Isner's typical first serve shooting at you—that you needed hawklike eyes to just glimpse it. While I can understand how countless hawk-eyed women could be offended by the bared nipples, it beats me that many guys were offended too. If the bared breasts of an extremely sexy woman would offend men, we should be extremely worried about the future of our species. What was the damage? What was the deal? Do all the parties have the freedom of choice? Ans. It was a wardrobe malfunction! Accidents do happen; it is an imperfect world. If it had been by choice, I would say, "Bravo, Janet! You have got a pair of seriously great-looking breasts! And thank you for showing them to me. You have made my day! Next time, please give us a little advance notice before doing that." Conclusion: I am not sure. My mind is still overwhelmed. What do you think?

The Highly Destructive Sex Beast—Blaming It on Women

There is a very good reason for us to fear sex. There is no doubt that sex can be very destructive and cause lots of hurt and misery. But that is due to our general ignorance. Ignorance will invariably open the door to let the bad, ugly sex in. Even at the present time when we know a lot about other branches of science, sex remains a confusing subject. Every city and every country in the world, regardless of how developed and how educated its people are, is still from time to time plagued by a variety of sexual transgressions, from rather mild to very serious. There are three classes of sexual offenses or moral misconducts. They are adultery, rape, and incest

Class I: Adultery

Domenic should have been a very happy man. He got everything that a man of his age could wish for. He was young, strong, and good-looking, and he was the only heir of a rich family. Other than a big house, he also had a wife of rare beauty. Domenic was quite content until he got involved with Gina. The two met at a social gathering. Like magnets of the opposite poles, the pair immediately became attracted to each other. Days after the party, the two were passionately entangled. The affair was kept secret at first, but after a while people began to talk. The gossip did not seem to bother Domenic or Gina. Domenic was often sighted visiting Gina's home in the early evening or during hours when most men were busy working.

No one would think twice that Domenic would fall for a woman like Gina. Why would someone give up French cuisine for meatballs? Gina was neither gorgeous, nor young. She was certainly not sophisticated. But Gina owned something few women did: she had a pair of aces and a Cleopatra-like body. Domenic had never been so happy and satisfied until he met the woman. Gina gave Domenic something no other women could: she made Domenic feel like the Great Caesar and the greatest conqueror ever lived in bed.

Gina was married to a man she loathed. She married him when she was young and her family had no money. Gina's husband was in his late forties, much older than Domenic, seriously overworked and overweight. He owned a restaurant that he had built from the ground up. Like most people that owned restaurants, he spent at least eighteen hours each day taking care of the business. If you wanted something done right, you had to do it yourself. The restaurant owner knew the secret of building a successful business.

The liaison between Domenic and Gina became known to Bruno, who was the youngest brother of the restaurant owner. Bruno knew very well what kind of woman his sister-in-law was. Several years earlier, Gina had invited Bruno for a dinner when her husband was working, which was almost always the case. She wore a dress that showed and highlighted her sexy body, her half-naked bosom, more than anything. Bruno left as soon as he was clear what his sister-in-law was up to. Bruno loved his brother like a father. He decided to take the matter in his own hands. It did not take Bruno too long to figure out when Domenic would show up again in his brother's mansion. He was ready. When Bruno kicked down the bedroom doors, he found, as expected, the naked pair in bed, with Domenic on top of his moaning and slithering sister-in-law. Bruno drew the sword, and soon the pastel bedroom was covered with patches of red of the lustful pair.

Bruno turned himself in. No one blamed Bruno for what he did. Most men even said they would have done the same in Bruno's place. Everybody blamed the pair, with Gina bearing almost all the burden. And above all, everyone cursed *sex* for destroying a fairytale marriage. Damn and curse you, son of Satan.

Case II: Sexual Assault—Rape

In a little village in the central part of India lived a family of six: the father, mother, and the four children. Harjit was the eldest son. Nina, fifteen, was the youngest daughter. Every way one would look at it, it was a very happy family. Like most families in the area, Harjit's family worked the land. The family was among the luckier ones. For generations, the family owned a couple of acres of good land. Everybody in the family contributed. Harjit, in particular, would make every father proud because he was both hardworking and reliable. Beyond doubt, Harjit would not only be the head of the family, he seemed destined to be the leader of the village. The young man had all the qualities of a leader.

Nina was rather innocent. Being the youngest and the only girl in the family, she was pampered by everyone, Harjit especially, and was spared from most of the hard chores. Besides helping her mother tidy up the house and cook, Nina often accompanied her mother to a nearby river to fetch water. Nina had a very mature body for her age. If things proceeded according to plan, Nina would be wedded to a princelike young man of a very wealthy family after harvest in the following year.

It was during an early summer afternoon that Nina went to fetch water alone because her mother was not feeling well. Besides being bored, there was little water left in the family's containers. Nina wanted to replenish the water so that she could make tea and prepare dinner for her father and brothers when they returned from the field. It was hardly chance that everyone in the family loved Nina. She cared for and loved each and every member of her family as well.

When Nina was on her way home with the filled containers, she was caught in a thunderstorm which happened all too suddenly. She got soaked before she could get to a nearby tree. With her wet clothes pressing against her body, Nina morphed into a goddess of erotic love, almost like a poster girl in wet T-shirt of the modern times. Nina had barely sat down when a strong muscular arm wrapped around her neck and brought her down behind a big tree. She screamed and was quickly stifled by her assailant with a piece of rag. Her attacker was none other than Parma, a young man in the same village, and a loner. The assailant quickly got on top of his prey and began punching Nina with his free hand. Nina tried to kick, scratch, punch, and wrestle away her attacker. It was futile. She was no match for the young man physically. In a desperate attempt to fight back, she sank her nails into the arms of her aggressor before she fainted.

The sun was shining brightly again when Nina regained her consciousness. She was shocked and dazed. She felt pain coming from every square inch of her flesh. The intense pain, however, was nothing compared to the horror of finding herself half naked from the waist down and her clothes torn. She tried to cover her body with the shattered garment; it was impossible. A suffocating shame, more than anything, had overwhelmed the once innocent and pure girl.

It was long after dark when Nina's three brothers came to the wood to look for the missing family member. Before they came, they had found out what had happened to their once loved sister. Someone in the village had spotted Parma returning home in a messy shape with his face and arms covered with scratches. It appeared that the loner had been attacked by a man-eater.

When Harjit kicked down Parma's door after pounding at it with no one answering, Parma was trying to escape from the back of the house. The brothers quickly caught up with the assailant. Harjit brought Parma down and overpowered the fleeing coward. It did not take the brothers too long to "persuade" the captive to tell the truth. The brothers, after having vented their anger on the villain who had destroyed their sister and shamed their family, finished him with their knives.

When the brothers spotted Nina, she was shivering—more from fear than cold—and crouching with her back against a tree, her knees tightly pressed against her body in a futile attempt to block her stained body from the sight of her brothers. Unfamiliar to Nina, there was no tenderness in the brothers' eyes; they were cold, harsh, disgusted, and even contemptuous.

Without a word, Harjit stepped forward and seized Nina's messy and filthy hair, which had lost all its shine and silkiness. The hair, which had once made the family proud, was like the purity of the young girl, utterly tainted. Nina found her face violently smashed against the dirt. She uttered a stifled moan as blood gushed out from several holes on her back while her body writhed among the fallen leaves. The pain her body had to bear was nothing compared to the despair of her shattered heart. As she exhaled her last breath, the cruel knowledge that she had been forever disowned by those she most loved lingered. She died with her eyes wide open. It was for the honor of the family that she must die. She knew it, and her brothers made sure of it.

Curse you, Parma. And above all, damn you, *sex,* for ruining a pure maiden and destroying everything.

Case III: Incest

The Huang family was to be envied. Huang Kwok-Chung was an exceedingly successful man even by the most stringent standards. Besides being a top-ranking government official, he was a renowned Confucian scholar like his father. And like every man of his status, Huang had several wives. By the time Huang was in his mid-forties, he had attained a rank and reputation above his father and most of his forefathers.

Huang had three sons and more daughters than he could remember or had time to remember. Typical of a man of his type, he rarely spent time with his children other than in some formal family gatherings, which only the sons could attend. And of all his children, Huang obviously favored the eldest son, Ming-Kin, who was the only son of his first wife, the matriarch, who was a daughter of one the emperor's brothers. Ming-Kin had the look that symbolized a noble Confucian and a tender temperament to go with it. He deserved every bit of his father's singular affection. Beyond doubt, he would grow up to be a man of honor and would prosper like the father. If there was a question about the young man's future, it would be how great he would become.

But no one should envy Ming-Kin. For sure he would one day inherit a very rich estate built by his family. But before the day came, he had to endure the ever-increasing expectation and pressure that had fallen upon him. When Ming-Kin began to learn to read and write, he had been keenly aware of his duty. He was quite sensitive, even as a child. Huang had never failed to use every chance to remind his most loved son about his duties and obligations to his family and the country. It was not an enviable position to receive all the attention of a high-achiever father. Following a typical Confucian tradition, Huang believed that being strict, firm, and stern were the proper ways to bring up his children. To Ming-Kin, the standard was even more stringent. Though Huang loved Ming-Kin dearly, he rarely showed his tender side. Again, Confucian teaching holds that being soft will be a sure way to spoil a loved one.

Though Huang spent little time with his other children, he paid close attention to Ming-Kin. Each day after work, Huang would drop by Ming-Kin's studio and make sure that the boy was studying. There were piles and piles of Confucian books in the studio. The father wanted to properly prepare his son to do even better than him in his future annual government exam. With his quality and proper grooming, Ming-Kin could win it all and become the champion, the father firmly believed. To be the champion not only was of utmost honor, it also guaranteed a prestigious and lucrative post handpicked by the emperor. For many, many centuries under the emperors, studying Confucian books to do well in government exams was the only reliable way for ordinary people to become prosperous. That is why even today every Chinese parent wants his child, the boy especially, to spend hours and hours studying each day. Studying is productive and playing a waste of time. The Confucian teaching has been deeply entrenched in Chinese culture. It was under such an environment that Ming-Kin had been brought up, spending practically all his waking hours locked up in his studio.

It was shortly after Ming-Kin's seventeenth birthday that Huang had to go to the capital to partake in an important project sponsored by the emperor. For Huang, it was the realization of a lifelong dream to be among the handful of the most noted scholars invited. He was on the road with his beloved mistress Madam Ou and a few servants the next day. Alas! Had Huang known that realizing his most treasured dream would bring the worst curse to his beloved ones and family, he might not have embraced the emperor's offer so eagerly. For no fame and glory would offset the grief and shame he was going to endure.

It was a rare break for Ming-Kin for the first time in his overburdened young life. It was at dawn that the family members gathered in front of the massive red front doors to bid farewell to Huang and his party. Ming-Kin stood in front of the matriarch and the other sons. Then, Ming-Kin kneeled and bowed to the father. Huang nodded and smiled with approval. The party began its journey. Just at the time the party was about to take off, a crow flew over, made several ugly cries, and dropped some filth in front of the carriage. It was a bad omen. Huang was a bit uneasy. But he had a will of steel; he would not let some superstition stop him.

The two-horse carriage not only carried his father away, it also took with it a heavy load from Ming-Kin. The young man admired his father, he also feared him. Even during the father's absence, the son somehow felt his watchful eyes. In Huang's absence, Ming-Kin became the acting head of the family.

It was several days after Huang's departure that a lingering drizzle had finally ended. After a long absence, the sun reappeared. The wet period had done wonders to the plants and the creatures around. The family's massive manicured garden sprang to life. Flowers of all colors and shades were trying to outdo each other in showing off and luring the many butterflies and bees to them. It was a beautiful spring day. A lax student would say *"springtime is never for studying."* There was not a cloud in the sky. Birds sang, and a persistent breeze kept sending bouquets of flowers to Ming-Kin's room, intently inviting the young master for a visit. So Ming-Kin obliged. It was pointless to sit in the studio when his mind and heart were not there. With his father being far, far away and not likely to return for months, there was no reason to stay in the studio all day long. After having resisted going out the whole morning, Ming-Kin decided to take a walk outside in the early afternoon. The young servant Ah-Bo followed the young master dutifully several steps behind.

As soon as Ming-Kin stepped out, all his guilty feelings were swept away. He had grown up in the family's sprawling mansion and yet he knew so very little about the garden. He started learning to read and write at a very early age, a couple of years ahead of most other children. Since then, most of his time had been consumed in the studio between the endless dull pages. He did it mostly to please the father. Like all Confucian followers, he believed in filial piety; his father's wishes became his commands. To observe and obey a father's wish without question were the duties and the noblest deeds of a son according to Confucianism.

The young master quickly and completely forgot all his worldly concerns. It was a new experience. He was enchanted by the many colors and forms in the impeccably kept garden. It was as if he had ventured into a fairyland. Then, came the laughter of a girl behind some tall hedges. Ming-Kin immediately quickened his steps ever so slightly toward the sound; he did not want to appear to be eager. To allow himself to be distracted by a girl, much less drawn to her, was certainly a despicable character defect according to Confucianism. A colorful butterfly fluttered by just before Ming-Kin could turn a blind corner to his right to get to the other side of the green wall. Almost at the same instant, a girl in a pale lavender dress bumped into him. The young master instinctively held on to her. Before Ming-Kin knew what to do, the girl gently pushed herself away from him. She quickly turned and hurried away, lowering her head as much as she could, trying to hide her embarrassment. That would have been the end of an innocent encounter. Alas! She turned her head and gave the young master a smile and made fleeting eye contact with him before she disappeared.

Ming-Kin was doomed the moment he saw the maiden's face. A girl of such beauty should only be found in heaven. And more than anything, the scent of the maiden kept lingering in the young man's mind long after she had left. It was a faint, sweet scent and yet it was so powerful, the young man could not rid his mind of it no matter how hard and how many times he tried. Ming-Kin finally gave in to the temptation. His stubborn resistance failed after fighting the losing battle for several unsuccessful days and sleepless nights. The maiden's smile and her sweet scent kept forcing themselves into and occupying his consciousness, making all his attempts to focus on the book useless. He decided to find out who the girl was. He was almost old enough to get married. He planned to ask his father's permission to marry her, and it should not be much of a problem.

"Young master, her name is Sue-Yee, the eldest daughter of Madam Ou," Ah-Bo replied. The servant's very courteous and soft answer sounded almost like a cracking thunder; it shook the young master to the core. The girl he had been so obsessed with was none other than his own sister! Maiden Ou was one of his father's four wives. Sue-Yee, without a shred of doubt, had to be his half-sister! Still, the young master could not stop thinking about Sue-Yee. He tried reason, morality, and his future and duties with his family, but none could help him. Just the opposite. The more he resisted, the stronger was the longing.

He was a highly disciplined man. He came up with a solution. He decided never to visit the garden again. Then, the two could not see each other. Given time, it would end. The young master felt a bit relieved after making the decision. However, he still could not focus on the book. Then, the maiden's image quietly came back. He could no longer control himself. Ming-Kin stepped out into the garden and walked to where he accidentally met Sue-Yee some days ago, hoping to catch a glimpse of the young maiden. He was disappointed. And time after time, he was again disappointed, only to return to the studio feeling gloomier.

As days went by, the young master had lost interest in everything. He kept playing back the images of the brief encounter in his mind. And more than anything, it was the scent of the girl that haunted him most, leaving him no peace in the nights and days that followed. He knew too well that even to allow himself to be slightly distracted by a girl was a great sin to the teaching of Confucius, a point his father had kept drilling into him. And the absolute worst of all, Sue-Yee was the very last girl in the world he should think about so passionately! He was a proud man; he carried all the family's hope. He was expected to be even greater than his father. How did he become the very person he used to deride and despise? Like an animal fallen into a mud pool, he was unable to free himself from the powerful grip of his shameful yearning no matter how hard he struggled.

After yet more days of wasted effort, Ming-Kin asked Ah-Bo to prepare the ink and the brush. He had made up his mind. Soon, the servant finished the preparations. The young master instructed Ah-Bo to wait outside. He then sat down and began to write several lines on a piece of paper. It was a poem.

A butterfly, in a spring day;
Such rare beauty, a flawless face;
Amid my earthly garden,
Dwells a heavenly maiden.

Ming-Kin read the poem several times before he carefully folded it up, knowingly not putting his name down. He then got an envelope, put the paper in, and sealed it securely. Again, he left the envelope blank and handed it to Ah-Bo. "Deliver the letter to the girl." And after a short pause, he added, "And if your head is to stay up there, you will not let anyone know about the letter, not even the littlest thing. Understand?" the young master ordered his servant in the sternest way. "Yes, young master, I fully understand. I do, I do," Ah-Bo replied. The servant then carefully tucked the letter in an inside pocket and hurried away. Ah-Bo knew the seriousness of the job. Like a faithful servant of his day, he never asked his master any questions. Ah-Bo was very faithful and loyal.

Ming-Kin had been pacing back and forth in his studio since his servant left him. He gave the letter to Ah-Bo when the sun was barely above the horizon. The sun had long passed its highest point. Besides being very anxious to see what would develop, the young master was also worried. He began to imagine all kinds of bad scenarios happening to the letter and its courier. It was very unlike Ah-Bo to take such a long time for a simple errand. Ah-Bo was a couple of years younger and the two grew up together as far back as Ming-Kin could remember. The two were more like friends than master and servant. Ah-Bo was always reliable. To a person anxiously waiting for an important answer, time was a merciless tormentor. And time kept on stretching. Ming-Kin finally decided to go out to look for Ah-Bo. Just as he opened the door, the young servant ran in like a wind. Before he uttered a word, he carefully searched an inside pocket to pull out a lavender envelope.

Ming-Kin's hands were quite visibly shaking and his heart was pounding like a war drum as he opened the letter. "Young master, I . . .," Ah-Bo was trying to explain. Ming-Kin signed at him to stop. He pulled out a piece of paper of the same color. A familiar fragrance greeted the young master as he unfolded the paper. It, too, contained a poem:

Is butterfly not frail like a young vine?
Thou, a towering pine.
Wish that my laughter,
Forever to please the master.

***

With the help of his faithful servant, Ming-Kin met with Sue-Yee the first time the following evening in a quiet corner of the big garden. In every which way, the two were perfectly matched and should belong to one another. What a shame, and through what wicked twists of fate that the two were born brother and sister! Ming-Kin vaguely sensed and had an uneasy hunch from the day he met Sue-Yee that she could be a very wrong person. He should have stopped any thought and cut any attempt to develop any form of friendship with her after he learned he and the girl were actually brother and sister. But he found himself powerless to fight a shapeless, persistent, and very powerful demon. Even after sending Sue-Yee the poem, one part of Ming-Kin was hoping that his half-sister would have more sense than him. He would have preferred Sue-Yee to despise him and be enraged, and thereby never talk to him. Instead, Sue-Yee had responded quickly and passionately. A most tragic fate was thus firmly locked.

It had been a handful of months since the two met. Then, the servants began to gossip: Sue-Yee was pregnant! And among the gossipers, a woman called Luk-Por started a rumor that Sue-Yee had been sighted with the young master in the garden and the studio. The rumor spread like a wild autumn fire; it threatened to engulf the eminent family. It was close to midnight that the silence and peace on the road leading to the Huang estate was abruptly shattered by a carriage drawn by two horses. Huang had been riding almost nonstop from the capital. He made it back home in five days for a distance that usually took him more than ten. Huang got a letter from the matriarch through the imperial express. He begged the emperor for permission to take a short leave as soon as he got the letter. Something very urgent at home needed his personal attention, he pleaded to the emperor without specifying the reason. His request was granted right away.

***

The central hall of the sprawling Huang estate strictly prohibited women and most men from visiting; it housed the memorial tablets of the Huang ancestors. The hall was also the place where extremely serious family matters were settled; it was the first time in many years the master had used it for such a function. The master and his matriarch were seated near the center of the hall. The master looked cold and stern while the matriarch buried her face crying. Behind them was a huge wooden table where a great number of candles and incense sticks were burning. Other than the first day of a New Year and a few very special dates, one would not find such vast numbers of candles and incense sticks in use. The shelves where the tablets were placed were adorned with many gold items showing the immense wealth of the family. It also revealed its deep roots. Kneeling with both knees down in front of the couple was a girl in lavender whose hands were tied behind her back. She lowered her head as much as she could, with her scattered shiny black long hair blocking her face. And judging from the size of her belly, she was a couple of months from full term.

"Who did it? Answer me truthfully, you worthless little slut!" The master did not raise his voice much. However, the venom of the voice would freeze the heart of any person who faced the demand. The girl remained silent. She lowered her head further as if to find a way to hide.

"Who did it? Answer me!" Huang stifled his roar as he tried to contain his rage. Again, Sue-Yee did not answer. Her slender body began to tremble slightly as if to hold back her emotion. One would never guess such a tender and meek girl could harbor a will of stone. She stubbornly and quietly refused to respond. It became apparently to the master that the girl would never talk. "Very well! May be this is the best. Take her away and have her locked up." The master turned to the head housekeeper and commanded, "Now, bring me Luk-Por." The housekeeper hurried away with a couple of servants. Perhaps it was the best scenario Huang could have hoped for. Sue-Yee's silence had made it much easier to salvage the potentially very destructive situation, Huang reckoned. The matriarch hinted in her letter that Ming-Kin might have something to do with the ugly incident; the master refused to believe it. Even it was true, he would try his best to cover it up and protect his heir. Though reasonably angry at his son, the master had no intention of punishing Ming-Kin harshly. His wrath was all directed at Sue-Yee. The girl was the source of all evils. She was going to die most shamefully for corrupting Ming-Kin, Huang had decided long before he got home.

The cup of tea next to the master was still warm when the cry of a woman begging for mercy was heard outside the massive closed doors, poignantly breaking the silence before daybreak. Then, a plump middle-aged woman was dragged in by the two servants. She was hurled down in front of the master. The woman hurried to get onto her knees almost at the same instant. She began repeatedly banging her head loudly against the wooden floor begging for mercy. "Stop the nonsense, woman. Now tell me what you know about the foul affair," the master commanded. The women felt a chill through her entire body; she began to shake uncontrollably. "Please have mercy, master. I don't know nothing. Please, please, I beg you, I beg . . ." Luk-Por knew too well that it was not the time to say anything. "So you won't tell me, will you?" the master said in a dreadful tone with a cold smile. "No, no, please! I won't say nothing again. Please, please, I beg you, I beg you!" Luk-Por resumed banging her head against the floor with renewed fervor, breaking open the skin on her forehead. A stream of blood began to flow down her face as she pleaded for mercy. "Very well. I'll show you mercy. But to make sure you won't talk again . . ." The master did not continue. Instead, he signed to the head housekeeper to take the noisy woman away.

***

It was dawn when the master got to his bedroom and was ready to take a short rest that he heard a sharp squeal of a woman breaking the silence of the estate. And dogs began to bark and howl, perhaps to signal the beginning of another dark day for the renowned family. Before the sun had risen above the treetops, almost every member of the family from an age of five up was already standing and waiting around the big pond that occupied a well-tended part of the garden. Most of family members were not yet fully awake; they were not used to getting up so early. When the master's order came to some of them in the morning, most were still in bed. The members gathered in groups, with several women whispering nervously as most of the men waited quietly without much expression.

Then, first to appear was Huang, who was closely followed by the head housekeeper and then a couple of servants. To most of the family members, it was the first time they had seen the master again since his months of absence. Huang appeared to have aged many years. Then came two men dragging a middle-aged woman with untidy hair. The woman's mouth was still dripping blood. The patches of blood all over her dress were still wet. At the end of the approaching party were two men carrying a bamboo cage usually for transporting swine to be slaughtered. It was Sue-Yee who was in the swine cage. Her hands were tied behind her back and she was struggling to stay on her knees inside the rocking cage. Instead of her favorite lavender, the maiden was wearing a two-piece outfit of crude material in off-white—the color of death. Her bare feet too were bound by ropes. To show a girl's naked feet to the public was the cruelest humiliation and the most severe punishment fitted for the foulest offense. The party stopped near the edge of the pond. After getting a nod from the master, the head housekeeper pulled out a piece of paper, cleared his throat, and read aloud, "For those who spread rumor to defame the family, be warned and take a lesson from Luk-Por. She will be forever expelled from the family." The housekeeper paused briefly and then continued, "And for any woman who fails to control her lust and shamelessly commits this most despicable act of ultimate filth, let her be your example!" The housekeeper ended the speech with his finger pointing at Sue-Yee.

As soon as the housekeeper finished reading, the two men who carried the cage proceeded to load the bamboo cage with several good-size stones. After that, they replaced the cover and sealed the opening securely. Having double checked, each man held on to an end. The two lifted up the cage and tossed it into the pond with a big swinging action. The cage made a big splash when impacting the water. It soon disappeared in the green, murky pond. And after several bursts of bubbles from the bottom, the surface became quiet again.

No one made a noise. And above all, Sue-Yee was quiet during the whole time. Nobody knew her facial expression because her head was closely tucked to her chest and her face was behind a veil of black hair. She noiselessly took her secret with her to protect the only lover she had ever known.

After everything was done, it became glaringly obvious that Ming-Kin, Ah-Bo, and Madam Ou were missing in the gathering. Huang hurried to see his son. He was not going to punish Ming-Kin and was prepared to let the whole thing go. No one was going to say anything about the foul incident; the master had given a stern order. The studio's door was locked. A servant first knocked and then pounded at the door repeatedly and there was still no answer. "Kick it down!" the master roared. Ming-Kin's lifeless body hanging from the ceiling was the first sight that greeted the master. The body was cold when the servants let it down. Ming-Kin had been dead a long time ago. Ah-Bo was nowhere to be found. Before the master knew what next to do, a servant ran hurriedly in, knelt, and reported to the master that Madam Ou had killed herself with poison.

Huang never did return to the capital; he got ill within a few days after. He soon passed away; he died devastated and without fulfilling a lifelong dream. The whole community condemned Sue-Yee. And above all, everyone scorned and spat at *sex,* for it had destroyed a promising young man and ruined a legendary family.

***

Sex had been blamed, and rightly so, for destroying productive men, most were at their primes, and some prominent members of the societies. (In the "good old days," women counted very little, if at all. Even nowadays some cultures still do not count women.) Bruno, Harjit, Ming-Kin, and the master Huang could have been Karl, Kwok-Keung, or Kurt. Rather than in Milan, Raigarh, or Shanghai, it could easily happen in Wakayama, New Orleans, or Timbuktu. The time, place, and the central characters involved could be different but the theme has remained the same: sex ruins young and productive men and wastes useful lives. Above all, sex destroys families, often seemingly happy families, together with the many innocent members like Domenic's wife and family, Harjit's parents and brothers, and members of the once prominent and respected Huang household. Families, more than anything, have been the most basic unit of a stable and functional society; they are the building blocks of a community and a country. Sex decays and rots the building blocks one at a time. The specialty of sex, it seems, is its passion for bringing families to ruin.

Imprisoning the Sex Beast

The Lawless Early Communities Ruled by Wild Sex

You may ask: why does sex hate families with such passion that it always seems to seek them out to destroy them? To answer the question, we have to know how and why families were created in the early human societies. The traditional family structure was likely to be created after many, many generations following large-scale farming. As discussed, farming had created a group of people in a community who did not have to farm at all and lived rather well. Most of these idle people were likely to be young men full of energy as well as brimming with testosterone. So what would the young men do with too much time on their hands and their guns loaded, so to speak? Well, they would naturally follow their hearts and would do what Mother Nature had intended them to. Does it make sense to you? Remember that males are primarily sperm delivery organisms in nature? Men are no different; they all are primarily Mother Nature's sperm delivery boys. Men, if Mother Nature is in total control, are born to have their sperm delivered to women! And the time was right, because none of the major religions or the great teachers had been born! Young people at the time did not have any moral sense; they were still very animal-like in their behaviors. I would not want to live in such bad old days despite being a man; yours truly is neither muscular nor gifted in fighting. It was perhaps one of the darkest periods of human history.

Testosterone's job, besides making sperm and building muscle, also makes its bearer very needy sexually and aggressive. An early community got a lot of horny and aggressive young men, and a short supply of available mature women because of the sexual appetite gap. What do you think would happen? It would be just like other animal groups such as lions, seals, and rams, would it not? Early humans, like all male mammals, were ruled by testosterone.

If there were newspapers or TV, each day the media would be flooded with so and so young man got killed together with the rest of his family in defense of his sister from a group of hooligans. A young mother was raped and killed with her lover, leaving two orphans. Or the Chans had burned down the Wong village in retaliation for several Chans being killed when the Wongs raided their village and kidnapped several of the Chan women several years earlier. Sex-driven killings were constantly draining a community of its productive men, often together with some women. If allowed to continue, it would gravely weaken a community, making it susceptible to outside invasion.

In those lawless societies, it was likely that the mortality rates of young men, women, and their children would be high. So young, productive men got killed fighting for women, women got raped and killed, and children were often left to care for themselves. The killing continued if there were still enough young people left. The wise, elderly people would likely be among the first who clearly saw the ugly side of unregulated or follow-the-heart sex. They saw that wild sex was continuously draining the cream of their community. It would not take King Solomon to see that sex was the problem, and unless something was done to stop it, it would forever bleed a society. Agree? The wise, elderly, too, during many times in their young lives, had done their fair share of sex-related fighting and killings; they would understand the problem. With their testosterone levels receding, they were able to reason more clearly; they knew that sex had to be tamed somehow! But it was likely to be the ruler of a community that had first declared war on wild sex. Why? He was the only person who had the power to do so. And he was also the party which had the most to lose if sex was allowed to roam freely.

Let me give you an example. When I was young, I lived with my mother in my native village. It was my job to take care of the chickens. Out of a newly hatched bunch, there were some males which at a certain stage would begin to assert their dominance and pick on other birds and cause all kinds of turmoil. We always got the male chickens neutered before they got too aggressive. A ruler depended on his subjects to provide for him; the subjects were his properties. For financial and military reasons, he could not afford to lose productive men and women from sex-driven squabbles day in and day out. When neutering his men was not an option, what would you do if you were in a ruler's shoes? How would you fight the sex beast? How would you fight a beast powered by testosterone? Because a ruler in those days knew nothing about biology or biochemistry, to them sex was like a shapeless malice with horrifying destructive power. Sex was a like a ghost or evil spirit that caused diseases. How would you fight an invisible enemy that always attacked by controlling your heart, your most vulnerable part, which also happens to be your real decision maker?

The Solution to Wild Sex and the Birth of Traditional Marriage and Family

It would be very difficult indeed. Because the evil had no physical form, you, the ruler, could pretty well forget about launching preemptive assaults at the enemy. Your only option would be putting up fences or walls in defense, and pray that your fence would be strong enough to hold back the mighty foe. So the rulers sought advice from the wise, who were likely to be priests or teachers. Surprisingly and most interestingly, the priests and the teachers in the different parts of the ancient and isolated world had all come up with almost the same solutions: (1) They decreed a moral code that sex was evil and destructive; it had to be contained. The moral code also declared that the sex evil dwelled in the bodies of women. (2) To contain, or more appropriately, to imprison this evil, a family structure was the solution. They had unanimously suggested building families to control the sex beast. And since they were convinced that the invisible evil dwelled in women, therefore controlling the sex evil could only be done through controlling women. Though the final shape, size, and packaging of their proposed models varied, the basic designs and architecture of a family had turned out amazingly similar. Let us try to rationalize why and how the two points in the moral view were established.

Point number 1: sex is evil and destructive. This point is quite valid, even according to today's knowledge. There is little doubt that sex can cause a lot of hurt to many unfortunate parties, primarily women and sometimes men, when sexual crimes are committed. When adultery breaks up a family, the innocent spouses and children often become collateral damage. The victims of rape are not just the raped women; they often include the family members and friends that love them. While one can recover from the physical hurt given time, the emotional scars last a long, long time and many can never recover from it.

At the time when the moral code was decreed, most of the offenses involving sex were likely to involve violence; rape and various sexual assaults were common. It would be common to have people killed in the process. Then there would be revenge that followed. The victims' family members and friends would want to get even. Fighting thus ensued. And the revenge could evolve into cycles with more and more people getting involved and killed. It was rather easy to see this ugly side of wild sex. And before there was morality, many sexual activities were wild sex.

Point number 2 that the sex evil dwelled in the bodies of women did not make any biological sense from what we know. Men are the animals obsessed with sex; they are Mother Nature's sperm delivery boys. To successfully perform their natural duties, men, whipped by their high levels of testosterone, are hungry for sex most of the time. Sometimes, a delivery boy's urge to have sex can be very strong and persistent, making it almost impossible to resist. Unfortunate for the sperm delivery boys, women, in general, are not as keen to have sex as they are. So at any given time and in any society there are likely far more very sexually hungry men than receptive women. This was true millions of years ago; it is still true today. The two factors became an explosive mix waiting to be ignited by the wrong circumstances. With our knowledge, we can clearly see that women were far less interested in sex and physically much less capable of committing any sexual crime than men. Then, how did they end up becoming the evil parties?

Though the labeling did not make any scientific sense, it did make perfect political logic. How? Let us see among the sexual offenders who were most likely to initiate an attack. For sure, they were those with the highest amount of testosterone. That was why they were so uncontrollably horny in the first place. They were also men with the biggest biceps and the most aggressive type—all because of their high testosterone. They, not surprisingly, were also very successful go-getters—also because of the hormone. Quite often, the rapists or assaulters were a ruler's powerful allies or trusted friends. A ruler was certainly one of them, the strongest and himself a regular rapist. When he was confronted by someone with a grievance that his daughter or partner got raped by one of the ruler's right-hand men or soldiers, who would the ruler side with? It would be a no-brainer, would it not? The guilty party would always be the victim, the assaulted woman. It was the woman who had made a man do it. *"If she had not so carelessly taken a bath in the river and let the man see her, none of it would have happened." "If she had concealed her body properly, the man would not have raped her."* Or, *"if she had not been too friendly with the man, he would not have taken it as a consent."* Etc., etc. In every case, it was a woman's fault.

Sounds crazy? Not really. It is still going on today. Take the sexual abuses of a number of football players at Penn State University in 2011 by the assistant football coach Jerry Sandusky for example. Many of Sandusky's colleagues knew about the abuses but had chosen not to tell the police. The incident led to the sacking of Joe Paterno, the head coach of the university, for failing to deal with it. Paterno was Sandusky's boss. He knew for sure what had been going on for a number of years. To protect his right-hand man, the much-loved eighty-four-year-old head coach of the Penn State Nittany Lions, the most successful coach in the history of college football, paid a very steep price. Many high-ranking officials of the university were also subsequently fired. Protecting your own men is considered loyal; loyalty has a high, very high moral value in every civilized society. If this kind of boy's club cover-up happened in the States, you can be sure it happens in Canada, and for that matter, happens in every corner of the world. Boys protecting boys by sacrificing women is nothing new; it happens with regularity today despite our much more advanced civilization. What do you think those ancient priests and teachers would do when they had to make a choice protecting the men or women? It was a common practice for bosses to protect their buddies in ancient times; the practice is still the norm in today's many governments or business organizations.

The label stuck quite easily. What else could women do in a world ruled by testosterone? Having successfully stuck the ugly label on women,

men could justifiably do what they really wanted. They wanted to turn every woman into a subclass citizen, a servant, a sex object, and even a slave. With the moral view established, the rulers, with the help of their priests and wise men, passed laws to enforce their power over women. They also created a prison called family to keep them in. A family, according to the wise and the pious, was universally propped up by three tenets. First, sex was allowed only between wedded couples. For men to have sex, they needed to first marry some women. Second, once a couple got married, it was for life. *"Till death do we part"* is still a very popular wedding vow; it has a very long root. Third, only certain people of authority—usually the fathers—could decide who could marry whom.

A family structure was an effective solution to the two most plaguing issues in the early societies. Under the system, young men were no longer allowed to follow their hearts and rape women whenever and wherever they wanted; they had to follow the rules. And a government was the enforcer of the rule. The design did drastically cut down sex-related fighting and killings. The system had also greatly reduced the number of single moms and children. From then on, there was no free sex for men; men had to pay a price to get their sperm delivered. They also had to protect and support their women and children. Gone were the days when men could hit and run; they were since held responsible. The system also gave men much, much greater legal power over women; women have since become the properties of their men. Through marriage, men legally owned their women.

The system had installed law and order for the first time in the wild ancient world. All in all a family design worked well. It stabilized a community, cut down waste of productive human lives, and allowed a community to prosper. For communities that did not have a family system, they continued to waste their most precious resources, and were, one by one, conquered and eliminated by those that got it. So a family system had become a must-have if a community was to survive and prosper.

The Problematic Family Structure

A family sustained by the three dogmas, while having solved the two most pressing problems in the early societies, also created some new ones. Among them, it had enraged the sex beast because the system targeted taming the testosterone-driven emotional animal. In essence, family declared war against the sex beast. Before there were families, the beast was humming along freely and doing what it had always done best, which was to make sure that sperm got delivered on target. Suddenly, families appeared from nowhere and tried to bar the beast from fulfilling its duty. If you were the sex animal, would you not get mad and try your best to hunt down the very thing that had irked you? And that, pal, is the reason why sex has loved nothing more than ruining families.

Confucius once said: "To eat and to have sex are both human nature." A young man's urge to have sex could be likened to a bull at its prime trying to break free from protective fences or walls. And guess who would win from time to time? And when the fences and walls were crushed by the beast, when morality failed, tragedies took place through adultery, rape, or incest, and claimed its casualties in human lives. From day one of its installation, the system had been problematic, like the lemon you once got from the car dealer!

Maybe we could console ourselves that it is not a perfect world, there is no perfect solution to the sex problem, and we have to accept the lesser of two evils somehow. It makes sense, does it not? And to give the wise and the pious credit, the solution was the best idea anyone could have come up with in those ignorant days. If the problem were limited to the occasional collapses of some fences and walls, perhaps we could put up with the patchy human toll that had come with it in exchange for the stability of a community. Fair enough? Were adulterers, rapists, and incestuous individuals getting killed, sometimes together with a number of innocent people ruined, the only problems of having a family structure? If it were the case, maybe we could still relax, watch the Olympic games on TV, eat our pizzas, drink our beers, and say, "Well, tough, isn't it?" Were the sinners and some innocent people getting killed the only bad thing coming out of a traditional marriage?

To answer the question, let us take another look at the way a traditional family was set up. Let us look at those married couples. First, who were those husbands and wives? Well, they were people who often knew absolutely nothing about each other before they were wedded. The strangers who by the supreme orders of their parents were bound together for good. What was wrong with that, you ask. It was wrong because the parents, in deciding the marriage for them, often did not take their happiness into consideration. To them, it was often a business deal most of the time. That had been and still is the way a typical family is set up in the old days of China, India, and still in most of the Islamic world nowadays. Try to imagine if you happened to be one of them. You preferred a blonde; she was a Snow White. You were chubby and would have chosen a plump man; he was a marathon runner type. You were a health nut; he loved steak, garlic, and potatoes, and got lethal breath. As you know, taste is a very personal thing. If you would not allow someone to buy clothes for you, why would you let someone choose your spouse? And there was another catch: a traditional marriage said, "Once you are married, you are in as long as you live." That is it, folks, whether you like it or not! This was hardly a satisfactory arrangement for either men or women, especially with the odds of getting the wrong type of spouse so high. And if you still remember, we men are sperm delivery boys; our job is to deliver our sperm to as many women as humanly, or often, financially possible. How could men, the ones who had created the family structure, be so stupid as to suggest something that resulted in greatly limiting their freedom?

Not to worry. There were plenty of ways out for men, especially if you happened to be rich or powerful. The priests and teachers were male too. They understood your concern and would not create a system which was not fair to men. There were many ways out. Number one, if a man was not happy with his first wife, he could always get another, another, and yet another. His power or wealth would be the limit. There are many cultures and religions that still sanctify polygamy for men. Number two, if a man could not afford more than one wife, he could always have sex with other women through adultery, rape, or other naughty things. And for those men who were not careful enough and got caught with their pants down or without, the penalty for man sinners often ranged from slaps on their wrists to some warnings or cautions: "Naughty boy, you must try to be more careful next time."

So for their inconvenience men had been handsomely compensated. In most, if not all, cultures, men were the head of families; they were to be unquestioningly obeyed by their wives. Family values of every culture has sanctified this right. Therefore, men got their sex objects, servants, or even slaves through the setup called marriage and family! Traditionally, husbands could rightfully demand sex from their wives anytime, whether the wives had headaches or not. And in an agricultural society, guess who would be doing most of the jobs in the field and at home? Even today, how many husbands would do their fair share of housework? Forget about diaper changing.

What if the wives would not take orders from their husbands? Do you think the husbands would sweet-talk their wives into it? Why waste time if you could simply beat them into submission? The laws were on your side. I don't know how many societies had laws against wife battering, certainly not in China under Confucianism. Not only was it legit, it was the right thing to do! Was China the only country that had condoned wife disciplining? You tell me.

So for a man, was it such a bad thing to let your parents arrange your marriage and lock you in for life with a wife that you might not like? I would say it was not a bad deal at all considering all the fringe benefits that came with it. To be fair—if there were such a thing in a man's world for women—I would say men got themselves the best deal ever! No other animal has come close to what we got from our women! That, my friend, is the reason why some men are still fervently defending and upholding the system in many places of the world. And to their credit, the system is still going strong. It makes me wonder why some women are also so wholeheartedly supporting the men in their quest, like the ex-Alaska governor who could see Russia from her state, according to a rumor.

Let us now consider what type of deal women got out of a traditional marriage. To start with, a woman's position had always been lower than her husband's. This was almost universal. There are similar teachings in different cultures that require women to submit to their husbands; it is considered virtuous. According to Confucius (it was no secret that the supreme saint had problems with women, particularly his wife), a woman should obey her father. Her marriage was to be arranged by her father, who often traded her like a commodity. After marriage, her husband would become her new boss who had absolute power over her. A woman had two roles: to bear the children of her husband and to serve the husband's every need. If she disobeyed, she would be lucky to be disciplined and beaten, the not so lucky ones got killed, justifiably. Long live Confucius! No wonder Chinese men worship you.

One may think that wife beating is a thing of the past. Think again. Even in today's most civilized communities like Toronto, wife beating is still very common. Wife beating does not usually make it to the news unless someone gets killed. Spousal abuses that appear on the news are only tips of the wife-battering iceberg. I don't have statistics, but I believe it will be very significant. I had seen it firsthand in a public park. It was really ugly and sickening. Having no place to turn to, a battered wife often has no choice but to return home and subject herself to the endless physical and mental torment. There is absolutely no place to hide for many of them even today. Some try to run away or get a legal separation from their possessive men, only to be stalked and hunted down like game by their abusive, possessive, and controlling husbands. Why do men still do such barbaric things to their women? I highly suspect that the old family concept has something to do with it. Under many religion based or Confucian moral systems, a man legally owns his woman.

What if you were a woman born at the time or in the wrong place today? I would say good luck, honey. Sorry, there was not much you could do. But if I were to give you some advice or suggestion, I would say no matter how hard it would be, grind your teeth, if that would help, and put up with it. If your husband wanted to have sex and you were not in the mood—and frequently you would not be in the mood because you needed to be tenderly worked into the mood—comply because you do not want to provoke him. It would not be nice to provoke a master who has more muscle than you. And if your husband beats you up just because he had an off day, it would not make the matter any easier for you to complain because it is the norm.

"So what should I do?" you, the woman, ask. Go to a church, if you are a Christian and try to be blameless and hope that you would go to heaven later. Our lives on earth, as you might have been taught, are no more than a short journey that would lead us to eternal happiness. So be patient, my child. Or, if you believe in Buddha, then you should try to suffer through it. Life, as you should know by now, is meant to be full of suffering. And if you do your part, you could hope to be born a man in your next life. "But life is too hard. I want to get out," you, the woman, insist. There would be no escaping it. Men run the world; you would soon be caught. It would be easier had you tried to escape from Alcatraz rather than your abusive husband. Your only way out is to kill yourself. It is not much of an option, is it?

Alas! Women, it is almost certain that you had given mankind farming; we should all share the fruit. Instead of being grateful, men had, out of selfishness, turned against you by imprisoning and even enslaving you. *Pray that I shall not be born a woman in my next life.* This prayer is said every morning by millions of Jews around the world.

And if you still have not learned, men have enslaved women, not by their superior intelligence, knowledge, or virtues, they have "earned" it the old-fashioned way through muscle. Muscle has not only ruled the animal world, it also rules human societies. Because men are animals run by the same testosterone, you are bound to be disappointed if you allow their seeming sophistication and occasionally nice mannerisms fool you. Marriage was often a prison, if not a deathtrap for women; it still is in many cultures.

It makes you wonder why women have been put into such a rotten situation in traditional marriage. It all started when the wise and religious men decreed that sex was evil and that the bodies of women were where the evil dwelled. From these they set up a family structure to control the evil; i.e., women. Accordingly, a man was the boss of his wife. He could get more than one wife but not vice versa, and could get away lightly for adultery and rape, not vice versa. Marriage and family were really designed to license legal ownership of women by men, like a government gives licenses to own dogs, houses, or cars. In case you doubt the marriage-ownership connection, how many love songs have you heard that have something like this? *You belong to me . . . You are mine,* or *I'll never let you go . . .* How romantic! I also have a hunch that men are more prone to singing such songs.

What does ownership imply? In a trip to Cuba many years ago, I bought a Venuslike sculpture made of solid and very heavy wood. I love the sculpture. I spent a lot of time looking at it, waxing it, and feeling it. It belonged to me. I had become possessive. Sometimes, I told my friends not to touch the sculpture. Nowhere in our society is a possessive emotion and instinct stronger than owning the wives. We would defend our women like a male lion defends its pride. Often, love has nothing to do with it. Is being possessive of another human being—wife or husband—a healthy attitude? A natural consequence of a possessive behavior that comes with ownership is to fully control what you possess, isn't it? Your automobile, for example. If you have fully paid for it, you can do anything you want with it, right? Or a tennis racket. It is not unusual to see players smash their rackets to vent their anger. They own the racket, they can do what they want with it. I don't know how many spousal abuses have originated from this possessive or "I own you" sentiment.

If I were a gal, I would be very wary if a man would tell me or sing to me that I belonged to him. I have once come across a poster which says,

If you love someone, let him/her free . . . I liked it at the time, I like it even more now. Come to think of it, this might have been the reason why my two exes have let go of me. Hmmm, maybe not . . .

Having checked the background, let us see whether or not the three old tenets of traditional marriage have any value in our societies. The objective of the first tenet was to stop men from killing each other over women. Thanks to progress and good law enforcement, in a modern society men seldom kill each other over women. And rapes have been greatly curbed by laws and education. And thank goodness women in civilized countries no longer get stoned to death or drowned in bamboo cages because they had sex outside wedlock. While no one openly condones it, women are no longer condemned for being promiscuous either, which should have been the case to begin with. Three cheers for woman's lib! Do we still need tenet number 1?

Tenet 2: Marriage was for life. Let us look at what functions the tenet had served. To be fair, it was to protect women and their children. You may not believe it, but in the "good" old days married women used to fare much worse than your like-new Cadillac; i.e., once it has been owned it loses serious value, and often the mileage has little to do with it. Our traditional value treated a woman as merchandize. Once a woman was married she was treated as soiled or tainted and worthless, and there would be no refund. To less civilized men, a married woman, or for that matter a woman having lost her virginity for whatever reasons, was considered like soiled underwear, a used toothbrush, or tainted blood, and to be treated like garbage. That is the reason behind the so-called honor killings. To allow a stained woman to live would be like displaying dirty undergarments for everyone to see. The system of treating sexed women like dirt was an important reason to lock the sperm delivery boys in for life, making them liable to pay support because those women were no longer good for circulation. In civilized societies, married women were no longer a subclass of human beings to their counterparts. Do we still need tenet 2?

The last reason I could think of in defense of marriage for life is to ensure the sperm delivery boys would support and protect their children. In fact, the welfare of children has been one of the most important reasons why people are still defending the traditional family values. Many supporters think that families with both parents are the best place and the only way to bring up healthy children. Their defense of family values is based on many unstated assumptions. And two of which are, first, the parents care about their children, and second, the parents love each other.

On one issue of the *Toronto Star* was a large picture of a family of three with a background of many smiling and approving people. The picture highlights a young clean-looking guy standing on the left, holding an impeccably groomed son (?). Standing next to the man is a *cover-girl* like woman (presumably the wife). And below the picture were two prominent lines that read: *We believe in Mom and Dad. We believe in marriage.* A job well done and a message cunningly delivered. It is the picture of the woman that had caught my attention and made me read the article subsequently. (I suspect that many female readers had also ended up reading the article because of the picture of the guy.) If all families were like that, yours truly would definitely vote for family. Speaking from experience, my father had spent in total less than a year with me when I was a child. And Mother, who looked after me, used to beat me up once in a while with reasons which I never agreed to and often didn't understand. And as far as I know, my family was not that odd. Lots of Chinese families are like mine. So is a family always the best way for the welfare of children? The answer, I guess, depends on as compared to what. Regardless, having a home surely beats having none.

My question again will be how many families you know are like the one shown in the picture, with caring and responsible parents who love each other (the couple surely looked that way)? I have no statistics, but based on the divorce rate in North America, plus couples that stay in marriage for various reasons than love (there should be a few, right?), I would think that the portrayed family is not the norm but a rarity. The portraiture is not unlike the hamburger pictures in fast-food outlets. They always show picture-perfect hamburgers; what you get is often very different from what you see! Call me stupid, I still buy hamburgers because of the pictures now and then.

Does a typical family provide the best environment for children to grow up in? How about families with parents who smoke and drink heavily? What kind of chance do their children have? How about parents that do not care much about their children and view them as parasites? How about parents that never see eye to eye? Or parents who are too busy with their careers to spend much time with their children? And the worst, how about parents who are professional welfare dependents—in some cases, not just for one generation? With so many unanswered questions, is a traditional family still the best deal for children? I would say get married for sex, for money, or just because it is there, but I seriously doubt it makes a good argument to do it for the children's sake. Should we reserve a big question mark on this one issue? If it is for protecting children, there should be a much better way of doing it. We shall discuss this topic again in a more thorough and makes-sense fashion in the governing part of the book.

The Impossibility for the Old Moralities to Solve the Sex Problem

Not knowing its biology, the morality of sex was an impossible problem for the priests and wise men of old to solve. That is why the solutions they came up with, their moral solutions, invariably claimed sex to be filthy, dirty, and beastlike behavior to be avoided. To make their moralities work, they also blamed women as the source of the evils. From their moralities, they justifiably locked women up in prisons called families. Because their views on sex were erroneous, their solutions were flawed. While solving the two most pressing problems, their solutions have created many new ones. Today, the problems their moralities had solved—men killing each other for sex and women being worthless once they got married—no longer exist in civilized countries; however, the problems that traditional marriage have created continue, making the lives of many (women in the not so civilized countries in particular) unbearable. And the claim that family structure is the best to bring up children in is at best very questionable.

There seems absolutely no more reason to hold on to the so-called family values. And with it comes the very question whether we should keep or get rid of the old moralities because of their many erroneous moral views, particularly on sex and the way they treat women. But it will not be an easy task, because with every existing view comes a religion and the god behind it. People will never give up their gods without a fight, often to a degree defying death. And many people—priests, pastors, clergymen, monks, and nuns—also have their livelihoods depending on their religions. On the other hand, status quo will only prolong the many unnecessary sufferings and miseries endlessly from their views. The old views are like malignant growths. It will be painful to remove them, but we have no choice if our goal is to bring happiness to our planet. We need to change how we decide moral right and wrong, particularly the moral view on sex.

A Bigger and More Complete Picture of Sex

It is difficult to change people's moral views, but it is not impossible. To change people's views, one must first make people understand that their views are wrong and how the mistakes arose in the first place. With absolute certainty, the errors had come from ignorance; the learned and wise of old who gave us the moralities were ignorant. With what they then knew, their views were the best humanity could offer at the time. To undo their errors, knowledge and understanding will be our most effective tools.

Science, though slow, has been gradually gaining on religions by replacing many once infallible and sacred beliefs with facts and proven theories. Christianity and the Catholic Church, for example, have been losing ground to science as a result. If science can win over Christianity, it can also trump other religions given time. I strongly believe (science) knowledge backed by rationality will be victorious. When that happens, we will have a better chance of healing the planet and bringing all living creatures a happier world. So let me try to share what I know about sex with you.

We have already mentioned that sex for humans is quite unique, because unlike any other organisms, except bonobo chimps, sex for humans serves two equally important functions: to reproduce and to bond the two sexes together during the difficult early stages of our evolution. The bonding function in us is far more important and intense than the peace-keeping function among the bonobo chimps.

Sex's Primary Function: Reproduction

For humans, the primary function of sex, like with all other living organisms, is to reproduce, to make new copies of us. If we look at the activities of a living organism—a plant, fungus, bacteria, or an animal—we can, without exception, group its activities into two phases: growth and reproduction. For a plant, to grow means to harvest the sun's energy, to absorb nutrients from its surroundings, and to use them to synthesize the various components of its body. For an animal, it means eating other organisms, alive or dead, to get the energy and materials for bodybuilding. If an organism can manage to get the required energy and materials to grow and at the same time avoid being killed—usually eaten by another animal—and reach sexual maturity, it reproduces. There is no exception to the rule.

Or we can say that the activities of all living things are directed to one goal, and the one goal is to get ready to reproduce so that the species can continue to travel through time. It is like a relay that, hopefully, will never be broken. Each organism is a participant in the relay. The DNA is the baton and the organism is its athlete; the organism's goal of existence is to pass the baton to its offspring. With each participant doing its best, a species can hope to continue to exist. The urge/drive to reproduce is one of the most powerful forces in the animal kingdom because the existence and survival of a species depend ultimately on it. Sexual urge among animals is so strong that it is often irresistible.

From this fact, we know that counting on morality to totally resist sex often ends in failure. Many religions, Catholicism in particular, have committed this blunder, which has cost them dearly. A better way is to work with our sex urge by managing it morally so that wild sex, which is the only harmful form of sex, will not happen. Managing our sex urge is a dependable, healthy, and beneficial solution. But before we can manage our sex urge, we need to first fully understand sex. And before we can fully understand, we must also get rid of the wrong beliefs that sex is shameful, dirty, and evil, and therefore never to be discussed in public. Sex is one of the activities linked directly to survival; it creates new lives. If life is sacred, then there is no reason to believe that the process leading to creating it would be shameful, dirty . . .

The take-home message from this part of discussion is sex is for reproduction, which in turn powers the survival of practically every species. For this reason, sex urge is exceedingly powerful, making it almost humanly impossible to resist it for a long period of time. Instead of fighting sex with morality, which is both unnecessary and often ineffective, giving way to wild and harmful sex, the better way is to work with it by managing it to prevent harmful sex from happening. Then, sex not only is harmless, it is healthy and beneficial and an ingredient for a happy life. It is unfortunate that most of our sex education has failed to deliver this most important message. The same failure occurs in most Biology 101.

Eventually, the question will be why have sex? Primitive creatures and many other organisms can still reproduce asexually, why go through the trouble? There is, in general, a lot of work involved before an organism can reproduce sexually, why do it the hard way?

Sexual Reproduction is a Gene-Shuffling Machine

With few exceptions, reproduction universally involves sex. Sexual reproduction provides the organisms of the new generation with gene contents totally different from their parents. It is a gene-shuffling machine through which the reproducing parents shuffle their genes before passing them on to the next generation. How? Sexual reproduction has two separate parts. Part 1 is the production of the sex cells, sperm or eggs, which are the gametes. Part 2 is the union of a sperm with the egg. Gametes are only produced in the sex organs of an organism through a special type of cell division called *meiosis*. It is during meiosis that the genes in a starting cell are randomly shuffled before producing the sperm or eggs. Meiosis, other than shuffling the genes in a parent's cell, also reduces the amount of DNA in a starting cell by half. Sperm and eggs are haploids. That is why meiosis is often called "reduction cell division."

In humans, we have twenty-three pairs of chromosomes, which are structures where the genes (DNA molecules) are located. Randomly shuffling the twenty-three pairs of chromosomes plus crossing over during meiosis help to produce an astronomical number of possible gene combinations from a parent's cell in the sperm or eggs thus produced. While all the cells in your body are practically the same in their gene contents, every gamete, a sperm or egg, is unique in the genes it has. Meiosis produces more combinations for genes than shuffling produces for a deck of cards.

Part 2 involves the union or fertilization of an egg by a sperm of the same species to produce a fertilized egg. Given time and chance, it develops into a new organism. Fertilization restores the amount of genetic materials to normal. It also determines the actual gene mix of the new organism out of the astronomical number of possibilities. If a couple produces two children during their marriage, only two of countless gene combinations are realized; the other combinations are wasted.

Sexual reproduction makes sure that no two children from a different fertilization are the same. That is why no matter how many children you and your wife are going to have, none of them will be genetically identical, except identical twins.

This brings up an interesting or daunting point. In the event of extreme climate change due to global warming, many existing organisms will not be able to cope and will die *en masse*. Then it will be up to the organisms of the next generation to find the solution based on the gene mixes they received at the time of fertilization, correct? Then, you will see the advantage of producing a huge number of offspring, like bacteria, fungi, or virus, because the sheer number of their "children" will give them a better chance to get the right gene mix for the new environment. Insects also will be more likely able to cope than any reptile, bird, or mammal. Humans in developed countries, because of our knowledge and technology, are likely to find solutions and survive. But will it be a beautiful world? Would you like to live on a planet without those lovely animals?

Sexual reproduction does not always require a male and its female partner to have any physical contact or intercourse. Many aquatic animals—sea urchins, for example—dump their gametes into the surrounding water where fertilization takes place. In flowering plants, their flowers are sex organs. They often contain both sex organs. A flower generally contains a number of stamens and a single carpel. A stamen is a male sex organ. It produces many pollens and each pollen contains a male gamete. A carpel contains the ovary of the flower, which contains the eggs, the female gametes. Before fertilization can take place, pollen needs to be delivered onto the stigma of a carpel of the same species. The delivery of pollen to the carpel is called pollination. It can be done either by animals or by wind. Again, the sex organs of the opposite sexes do not need to have any physical contact.

Sexual reproduction is extremely pricey because there will be a tremendous amount of waste as mentioned. It requires a lot of preparation—to grow and to mature—on the part of the participants before they can start to produce gametes. The preparations often take a lifetime for many. The cicadas that had caused so much unease for the CBC newsperson spend seventeen years in preparation. For fertilization to take place, the participants—the male animals in particular—often have to overcome huge hurdles before they can get the sperm to unite with the eggs so that the yangs and the yins can, once again, be made whole. Remember the gametes are haploid?

Why do living creatures go through so much trouble to have sex to reproduce? Can they not just mature and reproduce asexually like budding in yeasts or among *Hydras* for example? Asexual reproduction is very frugal and exceedingly economical and effective; there is hardly any waste in the entire process. And the result is 100 percent predictable. The new individual created will be genetically identical to the parent. Despite all these benefits, it has one shortcoming and that is new individual will be exactly the same, genetics wise, as the parent. This shortcoming eventually is going to cost the existence of the whole species. This is like a carmaker that only produces one model of car and exactly the same type of car year in and year out. Suppose the car is great in dry weather, what will happen if it rains? See the point?

The only reason for organisms to have sex despite its prohibitive cost that always comes with it is to provide Mother Nature with organisms that have many, many different genetic mixings/combinations to select from. It is exactly the same reason why carmakers often offer many different models, and keep changing the models every year to cater to many different needs and appetites. Why is it important to provide the many genetic mixings? Because each type of genetic mixing provides the organism a particular ability to do well in a certain environment, and there are many drastically different environments. Mother Nature also has a nasty habit of changing the environment constantly. Doing well in today's environment does not guarantee you will do well in it after a number of years. Worse, none of the earthy organisms can read Mother Nature's mind in order to deliver the gene mixes she wants in a changing world.

So what do they do to better their chances of meeting the Mother's cut? They provide a great variety of their gene mixings—as many as they can afford—and hope that some of the combinations can please the Mother. And sexual reproduction—meiosis together with fertilization— is the only device that can produce the gene mixings. That is why every creature on earth has sex. For the survival of the species, they can't afford not to. They don't do it just for fun, at stake is the existence of their kind. Sexual reproduction is a necessity to survival.

Let me give you another analogy. It is like your new boss asks you to get him a coffee and you have absolutely no idea how he takes it and you dare not ask. So what do you do? You buy every possible flavor from Starbucks. You don't know how he takes his coffee either, so you take several packs of sugar, including the sweeteners, a copious amount of cream, and every type of milk—homo, 2 percent, and skimmed milk. If you can afford it, you may consider buying a small, a medium, a large, and an extra-large coffee for each flavor to increase your chance of hitting it right because your future may depend heavily on the coffee. There is a big difference. You might never get fired for bringing the wrong coffee. A species, however, does not have such a luxury. You fail Mother Nature once, and you are out forever. It is like a special baseball game in which Mother Nature is the pitcher. She tosses the ball to you—fast ball, slider, off-pitch, etc.—and some of your players have to hit it to get on base every time!

Unfortunately for the earthy creatures, Mother Nature's tastes can be compared to that of a pregnant woman, it changes from time to time and place to place. To make her happy so that your species can avoid joining the dinosaurs, the organisms collectively must continuously come up with new combinations for her sampling. And this, my friends, is the only reason that almost every living organism has sex. Contrary to what you might have been brainwashed to think, sex has never been the source of filth or evil. How can it be filthy and shameful? It is a process to create life, and we all think that life is sacred. There is no logic; it is ignorance, pure and simple. Above all, the future of our species, and for that matter every species on the planet, depends on sex to give them the gene mixes. Beyond any doubt, to have sex is a life-and-death issue, and the fate of a species is directly tied to it—like it or not, or knowing what they are doing or not. Because of the importance, and when an organism is ready, there is no other priority higher than having sex for the organism, be it a plant or an animal, bacteria or fungus, etc. Biologically, the only ultimate mission of every living creature on the planet—mankind included—is to have sex, which naturally leads to reproduction.

If that is the case, what will happen to a creature after it has completed its assignment? Well, there should be no point for it to continue to exist only to prolong its miserable existence, should it? It may as well drop dead, right? And in fact, if one looks at all the organisms in nature, one will find that many organisms do drop dead soon after the sex act. Thus, the noisy cicadas were noisy no more shortly after mating. Nature does not believe in wastefulness like most wealthy Americans or

Canadians do. Come to think of it, it is not a bad deal at all to die shortly after sex, is it? I'll bet every cicada has died smiling.

For those that can mount the attempt many times, Mother Nature usually does not allow them to live out their potential reproductive years. They are seldom permitted to reproduce past their peak. With the exception of humans, other animals—lions, walruses, elephants, or rams, etc.—might as well forget about sex in their golden years. There will always be some younger and stronger newcomers waiting to make their contributions to the species' gene pool. There is an unspoken rule in nature—and every living organism understands it—and the rule is: have sex whenever, wherever, however, and at whatever price. Do it at the earliest possible chance you have. And if it costs your life, so be it. A male praying mantis is a good example; it often gets its head bit off by his hungry and very selfish "wife" during lovemaking. One would think the headless Romeo would stop immediately, right? Wrong. Rain or shine, head or no head, the mission has to be completed. They don't call it *mission impossible* for nothing. So the copulation continues unabated in its physical intensity. With the penis still firmly anchored, the headless body continues to writhe, twist, and convulse in every which way violently to squeeze out the last tiny bit of its seed. Only with death—and not before the last bit of semen is delivered—does it stop, but won't part. When it comes to wild and totally uninhibited sex, nobody—I mean absolutely nobody, the bad boys included—beats those praying mantises.

Strangely, civilized humans, through our supreme intelligence, have somehow concluded that sex should be avoided and intentionally denied when it is available. It is just so damn unfair to those male praying mantises and male black widow spiders! Regardless of how sex is done among organisms—and there are endless ways, and some are quite weird by human standards—the goal is to ensure that the sperm will unite with the egg. In more advanced animals, the sperm and the eggs—the gametes—are produced in two separate individuals that are called males and females. Even among hermaphrodites, an individual would seldom have sex with itself—we are not talking about masturbation. It is more desirable to exchange genes with another individual.

Guess which gender often has to deliver the gametes? You got it; it is usually the onus of the males to locate the females and deposit their sperm into her bodies. Among animals, a female often only has to signal that she is ready and receptive and the males will drop everything to rush to her before someone does. In the animal kingdom, there are very few males like Brad Pitt and Tom Cruise for whom getting laid appears to be the least of their problems. Men chasing women or males going after females are the norm. And depending on which species one belongs to, making the sperm deliveries to the females could be trickier and riskier than delivering flowers or pizzas—a praying mantis or black widow spider are good examples. It often requires great ingenuity, lots of risk taking, and often involves great sacrifices on the part of the males before they can complete the perilous mission. The survival of a species, as a rule, depends heavily on the brave, dutiful, and highly motivated males to get their jobs done.

To make sure that the males will do their jobs, won't get lazy, back down in the face of difficulty and danger or steep competition—it is all too frequent that too many eager, strong, and capable males are competing for the same opening—Mother Nature has made sexual urge among males so compelling that it is simply irresistible. And for those that keep doing their jobs well, the species will be rewarded with a new generation. Survival is a never-ending relay. The batons are the genes, the athletes are the continuous supply of new organisms that pass their batons on during sexual reproduction.

What Drives Men to Have Sex?

For many organisms, including most animals, sexual reproduction is driven by some hormones. But trees, grass, or fungi are not burdened by the stress of it like an animal is. Lucky for us and thanks to many hardworking biochemists, we know a lot about what drives mammals such as dogs, bulls, and humans to have sex. The driving force is, not surprisingly, sex hormones. Sex hormones for male and female are different, and each sex has a number of hormones working together like musicians in an orchestra before sex can take place. And since the males are the parties that have to make the sperm deliveries, they have to actively pursue sex. Let us first look at what drives men to want sex almost during all their waking hours, and often in their dreams, causing many young men much embarrassment.

For men, there are more than one hormones involved, but none is as important as testosterone. Let us look at what testosterone does to a man's body:

1. *Promotes the normal development and maintenance of the maleness hardware—including the organs, sperm production, and male secondary sexual characteristics, etc.*
2. *Stimulates protein synthesis and muscle growth in particular*
3. *Enhances competitiveness and aggressiveness*
4. *Gives sexual desire*

Pretty amazing, isn't it? It is amazing because the scheme is so exquisitely simple that it will be foolproof. One lousy chemical compound is all Mother Nature needs to drive men crazy to complete the assignment. If you look at those functions, it becomes glaringly clear that all testosterone does is make sure a guy under its influence will be superbly equipped for the job: he is loaded with sperm, he gets muscle, he gets the right attitude, and above all, he gets a burning desire! If you were to design a sperm delivery boy, how would you do it? I don't care if you are a rocket scientist, neurosurgeon, or a person with the IQ of Stephen Hawking, you just cannot do any better. That is why they call it a complete package! Nadal gets it, King James gets it, Arnold the ex-governor used to get it, and Mr. Clinton during his presidency most definitely also got it. Some people are just luckier. They simply get packages that are more complete than those of other mortals. Being better equipped certainly makes the job easier.

Testosterone Drives Women Crazy Too

Interestingly, testosterone not only is the desire hormone for men, it does the same trick on women also. Let me quote what Ms. Gill has to say in a program aired on March 15, 2002, on *The National*, a CBC TV program. I got the info from the Internet inadvertently.

> *Alexandra Gill was prescribed the drug (testosterone) for endometriosis. It didn't do a thing for the disease but it kicked her libido into overdrive. "It became a distraction. Sex was just always on my mind," says Gill. "I really don't*

understand how most men get through a normal day if this is the way they feel. How do they get up, go to work, focus on things? I just couldn't focus very well because I was always thinking sex, sex, sex."

Let me tell you, Ms. Gill, it ain't easy, believe me. Sex, too, is always on my mind. And by the way, Ms. Gill, the stuff you received was likely to be less than 10 percent of what's in a normal man's blood, and you think you got a bad deal. Try to think what we men have to endure every day, 24/7, and 365 days and horny nights from about fifteen to at least our mid-fifties. And for that reason, please, gals, believe me for your own good: men are animals, and sex, primarily, is what men want from you. Consider yourself warned by one of them.

Some may deny it, but it should not be a myth that sex is on the mind of most men most of the time, especially when meeting or sighting a sexy woman. How can it be otherwise when our minds are controlled to a great extent by our hormones? Testosterone is the boss. That is what men are: obsessed sperm delivery boys. You may be a president, prime minister, or a CEO of a Fortune 500 company, or for that matter, the president-elect of America, it still does not change the fact that your primary concern will be getting your sperm delivered. And that is why men are thinking with the wrong head most of the time! And some famous persons even lose control, grabbing women's private parts. That, my dear reader, should pretty much sum up what men really are, yours truly in particular.

To be successful in the sperm delivery business, a man needs women, the more the merrier, to agree to have sex with him—everybody knows this simple fact. Often, getting a woman to agree is the most difficult part for us delivery boys.

The Pathology of Love and Getting Married for Love a Stupid Idea

I have always been a fan of choosing my own spouse. I guess I have been seriously misled by fairy tales. Once they get married, they live happily ever after. Choosing my own wife will certainly beat letting my old man do the picking. But the fact is it may not be that ideal after all. Most marriages won't last more than two years in North America, where people make their own choices, according to some research. Me, for example, twice I have picked my own wives, twice the marriages have fallen apart. I married my second when I was in my early fifties—so much for the older the wiser. I have been scratching my bald head trying to understand why I have kept failing and have come up empty until I came across an article titled "The Pathology of Love" posted on June 14, 2004, by Sam Vakin. I began to see my folly. Thank you and thank you, Sam!

The followings are some highlights from the article:

> *. . . falling in love is . . . indistinguishable from a severe pathology . . . behavior changes (of people in love) are reminiscent of psychosis and, biochemically speaking, passionate love closely imitates substance abuse. British National Addiction Center said that love is addictive, akin to cocaine and speed.* (But we have covered that, haven't we?)

> *. . . The BBC summed it up succinctly and sensationally: "Events occurring in the brain when we are in love have similarities with mental illness."*

And once again, the culprit is testosterone:

> *A recent study in the University of Chicago demonstrated that testosterone levels shoot up by one-third even during a casual chat with a female stranger. The stronger the hormonal reaction, the more marked the changes in behavior, concluded the author . . . The hormone's readings in married men and fathers are markedly lower than in single males still "playing in the field."* (After all, marriage is not all bad, if one is to lessen the whipping of testosterone.)

Then I realized that I was not crazy for considering getting myself neutered many times over the years, each time after going through the frustration and heartache from looking for "love." With that scientific backing, I would declare all love-driven marriages null and avoid, not just the gay couples who live in Texas, Alaska, and Alabama, etc., because the men are likely to be intoxicated and impaired, albeit by their own hormone. Why not? If I can prove that I have made a deal when mentally impaired, do you think the contract is enforceable in court?

But the guy should not be set free lightly because he has caused serious emotional hurt to his woman. Like driving impaired, the husband, getting married under influence, if he is to be freed of a marriage contract, should be charged with reckless loving and causing harm to his victim and be liable for all sorts of damages. These findings not only throw light on my failed marriages, it should also answer those who propose marriage for life. Again, it should not have come as a surprise. It is exactly the way Mother Nature has designed men to be—obedient sperm delivery boys like soldiers, and faithfully carrying out the order without considering other factors. In order to enhance the survival of a species, we have to do it at all cost, including our sanity. In essence, Mother Nature is telling men and women and especially men: "Just do it!"

Yet Another Example of the Interest of a Species Trumps Its Individual's

Here is yet another example of how the interest of a species trumps those of its individuals, as first discussed in chapter 2. To prevent our intelligence from interfering with the chance to mate, testosterone, among the other things, also messes up our faculty to reason clearly. When the chance to reproduce comes, Mother Nature has made it the topmost priority for every organism (the most intelligent humans included) and giving them no choice but to obey, often disregarding the perils that follow. The sick bitch of Panama was an example, so were the millions of poor parents, the husbands in particular. For many of us, it is not that we are ignorant of the dangers of sex under certain circumstances—unwanted pregnancy, becoming a criminal, financial loss, getting infected, etc. However, we cannot always resist the urge. As a result, we get ourselves into a lot of subsequent headaches and heartaches. Of course, most of us know it will not serve our long-term personal interest to take the bait, but for the interest of our species we often bow to testosterone. The lust molecule is supreme. Under its influence, every man becomes a lunatic with only one goal in mind: do it, do it, do it . . . It has defeated some of our smartest and otherwise most disciplined guys.

For the good of the species, getting you, the unfortunate individual, into trouble will be Mother Nature's least concern.

As discussed, the reproductive part of an organism's life cycle is where we often find that the interest of an individual and its species' may not be, and are often not, in sync. There are few things in nature that jeopardize the welfare of an organism like producing progeny. Yet, all animals are powerless to resist their sex urge. If it better serves the interest of the species that male praying mantises should get eaten, then the Romeos must die. When the interests of a species and its individual organism are at odds, the interest of the species—i.e., to survive—will forever trump those of its individuals'. This is an important new principle of survival. This is another healthy reason we should fear sex because of its power.

Strangely, Mother Nature is not the only one pushing people to reproduce regardless of the consequences. The Catholic Church has been Mother Nature's eager accomplice. I cannot help but ask again: why has the church been pushing the freely reproduce and the marriage-for-life deals? Should we forgive the clergy because they know not what they are doing? If love is comparable to mental sickness—there are tons of scientific facts to support it—why does the clergy keep pushing innocent people into this trap? And if it is such a great deal, why don't they get married? Hmm . . . I smell fish! Not only the Christian churches, the WHO is pushing the same reproductive rights. The WHO is under the same human rights umbrella; it is full of ideals but seriously lacking foundation for claiming such rights.

Getting Married, the Hidden Dangers

Even under the most ideal scenarios, marriage is unlikely to last more than several years. There are a number of reasons that tend to erode even a happy start where a couple make their own choice, have time to know each other well by living together for a number of years before tying the knot, etc., etc. I have done all those. My two marriage still ended up broken—one after twenty-three years, the second began to disintegrate from the wedding day.

There are many reasons for marriage not to last. The first I can think of is the two sexes play different parts in a survival game. Men's primary role is to deliver our sperm to as many receptive women as possible. Men, by nature, are not designed to be faithful or happy with one woman; men are constantly looking for sex. Men get married for sex. Women, on the other hand, get married for security. As discussed, women in our lineage have gone through a very long and dark period of time when they were very vulnerable and needed protection and provision. When a woman chooses a man, the instinct she gets from that period of time is still active and leads her to choose a strong and aggressive man, a good protector and provider. We also know that a strong protector and provider is powered by none other than testosterone, which has a nasty side effect of making a man unfaithful. An irony, isn't it? On top, women are designed to be the primary givers and providers for their children. After a woman has a child, her priority will be shifted to her child, the husband often comes in second, sometimes a distant second. So the husband gets neglected. What would a frustrated sperm delivery boy do under this circumstance? Will he still be faithful and loyal to his wife if tempted?

So these primary differences will make a happy marriage drift apart. And a natural human instinct to take things for granted also gradually comes into play. The parts of him or her that used to excite you will be no more. If a couple stops growing together, finding new things to keep the warm feeling going, their love will soon be dead. It is quite common for a very good-looking couple to go separate ways. Brad and Angelina did go separate ways. You cannot get a more attractive-looking pair than that couple.

The last point is human nature is selfish. Unless a couple has the education, moral discipline, and care, one or both will begin to hurt one another when chances arise. For men, it is often another willing woman or money. For girls, it usually is money, the thing to give them security; it can also be another man. For sex education to be useful, potential lovers must be warned of the hidden dangers before they are allowed to commit to each other. It will certainly cut down on the amount of heartaches and headaches in a society. Be warned: the message is from someone who has failed twice and may not know what he is talking about.

Getting Married for Money or Career

Please don't get me wrong. A marriage contract still has great value under certain circumstances. The first one I can think of will be for sex. (Funny, sex is always on my mind; sex is always on my mind . . . tune by Willy Nelson.) My rationality for marriage would be like this:

> *Me, old and wrinkly*
> *She, young, gorgeous, with a sinfully delicious full body*
> *Marriage gives us both what we want:*
> *Me, an exclusive right to sex with her*
> *She, a lioness's share of my properties*

A traditional marriage will certainly guarantee me and her those goodies. To be sure, I will like nothing less than a society that harshly punishes adulterous women. And for animals like me, luckily there still are many such "perfect" societies. Other than getting married under the influence of love, there can be plenty of good reasons for people to do it, like for career advancement or business. And since these contracts are made by sober, willing, and well-informed parties, this type and this type of marriage contract only should be fully enforceable under law. Getting married does have value in modern societies! And I am not being cynical or satirical in saying that; I have the backing of science and many observed facts!

Why Sexual Intercourse?

Almost every adult knows what sexual intercourse is. But not many know what it is for. Sexual intercourse—a.k.a. coitus or copulation—is the insertion of a male's penis into a female's vagina for the purpose of safely delivering sperm. Though sexual intercourse is exceedingly pleasurable for humans, as discussed—and likely for all other animals too—the pleasurable part of sex is not the ultimate goal. The real goal of sexual intercourse is for safe sperm delivery. The pleasurable part is, again, Mother Nature's trick to make animals do it to ensure the survival of their species.

Why is it necessary for the sperm to be delivered into a female's body? Sexual intercourse is certainly an important adaptation to terrestrial dwelling. Aquatic animals like sea urchins, lobsters, fish, and amphibians, etc. can simply drop their eggs and sperm into the surrounding water where fertilizations take place. There is no sexual intercourse involved for these animals. Land animals have no such luxury. If they drop their gametes onto the land, the sperm and eggs will certainly all dry up within a short time after leaving the bodies of the animals. To protect the gametes, they must never be allowed to leave the protective environment of the animals. As a result, intercourse and internal fertilization is the rule for all land-dwelling animals; there is no exception. That is why all land animals have to have sexual intercourse before reproduction can be achieved. Though it is often fun for the animals, fun is the bait. Get it?

Sex's Secondary Function: Bonding Agent

At the risk of being obsessed with human centrism or species narcissism, we are truly a very unique kind from any angle you may choose to look at ourselves. It all began when a chimp was forced to walk on two feet, and ever since the many peculiarities in our species have not stopped popping up. And you can find a number of them in our sexual features and our sexual relationship between the two sexes.

The Unusual Sexual Features of Humans

One of our truly unique sex-related features is certainly the participation of men in bringing up a child. There is no male mammal, not even a single male ape, including those sex junkies the bonobo chimps, which takes part in caring for its children. And we do it willingly and out of choice. There are other male animals that take part in nourishing the young; they are found only among some birds. Not every kind of male bird takes up the chore either. Roosters, ganders, or peacocks don't take part in finding food or protecting the chicks at all. The jobs are left to the mother birds. But there is an interesting exception; it is a bird called cassowary in Australia and New Guinea. They are big flightless birds. It is the males that hatch the eggs, protect the chicks, guide them, and bring them up. The females are like "playgirls." They take off to hunt for more males after having raped her "husband" and laying a number of eggs for him to look after. They completely reverse the roles of a mother and father. I think women's lib should consider adopting the cassowary as their mascot.

Unlike mammals, the participation of male birds in bringing up families is not rare; there are a number of species that do so. The common examples are among birds of prey, birds that eat meat or fish, such as eagles, hawks, sparrows, penguins, and puffins, etc. It is a survival requirement for both sexes to participate. For these birds, finding enough food for the parent bird and its chicks is far too difficult for one parent to solo it; it needs both parents. For those who have not done it, I would highly recommend a reader to watch a documentary called *March of the Penguins* to appreciate the difficulties these birds face during reproduction. It is a 2005 French feature-length true story directed and cowritten by Luc Jacquet, coproduced by Bonne Pioche and the National Geographic Society. The survival game played by these birds is more than cruel.

The degree of involvement in bringing up children for men during our evolution was at least as deep as any of the birds', including those emperor penguins. Our men possibly began to get involved not later than at the *H. habilis* stage, if not at Lucy's type, according to our theory. It gradually intensified over a number of millions of years. By the time it got *to H. erectus*, the participation of men was vital if the mother-and-child pair was to survive the hardship the months before and the years after a child was born. Sex, the intense sexual pleasure from it, was the bonding agent Mother Nature employed to do the trick. That is the reason why we find so many unusual sexual features in our bodies as discussed. The intense sexual pleasure produced by the many sexual features combined also makes sex highly addictive, especially to men. Once he was hooked, he would not leave and would willingly look after his woman and child. Then, it was possible for our intelligence to continue to increase. It seemed to be an unavoidable development for a being forced to walk on two feet.

According to our theory, the females of our lineage had gone out of their way to make sex extremely pleasurable by lopsidedly contributing more features: constant receptiveness, big breasts, naked body, softer and smoother skin, forwardly tilted vagina, and occasionally be able to hit orgasm. For every one of our female ancestors, the ability to secure a caring man was a matter of life and death and therefore exceedingly competitive. That was why they were so eager to contribute more to make sex pleasurable. To be constantly receptive, for example, allowed her to keep her man sexually satisfied all the time and thereby hold on to him for the period she would need help. I hope sensitive readers will not call me a sexist. If you do, that is what I am. I have googled the term to confirm that I fit the many descriptions. But I am a sexist with a difference. I have the correct moral view to guide my every dealing with others. I don't intentionally hurt others. I always allow people, men or women, to choose.

Playing Hard to Get

But there was also a catch. For her to secure a man, she also needed to be less interested in sex. An irony, isn't it? There is a very significant gap between the sexual appetite or sex drive of men and women. In an ideal (sex) world, I would wish for a 50/50 distribution, meaning gals would be as horny as the guys all the time. Wouldn't it be yummy? But it won't work for Mother Nature during the time the mothers of our species needed help most. It would be too easy for the sperm delivery boys. And if life were like that, there would certainly be no need for some men to have credit cards, would there? Why has Mother Nature made it so hard for men to get laid? How does it serve her supreme purpose? Does the sexual gap serve any survival purpose?

I think there is a good reason and it was ultimately for our own good that the gap had to exist. To see how it had to exist, let us see where we would end up if there were no gap in the sexual appetite between men and women like in many mammalian species. Let us go back to the time shortly before *H. erectus*. If you remember, *H. erectus* was the stage if not earlier, in which bigheaded babies really created serious problems for their moms. So that the babies could safely pass through the birth canals, they were born prematurely. In short, both the mom and her baby needed the help of a capable selfless male—a husband and a father—for many months before and years after. Now, imagine the females of *H. erectus* were as easy as the males. It would not require the males to persuade the females into a receptive mood, would it? So they just mate and that would be it, would it not? There would be no need for a male to work for sex and thus there would be no chance for bonding, would there? So the female got pregnant and found herself hapless soon after, especially in the months before and the several years after the birth of her child. What do you think would happen to the mother-and-child pair in a barbaric time when meat was hard to come by? Would you give the pair more than 50/50 chance to survive? I would certainly not.

Had the females been as eager as the males, our human evolution would have stopped long before *H. erectus* stage, would it not? So does it make sense to you that human females could not afford to be as ready as males? So should we complain? It was a very small price to pay—buying lunches, paying for movies, etc.—in the name of improving our species, wasn't it?

To give the mother and baby pairs of our ancestral species any chance to survive, the gap had to exist I believe. It makes sense, does it not?

Let us see what the sexual desire gap had created in courting. Let us see what an *H. erectus* male needed or a modern man will have to do before he could/can get his sperm delivered. Assuming that the populations of sexually mature men and women are roughly the same, then there will be several times more men wanting sex than women at any given time and place. Under this circumstance, who would have to work for it, a loaded sperm delivery boy or a gal who is lukewarm about sex? It is a situation that boils down to whoever needs it more will end up taking the initiative, doesn't it? You want to go downtown and I am not so hot about the idea. Guess who will be driving and perhaps also buying the drinks? And if you happen to be unbearably horny (which is often the case when one is young and loaded) and your gal is not in the mood, what will you do? I would certainly try to be nice and charming, and hopefully my doing so could switch the gal's so-so mood into a receptive mode, would I not? Now you understand why guys are always buying lunches, paying for movies, or washing their girlfriends' cars—I used to do all those things. When rape is not an option, what other choice do you have besides being nice? If begging helps, I would do it. (Done it once; did not work.)

The gap was a built-in mechanism designed by Mother Nature to favorably select males with caring and patient temperaments, the crucial qualities required for a taxing job. And before a female would get aroused to a sexually receptive level, she had plenty of time to get to know her potential sperm donor. Through trial and error and by natural selection, the 10 to 1 ratio in the horny scale must have worked best to ensure bonding without creating too much difficulty before the guys would get fed up and say the hell with it to sex or resort to violence. We men all have our share of experiences with those impossible-to-get types. Horny we men are, salmonlike we are not. Does it make sense to you that the gap had to exist if not for today's developed societies?

Sexual Tension Existing in Every Society

The inequality in sexual interest always creates more, far more, sexually deprived men than women. It is a situation in India, Canada, Kenya, or whatever place you can think of. If you happen to be a male in China after the one-child policy, I wish you luck, because other than for waste disposal your organ will unlikely be employed in another intended function. The problems from the unequal sexual appetite began to surface in communities shortly after farming was established.

Being totally in the dark about survival—the related biology and the unique jumps in human intelligence during evolution, which, in all, is a huge body of knowledge—the priests, the wise men, and teachers did come up with similar bandage solutions. They all unanimously decreed that sex was a demon that dwelled in women's bodies. Sex was dirty, shameful, bad, and the root of all evils; something that should never be talked about in public, and to be avoided by virtuous persons as much as one could. Women, being the accomplices of this evil, were to be locked up in a system called family through arranged marriages. This type of moral view is still very strong and powerful. Even the very learned, men and women, do not question such a debased view of sex. With the erroneous views also come the many sexual problems; sexual assaults, rapes, adulteries, and incest are still plaguing our world with different degrees of severity. Together comes many innocent victims. Such an attitude often takes a toll on people, adults, and children.

Let me share with you a personal story. From the time when I was about eight years old, my foreskin, on the average, would get infected about twice a year for nearly ten years until I got circumcised. The infection caused the part to secrete some kind of gunk. I felt filthy and worthless from the infection. But the emotional burden was minimal in comparison to the physical pain. The yucky stuff would dry up in a couple of days and completely seal the opening as it hardened. Urination became a big problem. The urine had to force its way through the scar at several spots. It opened up fresh wounds and made a big mess each time. It was one of the most painful experiences. During the period, I dreaded going to pee and would avoid it at all cost—not a pleasant alternative either.

After several days, the infection would subside and the part began to heal. Another type of torment then began. The foreskin then became exceedingly itchy. At its most intense moment, I was confronted with two choices: to scratch or not to. Scratching it would give me badly needed relief, but the short break would come with a huge penalty later because it often worsened a bad situation. And worst of all, the unbearable itch usually came at night when I needed to sleep most. It took superhuman willpower to refuse to give in to it. The whole thing usually lasted about a week to ten days. When it was over, I would have to tighten my belt a couple of holes.

You may wonder why I didn't go to see a doctor. As a boy, I needed my mother to go with me. Then, the question becomes: why didn't I tell my mother? You are not pulling my leg, are you? I could not. From very young, I was conditioned by every senior person, Mother in particular, to keep my private part well concealed and never talk about it in the presence of girls and women. My mother had constantly reinforced the rule to make sure that I would never forget. Mother must have known my condition too because I had little energy and walked funny during the dreaded period. Lucky for me, she did not ask, and I would not divulge my condition.

I was hardly alone. I am sure every Chinese boy or girl has a similar sex-related horror story. For the girls, it will often be their first period. I remember Mother had once beaten the crap out of Sister for no obvious reason. I also clearly recall seeing some bloodstained tissues lying in a remote corner of her room before the incident. When I was a teenager, I had occasionally heard women whispering to one another about something called "dark ailments." It took me quite a while to know that they were referring to something that has to do with sickness in their private parts. "Dark ailments" are something they could not bring out and seek treatment for. That was why they were called "dark ailments." This attitude is still quite common today among Chinese women.

And I am quite sure that the Chinese are not the only people who treat sex as taboo. If I am to take a guess, I will say that easily over 95 percent of the world's mature adults hold such a view. And I am not talking about dummies and idiots who believe that women can get pregnant from eating an organ either. A great percentage of these people are highly educated and otherwise intelligent people, who also include some medical doctors. The common view is sex is ugly and shameful. You are not supposed to talk about it in public.

Sexual needs also create many poor families and perpetuate it endlessly. Yet, the Christian view still holds that procreation, regardless, is holy. Human rights also believe that it is every one's right to freely have children. It is a (God) given right. Unless we solve sexual problems, the world will continue on its miserable journey. And now, we have the tools to do so.

Changing Our Attitude on Sex

Or a more valid question will be should we treat sex as a wild beast at all? Must we fight it, imprison it, or even do without it? Does sex have to be viewed as an enemy which always wants to destroy us? Does it do any good to our mental health to label sex as dirty, unholy, or a behavior suited for animals? The answer to those questions should not have come only from the pious and religious, because they are likely to be totally ignorant and inexperienced when it comes to sex. That is why they are saints in the first place. Saints avoid sex and try hard not to do it. And their views often have no relevance to scientific findings.

That Sex is Dirty, Shameful, and the Root of All Evil Is Half True

Sexual problems began to plague human communities very early, possibly soon after farming communities began to form. The problems that sex created all belong to bad sex. What is bad sex? For bad sex to happen, one very important factor is always there: it is without the consent of the party targeted, usually the weaker sex, a woman. The victim is forced into it and thus has no choice. Bad sex is always an immoral act. The second factor for bad sex to happen is giving the sexual partner something unintended, such as a disease or making the gal pregnant. Under these two conditions, one or both parties will get hurt. Bad sex always ends up harming at least one party, whether intentionally or unintentionally. If it is an intentional hurtful act, it is immoral and should be criminal. Bad sex was the only form of sex that the wise, the pious, and the teachers ever knew. It was no accident and understandable that they had label it that way.

Because of their erroneous view on sex, billions of people today are misguided. Some even reject it as a pledge to be virtuous and pure. People who reject sex are misguided. Rejecting sex does not mean that you can totally get away from it. Rather, the person will have sex in a twisted or out-of-control manner when his sex urge trumps his moral restraints in their constant battle for supremacy. It is always when moral restraints fail that bad sex—rape, sexual assault, or attack on minors, etc.—takes place, often causing a lot of damage. Be very clear: bad sex will happen from time to time until we correct our view on sex, biologically and morally. Also make no mistake: very, very few people can continuously resist their sexual urge. When one's heart is always at odds with his mind over sex, bad sex will thrive, like lethal bacteria in environment lacking oxygen.

The Sad Story of Douglas Moore

Let me give you a real crime story to show what bad sex can do. It is a story about Douglas Moore, a pedophile, a suspected serial killer, and a monster, according to many people. According to a summary of events leading to his crimes, Moore had been sexually abused by his father over a period of six years from the age of seven. Moore grew up a violent person and a pedophile. He was first charged with sexually assaulting four teens when he was nineteen. To make a long, sad story short, Moore hanged himself in his cell at thirty-seven after he was arrested in connection to the death of three young men.

Criminals like Moore have given people yet another reason to fear, to expel, and to chastise sex. But very few people understand he was a victim of our erroneous moral view. I am sure that Moore is not the only abused turned abuser. Again, people who despise sex are likely to be those who only know the bad side of sex. Sex does have a beautiful side; it makes happy people and creates great lovers. Does sex deserve the way it has been treated by our society in general? Let us put things into perspective. If the number of people killed is a good measuring stick of the seriousness of a behavior, an offense, or a crime, let us see what the heavyweight killers are in our society. The gold and silver medals will certainly go to heart disease, cancer, and accidents caused by drunk drivers, some of which are certainly preventable. Beyond any doubt, nicotine and alcohol combined have killed many, many more people than wars or natural disasters. Then it begs the question why testosterone has been singled out for the bashing. Is it fair? It does not have any science backing.

How to Change Our Erroneous Sex View—The Important Messages

From scientific findings, there is absolutely no reason to treat sex as our enemy; it could be our most powerful ally and benefactor instead. Chinese liken sex to a lustful fire. I think it is quite appropriate. Fire can destroy, or it can benefit if under full control. Why don't we allow the fire of lust to burn brightly within certain moral constraints so that it will warm up many cold, cold hearts and help us to see the way to happiness? Sex should be treated as "food" for our mental health. Starving our body of the joy of sex is unlikely to make us whole. How many pictures of smiling and satisfied saints have you seen? I have never seen one. There is a reason for their serious and sad look, because they have been deprived of one of the most pleasurable things in the animal kingdom if you ask me. Do you know that Mother Teresa was very unhappy according to her own account? Not good, is it? The symptoms of sexual deprivation are quite well documented. People who are constantly deprived of sex—by choice or by circumstances—are likely to be frustrated, bitter, prone to get angry, and unhappy. They are no fun and definitely not cool. I would urge a reader to google it to satisfy himself. It is a widespread problem and a time bomb. It all comes from our erroneous views.

Sex is a Necessity

Education is the only way to change our erroneous views on sex. There are a number of important messages we should cover in our sex education. 1) Sex is a biological necessity directly linked to survival; continuously resisting it will be futile and harmful. The Catholic Church should learn through the many painful experiences in trying to mystify and vilify sex. How many priests have to continue to fall from grace before the church reevaluates its stand based on a scientific point of view? I am sure that every one of those who have fallen must have been trying his best to resist. In the end, their struggles have fallen short. Confronted by one of the most powerful forces in the living kingdom, many of them have been doomed from the day they committed to the pious course. Should we mercilessly condemn the fallen angels? Not if one understands the power of the "dark" force. If I were to be put under such unfortunate situations and be tempted, I cannot be sure that I could resist it. Let us face it, we are no match for the sex force if we choose to view it as our enemy. Fighting sex brings nothing but misery, a case in point we should learn from the Catholics.

Sex Can be Very Beautiful or Ugly; How to tell them Apart

The second equally important message to deliver will be sex has two sides: (1) a very beautiful and healthy side, and (2) a very ugly and harmful side. Teaching students to tell them apart is very important so that they can make the right choice and be benefited by sex, instead of making the wrong one and be hurt, often very seriously. Beautiful sex has two components: i) you always allow your partner to freely choose, and ii) both parties will ensure that they don't give the other party something unwanted, like a disease or pregnancy. Bad sex will be the opposite: giving the other no choice, and/or giving your partner something nasty. A reader can easily see that good sex is moral and bad sex is not.

I am a firm believer of healthy sex. To show you my point, let me give you a little story. When my elder daughter was at mid-teens, she asked my opinion about having sex at that stage. The following was what I told her. "Yes, you can enjoy sex as much as you want under the following conditions: (1) it is something you could do that all the time to do and are not pressured into it, (2) you don't get pregnant from it, and (3) you don't get infected with a disease either. Enjoy! You don't need my permission." It sounds redundant, but it is worth repeating because it is such an important message: bad sex was the only sex that the wise and the pious knew, and for the matter, that is the only thing about sex that people have learned. The ignorance has claimed many victims. Douglas Moore was certainly its victim, though many of us do not look at him this way. He was abused at a very young age by his own father, who in turn could be a victim himself. Sex being shameful and sinful prevents many victims from telling their stories. Unlike victims from other sources like violence or hunger, they have no place to go. They keep the feeling inside. However, they are unable to resolve the shame, and often blame themselves. At the same time, their sense of right and wrong has been turned upside down. They also harbor a lot of anger. Unresolved shame and anger eventually will become hatred. When a person is overwhelmed with hatred, he becomes very destructive and harmful to other people.

I feel sad for Moore, I also understand his anger. How could a person like him not be angry? By no fault of his own, he got hurt by his own father. An overwhelming shame which came from our view of sex would prevent him from talking to anyone. He therefore had to bear the shame and pain alone. Not able to heal the wound, he became angry. He was trapped. The unresolved anger became hatred. He first hated himself, but this would not be a solution. To get relief, he began to transfer the hatred and project it to others. At that stage, he would begin to look for victims, usually someone like him at the time he was assaulted. He was a victim that turned into an assailant. He was like a person infected by a disease and became a disease spreader.

We don't need to hate people like Douglas Moore, they would do it themselves. That was why he committed suicide—his only option to rid himself of his guilt and shame. I don't despise him. He should be pitied instead. He was a victim of the erroneous sexual views of our society. Is Moore an isolated case? I would urge a reader to research on sex victims turned predators. Please help to keep your eyes and minds open for those incidents. With more people helping, we can change the view.

Our erroneous view can lead to some cruel acts by some otherwise nice folks. In the village I grew up in, it was not unusual that during certain seasons a couple of dogs would mate in broad daylight in public. In some cases, there were two males to one bitch. How disgusting! Villagers would do all sorts of cruel things to break up the mating dogs by beating up the animals or by pouring boiling water onto their genitals. How exceedingly cruel! To most Chinese, sex is evil, dirty, and filthy. My mother had taught me the idea when I was a boy. I have, in turn, ignorantly passed the concept to my daughters, and they, unless learning otherwise, will likely teach their kids the same thing. It is like an heirloom to be passed from one generation to the next generation. And from what I see, they are actually passing my view to my grandsons. Chickens are coming home to roost.

Among Muslims, the erroneous view often leads to the tragic ending of a family member, often an innocent girl who has been raped. By no fault of her own, she was raped and left with a deep emotional scar. Instead of sympathy and understanding from those she loved and trusted, she was condemned to death by them to the so-called honor killing. The belief is also the reason that many justify mutilating female genitals to take away the sexual pleasure from girls. The list of cruelty from the wrong view continues . . .

Stephen Y. Cheung, Ph.D.

It Is Not Going to Be Easy

To correct our erroneous view is not going to be easy; it is all from ignorance. The number 1 reason it is not easy is bad sex is real. It keeps reminding people that it exists and continues to take its toll. The number 2 reason is the views have come from people's religions, which often claim that their views are from gods. When it comes to religions, there are many wishes that are associated with their beliefs. People would rather choose what they hope for than sanity. There are not many people who are prepared to give up their prospect of going to heaven and eternal life over reason. I was a Christian for several decades. For me to keep my faith, I often had to kill my rationality. Until we can untie this knot (the messy union of moral view and religion), people will keep choosing ignorance. Let me paraphrase something I have read: It is difficult to get people to understand something (sex) when their prospect of going to heaven depends on them not understanding it. Religions are often rationality killers.

The last reason I could think of is that people get their moral view when they begin to learn, at a very young age, at the time when the human mind is blank and extremely eager for information. At that stage, a mind is like a sponge, happy to absorb any kind of information/knowledge fed to it. And the people doing the feeding are also those we most trust and love. It would take more than reason to overcome such powerful and deep-rooted beliefs. I know sex is healthy and there should be no shame reading about it in public. For a person who wants to change people's view, one would expect that I'll be more courageous. But I can't read *Playboy* where people can see me reading it. What a chicken! It also shows you how difficult it will be to overcome it. I also find it hard to watch a steamy sex scene in movies with my daughters present. Despite the difficulties, the choice is up to us to make. We can either choose to embrace good sex with our bodies and minds and be blessed by it, or we can continue to totally reject sex and suffer. And the most stupid option according to science is to treat it as an enemy and keep it out of our lives. Saying "No" to good sex is hardly intelligent.

The Morality of Sex

Having discussed the biological background of sex, I hope a reader now can fully understand its importance. Having the right attitude toward sex is very important for a happy life, as discussed. It is time for us to use our new moral model to take a look at the morality of different forms of sex. After all, morality should decide whether a certain form of sex is acceptable.

Sex between Married Couples

According to traditional moral views, this form of sex is the only permissible form of sex. In Muslim countries, any form of sex outside wedlock is immoral, and its participants, especially a woman, if caught will be subject to severe punishment—to be stoned to death in the old days. In view of sex being a necessity and it being not readily available, the punishment is excessive.

Let us look at sex between couples whose marriages have been arranged. It this case, a husband can rightly demand sex from his wife almost at any time, whether she likes it or wants it or not.

Let us ask the three questions:

1. Whose interest does the sex serves?

   Ans. Mostly that of the husband.

2. Whose is getting hurt?

   Ans. If the wife does not want it and she has to comply, wouldn't she be a victim? Or, if she resists it and gets hurt by her husband, she would certainly be a victim, won't she?

3. Is freedom to choose available to both parties?

   Ans. In an arranged marriage, a woman has absolutely no choice; the choice belongs to a husband and him only.

Conclusion: We can clearly see from our morality that sex in an arranged marriage can be an immoral act because after that a woman has lost all her freedom. This brings up a question, should any country, including a developed one, bring up a law to legitimize a husband's right to demand sex from his wife despite her maybe not wanting it or even resisting it? Would it constitute rape?

Rape and Sexual Assault

This form of sex is beyond doubt immoral. If we ask the three questions, it will be clear that the rapist or assailant is forcing his will against an unwilling victim, usually a woman. In so doing, a rapist or assailant serves his only interest: intentionally hurting a victim. Freedom of choice is one-sided. It is immoral. If Trump did grab some women's pussies without their permission, the act was definitely sexual assault; the Golden Rule implies so. Yes, Mr. President-elect.

Adultery

In adultery, the couple doing it is both willing and doing it by free choice. But is it moral? If we only consider the adulterers, it would seem moral, wouldn't it? Who will be the victims? Adultery implies that one of the adulterers is married, then his or her spouse will be a victim. And it hurts like hell. I had the unfortunate fate of going through it once. If someone wants to know what hell is like, going through the pain of having an adulterous spouse will make you understand. One may justify adultery by blaming his or her spouse. If that is the case, there should be a more civilized way of solving the problems. After all, getting married is a pledge to be faithful, isn't it? When both adulterers have spouses, the situation will be messier. What if there are children involved and the two get divorced? After learning the hurts associated with it, I have since made a promise to myself not to do something so stupidly hurtful. Adultery hurts every party involved or related, often including the adulterers, and it is certainly immoral.

Incest

Incest is a sexual act between closely related individuals, a father and his daughter or between a brother and a sister. In nature, incest has been widely avoided in the animal kingdom. Male lions are forced to leave their pride when they reach maturity to prevent them from mating with a closely related lioness. Among groups of chimps, sexually mature females often have to go away to find a new group to live in. Though those animals don't know, their practices have the support of genetics: closely related individuals have many genes in common and the chance of getting a pair of defective, and often fatal, allele genes together is much higher than with unrelated individuals.

One might, for argument's sake, think incestuous couples that do not want children are moral: it is their free choice and no one is getting hurt. So what is the problem? In such a narrow sense, one might justify it if one really, really wants it. But I also think a moral view should, at the same time, promote the happiness and wellbeing of a society. In that case, one may ask what kind of society will it be if everyone does it? It won't be good, would it? In this consideration—and it is a valid one—incest should not be viewed as moral. Should we ban it? It depends on how widespread it is. The royalty of Ancient Egypt practiced incest; their children typically were short-lived. King Tut was one of the well-known tragic examples.

The Need to Legalize Prostitution

What is prostitution? The dictionary defines it as *a woman who has promiscuous sexual intercourse for payment, or a person who degrades his talents for money.* From the definition, you can immediately see the prejudice and bias: *a woman . . . promiscuous sexual intercourse.* Promiscuous means indiscriminate mingling or association, especially in having sexual relations with a number of partners on a casual basis or indiscriminately. Let me correct the definition: prostitutes are very discriminating. You need money, and some of them also need to be comfortable with their client before they allow you to do what you want to do. They are not promiscuous. Quite the contrary, women, when it comes to their sexual partners, are naturally very picky. Promiscuity only applies to men. Other than that, it is an interesting definition.

While the first part of the definition refers only to a woman, the *or* part also makes yours truly a prostitute because I have been "degrading" my talent for money most, if not all, of my life. After I got my PhD and having worked and taught in university and college for several years, I sold flowers for about ten years, and then sold real estate for commission for another twenty or so years. I did those things entirely for money. Wow, I am flattered. I did not know I would qualify to be a prostitute. The definition also turns practically each and every person—a banker, financial analyst, and a stock broker, especially— into prostitutes. Tell me who isn't degrading his/her talent for money these days? This is how capitalism works. Greed is great, remember?

Most people are not as twisted mentally as yours truly, who finds being labeled as a prostitute flattering. Calling someone a prostitute is often the ultimate insult. A prostitute is a woman who makes money by offering her body for sex, the most degrading, humiliating, and shameful way to make a living, according to the traditional morality. I once lived in a village that did not have a sewage system. Each day before daybreak, some women—always women—would come to collect human waste and carry them away. It was a shitty job literally. The women also got shitty pay practically. Nobody despises a waste collector, everyone scorns a prostitute.

Why does the word carry such a foul meaning? Why do most people treat a prostitute with such contempt? The answer certainly has to do with our traditional moral view on sex and a woman's role in a traditional marriage. The answer also clearly demonstrates how men would value a woman. Men used to look at a woman mostly as a sex object. Traditionally, a woman should and was only allowed to have sex with one and only one person, and that person is her husband. This rule does not apply to men. This belief has prevailed for thousands of years and is still going strong. Guess whose interest this rule serves? If a woman has sex with any person other than her husband—whether she is forced to or with her consent—she is considered soiled and deserves to be treated as such. In some cultures, soiled women have to be eliminated for the honor of the families. Now, consider a woman who knowingly offers her body for sex for the multitude; she is filthier than dirt and worse than leprosy. A prostitute also openly challenges the traditional value of a woman; it is a rebellion. And that is the reason why prostitutes have been treated this way.

420

Once a prostitute, a woman will be condemned by all. In most cases, there will be no turning back; the morality of our societies will not allow her to. She has to live in the underworld, to be raped, beaten, exploited, sucked dry, discarded, and die like a disowned cat. Though a prostitute works hard and is a human being; she is not entitled to any rights and practically is not protected by law. How many serial killings involving prostitutes have received high-profile attention like the kidnapping of a child? Prostitutes have no value, do they? In a serial killing committed by R. Pickton in 2002 in Vancouver, British Columbia, Canada, more than sixty prostitutes disappeared over the years and nobody seemed to be aware of them being missing. Who cares? Those were only prostitutes!

It is not only men—often the hypocrites—who have trashed prostitutes with deafening decibels; the voices of women can be as loud and merciless. Raymond clearly shows her feeling about prostitution in her article. I learned that the author is a professor and a longtime feminist activist against violence against women and sexual exploitation, as well as against the medical abuse of women. Dr. Raymond champions women's lib. I am quite sure that Dr. Raymond considers prostitution immoral and I wonder if she would ever consider a prostitute to be her bosom friend. Let me give Dr. Raymond some unsolicited point of view: unless you change your moral view about sex, women will forever be imprisoned. The old moral view is the tool which has been used to justify the way men treat women.

Let us put aside the sentimental stuff. Let us look at prostitution at another angle. An article named "Legitimating Prostitution as Sex Work: UN Labor Organization (ILO) Calls for Recognition of the Sex Industry," October 2003, provides a good starting point to look at the pros and cons of prostitution. The pros have been voiced by ILO, the cons by Dr. Raymond. Let us review some of the points in the article. Here is how it all gets started. In a 1998 report, the ILO, the official labor agency of the UN, recommended the economic recognition of the sex trade. The contribution of the sex sector to the gross domestic product in four countries in Southeast Asia had been substantial and deserved official recognition, the ILO cited. The ILO mentioned eleven points to argue in favor of the recognition, and to each and every one of those points Raymond has offered counter views. Please allow me to present the key points from both sides.

First, from the ILO:

1. *Prostitution is mainly economic in nature and the sex business has assumed the dimensions of an industry, and has contributed substantially to a nation's income and economy.*

2. *Recognition of the sector will allow governments to control the criminal elements of the industry in areas like organized crime, drug abuse, and child prostitution.*

3. *It will improve the working conditions, social protection, and entitle the worker the same labor rights and benefits as other workers.*

The ILO, however, admits that there are unanswered questions to the moral, religious, health, human rights, and criminal issues arising from the recognition. The inability to reconcile the moral matter becomes a fatal flaw to the ILO recommendation.

From Raymond, it can be summed up as:

1. *Recognition will institutionalize the buying and selling of women as commodities. And it legitimizes men's ability to put the bodies of women at their disposal.*

2. *Prostitution can be compared to slavery; it is abusive to women, condones exploitation of women, and violates their human rights.*

3. *Prostitution, besides being immoral, also subjects prostitutes to health hazards of unwanted pregnancies, miscarriage, multiple abortions and infertility; in addition, the prostitutes are also at high risk of being infected with deadly sexually transmitted diseases (STDs).*

4. *The recognition would be viewed as legitimized paid rapes and prostitutes are the victims.*

While the views from the two sides differ, both do agree that the move will likely worsen child prostitution. I might have missed some key points; but let us take it from here. The arguments, either in favor or against, can be grouped into two categories: the physical harm suffered by the prostitutes, and the moral degradation of this group of human beings. Let us first look at the opposing views.

The Physical Harm:

Let me quote: Human Rights Watch/Asia documents:

Most girls and women start out in the cheap brothels where they are "broken in" through a process of rapes and beatings . . . The Combination of debt bondage, illegal confinement and the threat or use of physical abuse force the women and girls into sexual slavery . . . The lives women in prostitution lead are hazardous and bordering on brutality. There are also many serious health issues such as diseases and unwanted pregnancy. Prostitutes are routinely exploited by pimps or organized crime; in some countries, they receive, on the average, 10 percent of the money paid for their "work," with the balance going to their bosses. Further, most of the prostitutes are drug addicts; they spend practically every penny they receive on drugs, thereby leaving them no choice but to continue selling their bodies. At the end of their short careers, they mostly end up very poor and without skill for other employment. Prostitution is a trap, which very few, if any, can escape.

I hope I have covered the major issues. Now let us see whether I can provide some suggestions. Ironically, the objections are all the reasons that we should legalize prostitution. It would solve all the problems, including the issue of child prostitutes. Let me explain. My first point is, whether you like it or not, and no matter how harsh a punishment one can dole out to prostitutes caught perpetrating the trade—stoning them to death for example—prostitution ain't going away in human societies. There is a strong biological reason for prostitution to exist. We can either beat it or join it, if beating it is impossible. Besides sexual urge being the most powerful force in the living kingdom and therefore impossible to contain, there is another reason which makes prostitution inevitable, and the reason is a big gap that exists in sexual appetite between women and men, as discussed. Men in general have much greater need for sex. The disparity in sexual appetites is a direct consequence of the levels of testosterone in the bodies of the two sexes. At an average, men have at least ten times as much of the stuff as women. Testosterone is nicknamed the (sexual) desire hormone. So at any given time, day, and place, there will be, on the average, at least ten horny men to one horny woman.

I might have oversimplified sex desire by relating it solely to the level of testosterone, but the existence of the big gap should be beyond doubt. The existence of the sexual appetite gap in our species has a long root, possibly arising from the need of our ancestral women to secure their men to provide them with protection and food during their pregnancy, as discussed. The existence of the sexual gap made bonding between the two sexes possible so that those bigheaded babies could be born prematurely, so that intelligence of our species could continue to increase. This gap, while having solved the most pressing problem at the time, has now left us with a big problem in every society and country. There is constantly a very high population of men under sexual deprivation. That is the reason behind most sexual crimes, and most of them are committed by men.

There are few things horny guys won't do for sex. I recently saw an apron in a kitchen store which says *I'll cook for sex.* It begs the question: who won't? But when you don't even have a girlfriend, what could you do? To many, paying a gal to get rid of the stress is an uncomplicated solution, isn't it? And this, pal, is the reason why prostitution existed, is happening, and will certainly continue until testosterone is tamed. Face it, horny guys not getting laid is a big social problem. I suspect that it is the root of road rage, bosses with rotten tempers, fathers who yell at their children, or surgeons that leave scissors inside their patients. If you are a lawmaker, how will you deal with these hidden hazards? Getting married will only take care of the sexual needs of a small number of males in the population, or it may not. How about those that do not want to get married, cannot afford to get married, or have no hope of getting girlfriends? How will you look after the sexual needs of people like Igor? Not to provide bachelors with accessible sexual outlets is not an option. Again, please keep in mind that sexual urge is one of the most powerful humanly desires. Not every man can continuously resist the relentless sexual-desire attacks and temptations. I don't have to give you statistics; you know it is true. If you are a guy and have been young or are still young and full of mojo, can you honestly tell me that the urge is no more than a passing nuisance? It can be quite stressful, can't it? The good will masturbate from time to time, the bad will commit minor sexual offenses, and the really ugly will break the law and end up gravely harming the most innocent and ruining many lives. I have no statistics, but do you think I am using scare tactics? In Toronto, which is one of the world's most livable cities, we have girls kidnapped, sexually assaulted, and killed on and off. Women being sexually assaulted will not even make it to the headlines. I believe legalizing prostitution is not an option, it is a necessity.

The Morality of Prostitution

Regardless of our previous arguments, the right and wrong of prostitution still hinge on two issues: (1) Is sex healthy or is it always evil and shameful? (2) Is prostitution immoral? From science, we know that sex is a necessity for a healthy body and a healthy mind. There is absolutely no reason to curb it. Then the focus will be how to promote it to take away all the harm from bad sex. According to science, sex can be very beneficial if done right. It is not evil or shameful.

Now, let us zero in on the most important issue: the moral issue of prostitution. Moral issue makes all the other concerns secondary. When looking at the morality of prostitution, let me be clear about certain things. In the following discussion, I shall be talking about mature women, who out of their own free choice and are well informed have chosen to exchange sex for money. We also assume that the earnings will all go to the sex workers who are not being exploited. Having said that, let us ask the three questions on trading sex for money:

1. Whose interest does it serve?

   Ans. Those of the prostitutes and their customers.

2. At whose expense?

   Ans. No one is getting hurt. It is a win/win situation. A sex worker gets her money; her customers get their needs satisfied.

3. Is free choice allowed in the parties involved?

   Ans. Yes, we have two willing and consenting parties. It is an arm's-length business transaction.

Conclusion: Prostitution is not an immoral act. Both parties choose to do it and both are benefited. My conclusion, according to the model, is that prostitution is a very beneficial thing and is therefore morally sound beyond any shred of doubt. Allowing prostitution serves a society well.

Now, let us look at the morality of those who disallow or oppose prostitution for various reasons, factual, philosophical, or religious. Again, let us use the three questions:

1. Whose interest does it serve?

   Ans. Those who oppose, because they hold that the profession is degrading to the women and are imposing their ill-based moral view upon the other.

2. At whose expense?

   Ans. The women who choose to earn their living by selling sex and their needy potential customers.

3. Is free choice allowed?

   Ans. The sex workers and their customers have no say in their decisions; prostitution is banned as a result and thereby deprives some women of earning their living, and the horny customers some badly needed outlets.

Conclusion: Disallowing and opposing prostitution based on weak or erroneous personal belief to the extent of banning it is immoral. Those opposed do it to serve their interests, philosophical or religious, at the expense of the prostitutes and the needy males by taking their outlets away. They impose their beliefs—i.e., their ill-found moral views—upon others. It is an immoral act.

Because there is a big gap in sexual desire between women and men, women are born with a commodity. They are controlling something that men want badly, something of value, and something that they can cash in for their own benefit if they should decide to do so at their sole discretion and free choice. Read my lips, it is a valuable asset and a commodity which they can make money out of. This, of course, will be garbage if you believe that (1) sex is an evil and shameful act that brings no benefits, and

(2) a woman should only serve one man, according to the old morality. A mature, well-informed woman, of her own choice, can do whatever she wants with her asset. She can freely give it to one man, lock it up and throw the key away, or market it to make a living. And above all, it will be win/win for her and her happy customers. It is something moral, just like being a good medical doctor, a stress therapist, or a mechanic. Yes, I am comparing a sex worker's line of work to that of a doctor, the most revered profession. So let us explore the way it could be done.

The To-Do List:

1. Changing the name: *Prostitution* carries a bad connotation because of its less than shiny history; the name should never be used. Calling a woman a prostitute is degrading, and is passing a moral judgment that is gender biased: men can screw around; women should not and cannot, or face dire consequences. I suggest that they should be called sex workers at entry level, kama sutraists at the next, and sex therapists at the top, etc.
2. Licensing: Besides getting the needed revenue, licensing allows the government to regulate and impose a strict standard on the industry, just like an auto garage, a medical office, or a restaurant. One of the regulations should definitely include banning high-risk sex. Regular physical exams on sex workers are required before renewing their licenses. I think the men who plan to use the service should also get medical clearance from their doctors to certify that they are not carriers of sexually transmitted diseases.

Some of the licensing requirements should be:

3. *Knowledge Requirement:* In Canada, all professionals need to take a number of courses and pass the exams. To be a real estate broker, yours truly has taken a number of classes designated by the controlling body. Sex workers should be no different. The courses should cover the following areas: i) what causes diseases, how do they spread, and how to control and prevent the spread of STDs; ii) learn to use birth control and stop unwanted pregnancy; iii) ethics, professional conduct, legal knowledge and legal rights, etc.

I am sure that there should be more worthy courses; those are the basic ones. I see the need for designing courses that meet the specific needs of sex workers. With knowledge, a sex worker will never be a medium to spread diseases. They also won't get exploited because they will know their legal rights. Because they are legit, they will enjoy the full protection of the law. One very important thing that comes with legalizing the sex trade: it will promote and allow only good sex. And it will attract more highly qualified women into the profession.

The Setup Requirements

The Netherlands and Germany are countries that have legalized the sex trade. I have visited the areas; I am not sure that I like the way it is done. Sex workers are displayed nearly naked in windows like merchandize. It lacks taste, and it has no class. In the end, it gives legalizing the sex trade a bad example. It cheapens women. If they ask me—and they should—it should be done like restaurants. Remember, Confucius says that sex and food are both human nature (needs). Sex outlets should also be set up to cater to different economical appetites. Of course, there should be fast-sex outlets like McDonald's, family restaurants like Swiss Chalet, and fancy French or Italian restaurants like . . . Well, sorry. I don't know any high-end ones. Regardless, the business premises should meet certain minimum health requirements, such as a shower that meets certain standards; supplies of condoms, mouthwash (very, very important, if you know what I mean), tissue paper, clean towels and sheets. The goal is to stop spreading STDs and all kinds of nasty diseases. The premises shall be inspected by government agents from time to time to ensure compliance, like a restaurant, garage, or medical office. The inspectors should be highly trained professionals. Other than ensuring compliance of the premises, they should also be able to give consultation and answer some questions the workers may have. It will further protect the workers. The goal is to make it safe for all parties, prevent exploitation of the sex workers, protect the rights of the sex workers, make it an enjoyable experience, and above all, allow a government to tap into a rich underground economy which should not be too far behind the dining industry. It should make cutting deficits much easier. It will be a win/win/win situation; you just can't do better than that, or be more moral than that!

The Not-So-Publicized Side of Prostitution

One would wonder what kind of existence an average sex worker would lead if she is not exploited. Let us look at some numbers. From what I have found out in Toronto (believe me, I know what I am talking about), an average sex worker charges anywhere from $80 to $200 per thirty-minute visit. A customer has to go to the worker's place, which is often located in some cheap rental high-rise. (Don't ask how I know, okay?) Some model-like gals command from hundreds to more than a thousand dollars for her service; they are located in more luxurious apartments or hotels. An average worker easily averages two or more customers a day depending on her asset, the day of the week, the economy, and whether or not SARS is still a threat. I once visited a popular gal at 10:00 a.m., I saw a senior waiting when I left. Some gals easily average five to ten customers a day. If we take $120 per visit, it will be around $700 per day—tax free and next to no overhead. Brutal, isn't it? I mean for guys and gals, you and me, who have to sweat to make a buck, which at the end of the day only nets you 65 cents or less per dollar depending on your bracket. Provided she works five days a week and takes a one-month vacation each year, a sex worker makes anywhere from $50,000 to the sky being the limit a year—again, if you still don't get it, tax free. It is lucrative; it turns even a regular Canadian family doctor green with envy. If the amount of money one makes should be a parameter to gauge respect, I would suggest that sex workers are not someone to be sneered at.

With the kind of serious money a typical sex worker makes, she does not have to worry about her livelihood in her old age. If she starts early, say at twenty, and averages $150,000 a year—again, tax free; which should be easy—and provided she manages her income carefully, say with an accountant, she can afford to quit at thirty-five at the latest—and they think freedom fifty-five is such a big deal! What would she do with her time? It is none of our business, is it? But if you have to know, she has got more options than most of us who work our butts off. Now you tell me, is it a bad way to make a living or what?

I know a couple of the gals who take vacations regularly. I wish I could do that at the time. So much so for the stereotype that all sex workers lead lives of being brutalized, raped, dying young and poor with STDs. Don't get me wrong. There are too many of the unfortunate ones. It happens because those poor women have no legal status. I am not trying to glorify sex work. It is just another way of making a living, like many of the jobs we do. I am only saying that money for sex can be a very healthy line of work for a healthy and moral society if it is legalized, and only if it becomes legal. And according to our new moral model, it is a highly moral line of work.

During the past several years after publishing the moral model, I have used every opportunity to sell legalizing prostitution. While most guys would agree that it should be moral, according to the model, most women had a problem accepting that. A common objection was why should anyone be forced to do something they don't like or hate? It is quite valid. I often told the girls that for at least twenty-some past years I had done something—selling flowers or real estate—I hated. I had no choice at the time. And how many people in any society are making a living by doing something they truly love? I am talking about a lot of government employees in Canada who get very good pay but call in for sick leaves at higher frequency than the private sectors. For many, life is still full of suffering, for one reason or another.

And of all the voices that object to prostitution, the voices of the feminists are certainly the loudest and most forceful. What an irony! They still don't know it is exactly the argument that religions have been using to imprison women. To continue banning prostitution is not to allow women to freely choose to do what they want with their bodies. How can you liberate yourselves if you still allow the old morality to handcuff you? As long as a woman still buys that sex is dirty, shameful, etc., she will never be free.

To sum it up, there is only one reason why many societies ban prostitution. It comes from a myth or at best a half-truth that sex is evil, dirty, and unhealthy. Also, women are to blame. With this myth comes the moral view that selling sex is immoral. This myth has no science backing; the moral view is outdated. Men not getting their sexual needs satisfied have been a problem for every society since the discovery of farming. It is still a big social problem nowadays. From our reasoning, there is no reason to continue to ban it. A happy society, a happy country, and a happy planet depend on a drastic change in our attitudes toward sex.

CHAPTER 18

The Molarity of some Life-and-Death Issues

Melwes Eating Brandes—The Morality of A Dark Free Choice

Let us take up what we have left off in a previous chapter, the case of Melwes eating Brandes. Is cannibalism moral? Let us apply the three questions.

1. Whose interest does it serve?

   Ans. The interest of Melwes primarily; it also serves the "victim's" interest, which is his wish to be consumed by another human.

2. At whose expense?

   Ans. At Brandes's expense.

3. Is free choice allowed?

   Ans. Yes. Both parties are mature persons, sober, under no duress, and well informed about what is going to transpire, if Melves's statement is to be trusted.

Conclusion: On the surface, the case, bizarre as it is, is certainly "moral" according to our model. Although Brandes paid with his life in the event, it was his choice to end his life that way. However, it was according to Melves that Brandes was clear-headed when making the choice. Should we trust Melves? Whose interest did the claim serve? And what if Brandes was not clear-headed? How could anyone be clear-headed in making a choice which cost his own life with nothing to gain? In light of how self-preservation is the top priority of all living organisms, anyone who chooses to end his life when not under duress is clearly sick in a certain way. Therefore, Melves should not be trusted and must be punished to deter future copycats; he was a criminal. The example does show us that freedom of choice can be quite tricky, especially when the victim has nothing to gain and the other party, the initiator, gets all the benefit.

There are many cases where people choose to expose themselves to the possibility of getting killed and are moral. For example, a mother chooses to die to save her child, a soldier decides not to flee from overpowering enemies, or a firefighter endangers his life to save a trapped few. Can you think of other examples where the sacrifice is moral and should be praised? Isn't sacrifice a clear example of freedom of choice, which results in the death of the person who makes the choice?

The Morality of Abortion

If there is a controversial as well as disturbing moral issue, the morality of abortion will top the scale. It is not for the fainthearted or for those who view the topic too painful to tackle. It is certainly not for those too young to vote, drive, or drink. Because of the emotional nature of the topic, participants in the discussion easily get upset and let their feelings take over. It is very difficult to explore the morality of abortion with reason; whether or not it is moral still depends on one's religious view, like the way people see the morality of sex. I shall try to use our new moral model to look at the subject.

To begin, please allow me to give you the stories of two mothers. The stories are also about their babies.

The Stories of Two Mothers
Mother A: She was a sad character in one of the most livable cities in the world.
Time: Approximately 10:00 p.m., January 2003
Place: A desolate square in front of the city hall of Toronto, at a dark corner under a set of open concrete stairs. A homeless man in the square was awakened by a police officer who shone a flashlight on him. "It was

very cold," the homeless man later told a reporter. The officer told the man that the police had found a baby who was only minutes old lying naked and uncovered on the littered and freezing cement surface. The police sought information from possible eyewitnesses on the incident. When spotted, the baby was barely conscious, with her umbilical cord still attached. She suffered a heart attack on the way to the hospital. Luckily, the baby managed to survive; she was under the care of the Children's Aids Societies.

The identity of the mother was unknown at the time the story broke. The woman was later located by the police and was found to be suffering from mental illness. Her identity was subsequently withheld.

Mother B: She was a noble character in a civilized community.
Time: September 1961
Place: A city in Italy
It was during the second month of her pregnancy with her fourth child that the woman was diagnosed with having a large ovarian cyst. Besides being painful, the fibroid could threaten her pregnancy. The thirty-nine-year-old pregnant woman was a mother of three. She had three choices to deal with her medical condition as suggested by the medical experts. Her choices were:

1. To undergo hysterectomy; i.e., to have her uterus removed together with the fibroid. The option would be fairly low risk for her, it would, however, make her infertile for the rest of her life as well as put an end to the developing fetus.
2. To terminate the pregnancy and then to have the fibroid removed. The option would not affect her fertility, but the procedure would be an abortion.
3. To specifically remove the fibroid by surgery while trying not to affect the fetus. The option had many possible medical complications and unacceptable risks which would gravely endanger the lives of both the mother and the fetus during the term of the pregnancy. There would be no guarantee that either the mother or her fetus would be safe. It would be the most unwise choice from a medical point of view.

Guess what? It was none other than option 3 that the mother chose. Not only that, the mother instructed the surgeon to direct all the efforts to save the fetus; i.e., if confronted with saving the mother or the fetus, save the fetus.

If a person knows nothing about the mother who had made the choice, one will conclude that the woman is mentally unsound or uneducated, and therefore had poor judgment. You cannot be more wrong. The mother was a practicing medical doctor; she fully understood the consequence of her options. She had chosen option 3 decisively and promptly. She died in 1962, one week after giving birth to a baby girl weighing nearly ten pounds, primarily from an infection incurred during the C-section to deliver the baby. The mother's name was Gianna Beretta Molla. She was canonized and made a martyred saint by the pope. (Information based on *www.gianna.org*)

Now, let us consider the morality of the events pertaining to the births of the two babies.

Mother A: The mother would have been immoral to abandon her newborn in double-digit sub-zero temperature and leave her to die. However, being mentally ill, she should not be held morally or legally responsible for her action.

Mother B was Blessed Gianna: Before we look at the morality of abortion with our model, let us see what the Catholic Church had to say about the case. The point of view is published in an article named "The Medical Circumstances and Generous Immolation of Blessed Gianna Beretta Molla During Her Last Pregnancy" by Rev. Tadeusz Pacholczyk. The article sums up the view of the Church most eloquently.

But before we look at the Church's point of view, let us get some background checked; an outsider may not see the fine points. The three options faced by Blessed Gianna represented three very different moral implications according to the Church, as I have learned from the article:

> Option 1: Had Gianna chosen to have her uterus removed, the morality of the case would have been considered under the aspect of a hysterectomy and not under the heading of an elective abortion, because the operation was not to target the fetus and the fetus would

not be touched during the surgery. In short, it would not be considered as feticide since the procedure did not involve doing anything to the fetus.

Option 2: *"This option, by requiring direct abortion, would be morally contraindicated."* Those are the actual words in the article.

Option 3. The choice aimed solely at preserving the (two-month-old) fetus at all costs. In practice, it was the riskiest and the least promising; it guaranteed the safety of neither the mother nor the fetus. It was almost foolish to choose the option outside religious consideration.

The following is a quotation of the author's moral view on Option 3:

Sadly, though, we live in an age where life and death decisions against the unborn child are made with an ever greater casualness, and pregnancies are terminated for reasons that can only be termed trivial. Blessed Gianna's example of heroic commitment to the life of her own child throws into clear relief the scandal of the easy-abort mentality of our day. She believed that the privilege of being a mother, of being a cooperator with God in bringing forth new life meant always defending and protecting her children, whether in or out of the womb, even to the point of giving up her own life on their behalf. Even though it is rarely to the point of death, every mother is aware of this profound maternal reality of being immolated and making great silent sacrifices on behalf of their children. (To immolate means to offer up, especially to kill, in sacrifice. I did not know the meaning of the word prior to reading the article.)

Bravo! Having presented the Church's view, let us consider the morality of the event using the model.

1. Whose interest does Option 3 serve?

   Ans. Primarily the Church's interest. One may argue that it also served the interest of the fetus. But from the article, I seriously doubt that the mother was doing it out of loving the unborn.

2. At whose expense?

   Ans. Primarily at Blessed Gianna's expense. And how about the three very young children deprived of a loving and caring mother? How about the husband who had to survive without a loving and much-loved wife?

3. Is freedom of choice allowed?

   Ans. Yes. Gianna, being a medical doctor, would fully understand the consequence of her choice, and was willing to make the choice. She was well informed and knew the risks. Had she known that the choice would end up costing her life, it would still be very unlikely that she would change her mind.

Conclusion: She was selfless and therefore moral because she had chosen to sacrifice herself. But I don't think she sacrificed for her fetus. It was her religious belief that she willingly died for.

Pushing Death

Which brings up the noble nature of sacrifice. Why do we all so highly praise someone who has sacrificed for us? There is little doubt that the Catholic Church's decision to canonize Gianna has a lot to do with her choice against abortion. Had she chosen option 1, she would be moral according to the Church's point of view and would not have died. With option 2, she might continue to have more than one child after the surgery. Had she and her fetus both died of complications with option 3, or had both of them survived, it would have been the end of her story and no sainthood. To be a Catholic saint, the mother and the mother alone must die. The author's repeated use of *immolation* and *immolate* says it all.

Why does sacrifice have such a noble place in our moral hearts? We highly praise those who sacrifice themselves because we get the benefit through their sacrifices. Sacrifice is a selfless act for those who give their lives away. But let us look at the morality of those who teach and encourage other people to make sacrifices for them.

1. Whose interest does it serve?

   Ans. Those who encourage it; in our case, the Catholic Church.

2. At whose expense?

   Ans. Those who have died for it; e.g., Gianna.

3. Is freedom of choice allowed?

   Ans. Yes. The martyrs knew what they were doing and had willingly chosen their course of action because of the Church's encouragement.

Conclusion: For a party to encourage others to sacrifice to serve its interest is an extremely selfish act. It costs the lives of the persons who make the sacrifice. In fact, such teaching is highly predatory; it knowingly kills the followers. Therefore, the teaching is more than immoral, it is evil. And for that reason, no loving or caring person should ever encourage it or promote it. The cases of suicide bombers come to my mind.

The irony of encouraging sacrifice is that it selectively kills men and women of the highest moral quality and those who will be most beneficial to a community had they continued to live. Sacrifice kills the true heroes and heroines like Blessed Gianna. Scumbags will never consider making a sacrifice. Sacrifice is often a one-shot deal; once committed, there will be no more for a person who does it. And for this reason, sacrifice could only be justified when the lives of many are in grave danger and there is absolutely no other solution. And even under such condition, it should be up to the person who faces it to freely decide.

There was a fire in a primary school in India. Many children perished in the fire in the classrooms while all the teachers safely escaped. If there were an occasion to make sacrifices, it would certainly be the time for some of those teachers. But then, every human being is born with an overwhelming interest to survive. Would you toss the first stone at the teachers for leaving the children behind? It is not our part to condemn, is it?

Sacrifice should never be taught or encouraged. It should only be the sole decision of the person facing it when the urge to do it would be so compelling that resisting it would be impossible. It is under this kind of circumstance, and only under such circumstances, that it should be justified and honored. The same goes to the soldiers who partook in the D-Day invasion during WWII or the firefighters who perished trying to save lives during the 9/11 attacks.

Having presented my personal point of view on sacrifice, let us look at Gianna's story again. You can call me Satan, but please allow me to ask the Catholic Church several questions. (If you still don't know, Satan's specialty, according to the Bible, is asking very inconvenient questions; he does not kill, rape, or steal.)

1. In making the sacrifice, how many lives did she save?

   Ans. The "life" of a two-month-old fetus. It was a one-to-one exchange at best, was it not?

2. How does Gianna's death serve her community?

   Ans. Gianna was a loving and caring mother of three, a loving wife, and a physician who dedicated her career to the welfare of her community. Her absence would certainly be sorely missed by her children, husband, friends, and the many needy patients. If there was a party whose interest was served, it was the Catholic Church's. So in essence a noble character died and many suffered as a result to benefit one organization. You tell me, is it a good cause to die for? I also question the motive of the Church in making Giana a saint. What message is the Church sending to its followers? Is the Church not encouraging more pregnant mothers in similar situations to do the same thing? How heartlessly selfish! If you ask me, a person believing in the same God, I really doubt that a loving God would encourage his children to sacrifice for him. If you are a parent, will you ask any of your children to die for your sake?

3. Did Giana have to die?

Ans. There was no compelling reason that she had to choose option 3. Other than terminating the development of a two-month-old fetus, which is forbidden by the Church, option 2 appeared to be a middle-of-the-road choice. If "*the privilege of being a mother, of being a cooperator with God in bringing forth new life,*" then option 2 would achieve and serve that goal much better. That being the goal, Gianna did not have to die and should not have died.

Of all the points made by Rev. Tadeusz Pacholczyk, the followings really bug the hell out of me. Let me quote again:

She believed that the privilege of being a mother, of being a cooperator with God in bringing forth new life meant always defending and protecting her children, whether in or out of the womb, even to the point of giving up her own life on their behalf. Even though it is rarely to the point of death, every mother is aware of this profound maternal reality of being immolated and making great silent sacrifices on behalf of their children.

Let us look at the so-called profound maternal reality in a biological context. If you ask any biologist about maternal reality, chances are he will tell you that maternal reality is to preserve the life of a mother at all cost. In nature, the life of a fertile female is priceless, because the survival of a species greatly depends on her. Almost without exception, mothers will not hesitate to abandon their brood when their lives are endangered. Selfish? Certainly, but it will be well served for the survival of a species. Like a Chinese saying: "By keeping a green hill, there will always be firewood." You just don't sacrifice a fertile female in the biological kingdom under any circumstances. If the marsupials had done it, there would be kanga-bloody-roos no more (I learned the proper pronunciation from someone Down Under). Same applies to tigers, rats, lioness, giraffes, dogs, cats, and chimps.

I have a feeling that the reverend does not understand much biology. It certainly explains why he has used the term *profound* in describing *maternal reality*. These words sound grand in religious writings, don't they? But really, maternal reality is not at all profound. It is one of the easiest and simplest principles in biology. The simple and shallow point about maternal reality is, for a species to survive, you just don't fucking sacrifice a mother. A mother and a fertile female is your king in a chess game! (No apology for my language.) Please don't mystify maternal reality. *Profound*-ing it is fancy packaging, intellectual garbage. It does not change the content; it is still garbage.

And one more unsolicited opinion for the pope and your wise guys. I think you guys have picked the wrong person to advertise prolife. Let me quote the words used in the article by the reverend: *Being faced with two morally acceptable options in the early stages of her pregnancy, she freely chose.* The English is so plain and simple that even a Chinaman whose mother tongue is not English can understand. Gianna *freely chose*, those are your own words! Now, you guys tell me honestly and according to your own words whether Blessed Gianna was prolife or prochoice. Yes, she freely chose. Her choice was to obey Catholic dogma. What do you think? For me, she had clearly, knowingly, and willingly chosen to sacrifice herself for her Catholic faith, part of which requires her to save her fetus at all cost. *"If you have to decide between me and the child, do not hesitate; I demand it, the child, save it."* These were Gianna's words instructing her husband. She said it to him in a firm voice and with a penetrating gaze, according to the article. Gianna was prochoice and had been prochoice in her entire inspiring spiritual life. Her choice is to unfalteringly follow her Catholic faith, which, if you ask me, was misguided. What do you think, honestly?

I have no doubt that it was God's will that Blessed Gianna was trying to observe and please. It was her free choice. Now, please allow me to ask the Church another very unpleasant question. Are you damn sure that it was the divine will that Gianna needed to die to save the fetus? Where does the Church get the idea that God would prefer to see a mother of three young children, a loving and loved wife, and a dedicated medical doctor die to save a two-month-old fetus? I believe in a loving and compassionate God. What kind of God do you guys believe in? Going to the extreme in promoting Gianna's sacrifice, whose interest does it serve?

Having questioned the Church, let me present my view on abortion. (I have warned you that I could be very evil, have I not?) *Caveat emptor:* yours truly's knowledge of the Bible is very, very limited. It was only some years ago that I learned that the Bible was written by human hands instead of being photocopies of lecture notes which the Almighty gave his students. I have been a Christian for more than forty years. I still pray to the God of Jesus, Moses, and Muhammad every day. I don't go to church anymore. And for that matter, I don't think a person needs to go through Christ to find God, as advertised and claimed by the Gospels. Let us not be fooled by the attempt to monopolize God.

There are several things I still firmly believe. God is loving and caring. He cares for and loves the human race *unconditionally*. He is neither a selfish nor insecure God that craves attention and gratitude from us. He is a confident God. If there is a reason that God has created us, the most intelligent species, it is to share his joy and knowledge with us through life, I believe. And for this reason, he encourages and facilitates the continuous development of intelligence in humans over the past eons. For those who are open-minded, he will enlighten them with wisdom. And for those who keep searching, he may allow them to see there is really no conflict between science and faith because he is the source of both. Because mankind is the crown jewel of his creation, he gives us, and us only, the freedom of choice. Reasoning is a gift to us. It is up to us to accept and to use it or reject the gift—again, it is our choice.

Having defined my position, please allow me to lead the way in exploring the morality of abortion. First, what the Bible has to say about the subject. Above all, how does the Christian Church come up with the idea that abortion is an absolute no-no. Again, let me remind you that your guide in this exploration is not an expert.

The Unwelcome Gifts

The first question will be: where else in the Bible, the Old Testament or the New, specifically mentions abortion and its prohibition? From what I have learned, there is no, absolutely no specific biblical verse that dwells on abortion. It should not have come as a surprise. The various chapters of the Bible were written thousands of years ago. In those days, human societies were sustained either by farming or herding, and a big family would be a blessing. There was no need to abort, and they did not know how to do it safely.

Until recent years, there was a standard blessing to all newly wedded couples in China, and that was: *wishing you hundreds of children and thousands of grandsons.* I received the blessing when I first got married. Lucky for me, the blessing was a dud. I only got two daughters. Unwanted pregnancies were something that gradually existed after the industrial revolution; it did not exist in biblical times. Because there is no specific biblical verse on abortion, it can only mean that the Church has somehow come up with the idea that it is wrong. Does it make sense to you? And since it is only an interpretation, a perception, or belief, there could be a discrepancy between the Church's view and God's mind. Sounds reasonable? To deny that a possible discrepancy will be like saying there is absolutely no mistake in our reading God's mind. Agree? I don't believe the Church would dare to say that. What do you think?

From what I have learned, the Church opposes abortion on the following grounds implicated in the various verses of the Bible:

1. The giving and taking of life is God's prerogative
2. Life is sacred and a precious gift from God; it is a reward, and
3. Abortion is murder

Have I missed any important reason?

Now, let us look at each of them one by one. First, is the giving and taking of (human) life God's prerogative? With the advances in the many medical fields nowadays, doctors not only routinely encroach on God's prerogative everywhere, every day, and right at this very moment, they are playing god all the time. Should we burn them alive on stakes? For me, I believe that God is the creator of all things, living and nonliving. I also believe that it is none other than God that gives us an extraordinarily high intelligence. If you can accept my assumption, then do we have the privilege to exercise our God-given intelligence? What type of God would he be if he gave us something and would not allow us to fully use it? If you give your loved ones something, would you specifically instruct them on how they could use it? "Son, I give you this cell phone. Remember, you can only use it to call me, your mom, and maybe a couple of your friends, and that will be all." And your son is a college student. God gives me life. Am I not allowed to spend my life the way I see fit? If I am not, I would be something created to serve him. I would be no more than an instrument or a slave. I am not sure it is such a romantic idea. If God had created us only to serve him, then he would be a slave master and not a loving God. Right?

When a mature woman gets pregnant by mistake, will God not allow her to decide whether or not to keep the baby? Does a mature woman, sober and not threatened, have the right to decide what will be good for her? The Church says that God would not allow it. What would you say? Should we put a question mark beside this issue?

Second, life is sacred and a precious gift from God; it is a reward. Have you ever visited any slum in a big city? If you have not, I would highly recommend it, provided you do it safely. Then, you may learn how lucky you are. I spent several early years in a slum area in Kowloon, Hong Kong, where the police did not dare to go alone. Each day, I saw dirty children younger than me left alone, with clothes full of holes and eyes with empty looks. Some at my age collected discarded bottles and cans to help their families; they often fought over the copper in discarded electric cables. If you tell those kids that their lives are sacred and precious, please stay for their answers. Guess what they would say to you? Have you come across something that is sacred? Where would you find the sacred items? They will be closely guarded and well taken care of and treasured, will they be not? How about the contention that life is a precious gift from God? What will you consider a precious gift? A woman may want a top-quality and hefty diamond ring, a Rolex watch, or at least a bottle of Chanel. A bouquet of roses, though beautiful, will not usually cut it. For me, I would ask nothing less than good health, or better still, wisdom. I once received a shirt with the color I hated, a collar two inches too small, and sleeves several inches too long. I sent the gift to the Salvation Army the next day. If life is indeed a precious gift from a loving and understanding God, why have so many women chosen to say "no" to the gifts, and in essence, thrown eggs onto the Almighty's face? And how come so many women abandoned their "gifts" as soon as they received them? What would you call something that people don't want or would rather leave behind? To the don't-wanters, it will be garbage, won't it be? If that is the case, then an unwanted pregnancy is not and cannot be a gift from God, can it? To claim it otherwise would be an insult to his divine intelligence, wouldn't it be? Yes, I am saying that the mothers who are irresponsibly procreating are guilty of littering our world with miserable humans. They degrade humanity by lowering humans to the rank of animals. Unwanted pregnancies have nothing to do with God. What do you think?

Some pastors will preach, "Don't worry and just go ahead to have as many babies as God will give you because God will take care of you and your babies." According to Matthew 6:26: *"Look at the birds of the air: they neither sow nor reap nor gather into barns, and yet your heavenly Father feeds them. Are you not of more value than they?"* I am sure this is one of those "don't worry, be happy" verses in the Bible that the priests and pastors use to encourage people to freely procreate. You and your babies then become God's responsibility, are they not? If God indeed is responsible for looking after every single one of his "gifts," how come there are so many TV commercials paid for by none other than those Christian groups that on the one hand sing and praise the gifts of life, and on the other hand beg you and me to send money to change the lives of the many starving, fly-infested, and haunting young faces? Are they not also implying that God is irresponsible?

What if babies are not gifts from God? What if babies are the products of our sexual activities? If that is the case, then will it not be our responsibility to decide whether or not to have babies? If we should decide to have babies, it will be our duty to see them through and take good care of them. Makes sense? Do you think it is fair to the Almighty that he gets all the "credits" for our irresponsible sexual intercourse? How would it glorify God to have so many unwanted, neglected, and unloved children become malnourished and die prematurely each day? You have to close your eyes or have elephantlike thick skins to continue singing such hymns, right? So should we, too, leave a big question mark beside the notion that babies are gifts from the Almighty? Suppose they were, do we not have the freedom to choose not to take them? If I give you a chicken foot (my favorite), do you have to accept it and eat it?

Third, is abortion murder? Let us see what the Jewish authorities have to say on the topic. I would like to bring your attention to the fact that the Jewish and the Christians worship the same God and share the same Old Testament. And if anyone is capable of interpreting the Old Testament, I think very few will match the Jewish authorities. An article named "Biblical Text on Abortion (elsegal@ucalgary.ca)" by a Jewish biblical scholar(?) has the following to say about abortion:

> *Whatever their position concerning the permissibility of abortion, virtually all Jewish authorities would agree that abortion is not to be classified as murder.*

In my experience with Jewish people (and I know quite a few scholars who are Jewish), they just don't fool around when it comes to this type of serious issue. Trust me, they know what they are talking about. You can say I am kissing Jewish butts, but abortion ain't murder according to the Jewish scholars. So should we put another "?" beside the contention that abortion is murder?

From what we have discussed, the Christian Church's stance on abortion being immoral is certainly more a belief than a valid moral or legal claim. Do you agree? And having established the point, let us look at the morality of abortion.

First, let us look at abortion from the point of view of those who are personally affected by the decision. Let us look at a mature woman who is well informed, sober, and not threatened, and for reasons that concern her only has decided to abort her pregnancy.

1. Whose interest does it serve?

   Ans. The woman's interest.

2. At whose expense?

   Ans. At the expense of a developing fetus.

3. Is freedom of choice allowed?

   Ans. Yes; it is the choice of the pregnant woman.

Conclusion: An abortion in the early stages of pregnancy mainly affects the aborting woman. I have not counted the developing fetus as a person, who certainly has no knowledge of its existence and who is unlikely to feel any emotional pain. Of course, we could argue till the sea has gone dry on whether or not a fetus is a person and we would be unlikely to come to an agreement. At this stage, calling a fetus a person is still a philosophical or legal point. It is unlikely to be aware of its existence. Its mind is still empty with absolutely no information in it, agree? The point is, if you don't know that you have something, you won't feel the loss and the feeling associated with it.

Abortion is not healthy. But like smoking alone, it does not harm any other party than the smoker. I view abortion as morally neutral. What do you think?

Next, let us consider those who not only oppose but also impose their will on the community by preventing abortion.

1. Whose interest does it serve?

   Ans. Those who oppose and impose their will on the other by stopping abortion. Some lunatics even resort to violence.

2. At whose expense?

   Ans. If they are successful, then they are doing it at the expense of those women who do not want children accidentally conceived.

3. Is freedom of choice allowed?

   Ans. Yes for those opposed, no for those who want to abort.

Conclusion: Opposing and preventing women who want abortions from doing it is self-serving at the expense of women who want it. They also impose their beliefs upon others, forcing others to accept their point of view, sets of values, or religious beliefs. At the end, guess who has to take care of an unwanted child? It is a selfish act which results in harming another party. It is therefore immoral to oppose abortion.

Let us not forget abortion kills a developing human and there is a certain degree of cruelty. If you are a doctor performing the procedure, it could trouble you. Abortion is a choice between the lesser of two evils; it will either be the pregnant mother's future or her fetus. Abortion is never poetic; it is a damage-control measure. After a mistake is made, one can either let it develop to the fullest, or put an end to the mistake ASAP. Abortion is cleaning up after wetting your pants and much worse; it is never a thing of beauty.

Based on the new moral model, abortion is neither moral nor immoral for those who choose it. It is a free choice affecting mainly an aborting woman and therefore should be a personal matter. It should be nobody's business. Smoking and drinking, especially drinking mothers during pregnancy, cause much more serious health and social problems than abortion. If one really cares about the wellbeing of a community, he/she should direct more of his effort to preventing those two evils. And for those who have prevented or stopped abortion, again, they are self-serving at the expense of others. It is immoral.

Suicide and Euthanasia

Suicide

What is the morality for someone to commit suicide? To explore the question, please allow me to give you a real story, a story about the last day of Yukio Mishima, a prolific Japanese writer. On November 25, 1970, the same day Yukio Mishima finished his last novel named *Sea of Fertility*, he, with the help of several members of his private army, "The Shield Society," took over a military base in Ichigaya and demanded the resignation of the then Japanese prime minister. He read a manifest to a crowd, trying to rouse them to rise up against the Japanese government. The audience jeered at him instead. What happened next was quite dramatic in every sense of the word. Mishima then shouted, "Long live His Majesty the emperor!" three times, and then committed *seppuku* (ritual disembowelment) before a group of reporters and followers at 12:15 p.m. To complete the ritual, Mishima's head was to be cleanly cut off by a designated follower. His follower tried three times, made a big mess, and failed. Another follower took over and finished the job and put an end to the drama.

So what does the story tell us about the morality of suicide? I guess the answer depends on what you believe, doesn't it? If you ask some Japanese people about Mishima's case, a number of them would likely approve it. If one believes that life and death are the prerogatives of God, the answer will be certainly "No, it will be a sin to commit suicide." Again, we have two drastically different answers for the same incident. Who is right and who is wrong? Is there a moral standard to look at suicide, particularly for those who have chosen such an act with reasons deemed important and valid to them, like waking up a nation? If one believes that he is dealing with his own life and the decision directly affects him and him only, can he freely choose to end his own life? According to my belief, he does have such a freedom, and the act will neither be immoral or moral. If one applies the three questions to suicide, the answers will point to a neutral act, like the case of abortion, smoking alone, or masturbating in private. I am neither condoning nor condemning it, I am just saying that we should respect the choices of those who have freely chosen to do it for a cause, to make a political statement, a religious belief, or for personal reasons. Considering every living creature does have a strong will to seek survival, committing suicide is against nature. Obviously the person seeking it has some psychological issue. It should be treated as a mental disease and a governing body should try to prevent it from happening. Sounds fair?

Euthanasia

I can see the reasons why some nonreligious people are against abortion, but I don't understand why people would object to euthanasia. Why do people fight euthanasia? I am not referring to people who fight it on religious grounds, I am talking about people who from their legal point of view genuinely worry that euthanasia could lead to abuses. The concerns are:

1. A gradual erosion of our value of "life"; it could make patients who are dependent on others to take care of them feel worthless
2. Subject seriously sick patients to abuse, such as physicians initiating the question of whether or not they would consider euthanasia as an option; by offering euthanasia as a choice, patients could feel guilty refusing it by thinking that they unnecessarily burden their loved ones, and
3. Legalizing euthanasia will be the starting point of a slippery slope which we do not know where it ends; it could cheapen life. In countries that have legalized euthanasia, there are cases, according to those who oppose euthanasia, of termination of lives without those patients' consent. These examples show that the slippery-slope scenario is real, according to those who oppose.

Granted legalizing euthanasia has the real danger of patients being abused and *cheapening the value of life*, if we really know what that means, but should we not allow it just because the potential dangers exist? If real dangers are the reason, then no government should have legalized the use of automobiles, consumption of butter, eggs, steaks with fair amounts of fat, smoking, and alcohol. Should we stop legalizing something just because of its potential dangers? If the answer is "yes," then a lot of activities like boxing, hockey, football, mountain climbing, and sex should all be banned. Not allowing something just because there are potential dangers sounds like the philosophy of a coward, doesn't it? The question we should be asking should be: is euthanasia moral? If it is, it should be allowed. And if not, it should be banned. It is as simple as that.

So why don't we apply the three questions?

1. Whose interest does it serve?

   Ans. Those who out of their free will have chosen to end their lives before their natural deaths.

2. At whose expense?

   Ans. At the expenses of those who have chosen it.

3. Is freedom of choice allowed?

   Ans. Yes.

Conclusion: Euthanasia, like abortion, smoking alone, does not harm any other person. It is a private matter, morally neutral, and should be respected.

On the other hand, let us look at the morality of those who oppose euthanasia by asking the three questions:

1. Whose interest does it serve?

   Ans. Mainly the interest of those who oppose legalizing it.

2. At whose expense?

   Ans. At the expense of those who choose it. In the case of terminally ill patients, it means the lengthening of their suffering, which could have been avoided.

3. Is freedom of choice allowed?

   Ans. Yes for those who oppose it, no for those who choose to do it.

Conclusion: Opposing legalizing euthanasia amounts to imposing one's beliefs upon others. It is self-serving—though with good intention—and therefore immoral nontheless. In addition, the opposition often causes lots of unnecessary suffering for those seeking it. Having got the morality issue out of the way, we can focus on preventing people from using euthanasia as a money-making tool by killing those who are unwilling to die. The focus becomes in what way we can legalize euthanasia without cheapening life, without making those who refuse to choose it feel guilty, and without making our society heartless? Once the goal is clearly defined, I think the legal minds are certainly able to come up with solutions. It may involve trial and error, but it can be worked out I believe.

To sum up, I would like to quote a statement made by a person who says "no" to euthanasia:

> A compassionate society cares for and loves each disabled, sick, and dying member of its community. Compassion means literally "to suffer alongside." We have to ask ourselves: "Are we a compassionate society?" If we are, we do not kill the weak, disabled, sick people. *We do not allow anyone to extinguish the life of another.*

It is so poetically beautiful. But allow me to ask one question. If it is genuinely the free choice of a person to want death, will it make us any more compassionate by not allowing it? I think the statement that *we do not kill the weak, disabled, sick people* has intentionally omitted a very crucial part, which is the free choice of those who wish to die. Why has the writer chosen to omit such an important part of the issue? Whose interest does it serve? We are not heartlessly slaughtering the disabled, the weak, and the sick like Hitler; we are just granting them their wishes to go peacefully in a setting they choose and at a time appropriate to them. If being compassionate means to suffer alongside, how many of those who oppose, including the person who has written those beautiful words, have suffered the physical and emotional pain of a terminal disease? Where are they when the terminally ill are moaning and writhing in pain? The sentiment is romantic, but those beautiful words seem empty and phony. Allow me to be devil's advocate and let me ask the person: riding the moral high horse with those empty words, whose interest does it serve?

At the time I was rewriting this part, the case of Dr. Donald Low broke the news. Let me quote some sections from the CBC Toronto news: Dr. Donald Low, the microbiologist credited with guiding Toronto through the 2003 SARS crisis, makes a final plea for Canada to change the law to allow assisted suicide . . . He was diagnosed with terminal brain cancer seven months ago and died on September 18. (Eight days after making the plea.)

> "I wish they could live in my body for twenty-four hours and I think they would change that opinion," he said. "I'm just frustrated not to be able to have control of my own life. Not being able to have the decision for myself when enough is enough."

A spokesperson from the Office of the Minister of Justice sent an email to CBC News on Tuesday saying that the government has "no intention" of reopening debate on the laws surrounding euthanasia and assisted suicide.

"I wish they could live in my body for twenty-four hours and I think they would change that opinion." This, I think, is the best response to those moral-high-horse riders. Risking being evil and malicious, but still in the spirit of the Golden Rule, let me put it this way. Since terminal illness will be a fact of life and some people are going to suffer this cruel fate, I hope that such fate would fall upon some of those who based on their unshared beliefs, ideals, or private agendas have strongly and most vocally opposed euthanasia, like the clergy, or the minister of justice, the prime minister, or president who have the power but choose to do nothing. Then, and only then, would they realize the kind of cruelty they have so

unnecessarily inflicted upon others. For me, I certainly pray that I shall be spared of this cruel fate.

Cloning, Stem Cell Research, and Genetic Engineering

Cloning Humans

Playing God can be very addictive. In recent years, doctors have made many deadly diseases harmless by surgery. They routinely bring dead people back to life. Has there been any complaint? Cheating death is not the only thing doctors do, they have begun playing with creating life! The success of cloning a sheep called Dolly has made cloning humans a matter of sooner or later. The pioneering British team has wasted no time to suggest banning the technique to clone humans. But that does not mean that some people won't try it. I am not sure that every country has laws against human cloning. But let us look at the morality of cloning humans.

1. Whose interest does it serve?

    Ans. Who would clone himself or herself? Some narcissistic and very rich and/or powerful people who could afford the cost, perhaps?

2. At whose expense?

    Ans. The cloned person. If Dolly is of any indication, there are many problems facing a clone. A clone could be like a child of a smoking or alcoholic mother; he/she could be born seriously handicapped. The clone is definitely a different person from the original. Other than sharing the same DNA, like identical twins, there is no sharing of knowledge or experience between the two.

3. Is freedom of choice allowed?

    Ans. "Yes" for the cloner, "no" for the clone.

Conclusion: Cloning humans without the permission of a governing body is immoral. It serves the interest of a cloner at the expense of the clone, which is another person, like a member of identical twins.

I don't see any benefit to cloning humans for society. Under conditions, which I cannot imagine, a government may want to clone an individual—another Einstein or Darwin, perhaps? In such a case, a committee consisting of a number of wise and learned should decide. Cloning humans should never be the decision of an individual. It should be a serious criminal offense for anyone to attempt it.

Stem Cell Research

The uric acid level in my blood is high. It is something I got from my parent. I had gout attacks several times in the past. For those who have the ailment, they certainly understand how painful a gout attack can be. Some doctors rate the pain to be as intense as that of a woman giving birth. I could have changed my diet completely; I have chosen not to. A cold beer and/or a glass of red wine washing down some peanuts are the perfect way to end a day. I take Allopurinol every day to combat the excessive uric acid. I have had very few attacks over the past thirty-some years. Allopurinol, I have learned, is a target-specific drug for the ailment without any apparent side effects to me; a drug designed for the purpose. For those who invented the treatment, I am forever grateful.

Of all knowledge pursuits, few are as noble as those targeted to improving our lives, those that aim at curing diseases in particular. With this belief, I certainly feel stem cell research, which aims at curing diseases, should be given high priority. But let us look at the morality of such research by asking the three questions.

1. Whose interest does it serve?

Ans. Mainly the general public, especially those who suffer serious ailments such as diabetes and degenerative illnesses such as muscular dystrophy, Alzheimer's or Parkinson's disease.

2. At whose expense?

   Ans. I don't think anyone is getting hurt if we obtain stem cells without killing a person; there should be a number of ways.

3. Is freedom of choice allowed?

   Ans. Since there is no victim, the question does not apply.

Conclusion: The research aims at benefitting the multitudes and harming no one; it is certainly moral.

Genetic Engineering

Like cloning a person, a government should be the only authority that has the power to decide genetic engineering. Before any lab is allowed to begin a research project, the lab should first submit a detailed proposal to a group of scientists who have the expertise in the subject to evaluate its pros and cons. After a favorable review, the project should then be studied by social scientists for its impact on the populace before granting permission. Again, the research should aim more at solving impending problems than for cosmetic reasons. All such research should aim at improving our health by curing certain diseases or improving our environment.

Stem cell research and genetic engineering are new territories. The fields promise great rewards; they also harbor great dangers. Like a Chinese saying: danger and opportunity come in pairs, and which one will show up often depends on our execution. There will always be a price for human progress. Sometimes it can only be done by trial and error. With intelligence and caution, hopefully we can cut errors to a minimum.

One of the many governing principles of *life* is *change*. With wisdom, hopefully we can shape the direction of the changes to where we want instead of leaving it to mutations. Are we playing God? Certainly. Would it be immoral? It depends on whose interest it serves and at whose expense. When in doubt, ask: whose interest does it serve?

CHAPTER 19

The Morality of Union Tactics and War

We have established a moral model that allows us to look at the moral rights and wrongs when two individuals or parties are involved. Is the model suitable for judging morality at a much bigger scale, like between two big groups or two countries? Up to now there has been no universal way to tell moral right and wrong in large-scale conflicts, such as a war between two countries, the fight between two religions, or the conflict between unions and their employers. Lacking a standard, right and wrong is often settled by muscles. Should we continue to do it the way lions and tigers do? In this chapter, we shall apply our model and see whether it will help.

More on the Concept of Self

To apply our model, we need to change the parties involved from individuals to big groups of people. How? By using the concept of *self.* Let us review the concept of self as first defined in chapter 5. While a living organism is a biological term, a *self* is a psychological term. It describes how a living organism behaves toward other objects or other living organisms in its environment. A self is defined by its boundary and interest. The two are related: the interest of a living organism dictates how it draws its boundary. An interest is always something that is related to its survival, either directly or eventually.

For a very complex organism like a human, a self can exist in many levels at the same time. I know this seems very confusing. Please allow me to give you an example to clarify the point. The best example will be using a person, a woman named Jane. To begin with, Jane is a self who does a lot of things to serve her interest only. She eats sensibly and exercises regularly to maintain good health. She goes to work every day to make money for self-support. Jane also listens to music, talks to friends, and keeps a cat. She does all those things to benefit only one person, and that person is Jane. Because all the activities serve the interest of Jane only, the *Jane-self* consists of one person. Then, Jane meets a guy called Steve and the two get married after dating for a couple of years. After getting married, Jane does a lot of things with Steve. Gradually, there are a few things that Jane does without considering Steve's interest, and so does Steve. Since the couple frequently shares a common goal and interest, we can say that Jane and Steve often become a new self, which we can call the *Jane-Steve-self*, which we call a couple. The *Jane-Steve-self* often guides the way they deal with other people and the outside world. Jane and Steve individually still do things just for the benefit of their separate selves; the Jane-self and Steve-self coexist with the Jane-Steve-self.

Once or twice a week, Jane goes to play tennis at a local club. Jane likes to play doubles. During a game, we can say that Jane and her double partner form the *Jane-and-partner-self* with a common goal/interest to win the game. When the game is over, so is the Jane-and-partner-self. Jane is a member of the tennis club, which has a goal to promote tennis. She becomes a member of the *tennis-club-self*. And we know that Jane is a citizen of Toronto, Ontario, Canada. Jane, therefore, is a part of *Toronto-City-self*, the *Ontario-self*, and the *Canada-self*, respectively. To sum it up, Jane the person can be a member of many selves depending on how her interest is defined at the time.

A country is a self-defined by the interests of its countrymen. The Catholic Church is a self-defined by the interests of the Catholics, etc., etc. In the case of a labor union, the union is a *self*-defined by the collective interests of its members. Having laid the groundwork, let us look at the morality of the conflicts between two large groups, the clashes of the titans.

The Morality of Union Tactics—Strike

Let us use the model to see the morality of a strike by the Canadian Union of Public Employees (CUPE) in Toronto in the summer of 2009. The followings are some statistics as well as the issues:

The number of CUPEs involved: 24,000 city workers

What services are affected: garbage pickup, recycling, water and sewer services, recreational services, museum and cultural services operated by the City of Toronto and some fifty-seven daycare centers

Issues: Job security, seniority and scheduling, along with some proposed changes to a sick-leave plan that would scrap employees' ability to bank unused sick-leave days and cash them out at retirement

The people suffer the loss of services: All 2.5 million Torontonians, including parents who depend on the city-run daycares and recreational services. These parents get more than the inconvenience of smelly neighborhoods, they have their schedules turned upside down, plus the financial loss to find replacements. The financial loss of 400 students who are hired to work in the Centreville. No garbage collection creates all kinds of problems and hazards for the residents.

Now, let us apply the three questions:

1. Whose interest does it serve?

Let me give you multiple choices: a) for every Torontonian, b) for the whole world, or c) for the CUPEs only.

2. Who is paying for it, meaning getting hurt?

Ans. All Torontonians, especially those mothers who depend on the daycares, people who need the recreation facilities, students who need the summer jobs to pay for their tuition, and people who depend on the tourism business, etc.

3.   Do CUPEs have the choice not to strike?

Do Torontonians have any choice? Who initiated the strike anyway?

So here is my take. The union, to get their demands, does not hesitate to hold the public hostage, costing all kinds of hardship and misery to millions of people. (Isn't inflicting hurt to the innocent always their greatest bargaining tool?) They try to get what they want through inflicting hurt, or at the very least, causing major inconvenience. The union has the choice, the public does not. Therefore, the union violates the golden rule. Furthermore, they are forcing it onto the public. It is clearly immoral.

I have learned from talking to a number of the striking CUPEs that they have been unfairly treated by the city in comparison to what other city unions, like the police, the firefighters, and the people in the housing department, etc. Several of them also brought up the millions of dollars some CEOs earned each year. One striker even mentioned Tiger Wood's income. The sentiment was the same: if those people can earn that much money, why can't the CUPEs? Their anger was quite genuine. They were angry to be singled out for the mistreatment *"The city is putting the knife to us,"* said the president of CUPE Local 79. The woman certainly had a way with words. But a sense of fairness? If you ask me, it is the other way around. The CUPEs have the Torontonians by their balls.

Are the CUPEs mistreated by the city? Do they have a case? Well, maybe, if they compare themselves to the other unions, like the police, the firefighters, and other city workers that get more out of the city. Yes, certainly, if they compare what they get to the CEOs' fat pays. And beyond any doubt, they should feel bad if they have to compare themselves to some star athletes. It is not a secret that many CUPEs compare their earnings to that of doctors. They also think that Walmart greeters are lesser people. They get insulted if anyone dares to compare them to those greeters.

Who were the striking CUPEs? What qualifications do they have to give them such high expectations? I met and talk to a number of them. A couple of them tried to intimidate me and left. Some talked to me, not convincingly pleading their case. One, in doing so, almost made me laugh. None impressed me with extraordinary intelligence. Many were high school graduates, therefore with average knowledge, which seems a generous assessment. Some were quite out of shape. None would have any hope to qualify in a Miss Canada or Mr. Universe contest. They were, like you and me, quite ordinary. Nonetheless, they think they deserve CEO treatment. These high expectations not only make them miserable, they drag the whole city into it! Help me, Almighty!

Do the CUPEs have a case? How are they compared to the workers in the real world (WITRW) or workers in the private sectors? First of all, job security. WITRW don't have job security, the CUPEs, unless they screw up big time, won't get fired. Second, the pay: CUPEs, on the average, earn 17 percent more in comparable jobs than WITRW. Third, the sick leave: some lucky WITRW have up to six days per year; some, none. CUPEs have eighteen days. Fourth, pension: CUPEs have government funded, fully indexed pensions. They can also make more contributions. A CUPE with thirty years of employment can retire at fifty-five like a CEO. That does not apply to WITRW. The ongoing global recession and the ups and downs in the stock markets will likely make retiring at sixty-five impossible for most WITRW. On top of the above, CUPEs enjoy many benefits that are not available to ordinary people.

There is one more. When a WITRW is not happy with his/her job, his/her only option is to quit. How many ordinary workers can go to the boss to demand a raise, more sick-leave days, or a better pension? CUPEs can. They do it through a strike. They hold the public hostage. They hurt the innocent until they get what they want. It is extortion. If you and me do it, we can get jailed. But it is legal for the CUPEs.

Am I jealous? Like hell I am. It's not just me. There are millions of WITRW like me. What makes the CUPE so especial that they need to be pampered? Am I angry? Yes, a little bit. What I am really mad at is our system. A governing body in a civilized society allows and even nurtures the union of government employees to exist and to operate, to the extent of repeatedly harming the taxpayers. Clearly, unions have grown from the protectors of workers during the early years after the industrial revolution against abusive employers into sponsors and enforcers that allow their members to exploit others. While it is debatable whether or not unions should be allowed in the private sectors, when it comes to government employees they should certainly be banned. I think the CUPEs do understand who pays them. By consistently engaging in immoral tactics, striking to inflict hurt upon the citizens who pay them, are they not biting the hands that feed them?

People by nature are selfish. Given the power to self-serve, they will abuse it. With serious clout in number, most unions have done just that. And that power has been too frequently abused by unions, causing lots of misery and hardship to the general public. Why do we need unions for the government employees? To protect the workers from their own government? Why do we give the CUPEs the exclusive right to exploit the public? Don't you think there is already too much nonsense? Don't you think we should outlaw the unions of government employees? Again, unions of government employees should be illegal and banned. There should be no place for government unions in any civilized country. Allowing them to continue to exist not only makes the lives of the citizens miserable from time to striking time, it also creates many unmotivated workers who, because of their superb job security, gradually become unproductive or lazy. From what I have observed, most lack incentive to serve the public interest; they have low working morale in general. The only thing that interests them is to look for excuses to further increase their benefit at the expense of taxpayers. Not only are they spoiled, many of them hate their jobs. That is why they need so many days of sick leave. Because they hate their work and can't afford to quit, many of them won't be able to compete in the real world; they miserably get stuck in the same positions year after year. They are also prompt to complain.

Clearly, unions have outlived their usefulness in civilized countries. Government employee unions should never have been allowed. What good do they bring to a society? Other than their selfish interest, whose interest does it serve? They are like foreskin or an appendix. They are nothing but trouble and a source of misery. But banning government unions can only be realized if we have a common moral ground. Lacking a common moral ground, some political parties will exploit it to serve themselves. In Canada, we have provincial and federal NDP parties which condone the unions. The first step to outlawing unions will be putting those politicians out of work. To pick the lesser of two evils, I would rather vote for a party I don't like than an NDP, a union protector. Allowing public unions to continue will forever create two classes of citizens: union workers who enjoy special privileges, and ordinary citizens, you and me, who go without. For any government that has difficulty balancing their budget, it may be time to look at the payroll of its employees. It is not a secret that government-run organizations are big money losers. Why? I think their employees have lots to do with it. When you know damn well that the employer can't fire you for laziness, you won't work hard. I would certainly not! It is in our nature.

The Invasion of Iraq

We are going to use the past invasion of Iraq by the Americans and Brits as example and use our moral model to judge the morality of the conflict. Is the invasion moral? Without universal moral criteria, it will depend on who you ask, won't it? If you ask a typical Republican, he would certainly tell you that Bush was doing the right thing morally and he would also back it up with a number of "good" reasons. If you ask a Muslim, you would likely get an opposite answer, also based on "good" reasons. It would be confusing, to say the least. When it comes to the moral right and wrong between countries at war, the final judgment has, historically, always belonged to the country that won the war. Had Hitler won, I am sure that the world would have a very different moral verdict on WWII today—the millions of Jews would have deserved their deaths, and the US and all the Allied countries would have been the evil countries. When it comes to international conflicts, muscle and muscle only decides morality, as it does among animals. If your enemy happens to be the Americans and your weapons are those from WWII, chances are you will be labeled as one of the axes of evil, to be hunted down and punished.

There is a great danger in letting muscle decide morality. Sooner or later it will destroy all of us in a global war when two parties at war are closely matched and each has plenty of WMD, like the powerful Soviet Union against the States. It almost happened during the Cuban crisis in 1962; it will certainly happen again if we still believe in using muscle to get what we want, like pursuing military supremacy by the Americans despite there being no imminent threat of war.

Letting muscle decide morality, other than the real danger of bringing untold disaster to our world, essentially makes us all animals morally. Although we have achieved a lot in science and have invented Star Wars–like gadgets, we have not proceeded much further morally from the stone ages. It is both sad and comical to see in the final episode of *Star Wars* that George Lucas's view of right and wrong, good and evil, is still essentially decided by muscle. And judging from the popularity of the movies, lots of Americans still embrace this form of justice.

There is a popular belief that we, the human race, despite our scientific and technological achievements, are not intelligent or smart at all. Some believe that dolphins are smarter. I have heard the comment a number of times, usually from the well-informed green people. There is a lot of despair among them about our future. I strongly disagree. Beyond any doubt, we are the most intelligent and the smartest species if you check the definition of intelligence again. Then, what is the problem that leads us to this mess? The answer is: our moral right and wrong are all screwed up. What defines a good person from a bad, or a beneficial person from a harmful one? It is not how intelligent or smart the person is; rather, it is his moral sense. If you study history, you will learn that some of the world's worst criminals were always some of the smartest people. Hitler was not a dummy, neither are the nastiest crooks in the business world like Madoff. To inflict the scope of hurt upon a society, a person needs to be both a genius and morally rotten. Mao was such a person.

Are we intelligent? Yes, beyond any doubt we are. Then, what is the problem? The problem comes from the fact that we are extremely smart but we don't have the correct morality to guide our intelligence. All the great technological gadgets are our tools. They can either do a lot of good or cause a lot of damage. It all depends on the morality of the user. Nuclear energy, for example, can be used to generate electricity or can be used to build bombs. Automobiles can be a great tool to move people around, or it can be deadly weapons; it depends on the drivers. Or, the Internet can be a great tool for communication and knowledge sharing; it can also be used to commit some financial crimes. Again, it depends on the morality of the user.

Intelligence, knowledge, and the power that comes from it can either be put to good or evil use; it depends on the one wielding the power. Yes, we are extremely intelligent; however, we lack the morality to use it. That is why our planet is deteriorating so quickly, because our moral sense is several thousand years behind our intelligence. We have lots of power, but we lack the morality to handle it. As a result, we have done a lot of bad. Human nature is selfish. Without the morality to guide it and control it, our intelligence will continue to wreck our planet. Isn't the current state of our globe a good argument? What countries are doing the most damage, the third-world countries or the most developed? Indonesia or the USA? The Congo or Canada?

Can we stop the global nightmare from happening? We can! And the first step is to establish an unambiguous and universal way to tell moral right from wrong. It should also be the way to control and even to encourage our selfishness. I believe we have found the way; the new moral view is the answer. With it, we can now tell which country is right and which is wrong in wars or pollution. It no longer depends on muscle or depends on who owns CNN. When we can see through the propaganda and identify the bad guys ourselves, there is hope in stopping them. Most civilized people, me included, still strongly believe that morally right will eventually triumph over morally wrong. Let us put an end to the dominance of muscle.

In the morality of the invasion of Iraq by the US and Britain, please allow me to ask the three questions:

1. Whose interest does the war/invasion serve?

   Ans. The choices are a) Iraqis, b) the nations of the world, and c) the US-Britain-self, the initiators.

2. At whose expense?

   Ans. a) Iraq-self, b) the nations of the world, and c) the US-Britain-self.

3. Is freedom of choice allowed?

   Ans. It was a) an Iraqi choice, b) unanimous choice of the world's nations, and c) the choice of the invading nations.

Conclusion: If you believe that the US and Great Britain were doing it for the sole benefit of the Iraqi people at a price tag of 4,000 American soldiers' lives and counting, and billions of US dollars, then the invasion was certainly a selfless act aimed at benefitting a foreign country who neither shares the same set of values nor a religious belief. If that was the case, the US and his bodybuilding buddy would certainly deserve our highest praise for their sacrifices, would they not?

Let us continue to assume that the US and his buddy were doing it for the sole benefit of the Iraqis by ridding the country of a cruel dictator and to install a democratic political system in its place as claimed, there would be another point needed to be satisfied, and the point was: was the invasion a response to the choice of Iraq as a country or its people? Did the majority of the Iraqis send an invitation to the US and his buddy pleading with them to come liberate them? Did such an invitation exist? If it did not, then the invasion was uninvited, wasn't it? It was forced upon the Iraqi people or the country, wasn't it? Then the question becomes: even out of good intention—we are giving the US and his buddy the benefit of the doubt and are assuming that they were indeed doing it for the Iraqis, like *everything we do, we do it for you*—does a party have the right to go into a country uninvited to break down the country's front door and destroy everything the country has just to do something alleged to be beneficial to the country? Look at Iraq today. Is it better off than it was under Hussein? Whose interest does the invasion serve? If good intention justifies an invasion, then we can and should seek out families with abusive husbands and fathers, break down the SOBs' front doors, apprehend the bastards, and beat them up. Can or should we not? Does a perceived good intention make an uninvited invasion moral? Above all, was muscle the only way to achieve the noble goal? The US and the Brits say "yes." What would you say? Or, the US and his buddy were doing it for the safety of the world to get rid of a madman who had stockpiled lots of WMD, weren't they? If it was indeed for the world, why did no one applaud? There were many nations that did not condone the invasion. Some of these nations include the otherwise close allies of the US like Canada and France. How about the position of UN on the invasion? As far as the UN was concerned, it was not legit. So it appeared that the invasion had absolutely nothing to do with international safety or benefitting the world. Do you agree? Did the invaders find any WMD? Nothing!

So where does that leave us? There could be one and only one reason, and that was the US and his buddy Great Britain invaded Iraq for their collective interests! What other conclusion could you come up with? Far-fetched? I know very little about politics, national or international, but let me quote some content from an article in the *Toronto Star* named

"America's New Rules" by a columnist called Lynda Hurst. (I don't have the date.)

> *Known officially as the National Security Strategy or the Bush doctrine . . . it makes it blindingly clear that the United States, by virtue of its military might and perceived moral values, now holds unprecedented supremacy on the planet . . .*
>
> *The doctrine . . . formally declares that the United States will not be defied either by friend or by foe.*
>
> *It claims the right to act unilaterally if challenged by the former (friend) and to strike preemptively against the latter if it alone perceives an "imminent" threat.*

I have read this *acting unilaterally* and *striking preemptively* policy of the US in other publications, including *Time*, so there should be no mistake about the existence of such US foreign policies. What really frightens me are words like *the right to act unilaterally* and *to strike preemptively if it alone perceives an imminent threat*. So it does not even have to be a proven threat like the Cuban missile crisis! In essence, by declaring *unilaterally* and *striking preemptively*, and *perceived threat*, the US is flexing its military muscles, daring, "We do not say you have to like it, neither do we need any solid proof. We shall impose our will upon any party, friends or enemies, as we see fit. Sue us!" It is the philosophy of a bully.

Imagine this scenario: the guy with the biggest biceps in your community, for some profound reason, perceives you, a wimp, as an imminent threat to him and therefore decides to beat you up. More, the guy also boasts his moral righteousness, and that God sides with him for giving you black eyes and a couple of broken ribs. Does it not make you puke? If this is in fact the doctrine of the US, then, we, members of a global community, have a big, big problem, don't we?

Again, due to my ignorance in politics, I have to rely on the words of those who make their living in the political field. But let us not rely our views too heavily on the opinion of one columnist. Let us look at some facts and global reactions to the invasion. Since the war broke out, there were numerous demonstrations condemning the invasion in many countries, such as Canada, France, Germany, and even within the US and Britain. Could all these people be wrong? I don't have any statistics, but I would bet my two aging nuts—my most valuable assets—that globally the number of people condemning the invasion far exceeds those condoning it. How about the view of the majority of the countries in the UN? The invasion certainly had nothing to doing with serving the Iraqi interest or that of the world. Eliminating the two leaves only one choice, and the choice is it served the interest of the two invading nations; i.e., the US and his buddy, not-so-Great Britain. Do you have other choices? What conclusion can you come up with?

So what was their motive? Motive is an intangible thing. There could be a number of theories for something so big. Surprisingly, the global communities were quite unanimous: the war was about oil. One sentence summed it up tidily: *If Iraq exported potatoes, we wouldn't see this.* Getting full control over a nation that produces lots of oil would make an enticing motive, would it not? It suddenly makes sense to me. Does it make sense to you that the invasion had nothing to do with morality, with liberating the Iraqis, or with weapons of mass destruction? Denying it is like the Americans' favorite expression: it is all bullshit, isn't it?

So to what moral conclusion does it lead us? Even if one chooses to believe that the US-led invasion was for the good of the Iraqis or for the safety of the world, it would still be morally guilty of imposing the American political will upon an unwilling party, would it not? The US violated the very belief its people held sacred, and that is Iraq's right to freedom of action and the rights of its people not to have their freedom morally infringed upon. (I learned the concept from *capitalism.org* by Ayn Rand.)

The US, by invading the country uninvited and on unfounded grounds, was like someone breaking into your home, wasn't it? So what do we have? We have two standards, don't we? One standard applies to the US's citizens, where the rights of freedom of action are guaranteed. The other applies to the Iraqis, who for some reason do not have the same right of freedom to decide for themselves. Even if one chooses to believe that the US invaded Iraq out of good intention, the invasion was still immoral because the US had given the Iraqis no choice. The US could not be ignorant of the violation. They are the people who champion freedom of action and freedom of choice.

But I don't think many people in the world community believe that the US and not-so-Great Britain invaded Iraq out of good intention. You don't need the political savvy of Kissinger to know that it was really oil that triggered the war. It was certainly not out of character for the US; it was consistent with its National Security Strategy, foreign policy, past behaviors, and the nation's insatiable thirst for the black fluid. The rhetoric was polished and beautiful, but who were they trying to fool? Should we assume that the US was invading Iraq for oil? With the assumption, let us look at the morality of the invasion.

1. Whose interest does it serve?

   Ans. Those of the US and not-so-Great Britain.

2. At whose expense?

   Ans. Certainly at the expense of the Iraqis and the country. Look at the destruction and the shape Iraq is still in many years after the invasion.

3. Is freedom of choice allowed?

   Ans. "Yes" for the invaders, "no" for the Iraqis.

Conclusion: If the invasion was indeed motivated by oil, then the US and his buddy were doing it for self-serving purposes at the expense of the Iraqis; it was selfish. The fact that the invading nations should be aware of the possible cost to the Iraqis but had chosen to ignore such a toll made their actions all the more evil in nature. The invasion was immoral beyond any shred of doubt. They were doing it for oil, let us not be fooled. Had Bush admitted that he was doing it for oil and not tried to justify it, I would at least respect him for his honesty and guts. It would be macho. With the military might of the nation, they could have proclaimed to the world, "Yes, we are going to invade Iraq for its oil. If you like it, join the party, like the Brits. If you don't, sue me!"

It is a dog-eat-dog world. After all, that is what military supremacy for. Why spend trillions of dollars for so-called self-defense if it does not bring a handsome return? What was really insulting was Bush, besides claiming the morality of the invasion, was dragging God with him through the mud. It insulted the intelligent, and more than anyone it insulted the Iraqis, who are also worshipping the same God. How dare you say that God was on your side? And since when has the Almighty been under Bush's payroll, taking a bribe and becoming your servant? Bush, you are an international bully who had absolutely no sense of moral right and wrong. You also have no shame.

Looking at the invasion from the various angles, I have no choice but to conclude that the Iraq invasion was not legit, according to the UN, and immoral according to the Golden rule and the freedom of choice. From what I have learned, the war mainly served the interests of the American oil companies. The blood of many innocents, including the Iraqis and Americans— soldiers and contractors—has been spilled. If the Iraqi oil would flow your way, each drop of the black liquid would be coated bright red. Other than the interest in oil, do you care about the other things?

The High Reward of War

Why have humans been so obsessed with war? It is because war has often been exceedingly rewarding for those who initiate it. After farming, mankind has learned that war can often be very profitable. An unavoidable consequence of farming was an unchecked population growth. It led to overcrowding and shortages of resources, both of which were certain to ignite war between communities. Though the population among farming communities tended to increase, the rates of the increase would not be the same. A seminal factor on the population growth rate in an early farming community would likely be the quantity as well as the quality of food a community could produce. The more food a community could produce, the more people they could feed. And the more animal protein a community had for consumption, the stronger its members would become. So the military muscle of a community was directly related to its level of success in farming. A more advanced farming community tended to run out of farmlands faster than an inferior one. Therefore, a superior farming community would be more likely to start a war than an inferior one.

The outcome of a war between an invading tribe and the invaded had often been long decided even before the actual fighting began. The tribe with an edge in its fighters would win. A superior farming community not only would have a greater number of fighters, the fighters would also be stronger. And since an invasion was driven by overpopulation, which was a consequence of successful farming, an invader rarely lost! Though likely to be ignorant of the fact at first, a successful farming community would sooner or later learn that invading a neighbor would often be a low-risk and very profitable business. On top of land, the invaders also got a lot of goodies that usually came with a victory. Beautiful young women were for the taking, together with houses furnished with fixtures and chattel, etc., etc. Like a lion that has tasted human flesh, successful invaders would quickly learn to love the yummy taste of war. It would be stupid to resist a high-yield and low-risk venture, as any investment advisor would tell you.

After the wide spread of farming, a farming community was unlikely to assault its neighbor unless they had to. Humans are selfish; we are not cruel, I believe. Early farmers were unlikely to start a war unless there was no other choice; they did it for survival. Then, something happened and changed the nature of the war game. Among an invading party, none would gain as much as a victorious leading soldier. Besides having the first pick of all the worldly goodies, he got fame and glory. At a very basic entry level, a leader would certainly become an overnight hero to his community. And if the head soldier happened to come from a community that had a written language, his name would go down in history and became immortal. Nowhere in our human societies has there been an honor higher than that regularly bestowed to a head soldier after winning a war. The more massive a war, the higher will be the honor. In big European cities, there are always grand statues of the country's heroes, most of them ride on horseback with swords hanging on their sides. Those were the past heroes; most were soldiers.

History is full of great soldiers such as Alexander the Great, Han Wu-Ti, Julius Caesar, Genghis Khan, Nelson, and Napoleon. They got money, power, women, and the utmost of worldly luxuries. On top, they became gods even during their earthly days. Since being god is the dream of every mortal, and war is the most foolproof way to attain it, very few men will turn it down given an opportunity. Churchill, for example, would have been just another obese man and a cigar-smoking politician without WWII.

War first began between two farming communities, and used to be survival driven. It was something that a community, collectively, would choose to do. It has evolved into a means for a leading few to attain fame, glory, and power. Genghis Khan was from a herding tribe in Mongolia. He conquered China, Asia, and most of Europe. Did he do it for survival? What the heck did some herding tribes with a combined population of less than a million want so much land for? Therefore, war, instead of something to be avoided, has become something highly desirable and sought after by ambitious kings, head soldiers, and statesmen. To kings and emperors, war was much more appealing than a red Lamborghini, something they desired.

Have you ever wondered who were those great kings and statesmen in history? In China, the two greatest emperors were from the Han Dynasty and the T'ang Dynasty. Both of them greatly expanded their empires through wars. Even today, all Chinese are proud to be called the heirs of Han or T' ang. The Chinese call themselves the Han or T'ang people. We all worship war heroes. Granted that wars have increasingly become tools to serve the interests of a very elite few, the question becomes what is the problem with creating some heroes? Could you imagine a world without heroes, or history without Alexander or Khan?

One of the problems of war is the very steep ticket price in innocent lives lost during the process, people in a defeated country for sure. There is a saying in Chinese: *the fame of a general is often built upon a mound of skeletons*—the higher the mound, the greater the fame. War, despite its steep price in human toll and properties destroyed, is often extremely enticing to a top few. Every ambitious leader will not mind triumphantly standing on his mound of skeletons, whether they be that of the enemy or his own people, if that is what it takes. More and more, it has been a top few who are willing to commit their people to war to serve their private interests. The toll in human lives will always be high, with the common people having next to nothing to gain, even for a winning country.

For a leading soldier, he will be rewarded with great fame if he wins. The moral right and wrong of war, unlike other issues—stealing, rape, murder—is very simple: winning is everything. If Genghis Khan had been defeated in his very first military outing, or Alexander had not advanced beyond Turkey, would they still be viewed as the great or the greatest? It is winning or losing, isn't it?

Has the picture changed today? Will a country start a war just to serve an elite few? With all the knowledge and information available in science, social science, and philosophy, and the populace getting more educated and smarter, one would think that people in today's civilized countries would go to war for better reasons than serving the interest of a very few, right? I am not so sure.

With this, let us look at the invasion of Iraq again by the so-called Allied army and we ask whose interest did it serve? The interest of the Americans or the interest of Bush and his friendly oil companies? It appeared that the war would benefit Bush most. What good would invading Iraq bring him? Of course, to get Bush any benefit, he had to win the war against Iraq, correct? So what were Bush's odds for winning? Too bad Las Vegas had not offered any odds before the invasion or I would have bet all my retirement saving on the US winning. I would do it for money. With Star Wars–like technology against a country with mostly handheld weapons, the US might as well have let Lenny Wilkens, the most losing coach in the NBA, be the commander and it would still win hands down. If winning was a certainty, then the question becomes what would the payoff be for the elite few? Bush's Repupblican Party would win easily in the next election, then the oil would keep flowing to the strongest guy and his body-builder buddy's tanks. Oh yes, let us not forget the broken doors, the holes in the family room, furniture and dishes . . . Those would need to be replaced. There would be shitloads of business and truckloads of money to be made after the victory. Guess who would get those fat contracts?

The scary part of the whole war in Iraq was the mentality of it. Leaders still look at war as an investment and view the inevitable loss of human lives—some of them undoubtedly will be their own people— as part of the costs of doing the business. "If we make money at the end of the day, it will be all that matters." The mound of skeletons was steadily piling up after the invasion. Though the invasion was quick and successful, the Americans and not-so-Great Britain were drawn into a messy fight with the insurgency. It was something that Bush and his advisors did not quite foresee. Before Bush could further pile up his mound of skeletons with his own soldiers and those of the Iraqis, his Republican government got defeated, leaving Bush's ambition unfulfilled and thus making him one of the many very so-so presidents. As for Tony Blair, the British prime minister who led his country into the immoral war, he resigned before his full term. His Labor Party got defeated by the Conservative Party in an election that followed. Pity!

Other Titanic Clashes

Other than the fighting between countries, one religion also fights another religion. Not only do Christians fight Muslims, Muslims fight Jews, or Hindus clash with Buddhists. Sometimes, members of the same religion also kill each other—all in the name of serving the same God. It makes you wonder, is it for God's sake that they fight or for their own self-gain? Imagine that you are God and your children are killing each other in your name, how would you feel? If one is not confused by their cunning rhetoric, it will be quite easy to see the real reason behind the killings: it is self-serving. One simply needs to ask whose interest it serves. The answer, if one exercises a bit of reason, will be glaringly clear and very consistent.

The wars between religions, like the wars between countries, also involve claiming morality by their participants. After all, religion, besides the business of serving God, is also about morality, isn't it? It can be extremely confusing when Christians are killing Muslims, or vice versa, and saying that they are doing it for the love of the (same) God, and claiming that it is a moral and holy war. How do we tell the morality of such a war? There is a way. By asking the three questions, we can tell. The model gives a clear verdict: *whoever starts a war against their neighbor to serve their own interest will be immoral.* The Golden Rule says so, and they also violate other people's right of free choice.

If there is one most universal trait among living creatures, it will be their tendency to fight and wage war against one another. Our inclination to wage war comes from our selfish nature, like that of other animals. We tend to choose the surest way to settle conflicts: it is by muscle, like animals do. There is a very dark side to using war to settle conflict. Unlike fighting among animals, it will kill us all one day. Unlike animals, we have the choice not to.

War is cruel and destructive. War no long serves the interest of a community; it serves the interest of an elite few. The planet will be better off without wars. The hope, I believe, pins on finding a universal code of morality and being bound by it. According to our moral model, a country that starts a war is always immoral, because it only serves the interest of the starter at the expense of the invaded. If everyone agrees on this same common moral ground like we agree the red light means stop and the green light means proceed, maybe there is hope that the fighting will be cut down, like the number of accidents on the road. Does it make sense?

CHAPTER 20

Moral Selfishness, the One and Only Tool to Build a Happy Planet

Given a selfish nature, what should we do with it? If we care about being moral, then we should not, according to the Golden Rule, hurt others for our own benefit. And you say it is fine and noble, but you also say that you have a mortgage and insurance to pay, a car loan to meet, and kids going to school. Can I be moral and still make money to pay my bills? And above all, you have seen many hurtful people, people who have no moral qualms doing very well and getting ahead by choosing to hurt others. Unfortunately, the Golden Rule, useful as it is, only tells us what not to do and what types of behavior are unacceptable. It does not tell us the to-do part. To make our model complete, we need the proactive part.

One would be tempted to change the negative tone of the Golden Rule to positive:

> *"Treat others in ways that you would find pleasurable."*
> *"Do to others what you would do to yourself."*
> Or *"What makes you happy, do it to your neighbors."*

So we can see the reverse side of the Golden Rule is not quite applicable. People don't have the same tastes, and not everyone likes licorice, bitter melon, or chicken feet. We need a new model for the to-do part.

Existing Religions Are the Source of the World's Problems, Not the Solution

One may suggest that human cultures are full of great teachers, why don't we use the teachings of the Bible, Buddha, or Confucius as our guideline for the to-do part? The problem with using these teachings will be that the moral standards set by them are often too high. Jesus preaches love and forgiving. Forgive others and keep forgiving until seven to the seventh order times, which will be an astronomical number. And that is just for one person. Plainly, it is impossible. How about turning the other cheek? It will be very stupid, if you ask me. Buddha is said to have given up his body to feed a hungry eagle. I don't know how he could survive the ordeal, but Buddha is Buddha of course. Ordinary folks like you and me would find it very hurtful and painful to try it. As for Confucius, every man should obey an emperor and then his father; individual rights do not exist. It is terribly outdated.

To be virtuous and blameless, according to most mainstream religions, you have to deny your bodily needs. Celibacy is often a requirement at an entry level. Sex, according to traditional moralities, is a big no-no if you want to be virtuous. Besides that, you have to deny your body the pleasure of juicy steaks, lobsters, BBQ duck, beers, and wines. I don't remember seeing an obese saint who regularly eats steaks and drinks beers, have you? All these are against our human nature. Some followers of their religions even add self-inflicted pain or hardship as an additional proof of piety. To be morally impeccable, you have to be very harsh on yourself. It is like keeping pace with an Olympic marathon champ in your daily jog. Do you still want to be saintlike? No thanks, from yours truly.

Other than their exceedingly high standards and therefore being very difficult to follow, the great teachers have also been wrong in many important issues. All of them have the wrong ideas about sex by labeling it as evil and by blaming it on women. This wrong concept has created millions and millions of unsatisfied people—women of course, and also men not having the outlet—at any given day in the past millennia. To blindly glorify procreation is another reason for the world's misery, as discussed. If those are not enough reasons to give up the traditional moral views, they have all failed to solve today's many new issues like same-sex marriage, euthanasia, stem cell research, cloning, etc. on top of the existing ones like war, pollution, and poverty. If one wants to follow the teaching of a religion, then the question will be which one? All the religions share a common feature, and that is only their particular god is the true god. And none of the gods are tolerant of the others. To uphold their gods, the followers of different religions often resort to killing to do the convincing. Religions are one of the important reasons for our divided planet; they are by nature anticooperation. And they are unintelligent, because science and reason usually have no place in religions. As long as we allow the teachings of religions to lead, there will be never-ending fighting and killing.

For the reasons we have covered, the existing religions are the source of most, if not all the troubles of our planet; they are not the solution. And we have argued that the tools to help us to achieve a happy planet are cooperation and intelligence, the two forces that have carried us through the millions of years of difficult evolution and made us gods. Any factor that impedes or weakens the growth of the two forces will be against our goal. Existing religions have to go before good things can happen to our sick planet.

The Possible Outcomes of Human Interactions

Let us be practical about morality and forget about being a saint or worry too much about going to heaven later. Suppose my humble goal is to focus on my life in this very world, to make a decent living and do it without hurting other people, and I also want to feel good about myself and about the things I do. Is it possible to always put my own interest first, to be self-centered or selfish, and still be moral? More precisely, is being moral and being selfish or self-serving compatible? Do we always have to do it the hard way, be selfless, to make sacrifices to be moral?

Having defined the goal, let us see whether our humble wish is attainable. But first, let us look at how many ways, in terms of benefit gain and loss, we can interact with others. To keep it simple, let us deal with a one-to-one situation. Let us assume that person A is the initiator in a dealing or doing business with person B, the receiver of the action, then each person will have an outcome of either winning/getting a benefit or losing/suffer a loss. In a normal interaction, it is very rare and hard to imagine that one person will be benefited or suffer a loss while the other is totally unaffected. We can then summarize the possible outcomes of the interactions between A and B in the following table.

	Person A (the initiator) wins	Person A loses
Person B (the receiver) wins	A wins; B wins (I)	A loses; B wins (II)
Person B loses	A wins; B loses (III)	A loses; B loses (IV)

There can only be four possible outcomes. Let us take a close look at each of them.

Case I: Win/Win

Both persons come out winning or getting benefits from the dealing or the interaction. In our society, there are many, many cases where two parties in their interactions keep benefitting each other. The simplest example will be a happy marriage between two caring and loving persons where each party takes care of his partner's interest in everything he or she does. The pair complements and enriches each other. Win/win is the most desirable interaction; it creates beautiful relationships between the parties involved.

It can also be between two good friends or business partners who share a common interest to build a successful business through working together. One takes care of the planning and bookkeeping while the other implements the business plan to make it profitable. At the end of the day, both partners are bringing home enough money to their families and are happy. Or it can be the relationship between a professional and his client. The professional provides a service and gets paid by his client; both parties get what they want and are benefited and happy. A win/win situation can also be buying a ticket to see a good movie like *Shrek*, the *Lord of the Rings*, or *Avatar*, which makes you feel good while the filmmaker makes a profit.

In moral consideration, a win/win situation is certainly moral because no one is getting hurt (still remember harmfulness determines morality?); rather, both benefit from the dealing. A win/win is a cooperating scenario where the parties share the same goal/interest and work toward it. A win/win situation is quite common in the living kingdom. For example, some species of algae provides benefit for itself and its hosts by living together with a *Hydra,* a fungus, or a *Euglena.* Cellulose-digesting bacteria that reside in the stomach of an herbivore such as a cow or horse benefit both parties. Or, a shrimp gets food by cleaning the teeth of fish such as a grouper or barracuda. It is win/win for both parties. It is called symbiosis.

Case II: Lose/Win

It is a very odd outcome for a person who is selfish in nature to do something which ends up hurting himself to benefit a receiving party. We call this kind of behavior sacrifice. Sacrifice usually comes from a mother protecting her child, or happens between lovers. In rare cases, sacrifice can occur between two strangers, like a person donating his/her kidney to someone who desperately needs it. Those are beautiful people. Sacrificing one's interest to benefit another person, though noble, is not always sustainable because it is harmful to the initiator. It is not something I advocate. Personally, I would avoid it unless there is absolutely no other way to save something/someone that is very dear to me. Still, I won't jump into it. Sacrifice is driven by love. It is a tough choice between self-preservation and preserving someone/something one loves, like a cause or belief.

Case III: Win/Lose

In this scenario, the initiator comes out ahead at the expense of the receiver of his action. If you look at the interactions between living organisms, a win/lose situation will certainly be the most prevailing interaction, whether they belong to the same species or of different kinds. And for that matter, whether it is between two animals, plants, fungi, bacteria, or viruses. Living organisms are selfish; to hurt others for self-gain is a natural behavior for selfish creatures. People are no different. Examples are countless. Let us begin with some families where a husband constantly abuses his wife by battering her, forcing her to do more than her share of work, or cheating on her. It can happen between a father and his son where the father sexually assaults his child, like the case of Douglas Moore. Or it can happen between brothers. City officials, provincial politicians, or government members who use their positions for their own benefits are the they-win-you-lose experts; they are rats.

There are at least five different categories in the I-win/You-lose exchange:

Exploitation

An exploiter knows the exploitee's weakness and keeps milking it for his unilateral gain. A weakness can be a compulsive gambling habit, craving for attention, an uncontrollable desire for sex, money, or a certain type of food. An exploiter gets the benefits, his exploitee pays heavily. Exploitation is usually not illegal or there will not be so many casinos in Canada. Yes, we Canadians are catching up and cashing it in like our big brothers, the Americans. In Halifax, Canada, we have an Internet black widow named Melissa Ann Shepard who used the Internet to lure elderly men, preying on their loneliness and killing them with a noxious substance. In general, men are quite susceptible to the lure of sex, and I can certainly attest to this fact.

Parasitism

In Canada, there is a population of mature and capable bodies who know the weakness of the social system very well and exploit it. They decide not to work and collect social benefits instead. They are parasites of our societies. A number of years ago, a Torontonian employee quit his/her job and went on welfare. According to the quitter, it did not make sense for him to work if he could get almost the same amount of money from welfare. So the person quit. Parasites can be found in a family, a relationship, or in a company. Parasites are lazy people. No doubt, parasites weaken the society they live in, like mosquitoes weaken their hosts. The fact that the Canadian government allows those parasites to keep on depleting the resources of the country shows a major misguided moral view of the country. Parasites are not always lazy and unemployed people. They can be the presidents or the top politicians, or for that matter, government officials. They are the corrupt type. They use their power to channel tax money for their own use and often favor those who pay them bribes. They hurt the people they are supposed to serve.

Predation

Predators are killers. They are truly animals in every sense of the term. Predators don't always immediately kill; instead, they cause huge irreparable damages to their victims and render them in a state not much better than death. They are clergy who sexually abuse the children under their care, pimps who rape and force prostitutes to work without paying them, or ex-husbands who stalk their ex-spouses and harm them.

Cheating

I think we all know what it means. Cheating always involves a misplaced trust, because you need to trust someone first before you can be cheated. Cheating usually happens between close friends, boys and girls in love, or husbands and wives. It can also happen to professionals and their clients—Jones and Madoff for example. So cheaters are specialists preying on those who trust them. On top of the material or financial losses, the victims often suffer serious emotional wounds that cannot be healed.

Old-Fashioned Bullying

Bullying or using muscle in getting what you want is the most common and preferred way in nature. A big grizzly bear does not have to do the hunting and killing, it simply waits for a pack of wolves to do it and then walk in to claim the carcass. Lions do it all the time to the hyenas and wild dogs. Bullying happens quite often in our societies too. Unlike among wild animals, bullying among people often has little to do with survival. It happens quite often in schools and sometimes ends up killing the bullied. Robbery is the most common form of bullying. The invasion of Iraq was bullying at an international level in which the US and the Brits attacked Iraq.

Under the above five categories of win/lose dealings, one can find some of the ugliest people—or more appropriately, animals—in our societies. The ugliest, no doubt, are the evil ones. *Evil* has often been used by politicians to describe their enemies, it was also a term often used by Mr. George W. Bush during his presidency to describe his enemies.

Like the many words we use, we don't always understand them. So let us define it. It may not be the same as what the ex-president was talking about.

Definition of Evil

What is evil? If you ask a Christian, like I once did, he will most probably tell you that Satan is evil, but that does not tell you much about evil, does it? If you check the dictionary, it means wicked, morally wrong, or something that is bad, etc., etc. I am not quite satisfied with the definition, are you? So please allow me to give evil a definition. Just being morally wrong does not make a person evil. If I am hungry and I steal some money from you to buy food, I shall be immoral but that will not make me an evil person, will it? We are selfish by nature; we would do things from time to time for self-serving purposes at the expense of others. I still cut others off, jump a queue when driving, or turn on the volume of my TV too loud, etc. It would be unfair to label such minor moral infractions as evil acts, wouldn't it?

To be truly evil, a person pursuing his self-interest needs to have absolutely no consideration for others. Evil is relentless selfishness. "Having absolutely no consideration of others" does not mean the perpetuator has no knowledge of the possible damage—he knows all too well, he just does not care. Sometimes, it is not the actual amount of damage to others that makes an act evil, it is the complete lack of consideration of the other party. The victim's loss or suffering does not even enter into the perpetuator's equation. Often, an evil act is so needless.

An evil act is something which often results in a lot of damage to a victim or victims, and which can never be justified. What makes an evil act so foul is that the act is so unnecessary. An evil act is certainly not for the survival of the initiator. An evil person knows the consequence of his action and has chosen to ignore it. An evil person is never an unsophisticated person, quite the contrary. To qualify as truly evil, a perpetuator is often very smart or clever. An evil person either does not care about the sufferings of his victims, or even takes delight in it. To satisfy his sexual desire, a rapist destroys the lives of the innocent without a second thought; Paul Bernardo is evil. To get a higher profit, a company knowingly pollutes the environment; that is evil.

Surprisingly or not surprisingly, one can find many evil people among politicians. We in Canada certainly have our share of evil ones. So that his political friends get paid, an official gives away millions of the taxpayers' money to fake projects. Canada's ex-prime minister Chretien's scandalous sponsorship was an example. And Chretien was trying to stop the inquiry. If that was not evil, I don't know what is. And more than one billion dollars of tax money was wasted by Dalton McGuinty in trying to save his party's two seats; that is evil. Above all evils, Mao Zedong, in trying to regain power, willfully launched the Cultural Revolution and thereafter killed millions of innocent Chinese people and wrecked the country. That was certainly evil at the highest level.

Now, let me ask Mr. Bush, on what grounds did you base your Iraq invasion? Was it an honest mistake, such as the existence of WMD and the alleged connection of Saddam to Bin Laden? If it was, you were only incompetent, and that would make you no more than a lousy president in this issue. But those were proven untrue; they were only excuses. In knowingly using the excuses, you had little consideration for the human toll—both American and Iraqi. And from your speech delivered to the UN Security Council on September 21, 2004, you had absolutely no remorse in pursuing your oil interest, which would benefit some elite Americans who have close ties with you, and allow the Americans to drive gas guzzlers. What would that make you morally? The war on Iraq was an evil act. What do you think?

I would also like to ask the Catholic Church, did you know that withholding a proper and formal apology to those sexually abused by your clergy would perpetuate the hurt? Not apologizing will make the hurt impossible to heal? Weighing between saving face and stopping the hurt of the many victims, you have chosen to allow the hurt to continue. What would that make the church morally? What has stopped you from apologizing? I don't think it is love. If you ask me, it is extreme selfishness and is downright evil and despicable. Who was ultimately responsible for refusing to apologize? It was under the reign of Pope John Paul II. On April 27, 2014, Pope Francis made history with the dual canonization of Pope John XXIII and Pope John Paul II. Pope John Paul II a saint? You have turned my sense of right and wrong upside down.

Stephen Y. Cheung, Ph.D.

Case IV: Lose/Lose

You may wonder why people would, by choice, engage in a lose/lose outcome. Why? The suicide bombers are a good example. It is sad that some people have to resort to such tragic tactics. It is certainly an immoral act because an initiator chooses to blow himself up as a way of killing his enemies, often including many innocents, to achieve his political gain. To a bomber, it is a shrewd business deal—one life for many more of his enemies and innocents. They call it sacrifice and glamorize it. Make no mistake, it is an evil act. Though a sacrifice for the initiator, a planned lose/lose situation is not powered by love, it is driven by hatred. It is a form of offense that always bears bitter fruits.

Let me tell you a story I heard. A man had been going to church for many years. Every time he went, he prayed that he could be granted one wish. One day, when he was praying, an angel appeared before him and said to him, "Behold, the Father has heard your prayers for these years. He sent me to grant you one wish, as you have so sincerely prayed for." The angel paused. Before the man could say anything, the angel added, "There is one stipulation." "What?" the man anxiously asked. "Whatever the Father grants you, he will double it for your worst enemy. Now, tell me, do you still want us to grant you the wish?" the angel said. Without hesitation, the man replied, "Yes, yes! Could you please chop off my left arm and left leg?" That, my friend, is vintage hatred. That is what drives lose/lose.

In the animal kingdom, no animal will engage in a lose/lose exchange as an offense. Even the bees and ants won't do it. It is a choice uniquely human. Other organisms hurt and kill; it is for survival, nothing personal. Hatred is distinctively human. Other animals can never afford such luxury.

From the different classes of interaction listed in the table above, we find that a win/win exchange does satisfy our goal. We can both be self-serving and moral. In other words, we can have our cake and eat it too. But then, there is an objection. We all know that cod liver oil, Brussels sprouts, and daily exercise are good for the health, but they are hardly palatable or enjoyable. Is win/win the best to serve my selfish interest? Say I am a relentlessly selfish guy and I don't give a damn to what happens to those who are unfortunate enough to cross my path. My question will be can I get further ahead by choosing a win-for-me-and-lose-for-the-other-guy outcome than the proposed moral win/win approach?

I can understand the individualistic view. We all get only one life to live, and if I don't believe in heaven and hell, and if I can screw other people to get rich and get away with it, why not? After all, many successful CEOs and politicians are doing just that, aren't they? Isn't it how Trump got elected? It is a valid concern, so let us deal with the question, and the question will be—and let us not get tied down by morality—to get the most payoff and selfish gain, what will be a person's best strategy? To choose win/win or win/lose? Do I understand your concern?

The win-for-me-only approach just won't work. According to the game theory and particularly the results from Axelrod's research on prisoner's dilemma, they have shown this strategy won't produce the highest benefit for you. Instead, the win/win or cooperating with the person you interact with will bring you the greatest benefit after many dealings. But we don't need theorists to tell us that win-for-me-only won't work. If you observe what goes around you, you will know that win-for-me-only approach not only will not work in the long run, you will, sooner or later, end up a criminal and get locked up. Win-for-me-only is a strategy for criminals. That is what criminals do; they hurt people for a living. Playing the win-for-me-only game can be very addictive. For a first-timer, he often gets an out-of-proportion profit by cheating the party he is dealing with. It makes you cocky, feeling superior and invincible. Like heroin, it is extremely difficult to walk away from. It is also like playing Russian roulette. If you keep screwing people, you will be making enemies all the time and the law will catch up with you when you least expect it. In developed countries, it is impossible to make a criminal living. The news is full of such "smart" people. Most of them are still behind bars. Even if you can walk away free—McGuinty and Chretien— you will leave behind a foul name. Is it worth it? And history is full this kind of smartasses scorned by people.

Let me share a story with you, a story of a guy called Lee. Lee was once a close and trusted friend of mine. Lee's forte was win/lose games. He was obsessed with winning whether it was a tennis match, or a low-stake card game between friends. To win, Lee often cheated by calling a ball out when it hit the line, or by manipulating the cards. Then, more than ten years ago, Lee was caught and charged for operating a number of grow-houses. He was also caught cheating on GST, money laundering, and income tax evasion. Because of the crimes, his wife got laid off (or fired?) from a very good job, the kind of job that got stock options and dental plan, etc. Lee was sentenced and locked up for a number of years. Because of his addiction to the win-for-me-only game, Lee hurt many property owners and people who did business with him. Above all, he hurt his family big time. Lee has two daughters and a son. And Lee has never missed a chance to proclaim his love for his family. "I'll do anything to make my kids happy," he often said. None of them were happy at the time. And they will likely bear the emotional scars for many years.

Win/Win Is Both Moral and Selfish

Win/win is certainly the choice if one wants to be successful in life in the long haul. Win/win produces two satisfied parties in every transaction or interaction, and therefore is easy to do and sustainable. It is sustainable because both parties will look forward to future dealings again with each other. To be sustainable is the key to becoming successful over a long period of time. Gradually, a person with a win/win strategy will develop a reputation, making him highly sought after for business. A win/win person makes new friends in his every business dealing. He will unavoidably be a happy person because he feels good about the things he does and about himself. He also gets a lot of positive feedback from people who have dealt with him. Therefore, win/win is also the strategy if one's goal in life is to seek happiness. Should there be other higher or more worthy goals?

On the other side of the coin, a person with a win-for-me-only approach to life will fail at some point, and often quickly. People who have suffered losses will stay away from him and will often warn others against dealing with the hurtful guy. He will have a bad reputation and find his life getting harder and harder because no one wants to deal with him anymore. And depending on the seriousness of the hurt he has caused, the police may also be after him. A win-for-me-only guy will sooner or later end up in jail, like Lee. Win-for-me-only will not last.

If win/win is such a great deal, why is it not the norm of human interactions? Why does win-for-me-only strategy still dominate most of human behaviors? There are two reasons. First, human nature is selfish. To be selfish means self-serving in order to self-preserve, he therefore naturally tends to hurt others like an animal does. Hurting others is often the easiest way to get what you want. It would be much easier to steal money from others than work the many hours to earn it. Cheating—using illegal drugs or taking a shortcut—makes winning a race easier if you can get away with it. To practice win/win, our natural hurtful inclination must be suppressed by strong self-discipline in order to achieve sustainable success. Self-discipline is not in our nature; it takes years of practice and a strong will. To be able to self-discipline is the first requirement for a person to do win/win habitually. Second, to get the necessary energy to sustain practicing win/win, one also needs to embrace selfishness. WHAT? I hear a reader exclaim in disbelief. That has often been the first reaction from the people I talk to. Please let me explain. By embracing selfishness, you will be easily and highly motivated to do something; to self-benefit is where the energy comes from. Lacking motivation is the reason that many ideologies has failed. This is why union government employees get lazy. And it is the reason why a Communist country will be poor. It is hardly surprising that people loathe selfishness. It has a rotten connotation in all societies and it invariably stands for hurtfulness or immorality. That is why popular moral teachings all want to suppress (hurtful) selfishness and any expression of it. To be virtuous, one often has to self-deny, and best of all, to be selfless.

Traditional teachings, therefore, are against our nature. To follow traditional morality is like going against a current. Do we have to go against our nature to be moral? Since our goal is to be moral and also to put our interest first, the question becomes: can we embrace our selfish nature and still be morally sound? The answer to the first is "no," and the second is "yes." Win/win is the only way to achieve it. According to our model, harmfulness is what determines immorality. In a win/win situation, every party wins and no one gets hurt. Since no one gets hurt, therefore it is moral. And in a win/win interaction, a person always considers his interest. It is therefore powered by self-interest, or simply, selfishness. Win/win is therefore both moral (both parties get the benefit) and selfish (the initiator always considers his own benefit) in nature. To do win/win is to guide and control our selfishness with discipline by suppressing the hurtful part and focus on boosting the beneficial part to make it moral. You need moral discipline. With morality vetoing the hurtful part, we can freely allow our selfishness to soar. Win/win and moral selfishness are the same thing under different names. Win/win is your goal, and moral selfishness is how you achieve it.

Moral Selfishness

From the above discussion, we have laid the foundation needed to formally introduce *moral selfishness*. If anyone cares to ask me, "What is the most important message of this book?" I would, without hesitation at all, reply, "It is to introduce *moral selfishness.*" It is the only solution to our planet's many troubles. I am very fortunate to be the bearer of this message.

Definition

What is moral selfishness? Moral selfishness is a simple concept. It has two equally important components: (1) to be moral, and (2) to be selfish, hence the name. Easy to understand, isn't it? They are the two legs that carry moral selfishness. Missing either one, it will be crippled. Let us take a look at each component.

To Be Moral: To Others and To Oneself

The first component of moral selfishness is to be moral. We have already defined what morality is. In a nutshell, it is 1) you never hurt others intentionally for self-gain, and 2) you allow others to say "no" or to choose, even if your intention is to benefit others. Within these two constrains, all your dealings will be moral. Simple, isn't it?

To be moral to others is only one part of moral selfishness. The other part is one also needs to be moral to himself for the things he does. For several years after I discovered moral selfishness, I used to think that we need only to be moral to others. How about to myself? Do I owe myself the same moral obligation? Then, it dawned on me that my initial thinking missed an important part. The missing part is one also needs to be moral when dealing with himself. Seems confusing, doesn't it? Confusing, because in discussing the moral issues when only the doer is affected and no others are involved we consider it morally neutral. Examples are smoking alone, masturbating in a private setting, or swearing at no one, etc. In cases involving only the doer, we think that morality does not apply. It is like a situation that one does not need morality when he is living in an island alone. The argument is certainly valid. It is nobody's business when a doer is doing something that does not affect others; an outsider should not say anything about it. However, to get the highest benefit from moral selfishness, the doer still owes himself the same moral obligation. He should ask himself the same two questions when he engages in a certain behavior: (1) in so doing, am I hurting myself? And (2) will doing it give me more free choices or options in the future? If I am hurting myself, like smoking without others present or getting drunk alone and not needing to drive afterward, my doing will still be morally neutral to others. However, the behavior will be immoral to me because I am knowingly and intentionally hurting myself. This is a new concept, and I hope a reader will take time to critically think about it. Do you think you owe yourself a moral obligation?

Question #2: In doing something, am I or am I not giving myself less options? People, like most animals, are lazy by nature. Most people won't find going to gyms to workout fun. In the gym I go to, there is a slogan posted by a trainer: *Did you know that 50% of people drop out of their programs in 6 months?* Not exercising regularly is to allow our body to deteriorate faster. And as a result, the person is more prone to several diseases that typically arise from inactivity. When your health deteriorates, you have lost a serious amount of physical freedom. Do you still remember how we define freedom? Or, you have a tendency to use your credit card without planning. It will, sooner or later, get you into all kinds of financial trouble. Debt is a very serious problem among millions of Canadians. Unless you can control your spending habits, you are going to lose lots of freedom with your debts. First to go may be your house. Then, your car. You will have to take the public transit or move around the very old-fashioned way by using your legs. Then your girlfriend also leaves. No money, no honey is quite real. I can also testify to that. If you have a habit of doing things that hurt yourself, or doing things that end up reducing your choices, you are not doing a very good job at being morally selfish. Does it make sense?

If we agree to add this new stipulation—i.e., a moral obligation to one's own self—then you can see that a morally selfish person is also a person who loves himself very, very much. He will be healthy. Not only will he not indulge in hurtful habits, he will proactively promote healthy living. To give himself more options in the future, he will continue to improve himself, like continue to learn new things and skills. When you are healthy and have more tools at your disposal, you will have more options than most people and will be a very happy person. Isn't that what a happy life is truly about?

To Be Selfish

I don't think we need to explain this one; it is in our nature. To be selfish, in essence, is to put one's own interest first. *Will it benefit me?* It will always be me first before I agree to do anything. If yes, then I'll do it, if nothing, then no thanks. My goal to be selfish is so that I'll be happy in whatever I do. Therefore, a selfish person's decision on whether or not to do anything—interacting with others or to be alone—depends wholly on whether or not it will make him happy or please him. To be happy, or work toward it, is always the compass of a selfish person's every deed. To pursue happiness should thus be the only guiding principle for doing anything for a 100 percent selfish person. Please note, to be selfish does not preclude "sacrificing" a doer's interest for the sole benefit of others. What? A selfish person making sacrifice? It is contradictory, isn't it? Not really. If a "sacrificing" act makes you happy, like donating millions of dollars to charity, giving blood, donating a kidney, it is no longer a sacrifice, is it?

We need to define *sacrifice*, don't we? *Sacrifice is doing something for the sole benefit of another person or persons; as a result, the doer suffers some loss, something of value to his survival. In a sacrifice, the doer often does not want to do it but is somehow manipulated to do it; he often does not feel happy doing it either.* So by this definition, if a person is happily giving away something of value to benefit others, it is no longer a sacrifice. If you are manipulated into it, you won't be happy and will truly fit the definition. You will find many religious people in this category; they are also called "saints." None of them look happy. The Catholic logo for sacrifice was Mother Teresa. She was quite miserable.

Please remember that pursuing happiness is the goal. If a "sacrifice" makes you happy, it is a good enough reason for a selfish person to it. It is certainly moral and admirable. That is why people out of their own free will happily donate blood or give away money to the poor. That is also why some lovers do what they do. The "sacrifices" make them happy; it is also an expression of love. For such acts to be sustainable, the doers need to be happy and choose to do it. His "sacrifice" is primarily to make himself feel good and happy. Isn't that what selfishness is about? It seems redundant, but it is worth repeating to get the concept right. After all, it is about pursuing happiness, a central point of doing moral selfishness, and a central message of this book.

To Be Moral to Our Environment

One last thing. To be truly morally selfish, one also owes our planet a moral obligation. It means protecting other beneficial species and to consciously reduce the amount of garbage and pollutants. I don't like to use the word "sin," but in considering our obligation to protect our environment, it should be a sin to engage in wasteful behaviors. Americans and Canadians are often guilty of wasting. I go to the gym almost every day. I have seen lots of waste among the members. It is not unusual to see people using more than three clean towels during a trip to the shower—it is just for the shower. By the time some finish, they have gone through quite a number of them. Needless to say, it takes a lot of water and electricity to clean and dry a towel. And many just let the hot water run and run when shaving or are stepping aside and let the water run when taking showers; they are just wasting it. It bugs the hell out of me. How much trouble is to turn the water off or on?

The logic for our moral responsibility to the environment is obvious. If we keep on harming our environment, it will come back to harm us sooner or later. Just for selfish reasons, we should do it. No one likes to live in a city where people litter, where the waters are polluted and full of garbage, where the air is harmful to breathe, and where there is not much wildlife except the undesirable kinds. Many big cities are like that. It is a simple reflection of the levels of morality of their citizens.

To sum it up, moral selfishness is powered by the love of one's own self and the care toward people we are interacting with.

Stephen Y. Cheung, Ph.D.

What If the Whole World Is Full of Morally Selfish People?

Would it be an ugly world? In *The Selfish Gene*, R. Dawkins has this to say: "*. . . an advocacy based simply on the gene's law of universal ruthless selfishness would be a very nasty society in which to live . . .*" We are not advocating ruthless selfishness, are we? Again, everybody knows only ruthless selfishness.

I am not an expert on ethics. Before writing this book, big names in ethics such as Kant, John S. Mill, or recently Ayn Rand—who interestingly has written *The Virtue of Selfishness* (1964)—meant absolutely nothing to me. So, buyer, beware! Having disclosed my ignorance, I tend to agree to one of the widely used measuring sticks in gauging the usefulness of a moral value—like lying, stealing, sacrificing, or reciprocity—and the measuring stick is: what if everybody is doing it?

So we ask: what if the world is full of morally selfish people? Will it be nasty? Let me start with myself as an example. After I discovered the way to decide morality, I have consciously followed the two rules: not to hurt others intentionally for self-gain, and always allow others to choose whether or not to participate. Then, I developed two rules for self-guidance: (1) never to leave a place in a worse condition after my visit, and (2) never leave a person in a worse shape after dealing with me. Being moral has made me a more likeable person, to others and myself. After visiting a washroom, for example, it usually takes me no more than several seconds to make sure that I have not left a mess. It is that easy to be moral. And gradually, it becomes a habit for me to consider the other party before a dealing or exchange. The golden rule–based morality makes me a more caring person. I like the new me very much. By starting with asking what is in it for me, I don't waste time doing things that don't interest me or does not make me happy. I simply say no. Before I knew this concept, I often did things that I would regret. A rather pretty woman I hardly knew once implored me, "Stephen, would you help me to move next Saturday?" I agreed. I almost broke my back without any benefits. Hated it! Or, "Dad, would you loan me $30,000?" one of my daughters asked me. I did and it caused me some sleepless nights because the sum was all I had in reserve and she kept postponing paying me back. Those were before I practice moral selfishness. No more since. If similar situations should arise again, I would say, "Honey, you know Dad cares and loves you very, very much. But no!" I would also decline with a smile to show no hard feelings. I shared it with my banker friend, Tony. He liked it very much and I think he has become a much happier dad.

If you don't protect your own interest, no one will. Human nature is selfish. Those who take advantage of you are often your relatives, especially those closest to you. Never ever forget that.

Morally Selfish Parents

What kind of parents are morally selfish parents? Would they leave their children in a car while going to shop on a hot summer's day or freezing winter's night? There are people who have actually done just that. For sure they are selfish, but they have no moral sense. Morally selfish parents are loving and caring parents instead. They plan before having children. As a result, they are able to provide each and every one of their children with enough time to care for and love them. They also have the financial capability to buy the things their children need. They won't stop caring about and loving their children even after they have grown up. As a result, their children will be fully equipped to become a productive and contributing citizen when they grow up. This is what I have observed responsible parents do in the past decades. Morally selfish parents are for sure responsible parents.

From *Predicting the Probability to Harm or Hurt* previously discussed, I have good reasons to believe that a very high percentage of the criminals are from immoral parents. Those parents are the source of criminals in every society. Should we make it illegal for immoral parents to have children? Whose interest does having neglected children serve? Who is paying for it? Whose choice is it?

A Morally Selfish Spouse

How about a morally selfish spouse? He or she will be the best lover you can have. He takes care of himself physically, financially, and mentally. So he is a fit person, with money to spend on luxuries, and he is at peace most of the time. Therefore, he is fully capable of taking good care of you, and will. He often goes the extra mile just to please you. When you are tired, he offers you a massage before you ask. He is understanding as well as observant. He anticipates your needs and provides for them. He is able to keep doing so because he is in such great shape all around. Above all, he will never cheat on you, because he knows how much it will hurt you. Same applies to a wife. In short, a morally selfish spouse is a caring and a nurturing spouse. A morally selfish spouse is the source of everyday happiness. A person with such a spouse is, beyond any doubt, the luckiest and happiest person in the world.

A Morally Selfish Friend

He will be a great friend to have. He always takes your interest into consideration, does he not? He always cares about you. Am I right? He will never do things that hurt you for his one-sided gain. Isn't it true? In short, you will always enjoy his company, right? The enjoyment is mutual because you also look after his interest. So without doubt, a person who is morally selfish is a great friend to have. He is the type of person who puts a smile on your face whenever you think of him. Who is your best friend? Isn't it the way your friendship works? A morally selfish friend is someone you can trust the safety of your family members with when in need.

A Morally Selfish Employer

How about a morally selfish boss? We all know what an immoral boss will do. He takes advantage of you whenever he can. He will exploit you if you let your guard down. He makes unwanted and inappropriate advances on women working under him. You hate him, don't you? But how about a moral one? What is a morally selfish boss? He knows that for his company to be successful he needs the best from you. How does he get the best from his employees? As a start, he will pay his employees what is fair instead of trying to squeeze them. He will provide a good environment to work in, meaning besides a healthy workplace also a culture of cooperation. He also protects his employees. Because he is well liked and loved, his employees will always happily give him their best. His business is bound to succeed.

A Morally Selfish Employee

And what is a morally selfish employee? You know he will look after his own interest first. He will never work for free or be underpaid. But if you are lucky enough to have him, he will look after your interest too. You can be sure that he is a professional, doing a thorough job, producing quality work during every one of his working minutes, being responsible, not abusing his power for personal gain, and being on time, etc., etc. You can trust him with your company and take long vacations and expect to come back to find the company running well. A morally selfish employee makes a great worker. You'll never lose money on this guy. He helps you to make money instead, far more than he is paid.

A Morally Selfish Politician or Government Official

A morally selfish government official? Well, based on the daily news, one wonders whether there is such an animal. It will be a very rare breed for sure. What is an immoral one? We know all too well, don't we? They are the ones that abuse their power. They are those who sell senate seats to the highest bidders. They hire contractors without public tenders. They use tax money to pay personal favors. In short, in whatever they do, they always put their personal interest or that of their party ahead of the taxpayers'. You also painfully know who they are, don't you? They are those who make you swear (you don't?). I do it all the time in such situation. They send your blood pressure shooting up.

Morally selfish politicians are the opposite. They are rare, extremely rare, but if you are lucky enough, one or two of them will appear in your country or local government. They are selfish because they do it primarily to make themselves happy. They enjoy serving their own interest, as well as those of who elected them—that is the reason they run. They are moral because they will never consciously abuse their powers or hurt the taxpayers. For sure, they won't waste billions of dollars to save two seats for their party, nor will they pay party favors with tax money. For whatever they do, they will look after the public interest ahead of their own. They make great clerks, mayors, governors, premiers, presidents, and prime ministers. They are the blessings of the human race, because they are moral and they always remember serving the public interest is their goal.

A World Full of Morally Selfish People

Now comes the most crucial question: what if the whole world is full of morally selfish people? Wow! It will be paradise, won't it? Just imagine! There will be no violence. No crime, no war, nothing! If you are a news broadcaster, you will be the most loved person because you will always be the bearer of good news. You don't even have to be good-looking for people to like you. (There is the reason why all networks hire good-looking people to broadcast the news.) No war means no need for soldiers, correct? And the budget for defense will be next to zero, right? There will not be much need for policing either, will there? How about healthcare, which has been such a big problem for President Obama? Since a morally selfish person treasures his own health, he will eat healthily, exercise daily, and have enough rest. Health will no longer be an election issue, will it? Since government employees are all morally selfish, governments will be much more productive and efficient. The people in that country will be much happier and much better served. So key to realizing a happy world, realizing *"make love, not war," "no country or border,"* moral selfishness is the solution and the only solution. Why? Because the golden rule–based morality has a built-in feature to make caring people. When a person cares, he will develop love gradually.

Personal Growth and Moral Selfishness

The year following my first divorce was the lowest point of my life. Shortly after coming out from a several-months-long depression, I began to seek advice and wisdom from books on self-improvement. One concept kept coming up, and it was the phrase *personal growth*. It is a very common term but few people understand it. I knew vaguely that it meant something good for the soul and the spirit. But then, what is a soul or spirit? After discovering the concept of *self*, it dawned on me many months later that personal growth and *self-growth* could be the same thing.

So what is self-growth? Self-growth literally means to enlarge one's self by stretching its boundary. A self is defined by an interest, and your interest is how you draw your boundary. How and where a person draws his boundary of self is what decides how he interacts with those around him. If you are outside the person's boundary, you will be treated as a rival or even an enemy. If you are inside, you are his ally, someone to be cared for or loved.

The question becomes how do we make a self grow? To grow means to enlarge, doesn't it? According to its definition, we can make it grow by enlarging its boundary to include more things or people, correct? Please allow me to explain the concept by using the development of a child and his self-concept. Please be warned that I am not an expert on child development and be very critical of my idea. I am not aware of any research that will support my idea because the idea is new. It makes sense based on what I know. When a child begins to be aware of the world around him and can tell the difference between what belongs to him and what does not, he has established a boundary and formed his concept of self. At the beginning, his self includes only himself and no other person. As a child grows and if he is well provided for and nurtured, his concept of self may increase to partly include some of his family members. His primary care provider, the mom, for instance, will be the first to be incorporated into his boundary. How can we tell? The most reliable indication will be the child's willingness to share something he loves with the person. For example, when a child begins to share with his mom his ice cream cone, a lollipop, or a teddy bear, the gesture is a good indication. Why is the willingness to share an indication of self-growth? Please allow me to explain. Let us go back to the definition of self again. The self of an organism is defined by an interest, which is its survival. Likewise, the child's self is defined by his interest, which is always immediately linked to his wellbeing and survival. To the child, an ice cream cone and a lollipop are food he loves, they are things that enhance and thus are of value to his survival. The child's selfish nature will make him keep those things for himself and himself only. Likewise the teddy bear he loves to play with. Why go against his selfish nature by sharing them? Why would a selfish person offer a valuable item to another person, a nonself? He never will if he considers the other person as a nonself. The child willingly does it because he has gradually and unknowingly included his mom as a part of his self. His mom by then is a part of him. Why the mom? Because according to the child-self, his mom, by providing him with food, love, and other comforts, is crucial to his survival. As a result, the child develops a positive emotion and a bond toward this provider, his mom. The positive emotion toward the mom causes the child to voluntarily stretch his self-boundary to include her.

In so doing, the self of the child has greatly enlarged. Self-boundary is a funny thing. Though it is abstract, it has a plasticlike property and can be stretched, but only by a positive, warm, or loving feeling. As long as a person has that warm and caring feeling toward the outsiders, his self will keep growing. On the opposite side, if a child does not receive enough love, care, or is constantly under stress due to not having enough, he will become increasingly hostile to his surroundings. His self will not grow; his self will only include himself.

Love and Care Will Make You Grow

We all have positive emotions—to like, care, or love—toward objects or persons that are important to our survival and will naturally stretch our self-boundaries to include them. Following this logic, the more people you like, care for, or love, the greater will your self-boundary be and the more willing you are to share something of survival value with those people. How much you are willing to share depends on the number of people you have incorporated within your boundary. Makes sense? People madly in love will completely include their lovers into their selves. At such level, there is nothing they won't share, they are even prepared to die to save their lovers. This connection between liking/caring for/loving and self-boundary does explain a lot of the seemingly selfless human behaviors despite our selfish nature, does it not? For example, why do people do volunteer work? Why do they donate blood or organs? Why did Jane Goodall spend her life among chimps? Why do people tend their gardens? Why do you spend time washing and polishing your car? A person does certain acts for something because he has a warm feeling toward it, caring about or loving it. Through liking, caring, or loving, a person will stretch his self-boundary to include the objects or persons partially or completely into his self. When the chimps were happy, Goodall felt the joy; when one of them was hurt, she hurt as much. Goodall's self-boundary has included the chimps.

So how do we explain these behaviors which seemingly go against our selfish nature? The way I see it, we are still selfish in giving blood and helping a friend. We have included them and treated them as a part of our selves, therefore we are actually doing it for our own selves. Does it make sense? At least it is consistent with our selfish nature, isn't it?

So a selfish nature is not such a bad thing after all, is it? It all depends on how we define our boundary or draw the line, doesn't it? Now, sit tight. I am going to shock you!

God Is Selfish and Must Be Selfish

Following the above logic, I dare say that God is selfish and he must be selfish. However, his self includes us. That is why God, despite a selfish nature, is capable of the greatest love. Does it make sense? Or do you want to burn me alive for the assertion and blasphemy?

Love Can Be Extremely Dangerous

Love, though beautiful and often highly praised, can be very dangerous. For a person who is insanely in love, his self-boundary will extend to completely include the loved one. But this can be one-sided. There is no guarantee that the one you love will reciprocate, like between Romeo and Juliet. Alas! To reciprocate is not always the rule in a real world. Too bad that self-boundary is not elastic; it makes a recovery from a love-gone-bad very difficult and often impossible. Even worse, what if someone you love continues to hurt you? Having included the person as a part of you, how do you sever him from you? To yank the person out of your mind and heart would be like pulling a part of you out, wouldn't it? That, my dear Romeos and Juliets, is why a failed relationship is always so painful. It is not only your heart that is broken, your *self* has also been ripped apart and left with a gaping hole.

Hatred Will Shrink You

On the other hand, people who are overwhelmed with hatred have shrunk their selves to the minimum; their selves exclude all other people. If you love the *Lord of the Rings* like me, you will immediately know Gollum is that kind of being. They truly are the very lonely type. They are also very dangerous, because they see other people as competitors or enemies who threaten their survival. They will never hesitate to harm other people given the chance. The worst type is those who hate themselves. From this self-hatred, they are prone to destroying themselves. But some won't go quietly; they often take the lives of innocent people together with them. Sounds familiar? How about the suicide bombers?

So what choice do we have? To care or not to care, to love or not to love? For selfish reasons, the "not to" would not be an option, would it? For a person to be happy and fulfilled, he doesn't really have a choice. Assuming that you agree with this assertion and want to be happy, how would you do it? The way to be happy, to develop positive emotions, or to stretch your *self*-boundary to include more people and living organisms is by practicing moral selfishness. Why? Because the moral part will always guide you to be considerate and to do something beneficial to others. When you get into the habit of being considerate, the positive emotions will gradually grow in you. It will also come naturally. The selfish part is to motivate you and give you the required energy. It is also to protect you from being exploited continuously. Because you love yourself, you won't allow anyone to keep hurting you.

Not Engaging Will Serve Your Self-Interest Better

I have been practicing moral selfishness in the past ten or so years since I discovered it. I have been tempted from time to time to break it for self-reasons or a lack of discipline. When someone yelled at me or verbally attacked me, I would, like a reflex, want to fight back and hurt the other person because self-defense is in my nature. To get even seems to be the norm for lots of people, even for the educated. Some cultures even embrace it. *Don't get mad, get even.* Or, *an eye for an eye.* That is the reason for the continuing conflict between Israel and the Arabs. But gradually, I discovered that getting even will not make me happy and certainly won't serve my long-term interest. Instead, it will make it worse, because the other party will then try to get even. The cycle will never end. Gradually, I have learned not to engage, though it has been very hard at the beginning. I have learned just to walk away, not to say a word or look at the person. It was not easy. For many decades, I was used to having the last word. Then, it got easier and easier. My days have also since been much more uneventful. When some driver showed me the bird and yelled at me—it rarely happens these days—I would turn my eyes away from him. I would tell myself that the guy could be under a lot of stress and was probably looking for someone to let out whatever was bugging him. I stayed away. I want to protect myself. I would not allow myself to be used as an outlet to vent his anger or frustration and end up getting hurt.

Following the Golden Rule, I tried not to upset people by saying bad things to them. Verbally attacking others is invariably for my personal gain and would be immoral no matter under what circumstance, the Golden Rule says so. It has become increasingly easier for me to control my temper. Gaining full control of my tongue takes discipline, discipline needs practice. As soon as I found out that someone is unreasonable, I would seek the first chance to exit before it gets really messy. Then, I would conscientiously stay away from that person. Yes, you can hurt me once but no more, because I won't allow you to. I am selfish. Nonengagement is the key. Why allow someone to upset me? Why engage? I have found the not-engaging rule very useful. I have since no enemies because I have refused to engage.

I also will not litter a place, not even on a dirty street. I usually hold on to my coffee cup, soiled napkin, or a Popsicle stick until I come across a garbage bin. Sometimes I have to walk close to a kilometer before finding one. Japan, for example, is a country that does not have many garbage bins around. It has been getting easier and easier. These are little things. They make me feel good about myself. I like the culture in some German cities: men sit down to pee. Though not manlike, it makes good environmental sense. Practicing moral selfishness has made me a much more likeable person—to other people and myself. Most of the time, my mind is at peace. Having actually followed moral selfishness, I can say with certainty that it is very doable. Even if we cannot change the world overnight or over years, a person still will gain a lot of happiness doing it. I can also testify to that.

Moral Selfishness and Competition

Is moral selfishness compatible with competition? We all understand to compete is to beat your competitors for self-gain. Isn't that against the Golden Rule and therefore immoral? One of my young Brit friends asked me when I was staying in a hostel in Copenhagen: "Both my best friend and I like the same girl. To conform to the Golden Rule, am I moral to compete with my friend? If I am successful, am I not hurting my friend big time for my benefit?" Or, "In shopping, am I moral to pick the best fruit among the many? Then, am I not leaving the not-so-good ones to others and hurting other shoppers?" How would you answer those questions? It is a matter of fair competition, isn't it? Fair competition is not only necessary for a society to stay healthy, it promotes progress and prosperity. Fair competition creates vibrant societies. It is a good thing for mankind provided it is done in compliance with rules and regulations. Without competition, things will become stagnant. When workers don't have to compete, like the case of the many Canadian government employees, they often lack incentive and gradually become lazy. That is why so many of them hate their jobs, are so lifeless, so not eager to work, and more prone to take sick leaves. Their attitude also causes big damages to the people they serve and their country. Competition is a rule of nature. A practicable moral model should also try not to violate the law of nature, like the way we should embrace selfishness and do so morally. In answering my young Brit friend's question, I also mentioned that if you would not compete, were you not unfair to the girl? What if she liked you, were you not taking her choice away from her without her consent and thus hurt her? He nodded and agreed. I felt like I was pretty wise.

Moral Selfishness vs. Individualism, or Rational Self-Interest

Shortly after publishing *Happy to Be Morally Selfish*, I had my first book show. A handful of visitors asked me whether I knew Ayn Rand's philosophy or not. I had no idea at the time, did not even know who she was. I did some reading after and found that there are quite a number of similarities between my *moral selfishness* and her *rational self-interest*. I also love the way she expresses individualism in her book *Atlas Shrugged (1957)* through a character called John Galt:

> *"I swear by my life, and my love of it, that I will never live for the sake of another man, nor ask another man to live for mine."*

For sure it is individualistic; it is also selfishness, meaning being self-centered. There are many differences: I am a biologist, I better understand what life is and have defined it in a generic way. From the definition, I have also highlighted a living organism's need for survival and in turn have related it to selfishness. How we deal with this natural selfishness is a main part of the book. The answer is by our new morality, which uses the presence or absence of harmfulness as the deciding factor, and also the only deciding factor. Luckily, the golden rule, though the many religions do not highlight it, has been precisely prescribed to deal with causing harmfulness.

Based on the Golden Rule, I was able to come up with two simple principles on causing harm and freedom to choose as deciding factors; the two principles allow me to decide what behavior is moral and what is not. The proposed three questions make applying the two principles exceedingly simple. The new model enables everyone to decide morality on his own and has thus given the public the power to decide on many important issues, such as abortion, same-sex marriage, or euthanasia, etc. For the first time, the book has also identified the source of problems of our planet and therefore given us hope of solving them. Again, the solution is moral selfishness. The book has presented a coherent and complete theory to fix the planet's problems. The arguments on the book are based on science and reason, where every worthy concept or idea has been clearly defined to avoid ambiguity that is common in many philosophical writings.

Rand used the term *rational self-interest*. She did not explain what is *rational;* it remains a vague concept. And lastly, moral selfishness does not preclude altruism like individualism does. The ultimate goal of selfishness is for a person to pursue happiness, I also believe. If being altruistic makes you happy, then it will be a good selfish reason. To be altruistic, one must care and love; the moral part of moral selfishness will guide you to grow the two warm feelings.

Why the Ugly Name?

A couple of friends, out of good intention, strongly opposed the *moral selfishness* name. To be *selfish* is ugly and insulting, they voiced. "Why not use something more acceptable, like self-love or moral individualism, etc.?" I have been seriously tempted to give up the *selfish* part of the name; it may help to sell the philosophy. I have decided to keep it instead after much self-debate. Why? Selfishness is an integral part that makes life possible. It is a fact. I am not going to deny or hide what is true, like I am Chinese, for example. Keeping the (ugly) name also serves to constantly remind us of our predisposition and tendency to hurt; to be aware of the danger serves to protect us and helps us avoid it. When you are in possession of something dangerous, like a radioactive substance or a deadly animal such as a viper, will you not choose to constantly warn yourself? A classmate of mine dating back to primary school jokingly said to me at an alumni dinner, "Ah, Wok (my nickname), now everybody knows you are selfish!" I smilingly replied: "Thank you. I sure am." Put it this way, I am no longer ashamed to admit that I am selfish. If you want to know, my email address is iamselfish9@gmail.com. The "9" means forever. People always smile when they learn it. Incidentally, if you have any comment on the book, you can email me. Be sure to include the title of the book so that it won't be deleted before I read it. Thanks.

PART IV

IMPLEMENTING THE CHANGE,
THE ROLE OF A GOVERNMENT
AND
BUILDING A HAPPY PLANET

CHAPTER 21

We Now Have All That Is
Needed to Fix the Problems

To fix our damaged planet and to build a happy world are the goals of this book. In part 1, we have identified the sources of our planet's problems; they all have come from us, the people of the world. We have discovered that 1) all lives are selfish and 2) people are the same. A selfish organism naturally hurts in order to survive; humans are no different. However, human selfishness is different from the selfishness observed in all organisms. We destroy our environment and kill many of the living organisms in it because our species has godlike power.

In part 2, which deals with the evolution of our species, we found the reasons why our species has become so powerful. Our species has relied on intelligence and cooperation instead of muscle to compete. Intelligence and cooperation have allowed us to keep inventing new and more powerful tools to solve our problems; tools have given us more power than muscle. That is how we have gained godlike power. However, we don't have the wisdom to exercise our power; we are cruel gods to other species. To fix our damaged planet and to build a happy world, we need to find that wisdom, which shall be our new tool. In part 3, we found that tool, again through intelligence and cooperation working together. The new tool is a new morality based on the Golden Rule. The Golden Rule makes common sense and is found in the teaching of every religion. The Golden Rule, though simple, is very rich in wisdom, which can guide us to fix our planet. It is the right tool because (1) it specifically targets human hurtful behaviors, though this important goal was not clearly known to the persons who introduced it. And (2) it is universal, every major moral view has a similar version of it. It makes it easy for the Golden Rule to be widely accepted.

From part 1 through part 3, we identified the source of the planet's troubles. We can count on our intelligence and cooperation to fix the problems. And we also found the new morality we need. Everything we need to solve the problems is there and ready. The last step is to actually use them to change our world.

In part 4, we are going to explore how to implement what we have established so far to work for us. It would be slow, but certainly it can be and will be done someday. There will be road blocks. The most important block is our world is so divided that to get every country to agree on human selfishness is the source of the problems, and to adopt the two Golden Rule–based moral principles as the cure will not be easy. Strong resistance will come from religious leaders, because to remain in power they need to keep things the same. They will use their influence to fight any new idea that would weaken their position. The religious leaders and their followers will be our greatest enemies.

Still, I am very hopeful. My experience from chatting with many highly educated young travelers tells me that I don't need to despair. There are a whole bunch of these young people out there in the different corners of the planet. My effort in the foreseeable future will be trying to reach them. And the timing cannot be better. We now live in a world powered by the Internet. Spreading the message through social media will be fast. I shall try to learn to do it properly. The young people will carry the torch and be the driving force in realizing the change. These young minds are fresh and are willing to accept new ideas. They, in general, also believe in science and reason over doctrines and dogmas. I also have this unshakable belief that reason will prevail over theology, and science will trump religious beliefs in the end. This has been the unstoppable trend since science was born.

I am also 100 percent sure that we can solve the problems yoking our planet in the future, because now with biology and physics we can clearly see the selfish nature of living organisms is behind it. And more than ever, we now have a clear target, which is human selfishness, to shoot at and we also have the morality to fix it. I hope through reason and science, which are the foundations of the thesis of our book, more and more people will support it. They will then influence the government to make the change. Though the driving force to realize the change for a better world needs to come from the people, it will be a government that can effectively make the change. A governing body has to take a leading role.

What role should a government take? A government's role should at least cover the following areas:

Promoting Intelligence and Cooperation

From the knowledge we have gained through the evolution of our species, I am absolutely sure that fixing our planet begins with the continuous emphasis on the growth of intelligence and the strengthening of cooperation among the people of the world. This should be our overall goals, and let us never lose sight of the targets. Both start with building individuals who will be intelligent and are willing to work with others in a community and a country. These individuals will be our building blocks for a happy world. They are also the ones to inspire others to make the change. Then, the government focus will be on how to make these intelligent individuals also seek cooperation with others. But before we discuss the "how to" part, we need to understand what constitute intelligence and cooperation so that we clearly understand what is to be achieved.

Intelligence

Intelligence, by definition, is the ability to solve problems. At an individual level, intelligence should enable the individual to more than just meet the minimums of survival. It should allow him to live comfortably and happily. Then, he needs knowledge, which includes a number of basic science subjects to understand the world he lives in and moral right and wrong. He also needs a marketable skill that will allow him to earn an income. All of these can be acquired most effectively by going to school.

An individual also has an obligation to participate in solving the problems plaguing our planet. The three pressing problems are wars, environmental deterioration, and poverty. Then, he needs science to understand the real issues and the correct morality to deal with them. Again, the most effective way to gain such knowledge is by going to school.

Cooperation

Cooperation is a willingness to work with others for our common good. To get people to cooperate, we need two things: to have the correct moral view and to identify what will divide people. The correct moral view is certainly the Golden Rule–based morality, because as discussed the morality makes hurting people for self-gain immoral. According to our morality, the only kind of interaction with others will be to seek win/win, which, in essence, is to cooperate.

Next is to identify the people dividers. There are a number of things that divide people, making them uncooperative and often hurt others.

The People Dividers:

Religions and the Question of Whether to Accept Muslim Refugees

There is no doubt in my mind that religions divide people. Religion alone often makes people enemies of one another. There are many religions in the world. Since the main business of every religion is to worship God—and each religion has its own god—there are as many gods as there are religions. What every religion often tries to push will be its god is the only true one. This is no small matter; it is a point worth fighting and even dying for. Many wars between religions have been just that. Religions are often the reason for people to go to wars, sometimes not just between people of different religions. The followers of the same Bible or Koran often kill one another in the name of the same god. Reason has no place among the followers of religions. Further fueled by human selfishness, religions become the warm beds for wars. Make no mistake, the fighting between the followers of different religions or of the same religion has nothing to do with serving God, it serves only the selfish interests of those leaders. As a result, the followers of different religions are invariably very intolerant of others. Religions are one of the important factors why our world has been so cut up.

But some religions are worse dividers than others. Islam, for example, is extremely intolerant. Though sharing the same Koran, Islam is divided into two main branches, Sunni and Shiite, and from them a number of sects. The Muslim world, which includes the Arabian Peninsula, Middle East, many countries in Africa, and some countries in Asia, is a divided and often violent world. Intolerance leads to violence. The most violent and barbaric Muslim organization, no doubt, is ISIS, which often quotes scripture from the Koran to justify its many cruelties. A Muslim country is often a poor country where science and technology cannot thrive, which in turn leads to few industries and stagnant economies as a result. Ideology instead rules all Muslim countries; ideology suffocates science and reason. When ideology rules, intolerance and barbaric behaviors become commonplace, and most of its people suffer. That is what we have seen, and it is not going to end as long as ideology continues to dictate right and wrong.

Islam, from my limited research, is a very problematic religion. The problems all arise from Muslims' blind following of the Islamic ideology. The violence and intolerance of Islam come from the many teachings in the Koran, which collectively are grouped under the Sharia Law. The Sharia Law is the moral foundation of Islam. In light of the millions of refugees, most of whom are Muslims, who are seeking new homes in the western countries in the recent years, each country should know Islam better before making the decision to take them in. Countries like Canada, Sweden, France, and Germany are very naive in thinking multiculturalism is a strength. They also base their decisions on Christian ideology or ideals from humanity and strongly feel that it is their obligation to lessen the sufferings of those Muslims by accepting as many Muslim refugees into their countries as possible. I would like to caution them and to consider the following about Islam. Based on the principles of moral selfishness, a person or a country should do things according to two guidelines: Is it moral? And is it selfish? To be moral, a person or a country in pursuing its own interest *must not* intentionally hurt other countries for self-gain, and also *never* force others into accepting something; i.e., allow the country at the receiving end to freely choose. The US and Russia are the two countries that often violate the two moral principles. And to be selfish, a country should also consider its own benefits in the long run.

There are several points to consider before accepting Muslim refugees. Consideration #1 according to moral selfishness will be is it immoral for a wealthy and fully capable country *not* to accept someone gravely in need or danger? Most of the wealthy countries under consideration are western countries that follow the values set by Christianity. According to the teaching of Jesus, it almost is an obligation to help the poor and needy. That is why so many of these countries feel obligated. But another way to look at it will be, and I quote, *"The poor you will always have with you,"* Mathew 26:11. Even Jesus needed to look after himself first occasionally. What does this incident tell you if you really want to be a good Christian? It tells you that you need to take care of yourself too; you don't always need to give to be moral. Jesus did not always sacrifice himself. If you do, when will you stop? Do you stop when you have nothing left? Again, is it your moral obligation to help others? If you don't, does it make you immoral? Most of the versions of the Golden Rule do not say you must help, most of them do say one thing: don't hurt others. To help and to give is a gift to someone, it is also love. Are we obligated to give if we don't feel like doing it? Or to love everyone that is in need?

People or countries get into trouble for one reason or other—laziness, bad luck, or being born into a problematic religion like Islam. Common sense dictates that if you are not the reason for their misery you really are *not* obligated to do anything. If you do, it will be a gift from you to them. I don't believe that anyone is obligated to give if you are unwilling to or have better use for the money. If any countries should be obligated to take the refugees in, the first country will be the USA (but that is not what Donald Trump is doing; the guy is very shrewd), and then the UK, Australia, and Denmark—the countries that took part in the Iraq invasion, the war that set the genie in the bottle free. Not Germany, France, Sweden, or Canada.

Consideration #2 will be for selfish reasons. To be specific, what benefit will it bring to my country to accept those Muslim refugees? For (selfish) national interests, I believe a country should always put serving the interests of its people first. The top, top priority of every nation should always be its own people. Helping or serving the needs of the refugees on grounds such as human rights of the Syrian people, humanity, empathy, generosity, love, etc., etc. should be much lower. Following this morally selfish philosophy, my primary concern as a politician in deciding any policy will be and should be: how will taking in refugees benefit my own countrymen? Does this rationality make sense?

For immigrants to be beneficial in a long run, the most important question will then be how easy will it be to fully integrate them into the societies that accept them? Immigrants are foreigners; they come with a different culture and morality. Can they or are they willing to adapt to their new country's (moral) values? In considering integrating immigrants into one's society, not all immigrants are equal. Some are effortless, some take more time, and some are next to impossible and they will cause more trouble than good.

America, Canada, and Australia are good examples of countries built by immigrants. The earliest immigrants to America and Australia were Europeans—Irish, Germans, Dutch, French, or English. The transition for those different immigrants to their new country was quite smooth and uneventful. Why? Most of them were Christian and from democratic societies, and therefore shared similar values. They also strongly believed in science. What had divided them was their nationality, which, in a new country, hardly matters. And after the fall of Saigon, there were a huge number of Vietnamese refugees that went to the States and Canada. I happen to know quite a few of them. Most of them have successfully integrated into their new homeland. Many of them make a very good living, and their children become professionals and share the Canadian values. During the last few decades, more and more Chinese immigrants have come to Canada. Again, you don't hear much about this group of newcomers causing out-of-proportion problems.

Immigrants are not the same in terms of the ease with which they are integrated. If the many recent violent incidents in many countries—Belgium, France, Germany, and the US—are any indication, the Muslims are a group that will likely give any receiving country more headaches than benefits in the long run. I am not saying all the Muslims would cause trouble and get involved in violence, no. The fact still remains that much violence has been carried out by Muslims. Is it my prejudice? Is it by pure chance that most of those unfortunate events were linked to Muslims? Or is there a reason to it making it unavoidable? To be precise, we ask, are there some teachings in the Islamic ideology that give reasons to its followers to engage in violent acts? I have been very puzzled as well as curious to find out and have done a bit of digging myself. Let me caution you again, my digging has been far from thorough. I have not followed the Islamic faith before writing this section. Be warned that I am not an expert and can be biased. If I am, I do have my reasons for my conclusion.

Why will Muslims be difficult to integrate? Is there anything in the teaching of Islam that gives them justification to use violence, often including harming and even killing the innocent? To answer those questions I googled *Sharia/Shariah Law*. *Shariah* in Arabic literally means a path to be followed (to water). It covers both personal moral guide and Islamic law. The most important two sources of Sharia come from the i) *Sunnah,* which is a record of the conduct and words of the Prophet Muhammad, and ii) the Koran, allegedly to be the words of Allah revealed to the Prophet. Shariah Law is thus divine and cannot be challenged, according to most Muslims. Shariah Law is the foundation of Islamic law; it guides every aspect of a Muslim's personal life and has three components: his belief that Allah is the only true God; his character development to be humble, meek, kind, and avoid traits like dishonesty or pride; and his actions, which dictate how a Muslim should worship God—prayer, fasting, pilgrimage—and dealing with others.

To give you an idea of what Shariah Law is about, please let me quote a copy of the law in the Internet from www.billionbibles.org/sharia/sharia-law.html. According to the source, Sharia Law includes the following:

- Theft is punishable by amputation of the right hand
- Criticizing or denying any part of the Koran is punishable by death
- Criticizing Muhammad or denying that he is a prophet is punishable by death
- Criticizing or denying Allah, the god of Islam, is punishable by death
- A Muslim who becomes a non-Muslim is punishable by death
- A non-Muslim who leads a Muslim away from Islam is punishable by death
- A non-Muslim man who marries a Muslim woman is punishable by death
- A man can marry an infant girl and consummate the marriage when she is 9 years old
- Girls' clitoris should be cut (Muhammad's words, Book 41, Kitab Al-Adab, Hadith 5251)
- A woman can have one husband, who can have up to four wives; Muhammad can have more
- A man can beat his wife for insubordination
- A man can unilaterally divorce his wife; a woman needs her husband's consent to divorce
- A divorced wife loses custody of all children over six years of age or when they exceed it

- Testimonies of four male witnesses are required to prove rape against a woman
- A woman who has been raped cannot testify in court against her rapist(s)
- A woman's testimony in court, allowed in property cases, carries half the weight of a man's
- A female heir inherits half of what a male heir inherits
- A woman cannot drive a car as it leads to *fitnah* (upheaval)
- A woman cannot speak alone to a man who is not her husband or relative
- Meat to eat must come from animals that have been sacrificed to Allah; i.e., be "halal"
- Muslims should engage in *Taqiyya* and lie to non-Muslims to advance Islam

There are more, but this will be enough to give a reader some ideas. Please note that Shariah Law does not exist in Koran so tidily organized and presented in its entirety like the way the Ten Commandments are recorded in the Bible. It is scattered throughout the Koran, which is to be expected. To be prudent, I also strongly urge a reader to google a topic such as Islamic treatment of women, abandoning Islam, stealing, or adultery to satisfy himself. Better still, get a copy of the Koran and actually read the verses. I have done some reading regarding getting revenge; it is condoned and it is there.

I am fully aware that the source is very likely from a Christian organization; it could be biased. But sometimes, it is a good way to understand Islam from information provided by a competing religion if you can trust the provider. Though I have abandoned my Christian faith, I still trust that true Christians are honest people. In the same way, I have also learned that the four Gospels of the New Testament were assembled hundreds of years after Jesus passed away from a Muslim publication, information you would never find in any Christian publication. Given the technology of those days in recording events, one can imagine that there should be some errors, facts which are also pointed out by the same publication. Again, take my opinion with a grain of salt. Be warned that there will be a lot of denials and lies from Muslims to defend almost every single one of those punishments or treatments because to engage in *Taqiyya*, i.e., to lie—is moral to defend Islam. Enough said.

Stephen Y. Cheung, Ph.D.

I was shocked by the overt sexism, or more appropriately, misogyny and by the degree of violence of those very excessive punishments to a number of infractions. I was also struck by its extreme intolerance. I used to think that Confucianism is bad for women; Muhammad makes Confucius looked like a gentleman by comparison. In an Islamic world, women are well below men in status and are not free. According to Shariah Law, men can morally, and justifiably, treat women like third-class citizens, beating them up, disowning them, or killing them for extramarital sex. I also learned from a different reliable source that Muslims practice female genital mutilations (FGM). FGM is cruel; it is aimed at taking away the sexual pleasure of those women. It is not the same as male circumcision. Shariah Law is how Islam, like every religion, imprisons women. Though every existing religion imprisons women, Shariah Law is the cruelest and most unfair. And while followers of many religions are getting out of such practices, many Muslims still hold on to them.

Shariah Law is violent from the many excessive punishments prescribed. I learned that a Muslim judge may not always demand the hand of a thief to be cut off, but the punishment is there and has been occasionally carried out. Most Muslims will defend this cruel punishment by saying it is rarely carried out, or only those unrepentant thieves will get the treatment. But the fact remains it is there, and there is no justification to punishing someone so harshly for stealing, often for survival. What kind of mind was behind it? No civilized society would do that!

If you count the number of death penalties in Shariah Law, there are six; criticizing or denying any part of the Koran or the words of Muhammad, for example, can get you killed. It is not a lie; it has happened from time to time. And, abandoning Islam, called apostasy, is punishable by death, so is leading a Muslim away from Islam. I have abandoned my Christian faith. Thank goodness that Jesus is boundlessly forgiving. The death penalty also applies when a non-Muslim male marries a Muslim girl, even if the girl is willing. That is the reason why many parents kill their daughters—not even for marrying, but for dating non-Muslim males. Honor killings have happened in Canada, France, Germany, the UK. It will happen again and again as long as some Muslims still follow Sharia Law.

Islam is also extremely intolerant. Shariah Law justifies killing people who don't share their beliefs, like Allah is the only true God. You can't even criticize or deny any part of the Koran or the teachings, the words or the blamelessness of Muhammad. Muhammad is the Islamic version of Jesus in Christianity. Unlike Jesus, this guy did not believe in love or forgiving; there is no mercy in this Islamic Messiah. To kill someone just because he doesn't share your value or belief is extremely intolerant. This is the reason why many Islamic fanatics like ISIS have done the many violent and senseless cruelties against humanity. They often cited the Koran when they were chopping off the heads of the innocent. The level of intolerance is barbaric.

As I did more digging, I also discovered that Islam is a religion of war, in stark contrast to many Muslims' claim that it is a religion of peace. There are some verses in the Koran that justify warfare with Christians and Jews in the Arab world. That Islam often glorifies fighting, war, and aggression should not be a surprise, because Muhammad was himself a warrior. Islam was established through many wars against the many nonbelieving local tribes. In this regard, Muhammad was the only starter of a religion who was a warrior. Jesus, Moses, or Buddha was not. Jesus and Buddha were truly peace-loving men. A warrior believes in muscle and the law of the jungle like an animal; reason or fairness has no place in Muhammad's logic.

This is one of the reasons why the Islamic world will always be violent and turbulent. Islam is a divisive religion. The religion itself is divided into two branches following Muhammad's death, the Sunni and the Shiite. The two sides have not been able to peacefully resolve their differences; each of them has tried to suppress, quash, or kill the other instead. They have been doing it, like Muhammad, by muscle. The fighting has been nonstop since. Here is another example of what human selfishness without the guidance of a correct morality can do; it is endless killing. The attitude of Muslims toward nonbelievers, the infidels, is even harsher. It is not a secret that Islam at one time had been spread by war. After a Muslim leader conquered a region, the male prisoners were often killed. However, others were given a choice to convert to Islam and be spared. When your other option is death, it is not much of a choice, is it?

A society ruled by an Islamic majority often treats its citizens differently, and a Muslim always gets better treatment than a non-Muslim. Malaysia is such a country that has established policies to discriminate ethnic Chinese. If a country accepts Muslims into it, there is always a danger in the future when their number has reached a point for them to flex their muscle and demand that things should be done according to Shariah Law. It has been attempted in Canada. Beware, Islam is not an accommodating religion; it is the most divisive.

The prime minister of Canada Justin Trudeau thinks that multiculturalism is a strength in arguing in favor of accepting Syrian refugees. He is either naive or is intentionally omitting an important assumption, and the assumption is that the Muslims are willing to work toward the same goal, the Canadian values, if you know what they are. Will Muslims be a cooperative force or divisive force in a western country? It is not a cooperative force from what we have seen so far, is it? If promoting cooperation between its people is the way to make a country stronger and richer, Islam is not that force, not likely. The "multiculturalism is strength" argument does not apply to Muslims.

In Islam, a believer often has no choice. Muslims don't have the choice to abandon Islam, and from birth their parents will strongly shape or force them into believing Islam. For those children that resist, guess what the parents will do? Once a Muslim, a person will always be a Muslim. Shariah Law will often trump the law of the land. Giving people no freedom to choose makes Shariah Law immoral according to our Golden Rule–based morality. Having no freedom to choose is quite evident in the penalty for apostasy. Once you become a Muslim, whether by choice or by birth, you have no choice but to stay. It is a trap; getting out is no longer an option.

On top, if you happen to be a Muslim woman, your freedom to choose is further restricted. You can't freely choose who you can marry, love, or even talk to. Your legal right is often halved compared to a man's. Whether you are a man or woman, you don't have a choice to exercise your reasoning either, especially when it comes to the content of the Koran or the many things Muhammad said and did. Sharia Law greatly limits, if not suffocates, a believer's reasoning. If you cannot use your reasoning, it kills your intelligence. There seems a general trend that a Muslim country will be very behind in science. When you are weak in science, your industries cannot grow and your people will be poor in general. This, together with the intolerant nature of Islam, are the reasons why there will always be waves of refugees from Muslim countries. When would you stop helping? The religion is a warm bed for chaos, a reason for never-ending poverty and therefore refugees.

Islam also condones revenge: an eye for an eye. The verse is in 2:194, and the punishment has been repeatedly and literally carried out. It sounds right and just on the surface: you pay up what you owe and help to balance the credit to the debit side. The problem will be that when a person is carrying out revenge, he will rarely be reasonable enough to take out the exact amount owed, it is often done with interest. The receiving end invariably feels violated and thus wants to get even. This vengeful mentality is the reason that once a war or conflict has been started there will be no end to it. The Sunnis have killed a number of Shiites; now, it is the Shiites' turn to get even. And so on, from now to eternity.

Be very careful when you come across Muslims. Some get offended easily and sometimes most innocently. I have learned it the hard way. I have since made it a policy not to engage. I accepted what had happened, learned my lesson, and walked away without saying anything or even looked at the guys. I have also decided never to have anything to do with them again.

Muslims, according to what I have learned from Shariah Law, which is the foundation of their morality, believe in an extremely intolerant, violent, misogynous, cruel, and tyrannical god, a god ruled by fear. That is the picture one gets according to the Koran and Shariah Law and the words of Muhammad. So should a western country like Germany, Sweden, the Netherlands, or Canada volunteer to accept many Muslim refugees? The answer is yes, if you don't have anything better to do with you euros or dollars and most of your own countrymen's needs have been well looked after. Yes, if you still think Muslims will enhance multiculturalism and will be easily integrated to be beneficial. Or it is still your moral obligation to mend something that is not broken by you.

What if you still want to do it? What if you can't fully integrate those refugees? From having no freedom to abandon the faith, most Muslims and their children will still be Muslims; their number can only grow. That is a fact, and from what we have seen. A significant number of Muslims will still adhere to Shariah Law. And it only takes a very small percentage, say 0.1 percent, of them to turn violent. That 0.1 percent can harm you, as the French, UK, Belgian, and German governments have painfully learned. Most of the terrorists are also homegrown. Why so ungrateful? You still can't believe it has happened. There is a reason, and the reason is that some of them, especially the young, educated, and the underemployed feel that they have been discriminated upon, whether it is real or imaginary.

To the discriminated, it is ugly. Discrimination fosters anger, and if unresolved, then develops into hatred. When it gets to this stage, the persons are ready to destroy and kill. Shariah Law readily gives them the moral grounds to do so. This is how I see the situation.

So do you still want to take many Muslim refugees in? Are the needs of all your countrymen taken care of and you don't have a better way to spend your euros? I know for a fact that Canada can ill afford to considering the many infrastructure that need repairing, the many homeless, the unemployed, the veterans, the needy seniors, the nation and millions of its people drowning in debt. If you want to appease your conscience, you can send money and materials to the refugee camps. Taking them in is stupid for the reasons given.

Let me put it in another way. If a country is likened to your home, will you take a stranger who doesn't share your values and who has a history of violence and intolerance into your home? And while some of your own family members need your help? If you still want to accept him, where are you going to put him? In the garage or basement? And you will never want him to come in the family room or eat with your family. You get around by car, he has to walk or take the public transit. You have a lot of luxury, he just manages to survive. In short, you are not treating them like your own. On one side, you show him your kindness and expect him to be grateful and start to contribute in the future. On the other side, you also discriminate him. Do you think they will remain grateful for your generosity, particularly those who are the second generation? If not, then you have created more headaches and heartaches than you can handle. *The guys are now in your home!*

The question remains, given that religions divide people, how should a government treat the various religions that already exist in a country so that they will not cut up a country and thus weaken the country? The answer will still be from our Golden Rule–based principles: (1) If the follower of a particular religion who, based on the teachings of his religion intentionally causes harm to a nonbeliever, he is immoral and has committed a crime. And depending on the seriousness of the harm, he must be punished. (2) If a follower, also based on the teachings of his religion, does not give people choice in certain matters, he is immoral. And again, depending on the seriousness, also needs to be stopped. If the followers of a religion keep violating the two principles, then I think it will be justified to ban the religion. If the followers of various religions can stick to these two principles, then and only then can multiculturalism and having multiple religions be a strength. Again, I think a government, for the good of the country, should try to eliminate a religion whose followers keep violating the two principles.

Race and Culture

Different race usually comes with cultural difference, which leads to unacceptable behaviors, which again leads to discrimination and division of people. The Chinese immigrants to America prior to 1965 were mostly poorly educated and came with some bad habits, like spitting and poor personal hygiene, to name a couple. As a result, they were discriminated against. I immigrated to Canada in 1968. I came with a bachelor's degree in science and used to be a high school teacher in Hong Kong. I went to British Columbia and I did not experience any in-your-face discrimination, most people were in fact quite polite. But that was only at the surface. I often got rejected with smiles instead. I still dislike Vancouver and British Columbia in general because of my initial bad experience.

Discriminating against people who look different and behave differently is, I think, in our gene, it has a long root dating back from chimps. Chimps discriminate against other chimps from a different group, often trying to kill chimps that don't belong. It has survival value. In our modern societies, however, such discrimination only weakens a society, and that is why every advanced society has laws to stop discrimination.

The discrimination arising from race and culture will gradually subside as the immigrants begin to adopt the values of their new country. Children growing up in a new country usually can be fully integrated. I have not come across any noticeable discrimination against me for years. My two daughters, both born in North America, have completely melted in and integrated into Canadian society. The Chinese, from my own example and from what I have seen, are great immigrants to have. Please forgive my advertisement for my own group of people; though mostly white in value at the core, my heart is still yellow.

Stephen Y. Cheung, Ph.D.

Income Levels

Poor and rich people don't normally mix, especially when the poor are clearly visible. The discrimination against the blacks is a serious problem in the US. The discrimination often results in blacks being gunned down for rather minor infractions or even for no obvious reason. The discrimination against the blacks has obviously come from their financially poor standings than other factors. As long as the huge gap in income level exists between the blacks and the other groups, especially the whites, no amount of propaganda in racial equality and against racial discrimination will make it go away.

High Crime Rate

Poor people are also more prone to commit crimes, especially when you are poor and are full of desires and wants but have no means to get them legally. It would be naive to blame the discrimination against the blacks only on the widespread poverty of this group. The discrimination is likely from the out-of-proportionally high crime rate among the young blacks. According to one source, *the blacks accounted for 39.4 percent of the prison and jail population in 2009, more than any other ethnic group. The incarceration rate of black males was over six times higher than that of white males, with a rate of 4,749 per 100,000 US residents.* So I have good reason to believe that the discrimination against the blacks, the males mostly, has come from the high rate of violent crimes they often engage in. Is it wrong to do so? It may not be right, but certainly the discrimination is based on the obvious facts. If you are a police officer, will you not treat a black male with more caution? If there is a violent crime and you are looking for suspects, will you not go to where you are more likely to get the guys? Is a decision based on past experience and facts for you to treat black males unfavorably unjustified? You will be very stupid if you don't, and you will soon be dead.

I am sure by just asking those inconvenient questions will make me a racist for many politically right minded. But I don't think being politically right is always a good thing. If being politically right is not to say anything bad about others, and to do so at the price of not bringing out the facts and allow ignorance to continue, I would rather choose being politically wrong. If people don't know the reason for a problem, and it has been a very serious problem, you will never be able to fix it. I have brought out the reason for the discrimination because understanding it is the first step toward solving it. If the blacks in America are to be free from discrimination, the government must try to eliminate the poverty that has plagued this group. And there is a way. Please read on.

Political Parties

It seems odd that the political parties of a country, something that a democratic system is based upon, should be the reason to divide people, and thus make it much harder for people in the same country to cooperate. In Canada, we have three big parties, the Conservative, the Liberal, and the NDP, each representing the interests of a group of people. NDP is known for its support of the labor sector, the unions especially. The Conservative is more for people that hold on to traditional values and is aligned with the Christianity. While the Liberals are more free thinking, perhaps?

The Americans are divided into two camps: the Democrats and the Republicans, each with its clearly defined policies. While the other dividers can be fixed by the correct moral view or by a committed policy, there appears no way to repair and to reunite people cut up by their parties. Having more than one party is currently a structural part of democracy, like life must be selfish to survive. As a result, you seldom see the Democrats fully and wholeheartedly support the Republicans, and vice versa. Some intrinsically good policies—gun control proposed by the Democrats, for example—are routinely vetoed by the Republicans. If cooperation is a positive force in a country, and for that matter, any community as we have so far emphasized, then maybe it is time for us to look at this system of having multiple parties to make democracy work. We shall discuss this point again in a later chapter.

The above are the more significant dividers of people I can think of, there may be more. How would a governing body deal with the people dividers? The answer, I believe, is still our Golden Rule–based morality, because the two principles together will guide people not to hurt others and to allow others to freely choose. If the people can do that, then having different ideas, views, or religious beliefs will be a beautiful thing and a strength. That is why having a correct moral view is so, so important if a country is to do well; i.e., to make happy people that live in harmony.

Educating the Citizens

The most effective way to promote the growth of both intelligence and cooperation among people is education—education, education, and education. To educate its citizens is therefore an important role of a government. Educating an individual has several parts.

Preparing a Child for Education

Educating a person begins when he is a child. It begins years before he goes to school. For education to be successful—i.e., for a person to learn what he is supposed to learn (in school)—a child needs to be properly prepared or primed by his parents or parent. The preparation starts right after a child is born by giving the child the care and love he needs. The care and love provider naturally is a parent, usually the mother. A better job can be done if both parents take part. If a child is well nurtured, he will begin to trust people around him, starting by trusting the parent or caregiver, and then extend to more people around him. When nurtured properly, it will lay the foundation for a child to trust his teachers when he goes to school, to follow the teachers' instructions and learn. A well-nurtured child is likely to be a healthy and happy child who is full of curiosity about the world around him. He will be an eager learner.

Supporting a Child in Learning

The preschool preparation of a child by his parent or parents is the first part. When a child goes to school, a parent needs to keep monitoring the child's progress to see how the child is doing. Is he keeping up? Is there any problem for him to fit in with other students? Keeping an eye on a child's progress and helping him if there is problem will make a child's experience in school much more enjoyable. An enjoyable experience will make learning in school much more fruitful.

Monitoring a child's progress includes spending time with him to do the homework, if any, during the earlier years. Providing a child with a home environment conducive to learning is also a must.

The Things Students Should Learn

Education is an important source of intelligence. It is a crucial part to equip him with the knowledge to make a decent living and to make an individual who will take part in fixing the planet. What do we need to teach an individual in school? Education, I think, should cover at least four areas: (1) To impart upon the individual the correct moral view, which is our proposed Golden Rule–based molarity. (2) A knowledge that an individual can count on to understand the world he lives in. That knowledge is the various science subjects, such as math, physics, chemistry, biology, and social science. 3) A skill that an individual can market to make a comfortable living. 4) How to cooperate with others. Missing any of the four will be a failure.

Let me explain each of the four points.

1. Why teach our Golden Rule–based morality? Because it is the morality, and is the only morality, which can teach a person how to properly and harmoniously deal with others around him and fix our planet's many problems, all of which are the consequences of human selfishness. The morality specifically aims at removing the harm caused by selfishness. Because the Golden Rule is universal, using it as the guideline of moral right and wrong will be easy for every religion and culture to accept.

   And by using the Golden Rule to decide right and wrong, we can build a legal system based on it. Such a legal system will be simple, clear, and unambiguous, and thus easy for every citizen to understand and follow. Thus, issues like abortion, same-sex marriage, or euthanasia, etc. which have divided the people in even the most advanced countries will no longer be issues. The laws based on the morality of the Golden Rule will truly serve the interests of people rather than the interests of a particular group.

From the Golden Rule–based morality, we can also develop a concept called moral selfishness. For reasons already discussed in the previous chapter, morally selfish people are the only hope to realizing a paradise on earth. No other moral view can do that; instead, they divide the world and will only bring war, environmental degradation, and perpetuate poverty. The existing moral views are the reasons why our world is in such a mess. Our moral view, because it forbids hurtful human behaviors, will also make people cooperate.

2. Why emphasize science? And not arts, music, or other branches of philosophy? Science is based on reason and facts. Math is the foundation of most science subjects. Math trains a person to reason; rationality, not blind religious beliefs, is the hope to solving our problems. Science subjects—physics, chemistry biology, and social science—are based only on verifiable facts and therefore very reliable information. To solve our problems and to heal our damaged planet, we need dependable information, not theology or myths. Science gives us a very reliable road map about how our world operates; it provides the information we can pick and choose to solve our problems. Science has now provided us with all the information and technology to solve our planet's problems.

3. To be able to acquire a skill to make a comfortable living is critical to having a productive and thus happy life. An employed person will be able to pay taxes and thus support his society or country, instead of being a dead weight to others.

During the many past dynasties in China, education was to exclusively study Confucius's philosophy and teachings. A typical Confucian scholar had no other knowledge other than Confucius's ideology. He was only good for two jobs: a post in the government or teaching Confucianism. Most of them had no idea how to solve people's problems. Those who could not work for a government (and there were too many), often found themselves without any skill for any employment and ended up living a poor life and died unfulfilled.

Many countries, the many developed ones included, still offer university subjects that give students very little hope of finding employments. Students often become unemployed after graduation and are stuck with rather substantial student loans. Their governments have certainly failed them by not guiding and providing them the education that will lead them to jobs. I don't think the goal of education should just be to satisfy some curiosity; it will be a waste without considering employment. Many wealthy countries like Germany, the Netherlands, and Sweden, etc. have educational systems which take students' future employment into account.

4. To impart upon students the value of cooperation should certainly be an inseparable part of a successful education. There should be two simultaneous approaches: reinforcement of cooperation and prevention of division. Teaching moral selfishness not only will provide the guidance, practicing the morality will keep reinforcing it. It will also help for an educational system to design activities that aim at reinforcing cooperation among students. We have already identified what will divide people, a responsible government should keep track of them to prevent people from straying and weakening the cooperation among them.

For a community or country to have intelligent and cooperative people does not happen by chance, a government needs to cultivate and work toward achieving them. A government, by building individuals who have the correct moral view, have strong knowledge in science, have marketable skills to earn comfortable livings, and are willing to work with others will be our building blocks for a paradise-like planet. If more and more governments and countries will adopt our moral view and take part in building those individuals, then our planet will be gradually and surely transformed into a paradise, a world without borders, war, pollution, or poverty. Our morality is the hope, and the only hope, to realize this beautiful dream. It is doable; I know for sure because I have adopted it and it has changed me into a better person.

To End War, Pollution, and Poverty

It will ultimately be government that should take a leading role in ending the big three that have been damaging and wrecking our planet. And the first step to achieving those targets must be for every government to decide to adopt the Golden Rule as the only moral decision maker. It is then and only then that our moral view on right and wrong can be unified, like the way the world's traffic signals have been unified. The Golden Rule–based morality is cultural neutral and targets only human hurtful behaviors and forbids them. It can be easily accepted by different countries and is effective in preventing damaging behaviors such as war, pollution, or having children irresponsibly, which is the reason that poverty exists. Let us spend some time to explain why adopting our moral views will enable us to achieve our goals to first heal our planet and then make it a paradise.

1. To Stop Wars: A war is invariably started by a leader of a country, sometimes to serve the interests of a country. But more often than not, a leader starts a war against another country or even his people to serve his interests or those of an elite few. The invasion of Iraq by the America-led allies was a good example. Bush could start the invasion because the majority of Americans did not see anything wrong with such a war. Same applied to the people in the UK, Australia, and Denmark. People did not and could not see starting a war against another nation is intrinsically an immoral act because their traditional moral views often glorified war. Every existing morality thinks it is OK to invade another nation or kill your enemy. As long as we still hold on to such a moral view, be it a Christian view, Islamic view, or Confucian view, war is often condoned by the people of an invading nation.

   Our Golden Rule–based morality says it is wrong to intentionally hurt another person or nation for self-gain. Period. It doesn't further qualify who that party will be. That person can be your enemy, morally you are still not allowed to hurt him. That country can be a Muslim country or Communist country with very different ideology, you will still be immoral if you start a war against it. That is according to the Golden Rule.

A reader should know by now that I have a strong dislike of Muslims because of the Sharia Law they follow. However, it does not justify me hurting any of them. It is OK if I choose not to deal with the group; it would be immoral if I act out my dislike for them by hurting anyone of them. That is what the Golden Rule is about: hurting others intentionally is rarely justified and is immoral.

If every country makes laws based on the Golden Rule, then the Golden Rule will be like the traffic light that decides the morality of a behavior. Then, if a leader of a country starts a war against another nation or against whoever, the whole world, including the people of the invading and the invaded nations, will see it as wrong, the invasion will be wrong like someone running a red light. When and only when every country on our planet has a Golder Rule–based morality will there be no more war. It is a situation worth working hard for, isn't it?

2. To Stop Polluting Our Environment: If the whole world has a common moral view—i.e., our Golder Rule–based morality— then, everyone will agree that polluting the environment is immoral and therefore wrong. Then, everyone will see producing oil from the tar sand is very polluting, is immoral, and boycott buying oil from Canada. This of course will not happen overnight. If we can keep mounting the pressure for Canada to stop, and when enough Canadians are against it because it is immoral, the change will come from the top. Then, electing a prime minister for Canada will significantly be decided by a candidate that will do more to stop pollution. To have any hope of stopping a highly polluting but also highly profitable industry, a government must take the lead to make laws to end it.

Same will gradually apply to our reliance on fossil fuel. When enough people realize that our reliance on fossil fuel is producing too much carbon dioxide and hurting many aquatic lives and is immoral, more and more people will support the switch to renewable forms of energy. With the production of carbon dioxide reduced, there will be a point when the green plants can fully recycle the harmful gas. We don't need to wean from fossil fuel completely as long as the use does not exceed the recycling capacity of plants.

Carbon dioxide is hardly the only pollutant we need to worry about. On top, we have industrial wastes that, besides laying waste to the land and water next to their sources, will eventually end up in the oceans. Unless stopped, the industrial wastes, like carbon dioxide, will build up to a level that begins to cause great harm to our planet.

For everyone to see polluting the air, the waters, or the land is wrong morally, we need a unified standard, the Golder Rule–based morality. When that happens, the various forms of pollution can be stopped because by then everyone will know it is wrong. We can clean up the environment in the future. Many of the European countries are taking steps in eliminating pollutants; they are setting great examples.

3. To End Poverty: Poverty, other than a source of suffering for billions, also spawns criminal activities. And poverty divides people. The reason, and the only reason, we have poverty in so many societies and countries is simple: people who are absolutely not qualified to have children keep producing them, like the Panamanian bitch discussed in a previous chapter. As a result, their children do not receive the love or even the basic care they deserve and need. As a result, they don't know what love or care is because they have never tasted it. And as a result, they, in turn, will not be able to give care and love to their children. The cycle goes on.

On top, the children from poor parents usually cannot and often do not get good education. They usually grow up without a moral sense or the skills to make a decent living. These children will have high probabilities to become criminals. Unless something is done by a governing body to break the cycle, poverty will self-perpetuate. The way to stop the cycle is to prevent unqualified parents from freely procreating. How? By recognizing that it is morally wrong to hurt others, their own children, whether intentionally or by ignorance.

Plain and simple: unqualified parents are hurting their own children. To satisfy their sexual needs, to get more government welfare money, or to gain fame in a rare case, parents produce children with very grim outlooks. The parents often have a choice while their children are forced into poverty, which often turn them into criminals. That is why those parents are immoral. Some may argue that those parents don't intentionally harm their children, they are just ignorant. But that does not make it acceptable, does it? So obviously it should be a government's job to educate those unqualified parents that they will be hurting their children by their inability to give them the things they need and it is wrong. The government should also educate the general public on methods for birth control and family planning.

But that is not what we see among the hundred-plus countries on the globe, from the top of the top countries like Japan and the Scandinavian countries, to the absolute worst like many countries in Africa. No government has looked at having children without the ability to provide for them as immoral or even a crime. How do most countries treat the unqualified parents? All of them still allow them to freely procreate, whether by choice or driven by Mother Nature. In rich countries, they support those planless and clueless parents with government subsidies. They treat it as the right thing to do. None of us up to now have seen it as an immoral act, and in some cases should be a crime, like women drinking heavily while pregnant.

While many poor parents have more children because of ignorance, many deliberately do so. Many do it for more subsidies from their governments. But the most blatant case belongs to a Californian woman named Nadya Suleman who, through a medical doctor's help, produced eight children. "What is wrong with that?" you ask. Considering she already had six children, was an unemployed single mom, was likely on welfare, and likely had been unable to provide her existing children with the care and love they needed to grow up into productive members of society, would anyone with any moral sense consider doing it? There is absolutely no reason for any caring parent in her situation to consider having more children. Not her. Why this madness? She had an idea in mind and that did not have anything to do with the happiness of her children. She wanted to break the record of giving birth to the most surviving children in a single pregnancy and to profit from it. Sadly, she was successful. On January 26, 2009, she delivered eight children in a single birth. This should be an ugly and sickening occasion. But this was not how the Americans saw it. Most took it as an occasion for celebration. Few, if any, thought of it as morally wrong and thus condemned the insane attempt.

This is what having a confused and outdated moral view will do to a society, even to the country having the most advanced scientific knowledge. What should be alarming was that she got a medical doctor to be complicit. Medical doctors are supposed to be highly intelligent professionals. It makes you wonder where was the moral sense of the doctor?

The "freely procreate" belief did not happen by accident. It has the blessing of the Christian church. In fact, all religions condone or at least don't think of it as immoral for unqualified parents to have more children. The collective ignorance of the religions is justifiable because they were all founded at times when we were very ignorant. But how can countries like the US, Canada, UK, and Germany remain ignorant today despite their advances in science, biology in particular? So the perpetuation of poverty is not just by ignorance of the poor parents, it has been sponsored by governments and promoted by religions, Christianity in particular.

How can that happen? Governments are run by politicians whose top priority is often not to solve the social problems of their countries. Rather, their main concern is to get elected and to serve their own interests. Many of them don't have the knowledge to see that it is wrong. Rather, they are, in general, very shrewd and clever by staying politically correct and not saying anything that may upset their voters. Even if they know—and that is a very big *if*—they have more important private agendas to serve than solving the problem of poverty.

So how do we stop poverty? The driving force, I firmly believe, has to come from the general public, especially the educated and people guided by reason, the scientifically inclined minds. Through our morality, they will see the immorality of free procreation and stop it. Before that happens, politicians will not join the force, a government will not take the lead, and poverty will go on and on.

Permit for Children

From the above discussion, we can clearly see that poverty comes from unqualified parents who keep having children. They do so either from ignorance or from an erroneous moral view held by their government. So the way to end poverty is quite simple: (1) A government must realize that for parents to have children but being unable to properly provide for them is hurting the children and is thus immoral, it must be stopped. (2) Educate the public about responsible parenthood; it should include planning and contraception. A government must first toss away the old, confusing, and often erroneous moral view and embrace the two Golden Rule–based moral principles, then we can certainly stop poverty in a relatively short time. By adopting the two principles, a government will immediately see free procreation is often immoral and must be stopped. It is like knowing stealing is immoral and must be stopped. Makes sense?

To effectively stop poverty, I would like to propose something called *Permit for Children*. Before parents can have children, they must first apply to a governing body for approval. When I first introduced this idea to a friend, she reacted very emotionally and was fiercely against it. The policy would give the government too much control. And to start doing that would soon jeopardize the freedom people have fought so much to gain were the reasons she objected. She had good reason to be upset and would not allow me to elaborate. The reaction of a German woman was more subdued, though the same unease existed. It immediately and painfully reminded her of Hitler's cruelty. Like a reflex, she did not like the idea at all. But unlike my friend, she chose to listen to my reasons.

First, I compared the idea of Permit for Children to needing a permit to practice law, medicine, being a mechanic, or almost every profession in any developed country. A permit is to ensure the person is qualified to do what he does, and more importantly, to protect consumers. She agreed. Seeing the positive response, I asked her, "Do you think parenthood does not need to be qualified?" I paused to allow her to chew over the comparison. "Do you think everybody is fit to be parent? If he or she is not, who will get hurt?" Noting that she was undecided, I therefore asked her the two questions to guide her along. Then, she said, "I guess not everyone is fit to be a parent. If not, the children will be harmed. And I knew some bad parents." She began to agree. "But isn't it a cold and heartless policy?" She disclosed what really concerned her. Then, I began to see where she was coming from and I could address her unease. "It depends on the execution and how it is implemented," I said. Instead of cold and heartless, it could be done with a lot of care and compassion. A government needs a lot of planning and preparation before making it a law. Above all, a government needs understanding and finesse to get it through. There should be stages in the execution.

Stage I: Educating the Public

By using tens or hundreds of everyday people's examples, make it abundantly clear that procreation without planning hurts their children because they are often deprived of the two most important things for them to grow up to be happy: i) the children often have the care and love they need taken away by irresponsible parents, and ii) they are likely to grow up with little education because the environment in their homes is not conducive to learning. The two messages should be delivered with absolute clarity so that everyone in a society will see this connection between irresponsible parenthood and poverty.

Regardless whether parents are ignorant, careless, or greedy, I don't think any of them would knowingly want to give their own children such a bad start in life that often leads to misery. Many just don't know. Besides educating the poor and ignorant, the educating stage also will get more and more people, even the religious ones, on side with the Permit for Children policy. If there is a human right (you know my very unpalatable view on the human rights)I think everyone should have the right to be born to responsible parents so that he does not have to start life at a disadvantaged position that often is impossible to overcome.

Stage II: Implementing the Law

Before making it law, a government should let the citizens know that irresponsible procreation is immoral. The only way to establish this argument is by adopting the two Golden Rule–based moral principles. Failing that, some people will still think life is sacred and it will be their duty to bring more lives into the world. Or the argument from human rights will prevail. The right that every human being should be able to freely procreate has no moral grounds. When exercising your "right" hurts someone—that will be the children in the case of irresponsible procreation—you should not and will not be allowed to have that right. If you have doubt, please check the definition of *freedom* in a previous chapter.

If we can all see irresponsible procreation as immoral, then we have the duty to stop that, just like stopping stealing, robbery, or rape. It will simplify the issue, will it not?

Stage III: Execution

In implementing Permit for Children as law, it would help if the government would employ both push and pull. I mean there should a penalty for violating it and reward or help for people following the rule.

Penalty for violation: Like being a doctor or legal advisor without a license, a violator could and should face certain penalties. To take away the child born without a permit should be considered, depending on the situation of the noncompliant parents. Again, tact is very important in doing so. You don't just go in and seize the child and leave the parents grieving. No, a compassionate government will never do that. If the media finds out, it would have disastrous results. You assign a social worker to follow, to discuss, to monitor the situation, and to gather information. At a certain point, it should be easy to make a decision on whether or not to do it. If yes, how to do it to minimize the pain of the parents.

The best way should be by talking some sense into the parents. The social worker would explain to the parents that it would not be to their benefit or their child's to continue. First of all, because the parents don't have the permit, they would not and should not receive any government grant for having the child. There would not be any benefit for them.

Because they don't have the resource, the child would become a big burden. At certain point, and if enough information is provided to the parents, they would eventually see their mistake of having the child and be willing to give him away for adoption—a choice that would benefit both parties. Again, the whole process will be done with understanding and empathy.

Benefits for Compliance: For those parents who first apply before having children, a government should encourage the compliance with some benefits. It should start from the pregnancy period. Not every pregnant woman knows how to take care of herself at this stage. A social worker should be assigned to each potential mom, teaching her the things she should know for a healthy pregnancy: what to eat and to exercise, etc. There should be quite a few things to learn.

The first few months following the birth of a child can be quite taxing for new parents. During the first few weeks after my first child was born, for example, her umbilical cord was drying up and began to fall off. My first ex did not know it was natural; she taped the cord to keep it in place. When I bathed my daughter, I smelled some rotting flesh. It came from her tummy. I soon found the tape and carefully removed it, and the rotting cord fell right off. I washed her belly button with some rubbing alcohol and dried the area; she was fine.

Giving a newborn a bath is another challenge. You don't want the water too hot or too cold. You also need to hold her securely so that she won't slip out of your hand and start drowning, at the same time without applying too much force to bruise her. Changing diapers will be another struggle. A baby usually doesn't cooperate to make it easy. Or, your child suddenly gets sick, which happened almost with regularity with my first child. How do you deal with it? Are you going to take the child to the ER and spend hours waiting in distress every time? There are many more things new parents need to learn.

To give parents who follow the rule some financial benefit will make them happy to comply. And it should not be too expensive to give new parents some free items—milk, formula, and diapers to make their life easier. Parenthood is a job no less important than any of the professions, most of us are not ready and are ill prepared for it. We can all appreciate some timely help and information to make it one of the most enjoyable experiences—for the parents and the child—instead of a stressful journey full of hits and misses.

By helping parents who apply, a government is also sending a message to the people: we care. We care because we, the government, like the parents, want your child to grow up happy and productive. You will not be alone in bringing up your child; we are here to help. This message will also help to make it easy for people to support the Permit for Children policy.

Then, the question will be: with the added costs to manage the permit and all the incentives, can a government afford it? There is hardly a country in the world that is not running a perpetual annual deficit, how does a country finance it? The same should apply to providing free education, and that is far more expensive. Despite the high price tag, no developed country has ever considered cutting corners on it. Why? A country cannot afford not to do so. Investing in children is always a sound policy. It is sound because it brings many benefits to a country. To invest in children is to increase their likelihood to be productive and to be good citizens; the flip side will be very costly. Not only will they not grow up gainfully employed, the chance for them to become criminals is quite high, as we have already agued in a previous chapter. It is exceedingly costly to process a criminal—the policing, the justice system, and then the jail time. So it will be far cheaper than not doing it.

Criteria for Granting a Permit

Whether the program will succeed or fail also hinges heavily on how a government would decide who will be granted a permit. Many people object to this idea because they fear that a government may use that as a tool to discriminate against certain groups of people and even use it as an excuse to exercise genocide. So the criteria must not have anything that is based on race or ethnicity. It should be quite easy to do given the issue is so well-known. The focus on the criteria should be how likely is it for the applicants to successfully bring up happy and productive citizens. Or are the applicants fit to be parents. This should be the only consideration.

The following are the points I can think of to qualify parents, there can be more. And how much weight each criterion carries should be carefully worked out by a government.

1. Do the applicants have the financial capability to provide for another child? Are they on welfare? If yes, for how long? Some readers may be turned off by using the financial situation as a deciding factor. I would say let us be realistic: not having enough money will certainly make it hard to meet a child's growing needs—food, shelter, clothing, and stationery supplies, which will likely include a computer. I grew up rather poor. When I went to primary school, my family lived in a ghetto in Kowloon, Hong Kong, for a few years. I never had my own room or a permanent bed. As a result, I grew up carrying an inferiority complex that took me many years to learn to deal with. It still resurfaces once in a while without my knowing. I still harbor this deep fear of not having enough money, a feeling my two daughters do not seem to share. There should be a cutting line at a certain financial point that some parents should wait for their situation to improve before being granted the permit. It will be for their good as well as their children's. People who are on perpetual welfare should never be allowed. Let their line be terminated together with the genes they are carrying. Having children should be a privilege, not a right.

2. How many children do the applicants already have? And if they have children, how well are the children doing? Children needs care and love, they also need their parents to guide them and impart upon them some moral sense and discipline. These things all take time. Without these, they will not be different from animals, running wild and undisciplined. They will be headaches and heartaches for anyone unfortunate to come across them. I am sure a reader has come across this type of children. Not good, is it? They are the ones who scream to get what they want, which is one of their preferred weapons in public.

3. What are the conditions of the home? Is it clean and tidy, or dirty and messy? A person's home is often a very reliable way to tell how well a person can look after things. He is going to look after his child the same way he looks after his home.

4. Is there any sign of an applicant's bad habits? Some serious bad habits are heavy drinking, chain smoking, or doing drugs. The bad habits not only will harm the person doing it, they shall also negatively impact the children. The signs left by bad habits are

difficult to hide. When unsure, the social worker can simply ask. Habitual heavy drinking women should never be allowed to have children, because they will irreversibly damage their children's brain during pregnancy and thus condemn their children to miserable lives, which for the males often end in jail, and for the women often in getting killed very young. So should the drug users be banned.

5. How stable is the applicant's financial situation? Or more precisely, to find out the employment history of the main breadwinner. Is he skilled or unskilled? Does he change jobs often and goes for stretches of time without a reliable income? When I first became a landlord, I used to get bad tenants who not only did not pay rent but often damaged the apartment intentionally. Then I began to use their employment history as a guide to decide. I have had no more bad tenants since. An employment history is the one thing a social worker should pay a lot of attention to. Again, a person who has been on welfare for a long time, say one or two years as the cutoff line (?), should never be granted a permit. Let the perpetual welfare recipients' lines end together with their problematic genes. A society will be much better off without those parasites.

6. Who will be looking after the child? Looking after a baby is a full-time job. It is important to make sure that someone, usually the mother, will be there for the child during the first few years.

Those are only some of the points I can think of. A government should do its own research and come up with a race-neutral list to establish a point system to base its decision on. The list should also be made known to the public as soon as possible, well before the policy will be implemented. The central message of the point system is to educate the public on what will constitute good parenthood. The policy is to protect the children's benefit, or give them the right to have the chance of happy futures. The only focus of consideration will be on the children, no one else. The central point of the system will be nondiscriminating, and focus at the likelihood of an applicant's chance to be a good parent.

Stephen Y. Cheung, Ph.D.

How do you decline an applicant?

With the point system well publicized, people who are serious about having children will be much better prepared. It will also greatly reduce unwanted or accidental pregnancies because it is law to have a permit before having a child. In breaking the law, there should be consequences, and people can no longer use their children to profit. Eventually, when people begin to see the good things that will come out of the system, more and more people will support it and poverty will be greatly reduced, if not totally eliminated. Then, every child born will start from a level playing field and has equal chance for a happy life. Regardless, there will be some unqualified applications to be turned down. How a government turns down an application is another place where tact and compassion will be appreciated. You don't just send a registered mail:

> *This letter is to inform you that your application has been turned down because you don't have enough points. Yours truly . . .*

That will be cruel and heartless. The same social worker who looks after the application should be the same person to deliver the news. And it should be done in person, by a visit to the applicant's home. There he/she can go through the application with the applicants and tell them why they failed, with all the points focused at the future of the applicant's child. Hopefully, the parents can see it the same way. With the point system, the social worker can also highlight the areas the applicants need to improve. And the rejection is not final, they can reapply when they feel they are in a much better situation. Heavy drinkers or chain smokers need to get rid of the bad habits that have failed them. The compliance of those points not only will benefit the applicants, but also their children, the society, and the country. It will be win/win/win.

The social worker may end the visit this way:

> *"You know the government cares about you and your child; it is mainly from considering your family's interests that we need to turn you down this time. But don't be discouraged. You now have a clear target to improve on. We would like to come to help you again when you feel you are ready. In*

the meantime, here is a number you can contact me at if you have questions."

That is what I call tact and finesse. Carefully planned and properly executed, the policy will be a tide turner.

Increasing Transparency and Fighting Corruption

Politicians and Government Employees Are Supposed to Serve People

It should be very obvious to everyone that the role, and the only role, of a government, and therefore the job of a politician or government employee, is to serve its citizens. Nothing more. Unfortunately, very, very few people can clearly see this simple point. In Brazil, Indonesia, and the Philippines, for example, politicians serve mainly their own interests and serving the people who elected them is often a distant second in priority. Worse, people in those countries expect their politicians to be corrupt and it becomes acceptable as long as a politician does so in "moderation." You can drink with moderation, but not with *getting more money*. It is an unquenchable thirst. Failing to see this simple point of serving people first makes the citizens vulnerable to be fooled and exploited by their cunning and clever politicians.

If a government adopts our moral guidelines, citizens will get into a habit of asking the three questions regarding the behavior of a politician: (1) Whose interest does the behavior serve? (2) Who is getting hurt? (3) Whose choice is it? By habitually asking the three questions and using our two moral principles, a citizen can quickly get the answers. Then, those who have the habit of self-serving and are corrupt will be ousted quickly.

Corruption and Lacking Information from a Government Go Hand in Hand

But getting people to habitually ask the questions is easier said than done, because before a citizen can answer those questions he will need information from the government and whether the information is readily available will be the deciding factor. How much information a government makes available to the public is a very reliable indication of how willing it is to serve its people. From the amount of information available or the degree of transparency one can easily gauge how corrupt the politicians, especially those at the top, will be. So the amount of information available to the public is a reliable indication of the degree of corruption of a government. Makes sense?

Let us see in our world whether the above is a valid statement. From my observation, there are, in terms of rich and poor, two kinds of countries: some are very rich and some are very poor. A reader can google those countries to satisfy himself with the names. There appears to be a strong correlation between the degrees of corruption of the politicians and the level of poverty of the people: the more corrupt they are the poorer the people. This is expected because corrupt politicians do not have any intention to serve their people. They are parasites of the country, feeding on their people, sucking them dry.

If You Are Ignorant, You Can Easily Be Fooled

How do corrupt politicians get away so blatantly with harming their people? The reason is quite simple: it is because their people are mostly ignorant. When a person is ignorant, he can easily be fooled. Let me tell you a story to show the point. I once traveled to a small town called Baños in Ecuador. Unlike most small towns, Baños has many foreign tourists because it offers many attractions. You can, for example, book a guided outing for several days to an Amazon forest. I took a rafting trip in a nearby river and it was easily the best of all the rafting trips I have taken, including the ones in British Columbia, Canada, Chiang Mai or Crabi, Thailand. The river has many rapids and abrupt turns; they toss a raft around violently and can throw a raft upside down at any stretch. The girl sat next to me among the several people sharing the raft was a young woman from New York. I could tell she was very, very scared. She kept asking the guide how soon the trip would end, which was unusual when you were expecting to have fun. Above all, she was really afraid that she would be thrown into the water—that happened a few times to people in the other rafts. She was gripping the rope so tight that her knuckles turned white.

Our guide was delighted to see her so frightened and decided to have more fun at the poor girl's expense. He began to tell the girl by stressing that if she fell there were many piranhas in the water. Most people know that a piranha attack is much worse than a shark attack. They kill you by tearing away your flesh in bits and pieces. If you were to be killed by fish and you could choose by which one, the last one would be by piranhas. The girl was scared, really scared; she was visibly shaking uncontrollably while trying to hold on tight to the rope on the raft. The guide just laughed and laughed.

I felt we needed to put an end to the joke. So I said to the girl, "You see how clean and clear the water is?" The girl nodded. "And also it is rather cold, isn't it?" The girl nodded again, also trying to figure out what I was leading to. "You will find very few fish in this kind of water, let alone piranhas. They live only in warm and murky waters and mostly in Brazil. Relax!" To show the water was safe, I dipped my hand in the water. She began to smile.

It should be obvious that ignorance comes from lacking education. The girl was from the States, and judging from her age, should have at least finished high school, if not college. So she was not that ignorant, she just did not have the knowledge of the killer fish. Most people in poor countries don't have high school or even primary school education. That is why they can easily be fooled by their politicians, those at the top especially. On the other hand, the people in rich countries are highly educated. Most have finished college or university, and it is free. Highly educated people are highly intelligent, making fooling them next to impossible. They will find out quickly and put those rotten politicians out of job.

Ignorance, Lacking Transparency, and Corruption All Come in One Package

From the observations, let us do a summary on the cause and effect between ignorance, lacking transparency, and corruption. Rotten politicians are like mosquitoes, they can only thrive in certain environments. The environment is a political system that provides next to no information about the doings of the government and thus the politicians. The people are kept in the dark, and that is why they can get away with harming the people they are supposed to serve. With these parasites, people will remain ignorant and poor. The ignorance of people will provide a warm bed for the corrupt politicians to thrive.

To stop corruption, the most effective way is obviously to increase the transparency of a government. But human nature is selfish. Do you think those corrupt politicians will volunteer to provide the information on how they steal from the people? Doing that would mean the end to their other lucrative incomes; they have to be forced by their people. But the people are mostly ignorant and will never start making such a demand. So we are back to square one. That is why Haiti, Indonesia, and many African countries will forever be stuck where they are.

Without doubt, the way to minimize corruption in a country is by increasing the transparency of a government, which in turn will lead to accountability. The more accountable a governing party is, the less will be the corruption. Then, and only then, will politicians be more willing to serve their voters. But the voters have to fight for it; to fight for it, people need education.

The Way to End Poverty in Countries Like Haiti

Is there any way to end corrupt and poor countries like Haiti, Laos, or Chad? Yes, on paper at least, for the many small and perpetually poor and corrupt (the two appear to be synonyms) countries. It will be for a conglomerate of advanced countries to take over the country, by force, most likely. But before the takeover, the "invading" countries would need to first establish and prove that the leaders of the targeted country are exceedingly corrupt and harmful to their people. The fact-finding mission should not be difficult given that those leaders are not very sophisticated and will leave many trails to their corrupt acts. Having established the facts, the nations would make known their intention to invade and to take over the country. Unlike the invasion of Iraq by the US-led allies, countries in the world would not object; rather, would support the invasion. The invasion would obviously not be for the self-interest of the aggressors; there is no oil in those countries. By asking our three questions, the answers would justify it. There would be little gain other than helping the harmed people to get rid of their politicians. Sure, there would be parties hurt, those would be the parasites. I don't think anyone would think it wrong to kill mosquitoes that are sucking up your blood. It would truly be a noble war and a holy one.

After the complete takeover, the nations would use their know-how to build a new accountable nation. It would be a beautiful win/win. The invading nations would get a chance to test and perfect a new political system to serve the people better; the poor people would get a chance to end poverty. The invading nations might not have to use force after all. After their intention to take over is made known, the leaders of the corrupt country would be smart enough to know that their defeat would be inevitable for a number of reasons: (1) their people would love to see them go, and (2) the huge gap in the military capability between the invaders and their country. A diplomatic solution by offering the president and a few top politicians a comfortable life by allowing them to keep some of their loot would persuade them to surrender. The leaders should be smart enough to make the choice. After a successful takeover, the invading countries should be very transparent in what they do in the new country to silence critics. This is the only kind of invasion I would condone. If you ask the three questions, you would find out that the nations had not started the war to self-serve; they did it for the people under corrupt leaders and to free the people from a never-ending poverty.

Adopting the Golden Rule Morality as the Foundation to Make Laws

Our discussions on ending war, pollution, and poverty all require a government to have a correct moral view that allows it to achieve those goals. None of the existing views can do that. There are a number of reasons for the collective inability of the existing moralities to solve the three big problems. 1) All the religion-based moral views are primarily to promote the worship of the god of that religion; preventing people from harming each other, at best, plays second fiddle in their moral views. 2) There is no reason given why a certain behavior is immoral; instead, a follower needs to follow the orders and commands given to them. 3) The teachers and priests that gave us the various moral views did not know that human nature is selfish and it is therefore the root of all hurtful behaviors. When a moral view fails to see hurtful behaviors should be its primary target, it will be at best ineffective to solve them. Those are the reasons why existing moral views can never stop war, pollution, and poverty.

Quite the contrary, in the existing views, war is often justified and even glorified. The idea of controlling pollution simply does not exist in any of the religion-based moral view. And poverty will never end because most religions condone and encourage having more children, regardless whether the children can be properly provided or cared for. On top, many of today's urgent issues, such as abortion, same-sex marriage, euthanasia, and genetic engineering, were not there when the moral views were formed. Thus, traditional moral views do not know how to handle them. Those issues continue to divide a country and thus weaken it.

We now, for the first time in human history, are very sure that human nature, like that of every living organism, is selfish and has a natural tendency to harm others. This new finding comes out from our generic definition of a living organism. The definition, with the help of physics, allows us to see a living organism always needs to self-preserve and to survive; survival always necessitates hurting other organisms. From this new knowledge, it is the belief of this book that the one and only purpose of a moral view is to prevent people from hurting one another, nothing else. With this lone target, we can focus on trying to find a solution. We are very fortunate because the solution actually exists. Not only does it exist, it is in the teachings of every religion; that solution is the Golden Rule. In essence, the Golden Rule in most religions says one thing: don't do anything that you will find hurtful when it is done to you. Or simply: *don't hurt others*. Though none of the authorities that gave us the Golden Rule knew it, the rule was to prevent people from hurting others. Sadly, the Golden Rule was only one of the many teachings in the old moralities. Not knowing human nature is selfish, it has been seldom used in lawmaking and has remained idle for centuries.

Because the concept of human nature being selfish is quite new—it was first introduced in 2005 in *Happy to Be Morally Selfish*—a reader should be concerned about how reliable this piece of information is, because our morality revolves around solving it. What if our concept is wrong and living organisms turned out to be really harmless? Then, the foundation upon which all the theses is built will be faulty and therefore will not stand. This is a valid concern.

If there is flaw in the development of the concept, it will certainly not have come from physics, more specifically the Second Law of Thermodynamics. It will have to arise from the definition we adopt, the definition of a living organism. I have checked and rechecked the simple definition many times after formulating it. I could not find any flaw in it. The definition more accurately and better describes the phenomenon that we call "life," it also fully explains every behavior we see among the great varieties of living things; i.e., no matter what organism it is and no matter what it does, one can be certain that it is doing it for self-preservation. Therefore, before our theory is disproven, it will still be a very valuable working assumption.

Our second concern will be how valid is the Golden Rule to prevent hurtful behaviors? Well, it gets me sold; I wholeheartedly believe it. And I have easily challenged over hundreds of people during the many past years on the validity of the Golden Rule as the moral guideline. None, absolutely no one has ever said to me that he or she would believe it would be OK to do something that he or she would find hurtful to others. The Golden Rule, more than the Second Law of Thermodynamics, has stood the test of more than two thousand years.

Based on the above reasons, I believe it is paramount for a governing body to adopt the Golden Rule as the only foundation on which to enact laws. It will greatly simplify the process to make it clean, tidy, and meaningful. The laws thus created will solve the problems in our sickened planet. With the two principles derived and by asking the three simple questions, an average person, not just the lawmakers, can decide that starting an invasion, polluting our environment, and irresponsible procreation are all wrong and need to be stopped. The up-to-now puzzling and difficult issues like abortion, same-sex marriage, or euthanasia should be legal. And free procreation should never be a right, and all parents need to be screened before they will be allowed to have children. None of that will happen before most of the governments, the more advanced nations in particular, adopt the Golden Rule–based morality. Stopping wars, pollution, and poverty all need to come from the lead of a government. We have also argued that for politicians to take up the leading role, the voters, the common people, have to want it and therefore force politicians to be on their side. It seems like a chicken and egg issue. Yes, I believe that a government should champion the change. However, the people are the ultimate driving force. Therefore, our focus is still at educating more people on the Golden Rule and for them to accept it as the only moral decision maker. That does not entirely depend on the participation of a government or politicians.

Writing this book and spreading the message is to do just that, a dreamer's quest to get the message spread and eventually get more believing readers to partake. Then, we can exert our united force and make politicians participate. We can then hope to fix the planet and turn it into a paradise. Then, it won't just be a dream; rather, it will be a doable endeavor.

If a government embraces our Golden Rule–based morality, it will, other than preventing future wars, polluting our environment, and poverty from happening, further increase the levels of intelligence and cooperation of the country by doing them through creating more citizens with higher qualities.

Let me explain.

To Enhance Intelligence

The Golden Rule is almost common sense, which is easily understood. It is not an ideology that often is built on arbitrary or even on shaky ground. It has stood the test of time and there is a lot of wisdom in it to help us to solve the many problems created by a selfish human nature. You can grow with the Golden Rule, especially through the two moral principles to decide right and wrong. From the principles, the book has developed a concept called moral selfishness. If intelligence is the ability to solve problems, then wisdom is the highest grade of intelligence, which allows one to solve problems that will be longest lasting and will bring happiness to most people. Moral selfishness is just that wisdom, to effectively and thoroughly solve the problems originated from human nature and which will bring happiness to most people and beneficial organisms.

To Enhance Cooperation

The first step to heighten cooperation is by stopping people from hurting others, by seeing a hurtful behavior as immoral. Then, and only after that happens, our attention can be focused on how to deal with others in a moral way. It leaves only one choice, and that is to seek win/win, which is the essence of cooperation. Our Golden Rule–based moral view, therefore, has a built-in mechanism to make people cooperate. If everyone agrees on our Golden Rule–based moral principles, we can still have different religions and the world will still be peaceful. For the world to have any hope of peace, the Golden Rule must never be superseded. *No one or religious teaching is above the Golden Rule.*

To Enhance the Overall Quality of Citizens

The way a government can achieve that will be by promoting moral selfishness. Moral selfishness is always to look after the interest of oneself and be moral. When applying morality in dealing with one's own self, a person will never intentionally hurt himself for short-term gratification. He will also do things that will give him more choices in the future. As discussed, a morally selfish person will be a positive force in a community or his country no matter what role he plays. Morally selfish people are the building blocks for a future paradise.

With morality as guide, a politician can be as selfish or self-centered as he wants and still make a great politician. There are many possible selfish reasons: he really loves serving people, to solve their problems, and to make his country better. Or he loves the good pay he will receive as a politician. Most countries pay their politicians handsomely, much better than comparable administrative jobs in the private sector in general. They are allowed to be selfish as long as they stay moral.

Paradoxically, moral selfishness is also the tool to make more caring people. According to how we have defined "love," to care is the first step to developing love. It is a paradox because when people talk about selfishness, people usually think about a character that is uncaring and hurtful. Not with morally selfish people. To be morally selfish, a person needs to be moral, and therefore always consider the benefit he will give when dealing with others. The benefit needs also to be fair. When a person has a habit of doing that, isn't he a caring person?

And a caring person will gradually, even without trying, become a more loving person. Beautiful, isn't it?

To Build a Paradise on Earth

Many people dream of a world without wars and borders. John Lennon was one of the dreamers. I am also that dreamer. The difference between me and the other dreamers is that I know how to do it. Many think that love is the answer to realizing the dream. But the problem is that most of the people who talk about love do not have any idea of what love is. Love is also against a selfish nature. They know love is something very beautiful and desirable. But their understanding is foggy at best. Love will help, but it is not the real answer. The answer is a correct morality. Without the right tool, their dreams can never be realized.

A borderless world has been achieved among the many countries in Europe. The reason those countries are able to do that is because they have rejected wars, and the financial gaps between people in those countries are not that extreme. Those nations also share the same religion and thus their moral views, and highly value science. But the situation in Europe is far from perfect, because the nations still lack the morality that will take them to a higher level of cooperation. Not knowing what is right and wrong, there is a ceiling to your intelligence.

For most governments to have a unified moral view is the very crucial first step before a thorough change can happen. Our world has unified traffic light signals and knowledge based on science. Both systems have been and are still fully embraced by people of different cultures and religions because they are culturally and religiously neutral. Our Golden Rule–based morality is in every way the same: it is culturally and religiously neutral. And similar to the knowledge in science, our theses are based on facts and reason. The traffic light signals and the knowledge from science have both done great things for the human race.

So will a unified moral view based on the Golden Rule, especially moral selfishness.

Before we end this chapter, let me clarify one thing. Many people, especially some highly educated and environmentally caring ones, blame our science and technology for the mess of the world. For the same reason, the followers of some Christian branches have avoided using many modern technologies. Their intention, though good and admirable, however, is misguided. Misguided because they have failed to see that it is none other than their erroneous moral view that is the problem. As a result, it is also those good-intentioned, educated, and caring people, who, by ironically holding on to their outdated and defective moral view, have made preventing and stopping the problems created by technology impossible. Often, they are also the ones that fight adopting the new moral view the fiercest. There will be many road blocks to remove. For a government to have any chance to switch to the Golden Rule–based morality, it must first believe it is the right path to take and be fully committed. The knowledge and the tools are there; it will be up to a government, especially its politicians to decide.

CHAPTER 22

There Is Something Very Wrong
with Our Democratic System

Intelligence and cooperation continue to operate in human societies, not by conscientious choice; rather, that has been the way our species does business. From the first human to now, there has never been a break when these two forces stopped to help us and get us through. If one cares to look at a human society, any society, primitive or advanced, he will, for sure, find the two forces in operation in almost every aspect of people's lives in that society. The two are entrenched in our DNA. These two forces have been behind the development and eventual adopting of a democratic system among most countries in the world, from the most advanced to the most corrupt. It has evolved from an intelligent decision of how to best serve people's interests. Cooperation also plays a prominent role to make it widely spread over the globe. When people learned that democracy made sense by observing the system in foreign countries, they copied it for their own country. Without this knowledge imported from western countries, China, for example, would very likely still be ruled by emperors today.

Democratic Government

What is a democratic government? There should be many definitions. To simplify things, I shall summarize it this way: The people of a country decide the policies of the country and all democratic governments put the interests of their citizens first; the role of a government is to best serve their people. Agree? The role of a government should be just that: to serve its people. It is how a government tries to realize this simple goal where it all begins to go south or sideways.

Everyone knows that a government is run by elected politicians. We all assume that 1) people know how to pick the most qualified politicians, and 2) the elected politicians will put serving the interests of people ahead of their own. We all know, after many, many disappointing elections and after picking the many, many wrong politicians, that the two assumptions are not based on solid grounds. As a result, the politicians that come out from an election often are ill-fitted for the job, or even worse, they have no intention of serving their people.

Do people know how to pick politicians who are qualified for the job?

The election of Justin Trudeau to be the prime minister of Canada is a classic example of people not knowing how to pick their top politicians. Don't get me wrong, I like the guy more than any of the previous prime ministers. He is a gentleman, good-looking, very well brought up, and a perfect face for the country. But to be a good prime minister, I think, would take more than looks and manners. He has little qualification to run the country. Though someone has argued in Trudeau's defense that he has more exposure to politics in his early years than anyone, granted, but to run a country, I think, would take more than how to handle foreign politicians. It takes substance. If you look at young Trudeau's résumé, he has little substance based on his employment history. In electing a politician, voters seldom consider his qualification for the job.

So how really do people in Canada—and for that matter, the people of all other countries—choose their politicians? Often not by their qualifications; that is a starter. Most of the people choose who they choose because they are sick and tired of the politicians of the previous government. The prominent parties in a country are often playing musical chairs waiting their turn for the party in power to screw up. Screw up the party sure will, usually in less than two full terms. So out of frustration and disgust, the voters will switch to another one, having forgotten how that party lost its governance previously. So the musical chairs game goes on and on. It is not just Canada that is playing this musical chairs game, all democratic countries have been playing this game too. Is it a sound logic to pick a country's politicians?

The inability to pick the most qualified politician is not just among the ordinary voters like you and me, some really famous and learned people like David Suzuki had the same difficulty in some elections, so difficult for him to pick that he gave up his right to vote and essentially let some morons decide for him. If that is true— and I hope I have not gotten it wrong—it will be very sad. The world's political system is good in generating willing and eager people to run for office, but are they qualified before they are allowed to run? Something is definitely very wrong about the current system.

How voters vote seems to depend on several irrelevant factors. One of them is how much they hate the incumbent governing party. This can be a deciding factor. For me in the last provincial election, I really hated McGuinty's guts. He had wasted more than a billion dollars of tax money to save a couple of his party's seats. Therefore, the Liberal Party candidate was automatically out. I also don't like the NDP's affiliation with the unions; the candidate was also automatically eliminated. That only left me with the Conservative candidate. It should not be the way to decide, but that was how it was done and I was hardly the minority. The other common way is how popular a candidate is. People often pick a well-known name for the job. Thus, Ronald Reagan got elected as president. And Arnold, also a movie star known for his huge biceps, got the job of governor of California. I don't know the logic of why being a famous movie star will make him a good president or governor. But that is how most Americans vote. Why not the qualifications? And a voter would say, "What qualifications?"

The number of lawn signs a candidate has is another reason, the one with the most usually comes out winning. The behavior of voters is not that different from that of animals in a herd; they follow each other. There is no clear logic in what they are doing other than they find safety in numbers. I have a friend who does the opposite by picking a candidate with the fewest signs, and the best candidate for him will be without any sign. "That way, I can't contribute to the mistake," he proudly defended this odd behavior. Other than the top candidate like a president, prime minister, or a premier, a voter usually knows next to nothing about the real person he votes for, often not even the face. So how do you and I decide? By the number of signs a candidate has, naturally.

In electing a top-level candidate like a president, prime minister or premier, voters have the chance to learn more about who they are. But to decide whether the candidate will be qualified is often a hit-and-miss affair. Even if a voter wants to learn more about a candidate, he simply doesn't have the pertinent information to decide. The information that a candidate provides is often nothing more than an advertisement and often lacks truth. Then, it often evolves into a mud-throwing contest, which makes every candidate look ugly. The mud they throw doesn't even have to be substantiated. It rewards the most ruthless attacker. Ugly and painful, isn't it? This was how Trump won. Or, at best, it will be a beauty contest, with the best-looking or one who makes the most beautiful promises coming out on top. It often evolves into a lying contest. The most daring liar wins. Everybody knows that politicians can change their minds. The promises are no different than those made by guys who lie to get women in bed. The guys know they lie, so do the girls. No one will hold the other accountable for the promises made in election. If the goal is to select the most qualified politicians, the election system in the free and developed world has often failed miserably. Yet, despite having so many sharp minds, no country has questioned the system.

Will the elected politicians put serving the interests of the voters first?

If this is the goal, the election system has failed even more badly than the first assumption. Let us not look at countries like Brazil, Peru, Indonesia, the Philippines, or some African countries, which have the tradition of producing corrupt politicians election after election. Let us look at advanced countries like the US, the UK, Canada, or Japan, etc. The presidents or prime ministers don't always put serving the people's interest first. In the best scenario, the politicians put their party's interest ahead. And regrettably, no one—not the leaders of the opposition parties or the voters—think that is wrong. That is why the Liberal Party chose J. Trudeau as the leader. I don't think his ability to best serve Canadians has ever crossed the minds of those politicians who did the picking. There was one and only one reason: Trudeau's chance to win—not based on merit rather than the name—would be highest. Then, the Liberal candidates, some Janes and Joes, can be elected. The Liberals only serve their own interest! Sacrificing people's interest is something those politicians are willing to make. The fact that Trudeau did win showed how Canadians made their choice in an election. Wrong, wrong, wrong; sad, sad, sad for a country like Canada.

Or let us look at the 2016 American presidential election and see whether the free election has produced a president who will put serving the country's interest first. If you don't know, America was the first country in the free world to use election to produce its first president in 1789. After adopting the system for close to 230 years and producing more than forty presidents, one would reasonably expect that the Americans should have perfected the election mechanism to produce a qualified president that would put the interests of the people first. Why? Because one of the many great things the Americans are known for is the high intelligence level of its people. They are known for innovations besides the ability to solve difficult problems, like landing people on the moon. The country also has the most top-notch universities and the level of know-how is beyond comparison. Notwithstanding, there is little doubt in my mind that the 2016 presidential election will go down in history as the ugliest as well as the most painful election to watch in the country's election history. And for that matter, will possibly be the very worst the developed nations have to offer.

It is ugly because the Republican candidate Trump did not win by substance. He won by two ugly tactics: attacks and lies, the weapons of choice employed mostly by the lowest of the low. You don't normally see this kind of tactic in a country with the highest intelligence, especially when choosing its top executive, and therefore made it so very painful to bear by those who knew better. And there should be millions of them. The fact that Trump used such dirty tricks and won has seriously eroded America's moral standing as well as its intelligence level among nations.

Trump has made the election so ugly and painful not only by his choice weapons, he has easily become the lowest president elected in moral standing among the nations, even if one includes the third-world countries. He has also made it so blatant and so shameless. Any presidential candidate would have withdrawn voluntarily following the disclosure of his many repugnant comments toward women and the sexual assaults he has admitted committing, though inadvertently. The guy lacks the most elementary sense of right and wrong! Trump, from the things he has said, appears to be a habitual liar. Many of the attacks he unleashed on the media have been proven groundless. No admittance or apology from him; instead, he often doubled down on those lies. He must have been the most faithful student in brainwashing that if you keep repeating the same lie over and over again, people would eventually start believing. It is sad that the people in a highly intelligent country have allowed that to happen.

Politics has always been dirty and ugly, especially during election time. But Trump has taken the duo to a new low. It is painful because millions of the voters were forced into a no-win selection, a situation of picking between the lesser of two evils—those were the actual words used by some voters. You knew it was wrong and were very unwilling, but you still had no choice but to put a check mark next to Trump's name. Some of them must have had wet eyes and blurred vision doing it. It did not help that a highly revered Christian theologian named Grudem guilt-tripped you by saying that not voting for Trump would be committing a sin against God. It was so mind-boggling that choosing a president should be so agonizing. Some of the voters must have felt that they were raped by their election system. If free election is to produce the most capable politicians to serve people's interest first, then the 2016 election was clearly a lie. Trump may be highly capable, but serving people's interest ahead of his?

The most relevant question will still be will Trump put people's interest ahead of his for a change? Or will a self-centered guy suddenly do that? If the past is of any indication, Trump's signature has been leaving a trail of people hurt by him. If anything, he is not known to be caring or considerate; instead, he symbolizes what ruthless selfishness will do. He is an animal in clothes. Trump has definitely broken the record for low morality and thus is indefensible. Not for Grudem, who has an off-the-chart IQ. He has cleverly found a way to trivialize Trump's many glaring blemishes. He convincingly argues that every human is a sinner and all candidates are flawed. While it is debatable that every human is a sinner, all candidates being flawed should be beyond doubt. By those clever words, he dares anyone to cast the first stone. From there, he even goes on to argue that Trump will be a morally good choice. One cannot help but shakes his head.

Alas! The forgiving (or clever?) pastor should know there is a big difference between flawed and rotten. And Trump is rotten to the core. If you want to know what evil is, you can see quite a bit of it from Trump even without trying. And the so many hurts he had purposely inflicted on people, to women especially, were so unnecessary and bordered upon cruelty. There is little doubt that Trump is ruthless and habitually immoral. By endorsing Trump, the pastor, in effect, is hiring a devil to protect God's (or more appropriately Christian) values; namely, to defend the unborn and make gay unions sinful. He is using meat to make a vegetarian dish. The contradiction is way beyond my comprehension. In effect, Grudem is okaying the end justifies the means. He is condoning going to bed with the devil in exchange for its service. The pastor may have, in the name of doing good, put Christian value a couple of notches down. Sad, isn't it? Sad because Grudem comes with credentials that represent the highest intelligence the human race has to offer. He is a Harvard grad and has a PhD from Cambridge. What more can you ask for?

Or there is the illusion that Trump would suddenly change (his character) and champion the cause of the people. "Trump has changed his mind before, why not this time?" Grudem challenged the doubters. Again, my dear pastor, there is a difference between changing one's mind and his character. Everyone changes his mind from time to time; I have yet to see someone suddenly change his character. Character takes years to build and develop; short of a miracle, no one has ever suddenly change his character, from selfish to selfless or from ruthless to caring. Never! You really don't know? Or just trying to outsmart the Americans?

There is absolutely no reason for Trump to change his character either. It has taken him seventy years to get to this stage, which according to him and most of the people that voted for him is working extremely well. If it is not broken, why fix it? Do you think Trump would think his way of doing business is broken? Not unless the sun starts rising from the west. Why would he? By being ruthless and self-centered, he has built himself a big fortune, even by American's standard. And don't forget, he has just got the biggest endorsement by the majority of the voters picking him for president! The majority of the Americans are saying to him, "You are my kind of guy, Mr. Trump. Keep it up." Anyone in Trump's position won't change. If anything, he is encouraged and will step it up. No! I'll bet everything that I value most against him changing his character and serving the interest of the people!

Then, the question will be how will Trump screw his countrymen? The obvious answer will be in conflict-of-interest dealings together with abusing his power. "In what area?" you continue to probe. Among Trump's too many flaws—foul-mouthedness, wandering hands (to women's forbidden body parts), arrogance, and bombast, etc.—the one that should really, really concern the American people will no doubt be his lust for money. Women will be a distant second. Let me quote something Trump has proudly proclaimed:

"Part of the beauty of me is that I am very rich. I'm really rich. Cash is king, and that's one of the beauties of the casino business."

"Fighting for the last penny is a very good philosophy to have."

"You can't be too greedy."

Frightening isn't it? Frightening because the guy does not think there is anything wrong with his belief. Frightening because he was not bluffing; he is actually going to do it. Those things are at least consistent with his past behavior.

And there will be too many chances for him to make lots of "pennies," truckloads of them. He need not fight for them either. They will be delivered to Trump's assigned accounts by those grateful executives that get the president's favorable treatment. To make America great again, for example, Trump can easily get the support of the hawkish Americans to increase the budget for defense. We shall be looking at trillions and trillions of dollars. Will Trump give those contracts out free? I would say very unlikely, not by a guy who glorifies greed.

I was a real estate agent for many years prior to become a writer. I used to make 5 percent commission for every double-ended sale. That was in real estate. But Trump is a president, I think he deserves more. Double at least? One percent of a trillion is 10 billion. You can do the simple math on the number of "pennies" the president is going to make. It will be safe to say that by the end of a full term, if not earlier, Trump can easily pass the other billionaires and become the richest man on the planet.

Military spending is hardly the only chance for the president to make the "pennies." There are those free-trade deals to be renegotiated, with Mexico and China, for example, where transparency is low and making those shiny "pennies" would be safe and easy. The big American corporations would love to have some part of the new free-trade pies and some of the executives will no doubt be Trump's buddies. They would know the president's appetite well and do the "right" thing for Trump without any prodding. "It is not what you know but who you know." It is all about connection in the business world and few are better connected than the president. Needless to say, there will be many willing and eager executives wanting to dump those "pennies" into Trump's depositories. I don't think Trump will be able to turn down those offers even if he wants to. Will a vulture walk away from a rotting carcass?

There must be more chances. Trump has not become a billionaire for nothing, and luck is unlikely to have a lot to do with it. While many may miss it, Trump can usually smell money in the most unlikely places. And he certainly is a man of principle; his principle revolves around the dough. His overheated passion for money makes him highly bribable.

The love of money to the extent of being greedy is hardly Trump's only character flaw. The man is known to be daring to the point of ruthlessness. He is not going to hesitate to harm the Americans if there is profit to be gained. Now he is given the greatest power any man on earth can ever have by the Christians. Suddenly, the genie is let out of the bottle. But this genie serves no master but himself; he is going to grant all his own wild wishes. He has the power and the know-how. Conflicts of interest, abuse of power, and corruption will very likely be Trump's legacy to the Christians that put him there. Sad days are coming to America, and there are already a number of ill omens during Trump's infant presidency. Instead of making America great again, Trump is going to shame the country to a never-before-seen level.

"It may be the best thing that ever happened to America."

I was on a plane from Medellin to Miami. An American was seated on my right-hand side. While waiting for takeoff, I was writing down some ideas on my notebook. The American was curious and asked, "What are you writing?" I usually get annoyed when people interrupt me writing, but not with this question. I love the question. It gives me the chance to talk to people about the book. He also happened to sit on the side where my good ear is—my left ear has gone 95 percent deaf for a number of years. I could hear him clearly. I gladly folded up my notebook and then the little table in front of me; I wanted the guy to have my full attention.

I started with introducing the two moral principles I developed. As expected, he fully agreed that they made good sense. Then, we talked about using the two principles and the three questions to decide moral issues like euthanasia and same-sex marriage. He marveled at how simple it was. After breaking the ice, we chatted freely. Unavoidably, our conversation took us to the presidential election. He was not happy with Trump at all, which was hardly surprising because he had earlier disclosed that he wasn't a Christian. After a short pause, he also added, "It may be the best thing that ever happened to America." In what way, he did not further comment. There was no joy in him saying that. Soon, our conversation was interrupted by takeoff.

I think I understand what he meant. The American Christians have made a mammoth mistake in hiring the devil himself to defend their principles, the principles they felt have come from God. The devil and God don't work together. And mistakes are expensive—that I can testify to because I am an expert. The Americans are going to pay dearly for electing Trump. But there is also an upside, I can also attest to that. It makes you think deep and hard and learn from it. *"That which does not kill you makes you stronger."* I would paraphrase it as *makes you wiser.* No doubt the mistake is going to cost the country big time, but it certainly won't kill the country. America is too strong and too resilient to be destroyed by this mistake, immense as it is. It will be a very painful, even core-shaking, wakeup call. When all is done and the tally added up, Americans will realize that they have a lot of hard thinking to catch up to. The country has the most intelligent minds and an enviable amount of resources in terms of knowledge, but they have allowed themselves to act like fools. Instead of reason, they have chosen to believe in doctrines and in so doing have chosen to choke their rationality. The mistake will wake up the intellectuals of the country; some may begin to question the existing system of choosing their leaders by election because the system has failed them repeatedly, and often disastrously.

If Trump's presidency is the best thing that ever happened to America, it will *not* be for making America great again. Instead, he will make America so ashamed that the country will need to rethink its system for choosing a president. More importantly, they may also want to find out why so many of them have abandoned reason and sanity to choose Christian doctrines instead. And perhaps only a character like Trump can deliver a mistake of this magnitude to wake up the nation. There is no doubt in my mind that America will regain its greatness someday. And ironically, it will be through Trump, a guy who used the slogan to run and win, though in the opposite way.

Is free election the best way to pick politicians for a country?

The answer will be: not if the goal of an election is to pick the most qualified politicians, and not if the goal is to choose candidates that are willing to serve people's interest first. And if the facts borne by the results of elections throughout the world are any indication, the system has thoroughly failed and often badly. In most democratic countries, the system becomes a lying, mud-slinging, or at best popularity contest. The most recognizable name wins. That is how Justin Trudeau won. And a Filipino boxer named Manny Pacquiao is aiming at the presidency of his country and his chance of getting it is quite high. If he gets there, and it is almost sure that he will get there, it will be interesting to see what kind of president he will make. If the country's history is any indication, he will be one of the corrupt ones. He may want to resist corruption. But will his buddies, those who help him to get there, allow him to? Will being a great boxer make him a good president?

Elections for the top jobs in every country often become hot contests for the ambitious and the egoistic to fulfill their selfish dreams; serving people's interest cannot be more remote from those candidates' minds. As a biologist, I believe that the kind of organisms that thrive in an environment is predicated by the conditions of that environment; water that lacks oxygen favors the growth of foul bacteria while beautiful organisms like trout and salmon have no chance. What kind of politicians does the free election system favor? The Americans may want to think about the answer when they wake up.

Is there a better way to pick politicians?

The present system of electing politicians is obviously a very bad design and has repeatedly malfunctioned. It needs to be fixed or even junked. The question becomes how? To start, Americans must clearly realize that the system is not working. Does it need to be replaced? Some fundamental changes must be implemented this time. Funny that almost every presidential candidate loves to use *change* as a slogan, but none have really done it. Most end up making minor adjustments. No! The system needs a fundamental change in design. For example, having more than one governing party—of two, three, or four—has not been the best way to serve the people. The multiparty system, at the very least, divides a country; it cuts people up into different groups that, by principle, refuse to even to listen to the other side. By principle, they oppose like a reflex. A veto often has nothing to do with the merit of the policy, it is governed by reflex. That is why no matter how much gun violence has happened, and has happened too regularly, the Republicans are not going to let any attempt to pass gun control go through. They can also justify it in a twisted logic. That is both scary and absurd for a country with so many intellectuals.

Having a multiparty system more than divides a country into conflicting groups and thus weakens a country. Far more than that, it creates some party faithful who would routinely pledge their loyalty to their party ahead of their country. What will be good for their party comes first and the country second. Again, this is why the young and inexperienced Trudeau was chosen by the party faithful of the Liberals. I am sure this does not happen only in Canada; it should be quite common among the advanced nations. It is obviously wrong but no one sees it that way. In so doing, the politicians ultimately put their own interest ahead of that of the people they are to serve. That is also why a party always dumps its incumbent leader like a piece of moldy bread after a disastrous election. His ability, past record, or competence will not save him. Why? "Because we can no longer count on the guy to bring us the bread." Every leader knows this cruel fact and is willing to play this game.

Having more than one party makes it almost impossible for any incumbent party to do any long-term planning, like building infrastructure, healthcare, or research facilities, etc. The best forecast a party can plan for is often no more than four years. Eight will be a stretch, and anything beyond will be dreaming. There is a reason for their collective short-sightedness, because there will be no guarantee that the party will keep winning. After Trump was elected, he immediately wanted to get rid of Obamacare. Is his decision based on research, being a Republican, or a personal dislike of Obama? To nullify a policy of a former governing party just because it was from the other party seems a tremendous waste and is hardly an intelligent decision. But this is often what parties are doing, the merit or the lack of it seldom has anything to do with it. Consider what would happen if a corporation were run like a country. How long would it last? Lacking long-term goals and to keep changing direction will be a recipe for bankruptcy.

The alternative to a multiparty system will be a one-party system or no-party system. I am also painfully aware that the world's one-party states, possibly with the exception of China, are quite unappetizing. Corruption, lacking transparency and thus accountability plague those states. Considering the many advantages of the no-party/one party system, maybe those defects that are often associated with the one-party state system can be fixed given the will to do so. Why throw the baby out with the bathwater? The way to fix the blemishes is by increasing transparency and accountability; it should be very doable.

Picking a leader for a country, for example, instead of by election can be first done by a committee specialized in picking the many candidates. Here is how it could be done: A group, say three to five experienced people chosen for this particular task will be in charge of searching the qualified candidates in the country, with each official coming up with one candidate. An official must clearly state his reasons for his choice and put them in writing for every citizen to see. This will satisfy the transparency and accountability requirements. At the end of the selection period, there will a number of available candidates for the public to choose from in an election. The candidate will then be allowed to campaign for the job in a certain format. Social media will be a great way for them to showcase their skill and knowledge, including their employment history. The official who picks a certain candidate will have the onus to verify the claims made by his candidate and be held liable and accountable. Then, the citizens can study each candidate before casting their votes. The focus of the whole election process will be to provide extensive verifiable information on every candidate so that the citizen can be better informed to make their decision. It will eliminate for the voters the trouble of learning about and qualifying each candidate themselves. I think this process will be far more reliable for picking the right president than the existing method. People like Donald Trump and J. Trudeau would have a difficult time getting through the system.

The above is only one of the many possible solutions. The goal is to build a workable system for picking officials/politicians for a country. The goal is to provide as much information to the citizens about the candidates as possible before they vote. If a proposed system is feasible, then experts in the political science field may want to continue to work on perfecting it. From time to time, they should ask: "Is the proposed system/model working?" If not, why? By doing it with a scientific attitude, which time after time has proven its worth, the world will have a much better system for electing politicians. It will be a much more livable world for sure.

Is Christianity Good or Harmful to America, and for that matter, to any country? The Troublesome Teachings of Jesus

Other than prodding Americans to reexamine their election system, the electing of Trump should also be a reason for die-hard Christians to do some serious soul searching about their (blind) faith in the Bible. I am against the many teachings of Jesus, and I am speaking from experience. Having been a sincere Christian who wanted to follow every one of Jesus's teachings for more than forty years, and having decided, after a long struggle, to walk away, I think I should be allowed to voice my opinion for reference. A reader should also know that I still firmly believe in the same God. In fact, my faith has been stronger and my relationship with God has been closer since I walked away from Christianity. I still pray to God, or more precisely, the same gods; they have nurtured, protected, taught, and shaped me for more than seventy-five years. This book is my witness to their existence and their love for me.

I shall discuss what I feel about Christianity in the following points based on the Gospels; they all show that many of Jesus's teachings are problematic:

i) The argument of the original sin has no grounds.

"Original sin, also called ancestral sin, is the Christian doctrine of humanity's state of sin resulting from the fall of man, stemming from Adam and Eve's rebellion in Eden, namely the sin of disobedience in consuming from the tree of knowledge of good and evil." ——Original Sin, Wikipedia

According to this definition and its explanation, our original sin—every human, no exception—has come from Adam and Eve's disobedience in consuming *from the tree of knowledge of good and evil*. The definition, from what I learned, appears correct. What it says bugs me. First, it is considered as a rebellion. Disobedience? Yes. Rebellion, I think, is an overkill. A more sensible way to look at the incident will be with a bit of understanding. Humans are very intelligent beings. As a result, our species is very inquisitive; we always want to explore new things, which is a natural consequence of having very developed frontal lobes.

Here in the garden was this tree of knowledge of good and evil. Would you, if you were Adam and Eve, not be tempted to eat the fruit, especially the fruit that promised to give you the knowledge of good and evil? If it was any other fruit, I might be able to resist the temptation. But a fruit that would give me knowledge of good and evil? I would die for it. Adam and Eve were like children and were naturally thirsty for knowledge. Like children, they would often do things that you have specifically told them not to. Nailing them with rebellion appears to be harsh and lacking understanding. Would a loving and understanding God do that?

Then, the question becomes: Why would the Almighty prohibit our ancestors from gaining the knowledge of good and evil? Isn't it the best thing a parent could ever give his children? If you are a parent and there is this wonder drug in the market that promises to give those who consume it knowledge of good and evil, would you not mortgage your house, if you have to, buy it for your Billy ASAP? The story makes gaining knowledge of good and evil appear so extremely sinful, even more than stealing, robbery, or rape. Should the Almighty be so angry for something Adam and Eve have done to satisfy their curiosity and to gain knowledge? And he was unreasonably very, very angry. *But the whole story was groundless!* Science tells us, based on facts collected from many different branches of science, our ancestor was a common chimp and Adam and Eve were no chimps. Jesus might not have known this fact and therefore had made a case out of nothing. By the way, the Jewish people share the same Old Testament; most, if not all Jews do not believe in the original sin. Obviously, original sin was Jesus's idea. Why did he invent something like that?

Even if the story were true, which was definitely not, it was still nonsense. Basically, it says if your parents, grandparents, or even great-great-grandparents committed a wrongdoing and they had been punished, you, their remote descendants, will still have to pay for it. How barbaric! It is beyond barbaric, it has to have come from *a sick mind*! The guy who has the gut to propose such a thing must be a mental case. Even crazier, his followers—the pastors, priests, and clergymen—are fervently selling this sin to you, and many (close to 2 billion people) are still buying it. It is beyond nonsense; it is pure madness.

The original sin is one of the many things that bug me. I always want to find out more about it from the experts who make their living studying the Bible. The son-in-law of my sister was a pastor. So during a Christmas dinner gathering I raised the question of original sin to the pastor, hoping that he would know much more than an average churchgoer like me. He began to explain it to me with a smile. Soon, I found out his understanding was not that different from mine; it was typically the same stale stuff. I also asked him why wanting to get knowledge of good and evil was such a big no-no. That was when the thing began to get awkward and everyone in the room became uneasy. My sister, who had been quiet the whole time interrupted, "Yuk-Ngai, just because you got a PhD you think you know everything? Don't be so arrogant!" She was visibly shaking when uttering those words. I knew it was time to shut the hell up. I also promised myself never to discuss the Bible with the Jesus followers again.

ii) Everyone who looks at a woman with lustful intent has already committed adultery with her in his heart.

"But I say to you that everyone who looks at a woman with lustful intent has already committed adultery with her in his heart," Matthew 5:28, English Standard Version.

Committing adultery with a woman for people in the Arab region and many parts of the ancient world was, and still is, a very serious criminal offense, a sin often deserving death for the lustful pair. But just by looking at a woman lustfully and already you are guilty? *If your right eye causes you to sin, gouge it out and throw it away. It is better for you to lose one part of your body than for your whole body to be thrown into hell,* Mathew 5:29. So though you have not actually done it other than just by having the lustful thought, you have already sinned and therefore should be punished and as a result. Not by a slap on your wrist, it will be to have your whole body thrown into hell forever and ever. It is just so sick, sick, sick.

In essence, and by the same logic, if you look at a guy hatefully you have already committed an assault against the guy. If you look at someone's money greedily, you have already committed a theft against him. Or, if you look at someone's iPhone and want to have it, you also have committed the theft. No country in the world will be so insane as to pass such laws. But this is exactly what Jesus was trying to nail you with: you are a sinner if you do it. From this piece of teaching I had always felt that I was a sinner because ninety-nine times out of a hundred, when I looked at a good-looking woman, especially a sexy one, I would immediately fancy having sex with her; still do at seventy-five. I have forgotten how many times I have asked the Heavenly Father for forgiveness just for this one. Even worse, I knew I would fall again while asking for pardon. I also was 100 percent sure that I would sin again and again because I was powerless to stop it. I had even planned to do it and then beg. I felt like such a phony.

Fate has it that of all the science subjects I had chosen to study biology and got a PhD in biophysics. One thing that I really understand well is biology. The knowledge helped me to later discover that all living organisms are selfish and are obsessed with survival. To survive, every living organism needs to self-serve and self-preserve. To self-defend and to get energy are for the preservation and survival of an individual organism, but to reproduce is for the preservation of the species. In fact, the goal of self-preservation of an individual organism is a preparation to preserve its own species. Reproduction, if you look at it that way, will be the goal for every living organism because the survival of a species depends solely on it. Reproduction serves to preserve a species. Because it is so important, the interest of reproduction often trumps the other interests, like self-defense or to get energy; i.e., to eat for animals. Among animals, reproduction is mostly control by sex hormones. When an animal is ready to reproduce, its sex hormones will peak, urging the animal to reproduce. Because reproduction often involves sexual intercourse, the urge to have sex among animals is one of the most powerful and the strongest force in nature in controlling the behavior of an animal when it is ready. Almost no animal can resist it.

The sexual behavior of humans is a bit odd as compared to the other animals, but sexual urge is still very strong and very persistent, especially among men. So it is quite normal and healthy for a man who is loaded with testosterone, young or old, to look at a woman lustfully, especially those with the perfect proportions—big and bouncy breasts, small waist, and full hips. It is an instinct well served. And a lustful thought is beyond our control regardless how strong-willed or discipline you are.Was Jesus immune? Not a chance if he was a man. He had facial hair, according to all his portraits, didn't he? Then he must have the male hormones. It would be difficult to explain how, despite having the male hormones, he would be immune from it. Something did not quite add up. Either he chose to lie or he was odd, biologically speaking, and therefore had no understanding of what we real men are going through. Did he know that it would be impossible for a healthy man not to look at a (sexy) woman lustfully? It is very basic stuff in biology. If he was who he claimed to be, the only son of the Almighty, an omnipotent and therefore omniscient God, he could not have been ignorant of so simple a biological fact! That leaves us with two possibilities: either he was a fake, or he knew but had chosen to intentionally nail the common folks with something they had no power to resist. Either way, it would be wrong, morally very wrong!

iii) Is God, according to the Bible's version, the God of love?

Point i and ii—and there are more—are enough to make everyone, especially a man, a sinner. This net of guilt cast by Jesus is so enormous that there is no escaping it. They serve only one goal: it is to make you believe you are a sinner. Then, the question will be why was Jesus so anxious to the point of fabricating a story or purposely overlooking a biological truth to make you feel guilty? What will be the take for him?

"For God so loved the world, that He gave His only begotten Son, that whoever believes in Him should not perish, but have eternal life," John 3:16, New American Standard, 1977.

Aha! The cat is finally out of the bag! Don't despair if you are a sinner—and every human will be. There is a way out. And the only way to save you from the eternal fire of hell is to believe in Jesus. He, by being nailed on the cross and have died for your sin, him and him only can save you. But to get the deal, you must 1) believe and confess that you are a sinner, and 2) believe that Jesus is the only son of God and only he can cleanse your sin. Simple and easy, isn't it? Want assurance? Here they are:

But if we walk in the Light as He Himself is in the Light, we have fellowship with one another, and the blood of Jesus His Son cleanses us from all sin, 1 John 1:7, and If we confess our sins, He is faithful and righteous to forgive us our sins and to cleanse us from all unrighteousness, 1 John 1:9

This is easily the greatest deal ever to offer to the human race! Basically, all you need to do is to raise your hand or nod when you are asked whether you are a sinner or not. And you will get an eternal life and will not have to fear the burning fire. And it is all free! You would be a moron not to take it. If it sounds too good to be true, it probably is. As you go deeper and deeper into the worship, it turns out that the deal was not at all that simple and easy. The things you need to do to qualify keep growing; the list gets longer and longer.

Increasingly, I felt more and more uneasy, burdened by my many sins, often having no control over them. I was supposed to have peace, but it was exactly peace that had left me. After many decades of feeling sinful and inadequate, it then got to a point that I must make a choice: to get eternal life and kill my sanity, or to choose rationality and say, "Hell, here I come." I have finally chosen sanity. On the day I rejected Jesus (I did not reject God), I said a prayer to God without ending it with *"In Jesus's name, I pray."* I just ended it with a simple *Amen*. I also said to God, "If not to believe in Jesus because I could not, based on rationality, and you would cast me into hell, so be it. Amen." At the time, I did not understand what love is. Now, having defined love, the ludicrousness of the whole thing is even more. Love is one of the most talked about and also the least understood thing. In my last trip to South America, I have challenged many of my young audience, asking them to define it for me. Some, after searching for a while, simply admitted they did not really know. Those who tried did not quite nail it. They all knew that it is something very beautiful, desirable, and precious to have. I usually told them, "If you don't know what it is, how can you find it?" Or, "How do you tell the guy is real when he tells you that he loves you, and not trying to get you in bed only to leave?" The second remark has never failed to get them interested and listen.

We have defined love in a previous chapter. In a nutshell, love must be shown in action by offering a free gift of value to a willing receiver. I am pretty sure that is the essence of love. If we can accept this definition, then let us see whether (the Christian) God really loves the world. *"For God so loved the world, that He gave His only begotten Son, that whoever believes in Him should not perish, but have eternal life."* The love is not free! There is a condition attached to receiving this "love": you must believe in Jesus as the one and only son of the Almighty. If the gift is not free, it is not love, is it? You won't get eternal life unless you believe in Jesus. To believe in Jesus means that you can never doubt anything he said, like you have original sin, something that you inherited from our nonexistent ancestors. You also have to admit that you have sinned whenever you looked at a woman lustfully, which is in our instinct and which is essential to keep our species around. None of them make any sense! Not only is the "love" not free, the price tag has turned out to be very hefty. You have to keep suffocating any rationality that pops up from time to time. Doubters will have a more difficult time entering the kingdom than rich people. Any street-smart person will tell you that before you can be cheated you will be asked to trust the cheater. In this case, you need to trust a number of things that really make no sense in exchange.

iv) Many teachings are beyond absurd.

Scriptures like *If your right eye causes you to sin, gouge it out and throw it away. It is better for you to lose one part of your body than for your whole body to be thrown into hell.* Or, *But I tell you, do not resist an evil person. If anyone slaps you on the right cheek, turn to them the other cheek also, Matthew 5:39.* You don't know whether Jesus was serious or not. If you take him seriously, many of his faithful will be blind or have their hands cut off. *Don't resist an evil person?* I would fight him every time if fleeing is not an option. *Turn the other cheek?* You may as well give him your iPhone and wallet. Or, if you are a girl, you may as well comply with whatever the guy wants from you. Even in my most fervent days, I would not do it. And I always told my daughters to take care of themselves and never let anyone bully or take advantage of them. I wonder what those clever and resourceful Christian theologians have come up with in Jesus's defense. It would be advisable to keep their mouths shut if I were in their shoes.

v) Love, forgiving, and sacrifice, the three sacred but flawed Christian values.

They are widely considered among the highest values; they are also very difficult to follow if you are serious about it.

Love is a very odd thing for a selfish being. For humans, it is exceedingly difficult to choose to love because it means you need to freely and willingly give away something of value for your survival to a receiver, sometimes a stranger. I don't think Jesus had any idea of its difficulty when he casually mentioned it to his followers: *But I tell you, love your enemies, bless those who curse you, do good to those who hate you, and pray for those who mistreat you and persecute you,* Matthew 5:44 I am not saying that love is impossible for us, but it is certainly not as easy as Jesus's teaches it to be. A person can be trained to love; the training is by following our moral selfishness. To follow the Golden Rule is to put yourself into a receiving party's position. To be considerate is the essence of care. When you keep caring, love will grow inside you.

All my audience agrees that love comes from care and is a stronger emotion than care. If you put care and love in an emotion scale from 1 to 10, and a higher value corresponds to a stronger feeling, then care will be between 1 and 3 and love starts from 5 to 10. At 10, a person would not hesitate to give away his life for a cause or a loved one. If a person is habitually caring and considerate, he will become loving also. It is inevitable, and I can testify to that. A morally selfish person will gradually become a more loving person. To be selfish and to freely give seem incompatible, but are they? When I first brought up the idea of moral selfishness to a friend, she challenged me, "Then you don't believe in giving?" I didn't know how to answer. After several months, I came up with an answer to myself, "A morally selfish person does not do anything that he does not feel happy about." If giving makes me happy, I will do it. Not for the other; rather, I do it for me. The answer certainly satisfies my own query. Then, recently, it also dawned on me that to be moral to others has already included giving, by giving others what they deserve, an amount that is fair, in a transaction.

Moral selfishness leads to happiness because you do things that make you happy. When a person is perpetually happy, I think he would be more generous, would he not? So in giving what people deserve or an amount that is fair, he will give a bit more unwittingly. If the argument on care and love makes sense to you, you would also agree that love can be cultivated. And the only sure way to cultivate love in a person is through moral selfishness, the principle we propose in this book to save our planet.

In short, love must come from within and must come naturally. It will never be as simple as by saying love your neighbor and even your enemies, and *viola*, there is your love! I seriously doubt whether Jesus understood what love was. You will never find it according to Jesus, because you don't know what it is and how to grow it. The only way that I know is by following the Golden Rule.

To forgive is another extremely tough thing to follow. To forgive, according to the Bible, is to wipe clean someone's transgression and look at the offender's eyes like nothing happened—no anger, not even a trace of it, and instead, with a smile. To forgive is to forget; the pair is inseparable. Can you do it? Will it be as easy as what Jesus said? I can forgive my daughters for their wrongdoings, or my mother's many abuses. They are close to me, and whether I will be happy or not depends a lot on how I handle their flaws. For selfish reasons, it would be better for me to find a reason or reasons to excuse them. It took time and effort; not easy. But to a stranger who intentionally put a dent on your car just because you parked a couple of times too close to his space, and he was not sorry for doing it and therefore would never apologize? You want me to say hello and chat with him cheerfully like nothing happened? The guy was lucky that I don't believe in getting even, because it will always lead to endless bad things. I don't do revenge because it will come back to hurt me. But to forgive him? Never! I would not even give him a chance to say hello to me.

Or you would insist that it is doable. "Hasn't Pope John Paul II forgiven his assassin?" Call me cynical, I can't honestly believe that was genuine. The pope has lots to gain. 1) It is not that hard to do. All that was required was for the Church to arrange a meeting between the two parties and invite the media to attend for a photo op. 2) Both the pope and the Church had a lot to gain, didn't they? For the Pope, the act would raise his virtue to a level belonging to saints. In fact, he was later beatified and canonized on 1 May 2011. I am sure the forgiveness he showed to his assassin had something to do with it. The Church also badly needed some positive PR after a string of proven guilty verdicts in sexually assaulting children committed by its priests and clergymen. It could very well be a show to advertise forgiveness. But if you were one of the tens of thousands sexually assaulted, could you forgive those animals in priest's clothes who had repeatedly hurt you? Also knowing that they had no intention to apologize and given a chance would not hesitate to do it again? It would be *harder than conquering Mt. Everest*! I really don't think Jesus knew what he was talking about when giving those sermons.

To sacrifice is another of those impossible (I am running out of adjectives—unthinkable, unachievable, impractical, or nonviable won't quite fit) concepts. It will be undoable because it is against our nature. And the one who heeds the teaching often is susceptible to being exploited. To be exploited, one has to blindly trust. To kill one's own rationality is often the prelude. This is exactly what Jesus's teachings are mostly about, to make a demand on his followers to kill their intelligence so that they can be manipulated and exploited if the situation calls for it. People who are misguided to habitually and mindlessly sacrifice their own interests are often left empty and bitter. Look no further than the most glorified sacrificer Mother Teresa. She was not a happy person according to her own words and had been pleading for help and getting none from the Church. The authority had good reason to deny her. To help her is to admit there is something wrong with sacrificing when it is carried to an excess. And she was synonymous with the virtue. To help her is to destroy that logo, something the Catholic Church would never even consider doing. And the refusal to help was not for the benefit of the poor misguided saint. Though joyless during most of her years living, Mother Teresa will be considered lucky because she did have lots of appreciation from her Church and admiration from the Catholics. She has enjoyed the fame that has come with it. She was a privileged person. The many suicide bombers are not so lucky. They were exploited by some Islamic egoists to achieve their quest for power. I think they have foolishly died for nothing. If you use our two moral principles and ask the three questions to obtain the answers, you can clearly see that encouraging people to sacrifice for you or your cause is immoral. To encourage people to die for you is evil. Moral selfishness is against sacrifice. There is no way to justify it.

From our discussion, it is not just one or two teachings that the Bible is wrong. If it is, it is excusable because it is written more than two thousand years too long ago. There are bound to be some mistakes by today's knowledge. It is the widespread of the toxic or senseless messages. For me personally, many of the major teachings of Jesus are to be classified in the sick and absurd category.

The question becomes: Did Jesus know exactly what he was doing? Or, was it by design? The impossibly high standard was to fail most, if not all, his followers. When you have failed, not just once or twice but repeatedly, it really shames you, or more appropriately, makes you feel inadequate and guilty. That may be exactly what Jesus had in mind. Then, you can be easily manipulated. Many people guilt trip, but Jesus has made a big career of it. Jesus has got to be the greatest guilt-trip artist that ever lived, by nailing people with an original sin that does not exist, by convicting you for having looked at a woman lustfully, and by deliberately setting those impossible moral standards.

To be a sincere Christian, I gradually harbored more and more guilt in my heart. I was hardly alone. According to Dr. M. Scott Peck, the author of *The Road Less Traveled,* many of his mental patients were Catholic. They were so overwhelmed with guilt that they could not function and had to seek help. When I read the patients' stories, I knew how badly I had been poisoned. Believing in Jesus was supposed to give me the peace and happiness I was seeking. They were exactly the two things that had been hopelessly drifting away from me. There was seldom a moment I had peace ever since I was baptized. Looking back, to walk away, to turn my back to Christianity was certainly one of the best things I have done for myself. Now, having been fully detoxed, I can see clearly how Christianity selects its prey. The many doctrines and dogmas are designed to kill a follower's rationality and reason. If you want to keep yours, then you are not for Jesus. It is a screen that discards people who want to trust reason more than blind faith. No wonder the Church is losing scientists on a wholesale scale. Christianity is hardly alone. Most religions demand blind faith from their followers. As a result, countries that allow their religions to play a major role in moral decisions are in general poor and often barbaric.

Wake up, America. The world needs your leadership.

Some Americans, especially those Republicans that voted for Trump, may object. They are pious Christians and their faith has a lot to do with the success of America. *In God we trust* has defined the strength of their nation, so they are convinced. But to give the Christian faithful all the credit is unfair, because the main engine that drives America is science and its many hardworking and sharp-minded scientists. America has the most top-notched scientists, which is the envy of the rest of the world. That is the reason America has Apple, Google, Microsoft, Facebook, and Tesla, etc. Is there even one of the innovators of those companies who is a Christian? I doubt very much. Is it time to redefine the strength of the nation? It should be *In science we trust.* I firmly believe that it is none other than our God(s) that has given us the rules and laws of science. Science and God are one.

If anything, the Christians are like a broken piece of metal that gets in the engine, and will, from time to time, slow down the engine. If electing Trump as the president *is the best thing that ever happened to*

America, it will be to warn the country that following the teachings of Jesus is harmful to the country because it makes people who should be intelligent and smart stupid by choice, by deliberately killing their intelligence. By electing Trump, the Americans will soon see what harm killing your intelligence and reason can do to the country. No doubt, having spent four years studying in UCLA and thus having had the chance to see the inner workings of this great engine of America and to learn the open-mindedness of many of its students and professors, I have reason to believe America should be the leader of the world and champion the world to a higher and happier level. But it has been just the opposite. From the many recent wars that America was involved in (and there were few that the country was not involved in), the country has been the troublemaker for the world's community. If America is the police of the world as they have often claimed, then it is certainly a dirty cop, often hurting other nations for its own gain.

There are reasons for America to behave so badly. Number one is of course human selfishness. Next is America is the strongest and the most powerful nation that lacks a correct moral view. And the third will be the country is often run by the Christians; the election of Trump should be a good example. For reasons stated, this is not a good thing for a country full of capable and brilliant scientists. The scientists should have more say than the Christians. But the scientists are a timid bunch, more concerned about getting funded for their little pet projects than having a vision to apply their know-how to make the world better. Many, if not the majority, prominent scientists actually refuse to get involved in politics or moral right and wrong discussions. With their voluntary withdrawal, they gave away their power and let the Christians decide the most important policies. Their voice is absent when some schools refuse to teach the theory of evolution. And instead, allow the young minds to be made stupid by the seven-day divine creation. It is so absurd that it should actually happen to the world's most intelligent country. But no one is laughing. One can only feel sad, not just for America, because the world has lost a rightful leader.

I am a dreamer, the most stubborn and the most hopeless type. I still believe that America will one day wake up and see the folly of the path the majority of its people are taking. They are not just your ordinary people, they are the ones with the most desirable human qualities, hardworking and kindhearted, who really want to do good. Alas! They lack the correct morality to guide them. In hoping to get eternal lives, they also foolishly allow their minds to be poisoned. They seem powerless to walk away from a promise that may be empty. Maybe the Trump presidency will do the trick. To wake up this great nation, a hefty price will still be a bargain.

If America can wake up—I am quite sure they will given time—and use reason again, they will soon see the many benefits of following the Golden Rule–based moral principles and adopt it. And if most Americans are morally selfish, can you even imagine what a beautiful start for the world it will be? I know I am dreaming, some of my friends even told me it will be impossible. But this dreamer will never give up this beautiful dream, because I am thoroughly convinced it is doable. I am also convinced that all the beautiful ideas of this book are from the authority above. There is a spiritual community caring for us, the human race; I have once actually experienced their presence.

If you think that moral selfishness makes sense, follow it. Better still, tell a friend. This will be the way and the only way to change our world. Amen.

An Afterthought   Does God Exist?

It sounds very odd and even self-serving that I should refuse to believe the many ideas in the book, beautiful, significant, and original as they are, have come from me. Yes, I am the writer, but the ideas don't belong to me. Rather, they have been communicated to me by a higher authority that we call God. This kind of claim has been made several times by several religious leaders before. Unlike those who have made the claim previously, I am not someone who would inspire respect. I am your everyday common male who loves beer, pizza, and often looks at pretty girls with lustful intent.

To be honest, I have never had any interest or intent to write this kind of book. It covers three big unrelated academic fields—human nature, morality, and the forces that have shaped human evolution, each of which would be difficult for a lone scholar to tackle and up to now have been unsolved. To be precise, I am not worthy of such a project; I absolutely don't qualify. This sentiment of *I don't own the ideas* has pervaded almost every page of my first self-published book in 2005, *Happy to Be Morally Selfish*, the book where most of the ideas of this book first come from. The girl who edited my manuscript was a graduate student working toward a PhD in psychology at the time. She commented, "Steve, you have a PhD; own up to your ideas." I have since rewritten the entire book three times and talked to over a hundred people about some of its more important contents. I have become more convinced that the ideas and theses are valid; they will be the tools to make our world a better place. But more than ever, I also adamantly refuse to take credit, or the blame if those theses and concepts prove to be faulty. I have strong reasons to believe that the ideas have come from God, not me. And the ideas have come to me in the oddest way: from a shameful mistake I have made. The mistake has forced me to think about my self-worth. It made me seriously doubt myself. Was I still a good person? I have never been confronted with such an overwhelming issue that has demanded an answer right away.

Knowing that I am a good person is very important to me. For the level of education I got, I have achieved very little. I have borne this guilt of underperforming ever since I decided to leave academia. If there is one thing I have always wanted and is within my grip, it will be to die knowing that I have been a good person. This goal is for me—not for heaven or hell. Even this humble wish has been threatened. As a result, I was compelled to think deep and hard for the ensuing several months. I wanted to know how bad a mistake I have made morally. It was during those months that the many ideas began to be revealed to me. They are original and very significant ideas. I began to write them down lest I forget. Then, the notes have later become the *Happy* book.

I feel deeply obligated to disclose my source. Not disclosing would be stealing, it would also make me very ungrateful. In doing it, I also know the risk well, but it is the right thing to do. I would rather face the consequence—a possible turbulent future of being the target of attacks from every direction. I have chosen to face them and have the peace of mind and heart rather than bear the guilt; it is the only right choice for me.

I did not see the true value of the *Happy* book for several years after I published it; I was still trying to grasp the many ideas. The concept of a *self*, for example, has proven a very difficult one. I have tweaked the definition several times trying to make it right. It was not until after the third revision that I was more or less happy with it. *Moral selfishness* is the other one. They both have layers and layers of meaning which I only began to see after letting them sit in my mind to age for many years. And how and why the part of evolution of human has come to me remained a big puzzle. There appeared no reason for me to do it at the time. It was not something that has ever interested me and I knew very little on the field. I began to play with the idea of writing the book after getting some new ideas of deciding moral right and wrong, the issue that got me thinking. The subsequent discovery of how the first self, which was also the first living organism, came to exist, and with it the concept of a self, has further reinforced my intention. The realization of how the first self came to exist was one of the few *eureka* moments in writing the book. From self comes self-serving, self-preservation, and thus selfishness. And selfishness always tends to hurt. Then, I decided that the knowledge and concepts were too important to let vanish.

But the materials I had at the time were far from enough for a book. I needed some more substance to bulk it up to make it more respectable. I somehow settled on writing the evolution of our line, not knowing how to fit the part into the overall scheme. Above all, how would I do it? After the decision, I then began to look for information. I happened to have a copy of *The Images of the Past* that I got months ago from a garage sale. I picked it up because the price was ninety nine cents, I could not walk away from such a great deal. The book gives me most of the information to further develop the theme! Strange and crazy, isn't it?

After publishing the *Happy* book, I was far from happy with it. The book is full of mistakes and defects. There are also gaps in the logic and arguments in the theses. Some points are often redundant. As a whole, it was not well organized and was poorly written, thus making it quite tiring to read. I often jokingly told people that the book was great in curing insomnia. I seriously doubt that any of the buyers finished reading it. Notwithstanding, it has taken me several years and easily several hours each working day with full concentration to finish. It has taken a toll on me, both physically and mentally. I was quite drained near the end. I needed to end the project, though reluctantly. I have mixed feelings about the book. On the one hand, it was not well written and full of glaring, simple, and careless errors. It could be, and deserved to be, done better. On the other hand, I loved the many ideas in it very, very much. The book was like my child. I was very proud of it despite its many flaws and inadequacies. It was also very odd because most of the concepts were quite alien to me and were not something that I had remotely cared about prior; the DNA of the book was definitely not mine. Somehow they were dropped into or popped up in my mind as I was deep in thought. Instead of the biological father, I feel more like its surrogate mother. I love it all the same and as much.

They are beautiful and significant ideas: the link between selfishness and survival, human nature or simplifying moral decisions by using the two principles derived from the Golden Rule, and the role sex has played to help our species through the most difficult times in evolution, for example, was each in itself a heavyweight academic topic. Each subject, up to the time, has remained little known and unresolved, despite many learned and sharp-minded having no doubt tried. Each problem would not be easy for one expert to solve, let alone a lone ex-biologist who was preoccupied with selling real estate to survive at the time. Each would demand the sharpest of minds and the most learned among the intellects—of that I was quite certain. So from the beginning I had very good reason to refuse to believe that the ideas were from me at all. They must have been the answers to my many prayers during those difficult hours.

I knew where I stood and have been very level-headed all my life; daydreaming has not been a part of my traits. Besides, I was too busy keeping my head above water, trying to make enough money to pay the seemingly endless bills. I could not afford to do it; I did not have the financial luxury to support such a venture. I knew it would be a cardinal sin for my career and a sure way to get me into a financial nightmare again. In a nutshell: I had none of the required knowledge and qualifications, did not have the financial resources, and above all, had absolutely no plan to or interest in changing the world. Rather, the book was then to serve as my memoir to save the precious knowledge I have gained from the ordeal.

I got it written, though far from perfect. It has turned out rather easy because most of its many ideas have come naturally. It seems odd, doesn't it, considering their originality and significance? They seemed to have been waiting for me. Most of my difficulties were from the struggle with English. It is not my mother tongue and it has never been my strong suit. English, especially in writing composition, was my most loathed subject in high school and college.

But there had been quite a few happy coincidences that helped me to finish the book. Having enough income for me to write for four years instead of the planned one from an unexpected source was one of them.

The few books with important information I needed just happened to be there ready for me was the other one. They were either from an earlier garage sale, a book clearance, or a casual visit to a library. *Images of the Past,* first edition (?), by T. Douglas Price and Gary Feinman; *The Wisdom of the Bones* by Alan Walker and Pat Shipment; and an article on "The Selfish Gene" by Richard Dawkins are examples. And just when I had been struggling for weeks to come up with a way to decide morality, the Golden Rule appeared on *the Toronto Star.* And there were more. I could not have planned those events even if I wanted to. They just timely and conveniently dropped onto my lap.

How could one explain all those highly improbable coincidences that had made finishing the book possible? How would one rationalize an amateur managing to write significantly and coherently on three different major academic fields? It would be almost as hard as life to begin in abiogenesis. For me, I see only one explanation: the ideas are from gods; I am merely their messenger. Writing the book was not just about struggling with English or getting the ideas organized for presentation, it has been a journey of continuous learning and discovery of new knowledge and wisdom. It has been very rewarding. There have been quite a few *eureka* moments that brought intense joy and satisfaction, which won't get washed away with the passage of years. Memory of those moments has made me proud. The book has made me feel I have not lived in vain.

After publishing the book, my goal was to spend a couple of years at the most to promote the book to fulfill my obligation as the receiver of this rare gift. I fully expected the book, because of its many original and significant ideas, to create a big impact after it was published. Nothing happened. The book had to be the worst seller for Amazon, which had carried it online for a while; the company had sold 0 copies. Disappointed and thinking that I had done my part, I was prepared to leave the book and go back to my old life. At the time, I have introduced the ideas to many people, sold and given away more than 100 copies of the book. What more could anyone ask from me? And more importantly, I needed to put my focus back on making money; my saving account was running low. But there is no walking away from it. Like the image of the woman in a recent failed romance, the many ideas of the book kept coming back to me, demanding my attention. Unlike the thoughts of the woman, they have not faded with the passage of years. They have grown stronger instead, popping up incessantly into my awareness and often in my dreams. Also different from a lost love, the book had always brought me joy and satisfaction. Sharing many of its ideas—human nature is selfish and the two rules to decide moral right and wrong, in particular—with a willing audience has always made me very happy. Though not as intense as sex, the feeling is equally strong and lasts much longer, to quote Stephen Hawking. Most of my audience have been recent European university graduates I met in hostels traveling. The list also includes a couple of science professors, psychologists, judges, engineers, and ordinary people. None could rationally deny that living creatures, including us, are selfish and naturally hurtful. All agreed and accepted that the proposed two principles from the Golden Rule are fair to decide morality; some marveled how easy and simple the principles are to use. One even went as far as saying that *simplicity is the ultimate sophistication.* I later found out that is from the great Leonardo da Vinci. That was the greatest compliment I have ever received. I don't deserve it, though it does give me the steroid to go on. From the feedback, I have become increasingly sure that ideas are sound; they also have provided me with the courage and the needed fuel to continue.

Then, before I turned seventy-five, about ten years after publishing the *Happy* book, while walking along the Malecon in Quayaquil, Ecuador, around noon it suddenly became clear to me that I have been chosen to bear and spread the message of the book. Then, the two failed marriages, the many career changes, and the heartaches and headaches I have gone through took on new meanings. All my resentment, regret and disappointments began to evaporate; instead, my heart was filled with gratitude. Those have been the trainings, the fire and water I was meant to go through to shape me for this important assignment. For that, I shall remain forever thankful. It also became very clear that my entire existence has been to prepare for this one and only mission: it is to spread the message of the book. It has become my quest, for the time being, a solo quest. This will be a very difficult quest as well as an impossible dream. I am to fight many mighty enemies—the world's religions, established moralities, closed-mindedness, and above all, selfishness itself. There will be lots of frustrations for me to bear and possible dangers to face. For I shall venture where the fearless dare not go, my quest is to right the moral wrongs and give the world a new morality that leads to peace and happiness. I must continue when I am drained. But I know if I persist, I'll one day reach the unreachable goal and our world will become a paradise.

Without the slightest doubt, this is meant to be my quest, to follow that goal no matter how treacherous and no matter how far. And it will be full of disappointments and rejections, and from time to time, self-doubt. But as long as my faith stays strong, my heart will have peace and calm despite repeated defeats. And I shall get back on my feet again after every fall. I am certain the world will be better for this, that one man, mocked and covered with scars, still strove with his last bit of courage to reach that unreachable star. (My adaptation from the lyrics by Joe Darion in *Man of La Mancha*. It best describes how I feel.)

According to the accepted wisdom, I am a very unlikely bearer of the message. I am pretty average in whichever way one would define success. For many that know me, I would better fit what people would call a failure. I have worked very hard to obtain a PhD from a highly respected university, only to give it all up after a short several years of trying. I have failed to land an assistant professorship in a university. I have gone through two "broken" marriages, and have switched careers—high school teacher, research associate, florist, real estate agent, and several short ventures—like Broadway actors changing their outfits. Most of my life has been just to survive. Even after self-publishing two books, I have gained very little financially or in recognition. Yes, no doubt, I have been a failure; reality has forced me to accept the shameful label. In fact, this was what my first ex called me in one of those frequent nasty verbal fights. I would have most likely gone to my grave bearing this label with disappointment and regret. But the book has changed all of that, at least for me. Through it, I was reborn and awakened late in life because I have acquired a new purpose. This is my quest, something I am to do. For it, I have been patiently prepared, shaped, and forged for decades, possibly from the day I was born. And I am most happy to accept this quest, to be the tool and the most unlikely fixer.

I am also keenly aware that making this claim, a groundless and highly offensive assertion, will be madness. That is what all con artists do. Even if the book gets noticed, it will certainly incur the rage of many authorities, who would feel my encroachment as a challenge to their claim to monopolize morality. They will attack me mercilessly and try to destroy the new theories, if not my body. Or I'll be ridiculed, a laughingstock and a fool who let his ego get way out of control. This may not be a bad thing at all. Quite the contrary, it could be a disguised blessing. Then, I can challenge the attackers to focus on destroying the theories and to find faults in the foundation upon which they are built, in particular, to disprove that life is unstable and therefore needs to be selfish, and the thesis on the two forces that have powered human evolution and made us strong are false. Or, to negate the two principles for moral decision: (1) that it is immoral to intentionally hurt others for self-gain, and (2) that it is wrong to give others no choice—both are derived from the Golden Rule. If they are successful, it will be the best way to cure my insanity and to set me free again. Either way, I'll be happy.

I am quite sure all the theses will prevail. They have been put through exhaustive questions and the rigorous tests during the past years by me. As a scientist, I am the theses' most merciless critic from day one and during every step in their development. This is the reason I believe I am not deluded, it is also the source of my courage. That is why I am so happy to launch the project and try to see it through. It is also the reason I have chosen to take this treacherous route in my quest.

Though my quest has just begun, to prepare me to this stage by first writing the book has been a rather long process. It started in the early 2000s and completed in mid-2017. During those years, there has been seldom a day that passed without me thinking about some parts of the book. I have rewritten the book in its entirety three times, each time with some new information I have discovered along the way, each time giving it a new name, and each time trying to find a more logical way to present its contents. It was not until I finished the current edition, *The Quest of an Unlikely Fixer,* that I am quite happy with the result.

If one should ask me what has been my biggest gain in writing the book, it would be very difficult for me to pick one. Either discovering the many original ideas, the rich source of wisdom from the Golden Rule, moral selfishness especially, or the two factors (one being sex) in helping our species through and to become godlike could easily justify the answer. All have given me indescribable satisfaction and have become my fountain of joy. No, great as they all are, none can be my answer. The answer, I would say, is certainly the journey itself. It has allowed me to know God, or gods better. From the knowledge and wisdom given to me and through what has actually once happened, I have become absolutely certain that Gods exist. I am blessed with such a rare and precious knowledge. I know for sure that there is, though beyond the proof of science, a whole community of caring and benevolent spirits out there looking after us and guiding us. I am also fully convinced that it has been none other than these spirits that have brought life to our planet and have shaped the evolution and eventually created us, the human race.

If one looks at the evolution of our species according to our theory, it could not have been a blind process dictated by random mutations. Rather, the creation of humans has been a planned development. *We are their proudest creation.* We have been created in their image, beings with high intelligence capable of appreciating and understanding nature and solving difficult problems. The problem we are to solve is how to handle our selfish nature so that despite being born with it we can still coexist with others—our own kind and other living creatures— harmoniously. For that, they have given us the Golden Rule.

The knowledge has become my guidance, strength, and source of peace and happiness. It also has brought a happy ending to the most important search of my life. Without knowing it, I have been searching for three things throughout my life. From an early age, possibly around five, I had begun to search for knowledge, trying to understand things. It was no coincidence that I should be interested in science. After turning twenty, I began searching for love, the love of a woman to be precise. And much later in life, possibly after sixty, I longed to know more about God. It happened almost at the same time after I decided to abandon Christianity. I was hugely disappointed by the God described by the Bible. God cannot be like that; I refuse to believe it. The search also paralleled to the time the many ideas of the book were given to me.

I have been handsomely rewarded for my search in knowledge; it allows me to understand the working of our planet, especially what we call "life" better. I still vividly remember while walking along a small path between the rice fields, possibly being no more than six at the time, that I was puzzled by a problem. If I deliberately changed my next step, say instead of stepping forward going backward or sideward, will it drastically change my future? Obviously, each step will produce its consequence, how will it change me? It was not until I turned sixty that I could answer that question with some certainty. The knowledge I got has given me a lot of joy; it lets me better understand biology and "life" itself.

The search for love has brought only disappointments so far. Some brokenhearted call it a fool's game. I would do it again given a chance, for I have no immunity against it despite repeated exposure and being stung each time. I would gladly have a spoonful of honey in exchange for a gallon of bitter medicine. It has not been a total loss. Though having suffered quite a bit, it still is a road worthy of taking. I have learned and grown up from the errors and pains; it has enriched me immensely. Through them I have lived a fuller life. No regrets.

To say that my search to know God has been very rewarding or satisfying will be a huge understatement. Writing this book has allowed me to find them. It gives me new meaning for my existence and a new perspective on all the past disappointments and "failures." I have gained a peace in heart and mind at a level never before possible, and therefore am so very grateful. I have been so tremendously blessed.

My conviction that gods exist has been based mainly on reason. And I have plenty of reasons. Other than the wonderful ideas in the book and how they have been passed to me as already mentioned, there is another equally important one: I have once actually been touched by their spirits. It happened in 1990 during summer at noon when the sun was shining brightly, and when I was reading a chapter in the Bible. I strongly and unmistakably felt their presence. I was overwhelmed by the indescribable warmth. I have also learned from my years of following Christianity that such a grace has been invariably and exclusively granted to less than a handful of God's prominent servants. I felt so very undeserving. And for about ten years since, I had kept hoping and waiting for gods to let me know how I could serve them. Nothing happened. So I kept wondering why did it happen to me. Why such a rare and very precious gift for someone so unworthy? It was not until several years after publishing the book that I began to play with the idea that I might be God's chosen messenger; it seemed to justify the rare grace. It also seemed to explain how I got those important ideas for the book. From all I knew at the time, the explanation has made more sense than other possibilities. And my belief has gradually gotten stronger as I better understood the many ideas of the book.

The rare and precious experience has been my strength during the too many moments of self-doubt. It also has kept reinforcing my belief that the path I am taking is worthwhile. It served to prop me up and stabilize me while I was shaky from the lack of progress in spreading the messages, especially from the repeated rejections of the book publishers. Gods must have known that I am a person of little faith and have granted me this special grace to carry me through. I thank them for the understanding.

Amen.

INDEX

P

"Pain: Mother Nature's Cruel Punishment" 62
Panamanian Bitch 21, 287, 528
parasites 26, 28-9, 71, 388, 478, 537, 540-2
Penicillium mold 26-7, 65
Permit for Children 531-3, 535
  criteria for granting 535
personal growth 494
photoautotrophs 24
pixilation of the mating cicadas, the 356, 356
pleasure principle 53
pleasure seeking see happiness seeking 53-6, 58, 65
"Population Jump" 264
power grip 91, 98, 152, 172
precision grip 152
Pripyat, city 77
probability to harm or to attack 298
projectile, the first 157, 159
puzzle of 1808, the 219
"Puzzling Big Penis, Big Breasts, Naked Body, and More . . ." 190

R

"Reciprocity Entreaty, The" 315
reflex arc 123
resilient planet, our 78-9
reward-punishment coupling 131
Russell's dilemma 332

S

sacrifice, definition 488
Second Law of Thermodynamics 13, 15, 67, 69-70, 544-5

self
  beginning 70
  definition 70, 72-3, 495
"Self and Cooperation" 183
self-preservation 26, 29, 41, 55, 69, 118, 123, 156, 183, 228, 271, 432, 569
self-serving 156, 184, 188, 211, 227, 317, 334, 336-7, 340, 446-7, 467, 472, 475, 480, 482
selfish-human-god problem vii
selfishness viii-ix, 41, 63-5, 283-4, 288-9, 291-3, 485-7, 489-90, 498-501, 505-6, 508-9, 523-5, 546-7, 573-4, 578-82
seppuku 447
sex, a necessity 413-14, 425
sex beast, the highly destructive 362
sex phobia, the big 355
sexual appetite gap 198, 377, 424
sexual desire or drive 358, 408, 426
sexual intercourse, function 404
sexual tension in every society 409-11
sexually transmitted diseases (STDs) 422, 427
short-day plant 118
stick
  life-changing tool 113
  magical tool 110, 113, 132
  walking aid 112, 156
  weapon 106-7, 112, 114
Stone Throwing to Spear 161
stress
  definition 55
  sexual 57-8, 179
suffering and survival 53

Printed in the United States
By Bookmasters